AN HISTORICAL VIEW OF THE ENGLISH GOVERNMENT

NATURAL LAW AND
ENLIGHTENMENT CLASSICS

Knud Haakonssen
General Editor

John Millar

NATURAL LAW AND
ENLIGHTENMENT CLASSICS

An Historical View of the English Government

From the Settlement of the Saxons in Britain to the Revolution in 1688

IN FOUR VOLUMES

John Millar

Edited by Mark Salber Phillips
and Dale R. Smith

Introduction by Mark Salber Phillips

The Works and Correspondence of John Millar

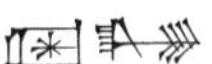

LIBERTY FUND
Indianapolis

This book is published by Liberty Fund, Inc., a foundation established to encourage study of the ideal of a society of free and responsible individuals.

The cuneiform inscription that serves as our logo and as the design motif for our endpapers is the earliest-known written appearance of the word "freedom" (*amagi*), or "liberty." It is taken from a clay document written about 2300 B.C. in the Sumerian city-state of Lagash.

Printed in the United States of America

10 09 08 07 06 C 5 4 3 2 1
10 09 08 07 06 P 5 4 3 2 1

Library of Congress Cataloging-in-Publication Data
Millar, John, 1735–1801.
An historical view of the English government,
from the settlement of the Saxons in Britain to the revolution in 1688/John Millar;
edited by Mark Salber Phillips and Dale R. Smith; introduction by Mark Salber Phillips.
p. cm.—(Natural law and enlightenment classics)
Originally published: London: J. Mawman, 1812.
Includes bibliographical references and index.
ISBN-13: 978-0-86597-444-9 (alk. paper) ISBN-10: 0-86597-444-6 (alk. paper)
ISBN-13: 978-0-86597-445-6 (pbk.: alk. paper) ISBN-10: 0-86597-445-4 (pbk.: alk. paper)
1. Constitutional history—Great Britain. 2. Great Britain—Politics and government.
I. Phillips, Mark, 1946– II. Smith, Dale R., 1969– III. Title. IV. Series.
JN117.M52 1812
942—dc22 2006011396

LIBERTY FUND, INC.
8335 Allison Pointe Trail, Suite 300
Indianapolis, Indiana 46250-1684

CONTENTS

INTRODUCTION

John Millar's first book, *The Origin of the Distinction of Ranks* (1771), is now regarded as a classic of eighteenth-century social inquiry, but comparatively little attention has been paid to the longer historical study that occupied Millar for much of the remainder of his career. Though less accessible than Millar's brilliant debut, *An Historical View of the English Government* (1787; 2nd ed. 1803) remains a work of real interest. Not only is it an important contribution to the historical and political literature of the time, but it also provides a fresh perspective on Millar's thought and intellectual context. If, to put it simply, the *Distinction of Ranks* shows us Millar's deep debt to Smith's teaching of law, *An Historical View* constitutes a sustained dialogue with Hume's *History of England* and is surely the eighteenth century's most serious response to that great work. Unlike so many of Hume's religious and political opponents, however, Millar shared most of the fundamentals of Hume's historiographical approach, and he presented his own "view" of British history from a position securely within the canons of Enlightenment historical thought.

Millar's *Historical View* and the Historical Views of the Eighteenth Century

An Historical View as we now have it appeared in two stages. In 1787 Millar published the first two books, which traced the history of English government down to the accession of the Stuarts. Millar intended to continue the work, but his political involvements at the time of the French Revolution distracted him from the task—or so his nephew and biographer, John Craig, suggests—and *An Historical View* was left incomplete at the time of his death in 1801. Among Millar's papers, however, Craig found a further section that carried the narrative as far as the Revolution of 1688 (now book 3), as well as a series of dissertations or essays that were apparently meant for a fourth book that would have continued the history down to his own day. Collecting these materials, Craig presented a new edition in 1803, in which the previously published books now made up the first half of a four-volume work.

Reviewing this posthumous publication in 1804, Francis Jeffrey painted a picture of John Millar as a typical figure of Scottish academic learning in his day. "To some of our readers, perhaps, it may afford a clearer conception of his intellectual character, to say that it corresponded pretty nearly with the abstract idea that the learned of England entertain of a *Scotish philosopher;* a personage, that is, with little or no deference to the authority of great names, and not very apt to be startled at conclusions that seem to run counter to received opinions or existing institutions; acute, sagacious, and systematical; irreverent towards classical literature; rather indefatigable in argument, than patient in investigation; vigilant in the observation of facts, but not so strong in their number, as skilful in their application."[1] The "leading principle" of Millar's thought, Jeffrey went on to explain, lying behind all of his ideas on history, law, and government, was that social institutions arise "spontaneously from the situation of the society" rather than from the exertions of individuals or the character of nations. "Instead of gazing, therefore, with stupid amazement, on the singular and diversified appearances of human manners and institutions, Mr. Millar taught his pupils to refer them all to one simple principle, and to consider them as necessary links in the great chain which connects civilized with barbarous society."

Jeffrey's summation of Millar's teaching points to the ambition of Scottish Enlightenment thinkers to fashion a view of society that would be both systematic and historical. It is not always appreciated, however, that to the same degree as the new historical orientation enriched eighteenth-century thinking about the social world, it also represented a sharp challenge to entrenched norms of historical writing—especially to the exclusive focus on narratives of public action typical of classical and humanist works. For all its continued prestige, in fact, the classical tradition no longer seemed to possess an adequate vocabulary for writing the history of the modern world. Without reference to commerce, manners, or the power of opinion, history

1. Francis Jeffrey, review of *An Historical View, Edinburgh Review* 3 (1804): 154–80. Jeffrey continued his discussion of Millar in his review of John Craig's *Life* (cited in note 6 below) in *Edinburgh Review* 9 (1806): 83–91.

could seem only a superficial enterprise, and yet none of these distinctive preoccupations of the Enlightenment had entered into classical historiography. Consequently, though the great historians of the ancient world continued to be admired as literary models, it was recognized that in a modern, commercial society historical writing needed both a wider social horizon and a stronger explanatory structure.[2]

This challenge was already implicit in the *Distinction of Ranks,* but it was far more acute in *An Historical View,* where Millar entered more fully onto the traditional territory of historical narrative. In this study of the evolution of English government, Millar not only confronted the historian's customary concern with politics and public life, but he also did so with a clearly polemical intention—namely to combat the narrative provided by David Hume, his great predecessor in the endeavor to write a philosophical history of Britain. No doubt it was to signal his independence from both his classical and Humean models that Millar decided to avoid titling his work a "history" and chose instead to call it a "historical view."

Millar's Life and Teaching

John Millar (1735–1801), the eldest son of a minister of the Scottish Church, was expected to follow his father's path, but he chose instead to make law his profession.[3] The crucial moment in Millar's education came with the arrival in Glasgow of Adam Smith, who began to lecture in rhetoric and moral philosophy in 1751. Smith's influence—first as teacher and later as colleague—decisively shaped Millar's subsequent work, providing the effective outlines of his own approach to jurisprudence. Millar's scholarly interests were also influenced by another pioneer of the historical approach to law, Lord Kames, who invited him to become tutor to his son. For two years

2. For a fuller discussion, see Mark Salber Phillips, *Society and Sentiment: Genres of Historical Writing in Britain, 1740–1820* (Princeton, N.J.: Princeton University Press, 2000).

3. The best brief summary of Millar's life and career is now to be found in the entry in the *Oxford Dictionary of National Biography,* ed. H. C. G. Matthew and Brian Harrison (Oxford: Oxford University Press, 2004). I am very grateful to Knud Haakonssen and John W. Cairns for allowing me to consult their work in manuscript. The pioneer research in this field was the work of William C. Lehmann, *John Millar of Glasgow, 1735–1801: His Life and Thought and His Contributions to Sociological Analysis* (Cambridge: Cambridge University Press, 1960).

Millar resided in Kames's household, where the "tutor of the son became the pupil and companion of the father."[4] In 1760 Millar was admitted to the bar, and, after a brief period of legal practice in Edinburgh, he was appointed in 1761 to the Regius Chair of Civil Law at Glasgow—a position he owed to the recommendation of both Smith and Kames and to the political patronage of Lord Bute. Glasgow was not the most propitious place from which to launch a career in law. It lacked the higher courts that made the law a central feature of Edinburgh's professional and intellectual life, and when Millar began his teaching, the number of students in law was very small. Despite these disadvantages, however, Millar proved an extremely successful teacher and soon acquired a large complement of students, making his university as "famous as a school for Law, as Edinburgh . . . for medicine."[5]

Beyond his teaching, Millar took a strong and public interest in politics. His central preoccupation was one that was strongly marked in the Whig tradition, namely the fear of royal encroachment, "whether in the undisguised shape of prerogative, or the more insidious, and perhaps more dangerous, form of secret influence."[6] Despite some advanced views (he was, for instance, sympathetic to republicanism), Millar remained at heart a Whig, not a radical. His allegiance was to the Rockingham Whigs and later to the leadership of Charles James Fox, to whom he dedicated *An Historical View.* He was an advocate of American independence and a fervent opponent of the slave trade. On the outbreak of the French Revolution, like many other Whigs, Millar welcomed what looked like a movement of constitutional reform, and he strongly opposed the war of the counterrevolutionary powers against France. Two anonymously published pamphlets opposing the war have been attributed to Millar. The *Letters of Crito, on the Causes, Objects, and Consequences of the Present War* (1796) seems almost certainly to be his work, while the *Letters of Sidney* may in fact be the work of Craig,

4. Alexander Fraser Tytler, *Memoirs of the Life and Writings of the Honourable Henry Home of Kames,* 2 vols. (Edinburgh, 1807), 1:198.

5. Robert Heron, *Observations Made in a Journey Through the Western Counties of Scotland in 1792,* 2 vols. (Perth, 1793), 2:418. On Millar's fame as a teacher of law, and on his teaching career more broadly, see the works cited in note 9 below.

6. John Craig, "An Account of the Life and Writings of the Author," appended to Millar's *Observations Concerning the Distinction of Ranks in Society* (Edinburgh, 1806); reprint, ed. J. V. Price (Bristol: Thoemmes Books, 1990), cii.

though heavily influenced by Millar.[7] "The real and ultimate object of the war," he argued repeatedly and insistently in the *Crito,* "has been invariably the preventing of a reform in our parliamentary representation; and this, it was thought, required a counter-revolution in France, by pulling down the new constitution, and restoring the ancient despotism."[8]

Millar's political position—a historical thesis as much as an ideological one—was clearly expressed in *An Historical View.* The Revolution of 1688, it was widely believed, had brought balance to the constitution, offsetting royal prerogative with the now unquestionable authority of the Commons. Millar was convinced, however, that the period since the Revolution had witnessed "the most rapid and alarming advances" in the influence wielded by the Crown and its ministers—a dangerous consequence of the expansion of government, the effects of commerce, and the financial dependence of great families on ministerial favor. Millar had long believed that the best way to limit the growing influence of the court was to trust in an aristocratic coalition in defense of liberty. The failure of the Whigs to regain power, however, and Pitt's success in manipulating the Commons had led Millar to rethink his position. Seeking other means toward the same end, he came to rest his hopes on a wider diffusion of political participation among "the middling ranks"—a body that seemed large enough to be independent of court favor and was now increasingly informed and enlightened about the principles of politics and economy. Nonetheless, Millar was no democrat, since he feared that a universal suffrage would only create a body of voters without the economic means or education to resist the manipulations of the great.

The "Lectures on Government" and *An Historical View*

Millar's primary academic duty was the teaching of Roman law, a responsibility which in part he turned into an opportunity to present a course on

7. For the attribution of these pamphlets, see Knud Haakonssen, *Natural Law and Moral Philosophy: From Grotius to the Scottish Enlightenment* (Cambridge: Cambridge University Press, 1996), 155–56.

8. *Letters of Crito e Letters of Sidney,* ed. Vincenzo Merolle (Rome: Giuffrè, 1984), 106.

natural jurisprudence modeled on the lectures of his mentor, Adam Smith.[9] For Millar's historical thought, however, the crucial course was that on public law, soon renamed as his "Lectures on Government."[10] Millar divided his lectures into three parts. In the first, "Of the Origin and Progress of Government in Society," he discussed the art of government with respect both to external defense and internal order and traced "its progress from the most rude and simple state of Society to the most improved." The broad civilizational history of this part points to many affinities with the *Distinction of Ranks,*[11] but the middle section of the course offered a survey of ancient and modern societies that anticipated many of the central themes of *An Historical View:* for example, the thesis that feudalism is a gradual, not a sudden, development; the division of English history into three stages (feudal aristocracy, feudal monarchy, commercial government); and the concern for the mixed effects of commerce on the balance of prerogative and liberty. Because of this correspondence, the set of lectures specifically devoted to English, Scottish, and Irish matters offers something like a brief guide to the contents of *An Historical View.* The approach here is more conventionally historical than the conjecturalism of the opening part, but Millar is also careful to explain that he had "pitched upon these governments, not only on account

9. Millar's career as a teacher of law was investigated by William C. Lehmann in two early articles: "John Millar, Professor of Civil Law at Glasgow (1761–1801)," *Juridical Review,* n.s. 6 (1961): 218–33; and "Some Observations on the Law Lectures of Professor Millar at the University of Glasgow (1761–1801)," *Juridical Review,* n.s. 15 (1970): 56–77. More recently, see the important studies of John W. Cairns, "John Millar's Lectures on Scots Criminal Law," *Oxford Journal of Legal Studies,* 8 (1988): 364–400 and "Famous as School for Law, as Edinburgh for . . . Medicine: Legal Education in Glasgow, 1761–1801," in *The Glasgow Enlightenment,* ed. Andrew Hook and Richard B. Sher, 133–59 (East Lothian: Tuckwell Press, 1995).

10. The course on public law was one of two presentations of Scots law and seems to have been aimed at a wider audience, not restricted to intending lawyers. See Craig, "Life and Writings," xlii–xliii; Haakonssen and Cairns, "John Millar," *Oxford Dictionary of National Biography.* As established by Cairns, the manuscript of the "Lectures on Government, 1787–88" (Glasgow University Library, MS Gen 289–91) derives fairly directly from Millar's own notes. (See Cairns, "John Millar's Lectures.") I am grateful to Knud Haakonssen for allowing me the use of his transcription of the "Lectures."

11. The "Lectures" present a broad approach to the history of civilization viewed in stadial terms. Thematically the organization is more similar to Adam Ferguson's *Essay on the History of Civil Society* (1767) than to the more focused inquiries of Millar's own work *The Origin of the Distinction of Ranks.* Though it is clear that this work bears a strong imprint of Smith's ideas, one wonders whether its organization might not also reflect Millar's need to distance himself from Ferguson's recently published work.

of their celebrity, or their connexion with ourselves, but as they illustrate different states of society." Finally, Millar devoted the last section of the course to what he called "the more practical part of the subject," namely the "Present State of Government in Great Britain." This material he evidently intended for a separate publication, some elements of which were among the papers Craig described.

The broad scope of the lectures allows us to see Millar's English historical materials in their widest framework. Readers of *An Historical View,* for example, will be aware of the fact that Millar introduces comparative elements in his approach to Europe-wide developments like feudalism. In Millar's hands, Scotland seems ready made for comparative perspectives, but French and other continental histories were also a frequent resource. Even so, the wider geographical horizon of the lectures gave Millar more scope to work out his sense of the unity of European experience and in that way make still more evident how broadly he approached his subject. At the same time, the lectures on English history are not only flanked by those dealing with other European nations, but also by those sections of the course (already mentioned) that took quite different approaches to its historical and political materials. This combination of approaches is especially important given the character of book 4, which is a set of historical dissertations without a unifying narrative. We will never know, of course, how Millar himself might have arranged the work if he had lived to complete it, but Craig's decision to include these dissertations seems all the more reasonable against the background of the lectures.

Millar's Historical Politics and the Critique of Hume

In a much-quoted passage from *An Historical View,* Millar called Montesquieu the Bacon and Smith the Newton of this new "branch of philosophy" (v.2, 404–5n). In relation to Hume, however, Millar was necessarily more divided, since in this quarter he felt philosophical allegiance and political criticism in equal measure. Much of *An Historical View* was intended as a rebuttal of what Millar took to be the royalist and authoritarian politics of Hume's *History.* And, looking beyond explicit ideological debate, it seems more than likely that some of *An Historical View*'s stylistic features—especially its austere avoidance of sentimental portraiture or picturesque narrative—represent a conscious turning away from techniques identified with

Hume and Robertson. The fact remained, nonetheless, that Hume was the preeminent exemplar of the Enlightenment's aspiration to write history in the systematic manner that writers of this period called "philosophical," and Millar salutes him as "the great historian of England, to whom the reader is indebted for the complete union of history with philosophy" (v.2, 418).

Ironically, Millar follows up his tribute with a point-by-point refutation in which he attacks Hume's well-known arguments for the absolutist character of the Tudor regime. Millar's sharp critique amounts to a general summary of their opposing positions, and in the shorter, first edition—where these arguments fell at what was then the end of the work—the impression would have been even stronger that Millar intended the entire work to serve as a refutation of Hume's politics. In some respects, however, the significance of Millar's counterargument becomes clearer when, with the addition of the politically charged third volume, this assessment of Tudor monarchy becomes the bridge to the turbulent period of the Stuart kings.

Hume had argued that an observer unbiased by Whig historical polemics would find little to distinguish English government under the Tudors from the absolutism of France in the same period, and he was even prepared to compare Elizabeth's rule to the government of Muscovy or the Ottoman Turks.[12] This was a deliberately provocative way of putting the case, but for Hume the stakes were high. He regarded the achievement of English liberty in the seventeenth century as the fortunate outcome of a blind struggle in which Parliament, not the Crown, was the principal innovator. In this context, establishing the absolutism of the Tudor regime gave him the foundation for overthrowing the Whig view that the Commons were simply defending ancient liberties against the ambitions of Stuart tyranny.

Millar is seldom specific in his citations, but on this occasion he answers Hume's case with unusual directness, and he mounts a series of arguments to show that even at the height of Tudor power—which he locates in the last years of the reign of Henry VIII—the government of England had never rested entirely in the hands of the Crown. Juries continued to operate, and

12. For Hume's polemic against Whig obfuscation of the absolutism of English government, see *The History of England, from the Invasion of Julius Caesar to the Revolution in 1688,* ed. William B. Todd (Indianapolis: Liberty Fund, 1983), 4:354. For a summary of his view of the absolutist tendency of Tudor rule, see *The History of England,* 5:557. For his comparisons of Elizabethan government to Muscovy and Turkey, see *The History of England,* 4:358, 360.

for the most part the judicial process remained free from interference. Most important, Parliament retained its role in legislation and its exclusive right to taxation. After Henry's death, what is more, the balance of the ancient constitution was fully reinstated, and no new parliamentary powers were required for the Commons to play its role as protector of liberty in the struggles that led to the Civil War.

To this point Millar's reaffirmation of the continuity of English liberties runs along lines long familiar in Whig historiography,[13] but his constitutionalism is modified by other, more systematic arguments drawn from the new form of inquiry which Hume had pioneered and to which his own work *The Origin of the Distinction of Ranks* had made such a signal contribution. In this context what was needed were historical explanations of a much more distanced and general character—potentially a problem when, as for Millar, the emphasis had to fall on English exceptionalism among European monarchies. "When we review the English constitution," he writes, ". . . it appears to illustrate the natural progress of that policy which obtained in the western parts of Europe, with such peculiar modifications, as might be expected, in Britain, from the situation of the country, and from the character and manners of the inhabitants" (v.2, 424). The philosophical historian's task, in other words, would be to show that England conformed to type, even if (as his political convictions led him to believe) it represented an exceptional case within the span of European polity.

Hume and Smith had provided the essential basis for a new interpretation of the shift in power in late medieval and early modern England. In their view, though a number of specific (or "accidental") factors were at work, the most general explanation (and therefore the most powerful) was to be found in the apparently innocent fact of a growing taste for luxury among the nobility.[14] The consequence was not simply that the nobility dissipated their

13. For a careful description of Whig interpretations and of Millar's place within this tradition, see R. J. Smith, *The Gothic Bequest: Medieval Institutions in British Thought, 1688–1863* (Cambridge: Cambridge University Press, 1987). See also the classic article of Duncan Forbes, "Scientific Whiggism: Adam Smith and John Millar," *Cambridge Journal* 7 (1953–54): 643–70.

14. "There were many peculiar causes in the situation and character of Henry VII. which augmented the authority of the crown. . . . But the manners of the age were a general cause, which operated during this whole period, and which continually tended to diminish the riches, and still more the influence, of the aristocracy, anciently so formidable to the crown." *The History of England,* 4:384.

wealth, but—more important—that their money flowed into the pockets of independent artisans and shopkeepers rather than going to the maintenance of the armed retainers who had been the basis of their military and political power. Eventually these changes would raise the status of the commons, but in the short term, the great beneficiary was the Crown. With the power of the nobility significantly diminished, and that of the Commons still in the future, "the sovereign took advantage of the present situation, and assumed an authority almost absolute."[15]

As a philosophical historian, Millar strongly endorsed this mode of reasoning from general causes, and he accepted much of its specific logic with respect to the underlying motives of political change in England. Of necessity, however, he stopped short of accepting Hume's absolutist conclusions, and he searched for other broad-scale causes which might explain the persistence of English freedoms against the pattern of other feudal monarchies.

For Millar, as for so many of his nineteenth-century successors, the clearest answer was to be found in the political and economic geography of the island nation. Politically, England's "insular situation" meant that England had little to fear from foreign invasion—a circumstance that was made still more secure by the Union of the Crowns in 1603, when England and Scotland were joined under a single ruler. As a result, the English king was deprived of the numerous opportunities enjoyed by neighboring princes "for signalizing his military talents, and for securing the attachment of his subjects" (v.2, 424). Among other things, this meant that England was slower to make use of mercenary arms and relied instead on its navies—a force much less adapted "to act as the tools of a court" (v.3, 496). Economically, too, England's island geography was decisive. From an early period, it encouraged trade and manufacture, giving "consequence to the lower order" and "by uniting their interest with that of the king, in opposing the great barons, disposed him to encrease their weight and importance in the community" (v.2, 425). And later, when trade was in full flower and feudal monarchy gave way to "commercial government," the king "found that he was unable to set bounds to those liberties, which his predecessors had endeavoured to promote, and was thence induced, though with infinite reluctance . . . to relinquish a part of his prerogative in order to retain the rest" (v.3, 498).

15. Ibid.

Conclusion

"He also made me read . . . many books which would not have interested me sufficiently to induce me to read them of myself," wrote John Stuart Mill, "among others, Millar's *Historical View* . . . a book of great merit for its time, and which he highly valued."[16] It is hard to imagine a book less likely to appeal to a young boy's interest in the past than the austerely unromantic history James Mill pressed on his precocious son, but it is also clear that by the time John Stuart Mill looked back on his early education, he felt that the *Historical View,* whatever its merits, belonged to a very different era. James Mill was indeed a great admirer of Millar's work, as he made clear in a long review article as well as in a number of references in the *History of India.*[17] The equivocal praises of the younger Mill, however, are more indicative of the book's fortunes in the new century. The posthumous edition of 1803 was followed by a corrected edition in 1812, which was then reprinted in 1818. Beyond this point, Millar's work gradually lost currency, only to be revived in recent times by a generation of scholars who have explored the ideas of the Scottish Enlightenment.[18] Too abstractly argumentative and unadorned to appeal to the historical sensibilities of the Romantic generation, too cosmopolitan for the nationalism of postrevolutionary Britain, the *Historical View* proved to be one of the last great examples of Enlightenment experimentation with philosophical history, and by the time a new program of systematic history was born in the mid-nineteenth century, its impulse would be directed by the ideas of Comte and Buckle, not those of Montesquieu and Hume.

Mark Salber Phillips

16. John Stuart Mill, *Autobiography,* ed. J. Stillinger (Boston: Houghton Mifflin, 1969), 7.

17. See James Mill's review in the *Literary Journal* 11 (1803), no. 6, cols. 326–34; no. 7, cols. 385–400; and Mill, *History of India,* ed. W. Thomas (Chicago: University of Chicago Press, 1975), 44–45n, 228–29n.

18. In addition to the works already cited above, see Michael Ignatieff, "John Millar and Individualism," in *Wealth and Virtue: The Shaping of Political Economy in the Scottish Enlightenment,* ed. Istvan Hont and Michael Ignatieff (Cambridge: Cambridge University Press, 1983); Colin Kidd, *Subverting Scotland's Past: Scottish Whig Historians and the Creation of an Anglo-British Identity, 1689–1830* (Cambridge: Cambridge University Press, 1993).

A NOTE ON THE TEXT

Given its length and its subject matter, *An Historical View* might seem a difficult work to introduce to a wider modern readership, but John Millar's strengths as a historian reside less in the detail of his researches than in the clarity, scope, and intelligence of his ideas. For the student who is relatively unfamiliar with the details of British history, we have identified names, places, and events that might otherwise be obscure, thereby making it easier to compare Millar's account with modern ones, wherever such comparisons might be helpful. Like most of his contemporaries, Millar is vague in his citations—so much so that John Craig, his nephew and first editor, found it necessary to apologize for his scholarly minimalism. We have attempted to remedy some of these deficiencies by identifying the more important and specific references. Our own additions to Millar's notes are enclosed in double square brackets, since Millar has used single square brackets for his own insertions. Further, we have provided a list of works mentioned by Millar (appendix 1) as well as a brief description of his principal sources (appendix 2). Note, however, that Millar's citations often do not indicate the edition used. From time to time, the notes refer readers to similar issues or ideas in Millar's earlier work, *The Origin of the Distinction of Ranks,* or in the works of Lord Kames, Adam Smith, David Hume, and Adam Ferguson, his chief mentors and peers in historical study. But in keeping with the general editorial policy of this series, we have avoided the temptation of didactic footnotes, leaving it to the introduction to provide a brief general background to Millar's work and intellectual career. In the new introduction, references to *An Historical View* are given using Liberty Fund page numbers. Typographical errors in the text have been silently corrected.

ACKNOWLEDGMENTS

We have been fortunate to have help and advice from a number of friends and colleagues. Knud Haakonssen has been not only a sympathetic general editor but also a very valuable reader and scholarly resource for all aspects of Millar's work. In preparing the notes, we have been much helped by the research assistance of Louise Stephens, Steve Takahashi, Michael White, and Heather Welland. Special thanks are due as well to Matthew Lauzon for his help during the last stages of editing. We are also grateful to Edward Hundert and April London for their reading of the introduction.

Mark Salber Phillips would like to express his deep appreciation to the Provost and Fellows of King's College, Cambridge, whose invitation to accept a visiting fellowship provided the ideal environment in which to complete this work.

We dedicate this book to Garry and Evelyn Smith and to the memory of Harry Tarley Phillips and Eva Juliet Salber.

ABBREVIATIONS USED IN THE NOTES

DNB *Oxford Dictionary of National Biography.* Oxford: Oxford University Press, 2004.

DR John Millar, *The Origin of the Distinction of Ranks.* Bristol: Thoemmes, 1990.

HE David Hume. *The History of England.* 6 vols. Edited by William B. Todd. Indianapolis: Liberty Fund, 1983.

HV John Millar. *An Historical View of the English Government.* London, 1803.

LJ Adam Smith. *Lectures on Jurisprudence.* Edited by R. L. Meek, D. D. Raphael, and P. G. Stein. Indianapolis: Liberty Fund, 1982.

TMS Adam Smith. *The Theory of Moral Sentiments.* Edited by D. D. Raphael and A. L. Macfie. Indianapolis: Liberty Fund, 1982.

WN Adam Smith. *An Inquiry into the Nature and Causes of the Wealth of Nations.* 2 vols. Edited by R. H. Campbell and A. S. Skinner. Indianapolis: Liberty Fund, 1981.

AN HISTORICAL VIEW OF THE ENGLISH GOVERNMENT

AN HISTORICAL VIEW OF THE ENGLISH GOVERNMENT

FROM THE
SETTLEMENT OF THE SAXONS IN BRITAIN

TO

THE REVOLUTION IN 1688.

To which are subjoined,
SOME DISSERTATIONS CONNECTED WITH THE
HISTORY OF THE GOVERNMENT,
From the Revolution to the Present Time.

BY JOHN MILLAR ESQ.

Professor of Law in the University of Glasgow

IN FOUR VOLUMES

VOL. I.

London:
PRINTED FOR J. MAWMAN, NO 22 IN THE POULTRY.

1803.
By T. Gillet, Salisbury-Square

ADVERTISEMENT

The Friends of Mr. Millar to whom he entrusted his Manuscripts, think they would be wanting in their duty, were they not to publish the following continuation of his Historical View of the English Government.

It was the intention of the Author, as will be seen in the following pages, to divide the history from the Accession of the House of Stewart, to the present time, into two periods: the first comprehending the history of those contests between Prerogative and Privilege, which, by the Revolution in 1688, terminated in a manner so honourable to the spirit of the nation, and so advantageous to the happiness and liberties of the people: the second containing the history of the rise and progress of the Influence of the Crown: an influence, which, though in some measure checked by the general diffusion of knowledge and the advancement of the arts, was likely, in the opinion of the Author, to become the more dangerous to the constitution, as its slow and insensible advances are less apt to excite attention.

Of these two parts of the general design, the <vi> first was left by the Author, in the state in which he apparently meant to give it to the public, and in which it now appears.—A great part of the materials for the history of the second period, as well as for an account of the present state of the English Government, had also been collected, and partly arranged by him: but considerable alterations on the manuscripts would be requisite, before these very important parts of the work could be offered to the public.

There were found, however, among Mr. Millar's papers several dissertations on subjects connected with the later history of the Government, Manners, and Literature of England, the substance of which it would appear he had intended to introduce into his work; these dissertations seem to contain so many ingenious and interesting speculations, that it has been judged proper to make them public, notwithstanding the unfinished state of the concluding Essay. <vii>

College, Glasgow.
14th March, 1803.

TO THE

RIGHT HONOURABLE

CHARLES JAMES FOX.[1]

SIR,

I shall, perhaps, be thought guilty of presumption, in wishing to draw your attention to the following publication. The truth is, it appears to me scarcely possible for any man to write a constitutional history of England, without having Mr. Fox almost constantly in his thoughts.

In delineating the progress of the English government, I have endeavoured to avoid those fond preposses-<viii>sions which Englishmen are apt to entertain upon the subject, as well as the prejudices peculiar to the two great parties, which the nature of our limited monarchy has produced. How far I have succeeded in this, must be left to the judgment of the public. But, whatever indulgence may be shewn to this work, the ambition of its author will not be gratified; unless he can procure in some degree, the approbation of a mind superior to prejudice; equally capable of speculation, and of active exertion; no less conversant in elegant literature, than accustomed to animate the great scenes of national business; possessed of the penetration to discover the genuine principles of the constitution, and of the virtue to make them an invariable rule of conduct. <ix> <x>

Impressed with the highest esteem for such a character, permit me to declare the satisfaction I feel from your steady perseverance in a system, which, by tending to secure the natural rights of mankind, has led to a reputation the most exalted, and the most grateful to a generous mind.

I have the honour to be,

SIR,

Your most obedient

Humble servant,

JOHN MILLAR.

College, Glasgow,

4th Dec. 1786. <xi>

1. Charles James Fox (1749–1806): a Whig statesman and one of the great parliamentary orators of his day. Fox's reformist policies included sympathy for the French Revolution, abolition of the slave trade, and support for political rights for Catholics and Dissenters.

CONTENTS[1]

1. The page numbers in the Contents are those of the 1803 edition.

INTRODUCTION

The great series of events in the history of England may be divided into three parts:[1] the first, extending from the settlement of the Saxons in Britain to the Norman conquest; the second, from the reign of William the Conqueror to the accession of the house of Stewart; the third, from the reign of James the First to the present time. The important changes exhibited in the state of the country, and in the situation of its inhabitants, appear, like a sort of natural boundaries, to mark out these different periods, and to recommend them as objects of distinct and separate examination.

The first period contains the conquest of England by the northern barbarians, the division of the country under the different chiefs by whom that people were conducted, the subsequent union of those principalities under one sovereign, and the course of public transactions under the Saxon and Danish monarchs.

The reign of William the Conqueror, while <2> it put an end to the ancient line of kings, introduced into England a multitude of foreigners, who obtained extensive landed possessions, and spread with great rapidity the manners and customs of a nation more civilized and improved than the English. The inhabitants were thus excited to a quicker advancement in the common arts of life, at the same time that the nation, by acquiring continental connections, was involved in more extensive military operations.

By the union of the crowns of England and Scotland,[2] upon the accession of the house of Stewart, the animosities and dissensions, with all their trou-

1. Millar identifies three broad periods of English history: (1) the Saxon Period (fourth century–1066); (2) the Norman Conquest to the accession of James I (1066–1603); (3) the Union of the Crowns to the time of authorship (1603–1801). Subsequently, he identifies these three periods with three successive constitutional forms: feudal aristocracy, feudal monarchy, and commercial government.

2. The accession of James VI, king of Scotland (r. 1567–1625), to the English throne in 1603 united the crowns of both countries in one person for the first time.

blesome consequences, which had so long subsisted between the two countries, were effectually suppressed. By the improvement of manufactures, and the introduction of a considerable foreign trade, England began, in a short time, to establish her maritime power, and to assume a higher rank in the scale of Europe.

The same periods are also distinguished by remarkable variations in the form of government.

Upon the settlement of the Saxons in Bri-<3>tain, we behold a number of rude families or tribes feebly united together, and little accustomed either to subordination among themselves, or to the authority of a monarch. During the reigns of the Anglo-Saxon princes, we discover the effects produced by the gradual acquisition of property; in consequence of which some individuals were advanced to the possession of great estates, and others, who had been less fortunate, were obliged to shelter themselves under the protection of their more opulent neighbours. Political power, the usual attendant of property,[3] was thus gradually accumulated in the hands of a few great leaders, or nobles; and the government became more and more aristocratical.

When the advances of the country in improvement had opened a wider intercourse, and produced a more intimate union, between the different parts of the kingdom, the accumulated property in the hands of the king became the source of greater influence than the divided property possessed by the nobles. The prerogatives of the former, in a course of time, were therefore gradually augmented; and the privileges of the latter suffered a pro-<4>portionable diminution. From the reign of William the Conqueror in England, we may date the first exaltation of the crown, which, under his successors of the Plantagenet and Tudor families, continued to rise in splendor and authority.[4]

About the commencement of the reign of James the First, great alterations began to appear in the political state of the nation. Commerce and manufactures, by diffusing a spirit of liberty among the great body of the

3. The idea that ultimately political power followed possession of property was an important theme in the political writings of James Harrington. On Harrington, see p. 569, note 35.

4. William I, the Conqueror: king of England (r. 1066–69), acceded to the throne after defeating Harold II (r. 1066) at the Battle of Hastings. William's reign marks the establishment of the House of Normandy in England (1066–1154). The successor dynasties were the Plantagenet (1159–1399) and Tudor (1485–1603).

people, by changing the system of national defence, and by increasing the necessary expences of government, gave rise to those disputes, which, after various turns of fortune, were at last happily terminated by the establishment of a popular government.

With reference to that distribution of property, in the early part of our history, which goes under the name of the feudal system, the constitution established in the first of these periods, may be called the *feudal aristocracy;* that in the second, the *feudal monarchy;* and that which took place in the third, may be called the *commercial government.*

Similar periods to those which have now <5> been pointed out in the English history, may also be distinguished in the history of all those kingdoms on the continent of Europe, which were established upon the ruins of the Roman Empire, and in which the people have since become opulent and polished. Thus the reign of Hugh Capet in France, and of Otho the Great in Germany, correspond to that of William the Conqueror in England; as those of Lewis XIII. and Ferdinand II.[5] in the two former countries, were analogous to that of James the First, in the latter.

In the following treatise, it is proposed to take a separate view of these periods of the English history, and to examine the chief differences of the political system in each of them. As the government which we enjoy at present has not been formed at once, but has grown to maturity in a course of ages, it is necessary, in order to have a full view of the circumstances from which it has proceeded, that we should survey with attention the successive changes through which it has passed. In a disquisition of this nature, it is hoped that, by considering events in the order in which they happened, the causes of every change will be <6> more easily unfolded, and may be pointed out with greater simplicity. As the subject, however, is of great extent, I shall endeavour to avoid prolixity, either from quoting authorities and adducing proofs in matters sufficiently evident, or from intermixing any detail of facts not intimately connected with the history of our constitution.

With respect to the Saxon period, which comes first in order, many writers appear to have looked upon it as too remote, and as affording a prospect too

5. Hugh Capet (r. 987–96): founder of the Capetian dynasty in France (987–1328); Otto I, the Great, king of Germany (r. 936–73) and Holy Roman Emperor (962–73); Louis XIII, king of France (r. 1610–43); Ferdinand II, Holy Roman Emperor (r. 1619–37).

barren and rude, to deserve any particular examination. But it ought to be considered, that the foundations of our present constitution were laid in that early period; and that, without examining the principles upon which it is founded, we cannot form a just opinion concerning the nature of the superstructure. To trace the origin of a system so singular in its nature may, at the same time, be regarded as an object of rational curiosity. The British government is the only one in the annals of mankind that has aimed at the diffusion of liberty through a multitude of people, spread over a wide extent of territory. The ancient republics of Greece and <7> Rome comprehended little more than the police of a single city;[6] and in these a great proportion of the people, so far from being admitted to a share in the government, were, by the institution of domestic slavery, excluded from the common rights of men. The modern republics of Italy, not to mention the very unequal privileges which they bestow upon different individuals, are inconsiderable in their extent. The same observation is applicable to the government of the Swiss cantons. In the Seven United Provinces of the Netherlands, the government can hardly be considered as more extensive; for, notwithstanding the confederacy by which they are connected, every particular province, and even every single town of any consequence, belonging to each, having the exclusive power of making or consenting to its own regulations, forms in reality an independent political system. By what fortunate concurrence of events has a more extensive plan of civil freedom been established in this island? Was it by accident, or by design, or from the influence of peculiar situation, that our Saxon forefathers, originally distinguished as the most ferocious <8> of all those barbarians who invaded the Roman provinces, have been enabled to embrace more comprehensive notions of liberty, and to sow the seeds of those political institutions which have been productive of such prosperity and happiness to a great and populous empire? To these questions it is hoped that, in the sequel, a satisfactory answer will be given. <9>

6. *Police* in this sense means civil order.

AN HISTORICAL VIEW OF THE ENGLISH GOVERNMENT

Book I

OF THE ENGLISH GOVERNMENT, FROM THE SETTLEMENT OF THE SAXONS IN BRITAIN TO THE REIGN OF WILLIAM THE CONQUEROR.

CHAPTER I

Preliminary Account of the State of Britain under the Dominion of the Romans.

The downfal of the Roman state, and the formation of those kingdoms which were built upon the ruins of it, may be regarded as one of the greatest revolutions in the history of mankind. A vast unwieldly empire, which had for ages languished under a gloomy despotism, was then broken into a number of independent states, animated with all the vi-<10>gour, but subjected to all the violence and disorder, natural to a rising and unsettled constitution. The arts and literature which had grown up in the ancient world were, in a great measure, overthrown; and a new system of political institutions, together with a total change of manners, customs, and ways of thinking, spread itself over the greatest part of Europe.

The plan of government, which the Romans adopted throughout the greatest part of their dominions, was uniform and simple. After that people had enlarged their city, as far as was convenient, by incorporating some of the neighbouring tribes, and had joined to it the possession of a considerable adjacent territory, they divided their future acquisitions into distinct provinces; in each of which they placed a governor, invested with almost unlimited authority. It cannot escape observation, that the Roman patriotism, even in the boasted times of the commonwealth, was far from being directed by a liberal spirit: it proceeded from narrow and partial considerations; and the same people who discovered so much fortitude and zeal in establishing and maintaining <11> the freedom of their capital, made no scruple in subjecting the rest of their dominions to an arbitrary and despotical government. The governor of every province had usually the command of the forces; and was invested with the supreme executive and judicial powers, together with the privilege of appointing the greatest part of the inferior officers, to whom the distribution of justice, or the care of the police, was intrusted. The oppressive taxes to which the inhabitants of the provinces were subjected, and the still greater oppression which they suffered from the arbitrary and illegal exactions of their magistrates are sufficiently known. The tribunals of Rome were at too great a distance to take a strict account of her provincial officers; and the leading men in the Republic, who expected, in their turns, to enrich themselves by the plunder of the provinces, were seldom disposed to enter very heartily into measures for restraining such enormities. The riches amassed by the offender afforded him, at the same time, the means of preventing any troublesome inquiry into his behaviour; and in proportion to the extent of his guilt, was commonly the degree of security which <12> he afterwards enjoyed. Cicero[1] affirms, that in the small government of Cilicia,[2] after saving to the public the amount of a full million sterling, which the former governors had applied to their private use, he had, at the end of the year, about twenty thousand pounds of clear gain.

But while Rome was thus extending conquest and slavery over the world, she communicated to the conquered nations her knowledge, and her refinement in the arts of life. The great military establishment maintained in

1. Marcus Tullius Cicero (106–43 B.C.): Roman orator, author of many philosophical and rhetorical works, including *On Duty, On the Orator,* and *Tusculan Disputations.*

2. Cilicia: a Roman territory in Asia Minor.

every province, in order to keep the inhabitants in subjection; the large body of civil officers necessary in the various departments of public administration; the numerous colonies, composed of Roman citizens, who settled in every part of the empire, and carried along with them the Roman institutions and customs; and, above all, the frequent resort of the chief provincial inhabitants to the capital of the empire, a natural consequence of their dependence; these circumstances produced an universal imitation of Roman manners, and throughout the dominions of Rome contributed to spread her language, arts, and literature. <13> These advantages compensated in some measure, and were sometimes more than sufficient to counterbalance, the loss of independence. Wherever the Roman dominion was established, the ruder parts of the world were civilized.

Among all the countries subdued by the Romans, none was in a more uncultivated state than Britain; and it is probable that no country derived greater advantages from her subjection. A great part of the inhabitants, before they were incorporated in the Roman empire, seem to have been strangers to agriculture, and to have been maintained chiefly by their herds of cattle. They were divided into small independent tribes, under their several chiefs, as commonly happens in that early state of mankind; and these little societies being much addicted to plunder, and for that reason frequently engaged in hostilities, a regard to mutual defence had occasionally produced alliances among some of them, from which a variety of petty princes, or kings, had arisen in different parts of the country.

The Roman administration of Britain does not appear to have been distinguished from that <14> of the other provinces at a distance from the seat of government. After the reduction of all that part of the island accounted worth the trouble of acquiring, the first great object was, to ascertain and preserve the conquest by a permanent military force. For this purpose the inhabitants were completely disarmed; and a standing army, composed, according to the lowest account, of three legions, amounting to upwards of thirty-six thousand foot and six thousand horse, was introduced, and regularly maintained.* These troops were distributed over the province, and placed in stations where their service could be most useful, either by overawing the natives, or by repelling the invasions of the unconquered tribes in the North. When not engaged in war, they were employed, according to

* Horsely Brit. Rom. Whitaker Hist. Manchester, v. i. b. i. ch. 6.

the usual practice of the Romans, in public works; in building and repairing these two northern walls, which at different times were intended as the boundary of the province; in constructing forts; in clearing the country of its forests <15> and marshes; and in opening a communication between different parts of it, by an uninterrupted chain of high roads.

There are said to have been, in the whole province, about a hundred and fifty Roman stations; which were connected with inferior fortresses, erected at convenient distances, and garrisoned with regular troops.* Each of these garrisons occasioned a resort of the neighbouring inhabitants, and probably gave rise to a sort of village or town, in which a promiscuous settlement was formed by Roman families, and those of the natives. The effect of such an intercourse, in the communication of manners and customs, may easily be conceived. In particular, as the military people were often rewarded by the public with landed possessions, their example could not fail to spread the knowledge and practice of agriculture, while their industry in the management of their estates contributed to beautify and improve the face of the country.

The connexion with Britain, which the soldiers of the British army acquired by living in <16> the country, was even seldom broke off when they were dismissed from the service. Though drawn originally from different parts of the empire, yet, having formed an attachment to the place in which they had so long resided, they were commonly disposed, in their old age, and when they had merited their dismission, to pass the remainder of their days in the province. The offspring of these people became natural inhabitants: and Britain, in this manner, was continually receiving fresh supplies of Romans, who compensated for such of the natives as, in the course of recruiting the armies, were naturalized into other provinces.

After establishing a sufficient military force to maintain her authority, the attention of Rome was directed to the suppression of internal disorder among her subjects, by the regular distribution of justice. The jealousy entertained by the first emperors had suggested an important regulation for limiting the dangerous power of their provincial governors. From the time of Augustus,[3] the provinces near the seat of the empire, as they enjoyed the prospect of tranquillity, were distinguished from such as were situated at a

* Whitaker Hist. Manchester, v. i. b. i. ch. 8.

3. Augustus (or Octavian): first Roman emperor (r. 31 B.C.–A.D. 14).

distance, and <17> on that account more exposed to disturbance. In the former, the governor was merely a civil officer, and had no direction of the forces; but in the latter, it was thought necessary that his authority should be rendered more effectual, by raising him to the head of the military, as well as the civil department.*

The president or governor of Britain was in the latter situation; having the command of the army, together with the supreme jurisdiction, and the appointment of inferior magistrates. In the courts held by all these officers, the laws of Rome were considered as the standard of every decision. Wherever the Romans extended their dominion, it was their constant aim to introduce their own jurisprudence; a system which was calculated to establish good order and tranquillity among the conquered people, as well as to promote the interest of the conquerors. The introduction of that system into Britain was more immediately necessary, to prevent those private wars, and to restrain those acts of violence and injustice, to which the inhabitants were so much <18> addicted. It is not likely, however, that an innovation of such importance was accomplished all at once. In the public administration of the province, the Roman magistrates assumed an absolute authority; but, in matters of private property, the British chiefs and petty princes appear, for some time after the conquest, to have retained their ancient jurisdiction, and to have determined the differences of their own tenants and dependants. But this jurisdiction became gradually more circumscribed, and seems at last to have been entirely annihilated. The continual migration of foreigners into the province, brought along with them the fashions acquired in other parts of the empire; while the multiplication and enlargement of the British towns, which, for the most part, were governed according to the policy of Rome, extended the influence of the Roman judges. The province of Britain is said to have contained about an hundred and forty towns, nine of which were of the rank of colonies; and the customs, as well as the notions of order and justice, which prevailed in those places of common resort, were easily propagated over the surrounding country. The <19> long continuance of the provincial government, and the progress of the natives in civilization, disposed them to neglect their original magistrates, and to court the favour of the ruling powers, by an immediate appeal to their protection.

To procure a revenue, not only sufficient for defraying the expences of

* Dio. Cass. 53.—Hein. ad. lib. i. dig. tit. 16. 18.

the civil and military establishments, but also capable of affording annual remittances to the emperor, was a third, and perhaps the principal object of his administration. The Britons were subjected to taxes of the same nature with those which were levied from the other provinces.* The proprietors of arable land paid an annual quit-rent, supposed to be equal to a tenth part of the fruits; and the possessors of pasture ground were also loaded with a duty, proportioned to the number of their cattle.† The customs and excise, in this part of the Roman dominions, are said to have been remarkably heavy;‡ but the impositions which excited <20> most complaint were, a poll-tax, and a duty upon funerals. These, being levied at a fixed rate, without any regard to the poverty or riches of the people, and having no immediate dependance on the prosperity of trade and manufactures, were most easily increased at pleasure, and therefore seem to have been the usual expedients for raising supplies, when every other taxation had been found ineffectual.§

The charge of collecting the revenue was committed to an *imperial procurator,* who had the superintendance of all the inferior officers employed in this branch of administration; and in Britain, as well as in the other provinces, the principal taxes were let to farmers for the payment of a yearly rent. From this mode of collection, so liable to abuse, and from the nature of the government in other respects, it may seem unnecessary to remark, that the Britons were exposed to grievous extortions. If the countries near the seat of the empire, and within the observation of the sovereign, were abandoned to the arbitrary measures of the <21> provincial officers, it cannot be supposed that those at a distance were in a better situation. Tacitus[4] mentions, in terms of the highest indignation, the unfeeling rapacity of the Roman officers in Britain; which, at an early period, excited a general revolt of the inhabitants.||

* See an account of the taxes throughout the Roman dominions, in Burman. de Vect. Rom.

† This tax upon cattle was called *Scriptura.*

‡ Strabo, lib. iv.

§ See the terms in which Boadicea is made to complain of the two last-mentioned taxes. Xiphilinus in Nerone.

|| Tacit. Agric. ch. 15.

4. Tacitus (ca. 56–ca. 120): Roman historian, an important source for the history of the Germanic tribes. His works include *Agricola* (ca. 98), a biography of his father-in-law and former governor of the Roman province of Britain; *Germania* (ca. 98), a comprehensive work on the Germanic tribes of central Europe; the *Histories* (105–8); and the *Annals.*

It is well known, that the cities and provinces under the Roman dominion were often reduced, by the demands of government, to such distress, as obliged them to borrow money at exorbitant interest: and that, by taking advantage of their necessities, the monied men of those times were enabled to employ their fortunes in a very profitable manner. In this trade, though prohibited by law, and however infamous in its own nature, the best citizens of Rome (such is the force of example) were not ashamed to engage. Seneca the philosopher,[5] whose philosophy, it seems, was not incompatible with the love of money, lent the Britons, at one time, above three hundred and twenty-two thousand pounds.* <22>

Were it possible to ascertain the extent of the revenue drawn from the province of Britain, we might thence be enabled to form a notion of the opulence and improvement attained by the inhabitants. Dr. Henry, who has made a very full collection of the facts mentioned by ancient authors concerning the provincial government of this Island, supposes that its annual revenue amounted to no less than two millions sterling.† But this is a mere conjecture, unsupported by any authority; and it should seem that no ac-

* χιλίας μυριάδας, quadrigenties sestertium; viz. £. 322,916. 13. 4. Xiphilinus in Nerone. [[The word *drachmae* is implicit in the Greek text, but the word is not actually there: ten million drachmae. A translation of the anecdote is found in Earnest Cary, *Dio's Roman History* (Cambridge, Mass.: Harvard University Press, 1961), 8:83. *Quadrigenties sestertium,* forty million *sesterces.*]]

† This supposition is built upon a calculation of Lipsius, who makes the revenue of Gaul amount to £. 2,421,875. This calculation is only supported by a passage of Cicero, quoted by Strabo, which mentions the revenue of Egypt, in the time of Auletes, the father of Cleopatra, as amounting to that sum; and by a passage in Velleius Paterculus, asserting that Egypt in taxes yielded *nearly as much as Gaul.* But the evidence arising from this is too slight, when opposed to the authority of Suetonius, and that of Eutropius; who say, that Caesar drew from Gaul only *quadrinenties,* £. 322,916. 13. 4. Supposing, however, the fact to be ascertained, that the revenue of Gaul was about two millions and a half, is there sufficient ground to infer from this that the revenue of Britain was, at least, two millions?—Lipsius de Magn. Rom.—Henry's Hist. v. i. [[Robert Henry (1718–90): Scottish minister and historian, author of the *History of Great Britain . . . Written on a New Plan* (vols. 1–5, 1771–85; vol. 6, 1793). Henry notes that "Though it is impossible to discover the exact value of the Roman revenues in Britain, we have reason to believe, that these revenues were very considerable. . . . If the calculations of Lipsius, concerning the Roman revenues of Gaul, be just, those of Britain could not be less than two million sterling annually." Vol. 1 (London, 1771), 238.]]

5. Seneca the Younger (ca. 4 B.C.–A.D. 65): Roman politician and author of works on philosophy, rhetoric, morals, and drama.

counts <23> have been transmitted by historians, from which the point can be determined.

The improvements made by the Britons in agriculture were such, as to produce a regular exportation of corn, for supplying the armies in other parts of the empire. Their houses were built in the same style of architecture; and many of them were adorned with statues and public structures, in the same taste of magnificence which prevailed in Italy. In this branch of labour, their mechanics were even so numerous, and had such reputation, as to be employed upon the neighbouring continent. In weaving cloth they appear also to have made considerable proficiency. We are informed, in particular, that linen and woollen manufactures were established at Winchester.*

The foreign trade of Britain, arising from her valuable tin mines, and for which the island was, at a very remote period, frequented by the Phenicians,[6] and other commercial nations of antiquity, is universally known. When this branch of commerce, together with those of <24> lead, wool, hides, and some other native productions, came to be secured of a regular market, under the eye and protection of the Roman magistrate, they were undoubtedly pushed to a considerable extent.

In taste and literature, the advances made by the Britons were no less conspicuous than in the common improvements of life. Even in the time of Agricola, "the youth of distinguished families," according to the great historian of that age, "were instructed in the liberal arts: insomuch that those who but lately were ignorant of the language, began to acquire a relish for the eloquence of Rome. They became fond of appearing in the dress of the Romans, and by degrees were led to imitate their vices, their luxury, and effeminacy, as well as their elegance and magnificence."†

The fashion of travelling for education, and of residing in Rome, and in other learned and polite cities of the empire, was early introduced among

* Henry's Hist. v. i. [[Winchester: an ancient town in Hampshire of importance to both the Romans and Saxons. Later the capital of Wessex, and subsequently of England.]]

† Tacit. Agric. c. 21. [[Gnaeus Julius Agricola (40–93): Roman statesman and soldier, governor of Britain 77–84. For a modern translation of this discussion in Tacitus, see *Agricola and Germany*, trans. Anthony R. Birley (Oxford: Oxford University Press, 1999), 17.]]

6. Phoenicians: an important commercial and maritime people of the eastern Mediterranean.

the Britons; who, in a noted passage of Juvenal, are mentioned as being indebted <25> to the Gauls for their eminent proficiency in pleading at the bar.* In Britain, as well as in other provinces, the utmost attention was given by government, to propagate the knowledge not only of the Latin and Greek languages, but of all those branches of science that enjoyed any reputation; and for this purpose, academies and schools, with public encouragement, are said to have been erected in the principal towns. From these different sources the Roman learning, in all its parts, was communicated to this Island; where it flourished for some time, and was afterward subjected to a similar decay as in all the other provinces of the empire.

The successive changes which happened in the political situation of the Roman empire produced alterations in the administration of all the provinces, as well as of Britain in particular. The despotical government of Rome, as it had been at first established, so it was afterwards entirely supported by a military force. In its original, therefore, it contained <26> the seeds of its destruction. As, by his tyrannical behaviour, the reigning emperor became naturally the object of detestation and resentment to his subjects, he was exposed to the continual hazard of insurrection, from the disgust or caprice of that army which he kept on foot for maintaining his authority. It was, at the same time, impossible that he should command in person the different armies necessary for the defence of the whole empire, or that he should prevent the general of every separate army from acquiring influence and popularity with the troops under his direction. The greatest and most veteran of those armies were unavoidably employed on the frontiers, where their service was most needed, and where their courage and activity were most exercised; and their leaders being too far removed from the chief magistrate to meet with any disturbance in forming their ambitious plans, were frequently in a condition to render themselves independent, or to open a direct passage to the throne.

But the independence of the opulent and leading men, in the distant provinces, was increased by another circumstance of still greater <27> importance. The first emperors, who possessed the extensive and rich countries

* Gallia causidicos docuit facunda Britannos.—Juv. Sat. 15. [["Eloquent Gaul has trained the pleaders of Britain." Juvenal, Satire 15.111; see *Juvenal and Persius,* trans. G. G. Ramsay, rev. ed. (Cambridge, Mass.: Harvard University Press, 1940; repr. 1969), 297. Juvenal (55–128) was a Roman verse satirist.]]

lately subdued by the Roman arms, enjoyed an immense revenue, and their influence must have been proportionably great; but the oppressive nature of their government, and the unbounded licence which they gave to the plunder of their subjects, could not fail to discourage industry, and of course to reduce the people to poverty and beggary. The extent of the Roman empire had, in the mean time, become so great, that the expence of maintaining forces on a distant frontier, with a view of making any farther conquest, seemed to overbalance the advantages which it might be supposed to produce. Adrian,[7] a prince no less distinguished for activity than wisdom, was induced to contract his dominions, and to abandon a part of what had been already acquired, that he might be able to preserve the remainder in greater security. Thus, while the old channels of public revenue were drained, no new sources could be provided to supply the deficiency. In this situation the emperor felt a gradual decline of his authority; and as he became less able to protect the inhabitants of the provinces, <28> or to punish their disobedience, they were more disposed to shake off their allegiance, and emboldened to follow the fortunes of any adventurer who found himself in a condition to disturb the public tranquillity.

For preventing these disorders, it was thought a prudent measure to associate different leaders in the supreme power. The first traces of this practice may be discovered about the time of Trajan and the Antonines;[8] who partly, as it should seem, from affection, and partly from political motives, adopted in their own life-time *a Caesar,* or successor to the crown. The same plan was farther extended by Dioclesian;[9] who divided the sovereignty between two emperors and two Caesars; and who seems to have thought that, to preserve the empire from falling in pieces, it was requisite to submit to the manifest inconveniences arising from the jealousy and bad agreement of so many independent heads. The emperor Constantine[10] rendered this division

7. Hadrian: Publius Aelius Hadrianus, Roman emperor (r. 117–138) who established frontier defenses for the empire, including Hadrian's Wall in Britain.

8. Trajan: properly Marcus Ulpius Trajanus, Roman emperor (r. 98–117); the *Antonines* is the collective name of certain Roman emperors of the second century, namely Antonius Pius (r. 138–61), Marcus Aurelius (r. 161–80), and Commodus (r. 180–92).

9. Diocletian: properly Gaius Aurelius Valerius Diocletian, Roman emperor (r. 284–313).

10. Constantine the Great: properly Flavius Valerius Aurelius Constantinus, Roman emperor (r. 306–37). He founded the new capital, Constantinople, on the site of Byzantium in Asia Minor (324–30).

more permanent, by erecting a great Eastern capital, which became the rival, and even superior, in opulence and dignity, to that of the west. <29>

In conformity to such views of dividing the sovereignty among those leaders who might otherwise be disposed to tear the empire asunder, subdivisions were made in those territories which had formerly composed a single province; and in each subdivision a chief officer was appointed, whose authority might serve to limit and circumscribe that of him who had the government of the whole. Thus the same prince who founded Constantinople, having disbanded the old praetorian guards,[11] whose power had long been so formidable, distributed the whole empire into four great *praefectures,* corresponding to the four joint sovereigns already established. Each praefecture he divided into certain large territories, called *jurisdictions,* under their several governors; and each jurisdiction he parcelled out into smaller districts, under the denomination of *provinces,* which were committed to the care of deputy-governors.

Britain, which originally formed a single province, but which, by the emperor Severus,[12] had been divided into two, was, according to this arrangement, multiplied into five provinces; and the *vicar* or governor of the whole, <30> enjoyed a paramount authority to that of its five deputy-governors.

The direction of the civil, and that of the military establishment, were, for the same reason, separated, and placed in different hands. After the dismission of the praetorian guard, and of its commander, two military officers were appointed, the one of which had the command of the infantry, and the other of the cavalry, throughout the empire; and under them the number of generals, in particular districts, appears to have been considerably increased. The Roman forces in this Island came, in the later periods of its provincial government, to be under the direction of three independent officers; the *duke of Britain,* who commanded on the northern frontier; the *count of Britain,* who conducted the troops in the interior parts of the country; and the *count of the Saxon shore,* employed in superintending the defence of the southern and eastern coasts, which, from about the beginning of the third century, had been exposed to frequent incursions from the Saxons.

11. The Praetorian Guard was created by Augustus to act as the emperor's private army in 27 B.C. Its size and proximity to the capital enabled it to become highly influential in deciding political contests. It was disbanded by Constantine in 312.

12. Lucius Septimius Severus: Roman emperor (r. 193–211).

All these precautions, however, by which the Roman emperors endeavoured to maintain <31> subordination and dependance in the different parts of their dominions, were ineffectual in opposition to the prevailing current of the times. The same unhappy system which tended to loosen the bands of government, contributed also to render the military establishment unfit for defence against a foreign enemy. As all power and distinction were ultimately derived from the army, it was the interest of every general to court the favour of the troops under his command, not only by enriching them with donations and emoluments, but by treating them with every kind of indulgence. The natural consequence of such a situation was the procuring to the soldiers an exemption from the laborious duties of their profession. Feeling their own consequence, the military people set no bounds to their licentious demands, and were rendered inactive and effeminate, in the same proportion as they became haughty and insolent. The heavy armour, which in former times had been used with so much advantage, was therefore laid aside, as too cumbersome and fatiguing; and the ancient military discipline, the great cause of all their victories, was at length entirely neglected. <32> It was thus that the Romans, being deprived of that superiority which they had formerly possessed, in their encounters with rude and ignorant nations, found themselves unable to resist the fierce courage of those neighbouring barbarians, who, about the fifth century, were invited to attack them by the prospect of plunder and of new settlements.

In this declining state of the Roman empire, the revenue of the provinces, by suffering a gradual diminution, became at length insufficient for the support of their civil and military establishments; and whenever any country had been reduced to such a degree of poverty as to be no longer able to repay the trouble and expence of maintaining it, good policy seemed to require that it should be abandoned. To such an unfruitful condition the distant provinces, and Britain more especially, appear to have been fast approaching, in the reign of Arcadius and Honorius,[13] when a deluge of barbarians, pressing on all sides, threatened the state with sudden destruction, and made it necessary to withdraw the forces from this Island, in order to defend the richer and more important parts of the empire. <33>

13. Flavius Arcadius, Eastern Roman emperor (r. 395–408), and Flavius Honorius, Western Roman emperor (r. 395–423), oversaw the Roman evacuation from Britain (407–10).

The situation of Britain, when thus deserted by the Romans, was no less new and singular, than it was alarming and unhappy. When mankind are formed into political societies, and have acquired property, they are usually provided with one set of regulations for repelling the attacks of their enemies, and with another for securing internal tranquillity. But the Britons, upon this extraordinary emergency, were left equally destitute of both. From the distrustful jealousy of Rome, they had been removed from all concern in military transactions, at least in their own country, and made to depend for their safety upon an army composed entirely of foreigners. In such a state they had remained for more than three centuries, enjoying the protection of their masters, without any call to exert themselves in their own defence, and cultivating those arts which tend to soften the manners, while they inspire an aversion from the dangers and hardships of a martial life. Thus the Britons, in their advances towards civility, lost the courage and ferocity of barbarians, without acquiring the skill and address of a polished nation; and they ceased to be warriors by nature, <34> without being rendered soldiers by discipline and education.

But the departure of the Romans from Britain was no less fatal to all the institutions of civil government. The governors and other officers, who directed the administration of public affairs, the farmers engaged in the different departments of the revenue, the magistrates of Roman appointment, who determined both civil and criminal causes, and who had now acquired a complete jurisdiction over the whole province, had no longer occasion to remain in a country which was totally abandoned by its master, and in which, by the removal of the army, they had lost the means of maintaining their authority. The courts of justice, therefore, were dissolved; the taxes were abolished; and all order and subordination were destroyed. Even private individuals, of Roman extraction, who had acquired estates in Britain, endeavoured to dispose of their fortunes; and by leaving the Island, avoided the storm that appeared to be gathering around them.

The disasters which followed were of such a nature as might be expected from the anar-<35>chy and confusion which prevailed in the country. The Scots and Picts,[14] who, in the northern part of the Island, had remained

14. The Scots, who began to raid the Scottish shore from Ireland in the third century, and the Picts, a group of probably Celtic origin, were a significant threat to the Britons in the post-Roman era. Though distinct through the better part of the Saxon period in

unconquered, and retained their primitive barbarous manners, took advantage of this favourable opportunity, to invade and plunder their more opulent neighbours. They met with little resistance from the Britons, who, giving way to their fears, and conscious of their inferiority, seemed to place their only refuge in the protection of their ancient rulers. The abject manner in which they, at different times, solicited that protection; the behaviour of their ambassadors, who in the presence of the emperor rent their garments, and putting ashes upon their heads, endeavoured to excite commiseration by tears and lamentations; the letter which they wrote to Aetius, the praefect of Gaul, inscribed *the groans of the Britons,* and in which they say, *the barbarians drive us into the sea, the sea throws us back upon the barbarians, and we have only the hard choice left us, of perishing by the sword, or by the waves;* these particulars, which are handed down by historians, exhibit the shocking picture of a people totally destitute of spirit, and unable to collect <36> resolution even from despair.[15] Upon two occasions they obtained from Rome the aid of a military force, by which their enemies were surprised, and repulsed with great slaughter; but the relief which this afforded was merely temporary, and they received a peremptory declaration, that, from the embarrassed condition of the empire, no future supplies of this kind could be spared.*

The consternation of the Britons, in this helpless condition, may easily be conceived, though in the rude annals of that period it is, perhaps, painted with some degree of exaggeration. Time and necessity, however, suggested the means of guarding against the evils to which they were exposed. The proprietors of land possessed a natural influence over the people whom they maintained upon their estates; and this was the source of a jurisdiction, which, during the subsistence of the Roman dominion, had been in great measure extinguished, but which, upon the dissolution of the Roman courts, was of course revived and rendered independent. The same influ-<37>ence

England, the Scots and Picts merged and evolved in the ninth century into the kingdom of Scotland.

* Gildae Hist.—Bedae Hist. Eccles.

15. Flavius Aetius (ca. 390–454): Roman general and consul. "The groans of the British" may be found in Gildas, *The Ruin of Britain and Other Works,* ed. and tr. Michael Winterbottom (London: Phillimore, 1978), 23–24; for the discussion in Bede, see *Bede's Ecclesiastical History of the English People,* ed. Bertram Colgrave and R. A. B. Mynors (Oxford: Clarendon Press, 1969), 47.

enabled these persons to call out their tenants to war, and to assume the direction of their conduct during a military enterprize. By these two branches of authority, a very simple form of government was gradually introduced. The whole country was broken into separate districts, according to the extent of territory in the possession of individuals; and fell under the civil and military power of so many chiefs, the most opulent of whom appear to have been dignified with the title of princes. By the efforts of these leaders, it is likely that private robbery and violence were, in some degree, restrained, and the people were encouraged to return to their tillage and ordinary employments, from the neglect of which, it is said, a famine had been produced. But their great object was to oppose the northern invaders. For this purpose they elected a general of their united forces, upon whom, after the example of the Romans, they bestowed the appellation of the *duke of Britain.* The same person presided in the assemblies held by the chiefs, in which the great affairs of the nation appear to have been determined.

After the government had remained for <38> some time in this channel, Voltigern,[16] one of the most opulent of their princes, was promoted to that high dignity; and upon a new alarm of an invasion from the Scots and Picts, he is said to have called a national council, in which it was agreed to solicit the assistance of the Saxons. As this measure was fatal in its consequences, it has been universally decried, and stigmatised as the height of imprudence; but we ought to consider that it proceeded from the same system of policy which has been practised and approved in all ages, that of courting the alliance of one nation, in order to form a balance against the formidable power of another; and the censures which, in this instance, have been so liberally bestowed upon the Britons, are a plain proof how ready we are to judge of actions from the good or bad success which attends them, or how difficult it is to establish any general rules of conduct; that will not appear grossly defective in a multitude of the particular cases to which they may be applied. <39>

16. Voltigern was the first high king of Britain (r. ca. 425–ca. 466 and ca. 471–ca. 480) in the post-Roman period. It is thought that Voltigern's decision to seek help from Saxon mercenaries was made ca. 449.

ꙮ CHAPTER II ꙮ

Character and Manners of the Saxons.

Of those barbarians who passed under the denomination of Saxons, and who, at the time when they were invited to assist the Britons, inhabited the northern parts of Germany, it is of little moment to ascertain the origin, or to trace the several places in which they had previously resided. The Germans, who subdued the western provinces of the Roman empire, have been supposed to possess a singular character among the rude inhabitants of the world, and to be distinguished by their eminent qualities and virtues. Such an opinion may be ascribed to the elegant description of that people by the masterly pen of Tacitus; to the great revolutions which they atchieved in Europe; and, above all, to that national vanity which is more extravagant than the vanity of individuals, because the multitude of persons who are influenced by the same weakness keep one another in countenance. But there is reason to believe that the ancient inhabitants of Germany exhibited the same <40> dispositions and manners, and adopted similar institutions and customs, to those which may be discovered in such barbarians, of every age or country, as have been placed in similar circumstances.

Deriving their chief subsistence from the pasturing of cattle, they generally possessed considerable wealth in herds and flocks; but as they were little acquainted with tillage, they seem to have had no idea of property in land. Like the early nations described in the Sacred History,[1] they were accustomed frequently to change their abode. Regarding chiefly the interest

1. This comparison of the manners of the Germans to those of the patriarchs in the Hebrew Bible recalls similar passages in the *Origin of the Distinction of Ranks,* where, for example, the biblical history of Jacob illustrates the manners of "those families or tribes of shepherds which were anciently scattered over the country of Arabia." *DR,* 348. For a similar use of biblical history in Adam Smith, see, for example, *LJ,* 405.

of their cattle, they often found it convenient to wander from one place to another, according as they were invited by the prospect of new pastures; and in their migrations, they were under no restraint, either from the cares of husbandry, or from the nature of their possessions.

But while the management of their cattle constituted the ordinary employment of these people, they were also frequently engaged in war. In common with all other barbarous nations, they were much addicted to theft and rapine. The right of property must be long <41> established, before the violations of it can be regarded as heinous offences; and it is necessary that men should be habituated to an extensive intercourse of society, before they are presented with sufficient inducements to sacrifice the immediate profits of fraud and violence, to the distant but superior advantages, derived from their living together upon good terms, and maintaining an amicable correspondence. The ancient Germans, inhabiting a country almost entirely overgrown with wood, or covered with marshes, were often reduced to great scarcity of provisions; and were therefore strongly instigated, by hunger and misery, to prey upon one another. Example, in such a case, found no difficulty to excuse or vindicate what custom had rendered universal.

The rude inhabitants of the earth appear, in all ages and countries, to have been divided into separate tribes and villages; a consequence of their hostile dispositions. When, from accidental circumstances, a family of such people had been planted, at so great a distance from their friends and acquaintance as to prevent all correspondence with them, its members, from inclination, as well as from a re-<42>gard to mutual defence, were usually disposed to live together, and to avoid much intercourse with neighbours by whom they were likely to be treated as enemies. If their multiplication rendered them too numerous to be all maintained under the same roof, they naturally subdivided themselves into different families, who erected their huts beside one another; and if at length their village had been so enlarged as to produce a difficulty in finding subsistence, they were led, by degrees, to remove that inconvenience, by sending out little colonies, with which, notwithstanding their distance, they frequently preserved an alliance and connection. The German tribes became larger and more extensive, according as, by the encrease of their cattle, they were enabled to live in greater affluence. In that part of Germany which was known to the Romans, there have been enumerated about forty different tribes or nations, many of which appear to have enjoyed considerable opulence and power. But concerning the number or extent of the villages belonging to each of these, little or no account can be given.

The political regulations established among <43> the ancient Germans were few and simple, and such as their situation could hardly fail to suggest. Every society, whether great or small, that had occasion to act in a separate military capacity, required a separate leader: for which reason, as every family was under the direction of the father, so every village had its own chief; and at the head of the whole tribe or nation there was a great chief or king. How far the king, or the inferior chiefs, enjoyed their dignity by election, or by hereditary descent; it may be difficult to determine; but their authority was far from being absolute. It was the business of every chief to compose the differences, and, probably, to command the forces, of that village over which he presided. The king too seems to have acted with their advice in the ordinary administration of public affairs; but in matters of great moment, such as the making of laws, or the trial of capital offences, he was obliged to procure the concurrence of a great council, composed of all the heads of families.* <44>

* "In pace, nullus est communis magistratus; sed principes regionum atque pagorum inter suos jus dicunt, controversiasque minuunt. Ubi quis ex principibus in concilio dixit se ducem fore—qui sequi velint prositeantur; consurgunt ii qui et causam et hominem probant, suumque auxilium pollicentur, atque ab multitudine conlaudantur: qui ex iis secuti non sunt, in desertorum ac proditorum numero ducuntur, omniumque iis rerum postea fides derogatur." Caesar de Bel. Gal. 6. § 23. [["In time of peace there is no general officer of state, but the chiefs of districts and cantons do justice among their followers and settle disputes . . . when any of the chiefs has said in public assembly that he will be leader, 'Let those who will follow declare it,' then all who approve the cause and the man rise together to his service and promise their own assistance, and win the general praise of the people. Any of them who have not followed, after promise, are reckoned as deserters and traitors, and in all things afterwards trust is denied to them." Gaius Julius Caesar, *De Bello Gallico,* 6.23. See *The Gallic War,* trans. H. J. Edwards (Cambridge, Mass.: Harvard University Press, 1966), 349. There is material omitted in Millar's Latin text.]]—"Reges ex nobilitate, duces ex virtute sumunt. Nec regibus infinita aut libera potestas; et duces exemplo potius quam imperio, si prompti, si conspicui, si ante aciem agunt, admiratione praesunt."——"De minoribus rebus principes consultant, de majoribus omnes: ita tamen, ut ea quoque, quorum penes plebem arbitrium est, apud principes pertractentur."——"Ut turbae placuit, considunt armati. Silentium per sacerdotes, quibus tum et coercendi jus est, imperatur. Mox rex, vel principes, prout aetas cuique, prout nobilitas, prout decus bellorum prout facundia est, audiuntur, auctoritate suadendi magis quam jubendi potestate."——"Licet apud concilium accusare quoque, et discrimen capitis intendere."——"Eliguntur in iisdem conciliis et principes, qui jura per

The general character of these barbarians was such as might be expected from their manner of life. It consisted not of many features, but they were distinctly and strongly marked. As in the carnivorous brute animals, obliged very often to fight for their food, and exposed to continual strife and contention in the pursuit of mere necessaries, their passions, <45> though excited by few objects, were strong, and violent. Their situation, at the same time, occasioned a wonderful similarity in the dispositions and habits of individuals. In every polished nation, the labour and application of the people is usually so divided, as to produce an endless variety of characters in those who follow different trades and professions. The soldier, the clergyman, the lawyer, the physician, the taylor, the farmer, the smith, the shopkeeper; all those who earn a livelihood by the exercise of separate employments, whether liberal or mechanical, are led, by the different objects in which they are conversant, to contract something peculiar in their behaviour and turn of thinking. But the ancient inhabitants of Germany had made too little progress in arts, to require that a single person should bestow his whole attention upon any one branch of labour, in order to acquire the usual degree of skill and proficiency in it. Every man therefore was accustomed to exercise indiscriminately the few employments with which they were acquainted. Every family built its own cottage, fashioned its own tools and utensils, managed its own cattle, and took precautions for its own <46> support and defence. Thus the whole people, being employed nearly in the same manner, and having no pursuits but such as were suggested by their most

---

pagos vicosque reddunt."—Tacit. de Mor. German. c. 7. 11. 12. [["They take their kings on the ground of birth, their generals on the basis of courage: the authority of their kings is not unlimited or arbitrary; their generals control the people by example rather than command, and by means of the admiration which attends upon energy and a conspicuous place in front of the line. . . . On small matters the chiefs consult; on larger questions the community; but with this limitation, that even the subjects, the decision of which rests with the people, are first handled by the chiefs. . . . when the mob is pleased to begin, they take their seats carrying arms. Silence is called for by the priests, who thenceforward have power also to coerce: then a king or a chief is listened to, in order of age, birth, glory in war, or eloquence, with the prestige which belongs to their counsel rather than with any prescriptive right to command. . . . At this assembly it is also permissible to lay accusations and to bring capital charges. . . . At the same gatherings are selected, among others, chiefs, who administer law through the cantons and villages. . . ." Tacitus, *Germania,* 7, 11, 12. See *Tacitus in Five Volumes,* vol. 1, *Agricola, Germania, Dialogus,* trans. M. Hutton, Sir W. Peterson, et al. (Cambridge, Mass.: Harvard University Press, 1970), 141, 147, 149, 151).]]

immediate wants, were trained up in an uniform sort of discipline, and acquired that uniformity of manners and customs,[2] which is commonly observed in persons of the same trade or profession. Even the nations inhabiting the most distant regions of that extensive country appear to have been no otherwise discriminated than by the different shades of barbarism and ferocity which the climate or situation, more or less favourable to improvement, might easily be supposed to produce.

Among people who are constantly exposed to the attacks of their neighbours, and who are almost continually employed in war, courage and other military qualities are naturally intitled to hold the first rank. There is an *active* and a *passive* courage, which may be distinguished from each other, as they seem to depend upon different principles, and are not always to be found in the same persons. The former is displayed in the voluntary encountering of danger, the latter in bearing pain and <47> distress with firmness and constancy. Valour, which demands a sudden and violent effort of resolution, may be regarded as a masculine quality; while fortitude, which, in many cases, is the fruit of calmer but more continued exertion, is often conspicuous in the weaker sex. In order that, with our eyes open, we may expose our lives to imminent danger, we must be excited by a strong desire of procuring esteem and applause, either from others, or from the reflection of our own minds. Efforts of this kind, it is evident, are most likely to be made in those countries where, from long practice, and frequent emulation in fighting, martial exploits have come to be universally admired, and looked upon by every one as the infallible road to honour and distinction. Fortitude under pain and distress may, on the contrary, be promoted by the opposite circumstances, by the want of sensibility, or by a conviction that our sufferings are beheld with unconcern and indifference. To complain or repine, in the midst of affliction, is an attempt to procure relief, or at least compassion, from others; and when we find that our complaints are disregarded, or treated with scorn and deri-<48>sion, we are led to exert our utmost resolution in order to smother and restrain them.

2. Millar's observations on the uniformity of manners in a society without the division of labor recall Smith's teaching. "The difference of employment occasions the difference of genius; and we see accordingly that amongst savages, where there is very little diversity of employment, there is hardly any diversity of temper or genius." *LJ,* 348. See also his observations on the ways the division of labor results in the differentiation of talents in *WN,* 1:28.

The savages, who live by hunting and fishing, are placed in a situation more favourable to fortitude than to valour.[3] Exposed by their manner of life to innumerable hardships and calamities, they are too much loaded by the pressure of their own wants and sufferings, to feel very sensibly those of their neighbours. They disdain, therefore, to solicit that sympathy, which they know by experience will not be afforded them; and having, from their daily occurrences, been long inured to pain, they learn to bear it with astonishing firmness, and even to endure every species of torture without complaining. As, on the other hand, they live in very small societies, and, in order to find subsistence, are obliged to remove their different villages to a great distance from one another, they are not apt to be engaged in frequent or extensive military enterprizes, nor to attain any degree of refinement in the methods of conducting their hostilities. The punctilios of military honour are unknown to them. They scruple not to take any unfair advantage in fighting, and can seldom be <49> brought to expose themselves in the open field. The unrelenting and blood-thirsty Indian of America is accustomed to lie concealed for weeks, that he may have a convenient opportunity of shooting his enemy, and may then with safety enter his cabin, to rob and murder the family.

Nations who subsist by pasturing cattle, as they live in larger societies, and are supplied with food in greater abundance, are more at leisure, and have greater incitements to cultivate their social dispositions. But their magnanimity, in bearing pain and affliction with apparent unconcern, is naturally diminished by their advancement in humanity; and according as individuals discover that their distresses meet with greater attention from their companions and acquaintance, they are more encouraged to display their sufferings, and to seek the tender consolation of pity, by giving way to the expression of sorrow and uneasiness. They are also likely to acquire a much higher degree of the military spirit. The wandering life of shepherds is the occasion of bringing frequently into the same neighbourhood a variety of stranger tribes; among whom any <50> accidental jealousy, or interference of interest, is apt to kindle animosity, and to produce quarrels and hostilities. In the frequent wars that arise from such a situation, and which are carried

3. Adam Ferguson, similarly, writes: "The principal point of honour among the rude nations of America . . . is fortitude." *Essay on the History of Civil Society,* ed. Fania Oz-Salzberger (Cambridge: Cambridge University Press, 1995), 90.

on with the ardour and ferocity natural to barbarians, the victors, having no fixed residence, are at full liberty to prosecute their success without interruption; and as, in every migration, such people are obliged to carry along with them their wives, and children, and servants, together with their herds and flocks, and even their furniture and utensils, a decisive battle never fails to reduce one tribe completely under the power of another. With the same ease with which the conquerors may pursue their victory, they can incorporate with themselves the vanquished party, and make use of their assistance in any future enterprize. Thus by repeated successes, and by a gradual accumulation of forces, a single tribe may, in a short time, become so powerful, as to meet with no enemy in a condition to cope with them, and be excited with great rapidity to overrun and subdue a vast extent of country. History is accordingly filled with the rapid and extensive conquests made by nations in <51> this early state of society; of which, in particular, there occur many celebrated examples among the Arabs and Tartars.

Such was the condition of the ancient Germans; of whom it is remarked by the historian, that they were less distinguished by their patience of labour, or by their capacity to bear the extremities of heat and cold, of hunger and of thirst, than by their active courage, and their ardent love of military reputation.* "They are more easily persuaded," says Tacitus, "to march against an enemy, and to expose themselves in the field, than to plough the earth, and to wait the returns of the season. They account it unmanly to acquire with sweat what may be procured with blood. When they engage in battle, it is a disgrace for the chief to be surpassed in valour; it is a disgrace for his followers not to equal the bravery of their chief; it is perpetual infamy to escape with safety, after the fall of their leader. To defend and protect his person, to devolve upon him the glory <52> of all their brave actions, is the principal point of honour. The chiefs fight for victory, their followers for the reputation and dignity of the chief."†

* Laboris atque operum non eadem patientia; minimeque sitim aestumque tolerare, frigora atque inediam coelo solove assueverunt. Tacit. de Mor. German. c. 4. [["Not correspondingly tolerant of labor and hard work, and by no means habituated to bearing thirst and heat; to cold and hunger, thanks to the climate and the soil, they are accustomed." Tacitus, *Germania,* 4. See *Tacitus in Five Volumes,* 1:137.]]

† Tacit. de Mor. German. c. 14. [[For a modern translation of this passage, see *Agricola and Germany,* trans. Anthony R. Birley (Oxford: Oxford University Press, 1999), 44. For a similar summary, also derived from Tacitus, see Ferguson, *Essay,* 96.]]

The same circumstances which gave rise to frequent hostilities between the members of different tribes, produced a strong attachment between the individuals belonging to each of those little societies. United by a sense of their common danger, and by their common animosity, against all their neighbours, they were frequently required by their situation to defend and relieve one another, and even to hazard their lives for their mutual safety. Living in a small circle of acquaintance, and having scarcely any intercourse with the rest of mankind, they naturally contracted such prejudices and prepossessions as tended to flatter their own vanity, and to increase their partial regard for that village or tribe of which they were members. But however warmly attached to their kindred and friends, it could not be expected that, in their ordinary behaviour, they would exhibit much delicacy or <53> refinement of manners. They were too little acquainted with the dictates of prudence and sober reflection, to be capable of restraining the irregular sallies of passion; and too little conversant in the arts of polished society, to acquire a facility of yielding up their own opinions, and of sacrificing their own inclinations and humours, to those of their companions. The head of every family, unaccustomed to bear opposition or controul, demanded an implicit submission and obedience from all its members. When he met with great provocation, it was not unusual for him to take away the life of a servant; and this was regarded as an exercise of domestic authority, for which he could not be subjected to any punishment.* Even the feelings of natural affection did not prevent the children from being, in like manner, subjected to the arbitrary power of the father, and from experiencing, on many occasions, the unhappy effects of his casual displeasure. Neither does the condition of the mother appear to have been <54> superior to that of her children: the little attention which, in a rude age, is usually bestowed upon the pleasures of sex, and the inferiority of the women in strength, courage and military accomplishments, deprived them of that rank and consequence which they enjoyed in a civilized nation. There is great reason to believe that the husband commonly bought his wife from her father, or other male relations, and that he considered her in the light of a servant or slave. If she

* "Occidere solent, non disciplina et severitate, sed impetu et ira, ut inimicum, nisi quod impune." Tacit. de Mor. German. c. 25. [["If they are killed, it is not usually to preserve strict discipline, but in a fit of fury, like an enemy, except that there is no penalty to be paid." Tacitus, *Germania,* 25. See *Tacitus in Five Volumes,* 1:169.]]

was guilty of adultery (a crime which, from the general simplicity of manners, was probably not very frequent, but which, by introducing a connection with a stranger, was highly prejudicial to the interest of the family) the punishment inflicted by the husband, was that of stripping her naked, turning her out of doors, and whipping her through the village.*

In the intercourse of different families, and in their common amusements, their behaviour <55> was suited to the spirit and disposition of a martial, but rude and ignorant people. Their military life, which was incompatible with industry, prevented the growth of avarice, the usual attendant of constant labour and application in every lucrative profession. Their employments were such as united them by a common tie, instead of suggesting the idea of a separate interest, or engaging them in that struggle for riches, by which the pursuits of every man are, in some measure, opposed to those of his neighbour. Their herds and flocks, in which their wealth principally consisted, being under the management and direction of a whole village or tribe, were considered, in some sort, as the joint property of all; so far at least, as to render individuals willing, on all occasions, to relieve their mutual wants, by sharing their goods with one another. Hence that hospitality and generosity which is so conspicuous among shepherd nations in all parts of the world. "No nation," says the author above quoted,[†] "is more hospitable than the Germans. They make no difference, in <56> this respect, between a stranger and an acquaintance. When a person has been liberally entertained in one house, he is conducted to another, where he is received with the same hearty welcome. If a guest, at his departure, should ask a present from his entertainers, it is seldom refused; and they will ask any thing of him with the same freedom. They are fond of making presents, which are scarcely understood to lay the receiver under any obligation."[4]

Their military operations, no doubt, required a violent, though an irregular and transient exertion; but upon the conclusion of an expedition they were completely at liberty to indulge themselves in rest and idleness. From

* Tacit. de Mor. German. c. 18. 19. The conformity of the German manners with those of other barbarous nations, in relation to the condition of women and children, I have endeavoured to illustrate, in a treatise entitled, *An Enquiry into the Origin of Ranks.* [[See *DR,* especially chap. 1, "Of the Rank and Condition of Women in Different Ages."]]

† Tacit. de Mor. Germ. § 21.

4. For a modern translation of this passage, see *Agricola and Germany,* trans. Anthony R. Birley (Oxford: Oxford University Press, 1999), 48–49.

these opposite situations, they contracted opposite habits, and became equally restless and slothful. When not engaged in the field, the warriors disdained to assist in domestic offices,[5] they even seldom exercised themselves in hunting; but, leaving the care of their cattle, and of their houshold, to the women and children, or to the old and infirm, they were accustomed to pass their time in listless indolence, having little other enjoyment but what they derived <57> from food or from sleep.* That from such dispositions they found great delight in convivial entertainments, and were given to great excesses in eating and drinking, may easily be supposed. By the pleasures of intoxication, they sought to dissipate the gloom of that languor and weariness with which they were oppressed, and to enliven the barren prospect which the ordinary course of their thoughts and sentiments was capable of presenting to them. For the same reason they were addicted to games of hazard; insomuch that persons who had lost their whole fortune at play would afterwards, it is said, venture to stake their liberty; and having still been unlucky, would voluntarily become the slaves of the winner.† The prac-

* "Quoties bella non ineunt, non multum venationibus, plus per otium transigunt, dediti somno, ciboque. Fortissimus quisque ac bellicosissimus nihil agens, delegata domus et penatium et agrorum cura foeminis senibusque, et infirmissimo cuique ex familia, ipsi hebent mira diversitate naturae, cum iidem homines sic ament inertium et oderint quietem." Tacit. de Mor. Germ. c. 15. [["When they are not entering on war, they spend [not] much time in hunting, but more in idleness—creatures who eat and sleep, the best and bravest warriors doing nothing, having handed over the charge of their home, hearth, and estate to the women and the old men and the weakest members of the family: for themselves they lounge about, by that curious incongruity of temperament which makes of the same men such lovers of laziness and such haters of quiet." Tacitus, *Germania,* 15. See *Tacitus in Five Volumes,* 1:153, 1:155.]]

—"Diem noctemque continuare potando nulli probrum." Ibid. c. 22. [["To make day and night run into one in drinking is a reproach to no man." Tacitus, *Germania,* 22. See *Tacitus in Five Volumes,* 1:165.]]

† Aleam (quod mirere) sobrii inter seria exercent, tanta lucrandi perdendique temeritate, ut cum omnia defecerunt, extremo ac novissimo jactu de libertate et de corpore contendant. Victus voluntariam servitutem adit. Quamvis junior, quamvis robustior, adligari se ac venire patitur. Ea est in re prava pervicacia: ipsi fidem vocant. Tac. de Mor. Germ. c. 24. [["Gambling, one may be surprised to find, they practise as one of their serious pastimes in their sober hours, with such recklessness in winning or losing that, when all else has been lost, they stake personal liberty on a last and final throw: the loser faces voluntary slavery: though he be the younger and the stronger man, he suffers himself to be bound and sold; such is their persistence in a wicked practice, or their good faith, as they themselves style it." Tacitus, *Germania,* 24. See *Tacitus in Five Volumes,* 1:167.]]

5. As Ferguson notes, "Every servile occupation they commit to women or slaves." *Essay,* 97.

<58>tice of gaming must have been carried to a high pitch, when fashion, even among such barbarians, had made it a point of honour to discharge a game-debt of that extraordinary nature. It is observable, that in countries where men have exhausted the enjoyments arising from the possession of great riches, they are apt to feel the same want of exercise and occupation, as in that simple age when they have not yet contracted those habits of industry by which wealth is acquired; and they are forced to make use of the same expedient to deliver them from that *taedium vitae,*[6] which is the most oppressive of all misfortunes. The opposite extremes of society appear in this respect to coincide; and excessive gaming is therefore the vice, not only of the most opulent and luxurious nations, but of the most rude and barbarous.

Among all the German nations, the Saxons, who appear to have been scattered over the pe-<59>ninsula of Jutland,[7] and along the neighbouring shores of the Baltick Sea, were the most fierce and barbarous, as they were most completely removed from that civility and improvement which every where attended the progress of the Roman arms. Their maritime situation, at the same time, had produced an early acquaintance with navigation, and had even qualified them to undertake piratical expeditions to several countries at a distance. They had, accordingly, long infested the coasts of Britain and Gaul; insomuch that in the former country it was found necessary to appoint a military officer, with a regular force, to guard against their depredations.

Making allowance, however, for such differences as might arise from this peculiarity of situation, their character and manners were similar to those of the other inhabitants of Germany, and, in general, to those of the wandering tribes of shepherds in every age or country.

Upon the whole, when we examine the accounts delivered by the best historians, concerning the ancient inhabitants of Germany, as well as the Saxons in particular, we find <60> nothing, either in their public or private institutions, or in their habits and ways of thinking, which we can reasonably suppose to have occasioned any peculiarity in the government established by the latter people in Britain. Whatever peculiarity therefore is observable in the Anglo-Saxon government, it must have arisen from causes posterior

6. Weariness of life.

7. Peninsula that forms part of Denmark.

to the migration of that people into Britain; from the nature of the country in which they settled; from the manner in which their settlements were formed; or from other more recent events and circumstances.

Some writers fondly imagine,[8] that they can discover, in the political state of the Saxons, while they remained in their native forests, the seeds of that constitution which grew up in England during the government of the Anglo-Saxon princes. With respect to those innate principles of liberty which have been ascribed to this people, it must be observed, that in proportion as mankind recede from civilized manners, and approach to the infancy of society, they are less accustomed to authority, and discover greater aversion to every sort of restraint or controul. In this sense the <61> Saxons may be said to have possessed a stronger relish for freedom than many of the other German tribes; as the present Indians of America, who are mere hunters and fishers, discover a still freer spirit than appeared among the Saxons. But as this love of liberty proceeds from the mere want of the common means of improvement, and from no original peculiarity of character, it is not likely to be retained by such barbarians, after they have opportunities of improving their condition, by acquiring property, and by extending the connexions of society. When the Saxons in Britain became as opulent as the German or Scythian tribes, who settled in other provinces of the Roman empire, there is no reason to believe, that in consequence of their primitive poverty and barbarism, they were with more difficulty reduced into a state of subordination, and submission to civil authority. The ancestors of almost every civilized people may be traced back to the most rude and savage state, in which they have an equal title to be distinguished, as men impatient of all restraint, and unacquainted with the commands of a superior. <62>

8. Many political writers traced English liberty to Saxon origins, a view that is often associated with the idea that the Norman conquest had deprived Englishmen for a time of this inheritance (a position sometimes referred to as "the Norman yoke"). Among those who, in quite different ways, emphasized the Saxon heritage were the Whig jurist William Blackstone (1723–80) and the Tory statesman Henry St. John, Viscount Bolingbroke (1678–1751).

CHAPTER III

Settlement of the Saxons in Britain.

The Saxons accepted with joy and alacrity the proposals made to them by the Britons; and it appears to have been stipulated, that they should immediately send a body of troops into Britain, to be employed in the defence of the country, and to receive a stated hire during the continuance of their services.* In consequence of this agreement, Hengist and Horsa,[1] two brothers, and persons of distinction among the Saxons, with about sixteen hundred followers, landed in the isle of Thanet, in the year 449; and having defeated the Picts and Scots, confined them, in a short time, within their ancient boundaries. The Saxon troops, immediately after, were stationed by Voltigern partly upon the confines of <63> the northern wall, and partly upon the Kentish coast, the two places that had been usually secured with garrisons under the late dominion of the Romans. In such a situation these auxiliaries, who formed the principal strength of the country, could hardly fail to perceive their own importance, and to entertain the design of extorting a permanent settlement from the inhabitants. With this view, Heng-

* Stillingfleet Orig. Brit.—Bede says, that the Saxons first took occasion to quarrel with the Britons, by demanding an increase of their *allowance,* to which he gives the name of *annona.* Hist. Eccles. lib. i. c. 15.

1. Hengist and Horsa (d. 488 and 455, respectively) were brothers who invaded England from Jutland. They are supposed to have landed on the Isle of Thanet at Ebbsfleet, on the Kentish coast of England. Millar's generalizing approach to the early historians can be compared with Hume's exasperation. Noting that the Saxon leaders, Hengist and Horsa, claimed descent from the god Woden, he writes: "It is evident what fruitless labour it must be to search, in those barbarous and illiterate ages, for the annals of a people, when their first leaders, known in any true history, were believed by them to be the fourth in descent from a fabulous deity, or from a man, exalted by ignorance into that character." *HE,* 1:17.

ist is said to have persuaded the Britons to hire an additional number of his countrymen, as the only effectual means for securing themselves from the future incursions of the enemy; and, upon an application for that purpose, was joined by a new body of Saxons, amounting to five thousand men. By this reinforcement he found himself superior to the disjointed and unwarlike forces of the country. Having therefore secretly concluded a treaty of peace with the Picts and Scots, and pretending that the articles of the original agreement, with relation to the pay of his troops, had not been observed, he ventured to throw off the mask, and openly to make war upon the Britons. His example was followed by other adventurers, among the same people, who, at the head of <64> different parties, allured by the hope of plunder, and of a new settlement, invaded the coasts of Britain, and endeavoured to penetrate into the country. Their attempts were crowned with success, and the most valuable part of the Island was at length reduced under their dominion. This great event, however, was not accomplished without a violent struggle, nor in less than a hundred and seventy years; during which time many battles were fought, with various fortune. It is remarkable that, notwithstanding their fears and pusillanimity, when first abandoned by the Romans, the Britons, in the course of their long-continued contest with the Saxons, defended themselves with more obstinate resolution, than, upon the downfal of the Roman empire, was discovered by any of the other provinces, though supported by the armies of Rome. The want of any foreign assistance was, in all probability, the cause of this vigorous and spirited behaviour; as it called forth the exertion of their powers, and produced in them a degree of courage and discipline, which the provinces enjoying the protection of the Roman government were not under the same necessity of acquiring. <65>

We have no full account of the circumstances attending the settlement of the Saxons in Britain; but we may form an idea of the manner in which it was completed, from the general situation of the people, from the imperfect relations of this event by our early historians, and from the more distinct information that has been transmitted concerning the settlement of other German nations, in some of the Roman provinces upon the continent of Europe.

The followers of any particular leader having gained a victory, became the masters of a certain territory, and enriched themselves with the spoil of their enemies. Willing to secure what they had obtained, they were led afterwards to offer terms of accommodation to the vanquished; with whom they appear, on some occasions, to have made a formal division of their land and other possessions. But even in those cases, where no express treaty of this nature had been formed, the same effects were produced, from the mere situation of the combatants; and upon the conclusion of a war, the parties were understood to have the property of the respective districts which they had been <66> able to occupy or to retain. Such of the Britons as had been made captives in war were doubtless, in conformity to the general practice of the ancient Germans, reduced into a state of servitude; but those who had escaped this misfortune resided in the neighbourhood of the Saxons, and often maintained a friendly intercourse with them.

The ambition, however, and avidity of these barbarians, incited them, at a future period, to renew their former hostilities; and these were generally followed by new victories, and by a farther extension of conquest. In this manner, after a long course of time, the country was completely subdued by these invaders; and the ancient inhabitants were, according to accidental circumstances, partly degraded into a state of slavery, and partly, by particular treaties, and by long habits of communication, incorporated with the conquerors.

From the declamatory representations of some early annalists, the greater part of historians have been led to suppose, that such of the Britons as escaped captivity were either put to death by their barbarous enemies, or, disdaining submission, and expecting no mercy, <67> retired into Wales, or withdrew into the country of *Armorica* in France, to which, from them, the name of *Bretagne* has been given. An acute and industrious antiquary, Mr. Whitaker,[2] has lately shown, I think in a satisfactory manner, that this extraordinary supposition is without any solid foundation. That many of the Britons were at that period subjected to great hardships, and, in order to save themselves from the fury of their enemies, were even obliged to quit their native country, may be easily believed; but that the Saxons were animated with such uncommon barbarity, as would lead them, in direct opposition to their own interest, to root out the ancient inhabitants, must appear highly improbable. Of the total extirpation of any people, by the most furious con-

2. John Whitaker (1735–1808): British historian and author of the *History of Manchester,* 2 vols. (London, 1771–75), as well as *The Genuine History of the Britons Asserted* (1773).

querors, the records of well authenticated history afford not many examples. It is known, at the same time, that no such cruelty was exhibited by any of the German nations who conquered the other provinces of the Roman empire; and it must be admitted, that the situation of all those nations was very much the same with that of the Saxons, as also that they were a people in all respects of <68> similar manners and customs. There is even complete evidence that, in some parts of the Island, the Britons were so far from being extirpated, that they were permitted to retain a certain proportion of the landed property; and it is remarkable, that this proportion, being a third part of the whole, was the same with that retained by the ancient inhabitants in some of those provinces, upon the continent of Europe, which were conquered by the other German tribes. Though, in other cases, the vestiges of such early transactions have not been preserved, it is highly probable that a similar division of the land was made, either by express contract, or by tacit agreement. There can be no reason to believe that the same Saxons would, in one part of the Island, exhibit such moderation and humanity to the vanquished people, and in another, such unprecedented ferocity and barbarity.

It is further to be observed, that the language which grew up in Britain after the settlement of the Saxons, and in which a large proportion of the *British* and the *Latin* tongues were incorporated with the *Saxon,* affords a sufficient proof that the inhabitants were compounded <69> of the different nations by whom these languages were spoken.

When the Saxons invaded Britain, they were entirely a pastoral people; but as they came into a country which had been long cultivated, they could scarcely fail to acquire very rapidly a considerable knowledge of agriculture. Having obtained a quantity of land that was formerly employed in tillage, and having procured a proportionable number of servants, already acquainted with the various branches of husbandry, it may easily be imagined that they would avail themselves of this favourable situation, for the prosecution of an employment so conducive to their comfortable subsistence.

In consequence of a general attention to agriculture, they must have been induced to quit the wandering life; since, in order to practise the employment of a farmer with any advantage, a continued residence upon the same spot is necessary. In the occupancy and appropriation of landed estates, those persons who had been most connected in war were most likely to become neighbours; and every little knot of kindred and friends were com<70>monly led to build their houses together, that they might be in readiness to assist one another in their labour, and to unite in defending their possessions. The villages of German shepherds were thus converted into villages of husbandmen, which, in proportion to the progress of their arms, and to their advances in improvement, were gradually enlarged and spread over the country. It should seem that, upon the first settlement of the Saxons, the whole people were distributed into little societies of this kind; and no individual was so opulent, that he could expect to live in security, without maintaining an alliance and intimate communication with others. This custom of resorting to villages, introduced by necessity, in times of extreme barbarism and disorder, is even at present retained by many of the farmers in England; although, from a total change of manners and circumstances, it is evident that a separate residence, upon their different farms, would often be much more convenient.

While the Saxons, by their intercourse with a more civilized people, were thus excited to a considerable improvement of their circumstances, the Britons were, from an opposite situa-<71>tion, degraded in the same proportion, and continued to sink in ignorance and barbarism. Engaged in a desperate conflict, in which every thing dear to them was at stake, and having to cope with an enemy little practised in the refinements of humanity, they were obliged, in their own defence, to retaliate those injuries which they were daily receiving; and by the frequent exercise of depredation, they became inured to rapine and injustice. The destructive wars, in the mean time, which were incessantly kindled, and which raged with so much violence in every quarter of the country, were fatal to the greater part of its improvements. The numerous towns which had been raised under the protection and security of the Roman government, and which now became the usual refuge of the weaker party, were often sacked by the victorious enemy, and after being gradually depopulated, were at length either laid in ruins, or left in the state of insignificant villages. In those times of universal terror and confusion, the ancient schools and seminaries of learning were abandoned, and every person who cultivated the arts subservient to luxury and refinement, was <72> forced to desert such useless occupations, and betake himself to employments more immediately requisite for preservation and subsistence. In the course of two centuries, within which the conquest of the more accessible and valuable parts of Britain was completed, the monuments of Roman opulence and grandeur were entirely erased; and the Britons who remained in the country, and who retained their liberty, adopted the same manner of life with their Saxon neighbours, from whom they were no longer distinguishable, either by the places of their residence, or by their usages and political institutions.

Those conquerors of Britain who received the general appellation of Saxons had issued from different parts of the German coast, at some distance from one another, and belonged to different tribes or nations: they have been divided, by historians, into three great branches, the *Angles,* the *Jutes,* and the *Saxons,*[3] properly so called. As the leaders of the several parties belonging to any of these divisions possessed a separate influence over their own adherents, and prosecuted their enterprises in different parts of the country, so they naturally <73> rejected all ideas of subordination, and endeavoured to acquire a regal authority; the result of which was, that, after various turns of fortune, no less than seven independent states, each under its own particular monarch, were at length established.

The followers of Hengist and Horsa, composed of Jutes, acquired a settlement in the east corner of the Island, and established their dominion in what is now the county of Kent. Different parties of the proper Saxons occupied a much larger territory, and laid the foundations of three different kingdoms. Those who, from their situation, were called the Southern Saxons, established themselves in the counties of Sussex and Surrey; the West Saxons extended their authority over the counties to the westward, along the southern coast; and the East Saxons took possession of Essex, Middlesex, and a considerable part of Hertfordshire. The Angles were still more numerous, and the territories which they occupied were much more extensive. By them was formed the kingdom of the East Angles, in the counties of Cambridge, Norfolk, and Suffolk; that of Northumberland, extending over <74> all the country which these barbarians had subdued, from the Humber to the Friths of Forth; and that of Mercia, comprehending the inland counties, which were in a manner included by the other kingdoms of the Heptarchy.[4]

In the western part of the Island, from the Land's-End to the Frith of

3. The Jutes and the Angles are believed to have come to Britain from the northern and southern parts of the Danish peninsula, respectively. The Saxons came from northern Germany.

4. The Heptarchy refers to the seven most significant English kingdoms of the later Anglo-Saxon period: Wessex, Kent, Sussex, Essex, East Anglia, Mercia, and Northumberland.

Clyde, the ancient inhabitants were still able to maintain their independence; and in this large tract of country were erected four British principalities or kingdoms; those of Cornwall, of South Wales, of North Wales, and of Cumberland. To the North of the Friths of Forth and Clyde the Picts and Scots retained their ancient possessions.

The changes produced in the manners and customs of the Saxons, by their settlement in Britain, were such as might be expected, from the great change of situation which the people experienced, in passing from the state of shepherds to that of husbandmen.[5] As in following the employment of the latter, they necessarily quitted the wandering life, and took up a fixed residence, they were enabled to acquire *property in land;* with which it is probable they were formerly unacquainted. The <75> introduction of landed property among mankind has uniformly proceeded from the advancement of agriculture, by which they were led to cultivate the same ground for many years successively; and upon the principle that every man has a right to enjoy the fruit of his own labour, became entitled, first, to the immediate crops they had raised, and afterwards to the future possession of the ground itself, in order that they might obtain the benefit of the improvement which their long cultivation had produced. In this appropriation, of so great importance to society, the Saxons in Britain were undoubtedly stimulated, and instructed, from the cultivated state of the country, as well as from the example of the people whom they had subdued.

This alteration in their circumstances had necessarily a mighty influence upon the conduct of their military operations. As a great part of their property was now incapable of being transported, the inhabitants of each village were induced to fortify, in some degree, the place of their abode, for the preservation of their most valuable effects; and therefore, in going out to meet an enemy, instead of carrying along with them their cattle, and other <76> moveables, and being accompanied by their wives and children, as well as by the aged and infirm (the usual practice in the pastoral life) none but the actual warriors had occasion to take the field. The immediate plunder, therefore, arising from a victory, was rendered more inconsiderable; and even

5. This description of the advance of the Saxons from wandering pastoralists to settled agriculturalists follows the stadial outline set out by Smith in *LJ,* 14–16, 404–9, and which forms a major theme of *Distinction of Ranks.* See also Adam Ferguson, *Essay on the History of Civil Society,* ed. Fania Oz-Salzberger (Cambridge: Cambridge University Press, 1995), 94ff.

this the victors were commonly obliged to secure at home, before they could conveniently undertake a new enterprize. Thus, after the settlement of the Saxons in Britain, they were less in a condition to carry on wars at a great distance; and they appear to have laid aside, for the most part, their foreign piratical expeditions.

The permanent residence of the people tended likewise to open a regular communication between different villages; the inhabitants of which, by remaining constantly in the same neighbourhood, were led by degrees to contract a more intimate acquaintance. From the acquisition of landed possessions, which by their nature are less capable than moveables of being defended by the vigilance and personal prowess of the possessor, the necessity of the public interposition, and of public regulations for the security of property, must have been <77> more universally felt. From these causes, it is natural to suppose that the connections of society were gradually multiplied, and that the ideas of justice, as well as of policy and government, which had been entertained by the primitive Saxons, were considerably extended and improved.

The introduction of landed property[6] contributed, on the other hand, to increase the influence and authority of individuals, by enabling them to maintain upon their estates a greater number of dependents than can be supported by persons whose possessions are merely moveable. The heads or leaders of particular families were thus raised to greater consideration; and, in the respective communities of which they were members, obtained more completely the exclusive direction and management of public affairs. The influence of the great leader, or prince, by whom they were conducted in their common expeditions, was proportioned, in like manner, to his private estate, and extended little farther than to his own tenants; for which reason, in the several kingdoms of the Heptarchy, the sovereign possessed a very limited authority, and the <78> principal powers of government were lodged in a *Wittenagemote,* or national council, composed of the independent proprietors, or leading men in the state.

Although the monarchs of these different kingdoms claimed an independent sovereignty, yet, in their struggles with the Britons, they often procured assistance from one another, and were combined against the ancient

6. Millar discusses the consequences of landed property throughout the *Distinction of Ranks.* See, for example, *DR,* 71–72.

inhabitants of the country, their common enemies. The direction of their forces was, on those occasions, committed to some particular monarch, who, in conducting their joint measures, was frequently under the necessity of calling a wittenagemote, or great council, from all the confederated kingdoms. Thus the idea of a permanent union among all the kingdoms of the Heptarchy, and of a leader, or chief magistrate, at the head of that large community, together with a set of regulations extending to all its members, was gradually suggested: according to the opulence or abilities of the different Saxon princes, they were, by turns, promoted to that supreme dignity; which became, of course, the great object of their ambition, and the source of those violent <79> animosities which, for a period of about two hundred years, continually subsisted among them. The most powerful of the states belonging to this confederacy were those of Wessex, Mercia, and Northumberland, to which the rest were gradually reduced into a kind of subordination; till at length, about the year 827, the several kingdoms of the Heptarchy were subdued by Egbert,[7] the king of the West Saxons, who transmitted to his posterity the sovereignty of those extensive dominions. The same prince extended his authority over all the Britons on the south side of the Bristol channel, and became master of a considerable part of Wales, and of the Cumbrian kingdom. From this time the distinctions among the different Saxon states were in a great measure abolished, and the several territories, united under Egbert, received the general name of England; as the people, from the union of the two principal nations, and in contradistinction to their countrymen in Germany, were called the Anglo-Saxons.

Several circumstances appear to have contributed to the accomplishment of this great revolution. With the bravery and military <80> accomplishments usual among the chiefs and princes of that age, Egbert, who had been educated in the court of Charles the great,[8] is said to have united an uncommon degree of political knowledge and abilities. His own kingdom, situated along the southern coast of Britain, was probably the most improved, if not the most extensive, of those which had been erected by the Anglo-Saxons. In almost all the other kingdoms of the Heptarchy, a failure of the lineal

7. Egbert, king of Wessex (r. 802–39): commonly recognized as the first king of a united England.

8. Charlemagne, or Carolus Magnus: king of the Franks (r. 768–814) and Holy Roman Emperor (r. 800–814).

heirs of the crown had given rise, among the principal nobility, to a contest about the succession: Northumberland, in particular, was weakened by intestine disorders, and in no condition to resist a foreign power; so that, by the conquest of Mercia, the only other independent state, the king of Wessex was left without a competitor, and found no difficulty in establishing an universal sovereignty.* <81>

There can be no doubt that the reduction of all these different kingdoms into one monarchy contributed to improve the police of the country, and to civilize the manners of the people. The scene of anarchy and violence which was constantly exhibited during the conquest of Britain by the Saxons was incompatible with any attention to the arts of civil life, and in a great measure extinguished the remains of Roman improvement. The beginning of the seventh century, which falls about the conclusion of that period, may, therefore, be regarded as the aera of greatest darkness and barbarism in the modern history of Britain. The advances, however, that were made, even after this period had elapsed, were very slow and gradual. So long as the country was divided into a number of petty states, independent of each other, and therefore often engaged in mutual hostilities, the persons and property of individuals were not secured in such a manner as to encourage the exercise of useful employments.

It appears, indeed, that the monarchs in several of those kingdoms were anxious to prevent disorders among their subjects, and, with <82> the assistance of their national councils, made a variety of statutes, by which the punishment of particular crimes was defined with great exactness. Such were the laws of Ethelbert,[9] and some of his successors, in the kingdom of Kent; those of Ina,[10] the king of the West Saxons; and Offa,[11] of the Mercians.† These regulations, however, were probably of little avail, from the numerous

* It must not however be supposed that the power of all the kings of the Heptarchy was at this period entirely destroyed; they retained a subordinate authority, founded upon their great property. The princes of Northumberland and Mercia still retained the title of *king;* and in the reign of Alfred we find them still claiming independence.—See William of Malmsbury.

† See the Collections of the two former, in Wilkins Leg. Anglo-Sax.—The laws of king Offa have not been preserved.

9. Ethelbert: king of Kent (r. ca. 560–ca. 616), the first English king to issue a law code.

10. Ina: king of Wessex (r. 688–726).

11. Offa: king of Mercia (r. 757–96).

independent states into which the country was divided; because an offender might easily escape from justice, by taking sanctuary in the territories of a rival or hostile nation; but when the different kingdoms of the Heptarchy were united under one sovereign, private wars were more effectually discouraged, justice was somewhat better administered, and the laws established throughout the Anglo-Saxon dominions were reduced to greater uniformity. We are not, however, to imagine that, from this period, the same regulations in all respects were extended over the whole English monarchy. The system of private law, being formed in good measure by <83> long usage, was necessarily different in different districts; and the customs which prevailed in the more considerable had obtained a currency in the smaller states of the Heptarchy. Thus we find that the law of the West Saxons was extended over all the states on the south side of the Thames,* while the law of the Mercians was introduced into several territories adjacent to that kingdom.† In a subsequent period a third set of regulations, probably a good deal different from the two former, was adopted in the northern and eastern parts of the country. <84>

* Called Westsaxenlaga.

† Called Mercenlaga. The inhabitants were denominated, from the kind of law which they observed. See Ran. Higden Polychron.—In France the Pays de Droit écrit and the Pays des Coutumes, were distinguished from a similar circumstance. [[*Pays de Droit écrit:* district of statute law (i.e., the south of France); *Pays des Coutumes:* district of customary law (i.e., the north of France).]]

ꕥ CHAPTER IV ꕥ

Similarity in the Situation of the Anglo-Saxons, and of the other Barbarians who settled in the Provinces of the Western Empire.—How far the State of all those Nations differed from that of every other People, ancient or modern.

During the same century in which the Anglo-Saxons began their settlements in England, the other provinces of the western empire were invaded by a multitude of rude nations, from Germany and the more easterly parts of the world. Allured by the prospect of booty, these barbarians had long made accidental incursions upon the frontier provinces; and having, by repeated successes, discovered the weakness of the Roman state, they at length endeavoured to gain more solid advantages, by settling in the countries which they had subdued. The Roman emperors were not only obliged to submit to these encroachments, but were even forced, in many cases, to enter into an alliance with those invaders, to employ them <85> as auxiliaries in the armies of Rome, and to bestow upon them landed possessions, upon condition of their defending the country. But these were merely temporary expedients, which in the end contributed to increase the power of the barbarians. Different swarms of these people advancing in succession, and pushing each other forward in quest of new possessions, continued to penetrate into the Roman dominions, and at last entirely overran and dismembered the western provinces. The Franks, the Burgundians, and the Wisigoths settled in Gaul.[1] Another branch of the Wisigoths established their

1. Gaul is traditionally represented as encompassing the approximate geographic area of modern France, less its easternmost territories. The migration of these Germanic

dominion in Spain. Africa became a prey to the Vandals. Italy, for a long time the center of Roman wealth, and of Roman luxury, invited, in a particular manner, the attacks of poverty and barbarism; and after it had suffered from the successive inroads of many different nations, a great part of the country was subjected to the Ostrogoths, and in a subsequent period, to the Lombards.

As the original manners and customs of all these nations were extremely analogous to those of the Saxons in England, and as their conquest and settlement in the western empire <86> were completed nearly in the same manner, it was to be expected that they would fall under a similar government. It has happened, accordingly, that their political institutions are manifestly formed upon the same plan, and present, to the most careless observer, the same aspect and leading features, from which, as in the children of a family, their common origin may clearly be discovered. They differ, no less remarkably, from all the other systems of policy that have been recorded in ancient or modern history. It may be worth while to examine, more particularly, the causes of the uniformity, so observable among all those nations, and of the peculiarities, by which they are so much distinguished from the other inhabitants of the world. In this view, there occur five different circumstances that seem to merit attention.

1. The settlement of the barbarous nations, upon the western continent of Europe, as well as in England, was effected by the gradual subjection of a more civilized people, with whom the conquerors were at length completely incorporated.

The rude and ignorant tribes who subdued <87> the Roman provinces, were too little connected with one another, and too little accustomed to subordination, to unite in prosecuting any regular plan of conquest; but, according as they were excited by provocation, or met with any encouragement, they made occasional inroads, with different degrees of success; and when they had overrun a particular district, they commonly chose to remain

---

peoples originated in Scandinavia and more generally northern Europe as populations in that area began to outstrip the available arable land. The arrival of the Huns from the east in 375 put further pressure on the Germanic tribes to migrate south and west. The Visigoths, or western Goths, and the Ostrogoths, or eastern Goths, were of special significance in the downfall of the Roman empire.

in the country, and frequently concluded a treaty of peace with the ancient inhabitants.

Having, on those occasions, become masters of a large territory, which had been long occupied in tillage, and having, by repeated victories, obtained a number of captives, whom they reduced into slavery, they found it an easy matter to employ their slaves in cultivating the land which they had procured. In this situation they soon made such progress in agriculture, as determined them to relinquish their wandering life, and apply themselves to the acquisition of separate landed estates. By their intercourse, at the same time, with such of the old inhabitants as retained their freedom, they necessarily acquired a variety of knowledge, and became acquainted with many of the com-<88>mon arts of life to which they had formerly been strangers.

It was not to be expected, however, that these barbarians would long remain at rest; or that they should have any difficulty in finding pretences for quarrelling with a people whom they meant to strip of their possessions. In a course of time, therefore, new animosities broke out, which were followed by repeated military enterprizes, attended with similar circumstances; till at last, by successive extensions of territory, and after several centuries had elapsed, the whole of the western empire was dismembered, and reduced under the power of these invaders.

The events by which this great revolution was accomplished, could not fail to produce very opposite effects, upon the ancient inhabitants of the country, and upon the new settlers. The former, while, in consequence of the violence and disorder which prevailed, and of their intercourse with the barbarians, they sunk very rapidly into poverty and barbarism, communicated in their turn to the latter a few great lines of that cultivation, which had not been entirely effaced among themselves. In the end, <89> those two sets of people were entirely blended together; and their union produced such a compound system of manners and customs, as might be expected to result, from the declining state of the one, and the rising state of the other.

The destruction of the Roman provinces struck out, in this manner, a sudden spark of improvement, which animated their victorious enemies, and quickly pervaded the new states that were founded upon the ruins of the western empire. In the earliest accounts of the modern kingdoms of Europe, we find the people, though evidently retaining very deep marks of their primitive rudeness, yet certainly much advanced beyond the simple state of the ancient Germans. Their husbandry, no doubt, continued for ages in a very low and imperfect condition, insomuch that extensive territories were often permitted to lie waste and desolate; yet such as it was, it procured the necessaries of life in greater plenty, and produced of course a more universal attention to its conveniencies. Their permanent residence in one place gave room and encouragement to the exercise of different employments, from which, during <90> their former migrations, they were in a great measure excluded. Their houses were built of more lasting materials, and rendered more commodious, than the moveable huts in which they formerly sheltered themselves. Particular persons, having acquired very great landed estates, were enabled, by the remaining skill of Roman artificers, to erect such fortresses as were sufficient to defend them from the sudden incursions of an enemy; and lived, in suitable magnificence, at the head of their tenants and domestics. The numerous, and opulent towns, which had been scattered over the dominions of Rome, though they suffered greatly in the general wreck of the empire, were not, however, universally destroyed or deserted; and such of them as remained, were frequently occupied and inhabited by the leaders of the conquering tribes. In these, and even throughout the whole of the country, that policy, which had become familiar to the old inhabitants, was, in many respects, continued; and in the early codes of laws, collected by the princes of the barbarous nations who settled in the western empire, we often discover a close imitation of the Roman jurisprudence. <91>

In these particulars, the situation of the modern states of Europe appears to have been a good deal different from that of every other nation, of whom any accounts have been transmitted to us. In many parts of the world, the rude inhabitants have continued unconnected with any other people more improved than themselves; and have therefore advanced very slowly in the knowledge of arts, as well as in the progress of the social life. From the remotest period of antiquity, the Arabs and Tartars have remained, for the most part, in a pastoral state; and are still almost entirely ignorant of husbandry. The Indians of America still derive their principal subsistence from hunting and fishing; and are in a great measure strangers to the invention of taming and rearing cattle. In early ages men are destitute of sagacity and reflection, to make use of those discoveries which fortune may throw in their way; and their improvement is much retarded by those habits of sloth which, being fostered by the primitive manner of life, are not to be overcome without extraordinary incitements to labour and application.

Among the instances, preserved in history, <92> of nations who have acquired a connection with others, by means of a conquest, we meet with none that are similar to those exhibited in Europe, during the period which we are now considering. The conquest in Asia, by Alexander[2] and his successors, was that of one opulent and civilized people over another; and produced no farther alteration in the Greek states, but that of inspiring them with a taste of Asiatic luxury and extravagance.

The first military efforts of the Romans were employed in subduing the small neighbouring states of Italy, whom they found in the same barbarous condition with themselves; and they had become a great nation, firmly established in their manners and political system, before they directed their forces against the refined and cultivated parts of the world. Besides, the Roman virtue disdained, for a long time, to imitate the talents and accomplishments of the people whom they had subdued.

China, and some other of the great Asiatic kingdoms, have been frequently overrun and conquered by several hordes of Tartars,[3] accidentally combined under a great leader: but the conquest, in these cases, was not carried on <93> slowly and gradually, as in the provinces of the western empire: it was completed by one or two great and rapid victories; so as, on the one hand, to prevent the learning and civilization of the vanquished people from being destroyed by a long-continued course of war and devastation; and, on the other, to prevent the conquerors, by long neighbourhood and acquaintance, from being incorporated with the former inhabitants, in one common system of manners, customs, and institutions. The final success, therefore, of the victorious army, produced no farther revolution, than by suddenly advancing their general, together, perhaps, with some of his principal officers, to the head of a great and civilized empire; of which the native country of the conquerors became only a tributary province.

The same observation is applicable to the dominion acquired by Mahomed,[4] and some of his immediate successors; which was not established

2. Alexander the Great, king of Macedonia (r. 336–323 B.C.): From 336 to ca. 325 B.C., Alexander engaged in the successful conquest of Asia Minor against the Persians and founded the port of Alexandria on the Mediterranean coast of Egypt.

3. Millar refers to the central Asian tribes now described as Mongols, who, under the leadership of Genghis Khan and Kublai Khan, conquered large parts of Russia, Iran, and China in the thirteenth century.

4. Muhammad (ca. 570–ca. 632): founder of Islam. In 629, after six years of combat, Muhammad gained control of Arabia.

by a gradual settlement of Arabian tribes, in the rich countries of Asia; but by a rapid conquest, that gave rise to no intimate coalition of the victors with those who submitted to the Mahometan yoke. No other <94> change, therefore, was produced in the state of the conquered nations, than what arose from subjecting them to a new religion, and to a new set of monarchs; while the wandering Arabs, the original followers of Mahomed, remained, for the most part, in their primitive state of barbarism. The conquest of the Saracens,[5] and of the eastern empire, by the Turks, had a greater resemblance to the progressive inroads of those who conquered the western provinces; but it was far from proving equally destructive to the former civilization of the conquered people, or from reducing them to the level of their barbarous conquerors.

2. The German or Gothic nations, who settled in the western part of Europe, were enabled, in a short time, to form kingdoms of greater extent, than are usually to be found among people equally rude and barbarous.

Of all the arts which contribute to improve or to embellish society, that of government requires the most enlarged experience and observation; for which reason, its progress towards perfection is proportionably gradual and slow. In that simple age, in which labour is not yet divided among separate artificers, and in which <95> the exchange of commodities is in a great measure unknown, individuals, who reside at a distance from one another, have no occasion to maintain an intimate correspondence, and are not apt to entertain the idea of establishing a political connection. The inhabitants of a large country are then usually parcelled out into separate families or tribes, the members of which have been led, by necessity, to contract habits of living together, and been reduced under the authority of that leader who is capable of protecting them. These little communities are naturally independent, as well as jealous of one another; and though, from the dread of a common enemy, they are sometimes obliged to combine in a league for mutual defence, yet such combinations are generally too casual and fluctuating to be the foundation of a comprehensive and permanent union.

But those barbarians who conquered the western empire were quickly induced, and enabled, to form extensive associations; partly, from the cir-

5. Historically, the term *Saracens* was broadly applied to Arabs. The Seljuk Turks conquered Asia Minor in the early eleventh century and defeated the Byzantine emperor in 1071.

cumstances attending the conquest; and partly, from the state of the country in which they formed their settlements. <96>

With respect to the circumstances attending their conquest, it is to be observed, that their tribes were far from being large or numerous, and that they overran and subdued a very large tract of country; in consequence of which, the members of the same tribe were enabled to occupy great landed estates, and came to be settled at a proportionable distance from one another. Individuals who had belonged to a small community, and who had been accustomed to fight under the same leader, were thus dispersed over an extensive territory; and, notwithstanding this change in their situation, were naturally disposed to retain their former connections and habits. The notion of uniting under a single chief, which had been established among the members of a wandering tribe of shepherds, continued, therefore, to operate upon the same people, after they had acquired ample possessions, and had reduced multitudes under their dominion.

The extent of the kingdoms, erected by those barbarous nations, was likewise affected by the state of each Roman province, in which their settlements were made. <97>

As every Roman province constituted a part of the whole empire; so it formed a distinct society, influenced by national views, and directed by a separate interest. Among the inhabitants of the same province, united by their local situation, by the ties of friendship and acquaintance, and even by that common system of oppression to which they were subject, a regular intercourse was constantly maintained. Those who lived in villages, or in the open country, carried on a variety of transactions with the several towns in the neighbourhood, where they found a market for their goods, and were supplied with those conveniencies which they required. The inhabitants of these towns, and of the whole province, were, at the same time, closely connected with the capital, where the governor resided in a kind of regal pomp and magnificence, and directed the various wheels and springs of administration. Here the public money, accumulated from different parts, was again distributed through the various channels of government; and hither men of all descriptions, the poor and the rich, the idle and the indus-<98>trious, were attracted from every quarter, by the views of profit, or pleasure, or of ambition.

The changes which at different periods were made in the political constitution of Rome, produced no great alteration, as has been already observed, either in the extent or condition of her provincial governments. The ancient boundaries of the provinces appear to have been generally retained under the later emperors; though, in order to secure the public tranquillity, they were often subdivided into particular districts, which were put under the direction of subordinate officers. The connections, therefore, between the several parts of the same province, were gradually strengthened from the length of time during which they had subsisted.

As, by the conquest of those countries, the ancient inhabitants were not extirpated, it is natural to suppose that their former habits of intercourse were not obliterated and forgotten; but, on the contrary, were in some degree communicated to the conquerors. They who had lived under the same government were still disposed to admit the authority of a single <99> person, and to remain in that state of union and subordination to which they had been accustomed. Particular chiefs having occupied the remaining towns belonging to a Roman province, were of course rendered masters of the adjacent territory; and he who had set himself at the head of the most powerful district, was in a fair way of becoming sovereign of the whole.

It may also be worthy of notice, that as the conquering tribes adopted a number of the Roman institutions, their principal conductor was frequently in a condition to avail himself of that authority, however declining, which the Roman government continued to maintain; and by assuming, or obtaining, the dignity which had belonged to the chief magistrate of a province, was enabled with greater facility to extend his dominion over the territories which had formerly acknowledged the jurisdiction of that officer. Thus we find that Clovis, who conquered a great part of Gaul, was, near the end of his reign, invested with the title of *consul,* and probably with that of *pro-consul,* by the emperor Anastasius; and that the posterity of Clovis were at the pains <100> to procure, from the emperor Justinian,[6] a resignation of all the rights of the empire over that nominal branch of his dominions.*

* Hist. de l'Etablissement de la Mon. Fran. par l'Abbe Du Bos. liv. 4. ch. 18. liv. 5. ch. 7.

6. Clovis, king of the Franks (r. 481–511); Anastasius I, Emperor of Constantinople (r. ca. 491–518); Justinian, properly Flavius Petrus Sabbatius Justinianus, emperor of the Eastern Roman (Byzantine) Empire (r. 527–65), who systematized the Roman law in the *Corpus Juris Civilis;* consul, one of the two most senior Roman magistrates elected annually under the republic as civilian and military rulers; proconsul, a former consul invested with authority *(imperium)* as a governor of a Roman province.

In like manner Theodoric,[7] the king of the Ostrogoths, who had been invested, in the eastern empire, with the title of *patrician* and *consul,* and who had obtained for himself and his followers a settlement in Thrace, was afterwards commissioned by the emperor Zeno[8] to conquer Italy, and take possession of the country.*

From these causes, countries at a great distance from one another were forced into a sort of political union: and the boundaries of a modern kingdom came, in most cases, to be nearly of the same extent with those of an ancient Roman province.

As Italy, which comprehended the numberless villas, and highly-cultivated pleasure grounds, belonging to the opulent citizens of Rome, was the object of more attention than those parts of the empire which lay at a greater distance, it was early subjected to a more ac-<101>curate police, and divided into smaller districts. It was distributed, by Augustus, into eleven *regions;* and in the time of the emperor Adrian that country, together with Sicily, Sardinia, and Corsica, included no less than seventeen divisions. The smallness of the districts into which it was thus broken by the Roman government had, no doubt, an influence upon the new arrangements which it underwent from the invasion of the barbarians; and made it fall more easily into a number of petty states, under the several dukes, or nobles, who assumed an independent authority.

In England, though the most part of the territories which had composed the ancient Roman province were at last united in one kingdom, yet this union was effected more slowly, and with greater difficulty, than in many of the other European countries. The settlement of the Anglo-Saxons was produced in a different manner from that of the other German nations who settled upon the continent of Europe. As the expeditions of the latter were carried on, for the most part, by land, it was usual for the whole of a tribe or nation to advance in a body, and after they <102> had defeated the Roman armies, to spread themselves over the extensive territory which fell under their dominion. The original connections, therefore, among the individuals of the conquering nation, co-operated with the circumstance of their set-

* Ibid. liv. 4. ch. 3.

7. Theodoric the Great: king of the Ostrogoths (r. 475–526). Theodoric secured Italy in the hands of the Ostrogoths by 493.

8. Zeno: Byzantine emperor (r. 474–91).

tling in the same province, to facilitate their reduction, either by conquest or confederacy, under one supreme leader. The naval incursions of the Anglo-Saxons were, on the other hand, made by small detached parties, collected occasionally by any single adventurer, who, for the sake of a precarious settlement, was willing to relinquish his kindred and acquaintance. The followers of every separate leader were therefore too inconsiderable to occupy great landed possessions; and as they invaded England at different times, and in different places, with scarce any previous concert, and with little attachment to one another, they discovered so much the stronger disposition to remain in separate states, and to preserve their primitive independence. From these circumstances, we may account for the division of England into so many independent kingdoms; which were not reduced under one monarch till between <103> three and four centuries after the first settlement of those invaders.

3. The great extent of the kingdoms that were formed upon the ruins of the western empire, together with the rudeness of the people by whom they were established, appears to have occasioned that system of feudal tenures, which is commonly regarded as the most distinguishing peculiarity in the policy of modern Europe.

The disposition to theft and rapine, so prevalent among rude nations, makes it necessary that the members of every family should have a watchful eye upon the conduct of all their neighbours, and should be constantly upon their guard to preserve their persons from outrage, and their property from depredation. The first efforts of civil government are intended to supersede this necessity, by punishing such offences, and enabling the individuals of the same community to live together in peace and tranquillity. But these efforts, it is evident, are likely to be more effectual in a small state than in a large one; and the public magistrate finds it much more difficult to extend and support his authority over a multitude <104> of individuals, dispersed through a wide country, than over a small number, confined to a narrow district. It is for this reason that government has commonly been sooner established, as well as better modelled, in communities of a moderate size, than in those which comprehend the inhabitants of an extensive region.

In proportion to the great number of people, and the great extent of territory, in each of the modern European kingdoms, the advances of authority in the public were slow, and its capacity of restraining violence and disorder was limited. The different families of a kingdom, though they acknowledged the same sovereign, and were directed by him in their foreign military enterprizes, were not, upon ordinary occasions, in a situation to feel much dependence upon him. Acquiring great landed possessions, and residing at a distance from the capital, as well as in places of difficult access, they were often in a condition to set the whole power of the crown at defiance; and disdaining to submit their quarrels to the determination of the civil magistrate, they assumed a privilege of revenging with their <105> own hands the injuries or indignities which they pretended to have suffered. When not employed, therefore, in expeditions against a public enemy, they were commonly engaged in private hostilities among themselves; from the frequent repetition of which there arose animosities and feuds, that were only to be extinguished with the life of the combatants, and that, in many cases, were even rendered hereditary. In such a state of anarchy and confusion, the strong were permitted to oppress the weak; and those who had most power of hurting their neighbours, were the most completely secured from the punishment due to their offences.

As the individuals of a nation were thus destitute of protection from government, they were under the necessity of defending themselves, or of seeking protection from one another; and the little societies composed of near relations, or formed accidentally by neighbourhood and acquaintance, were obliged to unite, in the most intimate manner, to repel the attacks of their numerous enemies. The poor were forced to shelter themselves under the influence and power of the rich; and the latter <106> found it convenient to employ a great part of their wealth, in order to obtain the constant aid and support of the former. The head of every family was commonly surrounded by as great a number of kindred and dependents as he was capable of maintaining; these were accustomed to follow him in war, and in time of peace to share in the rural sports to which he was addicted; it was their duty to espouse his quarrel on every occasion, as it was incumbent on him to defend them from injuries. In a family so small, that all its members could be maintained about the same house, a mutual obligation of this kind was naturally understood from the situation of the parties; but in larger societies it was rendered more clear and definite by an express agreement. A man of great opulence distributed part of his demesne among his retainers, upon condition of their performing military services; as, on the other hand, the small proprietors in his neighbourhood, being incapable of maintaining their independence, were glad to purchase his protection, by agreeing to hold their land upon the same terms. Hence the origin of vassalage[9] in Europe, the nature of which will be <107> more particularly explained hereafter. Every considerable proprietor of land had thus a number of military servants, who, instead of pay, enjoyed a part of his estate, as the reward of their services. By this distribution and arrangement of landed possessions, the most natural remedy was provided for the evils arising from the weakness of government. Men of inferior station, who singly were incapable of defending their persons or their property, obtained more security, as well as consideration, under their respective superiors; and the inhabitants of a large territory, being combined in societies, who had each of them a common interest, were in a better condition to resist the general tide of violence and oppression.

From these observations we may discover how far the connections between the superior and vassal, and the various parts of what is called the feudal system, are peculiar to the modern states of Europe, or belong to them in common with other nations.

In Greece and Rome, or in any of the small states of antiquity, there are few or no traces to be discovered of the feudal institutions. From the inconsiderable number of people <108> collected in each of those ancient states, and from the narrowness of the territory which they inhabited, the government was enabled, at an early period, to extend its protection to all the citizens, so as to free them from the necessity of providing for their own safety, by associating themselves under particular military leaders. If any sort of vassalage, therefore, had been introduced in the infancy of those nations, it appears to have been abolished before they were possessed of historical records.

In many rude nations of greater extent, both in ancient and modern times, we may discern, on the contrary, the outlines of the feudal policy. This, if we can trust the relations given by travellers,[10] is particularly the case at present in several of the kingdoms in Asia, and upon the southern coast of Africa. In these kingdoms, the number of barbarians collected under one

9. In the feudal system, a vassal was one holding lands from a superior on condition of giving homage or allegiance to a superior. Hence vassalage is defined as the actions of a good vassal.

10. For Millar's views on the proper use of travelers' reports, see *DR,* 12–13.

sovereign has probably rendered the government so feeble, as to require a number of subordinate associations, for the protection of individuals; but the coalition of different families being neither so extensive, nor produced in the same rapid manner, as in the modern states of Europe, the regulations <109> to which it has given occasion are neither so numerous and accurate, nor have they been reduced into so regular a system.

4. The custom of duelling, and the peculiar notions of honour, which have so long prevailed in the modern nations of Europe, appear to have arisen from the same circumstances that produced the feudal institutions.

The political establishment, in all those nations, was, for a long time, incapable of preventing the unlimited exercise of private hostilities; and every family, being exposed to invasion from all its neighbours, was obliged to be constantly in a posture of defence. In these circumstances, the military spirit of the people was not only raised to a high pitch, but it received a peculiar direction, and was attended with peculiar habits and opinions.

In a war between two great nations, when large and well-disciplined armies are brought into the field, there is little room for individuals to acquire distinction by their exploits; and it is only expected of them, that, like the parts of a complex machine, they should perform, with steadiness and regularity, the several movements for which they are destined; nei-<110>ther are those who belong to the opposite armies likely to entertain much personal animosity, the national quarrel being lost in that promiscuous multitude among whom it is divided. But in the private wars that took place between the several families of modern Europe the case was very different; for the number engaged upon either side was commonly so small, and they had so little of military discipline, that every single person might act a distinguished part, and in the time of action was left in some measure to pursue the dictates of his own bravery or prudence; so that a battle consisted of little more than the random combats of such particular warriors as were led by inclination or accident to oppose one another. The natural consequence of such a situation was to produce a keen emulation between the individuals of the same party, as well as a stated opposition, and often a violent animosity, between those of different parties. In a long course of hostilities, the same persons were often led to encounter each other; and having fought (perhaps on different occasions) with various success, were at length excited by a mutual challenge to a compara-<111>tive trial of their strength, courage, or skill. By repeated struggles of this nature a continual jealousy was kept up between the members of different families, who in prosecuting their quarrels became no less eager to support their military character, and to avenge any insult or indignity, than to defend their possessions.

The private wars between different families, which gave rise to mutual emulation and jealousy, as well as to violent animosity and resentment, continued in Europe for many centuries, notwithstanding that some improvements were made by the people in the common arts and modes of living. To assassinate those from whom great provocation had been received was, among the primitive conquerors of the Roman empire, a method of revenge pursued without scruple, and beheld without censure. By degrees however the love of military glory prevailed over the gratification of resentment, and those who aimed at maintaining the rank of gentlemen became ashamed of taking an unfair advantage of an enemy, which might imply a confession of inferiority in prowess; but thought it incumbent upon them, whatever was the quarrel, to invite him <112> to an open contest, in which the superiority might be decided upon equal terms. Thus the practice of *duelling,* the most refined species of private vengeance, was rendered more and more fashionable; and in every country of Europe, according to its progress from barbarism, assassination became less frequent, and was held in greater detestation. In Spain and Portugal, the least improved of those countries, it never has been completely extirpated; and the inhabitants have not yet attained that refinement of the feudal manners, which the rest of Europe, from a still higher pitch of improvement, are now seeking to lay aside.

So far was the government from restraining the custom of duelling, that the efforts of the civil magistrate tended rather to encourage it. Those who had sustained an affront thought it dishonourable to apply for redress to a court of justice; but when a dispute had arisen in matters of property, and had become the subject of a law-suit, it frequently happened, that in the course of the debate the parties, by their proud and insolent behaviour, affronted each other; which made them withdraw their cause from the court, in order to determine it by the <113> sword; the judge was unable to prevent this determination, but he endeavoured to diminish the bad consequences that might arise from it. By regulating the forms of the encounter, and superintending the ceremonies with which it was conducted, he availed himself of the punctilios of honour, which fashion had established, and restrained the friends of either party from interfering in the quarrel. Hence the *judicial combat,*[11] which has been erroneously considered by some as the origin of duelling, but which undoubtedly tended to support and extend the practice, by giving it the sanction of public authority. It has, accordingly, been observed, that as, in a judicial controversy, the most common provocation consisted in the parties contradicting each other in point of fact; so *giving the lye* has become that sort of offence, on account of which custom has rendered it most indispensably necessary to require *satisfaction* by fighting.

The institutions of *chivalry,* and the *jousts* and *tournaments,* were the natural appendages of the custom of duelling, or rather of that state of manners which gave rise to it.

In the battles of the feudal ages, men of <114> opulence and rank enjoyed many advantages over the common people, by their fighting on horseback, by the superior weapons and armour which they made use of, and above all, by that skill and dexterity which they had leisure to acquire. To improve these advantages was the great object of the gentry, who from their early years devoted themselves to the profession of arms, and generally became attached to some person of experience and reputation, by whom they were trained up and instructed, not only in the several branches of the military exercise, but in all those qualifications that were thought suitable to their condition. To encourage these laudable pursuits, a mark of distinction was bestowed upon such as had gone through a complete course of military education, and they were admitted, with peculiar ceremonies, to the honour of knighthood; from which their proficiency in the art of war, and in the virtues and accomplishments connected with that employment, were understood to be publicly ascertained and acknowledged.

Among the multitude of knights belonging to every country, who became professed can-<115>didates for fame, and upon that account rivals to one another, military sports, that afforded an opportunity of displaying those talents upon which the character of every gentleman chiefly depended, were of course the favourite entertainments. As these became the ordinary pastime among private persons, so they were exhibited, on particular occasions, by princes and men of high rank, with great pomp and solemnity. The *tournaments* were the greater and more public exhibitions, the *jousts* were those

11. Judicial combat was trial by battle in which the victor was also deemed to have won the court case.

of an inferior and private nature; to both of which all who enjoyed the dignity of knighthood were made welcome: they were also invited to that *round table,* at which the master of the ceremony entertained his company, and of which the figure is said to have been contrived on purpose to avoid any dispute concerning the precedence of his guests.

These public spectacles were begun in France under the kings of the second race;[12] and were thence, by imitation, introduced into the other countries of Europe. They are said to have been first known in England, during the reign of Stephen,[13] and to have been <116> rendered common in that of Richard the first.

There can be no doubt that these institutions and practices, by which badges of distinction were given to military eminence, and by which numbers of individuals were brought to contend for the prize of skill and valour, would contribute to swell and diffuse the idea of personal dignity by which they were already elated, and to inflame that mutual jealousy by which they were set in opposition to one another. The same opinions and sentiments acquired additional force from those extraordinary enterprises in which the people of different European countries were accidentally combined against a common enemy; as in the wars between the Moors and Christians,[14] and in the expeditions undertaken by the latter for the purpose of rescuing the holy sepulchre from the hands of infidels. The competition arising on those occasions among the numerous warriors collected in the same army, was daily productive of new refinements upon the military spirit of the times, and contributed to multiply and establish the forms and cere-<117>monies which, in every dispute of honour, were held indispensably necessary.

From these causes the custom of duelling has become so deeply rooted as, notwithstanding a total change of manners and circumstances, to maintain its ground in most of the countries of Europe; and the effect of later improvements has only been to soften and render more harmless a relict of ancient barbarity, which they could not destroy. In England, where the lower ranks of men enjoy a degree of consideration little known in other countries, the military spirit of the gentry has even descended to the common people,

12. The Carolingians, named after the first and greatest of the line, Charlemagne. His father, Pepin the Short, had deposed the last of the Merovingian kings in 751.

13. Stephen (r. 1135–41); Richard I (r. 1189–99).

14. Millar here refers to the Christian attempts to recapture Palestine from Muslim control during the Crusades of the eleventh to thirteenth centuries.

as appears from the custom of *boxing* peculiar to the English, by which they decide their quarrels according to such punctilios of honour as are dictated by the pure and genuine principles of chivalry.

In other ages and countries there is perhaps no instance of any people whose situation could lead them to entertain the same notions of military dignity which have been displayed by the modern inhabitants of Europe. The independent families or tribes of shepherds, in Tartary or in other parts of the world, have seldom <118> occasion to reside so long in the same neighbourhood as to create a stated opposition and jealousy between their different members. The nations of husbandmen, upon the southern coast of Africa, and in several parts of Asia, who have in some degree adopted the feudal policy, are too little advanced in civilization to admit of any refinement in their methods of executing revenge. In those ancient states that were most addicted to war, as in Rome and Sparta,[15] the people were early brought under the authority of government, so as effectually to prevent the exercise of private hostilities. A Roman, or a Spartan, therefore, was never under the necessity of supporting his military dignity, in opposition to his own countrymen; but was constantly employed in maintaining the glory of his country, in opposition to that of its enemies. The prejudices and habits acquired in such a situation were all of a patriotic nature. The pride or vanity of individuals was exerted in acts of public spirit, not in private animosities and disputes.

M. Voltaire[16] imagines that the practice of duelling, in modern Europe, has arisen from <119> the custom, among the inhabitants, of wearing a sword, as an ordinary part of dress; but the ancient Greeks, as we learn from Thucydides,[17] were, at an early period, accustomed to go armed; and there is ground to believe that the same custom has prevailed in all barbarous countries, where the people found themselves continually exposed to danger. The continuance of this practice in Europe longer than in other countries appears to be the effect, not the cause of duelling; or rather it is the effect of that

15. Sparta: a leading city-state of ancient Greece, distinguished by its military capability and strict morality.

16. François Marie Arouet de Voltaire (1694–1778): French philosopher, poet, and historian, author of works including the *Henriade,* the *Histoire de Charles XII,* the *Dictionnaire philosophique,* and the *Essai sur les moeurs.*

17. Thucydides (ca. 460–ca. 400 B.C.): ancient Greek historian and author of the *History of the Peloponnesian War.*

peculiar direction given to the military spirit, of which duelling is the natural attendant.

5. The same situation produced the romantic love and gallantry by which the age of chivalry was no less distinguished than by its peculiar notions of military honour.

The appetite of the sexes, which in the greater part of animals, nature has, for wise purposes, connected with exquisite pleasure, is in the human species productive of sentiments and affections, which are of great consequence to the general intercourse of society, as well as to the happiness of individuals. These two sources of enjoyment, though in <120> reality inseparable, and though the latter is ultimately derived from the former, are not always increased and refined by the same circumstances. The mere animal instinct seems to be strengthened by every circumstance that gives occasion to habits of indulgence; but the peculiar passions that nature has grafted on this enjoyment appear on the contrary to be raised to the highest pitch, by the difficulty attending their gratification; which, as it fixes the imagination upon the same object, has a tendency to exalt its value, and to debase that of every other in proportion.

In the ages of poverty and barbarism, mankind are commonly too much occupied in pursuit of mere necessaries, to pay much regard to the intercourse of the sexes; and their simple desires with relation to this point being easily gratified as soon as they arise, are not likely to settle with much predilection or preference upon any particular person.

The first great improvements that are made in any country, with respect to the means of subsistence, being calculated to multiply the comforts and conveniencies of life, enable the inhabitants to extend the circle of their plea-<121>sures, and to refine upon every enjoyment which their situation affords; the pleasures of sex become therefore, an object of greater attention, and being carried to a higher degree of refinement, are productive of more variety in the taste and inclination of different persons; by which they are often disappointed in the attainment of their wishes, and their passions are proportionably inflamed.[18] The introduction of property, which, being accumulated in different proportions, becomes the foundation of corresponding distinctions of rank, is at the same time the source of additional restraints upon the free commerce of the sexes. By the innumerable pretensions to

18. For a similar discussion of sexual appetite and social repression, see *DR,* 76–77.

dignity and importance, derived from the vanity of opulence, or the pride of family, individuals have often to surmount a variety of obstacles in order to gratify their passions; and in contracting what is accounted an unsuitable alliance, they are commonly checked and controuled, not only by the watchful interposition of their relations, but still more by the rules of propriety and decorum, which custom, in conformity to the state of society, has universally established. <122>

The effect of great wealth and luxury, in a polished nation, is on the other hand to create an immoderate pursuit of sensual pleasure, and to produce habits of excessive indulgence in such gratifications. In such a situation particular attachments are apt to be lost in the general propensity; and the correspondence of the sexes becomes, in a great measure, subservient to voluptuousness, or to the purposes merely of elegant amusement.

The passion of love, therefore, is likely to attain the highest degree of refinement in a state of society equally removed from the extremes of barbarism and of luxury.

The nations formed in the western part of Europe, upon the downfal of the Roman empire, appear to have continued for many centuries in that condition. They were possessed of such opulence, and of such improvements in society, as to stamp some value upon the pleasures of sex, without creating much incitement to debauchery. Their distinctions of rank, arising from the very unequal distribution of property, and the mutual apprehension and jealousy which a long course of private hostilities had introduced among different <123> families, occasioned, at the same time, in their whole correspondence, a degree of caution and distrust unknown in other ages and countries. The women of every family, as well as the men, were taught to over-rate their own dignity, and to look upon it as disgraceful to give any encouragement to a lover, whose rank and worth did not entitle him to a preference, in the opinion of the world, and in that of her own prejudiced relations.

As no man in that age was allowed to claim any merit, unless he had acquired a military reputation, the warrior who had been inspired with a youthful inclination could not expect any marks of regard, far less a return of affection, without signalizing his fortitude and prowess, by encountering a variety of hardships and dangers. Before he had in this manner deserved the favour of his mistress, it was held inconsistent with her character to divulge any impression she had received to his advantage; and the laws of delicacy required that she should behave to him on all occasions with distance and reserve, if not with insolence and scorn. By the delays, the disappointments, the uncertainty of success, to which he was thus <124> exposed, his thoughts were long engrossed by that favourite object; and the ardours of a natural appetite were at length exalted into a violent passion.

The romantic love, peculiar to the ages of chivalry,[19] was readily united with the high sentiments of military honour, and they seem to have mutually promoted each other. An accomplished character in those times required not only the most undaunted courage and resolution, supported by great generosity, and a contempt of every sordid interest, but also the most respectful regard and reverence for the ladies, together with a sincere and faithful passion for some individual. Persons possessed of these accomplishments, or who desired the reputation of possessing them, devoted themselves to the particular profession of protecting the feeble, of relieving the distressed, of humbling and restraining the insolent oppressor. Not content with ordinary occasions of acquiring distinction, there were some who thought it necessary to travel from place to place, with the avowed purpose of redressing grievances, and of punishing the injuries to which, from the disorderly state of the country, the unwar-<125>like and defenceless, but especially the female sex, were daily subjected.

It happened indeed in those times, as it naturally happens wherever mankind have been directed by fashion to admire any particular sort of excellence, that the desire of imitating the great and gallant actions of heroes and lovers, was often disfigured and rendered ridiculous by affectation, and became productive of artificial and fantastic manners. The knight-errant, who found no real abuses to combat, endeavoured to procure distinction by adventures of no utility, and which had no other merit but the danger attending them; as he who had never felt a real passion, tortured his mind with one merely imaginary, complained of rigours that he had never met with, and entered the lists, to maintain that superior beauty and merit which he had never beheld.

It is unnecessary to remark, that these institutions and customs, and the circumstances from which they proceeded, were peculiarly unfavourable to trade and manufactures. The Saxons in England, as well as the other nations who settled about the same time upon the <126> western continent of Eu-

19. For Millar's earlier discussion of chivalry, see *DR,* 79ff.

rope, though immediately after their settlement they had been excited to a considerable improvement in agriculture, and in some of the common arts of life, remained afterwards for ages in that hostile and turbulent state which gave little room or encouragement for the exercise of peaceable occupations. The manners introduced into those countries in early times being thus confirmed by long usage, have become proportionably permanent, and, notwithstanding the changes of a subsequent period, have left innumerable traces of their former existence. <127>

CHAPTER V

The State of Property, and the different Ranks and Orders of Men, produced by the Settlement of the Saxons in Britain.

The distribution of property among any people is the principal circumstance that contributes to reduce them under civil government, and to determine the form of their political constitution. The poor are naturally dependent upon the rich, from whom they derive subsistence; and, according to the accidental differences of wealth possessed by individuals, a subordination of ranks is gradually introduced, and different degrees of power and authority are assumed without opposition, by particular persons, or bestowed upon them by the general voice of the society.

The progress of the Saxon arms in Britain produced an appropriation of land and moveables, by all the free members of the community. Every warrior considered himself as entitled to a share of the spoil acquired by the conquest; and obtained a number of captives, <128> a landed territory, proportioned to his valour and activity, or to the services which he had performed. It is probable that the several conquering parties were seldom at the trouble of making a formal division of their acquisitions, but commonly permitted each individual to enjoy the booty which he had seized in war, and to become master of such a quantity of land, as by means of his captives, and the other members of his family, he was enabled to occupy and to manage. Such of the ancient inhabitants, on the other hand, as remained in the country, and had preserved their liberty, were in all probability understood to retain the property of those estates of which they had been able to maintain the possession.

There is good reason to believe that, for some time after the settlement of those barbarians in England, the landed estates acquired by individuals were generally of small extent. The Saxons were among the poorest and the rudest of the German nations who invaded the Roman empire; and Britain was, on the other hand, one of the least cultivated of all its provinces; at the same time that the progress of the conquerors in the appropriation of land <129> (which from these causes must have been proportionably slow and gradual) was further obstructed by the vigorous opposition of the natives, who seem to have disputed every inch of ground with their enemies.

We accordingly find that, from the beginning of the Anglo-Saxon government, the land was divided into *hides,* each comprehending what could be cultivated by a single plough. This, among a simple people, becomes a natural boundary to the possession of those who live in the same house, and are jointly at the expence of procuring that useful but complicated instrument of husbandry. The general estimation of the Anglo-Saxon lands, according to this inaccurate measure, points out sufficiently the original circumstance which regulated the extent of the greater part of estates. When, by the progress of cultivation, and by future successes in war, the landed property of individuals was increased, the ancient standard of computation remained; and the largest estates, by comparing them with the smallest, were rated according to the number of *hides* which they contained.* <130>

While the estates possessed by the Anglo-Saxons were small, they were cultivated under the immediate inspection of the owner, his kindred or servants, who lived in his own house, and were fed at his table. But when the territory acquired by any person became too extensive, and the members of his family became too numerous, to render this mode of living any longer convenient, a part of his land was parcelled out into different farms, and committed to the management of particular bondmen, from whom, at the end of the year, he required an account of the produce. A part of any great estate came likewise to be occupied by the kindred and free retainers of the proprietor, to whom, in return for that military service which they undertook to perform, he assigned portions of land for a maintenance.

Hence the distinction between the *in-land* of the Saxons, and the *out-land:* the former was what lay next the mansion-house of the owner, and was retained in his own hands; the latter, what lay at a greater distance, and was in the possession and management either of his retainers or servants.† <131>

* See Spelm. Gloss. v. *Hyda.*

† See Spelman on Feuds and Tenures by Knight-service, ch. 5. [[Millar refers to the

The *out-land* of every opulent person came thus to be possessed by two different sorts of people; the bond-men, who laboured their farms for the benefit of their master, and those freemen (most commonly his kindred) who had become bound to follow him in war, and upon that condition were entitled to draw the full produce of their possessions. The former have been called *villeins,*[1] the latter *vassals.*

Considering the right of the latter to the lands which they possessed, in contradistinction to that of the person from whom they derived their possession, the landed estates of the Anglo-Saxons have been divided into *allodial* and *feudal.*[2] The allodial estates were those of every independent proprietor. Over these the owner enjoyed a full dominion; and he had a right to alienate or dispose of them at pleasure. Upon the death of a proprietor, they descended to his heirs, according to certain rules of succession which custom had introduced; and they were not burdened with service of any kind in favour of a superior.

The feudal estates were those possessed by vassals upon condition of military or other ser-<132>vices: these were held originally during the pleasure of the superior, though it appears that custom had early secured the possession of the vassal for a limited time. When he had ploughed and sowed his ground, it was thought equitable that he should be allowed to reap the crop arising from his labour and expence. Thus a year came soon to be acknowledged as the shortest period, upon the conclusion of which he might be deprived of his possession. Even after this period it was not likely that a superior would think of putting away his relations and ancient retainers, with whose personal attachment he was well acquainted, and of whose valour and fidelity he had probably been a witness. The possessions, therefore, of the greater part of the vassals, though not confirmed by any positive bargain, with respect to the term of their continuance, were in fact usually retained for life; and even upon the death of the possessor were frequently enjoyed by his posterity, whom, out of affection to the ancestor, the superior

---

definitions in Sir Henry Spelman's *Treatise of Feuds and Tenures by Knight-Service* (1639). See *The English Works of Sir Henry Spelman* (London, 1723), vol. 2, chap. 5: "What Degrees and Distinctions of Persons Were Among the Saxons, and What Condition Their Lands Were," 12.]]

1. A class of serf entirely subject to a manorial lord.

2. Allodial lands were held in absolute ownership, in contrast to feudal lands, for which rents or services were due.

commonly preferred to a stranger, or to any distant relation. When the lands of a vassal had, by a positive <133> bargain, been only secured to him for life, or for a limited period, they were called *benefices.**

The differences which I have mentioned in the condition of estates, gave rise, most probably, to the celebrated distinction of *boc-land* and *folc-land.*[3] The former, comprehending the estates of the nobler sort, was *allodial,* and being held in absolute property, was conveyed by a deed in writing; the latter was the land possessed by people of inferior condition, who having no right of property, but holding their possessions merely as tenants, for payment of rents or services, did not obtain any written title for ascertaining their rights.†

It may be remarked that *boc-land* might belong either to the king or to a subject, and that it implied no obligation to feudal services, in the latter case, more than in the former. It is true that subjects who enjoyed *boc-land* were bound to defend the kingdom from enemies by sea or land, and to build or repair bridges and castles:‡ but these were services which they owed to the public as citizens, not to the <134> king as vassals. These duties were imposed by a general law of the kingdom, and were laid upon the possessors of *folc-land* as well as of *boc-land,* upon the clergy as well as laity, in short, upon all the free members of the community.§

Such was the original state of property in the Anglo-Saxon government; from the consideration of which, together with the early circumstances and manners of the nation, the inhabitants, exclusive of the sovereign, may be distinguished into three different ranks or orders.

1. The first and most conspicuous was that of the military people. It is probable that for some time after the settlement of the Saxons in England, this comprehended all the free men of the nation. The general character of those adventurers, and the views with which they invaded Britain, were such as disposed every man, who had the direction of his own conduct, to become

* V. Feud. Consuet. lib. i. tit. i. §. 1. 2.

† Spelm. on Feuds and Tenures by Knight-service, chap. 5.

‡ *Expedition, Burghbote,* and *Brigbote.*

§ See Spelman on Feuds and Tenures by Knight-service, chap. 8. 9. 10. 11.

3. Millar again cites Spelman's *Treatise,* which states that "[*boc-land*] carried with it the absolute inheritance and propriety of the Land, and was therefore preserved in writing, and possess'd by the *Thanes* and Nobler sort. . . . *Focland* was *Terra vulgi,* the land of the vulgar people, who had no Estate therein, but held the same (under such Rents and Services as were accustomed or agreed of) at the will only of their Lord the *Thane.*" *The English Works of Sir Henry Spelman,* 2:12.

a soldier, and to engage in every enterprize by which either plunder or reputation might be procured. These war-<135>riors, who in general were denominated *thanes,*[4] came soon to be arranged in two classes; the one consisting of those heads of families who had acquired allodial property; the other of such retainers as held lands, by a military tenure, either of the king, or of any other allodial proprietor. Both these classes of people were accounted gentlemen, and were understood to be of the same rank, in as much as they exercised the honourable profession of arms; though in point of influence and power there was the greatest disparity, the vassals being almost intirely dependent upon their superior. The soldiers of this lower class appear to have received the appellation of *less,* or *inferior thanes.**

2. The peasants composed a second order, greatly inferior in rank to the thanes of either class. They appear to have consisted chiefly of such persons as had been reduced into captivity during the long wars between the Britons and the Saxons, and had afterwards been entrusted by their masters with the management of particular farms; they were called *ceorls, carles,* or *churles.* Some of them, no <136> doubt, were kept in the house of their master, and employed in cultivating the land in his own possession; but the greater number were usually sent to a distance, and placed, as it happened to be convenient, upon different parts of his estate. The former being under his eye, and acting on all occasions from his orders, remained for a long time in their primitive servile condition; the latter, on the contrary, being withdrawn from his immediate inspection, had necessarily more trust and confidence reposed in them, and were thence enabled, with some degree of rapidity, to improve their circumstances. From their distance, the master was obliged to relinquish all thoughts of compelling them to labour, by means of personal chastisement; and as, from the nature of their employment, he could hardly judge of their diligence, otherwise than by their success, he soon found it expedient to bribe their industry, by giving them a reward in proportion to the crop which they produced. They were thus allowed to acquire property; and their condition became similar, in every respect, to that of the *adscripti glebae*[5] among the ancient Romans, to that of the pre-<137>sent colliers and

* Spelman, in the treatise above quoted.

4. In Anglo-Saxon England, thanes held land from their superior in return for military service.

5. To be tied to the soil; the condition of serfdom. Workers in Scotland's coal and salt mines were in a condition of virtual slavery until their emancipation in 1799.

salters in Scotland, or of the bondmen employed in the mines in several parts of Europe. In this situation some of them, by industry and frugality, found means to accumulate so much wealth, as enabled them to stock their own farms, and become bound to pay a certain yearly rent to the master.

It must be acknowledged, the writers upon Saxon antiquities have generally supposed that the *ceorls* were never in a servile condition; that from the beginning they were free tenants, forming a distinct class of people, and holding an intermediate rank between the villeins or bondmen, and those who followed the military profession. But this supposition, so far as I know, is made without any shadow of proof: it probably took its rise from observing that the free tenants, towards the end of the Anglo-Saxon government, were very numerous, without attending to the circumstances from which they obtained their freedom. It is not likely, however, that in so rude and warlike an age any set of men, who had not been debased by servitude, and restrained by their condition, would attach themselves <138> wholly to agriculture, and be either unfit for war, or unwilling to engage in it. If the *ceorls* had not been originally in some degree of bondage, they would undoubtedly have been warriors; and we accordingly find that when, from the circumstances above mentioned, they had afterwards acquired considerable privileges, they were advanced to the rank and employment of thanes.

Though the peasants were chiefly employed in agriculture, they were sometimes engaged in other branches of labour, as a collateral profession. From the poverty and rudeness of the country, for some time after the settlement of the Saxons in Britain, it may easily be imagined that little encouragement was given to mechanical arts, and that artificers and tradesmen were not of sufficient consequence to become a separate order in the community. Some mechanics, even in that simple age, were doubtless necessary to procure the ordinary accommodations of life, but the demand for their work was too narrow to occupy the sole attention of any individual. Such of the bondmen as had attained a peculiar dexterity in performing any branch of manual labour, <139> were naturally employed by the master in the exercise of it, and thus were led, by degrees, to make some proficiency in particular occupations. But they were not hindered by these employments from cultivating the ground; and they obtained a maintenance in the same manner with the other peasants, either by living in the house of their master, or by the possession of separate farms upon his estate. As these mechanical employments were accounted more unwarlike and contemptible than the exercise of husbandry, there was yet less probability that any freeman would be willing to engage in them.

3. A third order of men, who in this period of the English history became more and more distinguished, was that of the clergy. The numerous body of church-men introduced by the Christian religion, especially in the western part of Europe, the extensive power and authority which they gradually acquired, together with the peculiar views and motives by which they were actuated, amidst the disorder and barbarism of the feudal times, are circumstances of so much magnitude, as to deserve particular attention in tracing any modern system <140> of European policy. A few remarks, however, concerning the nature and origin of ecclesiastical jurisdiction, and the primitive government of the Christian church, will be sufficient, upon a subject that has been so often and so fully examined.

SECTION I

Of the chief Regulations attending the Establishment of Christianity in the Roman Empire, and in the modern Kingdoms of Europe.

After the Christian religion had been extended over a great part of the Roman dominions, it was at last, in the reign of Constantine, taken under the protection of government, and obtained the sanction of public authority. The uniformity of circumstances attending the introduction of this new religion, produced throughout the whole empire an uniform set of ecclesiastical regulations.

In every province, religious teachers had taken up their residence wherever they met with encouragement; and the country was, by degrees, divided into small districts, or pa-<141>rishes, in each of which a particular clergyman had gained an establishment.

As the inhabitants of a parish were accustomed to assemble at stated times for public worship, and were by that means united in a religious society, so the zeal with which they were animated in support of their religion disposed them to inspect the conduct and theological opinions of all their members. For the regulation of these, and of all their common affairs, the heads of families, belonging to every congregation, frequently held meetings, in which their pastor was naturally allowed to preside, and gradually obtained the chief direction of their measures. Even in secular matters, the people were disposed to be guided by his judgment; and when a controversy had arisen between individuals, he was esteemed the most proper person to compose the difference; which was therefore most commonly referred by the parties to his determination.

The advancement of Christianity opened a communication between the professors of this religion belonging to different parishes, who in like manner were accustomed to deliberate upon their common religious concerns. Some <142> particular clergyman became the ordinary president in those cases; and upon that account acquiring superior consideration and rank, was at length exalted to be superintendant, or bishop, of a large district or diocese. When these diocesan meetings were greatly multiplied, the attendance of the laity being found inconvenient, and appearing to them of less consequence, was gradually neglected, so that the business came to remain entirely in the hands of the clergy.

The minister of every parish was at first maintained by the occasional bounty of those who reaped the benefit of his instructions; and such was the attachment of the primitive Christians to their teachers, and to one another, that they cheerfully made contributions not only for that purpose, but also for the maintenance of their poor. In the declining state of Rome, when the decay of knowledge, by infusing a strong leaven of superstition, had corrupted the purity of the Christian religion, the clergy found means to obtain a more independent revenue, by persuading persons upon their death-bed to make donations to the church, in order to atone for their offences. <143> In the reign of the emperor Constantine, when Christianity became the established religion of the empire, testamentary bequests in favour of societies, which had formerly been prohibited by the Roman law, came to be permitted without controul; and from this time the fashion of leaving legacies to the church for pious uses became so universal, that the clergy were enabled to accumulate large estates, both in moveables and land.

The management of these estates, as of all other matters concerning religion, was naturally devolved upon the clergy of every diocese, who assumed a discretionary power of distributing the produce in such a manner as they thought most expedient, or most conformable to the purpose of the donors. As the bishop, however, acquired more influence in ecclesiastical meetings, he was in a capacity of appropriating to his own use a greater share of that revenue which fell under their disposal. His dignity became more conspicuous; and for supporting it a suitable estate was deemed necessary. His cathedral was enlarged and rendered more magnificent, a more pompous form of worship was introduced into it, and a <144> number of clergymen were appointed to assist in the religious services, or other branches of duty, that were supposed to belong to his department.

The rise of a bishop over the clergy of his diocese may be compared to that of a rude chief over the members of his tribe; as in both cases a superiority of station, derived from personal qualities, put it in the power of a single person to acquire superior wealth, and thence to become the permanent head or leader of a society: but the original pre-eminence of the chief arose from his military talents, that of the bishop, from the veneration paid to the sanctity of his character and profession. This makes the only difference in the nature of their advancement.

While those who had the direction of religious matters were thus advancing in opulence and power, there arose a new set of fanatics, who divided the esteem and admiration of the people, and were at length admitted into the clerical profession.

The erroneous notions entertained in the dark ages, concerning the Supreme Being; the supposition that he is actuated by anger <145> and resentment, in a literal sense, against those who transgress his laws, and that these passions are to be gratified by the mere suffering of his creatures; suggested to persons impressed with a strong feeling of their own guilt, and tortured upon that account with sorrow and remorse, the idea of submitting to voluntary penances, in order to appease an offended Deity, and to avert that future punishment which they were conscious of having deserved. From views of this kind, particular persons became disposed to retire from the world, and to deny themselves almost all the comforts and enjoyments of life: societies were afterwards formed, the members of which expressly bound themselves not only to submit to actual punishments, but to renounce all those pleasures and gratifications to which mankind have the greatest propensity, and for this purpose came under the vows of poverty, of chastity, and of obedience to the rules of their community. As Christianity took a firmer hold of the mind than any of the religions which had been formerly established, this perversion of its doctrines was attended with consequences proportionably more extensive. <146>

These misguided votaries to mortification[6] being originally poor, were

6. The reference is to monks and the monastic orders.

supported either by alms or by their manual labour; but their exemplary lives, and the austerities which they practised, having excited universal admiration, enabled them to follow the example of the secular clergy, by procuring donations from the people; and hence, notwithstanding the poverty still professed by individuals, their societies acquired the possession of great riches. The members of these communities were by degrees admitted into holy orders; and became no less instrumental in promoting the influence of the church, than in communicating religious instruction.

As the affairs of a diocese had fallen under the chief direction of a bishop, those of a monastery were conducted by an *abbot,* who presided in the meetings of the society, and who, by obtaining authority in consequence of that distinction, was at length permitted to assume the distribution and disposal of their property.

Although the authority and jurisdiction of the church in this early period of Christianity, and the subordination among different ranks of <147> churchmen, proceeded in good measure from the nature of the business committed to their care, and the influence derived from their profession, yet the general fabric of ecclesiastical government was likewise a good deal affected by the political circumstances of the Roman empire. The person exalted to the head of a diocese was very often the minister of the most considerable town of that district, who from the greater weight and importance of his flock enjoyed a proportionable consideration among his brethren of the clergy. As by the civil policy of the empire many of those districts were united in what, according to the later division of the country, was called a *province,* the clergy of this larger territory were led frequently to hold provincial synods, in which the bishop of the capital city, acquiring respect from his residence near the seat of government, became the regular president, and was thence exalted to the dignity and title of a *metropolitan* or *archbishop.* In the yet more extensive divisions of the empire, which were called *jurisdictions,* the clergy were induced, upon some occasions, to deliberate; and in those greater meetings the right of presiding <148> was claimed by the bishop, who resided in the same city with the governor of each respective *jurisdiction.* Hence there arose a still superior rank in the church, that of an *exarch* or *patriarch,* who obtained certain prerogatives over the clergy of that great division. Of all the patriarchs in Christendom those of Rome and Constantinople, the two great capitals of the empire, became soon the most distinguished, the former of which enjoyed a pre-eminence over all the clergy in the western, the latter over those in the eastern provinces.

Upon the conquest of the western empire by the barbarous nations, the ancient inhabitants, who had for a long time been declining in arts and knowledge, experienced at once a violent change of situation, and were suddenly plunged into the darkness and barbarism of their conquerors. As those conquerors, however, embraced the Christian religion, they submitted implicitly to the discipline of the church, and to all the forms of ecclesiastical government which they had found established. The Roman clergy, therefore, remained upon their former footing, and were far from losing any of their former privileges; they even en-<149>deavoured, amidst the general destruction of science, to preserve a degree of that literature which, in order to propagate and defend the tenets of their religion, they had been under the necessity of acquiring, and which was the great support of their influence and popularity. With this view, and for the instruction of the people, more especially of those that were to be admitted into holy orders, they erected schools in their cathedrals and monasteries, and thence laid the foundation of those communities, possessed of ecclesiastical powers and privileges, which have received the exclusive appellation of *colleges.*

From these two circumstances, from the gross ignorance and the consequent superstition of the people, and from the comparative knowledge and abilities of the clergy, the latter were enabled to reap the utmost advantage from their situation, and to acquire an almost unlimited ascendency over the former. Hence the doctrines of the church concerning her influence in the remission of sins, and concerning the distribution of rewards and punishments in a future state, came to be modelled in such a manner as was plainly calculated to <150> promote her temporal interest. From this period, therefore, the donations of land to the church were greatly increased, and the bishops, abbots, and other dignified clergymen,[7] who reaped the chief advantage from these benefactions, became possessed of estates, which enabled them in some degree to rival the greater thanes of the country. From the same causes the contributions made by every congregation for the support of their minister, were gradually augmented. To augment these contributions, and to render them permanent, the church employed the utmost address and influence of all her members. What was at first a voluntary offering came afterwards, by the force of custom, to be regarded as a duty. Having

7. *Dignified clergy* refers to the higher ranks of the clergy, or those holding "dignities" of the church.

gradually raised this taxation higher and higher, the clergy, after the example of the Jewish priests, demanded at length a tenth part of the annual produce of land, as due to them by divine appointment. Not contented with this, they in some places insisted upon the same proportion of the annual industry; and it came to be maintained, that they had even a right to the tenth part of the alms given to beggars, as well as of the <151> hire earned by common prostitutes in the exercise of their profession.* To inforce the obligation of submitting to these monstrous exactions, was for a long time, it is said, the great aim of those discourses which resounded from every pulpit, and of the pious exhortations delivered by each ghostly father in private. The right of levying *tythes,*[8] which was first established in France, and which afterwards made its way through all the western parts of Christendom, created to the church a revenue of no less value than what she derived from her landed possessions.† The tythes of every parish were collected by its own minister, but a large proportion of those duties came to be demanded from the inferior clergy by the bishop of the diocese.

When the provinces of the western empire were broken into a number of independent kingdoms, it might have been expected that the church establishment in those countries would experience a similar revolution, and that the clergy of every separate kingdom, being <152> detached from those of every other, would form a separate ecclesiastical system. It is not difficult, however, to discover the circumstances which prevented such a separation; and which, notwithstanding the various oppositions of civil government, united the church of all the western countries of Europe in one great ecclesiastical monarchy.

The patriarchs of Rome and Constantinople, of whom the one, as has been already observed, became the head of the western, and the other of the eastern part of Christendom, were in a different situation with respect to the establishment of their power and dignity. The patriarch of Constantinople, from his connection with the principal seat of government, appears for some time to have been exalted above his western rival, and to have enjoyed superior authority. But after he had attained a certain pitch of exaltation, the

* F. Paul's History of Benefices.

† The council of Mascon, in 585, excommunicated all those who refused to pay tythes. Ibid.

8. The tithe was an amount, comprising 10% of the annual produce of agriculture, considered proper payment for the support of the clergy or of religious establishments.

very circumstance which had hitherto promoted his advancement, tended immediately to stop the progress of it; for no sooner did he become an object of jealousy to the civil power, than the vicinity of the imperial residence contributed the more effectually to thwart and controul every pro-<153>ject for the extension of his privileges. The Roman pontiff, on the other hand, when he had risen to such opulence and dignity as might have excited the envy and disgust of the civil magistrate, was, by the dissolution of the western empire, freed from the troublesome inspection of monarchs, who probably would have checked the growth of his power; and being placed in the situation of an independent prince, was at full liberty to put in practice every politic measure which might either enlarge his temporal dominions, or extend his authority over that numerous body of clergy who already owned his supremacy.

It may further explain the history of the western church to observe, that while the bishop of Rome was thus in a condition to avail himself of that superiority which he had acquired, the circumstances of the clergy were such as made it their interest to unite in one body, and to court his protection. The character of churchmen was, from the nature of their profession, a good deal different from that of the laity, and incited them to very opposite pursuits. The former, in a military and rude age, were generally drawn from the inferior <154> ranks of life; at the same time that, from the prevalence of superstition, they possessed great influence over the minds of the people, and were daily advancing their claims to power and emoluments. By the ancient nobility, therefore, or leading men of every country, and still more by the sovereign, the haughtiness, the insolence, and the rapacity of these upstarts, was often beheld with indignation and resentment, and produced continual jealousies and disputes between those different orders; the latter endeavouring to maintain and to extend a set of immunities and privileges, which the former were no less eager to restrain. In such a contest the ecclesiastics of any particular kingdom were as much inferior to their adversaries in direct force, as they were usually superior in skill and dexterity; and their situation naturally pointed out the expedient of soliciting assistance from their brethren in the neighbouring kingdoms. That assistance they very seldom failed to procure. The controversy of every individual was regarded as the common cause of the whole order. By adhering to one another, however disjoined in point of civil government, they became sufficiently power-<155>ful, not only to avoid oppression, but even to defend their usurpations;

and by combining, like the soldiers of an army, under one leader, their forces were directed to the best advantage.

The opportunities which this great leader enjoyed, of augmenting his revenue, and of increasing his power, may easily be conceived. In the multitude of disputes which occurred between the clergy and laity in the different nations of Europe, the former, in order to obtain his protection, were obliged to submit to various taxes, and to the extension of his prerogatives. Hence the payment of the *first fruits,* and such other impositions upon the livings of churchmen, were established in favour of the holy see.

In like manner, during the wars that were carried on between the different potentates of Europe, the contending parties, finding that the countenance and approbation of the Roman pontiff would give great weight and popularity to their cause, were sometimes under the necessity of purchasing his favour, by ratifying his titles, and permitting the exercise of his claims over their subjects. From the same circumstances, the temporal dominions of the <156> pope in Italy were greatly enlarged, and his authority, as an independent sovereign, was recognized. Upon the conquest of Lombardy by the king of France, his holiness, who had thrown his whole influence into the scale of that monarch, was rewarded with a great proportion of the conquered territory; and, at the same time, was enabled to assume the privilege of conferring the imperial dignity upon the conqueror.[9]

The disputes among the clergy themselves, more especially between the secular and regular clergy, were another source of the papal aggrandizement. Every society of monks was subject originally to the bishop within whose diocese their monastery was situated; but as they advanced in riches and popularity, they were led to assert their independence; and in supporting their pretensions, having to struggle with the whole body of secular clergy, they were induced to court the head of the church, by such obedience and compliances as were likely to gain him over to their interest.

In the eastern church, where these causes did not operate in the same degree, neither the authority of the clergy, nor that of the <157> patriarch of Constantinople, rose to the same height. The payment of tythes, though it was there warmly asserted by churchmen, as well as in the west, was never inforced by public authority; nor was the head of the church in that part of

9. Charlemagne conquered Lombardy in 773 and was crowned by Pope Leo III in 800.

the world in a condition to establish such an extensive revenue as had been acquired by the Roman pontiff.

It may be observed, on the other hand, that the same circumstances which produced an independent ecclesiastical jurisdiction in Christendom, have been productive of similar effects in other religions, and in different parts of the world. Among illiterate nations, the clergy, by explaining the will of the Deity, or by directing mysterious rites and ceremonies, are naturally raised to great importance; and if many such nations profess a common religion, and maintain an intercourse with one another, their spiritual guides, by extending their ideas of a common interest beyond the bounds of a single kingdom, are easily reduced under one great ecclesiastical leader. Hence an independent system of church government is likely to arise.

This was formerly the situation of the Celtic <158> nations, who inhabited a great part of Europe: they were under the influence of a common religion, the ministers of which are said to have possessed a jurisdiction superior to that of the civil magistrate. These *druids* were, at the same time, united in one society, independent of the different political states to which they belonged; and were under the direction of a *chief druid,* who resided in Britain, and whose authority extended over the laity as well as the clergy, in all the nations of Celtic original.[10]

The authority of the grand *Lama* or *high-priest* of the Tartars, which is acknowledged by many tribes or nations totally independent of one another, had, in all probability, the same foundation. This ecclesiastical monarch, who resides in the country called Little Thibet, is also a temporal prince. The numerous clergy, in the different parts of Tartary, who acknowledge his supremacy, are said to be distinguished into different ranks or orders, somewhat analogous to those which take place in Christendom; and the ordinary priests, or lamas, are subjected to the authority of bishops, whose jurisdiction is subordinate to that of the sovereign pontiff. Without pretending to ascer<159>tain, with any degree of accuracy, the church-history either of the Celtic or Tartar nations, we cannot avoid remarking the general analogy that appears in the origin and constitution of all these different Hierarchies.

10. *Celts* is a broad term encompassing early non-Germanic peoples across northern Europe who were driven westward by the Germanic tribes into Gaul and Britain. Druids were an order of Celts of Gaul and Britain who according to Caesar were priests and teachers, but who figure in Irish and Welsh legend as magicians or soothsayers.

SECTION II

The Establishment of Christianity in Britain, under the Roman Dominion, and in the early Government of the Anglo-Saxons.

Christianity made its way into Britain, in the same gradual manner as into all the other parts of the Roman empire. It is supposed to have obtained a permanent footing in the country, under the government of Marcus Aurelius,[11] at which time a bishop of Rome is said, upon the application of Lucius, a British king,[12] to have sent over, to this island, several learned men, to preach and propagate the gospel. But whatever degree of credit may be due to this account, it is certain that, in the reign of the emperor Constantine,[13] this religion was taken under the protection of <160> government, in Britain, as well as in all the other provinces of Rome; and that it continued in this situation until the island was abandoned by the Romans. During this period the Christian church had received the same form as in all the other parts of the empire. Particular clergymen had obtained a settlement in small districts or parishes, according to the number and situation of the inhabitants.* Many of these districts were united under the inspection of a bishop, the minister of a cathedral church; and a metropolitan, or archbishop, was exalted over the whole clergy of a province. But though it is probable that this ecclesiastical establishment was modelled according to the situation of the great towns, and the chief divisions introduced by the civil government of the country; yet neither the number of the British prelates, nor the churches in which they were settled, appear to be known with any degree of certainty.† Men-<161>tion is made of three archbishops, who, it should seem, corresponded to three of the provinces, in the late arrangement which

* Gildas.—Also Whitaker, Hist. of Manchester.

† According to the monkish tradition, there were twenty-eight bishops in Britain, during the Roman government of that island. These corresponded to the twenty-eight considerable cities in the province. See Ranulph. Higden. lib. i.—This number of British cities is mentioned by Gildas, Bede, and others; and their names are transmitted by Nonnius.

11. For Marcus Aurelius, see p. 22, note 8.

12. Lucius: legendary British king, reputed to have written to Pope Eleutherius in the second century, desiring assistance in his conversion to Christianity.

13. For Constantine, see p. 22, note 10.

the Romans made of their British territories. The first resided in London; the second in York; and the third, whose jurisdiction extended over Wales, appears, at different times, to have had a different place of residence.* That the Hierarchy had early acquired a settled condition in Britain, and that its bishops held some rank among those of other churches, is evident from their sending representatives to the council of Arles, called in the year 314, and to other remarkable councils, that were afterwards convened in different parts of Christendom.†

The arrival of the Saxons in this island was productive of great disorder in the religious, as well as in the civil establishment. In those parts of the country which fell under the dominion of the Saxons, the Christian churches <162> were frequently demolished; the public worship was interrupted; and the clergy, in many cases, could neither be provided with a maintenance from the public, nor continue the regular exercise of their jurisdiction. The altars of Thor, and Woden, were often substituted for those of Jesus Christ; and the life and immortality which had been brought to light by the gospel, were obscured and eclipsed by the fictions of Hela's dreary abode, and Valhalla's happy mansions, where heroes drink ale and mead from the sculls of enemies whom they have slain in battle.[14]

Wherever the ancient inhabitants were able to preserve their independence, their ecclesiastical policy remained without any alteration. This was particularly the case in the whole western part of the island, from the southmost point of Cornwall to the Frith of Clyde; not to mention the country to the northward, which the arms of the Saxons had not penetrated. In the territories where that people had formed their settlements, there is ground to believe that, after the tumult and violence attending the conquest had subsided, the two nations frequently maintained an amicable <163> correspondence, were in some measure united in one society, and enjoyed the free

* Ranulph. Higden. lib. i. [[Millar cites Ranulf [Ranalph] Higden. See *Polychronicon Ranulphi Higden Monachi Cestrensis,* ed. Churchill Babington, 49 vols., Rolls Series (London, 1865–89; repr. Kraus, 1965), 2:110–13. Augustine changed the archbishopric from London to Canterbury when Pope Gregory died.]]

† Stillingfleet, Orig. Britan.

14. In Nordic mythology, Odin is the supreme god and creator. Thor is his son, the god of thunder, agriculture, and weather. Hela is the goddess of the dead, commonly represented as living in a cavern. Valhalla is the great hall of the gods in the Nordic pantheon.

exercise of their religion.* As their long neighbourhood produced, by degrees, a communication of civil institutions and customs, it was likewise, in all probability, attended with some approximation of religious opinions and observances; and in this particular, it can hardly be doubted that the regular and well-established system of Christianity, to say nothing of its genuine merit in other respects, would have great advantage over the unformed and loosely connected superstition of the barbarians. In the ardour of making proselytes, and in the capacity of propagating their tenets, the professors of the former must have greatly surpassed those of the latter; and it was natural <164> to expect that the Saxons in England would at length follow the example of all the rude nations, who had settled in the provinces upon the continent, by adopting the religion of the conquered people.

What laid the foundation for a general and rapid conversion of the Saxons, was an event, which happened about an hundred and fifty years after their settlement in Britain. Ethelbert, the sovereign of Kent, having married Bertha,[15] the daughter of a king of the Franks; this princess, already a Christian, made open profession of her religion, and brought over a French bishop to reside at the Kentish court. This incident suggested to the Roman pontiff, Gregory the great,[16] a man of unbounded ambition, the idea of converting the Anglo-Saxons to Christianity, and, at the same time, of establishing his authority over the British clergy, who had hitherto neither acknowledged the papal jurisdiction, nor yielded an exact conformity to the tenets and observances of the Roman church. For these two purposes, he gave a com-

* This was so much the case, that among the East Angles, according to the testimony of Bede, the Christian worship, and the Saxon idolatrous rites, were performed in one and the same church; such good neighbourhood was maintained between the two religions. "Atque in eodem fano et altare haberet ad sacrificium Christi et Arulam [[*sic:* arulam]] ad victimas daemoniorum. Quod videlicit [[*sic:* videlicet]] fanum, ex [[*sic:* rex]] ejusdem provinciae Alduulf, qui nostra aetate fuit, usque ad suum tempus perdurasse, et se in pueritia vidisse testabatur." Bed. Hist. Eccl. lib. ii. ch. 15. [["In the same temple he had one altar for the Christian sacrifice and another small altar on which to offer victims to devils. Ealdwulf, who was ruler of the kingdom up to our time, used to declare that the temple lasted until his time and that he saw it when he was a boy." *Bede's Ecclesiastical History of the English People,* ed. Bertram Colgrave and R. A. B. Mynors (Oxford: Clarendon Press, 1969), 191.]]

15. Bertha (d. after 601): queen of Kent.

16. Pope Gregory I, the Great (590–604).

mission to Augustine,[17] one of the monks of a convent at Rome, with about forty assistants, to preach and propagate the gospel in <165> Britain.* By the industry of these, and of succeeding missionaries, the Christian religion was, in the course of about half a century, established universally in all the kingdoms of the Heptarchy. The authority of the church of Rome went hand in hand with Christianity; and though the British clergy struggled for a considerable time to maintain their independence, and their peculiar doctrines, they were at length borne down by the prevailing system, and reduced into a subordinate branch of the Roman Hierarchy.†

The conversion of the Anglo-Saxons has been commonly regarded as an entirely new plantation of the gospel, in the territories which fell under the dominion of that people; and it seems to be imagined, that when Augustine entered upon his mission, there were no traces of Christianity remaining in those parts of the country. This opinion appears to have arisen, partly from the supposition, that the settlement of the Anglo-Saxons was <166> accompanied with a total expulsion of the ancient inhabitants, and partly from a disposition in subsequent ecclesiastical writers to undervalue that system of church-discipline and faith which had obtained in Britain, before it was fully subjected to the papal jurisdiction.

With respect to the general extirpation of the Britons, it seems to be a perfect chimera. Neither is there any reason to believe that they underwent any persecution from the Saxons upon account of their religion. The rude polytheism, professed by those conquerors, does not seem to have taken a firm hold of their minds, or to have inspired much animosity against foreign deities or modes of worship; and if, during the immediate conquest of the country, the British clergy were sometimes plundered or massacred, this, in all probability, proceeded from no peculiar enmity to their religion, but from the ferocity natural to barbarians, who, in the heat of a military enterprize, could not be expected to shew much regard to the distinction of characters

* Bed. Hist. Ecclesiast. lib. i. c. 23. 25.

† Bed. Hist. Eccles. lib. ii. seq.—Stillingfleet, Origin. Brit.—Henry's Hist. of Great Britain.

17. St. Augustine of Canterbury (d. 604): Italian churchman and first archbishop of Canterbury. Augustine's mission to Britain commenced in 596. For the discussion in Bede that Millar cites, see *Bede's Ecclesiastical History,* 69–73.

or professions. The effect of these disorders, however, was only partial and temporary. It appears that, even in those parts of the country <167> where the Saxons had remained the longest, the ancient church buildings were far from being entirely destroyed; for we learn from Bede,[18] that, upon the arrival of Augustine in Kent, he first preached in a church, which had been erected by the Romans in honour of St. Martin, and that soon after, when the monarch of that kingdom had been baptized, orders were given to build or *repair* churches, for the accommodation of the Christian missionaries.*

Upon the full restoration of Christianity in those parts of the country where it had been corrupted by the mixture of Saxon superstition, the religious establishments, which had been introduced under the dominion of the Romans, and which had always been preserved in the unconquered parts of the island, were completely revived; with this difference, that the British churches, in the degree of their submission to the papal authority, were brought into a greater conformity with the churches upon the continent. It is probable that the ancient parochial divisions had not been entirely lost; more especially in those districts, <168> which the Anglo-Saxons had but recently subdued when they embraced the religion of the former inhabitants.†

The number of bishops, it is natural to suppose, and the extent of their jurisdiction, were likewise directed, in some measure, by the antecedent arrangements in the provincial government of Britain; though, from the changes produced in the state of the country, many variations were, doubtless, become necessary. Of the three *archbishops,* who had formerly acquired a pre-eminence over the whole of the British clergy, one appears to have been sunk by the disjunction of Wales from the English monarchy; so that there came to be only two metropolitans under the Saxon establishment. The archbishop of the northern department resided, as formerly, at York; but the seat of the other, from the residence of Augustine, who obtained the chief ecclesiastical dignity, was transferred from London to Canterbury.‡

The revenue for maintaining the clergy was the same in Britain as in all the churches <169> acknowledging the jurisdiction of the Roman pontiff.

* Hist. Eccles. l. i. c. 26.

† Whitaker, Hist. of Manchester; and the authorities quoted by him.

‡ Ranulph. Higden. lib. i.

18. See *Bede's Ecclesiastical History,* 77.

It consisted, partly of contributions levied in every parish; and partly of landed estates, which the superstition of the people had led them to bequeath for pious uses: but the former of these funds remained longer than in the more southern parts of Europe, before it was converted into a regular tax, and exalted to a tenth of the whole yearly produce. <170>

CHAPTER VI

Institution of Tythings, Hundreds, and Counties.

In every nation it must be a great object to provide for defence against the invasion of neighbouring states; but in a rude age, the provisions requisite for this purpose are few and simple. The great body of the people are soldiers, willing and ready to take the field whenever their service is necessary. From the mutual depredations frequent among a rude people, they become inured to hardships, and familiar with danger; and having little employment at home, they are glad to embrace every opportunity of acquiring military reputation, or of enriching themselves with the spoil of their enemies. Every person, therefore, as soon as he is capable of using arms, is accustomed to the use of them, and acquainted with the simple manner of fighting practised among his countrymen; so that, as the chief magistrate finds no difficulty in raising troops upon any occasion, he is put to little or no trouble in training and preparing <171> them for those military operations in which they are to be engaged.

The appointment of certain leaders in particular districts, to collect the forces upon any emergency, and to command them in time of battle, seems to be all that is wanted, in such a situation, for putting a whole kingdom in a complete posture of defence. A few regulations of this nature, arising obviously from the circumstances of a barbarous people, were, at an early period, established among the Saxons in England, as well as among their neighbours upon the continent.

Every feudal superior was the military leader of his own dependents; but upon the settlement of the Saxons in Britain, the landed estates acquired by the greater part of individuals were at first so small as to render the number of their vassals inconsiderable; and the *allodial* or independent proprietors were therefore under the necessity, amidst the disorder that prevailed in those times, of associating for mutual protection and security. Different families, connected by the ties of consanguinity, or otherwise, found it expedient as well as agreeable to settle in the same neighbourhood, <172> that they might on all occasions be in a condition to assist one another. Thus the inhabitants came to be distributed into villages of greater or less extent, according to circumstances; and the members of every village, accustomed from their infancy to live together, and finding themselves united by a common interest, were led to acquire the strongest habits of intimacy and attachment. These little societies received the appellation of *vills, towns,* or *free-bourgs.*

As these villages were formed upon the plan of defence, and were frequently employed in the exercise of hostilities, there naturally arose in each of them a leader, who by having the privilege of conducting their military enterprises, obtained also a degree of authority in the management of civil affairs. To this person the name of *head-borough* or *borsholder* (a word supposed by some to be contracted from *borough's elder*) was commonly given.

According to the early policy of the Anglo-Saxons, each of their villages was divided into ten *wards,* or petty districts; and hence they were called *tythings* or *decennaries,* as their leader was denominated a *decanus* or *tything-*<173>*man.* This regulation appears to have been extended over all the kingdoms upon the neighbouring continent; and in all probability it originated from the influence of ecclesiastical institutions.*

As, upon the first establishment of Christianity under the Roman dominion, the form of church government was in some respects modelled by the political constitution of the empire; so the civil government, in the modern states of Europe, was afterwards regulated in many particulars according to the system of ecclesiastical policy. When the western provinces of the Roman empire were conquered by the barbarous nations and erected into separate kingdoms, the conquerors, who soon embraced the Christian religion, and felt the highest respect for its teachers, were disposed in many cases to improve their own political institutions, by an imitation of that <174>

* The term *free-burg* is sometimes applied not to the whole tything or village, but to each of those wards into which it was divided. [See the laws ascribed to William the conqueror. Wilkins, c. 32.] But more frequently a free-burg and tything are understood to be synonymous. See the Glossaries of Spelman and Du Cange, v. *Friborga.*

regularity and subordination which was observed in the order and discipline of the church.

In the distribution of persons, or of things, which fell under the regulation of the Christian clergy, it appears that, in conformity to the customs of the Jewish nation, a decimal arrangement was more frequently employed than any other. By the Mosaic institution the people were placed under rulers of thousands, of hundreds, of fifties, and of tens. A Jewish synagogue, corresponding to a modern parish, appears at a subsequent period to have been put under the direction of *ten elders,* of whom one became the chief ruler of that ecclesiastical division.* A tenth part of the annual produce was appropriated for the support of the Levites, as the same proportion of ecclesiastical livings was claimed by the high-priest. Hence we <175> find that in modern Europe, the members of a cathedral church, as well as those of a monastery, were divided into ten branches, each of which was put under a director, and the tenth of these persons, or *decanus,*[1] was intrusted with a superintendence of all the rest.† Hence too the modern institution of tythes, and the pretensions of the Roman pontiff, the Christian high-priest, to the tenth of all the revenues of the clergy.‡

When the western part of Europe, upon the dissolution of the Roman government, had been reduced into a state of barbarism, by which the inhabitants were necessarily divided into separate villages or small towns, each of <176> those little communities was naturally formed into one congre-

* Dr. Lightfoot's Harmony of the Four Evangelists, part 3. on Luke chap. 4. ver. 15.—Lewis's Antiquities of the Hebrew Republic, b. 3. ch. 21.—Goodwin's Moses and Aaron, b. 2. ch. 2.—also Vitringa Archisynagogus illustratus.—This author agrees with Dr. Lightfoot, in supposing that the *decem otiosi* [[Ten men of leisure. The reference is to John Lightfoot's *The Harmony of the Four Evangelists, Among Themselves, and with the Old Testament* (London, 1650), pt. 3, 115, who gives Hebrew rather than Latin.]], mentioned as requisite in every synagogue, were officers employed in the business of that society; though he differs as to the particular employments that were allotted to them.

† Burn's Eccles. Law.—Kennet's Paroch. Antiq.

‡ Though the distribution of persons and things according to *tens,* appears to have been immediately borrowed by the Christian clergy from the Jews, we find among many other nations a tendency to follow the same arrangement. Those natural instruments of notation, which every man carries about with him, the fingers, have probably been the original cause of the common arithmetical progression by *tens,* and of the general propensity to be governed by this number in the classification of objects.—The land-tax upon the ancient Roman provinces is said to have been a tenth of the produce.

1. Dean.

gation, and annexed to a single church. The same people who joined in public worship were also combined in their military expeditions; and the same arrangement, under different rulers, that had been adopted in the former capacity, was easily communicated to them in the latter. This division of a village, with the corresponding territory belonging to its inhabitants, into ten little *wards* or *districts,* probably arose in those European kingdoms which had first attained a regular form, and was afterwards extended to the Saxons in England, and to the inhabitants of other countries, who remained longer in a state of anarchy and confusion.

But while the members of every Anglo-Saxon town or village were thus intimately united, a connection of the same sort was gradually introduced between the inhabitants of a larger territory. Those who belonged to different towns or villages in the same neighbourhood had frequently occasion to assist one another against a common enemy; and in consequence of many joint expeditions, directed by a sense of mutual interest, were induced to <177> form a regular association, under a permanent military officer.

The extent of these associations was at first perhaps arbitrary and variable, but was at length settled in an uniform manner, according to the system of ecclesiastical policy which prevailed both in England and in other European kingdoms. Upon the principle which has been formerly mentioned, every ten churches of a diocese were united under an ecclesiastical inspector, who in England, in contradistinction to a similar officer belonging to a cathedral or monastery, was called a *rural dean.*[*] In like manner every ten villages or tythings, which were of the same extent with parishes, formed a military district, which obtained the appellation of a *hundred,* and its commanding officer that of a *centenarius* or *hundreder.*[†]

The connections of society being still farther extended, the members of different hundreds <178> were also associated for their common defence, and fell under the direction of a greater officer, called the *heretoch,* a title which, in the Saxon language, is synonymous with that of duke, and which appears to have been originally given to some of those leaders in the Heptarchy, who afterwards assumed the title of kings. The districts belonging to

* Kennet's Paroch. Antiq.—Burn's Eccles. Law. v. *Dean and Chapter.*

† Hundredus autem Latinè, says Ralph Higden, sive Cantredus, Wallicè et Hibernicè continet *centum villas.* [Polychronicon, lib. i.] [["A hundred, moreover, in Latin—or a cantred in Welsh or Irish—contains a hundred towns." Ranulph Higden, *Polychronicon,* 2:86.]]

these heretochs, which were greater or less according to accidents, and had been varied on different occasions, were gradually ascertained and established, so as at length to correspond entirely with the territories that were placed under the ecclesiastical jurisdiction of the several bishops. These districts were called *shires;*[2] and the officer who presided over them seems, at a later period of the Anglo-Saxon government, to have changed his title for that of *alder-man* or *earl.* It is a common opinion, however, that the heretoch and the alder-man were different persons, intrusted with different departments; and that the former was the chief military, as the latter was the chief civil officer of the shire.

In some parts of the country a smaller number of hundreds were associated, so as to com-<179>pose an intermediate district, called *lathe, rape,* or *trything;* and several of these districts were united in forming a shire. But this arrangement, peculiar to some shires, and depending upon the same principles with the divisions already mentioned, is of little consequence in our present view of the subject.

Such were the military institutions of the Anglo-Saxons; which appear to have arisen almost imperceptibly from the rude state of the country, from the natural divisions of the people, and from their progressive attempts in forming more extensive and permanent associations.

From the great deficiency of Saxon records, there are, concerning these institutions, many particulars, which remain in obscurity, and which have given rise to various disputes and conjectures. The earliest historians, who have said any thing upon this subject, appear, for the most part, to have lived at a period when these institutions had undergone many variations, and in several respects had fallen into disuse. They were, at the same time, ignorant annalists of a barbarous age; and their accounts, which appear to have been chiefly derived <180> from tradition, are short and unsatisfactory.[3] It seems to have been uniformly imagined by these authors, that the institutions

2. Administrative districts, consisting of a number of smaller districts called hundreds, united for purposes of local government.

3. In this usage, "tradition" does not carry its modern sense, but rather means orally transmitted stories: hence a weak form of evidence. Hume, similarly, writes: "Ingenious men, possessed of leisure, are apt to push their researches beyond the period, in which literary monuments are framed or preserved; without reflecting, that the history of past events is immediately lost or disfigured, when intrusted to memory and oral tradition." *HE,* 1:3.

above mentioned were peculiar to the government of the Anglo-Saxons; and that they were introduced by the singular policy of king Alfred, to whom the admiration of English writers has commonly ascribed every important regulation during the Saxon period. But it is now generally known, that the establishment of tythings, hundreds, and shires, was prior, in England, to the time of Alfred; and that it was not peculiar to this country, but was probably extended over all the barbarous nations who settled in the provinces of the western empire.

With respect to the establishment of tythings and hundreds, it has been the general opinion that the former consisted of ten families, and that the latter, of course, were composed of an hundred families. That such was the exact number of families comprehended in each of these divisions, the respective names affixed to them appear to have been thought sufficient evidence.

But when we examine this opinion, after all the pains that have been taken by late writers <181> to render it plausible, it seems to be attended with insuperable difficulties. To divide the whole people into military parties of ten and of an hundred families, without any regard to their places of residence, would mark a degree of art and contrivance hardly to be expected in a barbarous age: not to mention that it would be a most absurd regulation, as it would frequently separate near relations, and place them under the command of different officers, instead of uniting them under one common leader, with whom they had acquired a natural connection; for as the accidental collections of kindred and acquaintance, who lived in the same village or neighbourhood, could not be regularly composed of ten families, nor of any given number, they must of necessity have been split and jumbled with strangers, to make up the several tythings into which the people were thus artificially divided. If such a regulation ever had place in England, we must suppose that it was introduced by a political projector, neglecting, for the sake of a finical regularity, to avail himself of the usual sources of authority in a rude nation, and by a legislator invested with such absolute power, as might <182> render him capable of enforcing measures diametrically opposite to the natural course of things; a supposition which is neither applicable to the character nor to the condition of the early monarchs of Britain.

As the institution of tythings, together with that of hundreds, and of shires or counties, was not limited to England, but had place in most, if not all of the feudal countries, there is good reason to believe that it was not derived from artificial or distant views of policy, suggested to any particular prince; but that it proceeded from a concurrence of circumstances in the European kingdoms, by which it was recommended to the great body of the people.

That a tything was originally the same thing with a village, and that it did not comprehend any precise number of persons or families, may be concluded from this, that in the ancient law-language of England the words *vill, town, decennary,* and *tything,* have all the same signification.* If a tything have the same meaning with a vill or town, it is surely impossible that it can signify a collection of ten families only, without relation to the place of their <183> residence. Should we, on the other hand, suppose that a tything was regularly composed of so many families, the members of the same tything must frequently have resided in different towns or villages; in which case it would sometimes be necessary, in describing or pointing out those persons, to mention the *town* which they inhabited, as distinct from the tything to which they belonged; and these two terms therefore, so far from being synonymous, would come, upon such occasions, to be used in direct opposition to each other.

But what puts this matter in a yet more conspicuous point of view, is an early regulation mentioned by the English lawyers, that every tything should have a church, with celebration of divine service, sacraments, and burials.† If the limits of a tything, and of a town or village, were the same, such a regulation would naturally be established. Its establishment, on the other hand, affords complete evidence that a parish and a tything were of the same extent. But how is it possible to conceive that a parish comprehended only ten families? According to this doctrine every <184> eleventh house must have been a church, and the clergy must have composed the eleventh part of the whole people.

To obviate this objection, it is held by some authors that a family is not to be understood in a literal sense, but as comprehending all the vassals and tenants of a proprietor, who in some cases were pretty numerous. Admitting,

* Blackstone's Comment. Vol. I. Introd. § 4.

† Blackstone's Comment. Vol. I. Introd. § 4. [[Sir William Blackstone notes that "Tithings, towns, or vills, are of the same signification in law; and had, each of them, originally a church and celebration of divine service, sacraments, and burials; which to have, or have had, separate to itself, is the essential distinction of a town, according to Sir Edward Coke." *Commentaries on the Laws of England* (London, 1765), vol. 1.]]

however, this explanation in its fullest extent, it will only vary, instead of removing the difficulty. It would still be in vain to expect that a village or town should always contain exactly ten of these enlarged families, or even any number of tens; so that it would often be requisite to patch up a tything from the remnants of different towns or villages; and it would follow that these outcasts did not belong to the church in their neighbourhood, but, however dispersed over the country, and intermixed with other parishes, were united in one congregation, and were provided with a separate church and minister of their own.

The establishment of tythings, hundreds, and shires, was primarily intended for the mutual defence of the inhabitants, but it was likewise rendered subservient to other very salutary <185> purposes. When the people had been assembled in those meetings to engage in a military enterprize, or upon the conclusion of it to divide their booty, they had occasion to hear complaints of the injuries and disorders committed among themselves. Every feudal superior was the natural judge of his own tenants and vassals; but when a dispute had arisen between different allodial proprietors of the same tything, there was no single person possessed of sufficient authority to terminate the difference. The parties being independent of each other in point of property, and therefore masters of their own conduct, were under no necessity, in a matter of that kind, of submitting to the orders of any individual. They acted in the same manner with respect to the exercise of their civil rights, as with relation to peace and war. In both cases they considered themselves as free men, subject to no restraints, but such as arose from the nature of their confederacy, or were imposed by their common consent.

The same motives, however, which induced a village or tything to enter into joint measures for their defence against a foreign enemy, determined them also to take precautions for <186> composing animosities and differences among their own members. Roused by the danger of a quarrel which might be fatal to their union, and which might render them an easy prey to their neighbours, they readily interposed with all their influence to reconcile the parties, and to enforce their observance of the rules of justice. A judicial power was thus gradually assumed by every tything over the allodial or independent proprietors of which it was composed. The hundred, in like manner, came to exercise a power of determining the differences between the members of the several tythings, within the bounds of that larger district;

as the meetings of the shire established a similar jurisdiction over the different hundreds comprehended in that extensive territory. These courts took cognizance of every cause, whether civil or criminal; and as they enjoyed the sole jurisdiction, in the first instance, within the respective boundaries of each, they became naturally subordinate one to another; so that from the decision of the tything there lay an appeal to the hundred, and the sentences of this latter tribunal were reviewed in the greater meetings of the shire. <187>

These courts were held originally by all the allodial proprietors of each particular district; and the same persons had the same right of presiding in their judicial procedure, as when their meetings were called to deliberate upon military affairs.

It is probable that every kind of law-suit was at first determined in full assembly, and by a plurality of voices; but in the larger meetings of the hundred, and of the shire, it should seem that when the authority of those tribunals had been confirmed by custom, and their duty had become somewhat burdensome by the increase of business, convenience introduced a practice of selecting a certain number of their members, to assist their president in the determination of each particular cause. Hence the origin of *juries,* the precise date of whose establishment is uncertain, because it probably arose from no general or public regulation, but from the gradual and almost imperceptible changes, authorized by common usage in the several districts of the kingdom. The number of jurymen was for some time different upon different occasions; till the advantages of an uniform practice produced a general rule, which <188> determined that no less than twelve persons should be called in all ordinary causes.* <189>

* The custom of choosing twelve men for distributing justice, is frequently mentioned in the Anglo-Saxon laws. Thus, in a law of king Ethelred, it is said, "Et ut habeantur conventus in quolibet wapentachio, et exeant seniores duodecim thani, et prefectus cum iis, et jurent super sanctuarium quod iis in manus datur, quod nolent ullum innocentem accusare, nec aliquem noxium celare." [["And assemblies shall be held in each *wapentake,* and twelve of the leading thanes shall come forward together with the reeve, and they shall swear on holy relics placed into their hands neither to accuse any innocent man nor conceal a guilty one." A wapentake is a division of land in the Danelaw corresponding to the hundred. The Anglo-Saxon text can be found in *The Laws of the Kings of England from Edmund to Henry I,* ed. and trans. A. J. Robertson (Cambridge: Cambridge University Press, 1925), 65.]]—[Wilkins, p. 117.] In another law, ascribed to the same king, commonly called the *senatus consultum de monticulis Walliae* [[a decree

Concerning the institution of tythings, there is one regulation, connected with the administration of justice, that has been much taken notice of by historians, and has excited the admiration of all political writers: the members of every tything are said to have been responsible for the conduct of one another; and the society, or their leader, might be prosecuted, and compelled to make reparation for an injury committed by any individual.

If we look upon a tything as regularly composed of ten families, this branch of its police will appear in the highest degree artificial and singular; but if we consider that society as of <190> the same extent with a town or village, we shall find that such a regulation is conformable to the general usage of barbarous nations, and is founded upon their common notions of justice.

---

of the Wittenagemote concerning the mountain-dwellers of Wales; this is the title of the law as it appears in Lambarde, *Archaionomia, sive De Priscis Anglorum Legibus Libri* (Cambridge, 1644), 94]], it is enacted, for the mutual benefit of the English and Welch, that controversies between them shall be determined by twelve law-men, the half of whom shall be Englishmen, the other half Welchmen. [Wilkins, p. 125.]

These twelve persons correspond, it should seem, to the *Racimburgi* and the *Scabini,* who under the first and second races of the kings in France assisted in the decisions of the count and of the centenarius. [[The *Racimburgi* under the Merovingians were nobles assembled in groups of seven or eleven to assist the count in judgments in his court or to give their own judgments. The *Scabini* (in French *échevins*) succeeded them under Charlemagne in the eighth century. Robert Brady discusses the question in *A Complete History of England* (London, 1685), 1:76n.]]

It has been supposed by some authors that neither of these were upon the footing of modern jurymen, chosen out of the free men of a district for each cause, but that both were permanent assessors of the magistrate and members of the court. See Brady's complete Hist. of Eng.—Hickes's Diss. Epistol.

But that either these twelve men, or the Racimburgi or Scabini, were permanent members of the court, appears improbable, for the following reasons: 1. Because these twelve men were chosen among the *thanes;* and it is not likely that the same persons, of that rank, would subject themselves to the drudgery of being constant assessors to the magistrate. 2. The number of *Racimburgi* or *Scabini* appears to have been varied, according to the importance of the causes which they decided. This supposes a new election in each cause. 3. If there was a regular bench of assessors to the chief magistrate of a county, it is wonderful that no traces of that institution should be found at present, more especially in Scotland, where the county-courts have been continued upon the ancient footing.

Accordingly Horn, an author who lived in the time of Edward I. says expressly, in his *Mirroir de Justices,* that king Alfred put to death a number of his judges for deciding causes without a jury.

Among barbarians in all parts of the world persons who belong to the same family are understood to enjoy a community of goods, and to be all jointly subjected to the same obligations. In those early ages when men are in a great measure strangers to commerce, or the alienation of commodities, the right of *property* is hardly distinguished from the privilege of *using* or *possessing;* and those persons who have acquired the joint possession of any subject are apt to be regarded as the joint proprietors of it. At the same time, when a debt is contracted by one of several persons who have a perfect community of goods, it must of necessity be discharged from the common funds; and the obligation of every individual becomes therefore a burden upon the whole society.

After a family has been enlarged, and subdivided into different branches, their possessions are not upon this account entirely sepa-<191>rated, nor their notions of common property altogether effaced. Though the different families, who are thus formed into a tribe or village, reside in different houses, their neighbourhood allows them still to maintain a promiscuous intercourse; and their situation disposes them to act in concert with each other in all their important employments and pursuits. As, in their expeditions of war and hunting, they go out in a body, so, according to the primitive state of agriculture, they labour in the field, and gather in the harvest in common; and what has been acquired by their united exertions, before it is divided among them by consent, is naturally conceived to be the joint property of all.

It is no hardship, that persons connected in so intimate a manner should be liable for the obligations of one another; and when an individual has become bound to a stranger, who cannot easily know for whose benefit the debt was incurred, it seems reasonable that the creditors should be allowed to demand payment from the community, who alone have access to distinguish the rights of their particular members. <192>

But the greater part of the debts contracted in a barbarous age arise from injuries and hostilities: for which it is usual to make atonement by pecuniary compositions: and as in such cases it commonly happens, either that the offence was originally committed by a whole village, or, if it arose from a single individual, that the quarrel was afterwards adopted and prosecuted by the other members of the community, this appears a sufficient reason for subjecting them to a share of the punishment.

Thus, by the general custom of rude nations, the vengeance of the injured party for murder and other atrocious crimes is not confined to the guilty person, but is extended to his family, and even to the whole village or tribe of which he is a member. The prosecution of claims, founded upon this general custom, makes a considerable part of the history of mankind in the early periods of society. Traces of this primitive law of nations may be discovered even in some civilized countries; where, upon account of enormous offences, the criminal, together with his innocent children, and other <193> relations, have been condemned to one common punishment.*

Among the Jews, when a person was found murdered in the neighbourhood of a city, and the murderer was unknown, it seems to have been thought that the punishment might with justice be extended to all the inhabitants; who are, upon that account, directed to perform an expiatory sacrifice. "And all the elders of the city that is next unto the slain man, shall wash their hands over the heifer that is beheaded in the valley. And they shall answer and say, Our hands have not shed this blood, neither have our eyes seen it. Be merciful, O Lord, unto thy people Israel, whom thou hast redeemed, and lay not innocent blood unto thy people Israel's charge. And the blood shall be forgiven them."†

When it is customary to demand satisfaction from a whole village for the highest personal injuries committed by an individual, it cannot appear surprising that the same privi-<194>lege should be claimed upon account of the ordinary violations of property.

I am assured, from the most respectable authority, that, in the villages belonging to the Highlands of Scotland, a rule of this kind has been immemorially established. The stealing of cattle was formerly the only species of theft from which the inhabitants of that country could suffer any great prejudice; and when stolen cattle could be traced within the district of any particular village, the inhabitants were liable to repair the damage, unless they could point out the track of the cattle, passing again without their ter-

* See instances of this quoted by the acute author of The Historical Law Tracts. [[Millar's general reference is to Lord Kames, who noted that Egypt and Greece "deemed it unjust, that the innocent should suffer with the guilty, and that a child, common to mother and father, should lose its life for the crimes of the mother. We find no such similar instances while punishment is in the hands of individuals; for a good reason, that such regulations are incompatible with the partiality of man." *Historical Law-Tracts* (Edinburgh, 1758), 1:75–76.]]

† Deuteron. chap. xxi. [[Deuteronomy 21:6–8.]]

ritories. This law, which was founded merely upon long usage, remained in force at least as far down as the beginning of the present century.*

It was a custom, we are told, among the ancient Irish, "that the head of every *sept,* and the chief of every kindred, or family, should be answerable and bound to bring forth every one of that sept, and kindred under it, at all times, to be justified, when he should <195> be required, or charged with any treason, felony, or other heinous crime."† The Irish law, in this as well as in other particulars, was probably analogous to that of the other Celtic nations.

From the code of Gentoo laws published in 1776,[4] it appears that a similar regulation has been introduced among the ancient inhabitants of Indostan. If the footsteps of a thief have been traced, or if stolen goods are found, within a certain distance from any town, the thief is presumed to be concealed in it.—And whenever a robbery or theft is committed in the neighbourhood of any town or city, the *head-person* of that town or city is bound to make up the loss.‡

Upon some parts of the coast of Guinea,[5] the villages or towns, it should seem, are liable for the obligations of every sort contracted by any of their members; for we are informed, that when a person in that country neglects to pay a debt, the creditor is under no necessity of arresting the real debtor, but, in the district, where he resides, has the liberty of seizing, at <196> pleasure, such a quantity of goods as will satisfy the demand, leaving the sufferers to indemnify themselves in the best manner they can.§

About the middle of the thirteenth century it appears that the states of

* It does not seem to be supposed by historians, that the Saxon regulations concerning tythings were extended to a country so inaccessible as the Highlands of Scotland.

† Spencer's View of the State of Ireland. [[For this quoted passage, see Edmund Spenser, *A View of the State of Ireland,* ed. Andrew Hadfield and Willy Maley (Oxford: Blackwell, 1997), 42.]]

‡ Code of Gentoo laws, ch. 17. sect. 4. 6.

§ Hist. Gen. des Voyages. Mod. Univ. Hist.

4. *Gentoo* is an archaic term for Hindu. The publication of this law code was sponsored by Warren Hastings, then governor general of India. It states that "If the footsteps of a Thief may be traced for some little Distance, or if the Article stolen hath dropped for a little Distance, and afterwards no farther Sign can be found, then, whatever Town is near the Place where these Signs have for a little Way extended, the Thief shall be judged to lurk in that Town." *A Code of Gentoo Laws* (London, 1776), chap. 16, sect. 4.6, 257.

5. *Guinea* is a historical term for the West African coastline.

Germany had very generally adopted a similar practice; which is mentioned by historians as a proof of uncommon rudeness and barbarism.* <197>

The inhabitants of the same foreign country happening, at any one time, to reside in London, were formerly viewed in the same light; and any one of them might be prosecuted for the debts contracted by his countrymen. In a treaty between Edward the Second and Alphonso king of the two Castiles, it is agreed, that the merchants of Bilboa, and the other towns of Biscay, shall not for the future be arrested, nor have their goods distrained, for the debts of any Spaniard, for whom they have not become personally bound.† The small number of Spanish merchants residing in London, and the distance of their native country, made them appear as much connected as if they had been members of a single rude village or tribe.

This noted regulation concerning the Saxon tythings is therefore to be

* The following passage is quoted from Pfefel's Abrégé Chron. de l'Histoire d'Allemagne. "Je ne puis passer sous silence une autre nouveauté, qui prouve, on ne peut pas mieux, et le malheur de ces tems, et la barbarie des moeurs du siécle: c'est le droit *d'Otage.* [Jus obstagiorum] Rien de plus bizarre que ce droit. Un Souabe, un bourgeois d'Ulm, lésé par un Liegeois, ne se donnoit pas la peine de poursuivre sa partie, devant la justice ordinaire; il se contentoit de mettre la main sur le premier Liegeois qu'il pouvoit rencontrer, et le constituoit prisonnier à Ulm, c'est là qu'il faisoit juger sa cause, et *l'Otage* n'étoit point relâché que la sentence ne fût exécutée. L'histoire et les archives nous fournissent mille exemples de ces procès singuliers: et *Lehmann* rapporte que les citoyens de Spire ont fait déclarer par des lettres patentes, qu'ils n'étoient point sujets de leur Evêque, et que par conséquent l'on ne pouvoit les arrêter légitimement pour les causes que regardoient les sujets de ce prince." [["I cannot pass over in silence another extraordinary practice which furnishes the best possible proof both of the lamentable conditions of those times and of the barbarity of the customs of the century: that is the right to take hostages (*jus obstagiorum*). There is nothing stranger than this right. A Swabian, a burgher of Ulm, having been wronged by a citizen of Liège, did not bother to prosecute his opponent in court in the ordinary way; he merely laid hands on the first inhabitant of Liège that he could find and imprisoned him at Ulm. There he had his case tried, and the hostage was not released until the sentence had been carried out. History and the archives provide us with a thousand examples of these remarkable trials, and Lehmann reports that the citizens of Speyer caused a declaration to be made by letters patent that they were not subjects of their bishop and consequently could not be legitimately arrested for lawsuits involving subjects of that prince." Christian Friedrich Pfeffel, *Nouvel abrégé chronologique de l'histoire et du droit public d'Allemagne* (Paris, 1777), 1:453–54. This text is a paraphrase rather than an exact quotation.]]

† Anderson's History of Commerce. [[Edward II, king of England and Scotland (r. 1307–27); Alfonso XI, king of Castile and León (r. 1312–50). Millar cites Adam Anderson's *An Historical and Chronological Deduction of the Origin of Commerce,* 2 vols. (London, 1764).]]

regarded as the remains of extreme simplicity and barbarism, rather than the effect of uncommon refinement or policy; and in this view, it may be observed that, in consequence of some improvement in the manners of the people, the original obligation imposed upon every tything, to <198> repair the injuries committed by any of its members, was, in a period subsequent to that which we are at present examining, subjected to certain limitations. By a law which has been ascribed to William the conqueror, but which is probably of an earlier date, we find it enacted, that, if a crime is committed by any member of a decennary, who escapes from justice, his tythingman, with two others of the same tything, together with the respective tythingmen, and two others, out of the three neighbouring tythings, shall assemble to examine the state of the fact, and if the tything to which the criminal belongs is purged by the oath of these twelve persons, it shall be freed from the obligation to pay the damage.* The progress of government, by enlarging the general intercourse of society, contributed to diminish the peculiar connexion among the inhabitants of the same village, and made it appear an intolerable hardship, that they should, without distinction, be accountable for the misdeeds of one another. <199>

Beside the two branches of business which I have mentioned, the defence of the country and the decision of law-suits, that were canvassed in the Saxon tythings, hundreds, and shires, those meetings were accustomed to deliberate upon matters of still greater importance. They received complaints concerning such abuses in administration, or grievances, as had occurred within their several districts, and by introducing new regulations endeavoured to apply a proper remedy. Thus the heads of families or independent proprietors of every village, or tything, exercised a legislative power within their own liberties, but were liable to be controuled, in this respect, by the meetings of the hundred, which enjoyed the same power in a larger territory; and both of these were subordinate to the meetings of the shire, which possessed a legislative authority over all the hundreds of that extensive division. How the meetings of the shire were liable to be controuled by a still greater assembly, I shall now proceed to inquire. <200>

* See the laws collected by Roger de Hoveden, and said by this author to have been made by William the conqueror in the 4th year of his reign, with the advice of his barons, nobles, wise men, &c.

CHAPTER VII

Of the Wittenagemote.

By the gradual extension of intercourse between the different families or tribes of the Anglo-Saxons, and by the advancement of their political union, the inhabitants of larger territories were led to assemble for the regulation of their public concerns. As the freemen or allodial proprietors of a tything, of a hundred, and of a shire, determined the common affairs of their several districts, and were convened for that purpose by the tythingman, the hundreder, and the alderman; so the union of people belonging to different shires produced a greater assembly, consisting of all the allodial proprietors of a kingdom, and summoned by the king, the great military leader, and chief magistrate of the community. This national council received the appellation of the *mickle-mote,* or *Wittenagemote.*

During the continuance of the Heptarchy, each of the Saxon kingdoms had its own Wittenagemote; and there can be no doubt that <201> those national councils, though sometimes they might act in concert, were independent of one another. But when all the dominions of the Anglo-Saxons were reduced under one sovereign, the Wittenagemotes of each particular kingdom were dissolved, and there was formed a greater assembly of the same nature, whose authority extended over the whole English nation. The circumstances attending this important revolution are lost in obscurity; and we have no means of discovering with certainty, whether it was produced by the mere influence of custom, or by an express regulation. It is probable that when Egbert had subdued the different states of the Heptarchy, the members of every separate Wittenagemote were invited to that great council of the monarchy which was then established; and that, in consequence of this, they would scarcely think it worth while to continue their attendance in those inferior meetings with which they had formerly been connected.

Of the particular class or description of persons who composed the Saxon Wittenagemotes, either in the respective kingdoms of the Heptarchy, or in the monarchy which <202> was formed from the union of these, the historians of that period have given us little or no direct information. But, from a variety of circumstances, it appears highly probable that those ancient assemblies were composed of all the members of the community who enjoyed landed estates in full property; that is, of all those who had the appellation of the *Greater Thanes.*

1. From the state of the country after the Saxon conquest, these persons, being independent with respect to their possessions, were masters of their own conduct, and were under no necessity of adopting public measures to which they had not consented, or upon which they had not at least had an opportunity of deliberating and giving their suffrage. Without their advice and concurrence, therefore, the king could seldom adventure to transact any important national business; and from the frequent practice of consulting them, they were gradually formed into a regular assembly, and became an established branch of the constitution. The rest of the inhabitants were either *vassals,* whose benefices, if not held precariously, were secured to them only for a <203> limited period; or *peasants,* whose condition was yet more dependent and servile. That the king should find it necessary or expedient to summon either of these classes of people to his great council, cannot easily be conceived. Their support and assistance might be expected, of course, in the execution of every measure which had been approved by their superiors; and therefore the voice of the allodial proprietors of land might, on every public emergency, be regarded as the voice of the nation.

2. The usual designations given, by ancient authors, to those who sat in the Saxon Wittenagemote, seem perfectly to coincide with this idea of its constituent members. The persons present in that assembly, when they happen to be particularly specified, are commonly said to be the *bishops and abbots,* together with the *aldermen,* the *chiefs,* the *nobles,* or the leading men of the kingdom.* These expressions are peculiarly applicable to the allodial

* Principes, optimates, magnates, proceres [[aldermen, chiefs, great lords, nobles]], &c. See Spelman on Parliaments—Dr. Brady, Answer to Petyt—and the series of great councils before the conquest. Tyrrell's Bibliotheca Politica, Dial. 6. [[Millar cites, among others, the discussions of the Wittenagemote's composition in Robert Brady's *Introduction to the Old English History* (London, 1684), 7–10, and James Tyrrell's *Bibliotheca Politica: Or, an Enquiry into the Ancient Constitution of the English Government* (London, 1694). See 2nd edition (London, 1727), dialogue 6, 271–81.]]

proprietors of land. It is to be observed, that in <204> those times there was no such personal wealth as could create any authority; neither was there any distinction between what is now called a nobleman and a gentleman; but every individual, possessed of landed property, was a sort of leader, and maintained a degree of influence and rank corresponding to his fortune. The dignified clergy were distinguished by their profession, as the aldermen, or governors of shires, were by their office; for which reason, in speaking of the persons who composed the Wittenagemote, those two classes of men are frequently mentioned in particular, while the other proprietors of land are only pointed out by a general appellation expressive of their condition.

3. The same conclusion receives an additional support from the obvious analogy between the Wittenagemote, and the inferior meetings of the tythings, hundreds, and shires. These inferior meetings were plainly of the same nature with the great national council. The former deliberated upon the public affairs of the several districts to which they belonged: the latter, upon the public affairs of the whole nation. Both of these appear to have arisen <205> from the same circumstances; and probably the one was introduced in imitation of the other. It was because the chief magistrate of every inferior district had not, of himself, sufficient authority to execute public measures, that he was accustomed to call meetings of those inhabitants whose concurrence he thought was expedient; and it was upon the same account that the king was accustomed to assemble the great national council. There is great reason to believe, therefore, that all these meetings were constituted in the same manner; and, as it seems to be universally agreed, that the court of every tything, hundred, and shire, was composed of the respective proprietors of land in those districts; it can hardly be doubted that the constituent members of the Wittenagemote were the people of a similar description throughout the whole kingdom.

Lastly; The probability of this opinion is farther increased, when we examine the state of the national councils, which existed about the same time in the other European kingdoms. In all those kingdoms, the sovereign was under the necessity of transacting the more <206> important parts of the public business with the concurrence of a great proportion of his subjects; and the councils which he convened for this purpose appear, in every country, to have been composed of that part of the people who enjoyed a degree of influence over the rest of the community. Thus in France, the country of modern Europe in which the greatest number of particulars concerning the primitive government has been transmitted to us, the supreme concerns of the kingdom fell under the deliberations of the assemblies of the *field of march;* so called from the time of their principal meetings. From the accounts delivered by some of the French writers, these councils appear to have been composed of all the free men of the nation. According to others, they consisted of the leading men or nobility.* These accounts are, at bottom, not very different. In the early periods of the French monarchy, no person could be denominated free, unless he had the independent <207> property of land; and every landed proprietor was, in reality, a sort of chief or nobleman.†

In consequence of the disputes between the king and the people, that took place in England after the accession of the house of Stewart, there arose two political parties; the followers of which have maintained very opposite opinions concerning the constituent members of the Anglo-Saxon Wittenagemote. The supporters of the prerogative,[1] in order to shew that the primitive government of England was an absolute monarchy, and that the privileges enjoyed by the people have all flowed from the voluntary grants and concessions of the sovereign, were led to assert that the original members of the Wittenagemote were persons under the king's immediate influence and direction; from which it was concluded, that, so far from being intended to controul the exercise of his power, this council was called of his own free <208> choice, for the purpose merely of giving advice, and might of con-

* See Observations sur l'Hist. de France par M. l'Abbé Mably—and Memoires Historiques du Gouvernement de France, par M. le Compte de Boulainvilliers.

† Hinc haud aegre colligere est, unde nostri appellarent parliamenta procerum totius regni conventus.—Du Cange v. Parliamentum. [["From this it is not difficult to gather from what cause our countrymen called the assemblies of the nobles from the whole kingdom 'parliaments.'" Charles du Fresne, Sieur du Cange, *Glossarium ad Scriptores Mediae et Infimae Latinitatis,* 6 vols. (Paris, 1766), 6:175.]] The Salic laws are said to have been made with the consent of the *proceres* or the *optimates.*—And even charters from the crown usually bear, that they were granted *cum consensu fidelium nostrum,*—or *in nostra et procerum presentia.* Mably, ibid. [[With the agreement of our liegemen; in our presence and that of our nobles. Abbé de Mably, *Observations sur l'histoire de France* in *Oeuvres complètes de l'Abbé de Mably* (Toulouse, 1793), 1:270.]]

1. The reference is to those who aligned themselves with the royalist cause in struggles between the Crown and Parliament in the seventeenth century. Millar associates Hume with this royalist or Tory view. In fact, Hume makes very much the same point regarding later partisanship and its distorting effect on the historiography of the Saxons. See *HE,* 1:163–64, 174.

sequence be laid aside at pleasure. Hence it was contended, that beside the bishops and abbots, and the aldermen, both of which were supposed to be in the nomination of the crown, the other members of the Wittenagemote, who received the appellation of *wites* or *wise men,* were the lawyers or judges of the kingdom, who sat in the privy council, and were likewise in the appointment of the sovereign.*

Those writers, on the contrary, who defended the rights of the people, appear, from their eagerness in combating this opinion, to have been betrayed into the opposite extreme.[2] In their endeavours to prove the independent authority of the ancient national council, they were induced to believe, that, from the beginning, it had been modelled upon the same plan as at present; and that it was originally composed of the nobility, the knights of shires, and the representatives of boroughs.† <209>

It requires no great sagacity or attention, at this day, to discover that both of these opinions are equally without foundation. They may be regarded as the delusions of prepossession and prejudice, propagated by political zeal, and nourished with the fondness and credulity of party attachment. Nothing can be more improbable, or even ridiculous, than to suppose that the lawyers or judges of England were, immediately after the settlement of the Anglo-Saxons, a body of men so considerable as to compose the principal part of the Wittenagemote, and, from a title peculiar to themselves, to fix the general denomination of that great assembly. In a very rude age, the business of pleading causes is never the object of a separate profession; and the deciding of lawsuits does not form a characteristical distinction in the chiefs or leading men, who are occasionally employed in that manner. We may as well suppose that, in the period of English history now under consideration, the Anglo-

* Hume's Hist. of England, Appendix to Anglo-Saxon period.

† Sir Robert Atkyns' Power, Jurisdiction, and Privileges of Parliament,—Petyt, Rights of the Commons asserted.—Jani Anglorum facies nova.—Argumentum Antinormanicum.—Tyrrell's Bibliotheca Politica.—Lyttelton's Hist.

2. The reference is to those who took the parliamentary side in these struggles: hence, broadly to the Whig party and their controversialists and historians—here identified as Robert Atkyns (author of *The Power, Jurisdiction, and Priviledge of Parliament,* 1689); William Petyt (author of *The Antient Rights of the Commons of England Asserted,* 1680); James Tyrrell (author of the *Bibliotheca Politica,* 1694, and of *The General History of England, Both Ecclesiastical and Civil,* 1696–1704); and George, Lord Lyttelton (author of the *History of the Life of King Henry the Second,* vols. 1–4, 1769).

Saxon *wites,* or *wisemen,* were the physicians, <210> the surgeons, and apothecaries, or the mathematicians, the chymists, and astronomers of the country, as that they were the retainers of the law. We have surely no reason to believe that the latter were, by their employment, more distinguished from the rest of the community than the former.

Besides, if the *wites* are understood to be judges and lawyers, it will follow, that the ancient national assembly was often composed of that class of men exclusive of all others; for, in ancient records, it is frequently said, that laws were made, or public business was transacted, in a council of *all the wites* of the kingdom. But it is universally admitted, that the bishops and abbots, as well as the aldermen or governors of shires, were members of the Wittenagemote; from which it is a natural inference, that these two sets of people were comprehended under the general appellation of *wites.*

This may easily be explained. The term *wite* signifies, primarily, a man of valour, or military prowess; and hence a man of high rank, a nobleman.* It has been used, in a <211> secondary sense, to denote a *wise man,* from the usual connection, especially in a rude age, between military skill and experience or knowledge: in the same manner as *an old man,* or *grey-headed man,* is, according to the idiom of many languages, employed to signify a ruler or governor. As far as any conclusion, therefore, can be drawn from the appellation of Wittenagemote, or council of the wites, it is likely that this national assembly comprehended neither judges nor lawyers, considered in that capacity, but that it was composed of all the leading men, or proprietors of landed estates; in which number the dignified clergy, and the governors of shires, if not particularly distinguished, were always understood to be included.†

The other opinion is not more consistent with the state of the country, and the condition of its inhabitants. It supposes that in England, soon after the settlement of the Anglo-Saxons, the lower ranks of men were so <212> independent of their superiors, as to form a separate branch of the community, invested with extensive political privileges. This opinion supposes, in particular, that the mercantile part of the inhabitants were become a dis-

* Somner's Sax. Dict. v. *Wita.*

† By a law of king Ina, it is enacted, that if any person fought in the house of an alderman, *or of any illustrious wite,* he should pay a fine of sixty shillings. See Wilkin's Anglo-Saxonica, Leges Inae, c. 6.

tinct order of the people, and had risen to such opulence and authority as entitled them to claim a share in the conduct of national measures. There is not, however, the least shadow of probability in this supposition. Whatever improvements in trade and manufactures had been made in Britain, while it remained under the provincial government of Rome, these were almost entirely destroyed, by the convulsions which attended the Saxon conquest, and the subjection of a great part of the island to the dominion of a barbarous people. The arts which remained in the country after this great revolution, were reduced to such as procure the mere necessaries, or a few of the more simple conveniencies of life; and these arts were hardly the objects of a separate profession, but were practised occasionally by the inferior and servile part of the inhabitants. How is it possible to conceive, in such a state of manufactures, that the trading interest <213> would be enabled to assume the privilege of sending representatives to the great council of the nation? Even in those European states, whose advancement in arts was much earlier than that of the Anglo-Saxons, the formation of the trading towns into corporations was long posterior to the period we are now examining; yet this event must have preceded their acting in a political capacity, and consequently, their being represented in the national assembly.

But, independent of this consideration, which can hardly fail to produce conviction in such as are well acquainted with the early history of modern Europe; the fact in question may be determined in a manner still more decisive and satisfactory. If the representatives of boroughs, and the knights of shires, were constituent members of the ancient Wittenagemote, it is inconceivable that no traces of their existence should have been preserved in the annals of the Saxon princes. From the numerous meetings of that assembly, which are mentioned in many authentic records, and of which accounts are given by historians, who lived either in that period, or not long after it, a variety of expressions must have occurred, by <214> which the fact might be fully ascertained. Had it been a common practice for the towns and shires to choose representatives in the national assembly, is it possible to believe that this practice would never once have been alluded to upon any occasion whatever; or that, when mention is made so frequently, of the bishops and other dignified clergy, of the aldermen, of the wites, or leading men, who sat in this meeting, another part of its members, consisting of a class of people totally different from the former, would in no case, either from accident or design, have been pointed out in clear and unequivocal terms?

It cannot be disputed, however, that, notwithstanding the most diligent search into our ancient histories and records, by men of great industry and learning,[3] and eager to prove their hypothesis, not a single unambiguous expression, to that effect, has ever been found: and this observation is not limited to the time of the Heptarchy, but may be extended from the settlement of the Anglo-Saxons to the Norman conquest.

The attempts to prove that there were representatives of boroughs and shires in the Wittenagemote consist, for the most part, in <215> giving a forced interpretation to certain vague and general phrases, which happen to be employed by ancient authors, concerning the members of that assembly. The word *alderman,* for example, denoting a *ruler,* may be extended to the ruler, or chief magistrate, of a town, as well as of a shire; and therefore it is contended, that when the aldermen are mentioned in old records, as a constituent part of the national council, we are to understand the representatives of boroughs, as well as the governors of shires. It is, in like manner, asserted that, by chiefs, or leading men, and by wites, or wise men, the persons chosen to represent the commons are as properly described, as the nobility, or proprietors of land.*

According to this reasoning, the representatives of the commons, in every shape, and of every description, as they exist at present, though not separately mentioned, are included in almost every designation, applied to the ancient members of the Wittenagemote. How <216> far this mode of argument may be extended it is difficult to say. The *aldermen* and the *wites* have, each of them, the capacity of lord Peter's *bread,* containing the quintessence of beef, mutton, veal, venison, partridge, plum-pudding, and custard.

In the accounts given by ancient authors of those that were called to the national council, mention is made, in some cases, not only of the bishops,

* Tyrrell's Bibliotheca Politica, Dial. 6.—It seems to be the opinion of this author, however, that the existence of the knights of shires, in the Saxon Wittenagemote, is more doubtful than that of the representatives of boroughs.

3. In the *Bibliotheca Politica,* 1694 (dialogue 6, 281–307), James Tyrrell cites Matthew Paris and William of Malmesbury, among others, as providing arguments for the view that boroughs and shires had representatives; on the other hand, John Selden, Sir Edward Coke, William Lambarde, Sir Henry Spelman, and Robert Brady are credited with the opposite view.

abbots, aldermen, and chiefs, but also of the *people;* and the persons present are sometimes distinguished by the appellation of *a great multitude.** <217>

But it cannot escape observation, that if this proves any thing, it will prove too much: it will prove that all the inhabitants, even those of the lowest rank, instead of sending representatives, were personally allowed to vote in the national council. By the appellation of *the people* it appears that, on some occasions, the lay-nobles are understood, in opposition to the dignified clergy; and on others, the ordinary proprietors of land, in opposition to those of distinguished opulence. There is, at the same time, good reason to believe, that the multitude, said to have been present at some of those meetings, was partly composed of mere spectators, who might possibly, by their acclamations, testify their approbation of the measures proposed. <218>

There is produced an instance of a Wittenagemote, held by one of the kings of Mercia, in the year 811, in which a royal charter is said to have been

* Thus in the record of a Wittenagemote held by Ethelbert in 605, it is said, *"Convocato igitur communi concilio tam cleri quam populi."* [["Having therefore summoned a joint council of the clergy as well as of the people." Council of King Ethelbert in 605 in Sir Henry Spelman, *Concilia, Decreta, Leges, Constitutiones, in re ecclesiarum orbis Britannici* (London, 1639), 126–27.]]

A general council is said to have been held by Ethelwolf, in 855, *Praesentibus et subscribentibus Archiepiscopis et Episcopis Angliae universis, nec non Beorredo rege Merciae, Edmundo East-Anglorum rege, Abbatum et Abbatissarum, Ducum, Comitum, Procerumque totius terrae, aliorumque fidelium infinita multitudine, qui omnes regium chirographum laudaverunt, dignitates vero sua nomina subscripserunt.* [["With all the archbishops and bishops of England present as signatories, as well as Burgred, king of Mercia, Edmund, king of the East-Angles, and a countless multitude of abbots and abbesses, commanders, aldermen, and thanes from the whole land and other liegemen, who all praised the royal charter, the dignitaries signed their names in a true fashion." Spelman, *Concilia,* 350.]]

Canute, in the fifth year of his reign, is said to have held a great council, of his archbishops, dukes, earls, abbots, *cum quamplurimus gregariis militibus, ac cum populi multitudine copiosa.* [["with a great many common soldiers and a large multitude of the people." Spelman, *Concilia,* 534.]]

In some other instances, expressions of a similar nature occur; such as *vulgi consensus,* and *populo audiente et vidente.* [[*vulgi consensus:* the accord of the common people; *populo audiente et vidente:* before the eyes and ears of the people.]] [See the authors above quoted—as also Gurdon's History of the Parliament.] In many of these expressions a distinction is clearly pointed out between the members of the meeting and the inferior people that were merely spectators. It ought also to be remembered, that the greatest number of those general phrases, quoted for proving that the commons were represented in the Wittenagemote, are used only by writers after the Norman conquest; who, in translating Saxon laws, or in speaking of Saxon usages, may be supposed to accommodate their language to the ideas prevalent in their own times.

signed before "the Mercian chiefs, bishops, leaders, aldermen, *procurators,*[4] and relations of the sovereign, together with Cuthred the king of Kent, and Suthred the king of the East Saxons, and all those who were present in the national council."* As the members of the Wittenagemote had immemorially the privilege of appointing any person to act for them in their absence, it has been supposed, with great probability, that the *procurators* here mentioned were the proxies of absent nobles. In support of this conjecture, it is observed, that they are placed next in order to the nobles, and immediately before the king's relations.† <219>

But although there is no ground for believing that the representatives of the commons were ever admitted into the Wittenagemote, there can be as little room to doubt that, when the different Anglo-Saxon kingdoms were first united under one monarch, it composed a very numerous assembly. As, upon the settlement of the Saxons in Britain, few persons were in a condition to occupy large estates, the number of allodial proprietors was proportionably increased. It is probable that the estates of the greater part of individuals extended to no more than a *hide* of land, or what could be cultivated by a single plough, and that this property constituted the primitive qualification for voting in the several Wittenagemotes of the Heptarchy. We hear of no particular limitation in this respect, either in the reign of Egbert, or in any preceding period.

It has been imagined by some authors, that the privilege of sitting in the Wittenagemote was originally confined to such as possessed forty hides of land; a property of great extent, which few individuals, it is natural to suppose, could have an opportunity of acquiring; whence it seems to be inferred, that a small part only <220> of the landed gentry were admitted into the councils of the sovereign.‡ This opinion is founded upon a passage in the register of Ely,[5] which mentions a distinction in point of rank, enjoyed by

* *Merciorum Optimates, Episcopos, Principes, Comites,* PROCURATORES, *meosque propinquos, nec non Cuthredum regem Cantuariorum, atque Suthredum regem Orient. Saxon. cum omnibus qui testes nostris synodalibus conciliabulis aderant.* [Annals of Winchelcomb.]

† Gurdon's History of the Parliament.—In a charter of Athelstan, the *procurators* are also mentioned. But this charter was not granted in the Wittenagemote. [Ibid.]

‡ Dugdale's preface to his Baronage. Hume's Hist. of England, appendix to Anglo-Saxon period.

4. *Procurator:* a caretaker or official.

5. Ely: an abbey and bishopric in Cambridgeshire founded in the seventh century.

such of the nobles as possessed estates amounting to forty hides of land. But this passage refers to the state of the kingdom in the reign of Edward the confessor,[6] when property had been subjected to the most important revolutions, and government had widely deviated from its original institution. No inference can thence be drawn, concerning the primitive constitution of the national council; which must have arisen from the state of the inhabitants at the time when it was framed. How far the authority above mentioned is sufficient to justify that conclusion, with respect to the later periods of the Anglo-Saxon government, will fall to be afterwards examined. It is therefore highly probable that the Wittenagemote of the Anglo-Saxons was originally so constituted, as to admit a great proportion of the people into a share of its <221> deliberations: and it merits attention, that even such of the inhabitants as were excluded from this assembly, were either the slaves, or the tenants and vassals of those who sat in it. The former were thus placed under the protection of the latter. Men of inferior rank, though not formally represented in the national council, enjoyed, therefore, a degree of security from the influence of their master or superior, who had an interest to defend them from every injustice but his own, and whose jealousy was ever watchful to guard them from any oppression of the sovereign.

The *powers* exercised by the Saxon Wittenagemote[7] were such as might be expected from the independent situation, and the opulence of its members. It possessed a similar authority over the whole kingdom, to that of any tything, hundred, or shire, over its own subordinate division. In general, the Wittenagemote seems to have taken under its cognizance all those branches of government, which were of sufficient importance to merit its attention, and which, at the same time, could be directed, in consistency with the de-<222>lays arising from the deliberations of a numerous assembly.

1. It exercised, first of all, the power of providing for the defence of the kingdom, and of determining the public military operations.* This was, in all probability, the primary object in calling that assembly; and for which,

* Selden's Notes on Gov. of England, collected by Nath. Bacon, part i. chap. 20. and the authorities referred to.

6. Edward the Confessor (r. 1042–66).

7. For Hume's consideration of similar issues of Saxon government and manners, see his appendix 1 in *HE,* 160–85. For Millar's following reference to Nathaniel Bacon, see *An Historical and Political Discourse of the Laws and Government of England. Collected from Some Manuscript Notes of John Selden,* 4th ed. (London, 1739), 36.

according to the most ancient custom, it was regularly held twice in the year; in the spring when the seed-time was over, to resolve upon such expeditions as were thought expedient; and, in the autumn, before the harvest began, to divide the plunder. A people so rude as the early Saxons had little other business of importance but what consisted in the sowing and reaping of their grain; and were generally disposed to employ the greatest part of the summer, either in private rapine, or in hostilities against a foreign enemy. In the other kingdoms of Europe, the same seasons were observed for the meetings of the national council. We are informed that, in France, the vernal meetings were originally in the be-<223>ginning of March; but that afterwards, from greater attention, it should seem, to the cares of husbandry, they were delayed till the first of May.*

It may here be worth while to remark, that the power of declaring peace and war, which belonged indisputably to the Saxon Wittenagemote, affords complete evidence that its members were allodial proprietors of land; for, upon the supposition of their being the vassals of the crown, they must have been bound, when called upon, to attend the sovereign in war, and consequently their consent would not have been requisite in undertaking any military enterprize.

The same authority, by which military enterprizes were determined, made likewise a provision for carrying them into execution. As from the circumstances of a rude nation, every man was in a condition to furnish a number of soldiers proportioned to the extent of his property; it was a general law in the Saxon government, that the proprietors of land should be rated, for military service, ac-<224>cording to the number of *hides* which they possessed; and if any person refused to contribute his proportion, he was liable to forfeit his possessions, and to be deprived of the public protection.

The erecting and repairing forts and castles, as a defence against the sudden incursions of an enemy, and the maintaining a free communication, by roads and bridges, between the different parts of the kingdom, were objects of police which, in the same view, attracted the notice of the Wittenagemote, and for which individuals were assessed in proportion to their wealth. The magnificent works of this nature, which were executed by the Romans, in all the provinces of their empire, contributed much to facilitate the progress

* This change is said to have been made about the beginning of the second race of the French kings.

of their arms, and to establish their dominion over the conquered people. From their example, it is likely that the Saxons, in Britain, as well as the other nations, who settled upon the continent of Europe, were incited to improvements of this nature which they would not otherwise have thought of.

2. When the members of the Wittenagemote had been assembled, and when they had <225> settled every point relating to their martial operations, their attention was frequently turned to other objects of national concern. Whatever inconveniencies had been felt from the manner of conducting public business, whatever abuses had been committed in the administration of government; these were canvassed; and regulations were made for preventing the like evils for the future. It is not disputed that the Wittenagemote exercised a legislative power over the whole kingdom; and, of consequence, the power of repealing and altering the regulations introduced by the meetings of any particular tything, hundred or shire.* The imposition of taxes, the most important appendage of legislation, was likewise undoubtedly assumed by this great assembly, so far as taxes existed in that early period; but these were in a great measure unknown; the ordinary expence of government being defrayed out of the private estate of the king, and from the various emoluments annexed to the regal dignity. <226>

3. To this legislative power was added that of directing and controlling the exercise of the royal prerogative. Thus the demesnes of the crown were considered as not entirely the private estate of the king; but as in some measure the property of the public, which fell to be managed and disposed of under the public inspection. The alienation, therefore, of crown-lands, though proceeding in the name of the king, was not effectual without the concurrence of the *wites;* and hence royal charters were frequently granted in the Wittenagemote, and subscribed by a number of its members.†

The coining of money, in order to save the trouble of weighing and assaying the metals which pass in exchange, was a privilege early assumed by the king in the respective kingdoms of Europe; and even by the nobles or great proprietors of land in the territories under their jurisdiction. In the exercise of this privilege, great frauds had been committed on <227> many occasions, by debasing the coin below its usual standard; for preventing which abuses, the Wittenagemote, in England, appears to have superin-

* See the preface to most of the collections of Saxon laws published by Wilkins.

† Of this privilege of the Wittenagemote there occurs a remarkable instance in the reign of Egbert, in 836. Spelm. concil. t. i. p. 340.

tended the behaviour both of the king and of the nobles, and to have regulated the coinage throughout the whole kingdom.*

The members of this great council had no less authority in the government of the church than in that of the state. That they were early accustomed to take cognizance of the established religion, appears from what is related of Edwin king of Northumberland,[8] who being solicited to embrace Christianity, is said to have answered, that in a matter of such importance he would be determined by the advice of his wites and princes. In the Wittenagemote, all ecclesiastical laws were made; the king's nomination of bishops and other dignified clergy was confirmed; and their number, as well as the extent of their livings, was regulated.

The same national council gave sanction to the establishment of monasteries, and of the revenues with which they were endowed.† <228>

Not contented with directing the exercise of the executive power, the nobles and wites assumed, in extraordinary cases, the privilege of calling the sovereign to account for the abuses of his administration. Of this a remarkable instance occurs in the reign of Segebert,[9] a king of the western Saxons; who, for his tyrannical behaviour, and after he had treated with contempt the remonstrances of his people, was, by a general assembly of the nation, expelled [from] the kingdom; and another prince of the royal blood was elected in his place. This event is said to have happened in the year 755.‡

Lastly, when the members of the Wittenagemote had met to deliberate upon public business, they were accustomed also to hear complaints concerning such great quarrels and acts of injustice, as could not be effectually redressed by inferior judicatories, and to endeavour, by their superior authority, either to reconcile the parties, or to decide their differences. By frequent interpositions of this nature, that great council was at length formed into a regular court of justice; and became <229> the supreme tribunal of the kingdom; in which appeals from the courts of each particular shire, as well as original actions between the inhabitants of different shires, were finally determined. <230>

* Wilkins leges Athelstani.

† Selden's Notes collected by N. Bacon. part 1. ch. 20. and the authorities to which this author refers.

‡ Saxon chronicle.

8. Edwin, king of Northumbria (r. 616–33): converted to Christianity in 627.

9. Segebert, king of Wessex (r. 756–57).

CHAPTER VIII

State of the Sovereign in the primitive Anglo-Saxon Government.

The different parties of the Saxons, who invaded Britain, were each of them under the conduct of some adventurer, whose fortunes they had followed, either from personal attachment, or from a confidence in his abilities. After they had settled in the country, the same person continued to have the command of their forces, and became also the chief civil officer of the community. The longer he had remained in that high station, his possession of it was rendered more secure by the continuance of the same circumstances which had originally produced his elevation. His military talents, deriving lustre and importance from the distinguished point of view in which they were beheld, excited the admiration and respect of his followers; while the dangers with which they were surrounded, and a sense of their common interest, united <231> them in fighting under his banner. By every new expedition they became the more accustomed to submit to his direction; and the oftener they had found it necessary to solicit his protection and assistance, under those calamities to which they were exposed, they felt more sensibly the advantages derived from his favour, as well as the inconveniences arising from his displeasure.

In the early history of the Anglo-Saxons, the leader of every separate tribe or party, is accordingly represented as possessing a permanent office, with the title of *herotoch* or duke, in place of which that of *king* was afterwards assumed.

The king was in possession of a landed estate, acquired in the same manner with that of every inferior leader, by whose assistance the conquest had been made. As the booty arising from any successful enterprize, was divided among the free people or heads of families concerned in the adventure, and, as on those occasions, each individual obtained a portion, both of land and moveables, suited to his rank and abilities; it may easily be conceived that the property accumulated, in a <232> course of time, by the sovereign, would be much greater than that of any one of his subjects. His estate was naturally distributed among his dependents, according to the same plan which was adopted by every other landed proprietor. A part of it was bestowed upon his kindred or free retainers, under the condition of military service; and the remainder was cultivated by his villeins, or bondmen, for supporting the expence of his houshold. Over these two classes of people, he exercised the rights of a superior, and of a master. Throughout the rest of the kingdom, exclusive of his own particular estate, his authority was much more limited. Every allodial proprietor, unaccustomed to subjection, and supported by his own retainers, was more or less in a condition to maintain his independence; and those who had acquired considerable property, beholding with jealousy the superior dignity and pretensions of the king, were commonly ready to combine against him, either in resenting or opposing, whatever they deemed an infringement of their liberties.

The powers with which the sovereign came to be invested, either in the different states of <233> the Heptarchy, or in the subsequent monarchy which arose from the union of those kingdoms, were such as, in order to prevent confusion and promote the dispatch of public business, were tacitly devolved upon him, or as, from the nature of his situation, he had found encouragement to assume, and had, without opposition, been permitted to exercise. The dignity and office of the king, though higher in degree, were perfectly similar to those of the tythingman, the hundreder, and the earl; and he possessed nearly the same powers over the whole kingdom, which those inferior officers enjoyed in their own particular districts.

1. By having the command of the forces in the time of battle, the original source of his greatness, he was led to direct their movements on other occasions; to take preparatory steps for bringing them into the field; to suggest particular enterprizes, to plan the measures for conducting them, to execute treaties with foreign states, and in general to superintend the defence of the kingdom, and the whole course of its military operations.

2. In consequence of his being at the head of the military department, the king was led <234> also to exert his authority in suppressing internal disorders, in quelling tumults and insurrections, in restraining private rapine and violence, in seizing offenders, and preventing their escape from justice;

in a word, he obtained the province of maintaining the ordinary police of the country, and the security of its inhabitants.

3. As, from these two branches of power, he became the prime mover, and proposer of public measures, and as, in matters of great moment, the concurrence of the Wittenagemote was necessary; he acquired, of course, the exclusive privilege of calling that assembly, and of presiding in all its deliberations. The influence which he thence obtained, with regard to its determinations, may easily be imagined. The president of every numerous assembly has many opportunities of moulding the business that comes before it, into such a shape as will promote his own designs; more especially, if by the permanent enjoyment of that office, he has leisure to form a regular plan of management; and if, by having a discretionary power of calling the particular meetings, he may regulate his motions according as <235> the assembly happens, in different conjunctures, to be attended by different members. But while, by these favourable circumstances, the sovereign was capable of advancing his political interest, he enjoyed the additional advantage of superior opulence and dignity; which put him in a condition to intimidate, as well as to over-reach opposition. To a prince, therefore, possessed of much prudence, and of popular talents, it was not difficult, in ordinary cases, to procure the consent of the Wittenagemote to those measures which he thought proper to suggest; and the resolutions of that assembly, while they appeared to limit and controul the power of the crown, were at bottom, very often directed by the monarch, and rendered subservient to his will.

4. As the Wittenagemote enacted laws, distributed justice in the last resort, and regulated the administration of public affairs; so the duty of enforcing the decrees and regulations of that assembly, and, in general, the executive part of the government, were naturally devolved upon the king. That great officer, who conducted the military force of the kingdom, could hardly fail to assume the province of <236> causing the punishments decreed against offenders to be regularly inflicted, and of compelling every individual to fulfil the decisions of the law. The same person was led to procure information with respect to the commission of heinous crimes, and to direct that they should be prosecuted before the proper tribunals. In these employments, the sovereign acted as the head and representative of the community. In the same capacity, he obtained the nomination of many inferior officers in church and state; the privilege of coining money, and of superintending weights and measures; together with the exercise of all those powers which,

from their nature, could not be conveniently devolved upon a popular assembly.

These prerogatives, which, from the natural course of things, and probably without any formal or express regulation, were gradually annexed to the crown, became the source of such perquisites and emoluments, as more than compensated the trouble with which they were attended. The chief executive officer, who prosecuted a crime in the name of the public, had a plausible pretence, upon the same <237> account, for levying the fine or forfeiture arising from the conviction of the criminal. Besides, in government, as well as in religion, the bulk of men are commonly so engrossed by the image or picture, as to forget the original, and to bestow upon the representative the sentiments due to the object it represents. Thus the sovereign, who appeared to direct, and put in motion, all the wheels and springs of government, who enforced the laws, who vindicated offences, and took upon himself the whole burden of providing for the public safety, was apt to be considered as exercising, in his own right, those powers with which the community had invested him. Those laws which he enforced were conceived to be more immediately calculated for his own benefit: those officers whom he appointed were looked upon as the servants of the crown; and those crimes, which he prosecuted and punished, were regarded as crimes committed against him in particular, for which he was, therefore, entitled, of himself, to demand reparation.

The public revenue of the Anglo-Saxons, therefore, by which the rank of the sovereign was maintained, and out of which the various <238> expences of government were defrayed, consisted almost entirely of two branches; the original demesnes of the king, acquired in the same manner with the private estate of each allodial proprietor; and the various forfeitures and fines, whether of land or moveables, which, from time to time accrued, or were transmitted to him, as the head of the community. From this latter source he derived a continual accumulation of wealth. The disorder and violence, that prevailed so universally, gave occasion to the forfeiture of many rich individuals; and the king was commonly disposed to neglect no opportunity of seizing and improving such favourable conjunctures. In the greater part of crimes, as it frequently happens in the infancy of government, the criminal was not punished in a manner adequate to the purposes of public justice, but was admitted to atone for his offence, by making a pecuniary composition with the sufferer. In those cases, the king exacted a composition as well as the private party; and the profits arising to the crown, from the innumerable fines and amerciaments, to which this gave occasion, were one great cause of the <239> long continuance of that imperfect mode of punishing offences.

In this early stage of the constitution, the revenue above mentioned was sufficient for all the charges of public administration; which were then inconsiderable. There was no mercenary army to be paid by the king. The judges were either willing to determine differences among individuals, and to take cognizance of crimes, without any consideration for their trouble; or they obtained a compensation by exacting fees from the parties who came before them. Taxes therefore were almost entirely unknown. Their introduction belongs to the history of a more advanced period of society.

But even this primitive revenue of the crown appears to have laid a foundation for the Wittenagemote to interfere in the disposal of it; since the estate, acquired by the king, in the character of the chief executive officer, and as representing the community, was, in a proper sense, the estate of the public. This conclusion was not, indeed, applicable to the whole, though it undoubtedly was to a considerable part of the royal demesnes. But it was not <240> the genius of that age to make nice distinctions; and the interposition of the national council, in the management of some branches of the crown revenue, might easily be extended to others that were placed in different circumstances.

We find that, not only in England, but in the other states upon the continent of Europe, the arrangements which took place in the management of the king's household, and private estate, had necessarily great influence upon the government of the kingdom. According as the sovereign advanced in opulence and dignity, he was led to employ a greater number of servants in the several branches of his domestic oeconomy; and the same persons, who enjoyed the chief confidence of their master in that private capacity, became, in course of time, his ministers in conducting the business of the nation. In all the European feudal kingdoms, the management of the king's household was anciently divided into five principal departments, and fell under the inspection of so many great officers.

1. The first of these was the *steward,* or master of the household, called, upon the <241> continent, the *major domo,* the *mayor of the palace,* or *seneschall;* who had originally the care of the king's table. Upon him was naturally devolved the business of gathering in the rents of the crown lands:

for, as those rents were all payable in kind, and were intended for immediate consumption, it was most convenient, that they should be delivered into the hands of that person by whom they were afterwards to be laid out for the support of the king's family.

We may easily believe that, from the nature of his office, the master of the houshold was in a condition to acquire much influence over all the tenants and vassals of the crown. He was the person with whom they were obliged to settle their accounts; and who, from his minute acquaintance with their circumstances, was the most capable of giving his master information concerning them. He was, therefore, the person most likely to be employed in adjusting their differences with one another; and in consequence of his being the deputy judge upon the royal demesne, he came, at a subsequent period, to be intrusted <242> by the crown, with a similar power over the whole kingdom.*

2. As the collection and management of the victuals, with which the king's table was supplied, fell under the direction of the steward; so the care of the liquors was committed to a separate officer, the *cup-bearer,* or *butler.* In all the Gothic nations, persons of wealth and distinction lived in great splendor, and were much addicted to drinking; for which reason, it is not surprising that the accommodation of the sovereign, in this respect, was <243> exalted into a separate employment, and became an object of suitable importance.

3. The care of the chambers was committed to a third officer, the *chamberlain;* whose business it was to superintend the *lodging* of his master's family. As this officer was entrusted with whatever required to be locked up in the house, for the future service of the houshold, he seems, upon this account, to have become the keeper of the wardrobe, and, at a subsequent

* Spelman, v. major domo. This author supposes three different orders of *major domo* in the houshold of the Gothic monarchs. The first, who had the care of the king's table: the second, who presided over the whole houshold: and the third, who was employed under the king as chief executive officer of the kingdom. It seems evident, however, that these officers were originally derived from one, who, as he became great, appointed deputies to discharge the inferior branches of duty incumbent upon him.

In England the steward, in the king's houshold, is mentioned under the name of *Oeconomus* [[steward, i.e., the person in charge of running the household (from the Greek word for house, *oikia*)]] as early as the year 749. [See discourse on this office by Mr. Thynn in Hearne's Coll. of Antiquities.] But he does not seem to have acquired great power, as a minister of the crown, till the Norman conquest. [See same collection.]

period, when the crown rents were paid in money, the king's treasurer or superintendant of the finances.*

4. Another of the king's principal servants obtained the inspection of the stable, and was denominated the *comes stabuli,*[1] or *constable.* When, by the keeping of many horses, this department was rendered extensive, it appears to have been divided into two branches; the one belonging to the chief groom, or constable; and the other to the *mareschal,* or smith. It is difficult to mark the period when this divi-<244>sion was completed: nor is it an easy matter to ascertain the relative degrees of importance and rank which might then be annexed to these two kindred employments.

When the use of cavalry in war became frequent, we may easily suppose, that the persons, who had been accustomed to rear and manage the king's horses, would stand forth, as claiming superior distinction, and as having a peculiar title to be consulted. They were thus employed, under the sovereign, in conducting that important part of the troops; and, by an easy transition, acquired a jurisdiction in such controversies, as were either of a military nature, or had arisen in the army while it remained in the field.†

5. The writing of the king's letters, and the executing of the charters, or other deeds, that issued from the crown, became also the subject of a distinct occupation, that of the *secretary.* In those times, when the clergy had acquired great influence, and when a pro-<245>ficiency in the art of writing supposed an uncommon degree of literary education, the only person likely to be qualified for this employment was the *chaplain;* who might be considered as, in some degree, the keeper of the king's conscience; and who, from the nature of those religious offices which he performed, could seldom fail to acquire the confidence of his master.

When signatures were introduced, for ascertaining the authenticity of writings, the office of keeping the king's seal, and of appending it to his deeds, was committed to the same person who had been employed in writing them.

* It is probable that the butler [pincerna] was, for a long time, not separated from the steward; and in the early history of England neither he nor the chamberlain seem to have been much distinguished.

† This officer was known to the Anglo-Saxons under the name of *Stallarius.* [[Master of the horse ("staller").]] Spelm. Gloss. v. Constabularius. The mareschal seems to have been considered as the deputy of the constable.

1. Attendant in charge of the stable.

As in determining law-suits, it was found expedient, in many cases, to take down the sentence of the judge in writing, the secretary was naturally employed for this purpose; and became keeper of the records of the king's court. From this branch of his duty, he got the appellation of *chancellor;* which is said to have originally denoted a *scribe,* or *notary;* being derived from *cancella,* the place under the Roman government, allotted to persons <246> of that profession for carrying on their business.*

As this arrangement in the domestic administration of the sovereign, supposes considerable wealth and magnificence; it was probably of a later origin in England than in several of the kingdoms upon the continent. It is reasonable to suppose that the whole of the king's houshold was at first committed to one principal servant; whose business having been, by little and little, augmented and rendered more burdensome, was at length divided into these five different departments. A similar plan of administration, in a more limited sphere, was adopted by every great landed proprietor; who naturally multiplied his chief domestics, in proportion to the extent of his wealth; and often followed the example of the king, by dividing the affairs of his houshold into the same number of branches.†

The longer these great officers had been <247> established, they rose to higher degrees of consideration; and their authority was farther extended, from the superintendence of the king's houshold, to the direction and management of the kingdom. As, for the most part, they were originally chosen by the sovereign, upon account of their superior wealth, or abilities, which

* This officer is clearly distinguishable in the Anglo-Saxon government. Spelm. v. Cancellarius.

† Pasquier in speaking of these great officers of the houshold observes, that they were gradually established in the families of the great lords and gentlemen. "Parquoy estoient dessus tous, cinq estats plus estimez, le chancelier, grand chambellan, grand maistre, grand eschançon, que nos anciens appelloient grand bouteéller, et connestable. Nous estant par cecy monstrée une grand oeconomie: car aussi n'y a il maison qui vueille tant soit peu parôitre, en laquelle ces cinq estats ne se trouvent estre nécessaires, encore que ce ne soit avec tiltres de telle splendeur." Recherches de la France, liv. ii. chap. 12. [["For this reason there were five offices respected above all others: the chancellor, the grand chamberlain, the grand master, the grand cup-bearer, whom our ancestors called the grand butler, and the constable. Thus was the model of a grand household provided for us, for as a consequence there is no house with aspirations to put on even the smallest display in which these five offices are not felt to be necessary, albeit without titles of such magnificence." For a modern edition, see Etienne Pasquier, *Les recherches de la France,* ed. Marie-Madeleine Fragonard and François Roudaut (Paris, 1996), 1:436–37.]]

rendered them capable of supporting his dignity in the execution of the business committed to them; so the trust and confidence which he reposed in them, together with the share of public administration which they enjoyed, afforded them numberless opportunities of augmenting their private fortunes, and of increasing their influence. In proportion to their advances in wealth and <248> power, they were in a condition to render their offices more permanent. They were originally nominated by the king during pleasure; but that superiority, which had been the inducement to their first promotion, became commonly more and more conspicuous during the continuance of their employments. It was, therefore, seldom found convenient to displace them: and, even after their decease, the heir of that estate, which they had acquired, was naturally regarded as the person best qualified, and who had a preferable claim to inherit their dignity. By long usage, these offices were thus rendered hereditary in particular families. To this observation, however, the office of chancellor, in most European countries, is an exception. As the chancellor was unavoidably a clergyman, who held his rank in the church, and the estate connected with it, only during life, he had commonly neither any opportunity of securing the office to his family, nor any desire of annexing it to his ecclesiastical dignity.

Of the influence established by the great officers of the king's houshold, the political constitution of Germany affords a remarkable <249> instance. When the dominions of that empire, by the conquest of large territories in Italy, and in the southern part of France, had been so enlarged as to comprehend three distinct kingdoms, the emperor was induced, in that situation, to appoint three different secretaries.* The officers of his houshold were, upon this account, increased to the number of seven. In the progress of the German government, the power of these great officers advanced, as that of the emperor declined; and after the imperial dignity had become intirely elective, they assumed the privilege of *proposing,* to the national assembly, the successor to the crown; from which they at length proceeded to claim the sole right of electing him. Hence the origin of that precise number of persons who composed the primitive German *electors.*

The steward was originally the officer of the greatest importance in the

* The first was the secretary for Germany, properly so called; the second for Italy, and the third for Arles. It is remarkable that these chancellors, having become secular princes, their offices have been attached to their ecclesiastical dignity.

king's houshold; <250> because the supplying of his majesty's table with provisions was regarded as the chief concern of the family. We accordingly find that, in several countries of Europe, the person who enjoyed this hereditary office, attained a degree of rank and opulence which rendered him formidable to the sovereign. In France, the mayors of the palace, after having for a long time possessed the real power and authority of the crown, were at length emboldened to throw off the mask, and openly to mount the throne.

When the use of cavalry in war had become very extensive, and when that part of the feudal armies had the principal share in deciding the fate of battles, the constable, or marishal, was frequently in a condition to dispute the superiority with the steward or mayor of the palace. Thus, in Germany, when the throne happened to be vacant, the Elector Palatine, the mayor of the palace, was anciently appointed, for preventing the bad consequences of an inter-regnum, to be the *vicar of the empire.* But in a subsequent period, this high dignity was claimed by the elector of Saxony, the constable; and, after <251> violent disputes, and various determinations of the *diet,*[2] was at last divided between those powerful competitors.

In the ages of greater civility and improvement, when, from the complicated connexions of society, its laws became numerous and of difficult interpretation, and when, from the anxiety of individuals to ascertain their rights, the charters and writings proceeding from the crown were multiplied in proportion, the secretary, or chancellor, to whom the king committed that branch of business, was invested with powers of the greatest consequence, and therefore was exalted to the highest rank.

In those opulent and polished nations which have long been reduced under an equal and regular government; in which the impartial distribution of justice is looked upon as almost a matter of course; and in which the sovereign is accustomed to govern by influence, more than by the exertion of his prerogative; in such nations, the person who presides over the public treasury, who may be regarded as the substitute of the chamberlain, becomes the great channel through which the revenue <252> of the state is conveyed, and by which the authority of the crown is maintained.

It is hardly necessary to remark, that this distribution of the business in the king's household, into five departments, reaches far below the simple period of the Anglo-Saxon government which we are now considering. But,

2. The assembly of the Holy Roman Empire.

on the other hand, it merits attention, that when the exaltation of the sovereign had multiplied the occupations belonging to these different branches, it became expedient, in some of them, to appoint a variety of deputies; many of whom, in particular kingdoms, rose by degrees to such consideration and rank, as to appear no longer in a subordinate station, and even to make the origin of their appointment be forgotten. This circumstance must not be overlooked in perusing the enumeration, given by many historians, of the principal officers in the court, or houshold, of particular princes.

From the foregoing imperfect sketch of the powers of the sovereign, as well as of the constitution and privileges of the Wittenagemote, we may be enabled, notwithstanding the darkness of our ancient history, to form an idea of <253> the original English constitution. How remote this was from an *absolute monarchy,* must be apparent to every one, who considers that the privilege of legislation, together with that of determining peace and war, and even that of controlling the executive power, was lodged in the national assembly. Neither can this government be deemed in a high degree aristocratical; since the national council was composed, not of a small junto[3] of nobles, but of all the landed proprietors, comprehending a great proportion of the whole people. It seems, in fact, to be that sort of political system which is likely to be established in all rude and extensive countries; before a few individuals have accumulated so much wealth as enables them to domineer over their inferiors; and before the king, in consequence of his high station and prerogatives, has had leisure to acquire a revenue sufficient to overthrow and bear down any opposition that can be apprehended from the most opulent of his subjects. It cannot, however, escape observation, that, although the powers committed to the monarch by the early Saxon constitution were small, they were not accurately de-<254>fined; and that, in the exercise of them, he enjoyed, upon this account, a good deal of latitude. Accurate limitations of power, and a regular system of subordination, the fruit of experience and foresight, cannot be expected to characterize the institutions of a simple people, who are usually guided by their feelings more than by reflection, and who attend more to the immediate effects of any measure, than to its remote consequences. As the Anglo-Saxon princes were entrusted

3. From Spanish *junta,* a cabal, council, or committee. The term was applied by contemporaries to a small group of aristocratic Whig politicians who wielded great influence in a series of ministries at the turn of the eighteenth century.

with every branch of public administration, in which the Wittenagemote did not think proper to interfere; their conduct was directed, in a great measure, by particular conjunctures, and by the different unforeseen events which accidentally required their interposition. We need not be surprised, therefore, if in perusing the history of that period, while we discover strong marks of the weakness of the crown, we should also meet with some extraordinary exertions of the prerogative, and should at the same time observe, that these were suffered to pass without censure, or even without notice. It is a common source of mistake, among political writers, to con-<255>sider these extraordinary exertions as proofs of the ordinary state of the government; and to adduce as an illustration of the general practice, what is only the random and casual exercise of a power, not yet brought to a regular standard. We shall now examine the changes produced in the English constitution from the reign of Egbert to the Norman conquest. <256>

CHAPTER IX

Of the principal Events from the Reign of Egbert to the Norman Conquest.

While England, by the union of the different states of the heptarchy, was emerging from barbarism, and laying the foundation of a great and powerful kingdom, a new enemy involved her in a series of fresh calamities; and contributed to retard the progress of her improvements. The inhabitants of the northern part of Germany, who retained their ancient manners, and were still much addicted to piracy, continued to infest the coasts of Britain and France, and of such other European countries as, by some advancement in cultivation, presented an inviting prospect of plunder. About the reign of Egbert, several bands of those pirates, known by the general name of Danes, landed in England; and, after committing great ravages, were generally successful in carrying off their booty. Upon the death of that prince, whose vigour <257> had kept them under some restraint, their incursions became bolder and more frequent; they made their attacks in larger parties; and, having been often victorious over the forces that could be assembled against them, they were at length encouraged to form settlements in different parts of the country. From the time when the kingdoms of the heptarchy were united, to that of the Norman conquest; a period extending to about two hundred and fifty years, and comprehending a series of nineteen monarchs; the English were, with little interruption, engaged in a course of hostilities with those invaders; and subjected to perpetual inquietude and disorder. In the reign of Alfred,[1] the grandson of Egbert, the Danish arms had been so

1. Alfred the Great, king of Wessex (r. 871–99): the youngest son of Athelwolf, king of Kent and Wessex (r. 839–55), succeeded his elder brothers Athelbald, king of Wessex (r. 855–60), Athelbert, king of Kent and Wessex (r. 860–65/6), and Ethelred I (r. 865/

successful, and their acquisitions had become so extensive, as to threaten an entire conquest of the kingdom.

The history of that prince exhibits a pattern of the hero and statesman, equal to whatever is recorded of ancient patriotism, and even to whatever correct fiction has been able to suggest, in order to excite admiration and esteem. During the reign of Ethelred, his elder brother, by whom he was unjustly deprived of the <258> patrimony left him by his father, he discovered neither any marks of resentment for the private injury he had sustained, nor of what prevailed so universally among the princes of that age, an ambition to possess the crown; but with uniform alacrity seconded all the public measures of the king; and, while yet at an early period of life, displayed uncommon valour and talents, in opposing the enemies of his country. When he afterwards succeeded to the throne, his magnanimity and firmness were put to a severe trial in the school of adversity. Though he had been victorious over the Danes in many conflicts; yet the swarms of those invaders multiplied so fast; and from every quarter pushed their depredations with such rapidity, that the English, throughout the greater part of the kingdom, became quite disheartened, and submitted to the conquerors. His ancient subjects, the western Saxons, alone retained their fidelity, and supported the interest of their monarch: but these were incapable of resisting the torrent which broke in upon them, from the accumulated force of their enemies. After many fruitless efforts, and upon a sudden report of a new invasion <259> by a powerful body of Danes, that spread universal consternation, the king found himself almost entirely abandoned: and, being able no longer to keep the field, was obliged to disband his remaining adherents, and to provide for his present safety; he was even under the necessity of concealing himself by various artifices, and in mean disguises. The distresses to which he was exposed, and the private adventures which he met with, in that situation, appear not unworthy of notice; as they relate to a person of such eminence; and as the fate of England depended upon his surmounting the difficulties in which he was involved. In the garb of a common soldier he remained for some time unknown, in the house of one of his own herdsmen: upon which occasion, historians have mentioned a little incident, which exhibits a ludicrous picture of royalty placed in awkward circumstances with-

6–71). Alfred's reign is traditionally represented as an Anglo-Saxon golden age due to his military, administrative, and cultural accomplishments.

out being degraded by them. While the king was one day sitting by the fireside, and trimming his bow and arrows, the woman of the house, who had no suspicion of the quality of her guest, happened to be toasting bread; and, having occasion to go about some other affairs, <260> she found, at her return, that the cakes were burned; with which being greatly provoked, she heartily scolded his majesty, telling him, that though he neglected to turn her cakes, he was always very ready to eat them.

Meanwhile the royal demesnes became a prey to the Danish forces; who being no longer restrained by the apprehension of an enemy, gave a loose to their cruelty and rapacity. Alfred, reduced in this manner, to the condition of an outlaw in his own dominions, and having collected a few faithful followers, wandered for some time from place to place, finding shelter from the woods and marshes, which covered a great part of the country, and which were of difficult access even to the natives themselves. But his principal retreat was in the middle of an extensive morass, formed by the rivers Thone and Parret in Somersetshire; which was almost entirely surrounded with water; and which afforded great plenty of fallow deer, and other wild animals fit for subsistence. In this place the king took up his residence; and erecting some fortifications, remained for near the space of a twelvemonth. Here he had leisure to reflect upon the uncer-<261>tainty of human grandeur; to weigh the real value of all human enjoyments; and to revolve in his mind those benevolent and patriotic plans, by the execution of which he came afterwards to be revered by his countrymen, and has excited the admiration of mankind. From this retreat he made many secret excursions, in order to procure information or plunder, and to revive the drooping courage and spirits of his companions.

At length the earl of Devonshire, having suddenly attacked and routed a large party of the Danes, presented to Alfred a favourable opportunity of appearing once more in the open field, and of animating his subjects to hazard another attempt for the recovery of the kingdom. Amid all the difficulties and dangers to which this monarch was exposed, he appears to have uniformly discovered a mind cool and deliberate, resolute with caution, fruitful in expedients, and dexterous in executing such measures as the singular and desperate posture of his affairs made it adviseable to adopt. On this occasion he is said to have employed a stratagem, suited to the state of discipline in the armies of that age, and <262> which recals the memory of those military adventures related in the early periods of antiquity. In the disguise of a minstrel and fortune-teller, attended only by one companion, he visited the Danish camp; and supported the character with so much address, as to afford universal entertainment, and to pass through every quarter, not excepting even the general's tent, without incurring the least suspicion. Having thus procured every possible information, and having, by means of a previous intercourse with his nobles, suddenly collected a great body of his subjects, he found himself at the head of a powerful army, exulting in the recovery of their monarch, and eager to be revenged of their oppressors. With this force he fell unexpectedly upon the enemy; and entirely defeated them. His victory was so complete, that the Danes were incapable of any further opposition; and in a little time after were entirely subdued. Some part of them were driven out of the kingdom; the rest were under the necessity of submitting to such terms as he thought proper to impose.

The moderation and clemency of this prince, and the prudence which he displayed in the <263> improvement of these advantages, were no less conspicuous, than the vigour and abilities by which they were obtained. The Danes who submitted to him were sent to reside in East Anglia, Northumberland, and some of the neighbouring parts of the kingdom, where many of their countrymen had long been settled; and they were admitted to the enjoyment of the same privileges with his other subjects. By the zealous interposition of Alfred, they were also happily persuaded to embrace the Christian religion; a circumstance necessary to remove their prejudices against the ancient inhabitants, and to unite those different tribes of people in one community.

Upon the restoration of peace, the first attention of the monarch was employed in providing a fleet, sufficient to oppose any new invasion of the Danish pirates; in erecting fortifications upon the coasts more immediately exposed to their depredations; in making regulations for assembling the inhabitants upon any sudden emergency; in rebuilding the towns that had been destroyed; and in repairing the waste and desolation which the coun<264>try had suffered from a long course of rapine and violence.

To compile and publish a code of statutes is, in a rude nation, a measure of the highest utility, for instructing an ignorant people in those rules by which they are to be governed; and accordingly we find that this has been the great object of almost all the distinguished princes of an early period. It appears that Alfred bestowed much labour and time upon a work of this nature; of which the greatest part is now lost. It is probable, that, from the various feudal institutions and customs, which had prevailed either in England or upon the neighbouring continent, he selected such as were accounted the most beneficial, and most adapted to the peculiar circumstances of his time and country: and that, having established these regulations by the authority of his great council, he endeavoured, in the most effectual manner, to produce a degree of uniformity in law and government, throughout the whole of the kingdom.[2] We are not, however, to imagine, that all differences in the customs of different parts of the country were thus en<265>tirely abolished. On the contrary, we find that, in consequence of the new settlements in the northern part of the kingdom, a multitude of Danish customs had been introduced; and that the people were now distinguished into three great branches, according to the varieties in the system of private law, established among the Western Saxons, the Mercians, and the Danes.

But the promulgation of good laws is, for the most part, and especially in a country remote from civilization, a matter of less difficulty and importance than the vigorous and impartial execution of them. When a regulation is made, the beneficial objects, which it is intended to promote, are commonly surveyed in that distant and dispassionate view which admits the full exertion of patriotic affections; but when it comes to be enforced by the punishment of transgressors, it then frequently assumes a different aspect; and the interest of the public is likely to be obscured and counteracted by the private connections, and by the partiality and prejudice of individuals: not to mention that the splendor and eclat, which accompany the temporary interpositions of the <266> legislature, do not descend to the unremitting and laborious attention, to the painful and invidious task, of those inferior magistrates who render the law effectual. It was here that the genuine virtue of Alfred appeared most conspicuous. From the long course of depredation to which England had been exposed, that country was become a scene of the utmost license and disorder; exhibiting, on the one hand, a people fierce and barbarous in their manners, accustomed to live by robbery and violence; and on the other, a set of nobles, in reality the leaders of different pillaging parties, abusing that authority and jurisdiction with which they were invested, by protecting their adherents from punishment, and by oppressing those who had fallen under their displeasure. Yet such was the attention of

2. Alfred's law code was presented at some time between 878 and 885, and was an extensive revision of the law code issued in the reign of Ina.

this monarch to the inferior departments of government, so great was his vigilance in examining the conduct of judges, and his rigour in punishing them for malversation in office, that, in a short time, these evils were in a great measure removed, and an equal and regular administration of justice was introduced. In one year of his reign no fewer than forty-four magis-<267>trates, it is said, were put to death, for misbehaviour in their judicial capacity; a proof that corruption and licentiousness had risen to an amazing pitch. There can be little doubt, that in the accounts transmitted by historians, the accuracy and regularity of the police, established by Alfred, has been greatly exaggerated; but even these exaggerations, the usual effects of wonder and admiration, may serve to convince us, that he made great improvements upon the former system. We are informed that, in order to try the success of his institutions, he caused golden bracelets to be hung up near the highway; and that no person, such was the terror of the magistrate, adventured to touch them.

By the establishment of good order and tranquillity, the people were encouraged to follow those peaceable occupations which had been totally interrupted by the preceding disorders. The king was indefatigable in his efforts to promote manufactures, and to excite the industry of his subjects; by employing artificers in great public works; by inviting foreigners to settle in the country; and by rewarding the inventors of new arts. He con-<268>tributed, in a particular manner, to the extension of foreign commerce, by protecting it with his fleet, and by bestowing marks of his favour upon such as became eminent for their skill in navigation.

He was no less attentive to the encouragement of literature, not only by his patronage, but also by his example. His ardour, in this respect, was the more remarkable, as it surmounted the disadvantages he lay under from the neglect of his early education; for, among the anecdotes which have come down to us concerning the private life of Alfred, it is related, that he was twelve years of age before he had been taught to read; and that he first felt a desire of being instructed, in this particular, from the recital of certain pieces of poetry, with which the queen his mother was much delighted. Prompted, however, by a strong inclination for literary pursuits, he soon became, not only a proficient in the Latin language, and in such branches of learning as were respected in that age, but even a writer of eminence, both in prose and in verse. As a poet, he seems to have employed himself chiefly in translating, or composing, *fables,* or *apologues.* <269> These compositions are usually the first attempts, in a rude nation, to illustrate, by simple and familiar examples, the proverbs, or maxims for the conduct of life, which observation and experience have suggested, and which, as containing important information to an illiterate people, are frequently repeated, and appealed to, in ordinary conversation. The labours of this eminent statesman appear, in that particular, to have coincided with those of the first great teacher of morality among the Greeks.[3] It is probable that those two celebrated personages were directed in the choice of their subject by a similarity of character; and it may perhaps be suspected, that both of them were more remarkable for their philosophy and public spirit, than for their poetry.

Historians have mentioned the bodily accomplishments of Alfred, as corresponding to the extraordinary endowments of his mind. He was distinguished by the strength and activity, as well as by the dignity and gracefulness of his person; and while his dexterity and address, in martial exercises, excited universal applause, he gained the hearts of his subjects by an affable and engaging deportment. <270>

After all, though the history of this monarch may be accounted sufficiently authentic, to afford a solid conviction of his exalted merit; some allowance, no doubt, must be made for the colouring produced by that admiration which was due to his character, and which has been heightened by the remoteness of the period in which he lived. We need not be surprised, therefore, to meet with errors and prejudices, concerning his public transactions; and in particular, to find that he was supposed to be the author of several regulations, which he only revived, or brought to greater perfection than they had formerly attained. The great changes which he produced in the state of his country, by bringing it from anarchy and confusion into a degree of order and regularity, led his countrymen, in subsequent ages, to fix their attention upon him, as the person from whom they had derived the entire model of their constitution. He is thus held, by many historians, to have first divided the kingdom into tythings, hundreds, and shires, and to have introduced a peculiar system of policy connected with those divisions; though it seems now to be clearly proved, that these regulations <271> existed in England before his time, and that they extended to other European

3. Presumably Aesop. See p. 789, note 3. Hume, following the *Life of King Alfred* by Asser (d. 909), writes that Alfred both disseminated existing parables and invented others, while also translating Aesop. See *HE,* 1:80.

kingdoms. The institution of *juries* has, in like manner, been ascribed to this monarch; though there is good reason to believe that it arose from the general situation of the Gothic nations; and that it had a very early establishment in all of them. Alfred, in a word, has become the English Lycurgus;[4] and his interposition is the great engine which politicians have employed for explaining the origin of such particulars, in the English government, as have excited uncommon attention, and are too remote, in their beginnings, to fall within the limits of authentic history.

For near eighty years after the death of that prince, England appears to have been successfully defended against every foreign invasion; though she experienced a variety of disturbances, occasioned by the domestic quarrels and insurrections of the Danes and other inhabitants of the country. During this period we may distinguish the reigns of Edward the elder,[5] the son of Alfred, of Athelstan, and of Edgar, as remarkably vigorous; and as filled with exploits, which, if they make no very splendid <272> figure in the general scale of historical events, were, however, of considerable consequence to the peace and internal tranquillity of the kingdom.

Those princes are said to have adopted a measure, which, in that early age, appears extremely singular. They are said to have kept in pay a regular body of troops, collected from their Danish subjects; whose military character, it seems, was superior to that of the other inhabitants. Though the bulk of the people were not unfit for war, and, by their ordinary employments, were not hindered from taking the field upon very short preparation; yet the numerous piratical invasions to which they were exposed, and by which they were held in continual warfare, suggested the same sort of military establishment that has been found convenient in all civilized nations. The Danish families were employed, in preference to the English, from the same policy, which, in later times, made the inhabitants of Switzerland be engaged in the service of many European princes. As those mercenaries, however, were quartered about the country, and were probably not much under the controul of the <273> civil magistrate, they were guilty of many

4. Lycurgus is traditionally thought to have established Sparta's legal and governmental institutions in the ninth century B.C. Millar regards Lycurgus as an example of the mythic figure of the Legislator. For an earlier attack on this myth, including mention of both Lycurgus and Alfred, see *DR,* 6.

5. Edward the Elder, king of Wessex (r. 899–924); Athelstan I, king of Wessex (r. 924–39); and Edgar the Peaceable, king of Wessex (r. 959–75).

irregularities, and rendered themselves universally odious. They possessed all the power, and discovered, we may suppose, all the insolence of a standing army;[6] unrestrained by the watchfulness of a regular government, or by the influence of civilized manners. Hence the appellation of a *lurdane,* or *lord-dane,* which was bestowed upon them, came to be used as a term of reproach; and signified an idler and oppressor. Their situation led them, at the same time, to seek distinction, by the superior elegance of their dress and behaviour; and we are told, that they were accustomed frequently to change their cloaths, to comb their hair once a day, and to bathe or wash themselves every Sunday. By these effeminate arts they became the favourites of the women; and were so successful in their gallantries, as to debauch the wives and daughters of many noble families.* <274>

In the reign of Ethelred, a weak and pusillanimous prince, England was again infested by more numerous swarms of the Northern pirates; and at length was invaded by a formidable army under Sweyn, the king of Denmark, and Olave the king of Norway. Ethelred,[7] unable to resist these united forces, had recourse to the ineffectual and ruinous expedient of purchasing peace by the offer of a pecuniary composition; and when those princes had returned to their own country, he excited his English subjects, to gratify their

* "Habebant etiam ex consuetudine patriae unoquoque die comam pectere, sabbatis balneare, saepe etiam vestituram mutare, et formam corporis multis talibus frivolis adjuvare; unde et matronarum castitati insideabantur, et filias etiam nobilium concubinarum nomine detinebant." Chron. Joan. Wallingford. [["They had also from the custom of their country the habit of combing their hair every day, of bathing on Sundays, even of changing their clothing frequently, and of enhancing their physical attractiveness with many frivolous devices of this sort. By this means they laid snares for the chastity of married women and kept the daughters even of noblemen as concubines." *The Chronicle Attributed to John of Wallingford,* ed. Richard Vaughan (London: Royal Historical Society, 1958), 60.]]

6. In seventeenth- and eighteenth-century Britain, as well as in the American colonies in their struggle for independence, there was considerable fear that "standing armies" (i.e., professional armies maintained in times of peace) were an instrument of tyrannical government.

7. Ethelred II, the Unready: king of England (r. 978–1013, 1014–16). He paid this "pecuniary composition" or *Danegeld* to Svein I Haraldson, "Forkbeard," king of the Danes (r. 986–1014) and Olaf I Tryggvason of Norway (r. 995–1000). The St. Brice's Day massacre ordered by Ethelred occurred on 13 November 1002, and prompted the return of Svein I and Olaf I to Britain. Haraldson would reign as king of England by conquest for several months until his death in 1014, at which time Ethelred returned to power.

resentment against the Danes, by taking advantage of their security, and putting them to death in cold blood. The extent of this massacre, so disgraceful to the monarch, and to the nation, cannot easily be ascertained. The greater part of the historians consider it as extending to the whole of the Danish race at that time to be found in England; but the improbability of this, together with the authority of one ancient author, makes it reasonable to suppose, with Mr. Hume, that the slaughter was, for the most part, limited to those mercenaries against whom the rage of the populace was more immediately directed. <275>

To revenge an act of so much perfidy and cruelty, Sweyn, without loss of time, made another descent into Britain; and after destroying many of the towns, and desolating a great part of the country, he seems to have meditated an entire conquest of the kingdom. He did not live to complete his designs; but these were prosecuted by his son Canute;[8] who met with little opposition; and in a short time added the English monarchy to that of Denmark, which he possessed by inheritance. This prince, by his abilities, by the prudence and lenity of his administration, and by the extent of his dominions, was justly entitled to the appellation of *great,* which he has received from posterity. In England, after the first effects of the conquest were over, he endeavoured to procure the good-will of his subjects, by reducing the English and Danish inhabitants under the same laws, and by abolishing all distinctions between them. He published a collection of laws, which has been preserved.[9] After this monarch, two of his sons reigned successively in England; but, as they died without issue, the crown was restored to a prince of the Saxon line, known by the name of Edward the Confessor.[10] <276>

The conquest of England by the Danes appears to have been productive of no other political consequences, beside the interruption given to improvements, by the bloody and destructive wars with which it was attended. When Britain was deserted by the Romans, and fell under the Anglo-Saxon government, the country, which had made considerable progress in arts and

8. Cnut the Great: king of Denmark, Norway, and England (r. 1016–35), and son of Svein I Haraldson. Cnut conquered England in 1015, and gained entire control in 1016 after the death of Edmund II "Ironside" (r. 1016), with whom he had agreed to share the kingdom. He was succeeded by his sons Harold Harefoot (r. 1037–40) and Harthacanute (r. 1040–42).

9. Cnut's law codes, I and II Cnut, were issued in 1018.

10. Edward the Confessor (r. 1042–66).

civilization, was, of a sudden, reduced into a state of barbarism, and underwent a total revolution of its political system. By the Danish conquest, one set of barbarians were subjected to another, of kindred origin and manners; so that the sceptre was placed in different hands, without any alteration in the maxims by which it was swayed, or the authority by which it was maintained.

From the beginning to the end of the period, which is the immediate subject of this review, the circumstances of the kingdom were such, as contributed to render the government more and more aristocratical.

It has been already observed, that the landed estates, originally occupied by the Saxon conquerors of England, were of moderate extent; <277> for which reason there came to be a great number of allodial or independent proprietors. This was what might be expected, from the very limited power and opulence of the several heads of families who settled in the country, and from their want of the knowledge and experience requisite for the management of extensive possessions. During the continuance of their settlement, however, and the consequent improvement of their circumstances, the industry and abilities, or the good fortune, of individuals, were attended with gradual accumulations of wealth, and with proportional differences in the distribution of landed property.

From the reign of Egbert, when England became an extensive kingdom, the sovereign was necessarily removed to a distance from a great part of his subjects; who, for that reason, were equally beyond the reach of his protection, and of his authority. For putting a stop to those predatory incursions, by which the inhabitants of different districts were frequently harassing and injuring one another, the forces employed by the crown could seldom be brought to act, either with sufficient <278> quickness to relieve the sufferer, or with sufficient perseverance to chastise the offender. It was necessary, therefore, when the property of any person was invaded, or threatened with invasion, by a superior power, that the owner should not, in many cases, depend upon the interposition of the sovereign or public magistrate, but should endeavour to procure the immediate assistance of some of his neighbours. As the reciprocal acts of hostility, which were frequently committed, gave rise to hereditary feuds among particular families; so they occasioned, among other families in the same neighbourhood, a variety of combinations and alliances for mutual defence and security. When the parties, who thus formed a defensive alliance, had been exposed to the same difficulties, and expected to derive an equal benefit from their agreement, they were led to unite upon equal terms, and remained in a state of independence. Of the societies formed in this manner, we have many instances, both in England, and in the other countries of Europe.* <279>

But it happened more frequently that small proprietors, being exposed to continual oppression, and to every sort of injustice, from persons of greater opulence, were obliged to solicit the aid of one powerful neighbour, in order to shelter them from the attacks of another.[11] In such a situation they could not pretend to form an alliance upon the footing of equality; but were commonly reduced to the necessity of purchasing protection by the offer of submission and services. As they were to obtain, from their protector, the same advantages which he bestowed upon his ancient military servants, it was reasonable that they should, in like manner, acknowledge his jurisdiction, and contribute to the advancement of his power and authority. Thus, in some cases, by a formal agreement, in others, perhaps, by a long and uniform submission to the feudal services, many renounced that allodial property which they were no longer able to maintain; and, from the prospect of living in greater security, allowed themselves to be degraded into the state of military retainers or vassals.

From a similarity of circumstances, these transactions were often repeated in different <280> parts of the country, and were gradually extended over the whole kingdom. The more the demesnes of particular barons had been increased by such voluntary resignations, the remaining proprietors of small estates were the less able to retain their independence; and found it the more expedient to provide for their own safety, by incorporating themselves in some great feudal dependency. The allodial proprietors were, in this manner, continually diminishing; the landed property of England was daily accumulated in fewer hands; and the districts possessed by particular barons, who profited by the reduction of their neighbours into a state of subordination, were proportionably enlarged.

* They have been called *sodalitia, fraternitates.* [[Clubs; brotherhoods.]] Dr. Hickes, Diss. Epist. p. 21.

11. Millar contends the feudal tenures grew because smaller allodial (or independent) proprietors were forced to ask for aid from their more powerful neighbours, who granted protection on the basis of feudal service. As a result, feudal tenures increased at the expense of allodial ones, and, as more land was brought into fewer hands, the nobility consolidated its power.

By these changes, the nobility, it is evident, must have obtained more weight in the scale of government. While the landed estates of individuals were so small as barely to supply the necessaries of life, the owners were too inconsiderable to procure influence over others, and too numerous to prosecute an uniform plan for the advancement of their common interest. But in proportion as particular persons had acquired extensive possessions, they were ena-<281>bled to maintain a train of dependants and followers, directed on all occasions by the will of their feudal superior, and inured, by long habits, to scruple at nothing in order to gratify his ambition, or to exalt his dignity. From the smallness of their number, these great proprietors might, at the same time, be combined with more facility, in opposing the exertions of the prerogative.

The sovereign, we may suppose, was not an idle spectator of these alterations in the condition of his subjects. As every opulent baron obliged his poorer neighbours to become his vassals, the king also exerted himself in the protection of such as resided near the royal demesnes, and acquired over them the rights of a feudal superior. But the accessions acquired in this manner, to the revenue of the crown, and to the number of crown vassals, were probably not sufficient to counterbalance the vast accumulation of landed property under the lords of particular districts. We find accordingly, that about the reign of Edward the Confessor, a Godwin, earl of Wessex, a Leofric, duke of Mercia, a Siward, duke of Northumberland, with a few more barons, had become so powerful, as to be the objects of constant <282> alarm and jealousy to the crown, and in a great measure masters of the government.

The authority of the Anglo-Saxon princes was, on the other hand, weakened, in many cases, and prevented from acquiring stability by the defects of their title to the sovereignty.

The rules of succession to the crown appear, in all countries, to have been founded upon the same principles which govern the inheritance of private estates. According to the primitive notions of mankind, it was held, that, upon the death of any person, his estate should belong to his nearest relations, who, by being members of the same family, appeared to have the most intimate connexion with the family goods, of which they had formerly been a sort of joint possessors with the deceased. But in that state of the world, in which every family required a military leader to provide for their defence, the person invested with this office was by degrees permitted to assume the *management,* and at length to acquire the *property,* of that family-estate which was committed to his protection. Hence the right of *primogeniture* in succession; which, in opposition to the feelings of natural justice, has <283> been introduced from considerations of expediency. The eldest of the sons, being commonly the first who acquired experience and reputation in war, was, upon the death of the parent, admitted to be the leader and heir of the family; and when a general practice in his favour had once been established from the ordinary course of things, it was maintained by the force of custom, even in singular cases, where he had not the same superiority. In the succession to a monarchy there occurred a double reason for introducing this right of primogeniture; as the monarch was not only the leader and representative of the nation, but also the heir of that private estate, which had been the original source, and was the principal support of his dignity. But in kingdoms of great extent, and which had made but small progress in the arts of government, the indivisible succession of the crown was often maintained with greater difficulty than occurred in the transmission of private estates; because the several districts of an extensive monarchy, being at a great distance, and feebly united, were apt, upon the death of a monarch, to fall asunder, and to embrace the <284> party of those different members of the royal family, who might be tempted to aim at the sovereignty.

The rules of succession to the crown of England appear, in the period now under examination, to have been gradually advancing towards a regular standard; but were far from having yet attained a perfect uniformity. Among the nineteen princes who reigned from the union of the Heptarchy to the Norman conquest, we meet with no fewer than eight, who, according to the notions of the present age, must be regarded as usurpers; and several of these obtained the crown by titles, which, though considered as in some degree irregular, had not, in that rude age, been entirely exploded.

Instead of the eldest son inheriting the estate of a family, it is common, in early ages, that the children should be altogether supplanted by the brothers and other collateral relations; who, by having arrived at a greater maturity, and possessing superior prowess, are enabled to put themselves at the head of their kindred. Thus in many of the hordes, or petty nations, upon the coast of Guinea, the children are said <285> to inherit nothing from their father but his arms; his other effects are carried off by the older relations of the family. In the succession of the ancient kings of Numidia,[12] though a country far advanced beyond the state of primitive barbarism, the brother,

12. Numidia: an ancient country of northwest Africa (near present-day Algeria) that flourished in the first centuries B.C. and A.D.

as we are informed by Livy,[13] was preferred to the children of the preceding monarch. A similar practice may be discovered in several parts of the eastern world. It obtains at present in the Ladrone island;[14] as it formerly regulated the transmission of the crown in the kingdom of Siam, and in some dynasties of the Chinese empire. Of this preference of the brothers, or other relations, to the direct descendants, there are many traces in the early history of modern Europe; and among the Anglo-Saxon kings, even after the reign of Egbert, we meet with four instances of it; in the person of Alfred the Great, of Edred, of Ethelred, and of Edwy; the three first of whom succeeded to a brother; the last to an uncle; and all of them, in prejudice to the children of the predecessor. To these may be added, Edgar, surnamed *the Peaceable,* by whom Edwy his brother was dethroned.[15] <286>

According to the manners of a rude people, there is frequently little difference, with regard to the right of succession, between the children produced by a concubine and those who are born in marriage. It is the circumstance of living in the father's house, and having a sort of joint possession of the family estate, that is apprehended chiefly to bestow upon the children a title to the inheritance; and, in a country so destitute of refinement or delicacy, that the wife is indifferent about the fidelity of her husband, or is of so little consequence that her jealousy is not regarded, his bastards are likely to be often brought up under his own eye, and to receive a promiscuous maintenance with his legitimate offspring. This observation may be illustrated from the history of early nations, both ancient and modern, and in all quarters of the world. It is remarkable that, among the Israelites, in the time of their judges, the lawful children of Gilead had, apparently, no other way of preventing Jephthah, their bastard brother, from succeeding to the father's estate, than by driving him out of the family.* <287>

The strictness of morals introduced by christianity, contributed in Eu-

* See Judges, chap. xi. [[Judges 11:1–2, 4–11.]]

13. Livy, or Titus Livius (59 B.C.–17 A.D.): Roman historian, author of the *History of Rome* which he wrote in installments over the course of his life.

14. Ladrone Island: an older name for the Northern Mariana Islands in the west Pacific Ocean, east of the Philippines; Siam is an older name for Thailand.

15. Eadred (r. 946–55) succeeded his brother Edmund I, the Magnificent (r. 939–46); Ethelred II succeeded his brother Edward the Martyr (r. 975–78); Edwy (r. 955–59) succeeded his uncle Eadred and was himself succeeded by his younger brother Edgar, the Peaceable.

rope to diminish the privileges of bastard children. It does not, however, appear, that, even so late as the time of the Norman conquest, they were understood, in any European country, to be totally disqualified from inheriting estates. In England, not to mention the instances that might be collected among the kings of the Heptarchy, we find that Athelstan, the natural son of Edward the elder, was permitted to mount the throne, in preference to the lawful children of his father.[16]

The accession of Canute was merely the effect of conquest; though that prince endeavoured to support his claim by means of a stipulation, real or pretended, with the former king. Upon the restoration of the Saxon line, the nobles had acquired so much power as enabled them to dispose of the vacant throne. To their favour Edward the Confessor, who usurped the right of the lineal heir, was principally indebted for the crown; and the advancement of Harold had confessedly no other foundation.

By these numerous deviations from the re-<288>gular course of succession, the monarch was prevented from acquiring that accumulation of hereditary influence, which is the effect of an uninterrupted and long-continued lineal descent; at the same time that those princes who obtained the crown in an irregular manner were, upon that account, subjected to difficulties, from which they were obliged to extricate themselves by courting the nobility, and by making such concessions as tended to alter the balance of the constitution.[17]

From a singular incident, in the reign of the first Edmund, and which occasioned the death of that prince, we may easily discover that the Anglo-Saxon kings depended, in a great measure, upon the arbitrary assistance of their followers, for maintaining the dignity and authority of the crown; and were far from being provided with proper resources for securing a decent respect and obedience to their commands. "As Edmund, one day, was sol-

16. Edward the Elder, king of Wessex, had eighteen children by three wives, but the legitimacy of his first marriage, to Egwina, the mother of Athelstan I, is unclear. Thus, Athelstan's claim to the throne was legally less compelling than those of his clearly legitimate brothers.

17. The reign of Edward the Confessor, son of Ethelred the Unready, marks the restoration of the Saxon line upon the death of Harthacanute. Edward's accession was strengthened by the support of Godwin, earl of Wessex, chief among the nobles to whom Millar refers. Harold II, Godwin's son and chief adviser to Edward, rose to power after Edward's death by the influence of his father. William of Normandy contested his succession, and successfully invaded in 1066.

emnizing a festival in the county of Glocester, he remarked, that Leolf, a notorious robber, whom he had sentenced to banishment, had yet the boldness to enter the hall where he dined, and to sit at table with his attendants. <289> Enraged at this insolence, he ordered him to leave the room; but on his refusing to obey, the king, whose temper, naturally choleric, was inflamed by this additional insult, leaped on him himself, and seized him by the hair; but the ruffian, pushed to extremity, drew his dagger, and gave the king a wound, of which he immediately expired."* <290>

* Hume's History of England. [[For this quoted passage from Hume, see *HE,* 1:89.]]

CHAPTER X

Variations in the State of Tythings, Hundreds, and Shires.[1]

The resignations of land, made by allodial proprietors in order to procure the patronage and protection of a feudal superior, were moulded in a particular manner, and received a peculiar direction, from the institutions formerly mentioned, of tythings, hundreds, and shires, as, on the other hand, the state of these institutions underwent a great alteration from the progress of those resignations.

A tything was composed of a number of heads of families, who, possessing allodial property of small extent, and therefore having few dependants, found it convenient to live together in the same village or neighbourhood, for their mutual defence and security. The bulk of the free people, or allodial proprietors, appear to have been originally incorporated in the different tythings, throughout the kingdom; though it is probable at the same time, <291> that there were particular thanes, or military leaders, who, from their superior wealth and power, had no occasion to join in any tything; and who lived, in a state of greater independence and dignity, at the head of their own bondmen, or tenants and vassals. Beside the villages, therefore, which were composed of the freemen, and which had the denomination of tythings, there were others, composed of the dependants of a feudal superior, placed under his immediate jurisdiction and authority.*

1. On tythings, hundreds, and shires, see p. 97, note 2, and p. 99, the daggered note.

* See the laws ascribed to Edward the Confessor, published by Lambard and Wilkins. L. 21. is translated as follows: "Archiepiscopi, episcopi, comites, barones, *et omnes qui habuerint sacham et socam, thol, theam et infangthefe,* etiam milites suos, et proprios servientes, scilicet dapiferos, pincernas, camerarios, pistores et cocos, sub suo friborgo ha-

The primitive borsholder, or tythingman,[2] was elected by the freemen of the tything over which he presided; and at first was probably but little superior to them in opulence. By degrees, however, the rank which he enjoyed, <292> together with the influence, and the perquisites, which he derived from thence, enabled him to increase his fortune, and to extend his authority over the different members of the community. Upon his decease therefore, the person who inherited his estate, obtaining a great part of the weight and consideration of the predecessor, was naturally promoted to the same office; which after being continued for many generations in the same family, and bestowing upon the representative of it successive accumulations of property, was at last regarded as no longer elective, but as a permanent hereditary dignity. The borsholder came thus, in his own right, to demand military service from the members of the ancient tything; and to claim the privilege of being their judge both in civil and criminal matters. The tything, in short, was converted into a barony; and that voluntary combination of the inhabitants, intended for their mutual defence and security, was now lost in the more intimate connection between a superior and his vassals.

As the president of a tything advanced in the acquisition of this hereditary dignity, and found that his authority depended less upon <293> the consent of his original constituents, he became less attentive, we may suppose, to the inferior duties of his office; and the police of the village, in matters of small moment, was at length committed to a deputy. The remains of this inferior officer seem to be still preserved, in the annual election of a person to preside in each of the towns or parishes of England; who in some cases retains the old appellation of headborough, or tythingman; but who, from the branches

---

beant. Et item isti suos armigeros, vel alios sibi servientes sub suo friborgo. Quod si cui forisfacerent et clamor vicinorum de eis assurgeret, ipsi tinerent eos rectitudini in curia sua: illi dico qui haberent sacham et socam, thol et theam, et infangthefe." [["Archbishops, bishops, earls, thanes, and all those possessing sac and soc, toll, team, and infangthief shall have both their knights and their own servants, namely sewers, butlers, chamberlains, bakers, and cooks under their frank-pledge. And likewise they shall have their squires or others serving them under their frank-pledge. Accordingly if these persons commit an offense against anyone and a hue and cry is raised concerning them among their neighbours, the lords themselves—those, I mean, possessing sac and soc, toll, team, and infangthief—shall produce them for trial in their own court." See William Lambarde, *Archaionomia,* 144.]]

2. The "tythingman": the chief man of a tithing; later, it denotes a parish peace officer, or petty constable.

of business that have since devolved upon him, is more commonly called the *petty constable.*

Similar causes produced a change of the same sort in the condition of the *centenarius.*[3] This magistrate, like the tythingman, was originally chosen by the freemen of the district over which he presided; but as the richest man of the district was most likely to carry the election, so the longer any individual had remained in the office, he became, from the many opportunities it afforded of increasing his riches, the more secure of holding it for the future; and for the same reason, the heir of his private fortune, to whom he communicated his family interest, had likewise the pro-<294>bability of obtaining the same dignity in preference to every competitor. Thus the leader of the hundred was, through length of time, converted into an hereditary officer; and, from the superiority of his original office, was enabled to establish a permanent authority over the several tythingmen of his district. When these last had become the hereditary leaders of tythings, they were frequently reduced, therefore, into a state of feudal subordination to the hundreder. In other cases, the influence of this greater magistrate was exerted in bringing particular tythings under his immediate protection, and in checking and supplanting the tythingmen, who might otherwise have acquired a feudal authority in these little societies.

When the *centenarius* became a person of too much consequence to execute the inferior branches of business connected with his department, a deputy was appointed for that purpose; whence the office of the *high constable,* elected annually in those districts, appears to have been derived.

With respect to the alderman, or chief magistrate of a shire, it has been disputed whe-<295>ther he was originally nominated by the king, or elected by the freemen of the territory over which he presided. From what has been already observed, the latter of these opinions is much more probable than the former. Considering how little power was usually possessed by the sovereign in the infancy of government, not only among the Saxons, but in all the modern states of Europe; and considering that he had neither the nomination of the borsholder, nor of the *centenarius;* it is not likely, that he would assume the appointment of those who presided over the greater divisions of the kingdom.

It is universally admitted, that the Anglo-Saxon officers, who, in the early

3. The chief officer of a hundred.

periods of the Heptarchy, received the appellation of *Heretochs,* were elected by the people whom they were appointed to command. These Heretochs were the leaders of considerable bodies of the Saxons, who upon the settlement of their followers, became the governors of provinces; and of consequence they were in reality the same sort of magistrates with those who, upon the more accurate division of the country into shires, were better known by the name of <296> aldermen or earls. It is therefore highly probable, that the first aldermen were appointed in the same manner with their predecessors the Heretochs. By degrees, however, the chief magistrate of a shire was intrusted with the collection and management of several branches of the crown revenue within the bounds of his district; and for the execution of this part of his duty he became, of course, accountable to the king. This afforded the sovereign a pretence for interfering in the appointment; and, from the effect which his interference could hardly fail to produce, appears to have given him a negative upon the election.* How long the aldermen were appointed in this manner, it is not easy to discover: but from the same circumstances which had operated in the case of the tythingman, and of the hundreder; from the necessity of appointing the most opulent thane of a shire, who alone was able to command respect from <297> the inhabitants; and from the accumulation of property, and of interest, arising from the possession of that high station; the office was frequently continued in the same families; and was, in the end, annexed to them as a permanent dignity. We accordingly find, that, in the latter part of the Anglo-Saxon line, the aldermen, or earls, as they were then more commonly called, had in general become hereditary. In France it appears that the same change in the state of the *counts* and *dukes* was, in like manner, completed before the accession of Hugh Capet; which corresponds to the English period of the Norman conquest.

We may easily conceive that the hereditary governor of a shire, who had, in his own right, the privilege of assembling and commanding the forces, as well as of holding the chief tribunal for distributing justice, in that extensive territory, was possessed of great influence and authority; and that many al-

* In the reign of Alfred the earldoms were all held during the pleasure of the king. Asser. de gest. Alfredi. In the reign of Edward the Confessor they had a third part of all fines, forfeitures, and other profits of the shire, for their labour. Brady's Compleat Hist. of England.

lodial proprietors would find they had no better means of securing themselves from insult and depredation than by courting his protection. Even the leaders of hundreds, who had acquired a feudal superiority over their own districts, but who <298> had been placed in a station subordinate to the earl, were sometimes induced, by motives of interest, to become his immediate vassals, and to promise the same service and submission to him, which they exacted from their own military retainers. In particular tythings, more immediately situated within the sphere of his influence, the powerful protection of the earl superseded that of their own tythingmen, and, by a natural consequence, rendered the inhabitants more desirous of yielding homage and fealty to that superior magistrate, than to their own proper officers. In such cases the authority of the smaller magistrates was lost and swallowed up in that of the greater.

The advancement of the earl gave occasion to the appointment of an inferior officer, the *sheriff;*[4] upon whom was devolved the real business connected with the office. This officer was originally chosen by the free inhabitants, or allodial proprietors of the shire; though the extensive department committed to his care, and the great privileges with which he was invested, had the same tendency, as in the case of the chief governors, to vary the mode of his <299> appointment, and, in the course of time, to bestow upon him an independent authority.

It was in this manner that *allodial* was generally converted into *feudal* property, and that an enlarged system of military dependencies was at length established. The necessity of defence produced the primitive associations of tythings, hundreds, and shires, composed of allodial proprietors, with their respective bondmen or vassals. But, from the disorders of society, these combinations were too loose and feeble, to answer the purposes for which they were intended. To protect and rescue the individuals in each of these communities, it was requisite that their leader should be invested with greater authority than had originally been bestowed upon him; and that his associates or followers should become his permanent military servants. Tythings, hundreds, and even a considerable part of shires, were thus changed into fiefs; and the tythingman, the hundreder, and the earl, became the feudal superiors over such districts as found it expedient to court their protection.

4. The representative of royal authority in a shire, responsible for the execution of the law.

A subordination, too, was introduced among the lead-<300>ers of those districts; and the tythingmen of a hundred became frequently the vassals of the hundreder; as many of the hundreders belonging to a shire became vassals of that greater baron, the earl.

As these changes were produced very slowly and gradually, it is not surprising that they should be overlooked by contemporary annalists. The meetings of the tything, the hundred, and the shire, appear to have retained the same names, and to have transacted the same sort of business, long after the two former were entirely, and the last, in a great measure, converted into the courts of a barony. The alteration, in reality, consisted merely in a different shade of authority acquired by the leader or chief magistrate of those divisions.

It seems worthy of notice, that this conversion of allodial associations into feudal dependencies, while it promoted the aristocracy, was calculated to improve the police of the country.[5] When the tythingman, the hundreder, and the earl were exalted to the rank of hereditary barons, they were more capable than formerly of maintaining good order in their several districts; and, as every feudal su-<301>perior was responsible to the public for the conduct of his vassals and retainers, he had an interest to exert his authority in preventing rapine and violence. Unhappily, indeed, they were often too powerful to submit to this part of their duty; and, instead of repairing the injuries done by their dependants, were frequently disposed to screen them from the punishment due to their offences. <302>

5. *Police* in this sense means civil order. See p. 12, note 6.

CHAPTER XI

Changes produced in the Condition of the Vassals, and of the Peasants.

The members of every feudal dependency consisted of the military retainers or vassals, and of the peasants, or churles; both of whom, in the latter part of the Anglo-Saxon government, experienced a great alteration in their circumstances.

In that state of society which determined allodial proprietors to shelter themselves under the protection of a feudal superior, and by which the number of military retainers was therefore gradually augmented, the privileges belonging to this order of men were naturally increased; and their condition was rendered more secure and comfortable. The original vassals of any person were the members of his own family, who, from natural affection, and from ancient habits, were strongly attached to his interest, and upon whom, from a reciprocal regard, as well as from the consideration of <303> expediency, when they became too numerous to live in his own house, he voluntarily bestowed the possession of lands for their maintenance. As the superior had no reason to suspect that these men would ever be deficient in fidelity, or seek to withdraw their allegiance; so they entertained no apprehension that, while they were willing to fulfil their duty, they should ever be dispossessed of their lands. The intimate connexion between the parties, and the simplicity of their manners, made them place a mutual confidence in each other, and prevented their being apprehensive of any future disputes: so that neither the superior required any specification of the services to be performed, nor the vassal, any express stipulation, with respect to the duration or terms of his possession. Thus the original vassals, though, in fact, their land was commonly permitted to remain with them and their posterity, were properly no more than *tenants at will,*[1] and therefore entirely dependent upon the superior.

But when persons originally independent, had, with a view to certain advantages, allowed themselves to fall into a feudal subordination, <304> or had agreed to exalt an equal or a stranger to the rank of a superior, it could hardly be expected that these new vassals would be willing to hold their lands in so precarious a manner. Cautious of yielding any greater submission than their circumstances required, or suspicious of neglect or oppression from the person whom they had chosen for their protector, they naturally insisted, that the precise conditions of their tenure should be expressly ascertained; while the superior, distrusting the fidelity and attachment of men over whom he had no natural authority, and who submitted to him, perhaps, with reluctance, and from the mere pressure of temporary difficulties, was no less anxious to specify the nature of their service, and to secure the performance of it, by subjecting them, in case of negligence or disobedience, to severe penalties and forfeitures. From a variety of conjunctures, individuals might be laid under the necessity of submitting to harder conditions, upon some occasions than upon others; but, in general, when a feudal tenure was constituted by the consent of any allodial proprietor, it seems to have been expressly provided, that the fief should not only <305> remain with the vassal during life, but should descend, either to his heirs male, or to such of his heirs as were specified in the grant.

By the establishment of those hereditary fiefs, the vassal, instead of being a precarious tenant, became, in effect, the proprietor of the feudal estate, and the interest of the superior was reduced to a *reversion*[2] in default of the vassal's heirs, together with a right of levying, in particular cases, a variety of perquisites or casual emoluments. Of these casual emoluments or *incidents,*[3] as they are called, which might still accrue to the superior from the estate of his vassal, after it was made transmissible to heirs, the feudal writers have commonly enumerated seven different sorts.

1. Though fiefs had been rendered hereditary, yet, as every person who enjoyed them was liable for the feudal services, it was necessary that an heir,

1. Those whose rights to occupy the tenancy could be terminated by the feudal lord at any time.

2. In law, the legal return of an estate to the donor or grantor, or his heirs.

3. In law, refers to the management and disposal of the estate of a deceased person.

before he obtained the investiture, should solemnly undertake the performance of them, and come under an oath of fidelity to the superior. Upon the death of any vassal, therefore, the superior laid hold of the lands, and detained them in his possession, until the heir should claim a renewal of the <306> feudal engagement. This privilege gave rise to what is called the incident of *non-entry.*

2. When the feudal tenures were precarious, the sons of the vassals frequently endeavoured, by a present, to procure the favour of the superior, and to obtain the continuance of their ancestor's possession. Even after fiefs became hereditary, it still was found expedient to secure, by means of a bribe, what, though a matter of right, was not easily extorted by force; and the original arbitrary donation was converted into a regular duty, under the name of *relief.*

3. If the heir of a former vassal was incapable of performing the feudal service, he had no right to claim the possession of the fief. While he was under age, therefore, the lands were possessed by the superior; who, at the same time, from a regard to his own interest, if not from affection to the family of his old vassal, was induced to assume the guardianship and protection of the minor, his future military servant. Hence the complex burthen, and privilege, which went under the name of *wardship.*[4]

4. During the disorders which prevailed <307> under the feudal governments, it was of great consequence that the military vassals should not contract an alliance with the enemy of their liege lord; which might have a tendency to corrupt their fidelity. When fiefs therefore were secured upon a permanent footing, a provision was made against an event of this dangerous nature; and the vassals who married without the superior's consent, or who even refused to marry according to his desire, became liable to a pecuniary composition or penalty. Such was the incident of *marriage;* a perquisite suited to the rude and barbarous manners which occasioned its establishment.

5. Beside the ordinary revenue which the superior drew from his estate, he was accustomed, upon extraordinary emergencies, to apply to his vassals, and to request from them a contribution in order to relieve him from his immediate embarrassment. While they held their lands precariously, a request of this nature was equal to a command; since the superior might at pleasure seize upon the whole estate of his tenants. But when the vassals had

4. The guardianship and custody of the land and person of a minor.

obtained a more permanent right, it became necessary to settle the particular <308> occasions upon which those contributions were to be made, as well as the extent of the sum that might be demanded; and in this manner, *aids* or *benevolences*[5] came to be enumerated among the duties payable to a superior. Three cases are mentioned, in which, over all the feudal kingdoms, these contributions might be exacted; to redeem the superior from captivity; to portion his eldest daughter, at her marriage; and to defray the expence of making his eldest son a knight.

6. Though a fief had been rendered hereditary; yet, upon the total failure of heirs, it necessarily returned to the superior. The vassal might also forfeit his right to the lands, by his neglect to perform the feudal service, or by any violation of his duty. This forfeiture, or termination of the fief, was called an *escheat*.[6]

7. From the primitive state of the feudal tenures, the vassal had no title to alienate his fief, which he possessed as the wages merely of his military service. But when fiefs, by being transmissible to heirs, began to assume the appearance of property; when the general advancement of arts had rendered land more frequently an object of commerce; and when, <309> upon the suppression of the former disorders, the military service of the vassal was rendered of less importance, it became customary, by the payment of a sum of money, to compound with the superior for the privilege of selling the feudal estate. This produced the perquisite of superiority called the *fine of alienation.*

These feudal incidents may be considered as the remains of that absolute property of the fief, which the superior had formerly enjoyed; but which, with reservation of such casual emoluments, was now conveyed to the vassal.

After this new species of military retainers had become numerous, and had spread themselves over the country, it is natural to suppose that their privileges would, by the force of example, be communicated to the ancient vassals. The ancient feudal tenants, who, from the more extended connections of the superior, had probably become less the objects of his peculiar attention, and were not always treated with those marks of distinction to

5. Gifts or grants of money, often used in reference to forced loans or contributions levied by the king on his subjects.

6. An incident of feudal law whereby a fief reverted to the lord when the tenant died without leaving a successor to inherit under the original grant.

which they supposed themselves entitled, beheld with envy and jealousy the stability and security enjoyed by his new vassals; and were solicitous to hold their lands under the same permanent tenure. <310> A concession of this nature, by which the old and faithful followers of a chief were placed upon a footing of equality with strangers, could seldom be decently withheld from them; and in cases where he stood in immediate need of their assistance, was likely to be easily obtained. As these privileges were slowly and gradually introduced, and as they were often accelerated or retarded by the situation of particular baronies, not to mention a variety of accidental circumstances, it is impossible to mark the precise period at which their establishment was compleated; though it is probable that, before the Norman conquest,[7] they were extended to the greater part, if not the whole, of the ancient vassals.

While the incidents due to the superior were thus ascertained with accuracy, the interest of the vassals made it no less necessary, that the extent and duration of their military service should be exactly determined. In Britain, and probably in several kingdoms upon the continent, it was limited accordingly to forty days for each year; a period that might appear fully sufficient for those desultory enterprizes which the superior had occasion to <311> undertake. If ever he chose, after the expiration of this period, to retain his vassals in the field, he was under the necessity of procuring their consent, and was obliged to bear the charges of their maintenance.

The effect of these changes in the state of the military tenures could not fail to be discernible in the administration and government of every feudal dependency. Though it still was, no doubt, the interest of the vassals to avoid all contention with the superior, and to merit his favour by their fidelity and alacrity in the discharge of their duty, yet they were not under the same necessity of paying an implicit obedience to his commands. To whatever inconveniencies they might be subjected from the manner of levying the feudal *incidents,* yet, while they punctually performed their services, they could not, without gross injustice, be deprived of their possessions; and they had a right to follow their own inclination in the management of their private concerns. Sensible of this alteration in their circumstances, the superior was induced to be more cautious of disobliging them, to pay more deference to their opinions, to listen and give <312> way to their remonstrances, and,

7. Millar is concerned to argue that important features of the feudal system were generally in place before the Norman Conquest in 1066.

in public measures of importance, to act with their advice and concurrence. Thus, while the influence and power of the great lords was gradually extended by the multiplication of their vassals, their authority over each particular vassal was necessarily reduced; and they were obliged to exercise it with greater moderation, as well as to endeavour, by the arts of popularity, and even, sometimes, by pecuniary rewards and advantages, to gain the effectual support of their followers.

The improvements made in agriculture, produced alterations, of no less importance, in the state of the peasants or *churles.* The peasants, as has been formerly observed, were originally bondmen or slaves. But as from the nature of their employment, and from their living at such a distance as to be beyond the reach of the master's inspection, it was found expedient to excite their industry by bestowing upon them successive gratuities and privileges; many of them were enabled, at an early period, to acquire considerable property; and some of them were advanced to the condition of tenants, intrusted by the master with <313> a discretionary management of their farms. In the natural course of things, these tenants were afterwards raised to a still better situation. When, in consequence of some experience in husbandry, they were about to undertake an expensive melioration of their farms, common prudence required that they should be secure of the possession, for such a period as might afford them a reasonable prospect of a return for their labour and expence. By offering an advanced rent to the master, they sometimes prevailed upon him to make an agreement of that nature, and to grant them a *lease* for a certain number of years. From the improving circumstances of the tenant, he sometimes obtained, not only a right of holding the estate for life, but of transmitting it to heirs; and there appear to have been some occasions, though it is probable these were not very common, on which, by the payment of a full price, he was enabled to make an entire purchase of the lands.

Those churles who had acquired a landed estate transmissible to heirs, to be held for payment of a yearly rent, were denominated *soc-*<314>*cage vassals.*[8] From their employment and character, they were of an inferior rank to the military vassals; but they had the same permanent right to their estates.

8. *Socage* is a general term referring to the tenure of land by certain determinate services other than knight service. Hence, as Millar says, the socage vassal belongs to a rank inferior to those who render military service as knights.

They were also liable to the same *incidents of superiority;* excepting those of *wardship* and *marriage;* the former, because the superior was disposed to pay no attention to the education of such of his dependants as were employed merely in agriculture; the latter, because the alliances which they contracted were deemed of little consequence to him.

The churles who made a full purchase of a landed estate should have become allodial proprietors, and have acquired the rank and privileges of nobility; but the influence of ancient usage prevented so sudden and violent a change in the rank of individuals; and as the proprietor who sold his lands, was unwilling entirely to resign his dignity, so the purchaser had not the presumption to deprive him of it. To retain a faint shadow of the ancient connection, the latter became bound, as an acknowledgment of the superiority, to pay to the former an elusory annual duty, if ever it <315> should be demanded.* We find that, by a statute in the reign of king Athelstan, a churle who had purchased an estate consisting of five hides of land, with certain appendages, usually possessed by gentlemen of that fortune, was declared to have a right to all the *privileges of a thane;* by which those of a *lesser thane,* or military vassal, were probably understood.†

From this law, which demonstrates that the encouragement of agriculture was become an object of public attention, it may be inferred, that though in some cases the *churles* were enabled to acquire landed property, they had not been understood, upon that account, to obtain of course the privileges of the military people; since these were not conferred upon them without a special interposition of the legislature; nor even by that statute, except upon such as had accumulated a very considerable estate. Such was the original inferiority of the peasants, and so strong were the habits connected with their primitive condition, that <316> though they had been raised to independent circumstances, it was with some difficulty they were permitted to hold the rank of gentlemen, and procured the treatment suitable to men of that superior class.

The freedom acquired by a great proportion of the peasants, together with the advances in husbandry from which it proceeded, gave rise to an imme-

* This tenure has been frequently confounded with the ordinary soccage; but sometimes is distinguished by the name of *blanch.*

† Judicia civitatis Lundoniae. Wilkins, Leg. Sax. p. 70.

diate improvement in arts and manufactures. The first artificers[9] were villeins, or servants of the greater thanes; who happening to discover some ingenuity in the common mechanical arts, were employed by the master in those branches of manufacture, which he found requisite for his accommodation. The possession of their farms, according to the rude manner in which agriculture was then practised, did not hinder them from exercising this collateral employment. When these people began to be emancipated from their ancient bondage, they were at liberty to work, not only for their former master, but for every person who chose to employ them; and by working for hire, they drew a regular profit for their labour. A competition was then introduced among different workmen, <317> which contributed to promote their industry and skill; at the same time that the improvements which have been mentioned in the condition of the lower class of people, by increasing their opulence, produced an increase of demand for the ordinary conveniencies of life; and therefore afforded greater encouragement to the occupations by which those conveniencies were supplied. Particular branches of manufacture, or of labour, coming in this manner to be more in request, occasioned more constant employment to individuals; who, at length, found it their interest to abandon every other occupation, and to depend, for their livelihood, upon that single branch in which they had attained a peculiar proficiency.

A variety of trades and mechanical professions were thus introduced; and the artificers and labourers composed a separate order of men in the community. As these grew up and were multiplied, they became the chief part of the inhabitants in those villages where they resided; which were gradually enlarged into towns, of more or less extent according as their situation, or other circumstances, proved more favourable to manufactures. <318>

It is unnecessary to observe, that the separation of trades and professions,[10] among the different inhabitants, occasioned, of course, a degree of traffick or exchange of commodities. When the artisans, as well as the farmers, confined themselves to a single employment, they were able, by their own labour, to produce only one sort of commodity; and if they wanted any thing of a different sort, they had commonly no other method of procuring

9. An artificer is a craftsman, or artisan; a "mechanic."

10. This is one of a number of places in which Millar, following Smith, introduces the topic of the division of labor.

it, than by an exchange with the person who had produced it. This exchange was at first limited, we may suppose, to the inhabitants of the same town or village; but, according as different places began to excel in manufacturing goods of different kinds, it was extended to neighbouring towns, or to the more distant parts of the country. Upon the opening of such intercourse between places at a distance, the inhabitants found it, in some cases, inconvenient to go themselves to purchase the goods which they wanted, and had occasion therefore to employ some of their neighbours for that purpose; from which there arose, by degrees, a common *carrier,* upon whom this branch of business was frequently devolved. As this person acquired a little stock, he ad-<319>ventured sometimes at his own risk, to buy commodities in one place, with a view of selling them in another; and his employment was at length improved into that of a pedlar or travelling merchant.

Although these tradesmen and mechanics were no longer in a servile condition, they had still much dependence upon the original master, or feudal superior, of that village or town in which they resided. He defended them from the attacks of the military people around them; to which, from the turbulence and disorder of the times, they were greatly exposed; and which, from their unwarlike dispositions, they were of themselves but ill qualified to resist. He also encouraged and promoted their trade, by permitting them to hold *fairs* and *markets,* or stated seasons of rendezvous, between the merchants and customers of different places; by supplying them with warehouses, and with measures and weights, for the sale of their goods; and by such other kinds of assistance as, from the rude state of the country, and in the infancy of commerce, their circumstances made them <320> stand in need of. In return for these advantages, he levied from them such tolls and duties as they were able to bear; and of consequence augmented his revenue in proportion to the increase of their wealth.

According as the patron and protector of these manufacturing and trading towns was possessed of greater influence and power, their trade was likely to be the more prosperous and flourishing. Some of those towns, having sprung from the peasantry of the crown demesnes, were under the immediate patronage of the sovereign; others, being situated upon the estates of the greater thanes, were under the protection of those nobles. The former, it is evident, enjoyed a great superiority over the latter. The protection of no particular nobleman could reach beyond the limits of his own estate; but that of the sovereign extended, in some measure, over the whole of the kingdom: not to mention that the king, by residing occasionally in the towns of which he was the immediate protector, and which he was naturally desirous of encouraging, produced a resort of the nobility and gentry to <321> those places; and, by the expensive living incident to a court, created an additional consumption of their commodities.

The extent of the trade of England, before the Norman conquest, cannot, at this distance of time, be ascertained with any degree of precision; but there is reason to believe that it was not very considerable. Of this we need require no farther evidence than the small size of the principal towns in the reign of William the conqueror.* It appears, however, that, for more than a century before that period, the commerce and manufactures of the country had been making advances which attracted the notice of the legislature. By a law of king Athelstan it is enacted, that a merchant who, upon his own account, had made three trading voyages to a foreign country, should acquire the privileges of a thane.† Such extensive trade, it was probably thought at that time, <322> could be attempted only by a person of uncommon spirit, and in affluent circumstances; whose elevation, while it served as an incitement to commercial enterprize, might be regarded as no disparagement to the military people. In other statutes which have been preserved, of the same, and of subsequent princes, we meet with some of those fundamental regulations, which commonly have place in every country, upon the first efforts to introduce a regular commerce; such as the establishment of certain formalities in completing mercantile transactions;‡ and the appointment of a mint in the principal towns;§ together with that of a common standard of money, and of weights or measures.‖

* With regard to this point, see Doomsday-book—and Dr. Brady on Boroughs. [[Millar's general references are to the Domesday Book, the census that William commissioned in 1085 and completed 1086–87, and to Robert Brady. See *Domesday Book: A Complete Translation,* ed. Ann Williams and G. H. Martin (London: Penguin, 1992); and Brady, *Historical Treatise of Cities and Burghs,* 2nd ed. (London, 1704), which includes borough information during this period, 4–17.]]

† Et si mercator tamen sit, qui ter trans altum mare "per facultates proprias abeat, ille postea jure thani sit dignus." [["And if there nevertheless is a merchant who crosses the high sea three times using his own resources, he shall afterward be worthy of the privilege of a thane."]]—[Judicia civitatis Lundoniae. Wilkins, Leg. Sax. p. 71.]

‡ Wilkins, Leg. Sax. p. 80, 81.

§ Ibid. p. 59.

‖ Ibid. p. 78.

By the addition of artificers and tradesmen to the different orders formerly mentioned, the whole people of England came now to be distinguished into four great classes; which, from their differences in rank or employment, in characters and habits of living, were separated and kept at a distance from one another. <323> Those who exercised the honourable profession of arms, whether in the station of *greater* or *lesser* thanes, of superiors or vassals, thought it inconsistent with their dignity to engage in any lucrative occupation; and disdained to contract alliances with farmers or manufacturers.* The two latter orders of men, though nearly of the same rank, were by their situation prevented from living together, and led to acquire very different manners, and ways of thinking. The solitary and robust employment of the farmer was not apt to form a similar style of behaviour and accomplishments to that which was produced by the sedentary town-life of the manufacturer; and in a country where improvements had not been carried so far as to create an intimate correspondence among all the members of society, those two sets of men were not likely to exchange their professions. The children of the <324> farmers, as well as those of the tradesmen and mechanics, were commonly disposed to follow that way of life with which they had been early acquainted. They were even bred up in most cases, to their father's employment, before they could well have an opportunity of comparing it with any other. Not only were those two orders of men, in general, confined to their respective professions, but the mechanics, employed in the several branches of manufacture, frequently transmitted their occupations to their posterity; and continued them, for many generations, in the same families. The clergy, who formed a numerous and powerful body, were no less distinguished from the other three classes, by their peculiar education, by their separate views of interest, and by their professional character and manners. The celibacy, indeed, of the clergy, which, however, was introduced in England after the period that we are examining, prevented this order of men from being so entirely separated from the rest of the inhabitants, as might otherwise have been expected. When churchmen were prohibited from having posterity <325> of their own, it was nec-

* After the Norman conquest, we find that the superior lord was prohibited by statute to marry his female ward to a *villein* or a *burgess.* It is probable that the rank of the two last-mentioned orders of men had risen considerably, before this prohibition was thought necessary.

essary that their profession should be supplied from the other ranks of the society.

From the natural course of things, it should seem, that in every country where religion has had so much influence as to introduce a great body of ecclesiastics, the people, upon the first advances made in agriculture, and in manufactures, are usually distributed into the same number of classes or orders.[11] This distribution is, accordingly, to be found, not only in all the European nations, formed upon the ruins of the Roman empire; but in other ages, and in very distant parts of the globe. The ancient inhabitants of Egypt are said to have been divided into the clergy, the military people, the husbandmen, and the artificers; and these four descriptions of men were, by a public regulation, or more probably by the influence of custom, derived from the early situation of the country, kept invariably distinct from one another. The establishment of the four great *castes,* in the country of Indostan,[12] is precisely of the same nature. This division of the people, which goes back into the remotest antiquity, has been ascribed, by historians and po-<326>litical writers, to the positive institution of Brama,[13] the early, and perhaps fabulous legislator of that country; but, in all probability, it arose from the natural separation of the principal professions or employments in the state; as it has been since retained by that excessive indolence, to which the inhabitants of those warm and fertile regions are addicted, and which has hitherto checked their improvements, by producing an aversion to every species of innovation. <327>

11. Millar once again returns to both the subject and the essential method of his first book, *The Origin of the Distinction of Ranks.*

12. *Indostan* is an archaic name for the Indian subcontinent; *caste* refers to the traditional division of Indian society into several hereditary groupings, divided along social, religious, and professional lines.

13. The ancient *Laws of Manu* are traditionally believed to have been inspired by Brahma, the Hindu creator.

CHAPTER XII

The Influence of these Changes upon the Jurisdiction and Authority of the feudal Lords.

The advancement of the Anglo-Saxon vassals and peasants to greater security and freedom, and the separation of the trading people from the class of husbandmen, could not fail to limit the authority of the superior, and more especially to affect the state of his jurisdiction. When his military retainers held their benefices precariously, and when the other members of his barony were either bondmen, or merely tenants at will, he found himself under no restraint, in deciding their differences, and in punishing their offences; but after the former had obtained hereditary fiefs, and a great proportion of the latter had been exalted to the rank of soccage-vassals, he was obliged to relax his claim to their obedience, and to distribute justice among them with greater moderation and circumspection.

The retainers of every feudal superior were <328> bound, not only to the performance of military or other services, but also to assist him in maintaining good order and tranquillity within his barony; and therefore, when any of them complained of injustice from another, or was accused of a crime, the baron found it expedient, instead of deciding by virtue of his own authority, to call a number of his other vassals, and to proceed with their advice and concurrence in trying the cause. This expedient was the most equitable for the person concerned in the trial, as well as the best calculated for giving weight to the decision. The assessors of the judges were the *pares curiae,*[1] men of the same rank with one another, and with the parties; they were chosen occasionally, and varied in each cause, to avoid burdening any individual more than his just proportion; and they were commonly selected

1. "Peers of the court."

from the neighbourhood of the place where the accusation or dispute had taken its rise, that, from their own private knowledge, they might be enabled to form a better judgment of the facts in question.

Thus the trial by an *inquest,* or *jury,* which had formerly taken place in the tribunals of <329> the shire, and of the hundred, was introduced into those of a feudal barony. The causes, however, of this institution, in the former and in the latter, were somewhat different. A jury was found convenient, in the courts of the shire, and of the hundred, to supersede the attendance of all their members; and might be regarded as a sort of committee, in place of a full and regular meeting. In the courts of the baron, its interpositions became necessary, in place of the decisions formerly given by the judge himself, in order to supply his deficience in authority over vassals whose fiefs had been secured to them by a permanent right. A jury was therefore an institution less popular than that which had formerly obtained in the county or the hundred courts, but more so, than the mode of jurisdiction originally displayed in the courts of the baron. It is reasonable, at the same time, to suppose, that, when allodial proprietors had been changed into vassals, the custom of jury-trials[2] in the courts of the former, would facilitate the introduction of a similar practice in the judicial establishments of the latter.

That this form of trial obtained universally <330> in all the feudal governments, as well as in that of England, there can be no reason to doubt. In France, in Germany, and in other European countries, where we have any accounts of the constitution and procedure of the feudal courts, it appears that law-suits of every sort, concerning the freemen or vassals of a barony, were determined by the *pares curiae;* and that the judge took little more upon him, than to regulate the method of proceeding, or to declare the *verdict* of the jury.

The number of jurymen was originally varied in each cause, according as the opulence and power of the parties, or the magnitude of the dispute, rendered it more or less difficult to enforce the decision. So little, after all, was the authority of the court, that, in many cases, the party aggrieved by the verdict assumed the privilege of challenging the jurymen to single combat.* From the progress of regular government, and in consequence of the disposition among mankind to be governed by general rules, a certain number of jurymen became customary in ordinary <331> causes; and at last was

* Spirit of Laws.

2. For Smith's teaching on the same subject, see *LJ,* 283–87, 425–26.

universally established. From accidental circumstances, of little importance, a different number has been established in different countries; as that of twelve in England and fifteen in Scotland.

With respect to the time when trials by jury were first introduced into the court of every feudal barony, we are left in the same obscurity, as concerning their previous introduction among the allodial proprietors, in the courts of the hundred and of the county. But considering the circumstances from which the superior was induced to adopt this mode of procedure, there is ground to believe that it arose upon the establishment of hereditary fiefs, and became gradually more universal, according as the number of the feudal tenants, who had obtained a perpetual right to their possessions, was increased.

In this view, it seems probable that the practice of juries, in the baron-courts, was not very common in England till near the end of the Anglo-Saxon government. In the opinion of some antiquaries,[3] the first vestige of a jury-trial, in the English history, is posterior to the Norman invasion; a mistake <332> which appears to have arisen from the supposition, that before this period hereditary fiefs were unknown in England.

Though the fact seems now to be admitted, that jury-trials were established in the baron courts of every feudal kingdom, yet the origin of that institution has been the subject of much doubt and controversy. Some authors have thought that jurymen were originally *compurgators,*[4] called by a defendant, to swear that they believed him innocent of the facts with which he was charged. In the church courts, a person accused of a crime was understood to be guilty, unless he could clear himself by what was called the *oath of purgation;* and in some cases, unless his own oath was confirmed by that of a number of other persons acquainted with his behaviour. The injustice of this general presumption of *guilt,* the very opposite of what should be entertained in every court of justice, was the less observable, as the consequence of it was merely to draw upon the guilty person a spiritual admonition, or censure, for the good of his soul. From the influence of ecclesiastical procedure, the same rule, however, was after-<333>wards adopted in the temporal courts; where it came to be much more oppressive.

3. Here as elsewhere Millar tends to emphasize the continuity of English institutions, pre- and post-1066.

4. A compurgator was a witness to the character of the accused (or, in religious courts, to his orthodoxy).

But the province of *compurgators,* in those courts, and that of *jurymen,* were so totally different, as to make it scarcely possible to conceive that the latter could arise out of the former. Compurgators were merely witnesses; jurymen were, in reality, judges. The former were called to confirm the oath of the party, by swearing, according to their belief, that he had told the truth: the latter were appointed to try, by witnesses, and by all other means of proof, whether he was innocent or guilty. Compurgators, for this reason, were called by the party himself: the jury, on the contrary, were named by the magistrate.

In consequence of the different departments, occupied by these two descriptions of men, it should seem that, in most of the feudal governments, they existed at one and the same time; and that juries were accustomed to ascertain the truth of facts, by the defendant's oath of purgation, together with that of his compurgators. We can have no doubt that this was formerly the practice; since it is, <334> even at present, retained by the English, in what is called the *wager of law.*[5]

There are two particulars in which we discover a resemblance between the procedure of compurgators and of jurymen; whence, in all probability, the opinion abovementioned has arisen. Both of them were obliged to swear, that they would *tell the truth;* and both were subjected to confinement until they had given their declaration. But these regulations concerning jurymen afford no proof that they were ever considered in the light of compurgators. According to the simple idea of our forefathers, guilt or innocence was regarded as a mere matter of fact; and it was thought, that no man, who knew the real circumstances of a case, could be at a loss to determine whether the culprit ought to be condemned or acquitted. It was, at the same time, suspected, that individuals drawn occasionally from the common mass of the people, to give judgment in a law-suit, might be exposed to improper influence; for which reason precautions were taken to prevent their having the least intercourse with the parties or their connexions. <335>

As to the unanimity required in the English juries, a circumstance in which they agree with the ancient compurgators, it has not been universally established in the feudal governments. President Montesquieu,[6] at the same

5. An offer to make an oath of innocence or nonindebtedness, to be supported by the oaths of compurgators.

6. Montesquieu, Charles Louis de Secondat, baron de (1689–1755): French philosopher and jurist whose most influential works include the *Lettres persanes* (1721) and *De*

time, accounts for it, from a point of honour observed by the *pares curiae* in their judicial decisions, that they should agree with one another in pronouncing a verdict; because they were obliged to fight either of the parties who might give them the lie.

The same form of procedure which took place in the administration of justice, among the vassals of a barony, was gradually extended to the courts held in the trading towns. Notwithstanding the freedom acquired by the mercantile people, they still submitted to the jurisdiction of that person to whom they were indebted for protection, and were reduced by him under a system of government, similar to that which he established among his vassals. In as much as they held lands, for which they paid him a certain rent, they were in reality a species of feudal tenants.

The ancient jurisdiction of the greater thanes, or feudal superiors, came thus to be <336> exercised in two different courts. The one, in which causes were determined with the assistance of a jury, took cognizance of the military and soccage vassals, together with the inhabitants of the trading towns, under the protection of the superior. The other, which proceeded without that formality, was held for the trial of such members of the barony as were still in a state of greater dependence. The former is that which, according to some authors, was properly called the *court-leet;* being the court of the Liti, or free people. The latter, in which the superior retained his ancient authority, received by way of distinction, it is said, the general appellation of the *court-baron.**

---

l'esprit des lois (1748). Montesquieu's comparative study of the "spirit of the laws" was a foundational text for the writers of the Scottish Enlightenment.

* Bacon's discourse on the government of England, collected from the MS. notes of Mr. Selden, chap. 33. Also The Mirror. [[Both are courts with lesser jurisdiction. The court leet was held periodically within a hundred or lordship, before the lord or his steward. It had jurisdiction over petty offenses and civil affairs. The court baron was an assembly of the freehold tenants of a manor under the presidency of the lord or his steward. Such a court had jurisdiction in civil actions arising within the manor. Millar's note again cites Nathaniel Bacon's discussion: see his *Historical and Political Discourse,* 4th ed. (London, 1739), 49.]]

"Liti ac Litones idem ac Lassi et Liberti censentur." Muratori Ant. Med. Aevi. tom. i. dissert. 15. [[*"Liti* or *Litones* are considered to be the same as *Lassi* and freedmen." Lodovico Antonio Muratori, *Antiquitates italicae medii aevi* (Milan, 1738; repr. Bologna, 1965), vol. 1, diss. 15, 866. *Liti* (also called *Litones*) are serfs among the Franks, tied legally to the land but not subject to being bought and sold like slaves. *Lassi* are also serfs among

It is worthy of notice, that the king, considered as a feudal superior, was in the same circumstances with the greater thanes; and that, by the gradual multiplication of his vassals, his authority over them underwent a <337> similar limitation. The same regulations, therefore, concerning the distribution of justice by the intervention of juries, with the same distinction in this respect between his vassals and bondmen, were introduced into the baron courts of the king, as into those of the nobility, or such of his subjects as retained their allodial property.

The improvements which I have mentioned, in the state of the feudal courts, could not fail to produce a more equal and impartial distribution of justice; and this circumstance, together with the general advancement of civil society, contributed to increase the business of those tribunals. From the greater diffusion of property among the people of inferior condition, law-suits became somewhat more numerous; and from their being frequently decided by men of the same rank with the parties, were likely to procure a fuller and more deliberate hearing. As the exercise of jurisdiction was thus rendered more tedious and burdensome, the great lords, as well as the king, who had been accustomed to preside in the trial both of civil and criminal causes, within their several baronies, were less <338> disposed to give the necessary attendance; and by appointing deputy judges, endeavoured to relieve themselves from a great part of the labour. The same circumstances which gave rise to these inferior officers, contributed afterwards to enlarge their powers; and from the negligence of their constituents, who seldom interfered in controuling their decisions, and at last intirely abandoned the employment of judging, they became the ordinary magistrates in the several demesnes or territories committed to their direction.

The transference of jurisdiction, from the primitive judges to their deputies, laid a foundation for one of the most important alterations in the system of judicial policy. The *executive* and *judiciary* powers, with which every feudal baron was originally invested, were in this manner separated from each other; and the exercise of the latter became the sole occupation of particular persons; who, upon that account, were likely to give greater application, as well as to acquire more experience and knowledge in the determination of law-suits. The judges of a barony, though nominated by the

---

the Saxons, while *liberti* are freedmen (manumitted or freed slaves), whom Muratori argues are subject to limitations on their freedom.]]

baron, had necessarily their <339> own views of right and wrong; and having a character to support, might be supposed, in some cases, to conduct themselves without regard to the interest of their constituents. It happened likewise from the natural course of things, that as the most opulent vassals were found the best qualified for maintaining the dignity of a judge, the same persons were frequently enabled to secure the office during life, and even sometimes to render it hereditary. In either case the judge became in a great measure independent of the feudal lord from whom his authority had been derived. It must be acknowledged, however, that long after the period which we are now examining, the king's judges continued under a precarious appointment.

A distinguished political author has pointed out the separation of the judicial power from the king's prerogative, as one of the great sources of the liberty enjoyed by the subjects of Britain.[7] To those who speculate upon the conduct of human affairs, it is amusing to discover, that this important regulation was neither introduced from any foresight of its beneficial consequences, nor extorted from the <340> monarch by any party that were jealous of his power; but was merely the suggestion of indolence; and was adopted by the king, in common with other feudal superiors, to relieve them from a degree of labour and attention which they did not chuse to bestow. It was, in reality, a consequence of the general progress of society, by which employments of every sort, both liberal and mechanical, have been distributed among different individuals, and have become the object of separate professions and trades.

As soon as the business of a judge became the sole employment of particular persons, it was necessary that they should obtain a maintenance in return for their labour. This was acquired without any difficulty, from the very exercise of their profession; as the superior by whom they were appointed, empowered them to exact a fee or perquisite from every party whose cause they had occasion to determine. These exactions, which came to be fixed, in every step of judicial procedure, according to the degree of trouble it was understood to produce, were not only sufficient for maintaining the judge, but afforded also an emolument to <341> the superior, who demanded from his deputy a strict account of the fees he had levied. To prevent any embezzlement in this respect, a clerk was appointed to sit in court along with

7. Presumably a reference to Montesquieu.

the judge, and to keep a record of judicial proceedings. Such was probably the first intention, not only in England, but in all the feudal countries, of recording the decisions of a judge; though the practice was afterwards made subservient to other purposes of the highest utility.

Of the fees, or perquisites, drawn by the judges under the appointment of the crown, the sovereign acquired a considerable proportion, which formed an additional branch of the public revenue.

From this method of maintaining judges, they had obviously an interest to increase their perquisites by encouraging law-suits, and multiplying the forms of judicial procedure. Hence there occurred a new reason for the interposition of juries in the court of a barony; that they might prevent the unreasonable delay of justice. It may, at the same time, perhaps be admitted, that the interested activity and vigilance of the magistrate was, in that <342> early and rude age, more beneficial in preventing disorder and violence, than it was hurtful, either by promoting litigiousness, or by introducing tedious and absurd formalities into the system of judicial discussion. <343>

CHAPTER XIII

Of Ecclesiastical Courts.

While the nobles were gradually extending their power, and reducing that of the sovereign, the ecclesiastical order was advancing, with hasty strides, to the establishment of an authority independent of either. The barbarism and superstition that succeeded the downfal of the Roman empire, and the system of ecclesiastical government erected in the western part of Europe, had a uniform tendency, as has been already observed, to increase the wealth and influence of the church. Were we to consider merely the progress of superstition, we should expect that the usurpations of the clergy would be most rapid in those European countries, which were at the greatest distance from the incitements to cultivation, and in which the ignorance and simplicity of the inhabitants disposed them to follow more implicitly the direction of their spiritual guides. But the fact was other-<344>wise. The kingdoms in the neighbourhood of the pope's residence, and of his temporal dominions, were nearer the center of that artful policy, which by taking advantage of conjunctures, exalted no less the power and privileges of the church than the dignity and authority of her leader. Thus the right of levying the *tythes,* that enormous imposition for the support of the clergy, and which marks the prodigious extent of ecclesiastical influence, was introduced in France, and over a great part of Italy, as early at least as the time of Charlemagne; which corresponds to that of Egbert among the Anglo-Saxons; and the same tax was afterwards extended, by degrees, to the other countries of Europe. It appears to have been finally established in England, during the reigns of Alfred and of Athelstan; patriotic princes, who, doubtless, found themselves under the necessity of giving way to the current of the times, by submitting to such an oppressive exaction.

The increasing opulence of the clergy, as it was an effect of the blind zeal, and the general debasement of the people, so it was accompanied by a corresponding perversion of <345> religious opinions, and by an increase of superstitious observances. The real virtues of society, whose intrinsic value recommends them to our observance, and which frequently appear to cost us nothing, came to be little esteemed, in comparison of penances and mortifications; from which nature is disposed to shrink; and which are submitted to, for no other purpose, but that of appeasing the wrath of an offended deity. These last were accounted highly meritorious in persons of every description; but were thought more especially suitable to the profession and character of churchmen; upon whom it was incumbent to set an example to others. The monks, in particular, who, by their original institution, had no other means of distinction, were incited to procure admiration by the austerity of their lives, and by the severe and painful discipline which they underwent. As they advanced in reputation and popularity, they acquired more numerous and wealthy establishments; their influence in religious matters became proportionably extensive; and they not only rose to great consideration in the government of the church, but frequently, too, <346> interfered in that of the state. From the continent of Europe, the same practices, and ways of thinking, were communicated to Britain; where, about the middle of the tenth century, we find St. Dunstan,[1] at the head of the regular clergy, possessed of such power and credit, as enabled him to controul the administration of government, and even to dispose of the crown.

Among the several branches of mortification imposed by the monastic rules, that of celibacy, or a total abstinence from the intercourse of the sexes, was deemed the most important; whether on account of the difficulties which must be surmounted in counteracting the most violent propensities of nature; or on account of that variation of temperature in the human frame, which, however irresistible those propensities may be at certain seasons, yet, on other occasions, renders the indulgence, or even the expression of them, an object of aversion and disgust. This, therefore, became now the usual topic of declamation to the English monks; who, finding the secular clergy to be their great rivals in the public esteem, and being impatient of that superior authority which they possessed, in-<347>veighed against their married life, as inconsistent with the purity of a christian pastor; representing

1. St. Dunstan (ca. 909–88): counselor to Edmund, Eadred, and Edgar the Peaceable, who appointed him archbishop of Canterbury (959–88).

their wives in the light of concubines or prostitutes, and their children as bastards. Though the doctrine inculcated by these fanatical zealots was not carried into execution until a subsequent period, it appears, even at this time, to have been approved and supported by the general voice of the people.

From the situation of the Christian clergy, and from the influence and authority which they enjoyed, they were led early to assume the cognizance of judicial business, and to form a number of tribunals for the exercise of their jurisdiction. Even before the time of Constantine, when they received no protection or countenance from the civil government,[2] they were accustomed to enquire into the faith and manners of christians, and, after repeated admonitions, to *excommunicate* those individuals who persisted in opinions, or practices, which the church had condemned. This jurisdiction was at first exercised by the clergyman, together with the most respectable among the laity, of each particular church; but when the zeal of the latter, from the greater exten-<348>sion of the gospel, had begun to slacken, they became weary of interfering in such matters; and as they gradually lost their privilege by disuse, the business remained entirely in the hands of the former. When a number of churches were afterwards united in one diocese, the clergy of that latter district, under the authority of the bishop, exercised a jurisdiction of a like nature over the whole of the inhabitants. In the meetings that were called, however, for this purpose, after the introduction of wealth had produced very different degrees of rank among churchmen, the parochial, or inferior clergy, were by degrees overlooked, or endeavoured to excuse themselves from attendance; and the care of maintaining ecclesiastical discipline, throughout the diocese, was appropriated to the bishop and clergy of his cathedral church. This diocesan court, which, from a perfect uniformity of circumstances, was formed upon the same plan in every diocese of the kingdom, was every where liable to the review of a similar court, in a still more extensive district, convened by the archbishop; and from the decrees of this last, at a period when the papal authority had <349> arrived at its height, there lay an appeal to the Roman pontiff.

Together with this judicial authority, which was properly of a spiritual nature, the christian clergy came also to be invested with a temporal juris-

2. Emperor Constantine's Edict of Milan (313) gave civil rights and toleration to Christians throughout the empire.

diction.[3] After the christian religion was taken under the protection of the Roman government, and after the fashion of making donations to the church, for pious uses, had become prevalent, the dignified clergy, both secular and regular, as has been formerly mentioned, were enabled to acquire great landed estates. These, upon the settlement of the Gothic nations in the western part of Europe, were gradually reduced under the same feudal policy that obtained in the landed property of the lay-barons; and a great proportion of the lands of every bishop, or abbot, was commonly distributed among his villeins or vassals; over whom he exercised the jurisdiction and authority of a temporal lord and superior. The estate, or benefice, which from the piety of well-disposed persons, or from whatever cause, had been mortified to the church, and had come into the hands of some particular church-<350>man, was afterwards, in like manner as happened to the other fiefs of the kingdom, increased by the voluntary submission of neighbouring small proprietors; who, in order to purchase his protection, resigned their allodial property, and became his vassals. As the dignified ecclesiastics were not only possessed of a degree of influence corresponding to the extent of their benefices, but were supported by the spiritual arm of the church, they were often better qualified than many of the nobles, to secure their dependants from oppression; and of consequence the opportunities of augmenting their wealth, by an artful interposition in behalf of the inferior people, were proportionably more frequent.

In those circumstances, a bishop came to be invested with a civil as well as an ecclesiastical jurisdiction; the one extending to the people who lived upon his own estate; the other to all the inhabitants of his diocese. By virtue of the former, he punished the crimes, and determined the pecuniary differences of his tenants and vassals. In consequence of the latter, he enquired into the opinions and be-<351>haviour of such as were under his direction in religious matters; and censured them, either for heresy or immorality.

It required no great penetration to discover, that this temporal jurisdiction of the bishop might be extended, under cover of the spiritual jurisdiction. Every crime; every transgression of a rule of justice, whether of a public or private nature, may be considered as a sin, or as an offence in the sight of God; and in that view it might, consistently with the system of church-

3. The clergy, and especially the bishops, acquired civil and political powers, in addition to their spiritual authority.

discipline, become an object of ecclesiastical censure. Whatever, therefore, could be the ground of an action before the civil magistrate, might be brought, at the same time, under the cognizance of the spiritual judge. The professed purpose of the former was, indeed, very different from that of the latter, who pretended to act merely with the view of promoting the good of the party in a future world. But when the church had acquired great authority over the people, it was not difficult for the ecclesiastical judge to frame his sentences in such a manner as to affect also the interest of men in the present life. In making atonement for a sin, the <352> offender might be ordained to indemnify the injured person, or even to submit to a public punishment.

This extension of ecclesiastical jurisdiction was made with greater or less rapidity, in different parts of Christendom, and with regard to persons or causes of different descriptions. It began with regard to the clergy themselves.

To maintain the dignity and credit of the church, it was necessary that she should pay the utmost attention to the behaviour of her own members, and be careful to avoid scandal, by censuring their offences with impartiality and rigour. She found, at the same time, the least difficulty in compelling churchmen to obey her decrees; for, as soon as the Christian Church had come to be established by law, the excommunication of a clergyman must have inferred a forfeiture of his benefice; since a person, who had been cast out of the society of christians, could not consistently be permitted to hold any ecclesiastical dignity or employment. From the severe discipline, which the church exercised over her own members, it became customary to exhibit com-<353>plaints against them before the ecclesiastical, rather than before the civil judge, and to prosecute them in the church court, either for private debts, or for public offences.

After this practice had become general, it was regarded by churchmen as a matter of privilege. The peculiar functions and character of a clergyman required a peculiar delicacy, it was pretended, in judging of his conduct, which could not with propriety fall under the cognizance of the civil magistrate, and of which the clergy themselves were the only competent judges. In the progress of church power, this exemption from the jurisdiction of temporal courts was gradually established through the greater part of Christendom. It was introduced in the diocese of Rome by a law of Alaric,[4] which

4. Alaric II: Christian king of the Visigoths (r. 484–507), who issued in 506 a code of laws known as the *Breviarum Alaricanum.*

provided that the clergy of that district should only be prosecuted, in the first instance, before their own bishop; but from his decision an appeal was admitted to the civil magistrate. In the Eastern empire, the inferior clergy obtained a similar privilege, in civil actions, by a law of the emperor Justinian; though, in criminal causes, not properly ecclesiastical, <354> they might still be prosecuted either in the spiritual or temporal court. The higher orders of churchmen, however, together with nuns, were, by the regulation of this emperor, permitted, in all cases, to decline the jurisdiction of laic judges.*

When the exemption of the clergy from the jurisdiction of the civil magistrate, which, with the exception of a few causes, became universal in the Western part of Europe, had been completely established, the church was, in reality, independent of the state; since, whatever regulations were enacted by the legislature of any country, they might, with safety, be disregarded by churchmen, who could not be punished for the violation of any law, unless they thought proper to enforce it by their own courts.†

The power of the church, in the administration of justice to her own members, was followed by a similar jurisdiction over the laity, in those lawsuits by which her own <355> interest might, in any degree, be affected, or which appeared, however indirectly, to have an influence upon any ecclesiastical matter. But, in England, this encroachment upon the province of the civil magistrate was posterior to the Norman conquest: and therefore does not fall under our present consideration. During the government of the Anglo-Saxon princes, the clergy did not claim a separate cognizance in the temporal causes of the laity; but they laid the foundation of such a claim, in a future period, by assuming a privilege of assisting the ordinary magistrates in the determination of such causes. The extent of a diocese being the same with that of a shire, the bishop sat along with the earl or sheriff, as a judge, in the county courts; and the rural dean, whose ecclesiastical district coincided with the hundred, appears, in like manner, to have been associated with the *centenarius,* in the determination of such differences as arose among the people of that division. It is not improbable that the union of the civil and ecclesiastical powers was carried still lower, and that the parson of a parish was accustomed to judge along with the tythingman, in the <356>

* V. Nov. 83.—123.—79. Also Gianone, Hist. of Naples.

† There were certain great crimes, such as high treason, and sacrilege, to which this exemption did not extend.

court of the decennary: this is what might be expected from the correspondence between the limits of a parish and a tything, and from the analogous practice in the superior courts; though the accounts transmitted by early historians are too vague and general to afford any positive evidence of the fact.

This arrangement of the Saxon tribunals was a natural consequence of the influence possessed by the spiritual and the temporal governors, in the territories over which they presided. It seems, at the same time, to have been esteemed a wise regulation; in as much as by uniting the opinion of those two officers, in the distribution of justice, it was likely that the decisions would be tempered in such a manner, as might correspond to the interest, and the views, of every set of men in the community. The experience and foresight of that age was too limited to discover the inconveniency of confounding the plain and accurate rules of justice, with the intricate subtleties of casuistry, which naturally introduce themselves into the judgments of a spiritual director: not to mention the danger of committing a share of the judicial power, in those <357> times of ignorance, to a set of men, who, by their superior education, were likely to be an over-match for the civil magistrate, and who, by their situation, having acquired a separate interest, were led to seek their own aggrandizement at the expence of the great body of the people. <358>

CHAPTER XIV

Alterations in the State of the Wittenagemote.

The progressive changes in the state of property, and in the constitution and circumstances of the people, of which an account has been given, must have contributed, in many particulars, to alter the constitution and procedure of the Wittenagemote. As this national counsel was composed of all the allodial proprietors of land, whose estates, according to the primitive distribution of property, were generally of small extent, there can be no doubt that, upon the union of the different kingdoms of the Heptarchy, it formed a very numerous, and, in some degree, a tumultuary meeting. The measures which came under its deliberation were proposed, it should seem, by such of its members as were distinguished by their influence or abilities; and its determinations were signified, not by collecting exactly the number of suffrages, but by a promiscuous acclamation, in which the <359> by-standers, it is not unlikely, were accustomed frequently to join with those who had the right of voting. This, in all probability, is what is meant by the early historians, when they speak of the *people* being present in the ancient Wittenagemote, and of their *assisting,* and *giving their consent,* in forming the resolutions of that assembly.

It cannot escape observation, that this early constitution of the national council, while it contained a mixture of democracy and aristocracy, was, in some respects, favourable also to the interests of the crown. In so numerous and disorderly an assembly, there was great room for address, in managing parties, and in conducting the subjects of public deliberation; so that the king, the chief executive officer, had many opportunities of promoting the success of a favourite plan, as well as of parrying, and removing out of sight, those measures which were disagreeable to him.

The frequent resignations of land which, during the progress of the Saxon government, were made by the small allodial proprietors, in order to shelter themselves under the protection of a feudal superior, necessarily withdrew those <360> individuals from the Wittenagemote; and reduced them under the jurisdiction and authority of that particular thane whom they had chosen for their protector. As they became his military servants, they were bound, on every occasion, to espouse his quarrel, and to follow his banner. They were bound, at the same time, to attend his baron-court, and to assist in deciding causes, as well as in making regulations, with regard to his vassals. In consistency with that subordinate station, they could not be permitted to sit in the same council with their liege lord, to deliberate with him upon public affairs; but, on the contrary, were understood to be represented in the Wittenagemote by the person who had undertaken to protect them, and to whom they owed submission and obedience.

Thus, according as the vassals of the nobility, throughout the kingdom, were multiplied, the constituent members of the Wittenagemote became less numerous; and the right of sitting in that assembly was more and more limited, to a few opulent barons, who had acquired the property of extensive districts, <361> and reduced the inhabitants under their dominion.

This change of circumstances was no less unfavourable to the king, on the one hand, than it was, on the other, to the great body of the people. For although the vassals of the crown were, by the gradual resignations of allodial property, increased in the same, or even in a greater proportion than those of particular noblemen, the sovereign was not thence enabled to preserve his former weight in the determination of public measures. The more the national council had been reduced to a small junto of nobles, it was the more difficult to impose upon them, or by any stratagem to divert them from prosecuting their own views of interest or ambition. By the accidental combination of different leaders, they sometimes collected a force which nothing could resist; and were in a condition, not only to defend their own privileges, but even to invade the prerogative. It was often vain for the sovereign, in such a situation, to appeal to the sword from the decisions of the Wittenagemote. Those haughty and ambitious subjects were generally prepared for <362> such a determination; and, as they came into the assembly, supported by their vassals, armed and ready to take the field, they got frequently the start of his majesty. To give way, therefore, to their demands, and to wait for some future opportunity of recovering what had been yielded, was in many cases unavoidable.

In that early period of the Anglo-Saxon state, when the allodial proprietors were numerous, and when their estates were generally small, they were understood to be all of the same rank and condition. Although some persons might be distinguished above others, by their abilities, or military reputation, the superiority derived from thence, being accidental and temporary, was not productive of any permanent authority or privileges. But when, from the causes which have been mentioned, a few great lords had become masters of an extensive landed property, their exaltation in power and dignity was a necessary consequence. Those individuals, on the contrary, who remained in the possession of small estates, though by any fortunate concurrence of events they had been enabled to retain their independence, were degraded in proportion to <363> their poverty. They could maintain but few retainers to support their influence. Hardly in a condition to defend themselves, and afraid of every contest which might endanger their property, and their personal safety, they were deterred from claiming political consideration, and from interfering in public business. It was their interest to live upon good terms with their neighbours, and, by their peaceable and inoffensive behaviour, to shun every ground of jealousy and resentment. If they came into the Wittenagemote, their voice was but little heard; or if they ventured to differ from others, of greater opulence, it was likely to be treated with neglect, or with derision. They had but small encouragement, therefore, to attend the meetings of that assembly; where, at the same time that they incurred an expence not suited to their fortunes, they were subjected to continual mortification, and were incapable of procuring respect. In these circumstances, it is probable that the allodial proprietors, whose estates were inconsiderable, appeared but seldom in the Wittenagemote; and that, unless upon extraordinary occasions, when great unanimity was of the highest importance, <364> their absence was either dispensed with, or in a great measure overlooked.

It was to be expected that this very unequal distribution of property, as it produced a real difference in the consideration and importance of individuals, would come at length to be accompanied with corresponding marks of distinction; and that so much wealth as enabled the possessor to live according to a certain standard of magnificence, might become the foundation of suitable dignity. Thus, in the latter part of the Anglo-Saxon government, such of the nobles as enjoyed an estate, extending to forty hides of land, were distinguished in rank and condition from those who possessed an inferior property. This appears from a passage in the register of Ely, in which mention is made of a person who, "though he was a *nobleman,* could not be numbered among the *proceres,*[1] because his estate did not amount to forty hides of land."* <365>

From this passage, political writers have been led to advance two conjectures, to which it gives no countenance whatever. They consider the rank or privileges, attached to the possession of forty hides of land, as having existed from the original settlement of the Anglo-Saxons; although the writer of that passage speaks only, and that by the by, of what was established in the reign of Edward the confessor. They also maintain, that persons whose estates were below forty hides of land, were entirely excluded from the right of sitting in the Wittenagemote. But the passage referred to makes no mention of the right of sitting in the Wittenagemote, nor gives the least hint concerning it; but only points out the extent of property which entitled a person to be ranked among the *proceres.* There is no reason to believe, either from this, or from any other ancient author, that, even in the latter part of the Anglo-Saxon government, the proprietors of such great estates were the only members of the national assembly; though it is, no doubt, highly probable, that they would be more apt, than persons of a lower station, to give a punctual attendance upon its meetings. <366>

The superior dignity, however, enjoyed, in the reign of Edward the confessor, by such of the nobility as were possessed of a certain extent of property, is the more worthy of attention, as it became still more remarkable after the Norman conquest, and laid the foundation of that noted distinction between the *greater* and *smaller* barons, which was productive of important changes in the constitution.

As the Wittenagemote was diminished by the reduction of many allodial

* Habuit enim (speaking of the abbot of Ely) fratrem *Gudmundum* vocabulo, cui filiam praepotentis viri in matrimonium conjungi paraverat. Sed quoniam ille quadraginta *hidarum* terrae dominium minime obtineret, licet *nobilis* esset, inter *proceres* tunc numerari non potuit; eum puella repudiavit. Historia Eliensis, lib. ii. cap. 40. [["For he had a brother by the name of Gudmundus to whom he had made preparations to marry the daughter of a very powerful man. But since Gudmundus did not possess an estate of forty hides, even though he was a noble he could not be counted among the greater thanes, and so the girl rejected him." For a modern edition of the History of Ely and the above passage, see *Liber Eliensis,* ed. E. O. Blake (London: Royal Historical Society, 1962), 167.]]

1. Chief men, nobles, magnates.

proprietors into a state of vassalage; it may be questioned whether it did not, on the other hand, receive a gradual supply of new members, by the advancement of the *churles,* who, in consequence of the law of king Athelstane, were, upon the acquisition of five hides of land, admitted to the privileges of a thane. Concerning this point the following observations will occur. 1st. That though many of the peasants appear, in the latter periods of the Anglo-Saxon government, to have become free, and even opulent, it is probable that they held their possessions upon the footing of vassalage, rather than of allodial property; in consequence of which, they could only be ranked, from the <367> law above-mentioned, among the *lesser thanes,* who had no right of sitting in the Wittenagemote: 2dly, Supposing that any of these churles acquired allodial estates, and that they were strictly entitled to a voice in the Wittenagemote; yet, about the time when this privilege was bestowed, a much greater property than five hides of land, the quantity specified in the law of king Athelstane, was required for giving the proprietor any weight or consideration in that assembly, or for making his attendance upon it a desirable object. This was a privilege, therefore, which they would be more apt to decline from its inconveniencies, than to exercise, or to boast of, on account of its advantages.

It may also be a question, whether those merchants who performed three voyages into a foreign country, and who, by another law of the same prince, are said to have obtained the rights of a *thane,* were admitted into the Wittenagemote. But, as these mercantile adventurers were not required to possess any estate, real or personal, it is not reasonable to suppose that they could be allowed to participate, with the ancient nobility, in the delibe-<368>rations of the supreme national council. It has already been observed, that by the privileges of a thane, bestowed as an encouragement to a certain degree of enterprize in trade, were probably understood those of a *lesser thane,* or vassal; who, though not a member of the Wittenagemote, was of a condition greatly superior to that of the original peasants and mechanics.

As it does not appear that individuals among the merchants had, independent of any landed estate, the privilege of sitting in the Wittenagemote; so there is no evidence that, collectively, the trading interest were, even in the latter part of the Anglo-Saxon history, entitled to send representatives to that assembly. Of this we may be satisfied from the particulars, relative to the constitution of the national council, which have been formerly mentioned. The facts which were then adduced, in order to shew that in the

Saxon Wittenagemote there were no representatives, either from towns, or from the small proprietors of land, appear conclusive with regard to the whole period of the English government before the Norman conquest. If the <369> original constitution of that assembly admitted of no representatives from either of those two classes of men, it must be supposed, that the subsequent introduction of them, more especially if it had happened near the end of the Saxon period, when historical events are better ascertained, would have excited the attention of some historian or other, and have been thought worthy of transmission to future ages. But upon this point, of so much importance in the political system, and so unlikely to pass without notice, the later as well as the early Saxon historians are entirely silent.

The advancement of arts and manufactures, towards the end of the Saxon line, was, indeed, so considerable, as to have enlarged particular towns, and to have exempted the inhabitants from those precarious duties and services to which they had anciently been subjected. They were permitted to form *societies,* or *gilds,* for the benefit of their trade; which appear to have at length suggested the practice of incorporating the whole of a town with particular privileges and regulations.* By a series of progressive improvements, the trading people were thus gradually prepared <370> and qualified for that political consideration which they afterwards acquired by the establishment of representatives in the national council. But the acquisition of this important privilege was the work of a later period, when they rose to a higher pitch of opulence and independence.

The original meetings of the Wittenagemote in England, as well as those of the national council, in most of the kingdoms upon the neighbouring continent, appear, as was formerly observed, to have been held regularly at two seasons of the year; at the end of spring, for deliberating upon the military operations of the summer, and at the beginning of autumn, for dividing the fruit of those depredations. The same times of meeting were, for similar reasons, observed, in the courts belonging to the several shires and baronies of the kingdom. But as, in England, from her insular situation, military enterprizes against a foreign enemy were less regular than upon the continent of Europe, those meetings fell soon into disuse; and as, on certain great festivals, the king was accustomed to appear, with great pomp and solemnity, among his nobles; it was found convenient, on those oc-<371>casions, to call

* Madox firma burgi.

the Wittenagemote. Hence the meetings of that council came to be held uniformly at three different seasons; at Christmas, at Easter, and at Whitsuntide.[2]

The increase of the national business, particularly with respect to the distribution of justice, a consequence of the gradual progress of authority in the public, made it necessary that the Wittenagemote should be held more frequently than in former times; and therefore, in any extraordinary exigence, which arose between the different festivals above mentioned, a particular meeting of that council was called by the king. Thus there came to be two sorts of Wittenagemote; the one held by custom; and at three stated periods; the other called occasionally, by a special summons from the king.[*] Both were composed of the same persons, if they chose to attend; but commonly a much less regular attendance was given in the latter than in the former. At the occasional meetings of the great council, such of the nobility as lived at a distance were seldom at the trouble of appearing; and the business, of course, devolved upon those mem-<372>bers who happened to be in the king's retinue, and who might be said to compose his privy council.

For this reason, the occasional meetings of the Wittenagemote usually confined themselves to matters of less importance than were discussed in the old customary meetings. The chief employment of the former was the hearing of appeals from inferior courts: but legislation, and other weighty transactions, were generally reserved to the latter.

If, however, it was found necessary, in the interval between the three great festivals, to deliberate upon public business of importance, the king issued an extraordinary summons to his nobles; in which he expressly required their attendance, and specified the cause of their meeting.[†]

It may here be proper to remark, that the smaller occasional meetings of the Wittenagemote appear to have suggested the idea of the *aula regis;*[3] a separate court, which, after the Norman conquest, was formed out of parliament for the sole purpose of deciding law-suits.

As the occurrences which demanded the immediate interposition of the Wittenagemote <373> could not be foreseen, the king was led to determine

* The former were called *courts de more,* being founded upon immemorial custom.

† Gurdon's History of the high court of Parliament.

2. The season of Whit Sunday (fifty days after Easter) and the days immediately after, a celebration of the descent of the Holy Ghost.

3. Court of the royal household. The *aula regis* or *curia regis* was the grand justiciary established by William at the conquest.

the particular cases in which the deliberation of that assembly was requisite; and in the exercise of this prerogative, he was originally under no restraint. The powers exercised by the crown seem, at first, to have been all discretionary; and to have remained without limitation, until experience had shewn the danger of their being abused.

We shall afterwards have occasion to observe, that, under the princes of the Norman and Plantagenet race, the ancient and regular meetings of the national council were more and more disregarded, and at length entirely disused; in consequence of which the whole parliamentary business came to be transacted in extraordinary meetings, which were called at the pleasure of the sovereign. The attempts to limit this important branch of the royal prerogative will be the subject of future discussion.

Conclusion of the Saxon Period.

Such appear to be the outlines of the English government under the administration of the Anglo-Saxon princes. To the subjects of Britain, who consider the nature of their <374> present constitution, and compare it with that of most of the nations upon the neighbouring continent, it seems natural to indulge a prepossession, that circumstances peculiarly fortunate must have concurred in laying the foundation of so excellent a fabric. It seems natural to imagine, that the government of the Anglo-Saxons must have contained a proportion of liberty, as much greater than that of the neighbouring nations, as our constitution is at present more free than the other European governments.

When we examine, at the same time, the state of our country, in that remote age; the uniform jurisdiction and authority possessed by every allodial proprietor; the division of the country into various districts, subordinate one to another; the perfect correspondence between the civil and ecclesiastical divisions; the similarity in the powers exercised by the meetings of the tything, the hundred, and the shire, in their respective territories, and those of the Wittenagemote over the whole kingdom; the analogy between the office of the tythingman, the hundreder, and the earl, in their inferior departments, and that of the sovereign in his more exalted station; when, <375> I say, we examine these, and other particulars relating to the Anglo-Saxon government, in which we may discover so much order and regularity, such a variety of regulations, nicely adjusted to one another, and calculated for the most beneficial purposes; it is natural to suppose, that the whole has originated in much contrivance and foresight; and is the result of deep laid schemes of policy.

In both of these conclusions, however, we should undoubtedly be mistaken. When we look round and examine the state of the other European kingdoms about the same period; and when we observe, in each of them, the close and minute resemblance of its political system to that of England, how little soever the apparent intercourse of the inhabitants; we feel ourselves under the necessity of abandoning our former supposition, and of acknowledging that the regulations established in all of these countries proceeded from no artificial or complicated plans of legislation; but were such as occurred successively to the people, for the supply of their immediate wants, and the removal of incidental inconveniencies; in a word, every where, a kind of natural growth, produced by <376> the peculiar situation and circumstances of the society.

Neither was the Anglo-Saxon government calculated, in any peculiar manner, to secure the liberty and the natural rights of mankind. The sovereign, indeed, in the long period during which this government subsisted, and through all the successive alterations which it underwent, was at no time invested with absolute power. The supreme authority in the state was originally possessed by a numerous body of landed proprietors; but the rest of the community were either slaves, or tenants at the will of their master. The number of those who enjoyed a share in the government was afterwards greatly diminished: at the same time that, upon this advancement of the aristocracy, the lower part of the inhabitants became somewhat more free and independent. The encrease of political power in men of a superior class was thus compensated by some little extension of privileges in the great body of the people.

END OF VOL. I.

AN

HISTORICAL VIEW

OF THE

ENGLISH GOVERNMENT

FROM THE

SETTLEMENT OF THE SAXONS IN BRITAIN

TO

THE REVOLUTION IN 1688.

To which are subjoined,

SOME DISSERTATIONS CONNECTED WITH THE HISTORY OF THE GOVERNMENT,

From the Revolution to the Present Time.

BY JOHN MILLAR ESQ.

Professor of Law in the University of Glasgow

IN FOUR VOLUMES

VOL. II.

London:

PRINTED FOR J. MAWMAN, NO 22 IN THE POULTRY.

1803.

By T. Gillet, Salisbury-Square

CONTENTS[1]

Book II.

OF THE ENGLISH GOVERNMENT FROM THE REIGN OF WILLIAM THE CONQUEROR, TO THE ACCESSION OF THE HOUSE OF STEWART.

1. The page numbers in the Contents are those of the 1803 edition.

AN HISTORICAL VIEW OF THE ENGLISH GOVERNMENT.

Book II

OF THE ENGLISH GOVERNMENT FROM THE REIGN OF WILLIAM THE CONQUEROR, TO THE ACCESSION OF THE HOUSE OF STEWART.

The political history of this extensive period may be subdivided into three parts;[1] the first extending from the Norman conquest to the end of the reign of Henry the third; the second, from the beginning of the reign of Edward the first, to the accession of Henry the seventh; and the third, comprehending the reigns of the Tudor family. In each of these parts we shall meet with progressive changes in the English constitution, which appear to demand a separate examina-<2>tion, and which, being analogous to such as were introduced, about the same time, in the other European governments, may be regarded as the natural growth and development of the original system, produced by the peculiar circumstances of modern Europe. <3>

1. Millar's subdivision of this period comprises three eras: (1) 1066–1272; (2) 1272–1485; (3) 1485–1603.

ꕥ CHAPTER I ꕥ

The Norman Conquest.—Progress of the feudal System.—View of the several Reigns before that of Edward I.—The great Charter, and Charter of the Forest.

William the conqueror ascended the throne of England, partly by force of arms, and partly by the voluntary submission of the people. The great landed estates, acquired by a few individuals, towards the end of the Saxon government, had exalted particular nobles to such power and splendor, as rendered them, in some degree, rivals to the sovereign, and even encouraged them, upon any favourable emergency, to aspire to the crown. Among these, under the feeble reign of Edward the confessor, we may distinguish Godwin earl of Wessex, who had become formidable to the monarch; and, after the death of that earl, his son Harold, who, at the same <4> time that his possessions were not less extensive than those of his father, being endowed with superior abilities, and much more amiable dispositions, appears to have attained a degree of influence and authority which no English subject had ever enjoyed. He became, of course, an object of jealousy to Edward; who, in the decline of life, and having no children, was anxious to exclude this nobleman from the throne, by securing the succession to one of his own kindred. Edward himself was properly an usurper, having seized the crown to the prejudice of his elder brother's son, the undoubted lineal heir.[1] This prince being now dead, the right of inheritance devolved upon his son, Edgar Atheling, whose

1. Edward the Exile: son of Edmund II (Ironside), who was sent from the country at the accession of Canute. Edward the Exile's son, Edgar the Atheling, was in fact proclaimed king of the English in the brief period in 1066 between the death of Harold II and the accession of William the Conqueror.

tender age, and slender abilities, appeared to disqualify him, in such a critical conjuncture, for wielding the sceptre over a fierce and turbulent people. In those disorderly times, the line of hereditary succession, though not intirely disregarded, was frequently broken from particular accidents: persons incapable of defending the sovereignty, were commonly deemed unworthy to obtain it; and the recommendation, or *will,* of the reigning prince was always <5> held to be a strong circumstance in favour of any future competitor for the succession.

Edward the confessor had resided four and twenty years in the court of Richard the second,[2] duke of Normandy, his maternal uncle; by whom, in the short reign of his brother Edmund Ironside, and during the usurpation of the Danish monarchs,[3] he was generously educated and protected. By remaining, for so long a period, in a foreign country, where he was caressed, and treated with every mark of distinction, the English prince was led to form an attachment to the people, whose progress in arts, government, and manners, surpassed that of his own countrymen; and he ever retained a grateful remembrance of the hospitality and kindness which he had experienced in the family of his kinsman. When he mounted the throne of England, a communication was opened between the two countries; and an intimate connexion subsisted between the respective sovereigns. Multitudes of Normans resorted to the English court, in expectation of preferment; many individuals of that country obtained landed possessions in England; and many were promoted to offices of <6> great dignity, both in church and state. These foreigners, who stood so high in the favour of the sovereign, were imitated by the English in their dress, their amusements, their manners, and customs. They imported also the French language; which had for some time been adopted by the Normans; and which, being regarded as a more improved and elegant dialect than the Saxon, became fashionable in England, and was even employed, it is said, in the writings and pleadings of lawyers.

The dutchy of Normandy having descended to William,[4] the natural son of Robert, and nephew of Richard II. the affections, as well as the policy of Edward, made him cast his eyes upon that prince, his nearest relation by the mother, and the most able and accomplished warrior of his time, as the most

2. Richard II, Duke of Normandy (r. 996–1026).

3. The Danish occupation of the English crown, 1016–42.

4. William the Conqueror. See p. 10, note 4.

proper person to succeed him in the throne. His illegitimate birth, was, in that age, an objection of little moment; since it had not prevented him from inheriting the dukedom of Normandy; and since a similar stain is observable in the line of our Saxon kings. Some historians have asserted, that the English monarch actually made a *will,* by which he be-<7>queathed his crown to the duke of Normandy; and that this deed was even ratified by the states of the kingdom. But whether such a transaction was really executed, appears extremely doubtful. It is certain, however, that Edward had publickly declared his intentions to this purpose; that William, in consequence of such declaration, had openly avowed his pretensions to the crown of England; and that Harold himself, being upon a visit to the Norman court, and having received a promise of the duke's daughter in marriage, had taken a solemn oath to support his title. An artifice which was put in practice, with relation to that oath, in a contract between two of the most conspicuous personages of the age, is worthy of attention, as it exhibits a ludicrous picture of the superstition to which the minds of men were then universally subjected. William secretly conveyed under the altar upon which Harold was to swear, the bones of some of the most revered martyrs; and after the oath was taken, shewed the relics to the affrighted nobleman; who discovered, with equal concern and indignation, that he was ensnared into a much stronger obligation than he had <8> intended; and that his future breach of promise would be productive of more fatal consequences than he had been aware of.

By what species of casuistry Harold afterwards endeavoured to satisfy his conscience with respect to the violation of this oath, which had, indeed, been in some degree extorted from him, we have no information; but, in fact, he neglected no opportunity of increasing his popularity, and of strengthening his connexions among the nobility; so that, upon the death of Edward, he found himself, before his rival could take any measures for preventing him, in a condition to obtain possession of the throne, and to bear down every appearance of opposition. The duke of Normandy was not of a temper to brook this disappointment, and tamely to relinquish his pretensions. He collected a great army, composed not only of such forces as could be levied in his own dominions, but of all those desperate adventurers whom the prospect of plunder, and of military reputation, allured to the standard of so celebrated a leader. The battle of Hastings,[5] in which Harold and his prin-

5. The Battle of Hastings took place in 1066.

cipal adherents were slain, put an end to the strug-<9>gle, and left the victorious general without a competitor. This decisive action was followed by a speedy submission to his authority; and the chief of the nobility and clergy, together with Edgar Atheling himself, having made an offer of the vacant throne, he was crowned at Westminster Abbey, with the usual solemnities. It is worthy of notice, that, on this occasion, he took the same oath which had formerly been administered to the Saxon kings, "that he would maintain the ancient fundamental laws of the kingdom"; to which there was added a particular clause, suggested by the peculiarity of the present circumstances, "that he would distribute justice impartially between his English and his Norman subjects."[6]

The crown of England having thus been transmitted to a foreign family, William, according to the barbarous Latin of those times, received the title of *conquaestor;* which has, without much propriety, been translated the *conqueror.* It imported merely an *acquirer,* in contradistinction to a person who inherits by lineal descent, corresponding to the sense in <10> which, by the present law language of Scotland, *conquest* is opposed to *heritage.**

Whether the accession of this monarch is to be considered in the light of a real conquest by force of arms, unsupported by any other circumstance, would be a frivolous question, were it not for the serious and important consequences which have, by some authors, been connected with that supposition. It is maintained, that if William intirely conquered the kingdom, he could be under no restraint in modelling the government; that he, ac-

* "*Conquestus* id quod à parentibus non acceptum, sed labore pretio vel parsimoniâ comparatum possidemus—Hinc Guliel I. *conquestor* dicitur que Angliam conquisivit, i.e. acquisivit, PURCHASED; non quod subegit." [["An acquisition: that which we possess not as an inheritance from our parents, but which we have obtained by working, purchasing or saving.—Hence the name of Conquestor (Acquirer) is given to William I, who acquired England, i.e., purchased ("acquisivit") it, not because he subjugated it." The quotation is from Sir Henry Spelman's *Glossarium Archaiologicum* (London, 1687), 145. The reference is to Sir John Skene, *De Verborum Significatione* (Edinburgh, 1681): under the entry "Conquestus," Skene makes a distinction between property that is a "conquest" under Scottish Law and a "heretage."]] Spelm. Glossar. v. Conquestus. See also Skene, de verbor. sign.

6. James Tyrrell reproduces the Saxon royal oath (in Latin) in the general introduction to his *General History of England, Both Ecclesiastical and Civil* (London, 1704), 1:lviii. Millar's translated quote is likely from this source.

cordingly, overturned altogether the ancient constitution;[7] and in place of that moderate system which had grown up under the Saxon princes, introduced an absolute monarchy. The supposition itself is no less remote from truth, than the conclusion drawn from it is erroneous. It was the party of Harold only that was vanquished by the arms of the Normans; and had <11> it not been for the usurpation of that nobleman, William would probably have met with no opposition to his claim. After the defeat of Harold, there was, beside the duke of Normandy, no other candidate able to hold the reins of government. Even supposing William to have completely conquered the whole of the English, his conquest, surely, was not extended over those Norman barons, the associates and companions of his enterprize, to whom he was chiefly indebted for his success. When those powerful chieftains obtained possessions, in England, proportioned to their several merits, and became grandees of the kingdom, it is not likely that they would willingly relinquish the independence which they had enjoyed in their own country, or that they would regard the assistance they had given to their duke, in raising him to be a great king, as a good reason for enslaving them.* <12>

But, however this be, nothing is more clear in point of fact, than that William was far from wishing to hold himself up to the people of England in the light of a conqueror. Like every wise prince, who has employed ir-

* The dutchy of Normandy was at that period governed like most of the other feudal countries of Europe; and the duke, at the same time that he was a feudatory of the king of France, enjoyed a very moderate authority over his Norman vassals. In particular, he could neither make laws, nor impose taxes, without the consent of the barons, or principal land-holders of the dutchy. This appears from the Latin customs of Normandy, printed at the end of the old French edition of the *Coustumier de Normandy;* in the preface to which it is said; "Quoniam leges et instituta quae Normanorum principes, non sine magna provisionis industria praelatorum, comitum, et baronum, nec non et caeterorum virorum prudentum consilio, et assensu, ad salutem humani foederis statuerunt." [["Since the laws and statutes which the dukes of Normandy, along with the great and diligent foresight of the prelates, the counts, and the barons, as well as the advice and consent of other prudent men, decreed for the preservation of human society. . . ." See James Tyrrell's *Bibliotheca Politica* (London, 1694), 727.]] [Tyrrel's Bibliotheca Politica, dial. 10. Also many instances of Norman great councils, collected by Brady.]

7. The reference is to the idea of the "Norman yoke"—the notion that the Norman conquest had destroyed an earlier constitution more favorable to liberty. In the pages that follow, Millar is concerned to establish the continuities bridging the two periods, in part by arguing that the major social changes "had been gradually ripened and prepared" under the later Anglo-Saxon kings.

regular and violent measures for obtaining the sovereignty, he endeavoured as much as possible to cover every appearance of usurpation; and was willing to exercise his power in the manner most likely to secure the continuance of it. He was active in restraining his Norman followers from committing depredations on the English, and in preventing disputes between the individuals of those different nations. The partisans of Harold, who had distinguished <13> themselves by supporting his cause in the field, were, doubtless, deprived of their possessions; but the rest of the English, who submitted to the authority of the monarch, were treated with marks of his favour and confidence. Many of those who had been in arms against him, were overlooked or forgiven; and the people in general received assurances of his protection. London, and the other cities of the kingdom, were confirmed in their immunities and privileges. Even Edgar Atheling himself, the lineal heir of the crown, was permitted to live in safety, and to retain the estate and honours which had formerly been conferred upon him. Justice was every where administered, not only with great impartiality, but by tempering clemency with severity; and, the public tranquillity being thus, in a short time, perfectly restored, the government under the new sovereign proceeded, without interruption, in its former channel.* <14>

* Several historians, who write near that period, consider William's advancement to the English throne as the effect of a formal election. William of Poictou, this king's chaplain, gives the following account of it: "Die ordinationi decreto locutus ad Anglos concedenti sermone Eboraci Archiepiscopus, sapiens, bonus, eloquens, an consentirent eum sibi dominum coronari inquisivit; protestati sunt hilarum consensum universi minime haesitantes, ac si coelitus unâ mente datâ, unâque voce, Anglorum, quam facillime Normanni consonuerunt sermocinato apud eos, ac sententiam praecunctatorium Constantini Praesule, sic, *electum* consecravit Archiepiscopus," &c. [["On the day fixed for the coronation, the archbishop of York . . . wise, good and eloquent, addressed the English, and asked them in the appropriate words whether they would consent to him being crowned as their lord. They all shouted their joyful assent, with no hesitation, as if heaven had granted them one mind and one voice. The Normans added their voice most readily to the wish of the English, after the bishop of Coutances had addressed them and asked their wishes. . . . When William had been elected in this way the archbishop . . . consecrated him." *The Gesta Guillelmi of William of Poiters,* ed. and trans. R. H. C. Davis and Marjorie Chibnall (Oxford: Clarendon Press, 1998), 150–51.]]

Odericus Vitalis, who lived in the reign of William Rufus, speaks of the same event as follows: "Dum Aldredus Praesul alloqueretur Anglos, et Godofredus Constantiniensis Normannos, an concederent Gulielmum regnare super se, et universi consensum hilarem protestarentur unâ voce non unius linguae locutione." [[". . . when Archbishop Ealdred asked the English, and Geoffrey Bishop of Coutances asked the Normans, if they would

But though the constitution was far from being converted into an absolute monarchy, by virtue of an immediate conquest, a considerable change was, about this time, introduced, both in the state of landed property, and in the authority of the sovereign. For this change, the country, during the latter part of the Anglo-Saxon government, had been gradually ripened and prepared. When by the frequent conversion of allodial into feudal estates, the small proprietors of land were at length reduced <15> into the condition of military servants, those great lords, who remained at the head of extensive districts, were brought into a more direct opposition and rivalship to one another. Their estates, by gradual enlargement, were become contiguous; and those intermediate possessors, whom they had formerly been employed in subduing, were now distributed upon either side, and ready to assist their respective superiors in their mutual depredations. Those hereditary fiefs, which had been scattered over a multitude of individuals, were now concentered in a few great leaders; who felt a stronger incitement to the exercise of reciprocal hostilities, as well as the capacity of prosecuting them with greater vigour and perseverance, according as their power, together with their pride and their ambition, had been augmented. The public magistrate was often unwilling to interfere in reconciling their differences, and was even pleased to see their force wasted and broken by their mutual ravages. The greater nobles were thus permitted to injure and oppress one another at their own discretion; and, being exposed to such difficulties and distresses as had formerly been sustained by <16> the proprietors of small estates, were obliged to extricate themselves by similar expedients. They endeavoured to provide against the dangers which threatened them, from the invasion of some of their neighbours, by forming an alliance with others; or, if this resource had proved ineffectual, by courting the favour and soliciting the protection of the king. Nothing less than the power of the crown was capable,

---

accept William as their king, all of them gladly shouted out with one voice if not in one language that they would." *The Ecclesiastical History of Orderic Vitalis,* ed. and trans. Marjorie Chibnall (Oxford: Clarendon Press, 1969), 2:184.]]

Gul. Gemeticensis, in his history of the dukes of Normandy, agrees with the two authors above quoted, "Ab omnibus," says he, "tum Normannorum, quam Anglorum roceribus [[*sic:* tam Normannorum, quam Anglorum proceribus]] rex *est electus,*" &c. Tyrrel's Bibliotheca Polit. dial. 10. [["was elected king by all magnates, both of the Normans and the English." *The Gesta Normannorum Ducum of William of Jumièges, Orderic Vitalis, and Robert of Torigni,* ed. and trans. Elisabeth M. C. van Houts (Oxford: Clarendon Press, 1995), 2:170.]]

in many cases, of delivering them from their embarrassment; and, in order to procure that relief which their situation required, it was necessary that they should promise, upon their part, a return of good offices. If they were anxious to enjoy that security which he bestowed upon his immediate retainers, they could not decently withhold from him the same homage and fealty, or refuse to perform the same services. They found, in a word, that it was expedient for them to resign their allodial property, and to hold their estates by a feudal tenure as vassals of the crown.

The political theatre, at that time, exhibited a frequent repetition of the same parts by different actors. Those opulent individuals, who had formerly been in a condition to oppress <17> their neighbours, and force them into a state of dependence upon the sovereign, were, by a different combination of rival powers, or by an alteration of circumstances, rendered, on other occasions, incapable of maintaining their own independence; and being, in their turn, induced to supplicate the interposition of the crown in their favour, were obliged to purchase it by the same terms of submission. As these resignations of land were in the highest degree advantageous to the sovereign, we can have no doubt that the influence of the court would be uniformly exerted, and that every possible artifice would be employed, in promoting them. The great nobles were thus rendered subordinate to the crown in the same manner as the inferior free people had become subordinate to the nobility;[8] the whole kingdom was united in one extensive barony, of which the king became the superior, and in some measure the ultimate proprietor; and the feudal system, as it is called, of which the foundations had been laid several centuries before, was at length entirely completed.

From the state of England, about the accession of the Norman race of kings, a change <18> of this nature was likely to have happened; though it was, undoubtedly, promoted and accelerated by the peculiar circumstances of William the conqueror. From the great abilities of that prince, as well as from the manner in which he ascended the throne, he became possessed of uncommon personal influence; and, by his uniting the dutchy of Normandy to the crown of England, the royal demesnes, and the public revenue, were greatly extended. But above all, the numerous forfeitures, incurred by the

8. Millar's view is that the extension of feudalism, more than the fact of military conquest, created the conditions that shifted power toward the crown. Similar changes occurred across much of western Europe, without the impulse of conquest.

partisans of Harold, and by such as were incited to acts of rebellion, during the course of William's reign, enabled the sovereign to acquire a prodigious landed territory in England; part of which he retained in the possession of the crown; and the rest he bestowed upon his favourites, under condition of their performing the feudal services.

It must not be overlooked, that this feudal policy was extended to the greater ecclesiastical benefices, as well as to the estates of the laity. The bishops and abbots became immediate vassals of the crown; and, though not bound to the king for personal service in war, were obliged to supply him with a number of mili-<19>tary tenants proportioned to the extent of their possessions. Notwithstanding the great influence of the clergy, supported by the Roman pontiff, who strongly remonstrated against this innovation, yet, as ecclesiastical benefices were enjoyed only for life, those churchmen who expected preferment from the crown were, without much difficulty, prevailed upon to accept of a benefice, under such general conditions as now began to be imposed upon all the great proprietors of land.

The change which was thus effected in the state of the great nobles, was far from being peculiar to England. It was extended, nearly about the same time, over all the kingdoms in the western part of Europe; and in most of them, was the result of no conquest, or violent effort of the sovereign, but appears to have proceeded from the natural course of the feudal governments.

In France the great barons appear to have become the immediate vassals of the crown, in the time of Hugh Capet; whose reign began about eighty years before the Norman conquest; and who obtained the regal dignity, without any appearance of disorder or violence, <20> by the free election of the national assembly. The feudal institutions having been completed in that kingdom, of which Normandy constituted one of the principal baronies; it is likely that William, when he came into England with a train of Norman vassals, found it the more easy to establish that system, because his followers had already been acquainted with it in their own country.

In the German empire many powerful barons became vassals of the emperor, as early as the reign of Otho the Great; who had likewise been advanced to the sovereignty, not by force of arms, but by the voice of the diet. From particular causes, however, the feudal subordination of the nobility was not rendered so universal in Germany as in other European countries.* <21>

* Concerning the time when the feudal system was introduced into England, authors

By this alteration in the state of landed property, the power of the crown was undoubtedly increased; but it was not increased in so great <22> a proportion as at the first view may perhaps be imagined. When the allodial estates of the great lords were converted into fiefs, they were invariably secured to the vassal and his heirs. The power and influence of those opulent pro-

---

of great note have entertained very different opinions. [[See the discussions in John Selden, *Titles of Honour* (London, 1614), 300–302; Matthew Hale, *The History of the Common Law of England* (London, 1713), 107, 223–25; William Dugdale, *The Baronage of England* (London, 1675), vol. 1 preface, unpaginated; and Henri de Bracton, *On the Laws and Customs of England,* vol. 2, ed. G. E. Woodbine and trans. S. E. Thorne (Cambridge, Mass.: Harvard University Press, 1968), 37–38. On Bracton, see p. 354, note 15.]] Lord Coke, the judges of Ireland who gave their decision upon the case of defective titles, Mr. Selden, the author of the *Mirroir des Justices,* and many others, suppose that it was established under the Anglo-Saxon government. Lord Hale, Mr. Somner, Camden, Dugdale, Matthew Paris, Bracton, maintain that it was unknown before the Norman conquest.—Sir Henry Spelman, in his Glossary, seems to hold this last opinion; but in his posthumous treatise he explains his meaning to be, only that fiefs did not become *hereditary,* so as to yield feudal incidents, before the reign of William the conqueror. The opinion which I have delivered above seems to account for these opposite conjectures. It seems impossible to deny that there were fiefs among the Anglo-Saxons: on the other hand, it appears equally clear that there were many allodial estates principally in the hands of the great nobility. Nothing therefore remained for William, towards completing the feudal system, but the reduction of these last into a state of vassalage.

We find accordingly, that, in the twentieth year of his reign, this monarch, having finished a survey of all the lands in the kingdom (except those of Northumberland, Cumberland, and Westmoreland) summoned all the great men and land holders, to do homage and swear fealty to him. The expression used in the Saxon Chronicle, in mentioning this fact, is, *Proceres, et omnes praedia tenentes, se illi subdedere, ejusque facti sunt vassalli.* [["The nobles and all those who were in possession of estates submitted themselves to him and became his vassals." (Anglo-Saxon Chronicle, year 1086). A recent translation of the Anglo-Saxon text may be found in *The Anglo-Saxon Chronicle,* trans. Michael Swanton (New York: Routledge, 1998), 217.]] Having become vassals of the crown, at that time, it may be inferred they were not in that condition formerly. It is further probable, that the twenty years which had elapsed, since the accession of William, were occupied in bringing about this great revolution; for if the great men had been crown vassals during the Saxon government, it was the interest of this prince not to delay their renewal of the feudal engagement by their swearing fealty to him as soon as he came to the throne.

From Doomsday-book, which is now happily laid open to the inspection of all the world [[Millar may be referring to *Domesday Book,* 2 vols. (London, 1783), or Robert Kelham, ed., *The Domesday Book Illustrated: Containing an Account of That Antient Record* (London, 1788).]], this fact is made still more certain, as innumerable instances occur of landholders, who are said to have held their lands *allodially,* in the reign of Edward, the preceding king.

prietors were therefore but little impaired by this change of their circumstances. By their tenures they were subject to the jurisdiction of the king's courts, as well as bound to serve him in war; and they were liable for various *incidents,* by which his revenue was considerably augmented; but they were not in other respects dependent upon his will; and, while they fulfilled the duties which their condition required, they could not, with any colour of justice, be deprived of their possessions. Neither was the sovereign capable, at all times, of enforcing the performance of the feudal obli-<23>gations; but from the power of his great vassals, or the exigence of his own situation, he found it necessary, in many cases, to connive at their omissions, and even to overlook their offences.

The reign of William the First was filled with disquietude and uneasiness, both to the monarch, and to the nation. About six months after the battle of Hastings, he found the kingdom in such a state of apparent tranquillity, that he ventured to make a visit to Normandy; in order, as it should seem, to receive the congratulations of his ancient subjects. He probably intended to survey his late elevation from the most interesting point of view, by placing himself in the situation in which he had planned his undertaking, and by thence comparing his former anxious anticipations with his present agreeable reflections. William is, on this occasion, accused by some authors of having formed a resolution to seize the property of all his English subjects, and to reduce them into the most abject slavery.[9] He is even supposed to have gone so soon into Normandy, for the purpose of giving them an opportunity to commit acts of rebellion, by which a pre-<24>tence might be afforded for the severities which he had purposed to execute.* But, as this has been advanced without any proof, so it appears in itself highly improbable. It is altogether inconsistent with the prudence and sound policy ascribed to this monarch, not to mention the feelings of generosity or justice, of which he does not seem to have been wholly destitute, that he should, in the beginning of his reign, have determined to crush and destroy the English nobility, merely for the sake of gratifying his Norman barons; since, by doing so, he must have expected to draw upon himself the hatred and resentment of the whole kingdom, and to incur the evident hazard of losing that crown which he had been at so much trouble and expense in acquiring. Although

* Hume's Hist. of England.

9. See Hume, *HE,* 1:194.

William was, doubtless, under the necessity of bestowing ample rewards upon many of his countrymen, it was not his interest that they should be enriched, or exalted beyond measure. Neither was he of a character to be guided by favourites, or to sacrifice his authority to the weakness of private affection. When he found himself seated upon the English <25> throne, it is natural to suppose that he would look upon the dutchy of Normandy as a distant province, or as a mere dependency of the crown of England; and that he would be more interested in the prosperity of the latter country than of the former, as being more immediately connected with his own dignity and reputation. Upon his return from Normandy, William, accordingly, exerted himself in putting a stop to those quarrels which, in his absence, had broke out between his English and his Norman subjects, and in giving redress to the former, for those injuries which they had sustained from the latter. In particular, he endeavoured, every where, to restore the English to those possessions from which they had been expelled, through the partiality, or want of authority in those persons with whom he had left the administration of government.

Several circumstances contributed to render this monarch unpopular, and have subjected his conduct to greater clamour and censure than it appears to have merited.

1. The jealousy with which the English beheld the Normans, whom they looked upon as intruders, and who became the ruling party, <26> gave rise to numberless disputes, and produced a rooted animosity between them. The partiality which, in such cases, might frequently be discovered, and perhaps was oftener suspected, in the sovereign, or in those to whom he committed the inferior branches of executive power, inflamed the passions of men who conceived themselves loaded with injuries, and excited them to frequent insurrections. By the punishment, which fell unavoidably upon the delinquents, and which could not fail to be regarded by their countrymen as rigorous, new discontents were occasioned, and fresh commotions were produced.

To the aversion which the English conceived against William, as a Norman, and as the friend and protector of Normans, they joined a strong prejudice against those foreign customs which he and his followers had imported. Devoted, like every rude nation, to their ancient usages, they were disgusted with those innovations which they could not prevent; and felt the utmost reluctance to adopt the peculiar manners and policy of a people by whom they were oppressed. The clamours propagated against particular laws of William <27> the conqueror, which were considered as the most oppressive, may serve to demonstrate, that his subjects had more disposition to complain than there was any reason to justify. It appears that the origin and nature of some of these laws have been grossly misunderstood and misrepresented. The regulation, for instance, that lights should be extinguished in every house by eight in the evening, for the execution of which, intimation was given to the public by the ringing of a bell, thence known by the name of the curfew, has been regarded as the most violent exertion of tyranny; and the most incontestable evidence, not only that William was determined entirely to break and subdue the spirit of the English, but that he was held in continual terror of their secret conspiracies. It is now generally understood and admitted, that this was a rule of police established in the greater part of the feudal nations; as by the extreme sobriety which it enforced, it was peculiarly adapted to the circumstances of a simple people. Another law, the source of much complaint, and deemed an intolerable grievance, was, that when a Norman was robbed or slain, the hundred, within <28> whose territory the crime had been committed, should be responsible, and subject to a pecuniary punishment. This regulation, which, in all probability, had become necessary, from the multitude of Normans that were daily assassinated, was originally of Saxon institution, and was only accommodated in this reign to the exigence of the times.

2. The extension of the prerogative, by reducing the allodial proprietors of land into a state of vassalage under the crown, was likewise, we may suppose, the ground of dissatisfaction and murmuring to those great barons, who found themselves deprived of their ancient independence, and were exposed to much vexation from those various *incidents,* the fruit of the feudal tenures, that were now claimed by the sovereign. The discontent arising from this cause, and the desire of recovering that condition which they had held under the Anglo-Saxon princes, was not limited to the English nobility; but was readily communicated to those Norman chiefs who had obtained estates in England, and were naturally animated with the ambition of supporting the privileges of their own order in opposition to <29> the claims of the sovereign. One of the most formidable insurrections, during the reign of William the First, appears to have been excited and conducted by some of

the principal Norman barons; and to have proceeded from the impatience of those individuals under that recent authority which the crown pretended to exercise.[10]

3. Another circumstance which contributed, no less than either of those which have been mentioned, to render William unpopular, was the resentment of the clergy, whom he greatly offended by his exactions from them, and by his opposition to the progress of ecclesiastical authority. As the clergy possessed great influence over the people, so they were the only historians of those times;[11] and in estimating the character of any particular prince, they seem to have had no other criterion but the liberality and favour which he displayed to the church. According to his dispositions in this respect, they appear to have extolled or depreciated his virtues, to have aggravated or extenuated his vices, and to have given a favourable or malignant turn to the whole of his behaviour. From these impure fountains the <30> stream of ancient history contracted a pollution, which has adhered to it even in the course of later ages, and by which it is prevented from reflecting a true picture of the past occurrences.

After all, it cannot be controverted, that this monarch was of a severe and inflexible temper; and that he punished with rigour every attempt to subvert or to disturb his government. That he was rapacious of money, as the great instrument for supporting his authority, must likewise be admitted. Among other exactions, he revived a tax, no less hateful than singular, known to the English by the name of *Dane-gelt,* which had been abolished by Edward the confessor. It appears to have arisen from an extraordinary contribution, which the Anglo-Saxon kings were under the necessity of levying, to oppose the inroads of the Danes, or to make a composition with those invaders. According to the maxims of prudence, common to the princes of that age, William was not content with providing a revenue sufficient to defray his annual expence; but accumulated a large treasure for the supply of any sudden or extraor-<31>dinary demand. That he exterminated, however, the whole English nobility, or considerable proprietors of land, or that he stripped them of their possessions, as has been asserted by Dr. Brady[12] and

10. Millar is likely referring to the insurrection of William's brother Odo and his son Robert in 1088.

11. For similar remarks by Hume, see *HE,* 1:25.

12. Robert Brady (d. 1700), English historian and royal keeper of the records. Brady's

by some later writers, from the authority of some declamatory and vague expressions in one or two ancient annalists, there seems no good reason to believe.* <32>

---

focus was the history of English feudalism, a subject of much political significance in the years surrounding the Glorious Revolution of 1688. Brady's most important works were the *Introduction to the Old English History* (1684), the *Complete History of England* (1685), and the *Historical Treatise of Cities and Burghs* (1690).

* This point has been the subject of much disquisition and controversy. See Petit's Rights of the Commons asserted—Atwood's Janus Anglorum ab Antiquo—Cook's Argumentum Antinormanicum—Tyrrell's History—and Bibliotheca Politica, dial. 10. On the other side of the question, Dr. Brady's History, and his various political treatises. [[Among Millar's sources concerning the matter of the extermination of the English nobility by William the Conqueror are Robert Brady, *Complete History of England* (London, 1685), 1:185–216, especially 192–93; James Tyrrell, *Bibliotheca Politica* (1694), dialogues 6 and 10; 305, 518, 523, 527, 546; William Petyt, *The Antient Rights of the Commons of England Asserted* (London, 1680), 17–18, 21–22, 29; William Atwood, *Jus Anglorum ab Antiquo* (London, 1681), 2–3, 33–39.]]

From an inspection of Doomsday-book, it cannot be denied, that William the first, before the end of his reign, had made prodigious changes in the landed property of England, and that very large estates were conferred upon his Norman barons, who had the principal share of his confidence.—But, on the other hand, it seems equally clear, that a great part of the landed property remained in the hands of the ancient possessors. Whatever burdens were imposed upon the church, it is not alleged that the clergy, or that any religious societies, which had been established under the Anglo-Saxon government, were deprived of their property. These ecclesiastical estates were of great extent, and the tenants, or knights who held of the church, were numerous and powerful. Of 60,215 knights' fees, computed to have been in England not long after the conquest, no fewer than 20,015 are said to have belonged to churchmen. It must be owned, however, that when vacancies occurred in church livings, they were most commonly bestowed upon Normans.

With respect to the laity, there are great numbers mentioned in Doomsday-book, as having held estates in the reign of Edward the Confessor. This is so palpable, that even Dr. Brady himself, in his answer to the Argumentum Antinormanicum, seems to abandon his assertion, that the English were deprived of their possessions, and contents himself with maintaining, that the nature of their property was changed, by their being reduced into the subordinate state of vassalage.

But even here the fact seems to be misrepresented, and in the list of crown vassals recorded in Doomsday, we may discover great proprietors, who held lands in England before the conquest: such as, *Radulfus de Mortimer*—*Hugo de Porth*—and even in this number we may reckon the *Earl of Moreton,* who, though a Norman, had, along with many others, obtained English possessions in the reign of Edward the Confessor. Among those crown vassals, it seems difficult, in many cases, to distinguish the names of the Norman from those of the Anglo-Saxon families; but there are many which appear to

When, at the same time, the situation of William, and the difficulties which he was <33> obliged to encounter, are properly considered, it must on the one hand be acknowledged, that the rigours imputed to him were, for the most part, excited by great provocation; as, on the other, it may be doubted, whether they were not in some degree necessary for reducing the country into a state of tranquillity; and whether a sovereign, endowed with greater mildness of disposition, would not have probably forfeited the crown, as well as involved the kingdom in greater calamities than those which it actually suffered.

William Rufus,[13] the second son of the Conqueror, succeeded to the throne, in preference to Robert his elder brother, from the recom-<34> mendation of his father; from the influence of Lanfranc,[14] the archbishop of Canterbury; and from his being, at his father's death, in England to support his claim, while his brother was at a distance. His reign exhibits the same aspect of public affairs with that of his father; the internal discord of the nobles; their frequent insurrections against the sovereign; with his correspondent efforts to keep them in subjection. As by the succession of this prince, the dutchy of Normandy, which was bequeathed to Robert by his father, was detached from the crown of England, many of the Norman barons, foreseeing the inconvenience that might arise from a division of their property under different sovereigns, endeavoured to prevent his establishment, and raised a rebellion in favour of Robert. But the same circumstance, which rendered the advancement of William so disagreeable to the Normans, made this event equally desirable to the English, who dreaded the continuance of a connexion, from which, in the late reign, they had experienced so much uneasiness and hard treatment. By their assistance, the Nor-

---

have been appropriated to the latter. Such as, *Oswald, Eldred, Albert, Grimbald, Edgar, Edmund, Alured.*

It is said, indeed, by William of Malmsbury and Henry of Huntingdon, that, about the end of William's reign, no Englishman was either a *bishop,* abbot, or earl, in England.

We may add, that, supposing the whole of the English to have been extirpated by William the Conqueror, it would not thence follow that his government became absolute. For what motive could have induced his Norman barons, now become English nobles, and possessed of immense estates, which were secured to them in perpetuity, to acquiesce in any violent extension of the prerogative, to which neither the nobility of Normandy nor of England had been accustomed?

13. William II, Rufus (r. 1087–1100).

14. Lanfranc (ca. 1005–89), archbishop of Canterbury from 1070.

man rebels were soon defeated; the estates <35> of the greater part of them were confiscated; and the authority of the king was completely established: a proof that, in the reign of the Conqueror, the English nobility or considerable land-holders were far from being extirpated; and that their power was not nearly so much impaired as has been pretended.*

Not long after, the king passed over into Normandy, with an army, in order to retaliate the late disturbances which had been promoted from that quarter; but before hostilities had <36> been pushed to any considerable length, a reconciliation, between the two brothers, was effected, by the interposition of the principal nobility in both countries; and a treaty was concluded, by which, among other articles, it was agreed, that, upon the death of either, without issue, the survivor should inherit his dominions. Twelve of the most powerful barons on each side became bound, by a solemn oath, to guaranty this treaty: a circumstance which, as Mr. Hume observes,[15] is sufficient to shew the great authority and independence of the nobles at that period. Nothing can afford fuller conviction, that neither this king nor his

* The expression used on this occasion by William of Malmsbury, is, "Rex videns Normannos pene in una rabie conspiratos, Anglos probos et fortes viros, *qui adhuc residui erunt* [[*sic: erant*]], invitatoriis scriptis arcessit; quibus super injuriis suis queremoniam faciens, bonasque leges, et tributorum levamen, liberasque venationes pollicens, fidelitati suae obligavit." Ordericus Vitulis says, "Lanfrancum archiepiscopum, cum suffraganeis praesulibus, et comites *Anglosque naturales,* convocavit; et conatus adversariorum, et velle suum expugnandi eos, indicavit." [["He (the king) when he saw the Normans almost to a man united in this mad conspiracy, sent a letter of invitation to all the English, good men and true, who yet remained; and complaining of his wrongs, bound them to his service, with the promise of good laws, lighter imposts, and freer hunting." William of Malmesbury, *Gesta Regum Anglorum: The History of the English Kings,* ed. and trans. R. A. B. Mynors, R. M. Thomson, and M. Winterbottom (Oxford: Clarendon Press, 1998), 1:546; "He . . . therefore summoned Archbishop Lanfranc with the suffragan bishops and earls and the native English, and gave them an account of his enemies' uprising and his own determination to overthrow them." *The Ecclesiastical History of Orderic Vitalis,* ed. and trans. Marjorie Chibnall (Oxford: Clarendon Press, 1973), 4:124.]]

Dr. Brady, whose system led him to maintain that none of the native English retained considerable property in the end of the reign of William the Conqueror, labours to prove, that, by the *Angli Naturales,* and the *Angli qui adhuc erant residui* [["the native English" and "the English who yet remained." The argument that these terms cannot refer to Anglo-Saxon English appears in Robert Brady's *An Introduction to the Old English History* (London, 1684), 7–8 of the glossary at the end, which is separately numbered.]], Normans, or Frenchmen, who had settled in England, are to be understood, in opposition to such as lived in Normandy, or were but recently come from that country.

15. For Hume's account, see *HE,* 1:232.

predecessor, though they undoubtedly extended their prerogative, had been able to destroy the ancient aristocracy, and to establish an absolute despotism.

The reunion of Normandy with the dominions of the English monarch was, however, more speedily accomplished, in consequence of an event, by which, at the same time, all Europe was thrown into agitation. I mean, the *crusades;*[16] which were begun in this reign, towards the end of the eleventh century, and continued for about two hundred years. The <37> causes which produced those expeditions; the general superstition of the age, by which Christians were inspired with a degree of phrensy to deliver the holy sepulchre, and the holy land, from the hands of infidels; and the ambitious designs of the Pope, supported by the whole Western church, to extend the dominion of Christianity over both the religion and the empire of Mahomed; these circumstances inflamed most of the princes of Europe with an eager desire of signalizing themselves in a war, from which they had the prospect, not only of the highest reputation and glory in this world, but of much more transcendent rewards in the next. Such motives were peculiarly calculated to work upon the gallant, thoughtless, disinterested character of Robert, the duke of Normandy; who, in the same proportion as he was deficient in political capacity, seems to have excelled in military accomplishments, and to have been possessed with all those religious sentiments, and those romantic notions of military honour, which were fashionable in that age. Embarking, therefore, in the first crusade, and being under the necessity of raising money to equip him for that extraordinary enterprise, he was prevailed upon to mortgage, <38> to his brother the king of England, the dutchy of Normandy, for the paltry sum of ten thousand marks. William Rufus took no part in that war, and seems to have beheld it with perfect indifference. He was upon bad terms with the clergy, whose resentment he incurred by the contributions which he levied from them; and he has, partly, we may suppose, for that reason, been branded even with irreligion and profaneness. His covetous disposition allowed him to entertain no scruple in taking advantage of his brother's necessities; and, being immediately put in possession of Normandy, his authority, by this extension of territory, and by the distant occupation thus given to Robert, was more firmly established.

This monarch, after a reign of thirteen years, having been killed acciden-

16. The Crusades were a series of wars undertaken by European Christians between the eleventh and fourteenth centuries to recover the Holy Land from Islam.

tally, by an arrow aimed at a wild beast, was succeeded by his younger brother, Henry;[17] who immediately seized upon the treasure of the late king, and obtained possession of the throne. The duke of Normandy was at this time in Syria, where he had gained great reputation by his valour. It was to be expected, that, as soon as he should be informed of these transactions, he would take vigorous measures for supporting <39> his title to the crown of England. Few of the English princes have appeared at their accession to be surrounded with greater dangers and difficulties than Henry the first; but his capacity enabled him to encounter them with firmness, and to extricate himself with dexterity.

During many of the reigns that succeeded the Norman conquest, we find that the demands of the nobility, in their disputes with the sovereign, and the complaints of such as were discontented with the government, were pretty uniformly confined to one topic, "the restoration of the laws of Edward the confessor." But what particular object they had in view, when they demanded the restoration of those laws, it is difficult to ascertain. That they did not mean any collection of statutes, is now universally admitted; and it seems to be the prevailing opinion, that their demand related to the system of common law established in England before the Norman conquest. From what has been observed concerning the advancement of the feudal system in the reign of William the first, it appears evident, that the nobility had in view the recovery of the allodial property, and the in-<40>dependence, which they had formerly enjoyed. They saw with regret, we may easily suppose, the late diminution of their dignity and influence; and submitted with reluctance to the military service, and to the other duties incumbent on them as vassals of the crown. The feudal incidents, which were levied by the crown-officers, and of which the extent was not ascertained with accuracy, were, in particular, the source of much vexation, and gave occasion to many complaints. Of these complaints the success was generally proportioned to the difficulties in which the sovereign was involved, and the necessity he was under of purchasing popularity by a redress of grievances.

As Henry the first was exposed to all the odium attending an open and palpable usurpation, and was threatened with an immediate invasion from the duke of Normandy, the acknowledged heir of the crown, he endeavoured to secure the attachment of his barons by yielding to their demands;

17. Henry I, Beauclerc (r. 1100–1135).

and, in the beginning of his reign, he granted them a public charter of their liberties, by which the encroachments of prerogative made in the <41> reign of his father, and of his brother, were limited and restrained. When we examine this charter, the first of those that were procured from the English monarchs after the Norman conquest, we find that, besides containing a clause with respect to the privileges of the church, it relates principally to the incidents of the feudal tenures.[18]

One of the most oppressive of these was *wardship;* by which the king became the guardian of his vassals, in their minority, and obtained the possession of their estates during that period. It is probable that this important privilege had not, in the case of crown-vassals, been yet fully established; since the guardianship of them is, in the charter of Henry the first, relinquished by the king, and committed to the nearest relations.*

The *relief,* or composition, paid by the heir of a vassal, in order to procure a renewal of the investure, was not given up by the sovereign; but the extent of this duty appears to have been settled, with a view of preventing oppression or dispute in particular cases.† <42>

The incident of *marriage,* by which, in after times, the superior was entitled to a composition, for allowing his vassals the liberty of marrying, seems, by this charter, to have extended no farther than the privilege of hindering them from forming, by intermarriages, an alliance with his enemies.‡

Upon the whole, the parties appear to have intended, in this famous transaction, to compound their differences. The feudal superiority of the crown is permitted to remain; while the nobles are, on the other hand, relieved from some of the chief inconveniences which had resulted from it; and, after the regulations particularly specified, the charter contains a general clause, in which the king promises to observe the laws of Edward the confessor, with such amendments as William the first, with the advice of his barons, had introduced. Copies of this deed were sent to all the counties of England; and deposited in the principal monasteries, in order to preserve the memory of an agreement, by which the prerogative of the crown, and the rights of <43> the people, in several important articles, were ascertained and defined.

* The charter of Henry I. published by Blackstone.

† Ibid.

‡ The charter of Henry I. published by Blackstone.

18. The Charter of Henry I was an elaboration on the traditional oath of coronation.

The popularity which Henry acquired by these prudent concessions, enabled him to defeat the ill-concerted enterprizes of the duke of Normandy; who, becoming the dupe of his brother's policy, was persuaded to resign his present claim to the crown, in consequence of an agreement similar to that which had formerly been made with William Rufus, that, upon the death of either of the two princes without issue, the survivor should inherit his dominions. Not contented with the quiet possession of England, Henry soon after invaded Normandy; gained a complete victory over Robert, and reduced the whole country into subjection. The duke himself, being taken prisoner, was carried over to England, and detained in custody during the remainder of his life, which was eight and twenty years. It is added by some authors, that he lived the most part of this time in utter blindness; having, on account of an attempt to make his escape, been condemned to lose his eye-sight. The character of these two brothers appears to exhibit a striking contrast, in the virtues of ge-<44>nerosity and private affection, as well as in activity and talents for public affairs; and the unfortunate duke of Normandy was no less distinguished by his superiority in the former, than by his inferiority, or rather total deficiency, in the latter.

During a reign of thirty-five years, Henry conducted the administration of government, with constant moderation, and with uninterrupted prosperity. He was attentive to the grievances of his people, vigilant in the distribution of justice, and careful to levy no exactions without consent of the national council. From the progress of ecclesiastical usurpation, he was involved in disputes with the church; but in the course of these he conducted himself with such address, as not only to avoid the resentment, but, in the issue, to become even the favourite of the clergy. His character has, of consequence, been highly celebrated: at the same time, when regarded only in a public view, it seems to merit all the praises with which it has been transmitted to posterity.

Henry left no legitimate sons; and only one daughter, Matilda; who had been first married <45> to the emperor, and afterwards to the earl of Anjou, by whom she had children. Setting aside the consideration that her father was an usurper, she had, according to the rules of succession in that period, by which females were beginning to inherit landed estates, the best title to the crown; but a great part of the nobility were in the interest of Stephen, a younger son of the count of Blois, and grandson, by a daughter, of William the conqueror. This nobleman, who had long resided in England, and was distinguished by his popular manners, had procured many partizans; and was probably thought the fitter person to wield the sceptre.* After obtaining possession of the sovereignty, he immediately called a parliament at Oxford, in which he granted a charter, confirming all the privileges contained in that of his predecessor; and in the presence of the assembly he took an oath to maintain them; upon which the bishops and peers recognised his authority, and swore fealty to him.† The policy of this monarch was <46> not equal to his bravery. During the long contest in which he was engaged with Matilda,[19] and her eldest son, Henry, he was generally unfortunate; and, in the end, was obliged to yield the reversion of the crown to the latter.

Henry the second,[20] who succeeded, in right of his mother, but who irregularly mounted the throne in her life-time, had excited sanguine expectations of a prosperous and brilliant reign. To the early display of great activity and abilities, he joined the possession of more extensive dominions than had belonged to any English monarch. Upon the continent he was master of Normandy, Britany, Anjou, Guienne, and other territories, amounting to more than a third of the whole French monarchy. He was, at the same time, a descendant, though not a lineal heir, of the Anglo-Saxon monarchs; his grandmother, the wife of Henry the first, being the niece of Edgar Atheling; a circumstance which contributed not a little to conciliate the affection of the English. Notwithstanding these advantages, his administration, though full of vigour, was clouded with misfortunes. Having conceived the design of repressing the incroachments of the <47> church, and wishing to execute this in the smoothest and most effectual manner, he promoted to the see of Canterbury his principal favourite, Thomas a Becket,[21] by whose assistance he expected that the direction of his own clergy would be infallibly secured. This prelate, however, happened to possess a degree of ambition, not inferior to that of his master; and no sooner found himself at the head of the English

* Daniel's Hist.

† Ibid. Blackstone, History of the Great Charter.

19. Matilda (1102–67) was first married to Henry V, Holy Roman emperor (r. 1111–25), and in 1128 married Geoffrey Plantagenet of Anjou (1113–51). Stephen (r. 1135–54) was the nephew of Henry I.

20. Henry II (r. 1154–89).

21. Thomas à Becket (1118–70) was created archbishop of Canterbury in 1162. Becket was murdered by four of Henry's knights in late 1170. Henry did not order Becket's death but nevertheless was held accountable. Becket was made a saint in 1173.

church, than he resolved to dedicate his whole life to the support of ecclesiastical privileges, and of the papal authority.

The particulars of that controversy, which terminated so unfortunately, and so disgracefully, to the king, are known to all the world. The greatest monarch in Europe, reduced to the necessity of walking three miles barefooted, to the tomb of *Saint Becket;* prostrating himself before that shrine, and lying all night upon the cold pavement of the cathedral, in prayer, and with demonstrations of the deepest penitence, for having offended a man from whom he had received the highest provocation; and, after all, submitting to be scourged by the prior and monks of the neighbouring convent; besides yielding up implicitly all those points <48> which had been the original cause of the contest: such an unusual and humiliating spectacle cannot fail to excite singular emotions; and it is believed that few readers can peruse this part of our history without visible marks of indignation.

That ecclesiastical tyranny is more extensively mischievous than civil, is indisputable; and that the former should therefore raise greater indignation than the latter, is reasonable. There may be ground for suspecting, however, that our feelings, in the present instance, proceed from a natural bias or prejudice, more than from any such rational or liberal views. The ambition of St. Becket, though accompanied with superior steadiness and intrepidity; and though it may be considered as a purer principle of action, by pursuing the aggrandisement of his own order more than of himself; yet is less calculated to dazzle the imagination, and to seize our admiration, than that of a Caesar or an Alexander,[22] who makes his own will the law of his conduct, and who scruples not to tread upon the necks of his people.

Besides the feudal incidents formerly mentioned, which were a sort of rights reserved by <49> the superior, upon his granting fiefs in perpetuity, there was another pecuniary payment, which grew up in course of time, from the regular duty of military service. As, in many cases, the performance of this duty became inconvenient for the vassal, he was led to offer a sum of money in place of his personal attendance in the field; and such a composition was generally acceptable to the sovereign; who, by means of it, was enabled to hire a soldier more perfectly subject to his direction. The sum

22. The sense here is that Julius Caesar and Alexander the Great are to be seen as examples of civil tyranny, a form of political injustice which is less "extensively mischievous" than Becket's "ecclesiastical tyranny."

payable by the vassal in place of military services, the extent of which was at first determined by an agreement with the king in each case, was denominated a *scutage.* In England, the practice of levying scutages became very general in the time of Henry the second; when the connexions of the sovereign with France gave rise to more expensive enterprizes than had formerly been customary; and consequently induced the crown vassals more frequently to decline their personal attendance.

In this reign the conquest of Ireland, as it is called, was begun and compleated.[23] As that island had never been conquered, or even invaded, by the Romans, it retained, with its in-<50>dependence, a total ignorance of those arts, and of that civilization, which every where accompanied the Roman yoke. It seems, on the other hand, to have escaped, in a great measure, the fury of the Saxons, Danes, and other northern invaders; who never penetrated into that country, but only committed occasional depredations upon the coasts, where they formed some small settlements, and built several towns. Thus, while the greatest part of Europe was, for several centuries, thrown into convulsions by the repeated irruptions of the German or Scythian nations,[24] Ireland was, by reason of its situation, exposed to little disturbance or commotion from any foreign enemy; and the inhabitants were seldom engaged in any military enterprizes, but such as arose from their own private quarrels and depredations. It is therefore highly probable, that, for some time after that country was first inhabited, and while the several families or petty tribes, to whom by its fertility it afforded an easy subsistence, were not much crowded together, they enjoyed more tranquillity than the other barbarians of Europe, and, of consequence, were less counteracted and restrained in those <51> exertions of generosity and friendship, to which, among people who live in small societies, and are strangers to industry, and to the concomitant habits of avarice, there are peculiar incitements. That they might, upon this account, acquire a considerable share of that refinement which is attainable in the pastoral ages, it is natural to suppose; and that they actually did so, the specimens of Celtic poetry, lately

23. For a review of Irish affairs, see vol. 4, chap. 1.

24. Scythia: an ancient region of Eurasia, extending from the Danube on the west to the borders of China on the east. The Scythians were nomadic conquerors who spoke an Indo-Iranian language.

published,[25] which have been claimed respectively by the Irish and by the inhabitants of the West Highlands of Scotland, both of whom may, in this case, be considered as one people, appear incontestible evidence. The authenticity of these publications has, indeed, been called in question; but it would require an equal degree of scepticism to doubt, that the groundwork of them is genuine, as it would of credulity to believe, that they are the original production of any modern publisher.

According as Ireland became gradually more populous, a greater number of families came to be united in particular principalities; the leaders of which being actuated by larger views of ambition, found more frequent pretences for quarrelling with each other; and their sub-<52>jects or followers, being thus involved in more numerous acts of hostility, or in such as were productive of greater violence and outrage, the manners of the people in general were, of course, rendered more ferocious. The whole island came at length to be reduced into four or five extensive districts, under so many different sovereigns; one of which frequently claimed a sort of authority or pre-eminence over all the rest.

After the English monarchy had come to be connected with the continent of Europe, and to interfere in its transactions, it was natural for the king of England to entertain the ambition of adding to his dominions a country so commodiously situated as Ireland, and which appeared to be so little in a capacity of making resistance. Henry the second is accordingly said to have taken some steps for executing a project of this nature, when application was made to him for protection, by Dermot the king of Leinster, who had been driven out of his dominions. In virtue of a bare permission from the king of England, two needy adventurers, Fitzstephen and Fitzgerald, and afterwards Richard, surnamed Strongbow, likewise <53> a man of desperate fortune, to whom the two former acted in a kind of subordination, landed with a few followers in Leinster; defeated any force that was brought in opposition to them; besieged and took several towns, and formed a settlement in the

25. The Scottish historian and philologist James Macpherson (1736–96) published what he claimed to be translations of the poems of Ossian, an ancient Gaelic poet and warrior. Those who disputed the authenticity of the poetry pointed to (among other things) the refined sentiments attributed to these heroes of a primitive time. Millar acknowledged the dispute, but believed the work to be built on genuine foundations and argued that this sort of refinement was not out of place among pastoral people.

province.[26] Upon receiving information of their progress, Henry, inflamed, as it should seem, with jealousy of their success, hastened immediately to take possession of the territory which they had subdued; and coming over to Ireland, received the submission of several chiefs or princes of the country, who, dreading the effects of his power, were anxious to avoid any contest with him.[27]

Neither Henry himself, nor his successors for several centuries, appear to have derived any substantial benefit from this acquisition. Their authority was confined to that narrow district inhabited by the English; and even *there* was more nominal than real; for the English inhabitants, harassed by continual inroads from their neighbours, and receiving a very uncertain and casual support from England, were, on many occasions, tempted to throw off their allegiance, and were seduced to imitate the <54> barbarous manners and practices of the natives.

Henry, in the latter part of his life, was rendered unhappy by domestic misfortunes. A conspiracy was formed against him, by his queen and sons, which became the source of repeated insurrections, accompanied with several very formidable invasions from the neighbouring powers.[28]

Though the king was successful in repressing these disorders, and in defeating all his enemies; yet the obstinacy with which his children persisted in their unnatural attempts, appears to have impressed his mind with deep sentiments of melancholy and dejection. From the difficulties, at the same time, with which he was surrounded, he found it highly expedient to court the good-will of his subjects, not only by a careful attention to the police of the kingdom, and by an equal distribution of justice, but by granting a new charter in the same terms with that of Henry the first.*

* Blackstone, History of the Great Charter.

26. Diarmid Macmurchada, king of Leinster, offered to become Henry's vassal in exchange for assistance in regaining his Irish kingdom. The "needy adventurers" Millar refers to were Robert Fitzstephen (d. ca. 1183) and Maurice Fitzgerald (d. 1176). Richard Strongbow is another name for Richard Fitzgilbert, earl of Pembroke (d. 1176), who in 1170 answered Diarmid's call for help by taking Waterford in the south of Ireland.

27. Henry's conquest of eastern Ireland took place in 1171.

28. In 1173, two of Henry's sons, John and Richard the Lionheart, along with his wife, Eleanor of Aquitaine (1122–1204), rebelled against their father with the assistance of Phillip II Augustus of France (r. 1179–1223) and William the Lion of Scotland (r. 1165–1214). Richard again rebelled against his father with Phillip II in 1188.

Richard the first,[29] who succeeded his father, was entirely engrossed by the love of military <55> glory; and the short period, during which he held the reins of government, was, for the most part, employed, either in preparations for a magnificent crusade, the fashionable atchievement of that age, or in oppressive exactions, to relieve him from the burdens which he had incurred by that unfortunate enterprize.

The character of John,[30] his brother and successor, is universally known, as a compound of cowardice, tyranny, sloth, and imprudence. This infatuated king was involved in three great struggles, from which it would have required the abilities of his father, or of his great grandfather, to extricate himself with honour; but which, under his management, could hardly fail to terminate in ruin and disgrace.

It is observed by Mr. Hume, with his usual acuteness, that the extensive territories which the kings of England, at this period, possessed in France, were the source of much less real than apparent strength;[31] and that, from their situation, they were filled with the seeds of revolt and disobedience. In the ordinary state of the feudal tenants, the vassals of the nobility were much more attached to their immediate superior, by whom they were most commonly <56> protected, and with whom they maintained an intimate correspondence, than with the sovereign, who lived at a distance from them, and with whom they had little connexion. The power of the king, therefore, depended, for the most part, upon the extent of his own demesnes; and in every quarrel with his nobles, it was to be expected that all their vassals would take party against him. But in the dominions which the king of England held in France, these circumstances were completely reversed; and his immediate vassals, by their situation, were less capable, on any emergence, of receiving protection from him, than from the French monarch, their paramount superior: not to mention, that they regarded the king of England as a foreign prince, whose interest was commonly very different, and sometimes diametrically opposite to that of their native country. Their affections there-

29. Richard I the Lionheart (r. 1189–99) left England in 1190, one year after his coronation, and did not return until 1194. The same year he promptly left for France, never to return.

30. John, Lackland (r. 1199–1216).

31. In what follows, Millar echoes Hume on the French territories: "their immediate lord was often at too great a distance to protect them; and any disorder in any part of his dispersed dominions gave advantages against him." *HE,* 1:299–300.

fore were gradually alienated from their immediate superior; and transferred to their sovereign; who, it was natural to suppose, might, some time or other, availing himself of his advantageous situation, be enabled to wrest those dominions from his rival. This accordingly hap-<57>pened in the beginning of the present reign. As John was advanced to the throne in preference to Arthur,[32] the son of his elder brother, and consequently the lineal heir, and as he had incurred great odium in a war with that prince, whom he defeated, and was afterwards believed to have murdered; Philip Augustus at that time king of France, seized the opportunity of interfering in a dispute, which afforded so fair a prospect of acquiring popularity, as well as of promoting his interest. Having called a national council, he procured a declaration, that the king of England, by his behaviour, had forfeited Normandy, and the other territories which he held in France;[33] and in the greater part of those territories, this decree, from the concurrence of the inhabitants, co-operating with the power of the French crown, was easily carried into execution.

This disaster was followed by a contest with the Roman pontiff, concerning the right of electing the archbishop of Canterbury; in which John was, if possible, still more unsuccessful. In order to remove the papal excommunication which had been inflicted upon him, he was laid under the necessity, not only <58> of abandoning the points in dispute, but of surrendering his kingdom to the pope, and submitting to hold it as a feudatory of the church of Rome.[34]

The contempt which this abject submission of their sovereign could not fail to excite in the breast of his subjects, together with the indignation raised by various acts of tyranny and oppression of which he was guilty, produced at length a combination of his barons, who demanded a redress of grievances, and the restoration of their ancient laws. As this appeared the most favourable conjuncture which had occurred, since the Norman conquest,

32. Arthur, duke of Brittany (1187–1203), was the son of Geoffrey II of Brittany and the grandson of Henry II. It is alleged that he was put to death by his uncle, King John, as a superior claimant to the throne.

33. King John had ceded almost all of his French territories to Philip Augustus by 1206.

34. This controversy revolved around King John's rejection of the new archbishop of Canterbury, Stephen Langton, in 1207. John was excommunicated in 1208 as a result of his rejection. By an agreement with Pope Innocent III (ca. 1198–1216), John agreed to convert England into a fiefdom of the papacy, thereby gaining needed papal support against the nobility and the French.

for limiting the encroachments of prerogative; the nobility and principal gentry were desirous of improving it to the utmost; and their measures were planned and conducted with equal moderation and firmness. The king attempted, by every artifice in his power, to frustrate their designs. He endeavoured by menaces to intimidate them; and, by delusive promises, to lull them asleep, in order to gain time for breaking their confederacy. When all other expedients proved ineffectual, he made application to the pope as his liege lord; and <59> called upon his holiness to protect the rights of his vassal. The barons were neither to be deluded nor terrified from the prosecution of their purpose. Finding that their petitions were disregarded, they rose up in arms, and proceeded to actual hostilities.[35] The number of their adherents was daily increased; and the king who retired before them, was deserted by almost all his followers; till at last there were only seven lords who remained in his retinue. All further opposition, therefore, became impracticable. At Runnemede, a large meadow between Windsor and Staines; a place which has been rendered immortal in the page of the historian and in the song of the poet; was held that famous conference, when the barons presented, in writing, the articles of agreement upon which they insisted; and the king gave an explicit consent to their demands.* The <60> articles were then reduced into the form of a charter; to which the king affixed his great seal; and which, though it was of the same nature with the charters obtained from the preceding monarchs, yet, as it was obtained with diffi-

* ——— "Hail Runny-mead!
Illustrious field! like Marathon renowned!
Or Salamis, where freedom on the hosts
Of Persia, from her radiant sword shook fear
And dire discomfiture! Even now I tread
Where Albion's ancient barons won the pledge
Of independence. ———
——— O gallant chiefs! whether ye ride the winds,
Bound on some high commission to confound
The pride of guilty kings; or, to alarm
Their coward spirits, through the realms of night
Hurl the tremendous comet, or in bowers
Of blooming Paradise enjoy repose;
I ween the memory of your patriot zeal
Exalts your glory, and sublimes your joys."
RICHARDSON

35. The baronial rebellion began in May 1215.

culties which created more attention, and as it is extended to a greater variety of particulars, has been called, by way of distinction, *the great charter of our liberties.*[36]

As the feudal superiority of the crown, over the nobles, together with the various casual emoluments, or *incidents,* arising from that superiority, had now been established, with little or no interruption, ever since the reign of William the conqueror; it would probably have been a vain project to attempt the abolition of it. The chief aim of the nobility, therefore, in the present charter, was to pre-<61>vent the sovereign from harassing and oppressing them by the undue exercise of those powers, the effects of their feudal subordination, with which he was understood to be fully invested. The incidents of wardship, relief, and marriage, notwithstanding the provisions in the charter of Henry the first, had continued the subject of much controversy; for the removal of which, the nature and extent of those feudal perquisites were more particularly defined and explained. With regard to the practice of levying *aids* and *scutages,* it was provided that the former should not be demanded, unless in the three cases established by the feudal customs, to redeem the sovereign from captivity, to portion his eldest daughter, or to make his eldest son a knight; and that the latter should not be imposed in any case without the authority of parliament.*

The jurisdiction exercised by the king, as a feudal superior, was another source of oppression, for which a remedy was thought requisite; and several regulations were introduced, in <62> order to facilitate the distribution of justice, to prevent the negligence, as well as to restrain the corruption, of judges: in particular, it was declared, that no count or baron should be fined unless by the *judgment of his peers,* and according to the quality of the offence.†

While the barons were thus labouring to secure themselves against the usurpations of the prerogative, they could not decently refuse a similar security to their own vassals; and it was no less the interest of the king to insist upon limiting the arbitrary power of the nobles, than it was their interest to

* Blackstone's edition of king John's Magna Charta, § 2, 3, 4, 6, 12, &c.

† Blackstone's edition of king John's Magna Charta, § 21.

36. King John signed the Great Charter or *Magna Carta* at Runnymede on June 15, 1215. Throughout what follows, Millar cites Sir William Blackstone's edition: *The Great Charter and Charter of the Forest . . . to which is prefixed . . . the history of the charters* (Oxford, 1759).

insist upon limiting that of the crown. The privileges inserted in this great transaction were, upon this account, rendered more extensive, and communicated to persons of a lower rank, than might otherwise have been expected. Thus it was provided that justice should not be *sold,* nor unreasonably *delayed, to any person.** That no freeman should be imprisoned, nor his goods be distrained, unless by the *judgment of his peers,* or by the law of the land;† and that even a <63> villein should not, by any fine, be deprived of his carts and implements of husbandry.‡

It is worthy of notice, however, that though this great charter was procured by the power and influence of the nobility and dignified clergy, who, it is natural to suppose, would be chiefly attentive to their own privileges; the interest of another class of people, much inferior in rank, was not entirely overlooked: I mean the inhabitants of the trading towns. It was declared, that no aid should be imposed upon the city of London, unless with consent of the national council; and that the liberties and immunities of this, and of all the other cities and boroughs of the kingdom, should be maintained.§ To the same class we may refer a regulation concerning the uniformity of weights and measures, and the security given to foreign merchants, for carrying on their trade without molestation. The insertion of such clauses must be considered as a proof that the mercantile people were beginning to have some attention paid to them; while the short-<64>ness of these articles, and the vague manner in which they are conceived, afford an evidence equally satisfactory, that this order of men had not yet risen to great importance.

In order to diffuse the knowledge of the charter over the kingdom, and to ensure the execution of it, a number of originals was made, and one of these was lodged in every county, or at least in every diocese; twenty-five barons were chosen, as guardians of the public liberties, and invested with power suitable to the discharge of so important a trust; and the nobles farther required, that, in the mean time, the city of London should remain in their hands, and that the Tower should be put in their possession. The king consented to these measures; though nothing could be farther from his intentions, than to fulfil the conditions of the charter. No sooner had he obtained

* Ibid. § 40.

† Ibid. § 39.

‡ Blackstone's edition of king John's Magna Charta, § 20.

§ Ibid. § 13.

a bull from the pope annulling that deed, and prohibiting both the king and his subjects from paying any regard to it, than, having secretly procured a powerful supply of foreign troops, he took the field, and began without mercy to kill and destroy, and to carry devastation throughout the estates of all those who had any <65> share in the confederacy. The barons, trusting to the promises of the king, had rashly disbanded their followers; and being in no condition to oppose the royal army, were driven to the desperate measure of applying to Lewis, the son of the French monarch, and making him an offer of the crown. The death of John, in a short time after, happened opportunely to quiet these disorders, by transmitting the sovereignty to his son Henry the third, who was then only nine years of age.[37]

Under the prudent administration of the earl of Pembroke, the regent, the young king, in the first year of his reign, granted a new charter of liberties, at the same time that the confederated barons were promised a perpetual oblivion for the past, in case they should now return to their allegiance.[38]

It is observable, that a copy of this deed, with some variations, was also transmitted to Ireland, for the benefit of the English inhabitants of that island; who, it was justly thought, had an equal right to all the privileges enjoyed by their fellow-subjects in Britain.

The following year, when peace was concluded with Lewis, and the public tranquillity <66> was restored; this charter was renewed, with additions and improvements; and, as the charter of king John contained one or two clauses relating to the forest laws, these were now extended, and made the subject of a separate instrument, called the *Charter of the Forest.*[39] The two deeds, into which the original great charter came thus to be divided, were again renewed, with some variations, and confirmed, in the ninth year of Henry the third, when the king was, by a papal bull, declared of age, and began to hold the reins of government.[40]

The charter of the forest, how insignificant soever the subject of it may be thought in the present age, was then accounted a matter of the highest

37. Henry III (r. 1216–72) was the first English monarch crowned in his minority.

38. William Marshal, the first earl of Pembroke (d. 1219), was instrumental in subduing the rebellious barons, issuing the 1216 charter, and restoring order to the kingdom.

39. The Charter of the Forest was issued in 1217 and confirmed in 1225.

40. Henry assumed full authority in 1227, after the regency of Hubert de Burgh (1219–27).

importance. The Gothic nations, who settled in the Roman empire, were, all of them, immoderately addicted to the diversion of hunting; insomuch that this may be regarded as a peculiarity in their manners, by which they are distinguished from every other people, ancient or modern.* It arose, in all probability, from their having acquired very extensive landed estates, a great part of which <67> they were not able to cultivate; and from their continuing, for many centuries, in that rude and military state, which disposed them to bodily exercise, while it produced such a contempt of industry, and profound ignorance of the arts, as were the sources of much leisure and idleness. The free people, or gentry, commonly allotted to hunting the most part of the time in which they were not engaged in war; and the vassals of every chieftain, or feudal superior, were usually his companions in the former occupation as well as in the latter. Every independent proprietor, however, endeavoured to maintain the exclusive privilege of killing game upon his own grounds; and, having set apart, for the purpose of this amusement, a large portion of uncultivated land, under the name of a *forest,* he denounced severe penalties against his vassals, as well as against every other person, who should hunt upon it without his consent. The sovereign in each kingdom enjoyed the same privilege, in this respect, with the other allodial proprietors; though it appears to have been originally confined within the limits of his own demesnes. The completion of the feudal system, however, by reducing the great <68> lords to be the vassals of the crown, rendered the sovereign the ultimate proprietor of all the lands in the kingdom; and the privilege of hunting, being thus considered as a branch of the royal prerogative, was not understood, without a special grant in their charter, to be communicated to his vassals. Upon the same principle that the king was alone entitled to kill game within his dominions, he assumed the exclusive privilege of erecting lands into a forest; by which they were appropriated to the diversion of hunting: at the same time, for preserving the game in the royal forests, a peculiar set of regulations came to be established; and particular officers and courts of justice were appointed for executing such regulations, and for trying offences committed against them.

The diversion of hunting became still more fashionable, and was carried to a greater height in England, than in the countries upon the continent of

* Muratori, Antiq. Med. Aev. tom. ii. diss. 23.—The Romans generally employed their slaves in hunting. Ibid.

Europe. The insular situation of Britain enabled the inhabitants in a great measure to extirpate the fiercer and more hurtful species of wild animals; so as to leave no other but those which, placing their whole safety in flight, directed the attention of the people to <69> the pleasure merely of the chase. Hunting, therefore, in Britain, came to consist in a long and intricate pursuit, admitting the display of much art and skill; while, upon the continent, it was often a sort of combat with wild animals, requiring only a momentary exertion of strength and courage, or at most, of military dexterity. As the inhabitants of this island were, besides, less engaged in distant wars than the other European nations, they had, upon that account, more leisure to employ themselves in rural sports. It has farther been alleged, that Britain was anciently famous for its breed of slow hounds,[41] a species of dogs peculiarly fitted for the improvement of the chase; but whether this ought to be regarded as one cause of the national propensity to this diversion, or rather as the effect of it, there may be some reason to doubt. It is more probable that the English were led early to cultivate the breed of slow-hounds, because they were much addicted to that mode of hunting which required those animals, than that this kind of dogs, from something unaccountable in the nature of our soil and climate, were <70> the original and peculiar growth of our country.*

We may remark, by the way, that the English manner of hunting, and their fondness for that sport, has been the cause of another peculiarity, their passion for horse-racing. When hunting came to consist entirely in a pursuit, there was a necessity that the company should, for the most part, be on horseback; and when different sportsmen were engaged in the same chase, they had frequently occasion to vie with one another in the swiftness of their horses; which naturally produced a more formal trial, by running in a stated course; while the improvement of this latter diversion excited the people to cultivate that breed of race-horses which is now reckoned peculiar to the country.

During the whole period of the Anglo-Saxon government, the great lords, who possessed allodial estates, appear to have enjoyed the privilege of hunt-

* That England was anciently famous for its breed of slow-hounds, appears from Strabo, c. 4. The French, under the kings of the Merovingian race, were accustomed to procure hunting dogs from England. Velly's Hist. vol. i.

41. A sleuth-hound, pointer, or tracking dog.

ing upon their own <71> ground, independent of the sovereign.* But, in consequence of that feudal superiority over the nobles, which was acquired by the crown upon the accession of William the first, it became a maxim, that the killing of game was a branch of the royal prerogative, and that no subject had any right either to possess a forest, or even to hunt upon his own estate, unless by virtue of a charter from the crown.

In this part of the prerogative, William the conqueror, and his immediate successor, are said to have committed great abuses. As those princes were excessively addicted to the amusement of hunting, they laid waste very extensive territories, in different parts of England, in order to convert them into forests; having, for that purpose, demolished many houses, and even villages, and expelled the inhabitants. New and savage penalties were inflicted upon <72> such as encroached upon the king's game, or committed any trespass in his forests; and the laws upon this subject were executed in a manner the most rigorous and oppressive.

It may, indeed, be suspected that these abuses have been somewhat exaggerated. The extension of the prerogative, with respect to the privilege of hunting, must have been highly offensive to the nobles; and could hardly fail to excite loud complaints, together with some degree of misrepresentation, against the proceedings of the crown. The erection of great forests, even though these had been confined within the demesnes of the king, was likely of itself to occasion much popular clamour; as in our own times, the change of a large estate from tillage to pasturage,[42] by which many tenants are deprived of their livelihood, is frequently the source of much odium and resentment. There is reason, however, to believe, that these exertions en-

* By a law of Canute the Great, whose authority was more extensive than that of his predecessors, the right of the nobles to protect the game upon their own grounds seems to be laid under restrictions. The words are, "Volo ut omnis liber homo, pro libito suo, habeat venerem, sive viridem, in planis suis super terras suas, sine chacea tamen, et devitent omnes meam, ubicunque eam habere voluero." [["It is my will that every free man shall have the right to hunt, or the right to cut wood, as he wishes on his own fields on his lands, without, however, a chase, and that everyone shall avoid my chase wherever I wish to have it." The Anglo-Saxon original is to be found with a translation in *The Laws of the Kings of England from Edmund to Henry I,* ed. and trans. A. J. Robertson (Cambridge: Cambridge University Press, 1925), 215. A "chase" is an area of forest granted by the king to a subject that is exempt from some of the royal forest laws and over which the subject exercises jurisdiction.]]

42. The reference is to the Highland clearances, which made such large and devastating changes to the agricultural life of the Scottish Highlands in the eighteenth century.

croached, in some cases, upon the private property of individuals, and were, therefore, no less unjust than they were unpopular.

The charter of the forest contained a variety of salutary regulations for mitigating the seve-<73>rity of the laws upon that subject, for the rectification of the former abuses, and for preventing the future encroachments of the sovereign. In the proceedings against those who trespassed upon a forest, a greater degree of regularity was introduced; and capital punishments were, in all cases, abolished. The invasions of private property, by erecting a royal forest, except upon the demesnes of the crown, were prohibited; and it was ordained that all the lands belonging to particular persons, which, from the reign of Henry the second, had been included within the boundaries of a forest, should be *disaforested,* and restored to the owner.*

The long reign of Henry the third, from the feeble character of that monarch, and from the injudicious, the inconstant, and the arbitrary measures which he pursued, according to the different favourites by whose counsel he happened to be governed, was filled with insurrections and disorders; and in the latter part of it, the rebellion, conducted by the daring ambition and great abilities of Simon Montfort, the earl of Leicester,[43] had reduced <74> the sovereign to the most desperate situation, and threatened to deprive him of his crown; when his enemies were unexpectedly and completely defeated, by the intrepidity, steadiness, and good fortune of his son Edward. During the course of these commotions, Henry, in order to appease his barons, granted, more than once, a renewal of the great charter, and the charter of the forest. He also swore, in the most solemn manner, to preserve them inviolable; an oath to which, after he was relieved from the present embarrassment, he appears to have shewn little regard.

We may here take notice, though it falls beyond the period which we are now considering, that another solemn confirmation of these charters was afterwards obtained in the vigorous and successful reign of Edward the first.[44]

* See the Charter published by Blackstone.

43. Simon de Montfort, earl of Leicester (ca. 1208–65) was Henry's brother-in-law, and a powerful baron. Hostilities broke out in 1264, and, despite some successes, Henry was defeated and captured by Montfort at the Battle of Lewes.

44. Edward I, king of England (r. 1272–1307), defeated the baronial army at the Battle of Evesham in 1265.

1. When we take a view of these great transactions, and endeavour to estimate the degree of attention which they merit, their number, their similarity, and the long intervals of time at which they were procured, are circumstances which cannot be overlooked. Had one charter only been granted by the sovereign, on a singular occasion, it might well be sup-<75>posed to have arisen from a concourse of accidents, and from partial views. Instead of expressing the opinions entertained by the king and his people, concerning the rights of either, it might, in that case, have been the effect of a mere casual advantage, which the one party had gained over the other; and, so far from displaying the ordinary state of the government at that period, it might have exhibited the triumph and injustice of a temporary usurpation. But those important stipulations, not to mention the frequent confirmations of them in a later period, were begun and repeated under the reigns of six different monarchs, comprehending a course of about two hundred years; they were made with princes of extremely different characters, and in very opposite situations; and though, by the insertion of different articles, those deeds were gradually expanded, and accommodated to the circumstances of the times, yet their main object continued invariably the same; to limit those abuses of prerogative, which, from the advancement of the feudal system, and from the nature of the monarchy, were most likely to be committed. Taking those charters, therefore, in connexion <76> with one another, they seem to declare, in a clear and unequivocal manner, the general and permanent sense of the nation, with respect to the rights of the crown; and they ascertain, by express and positive agreement between the king and his subjects, those terms of submission to the chief magistrate, which, in most other governments, are no otherwise explained than by long usage, and which have therefore remained in a state of uncertainty and fluctuation.

2. It seems to be a common opinion, that, by these charters, the crown was deprived of many of those powers which had been assumed by William the conqueror, or by his son William Rufus, and the constitution was brought nearer to that equal balance, which it had maintained under the direction of the Saxon princes. In particular, by the charter of king John (for the preceding charters have been in a great measure overlooked) it has always been supposed that the bounds of the prerogative were greatly limited.[45] But upon examination it will be found, that this opinion is contrary

45. Edward confirmed the Charters in 1297. The "prerogative" in this sense refers to the peculiar rights and privileges of the monarch.

to the real state of the fact. During the whole period which we are now considering; that is, <77> from the Norman conquest to the time of Edward the first; while the barons were exerting themselves with so much vigour, and with so much apparent success, in restraining the powers of the crown, those powers were, notwithstanding, continually advancing; and the repeated concessions made by the sovereign, had no farther effect than to prevent his authority from increasing so rapidly as it might otherwise have done. For a proof of this we can appeal to no better authority than that of the charters themselves; from which, if examined according to their dates, it will appear, that the nobility were daily becoming more moderate in their claims; and that they submitted, in reality, to a gradual extension of the prerogative; though, by more numerous regulations, they endeavoured to avoid the wanton abuses of it. Thus, by the great charter of Henry the third, the powers of the crown are less limited than by the charter of king John; and by this last the crown vassals abandoned some important privileges with which they were invested by the charter of Henry the first.

In the charter of Henry the first, *the inci-*<78>*dent of wardship,* the severest and most oppressive of all the feudal incidents, is relinquished by the sovereign; and the heirs of a vassal being thus allowed to continue the possession of the fief, during their minority, that is, at a period when they could not perform the feudal service, were in a great measure restored to that allodial property which, before the Norman conquest, their predecessors had enjoyed. But, in the reign of king John, the incident of wardship had taken such root, that the crown vassals no longer thought of disputing the continuance of it; but were satisfied with procuring some regulations to prevent abuses in making it effectual. From this period, therefore, the nobles must be understood to acknowledge that they had no other claim to the enjoyment of their estates than as a consideration for the performance of military service.

According to the charter of Henry the first, the *incident of marriage* extended no farther than to prevent the crown vassals from marrying any woman, with whose family the superior was at variance; a restriction which was not likely to be very oppressive, and which was in some degree necessary for maintaining the <79> public tranquillity. But in the time of king John this incident had been so much enlarged, as to imply a right in the superior to prohibit his vassals from marrying without his consent, and even to require that they should marry any woman whom he presented to them. In the charter of that prince, therefore, it is provided, that the heirs of a vassal shall be married without *disparagement,* that is, they shall not be required to contract unsuitable alliances; and, to secure them from imposition or undue influence, in a matter of this kind, it is farther stipulated, that before they contract any marriage their nearest relations shall be informed of it.

The charter of king John may, on the other hand, be compared with that of Henry the third, in relation to *aids* and *scutages,* a sort of indirect taxes, from which a considerable part of the crown revenue was derived. By the charter of John, the exclusive power of imposing those duties is committed to parliament; but that of Henry the third is entirely silent upon this point; and leaves the monarch under no restraint in imposing such burdens by virtue of his own prerogative. It is true, that the former limitation upon this part of the prero-<80>gative was afterwards renewed in the reign of Edward the first.*

What I have observed concerning the variations in the series of great charters, does not seem applicable to the laws of the forest. The violations of private property, committed in this respect by William the first, and his successors, were too notorious to be seriously defended; and therefore, notwithstanding the general progress of monarchy, it was thought necessary to remove these abuses, and to guard against them for the future.

3. Whoever enquires into the circumstances in which these great charters were procured, and into the general state of the country at that time, will easily see that the parties concerned in them were not actuated by the most liberal principles; and that it was not so much their intention to secure the liberties of the people at large, as to establish the privileges of a few individuals. A great tyrant on the one side, and a set of petty tyrants on the other, seem to have divided the kingdom; and the great body of the people, disregarded and oppressed on all hands, were beholden for any privileges be-<81>stowed upon them, to the jealousy of their masters; who, by limiting the authority of each other over their dependants, produced a reciprocal diminution of their power. But though the freedom of the common people was not intended in those charters, it was eventually secured to them; for when the peasantry, and other persons of low rank, were afterwards enabled, by their industry, and by the progress of arts, to emerge from their inferior and servile condition, and to acquire opulence, they were gradually admitted

* 34 Edw. I. stat. 4. cap. i.—Also 25 Edw. I. 2, 5, 6.

to the exercise of the same privileges which had been claimed by men of independent fortunes; and found themselves entitled, of course, to the benefit of that free government which was already established. The limitations of arbitrary power, which had been calculated chiefly to promote the interest of the nobles, were thus, by a change of circumstances, rendered equally advantageous to the whole community as if they had originally proceeded from the most exalted spirit of patriotism.

When the commons, in a later period, were disposed to make farther exertions, for securing their natural rights, and for extending the blessings of civil liberty, they found it a singular <82> advantage to have an ancient written record, which had received the sanction of past ages, and to which they could appeal for ascertaining the boundaries of the prerogative. This gave weight and authority to their measures; afforded a clue to direct them in the mazes of political speculation; and encouraged them to proceed with boldness in completing a plan, the utility of which had already been put to the test of experience. The regulations, indeed, of this old canon, agreeable to the simplicity of the times, were often too vague and general to answer the purposes of regular government; but, as their aim and tendency were sufficiently apparent, it was not difficult, by a proper commentary, to bestow upon them such expansion and accommodation as might render them applicable to the circumstances of an opulent and polished nation. <83>

CHAPTER II

In what Manner the Changes produced in the Reign of William the Conqueror affected the State of the national Council.

The changes in the state of landed property, arising from the completion of the feudal system, in the reign of William the first, were necessarily attended with correspondent alterations in the constitution and powers of the national council. The Saxon Wittenagemote was composed of the allodial proprietors of land; the only set of men possessed of that independence which could create a right of interfering in the administration of public affairs. The number of these, having been originally very great, was gradually diminished, according as individuals were induced, from prudential considerations, to resign their allodial property, and to hold their estates of some feudal superior. But in the reign of William the conqueror, when the most powerful of the nobility, those who alone had hitherto retained their allodial property, became at last the immediate vassals <84> of the crown, the ancient Wittenagemote was of course annihilated; since there no longer existed any person of the rank and character which had been deemed essential to the members of that assembly.

As, during the government of the Anglo-Saxon princes, every feudal superior had a court, composed of his vassals, by whose assistance he decided the law-suits and regulated the police of his barony; so the king, considered in the same capacity, had likewise a private baron-court, constituted in the same manner, and invested with similar powers. In that period, however, the former of these courts, being held by allodial proprietors, acknowledging no farther subjection to the king than as chief magistrate of the community, were totally independent of the latter. But in the reign of William the conqueror, when the whole of the nobility became vassals of the crown, they were incorporated in the king's baron-court, and the jurisdiction which they exercised in their own demesne was rendered subordinate to that of the king as their paramount superior. The several districts, which had formerly been divided into so many independent lordships, <85> were now united in one great barony, under the sovereign; and his baron-court assumed, of consequence, a jurisdiction and authority over the whole kingdom. Thus, upon the extinction of the Wittenagemote, there came to be substituted, in place of it, another court or meeting, similar to the former, and calculated for the same purposes, though constituted in a manner somewhat different. To this meeting, as the Norman or French language was now fashionable in England, and even employed in public deeds and legal proceedings, the name of *parliament* was given; as the meeting itself corresponded, not only to the assembly known by the same appellation in France,[1] but to the national council of all those European countries in which the feudal system had attained the same degree of advancement.*

The English parliament, though its members appeared under a different description, <86> comprehended in reality the same class of people who had been members of the ancient Wittenagemote. It was composed of all the immediate vassals of the crown; including the dignified clergy, and the nobility, whether of English or of French extraction. The wealth of these persons, from the successive accumulations of property before, and in the reign of William the conqueror, must have been prodigious. From the survey in doomsday-book[2] it appears, that, about the end of William's reign, the immediate vassals of the crown were in all about six hundred: so inconsiderable was the number of baronies, whether in the hands of laymen or ecclesiastics, into which the whole territory of England, exclusive of Wales, and the three

* It has been alleged, that the name of parliament was bestowed upon the English national council even in the reign of Edward the confessor, at which time the French language began to be fashionable in England.—Discourse on the English government, published by Nathaniel Bacon.

1. In France, the *parlement* was a judicial body, growing out of the royal feudal courts.

2. The Domesday Book of 1086 was the result of a royal survey intended to collect information on the population and stock of each borough or village in the realm.

northern counties, and exclusive of the royal demesnes, had been distributed.* <87>

Notwithstanding the vassalage into which the barons had been reduced, their influence was but little impaired; and, though changed in outward appearance, they continued to maintain that authority which great landed estates will always procure. By the nature of their tenures, their property was not rendered <88> more precarious than formerly; but merely subjected to certain burdens or exactions in favour of the king. As vassals of the crown, their dependence upon it was even slighter than that of the inferior hereditary vassals upon their immediate superior; and from their number, their distance, and their vast opulence, the king was less able to retain them in subjection. Standing frequently in need of their support and assistance, he found it highly expedient to avoid their displeasure, to consult them in matters of a public nature, and to proceed with their approbation. In their new capacity, therefore, they still assumed the privilege of controlling the abuses of administration; and in directing the great machine of government, their

* The separate baronies in the different counties, including the lands in the crown demesne, amount in all to 1462. But as the same persons were often possessed of estates in many different counties, it is a matter of some labour to distinguish the exact number of separate proprietors. For example, the king himself held lands in every county except Shropshire.—Comes Moritoniensis possessed baronies in 20 counties.—Comes Eustachius, in 11.—Comes Rogerius, in 13.—Willelmus de Warenna, in 12.—Edwardus Sarisberiensis, in 9.—Willelmus filius Ansculfi, in 11.—Hunfridus Camerarius, in 9.—Comes Alanus, in 11.—Comes Hugo, in 21.—Ernulfus de Hesding, in 10.—Radulphus de Mortemer, in 13.—Episcopus Cantuarensis, in 8.—Episcopus Baiocensis, in 17.—Episcopus Wentoniensis in 11.—Abbatea Westmonasterii, in 14.—Episcopus Lincolcensis, in 9. [[Comes: count; Episcopus Cantuarensis: archbishop of Canterbury; Episcopus Baiocensis: bishop of Bayeux; Episcopus Wentoniensis: bishop of Winchester; Abbatea Westmonasterii: Westminster Abbey; Episcopus Lincolnensis: bishop of Lincoln.]]

After a pretty accurate scrutiny, it is believed the separate crown-vassals, recorded in doomsday-book, are not above 605, though they may possibly be one or two below that number. Of these, the ecclesiastical vassals, including the different sorts of religious societies, amount to about 140. It is to be observed, however, that some of these appear to have belonged to Normandy, though they possessed lands in England.

It is evident that the power and influence of the crown-vassals, in the reign of William the conqueror, must have been great in proportion to the smallness of their number, and the vast extent of their property.

power was little inferior to that which had formerly been possessed by the Wittenagemote.* <89>

The power of declaring peace and war was from this time, indeed, regarded as a branch of the royal prerogative. It was a principle inseparably connected with the feudal polity, <90> that the vassals of the king, as well as those of every subordinate baron, should be liable for military service to their liege lord, and should be ready to attend him in the field whenever he chose to call upon them. To determine the particular quarrels in which he should engage, and the military enterprises which he should undertake, was his province, not theirs; and, provided their attendance was not more burdensome than their duty required, it was understood to be a matter of indifference to them, against what enemy they should happen to be employed. The discretionary power, which came thus to be assumed by the king, as the great feudal superior of the kingdom, was, at the same time, supported by the consideration of its expediency. During the numerous invasions customary in the feudal times, it was necessary, upon any sudden emergency, that the leader of a barony should take his measures upon the spot; and that

* That parliaments were frequently held by William the conqueror, and by his son William Rufus, as well as by the succeeding monarchs, is indisputable. In the fourth year of William the conqueror, the laws of Edward the confessor were confirmed by a great national council. [R. Hoveden. Annal. Also Selden, Spicilegium in Eadmerum.] It is doubtful whether this was the same parliament which confirmed the collection of Edward the Confessor's laws, preserved by Ingulphus, the abbot of Croyland, and secretary to William the First. Selden, ibid.—Another parliament was held in 1070, for terminating a dispute between the archbishop of York and the bishop of Worcester.—*Coram rege et dorobuniae archiepiscop. Lanfranco, et episcopis abbatibus, comitibus, et primatibus, totius Angliae.* [["In the presence of the king, Lanfranc, archbishop of Canterbury, and the bishops, abbots, and noblemen of all England."]] Dr Brady's Tracts.—Another parliament is mentioned in 1084, for changing the canons of Durham into Monks—*Praesentibus omnibus episcopis et baronibus meis.* [["In the presence of all my bishops and barons." See Brady, *An Introduction to the Old English History* (London, 1684), appendix, 54.]] Ibid.—See also in the same author, the instances of national councils convened by William Rufus.

The whole territory of England not having been united as the feudal barony of the king, till near the end of the Conqueror's reign, his parliament or baron-court could not, before this period, be properly invested with an authority over the whole kingdom. It is probable, however, that this circumstance was overlooked; and that, as a great part of the nobility, soon after the conquest, were become vassals of the crown, they were called, in that capacity, to the national council; while others, who still retained their allodial property, might be willing perhaps, without regarding the difference of their situation, to join in the deliberations of that assembly.

without consulting his vassals, he should proceed to repel the enemy by force of arms. To call a council, in such a case, would be to lose the critical moment; to waste, in deliberation, the proper season for action; and, for the sake <91> of a punctilio, to involve the whole community in utter destruction.

This may be accounted the chief difference between the Anglo-Saxon and the Anglo-Norman government. In the former, the power of making peace and war was invariably possessed by the Wittenagemote, and was regarded as inseparable from the allodial condition of its members. In the latter, it was transferred to the sovereign: and this branch of the feudal system, which was accommodated, perhaps, to the depredations and internal commotions prevalent in that rude period, has remained in after ages, when, from a total change of manners, the circumstances, by which it was recommended, have no longer any existence.

The legislative power was viewed in a different light. New regulations generally took their origin from a complaint of grievances, made to the sovereign, the great executor of the law, and accompanied with a request, that, in the future administration of government, they might be redressed. The privilege of preferring such petitions, or at least that of de-<92>manding a positive answer to them from the sovereign, was anciently appropriated to the Wittenagemote; and, upon the dissolution of that assembly, was devolved upon the Anglo-Norman parliament. In every subordinate barony into which the kingdom was divided, the vassals exercised a similar privilege with respect to the conduct of their own superior. A public statute was, according to this practice, a sort of paction or agreement between the king and his vassals, by which, at their desire, he promised to observe a certain rule of conduct; and in which, therefore, the consent of both was clearly implied. No such rule was ever thought of without the previous request of parliament, nor was it ever effectual to bind the parties, unless the sovereign acceded to the proposal.

The supreme distribution of justice was likewise a matter of such consequence as to require the interposition of the crown-vassals; and therefore constituted another privilege of the Anglo-Norman Parliament. How this branch of business came, in ordinary cases, to be devolved upon an inferior court, with re-<93>servation of an ultimate controlling power in the parliament, will be the subject of a separate inquiry.

Taxation is properly a branch of the legislative power; since every rule that is made, with respect to the payment of taxes, is a law which directs and limits the future administration of government. This branch of legislation is in itself of greater importance, and it is more likely to be abused, than any other; because every member in the community has an interest to avoid all public bargains, and to roll them over upon his neighbours; while the chief executive officer, or whoever has the management and disposal of the revenue, is interested to squeeze as much as he can from the people. We may easily suppose, therefore, that as the vassals of the crown, after the Norman conquest, assumed the ordinary exercise of the legislative power, they would not be disposed to relinquish that peculiar branch of it, which consisted in the imposition of taxes; and there is, accordingly, no reason to doubt, that, as far as it could exist in that period, the power of taxation was immediately transferred <94> from the Wittenagemote of the Saxons to the Anglo-Norman parliament.

But in that age, there was little occasion for exercising this power; few taxes being then, directly at least and avowedly, imposed upon the nation. The chief support of the crown was derived from a revenue independent of the people; and when additional supplies became requisite, they were obtained, either by means of a private bargain, for a valuable consideration; or under the mask of a gift or voluntary contribution.

At a period when mercenary armies were unknown, and when the administration of justice, instead of being a burden upon the crown, was the source of emolument, the royal demesnes, which, after the accession of William the first, became prodigiously extensive, together with the profits of amerciaments and fines, and the common feudal rents and incidents arising from the estates of crown-vassals, were fully sufficient to maintain the dignity of the sovereign, and to defray the ordinary expence of government. This ancient revenue, however, was gradually improved, according to the <95> increasing charges of government, by the addition of *scutages, hydages,* and *talliages.*

The first were pecuniary compositions paid by the crown-vassals, in place of their military service; and, being settled, in each case, by a stipulation between the parties, had no resemblance to what is properly called a tax. It was always in the power of the vassal to insist upon such terms, with respect to this composition, as he judged expedient, or to avoid the payment of it altogether, by performing the service for which he was originally bound. The sum paid was a voluntary commutation: and therefore it must be understood that he who paid it thought himself a gainer by the bargain.

Hydages were due by the soccage-vassals of the crown; who, beside their constant yearly rent to their superior, were bound to supply him with carriages, and to perform various kinds of work. As these were, by their nature, somewhat indefinite, they came to be frequently exacted by the crown-officers in an oppressive manner; and, when the vassal rose to a degree of wealth and independence, he was willing to exchange them for a pecuniary <96> payment, which might, at the same time, yield more profit to the crown. Of this payment the extent was originally fixed, like that of the scutage, by an agreement in each case between the parties.

Talliages were paid, in like manner, by the inhabitants of towns in the king's demesne. As the king protected his boroughs, and bestowed upon them various privileges, with respect to their manufactures, so he levied from them such tolls and duties as they were able to bear. According as those communities became opulent and flourishing, their duties were multiplied, and rendered more troublesome and vexatious; from which it was at length found convenient that they should be converted into a regular pecuniary assessment.*

The trade of the country, however inconsiderable, became also the means of procuring some revenue to the sovereign. Persons engaged in this employment, standing in need of the protection of government, and being also frequently destitute of conveniencies for trans-<97>porting and vending their goods, were not only protected, but even sometimes provided with warehouses, and with measures and weights, by the king; who, in return, demanded from them, either a part of their commodity, or some other payment suited to the nature of the benefit which they had received. A similar payment was demanded by the king upon the passage of goods from one port of the kingdom to another. To the duties which came thus to be established by long usage, was given the appellation of *customs.* Having arisen from the demands of one party, and the acquiescence of the other, they were in reality founded upon a sort of stipulation or mutual agreement.

When all these branches of revenue proved insufficient, the king upon any extraordinary exigence applied for an *aid,* or general contribution from his vassals. We find that aids are enumerated among the feudal incidents; but, exclusive of the three cases formerly mentioned, whatever was

* The name of talliage is frequently extended to every pecuniary contribution levied by the superior from his vassals.

contributed in this manner, appears to have been regarded in the light of a free gift; and, according to this view, came afterwards to be denominated a *benevolence*.[3]

Though none of those duties, which were <98> levied by the express or implied consent of parties, could with propriety be considered as taxes, they became in reality the source of much oppression and injustice. It was dangerous to refuse the sovereign, even when he demanded a thing to which he had no right. It was difficult to make an equal bargain with a person so greatly superior in power and influence. By adhering strictly to their privileges, and by incurring the resentment of the king, the people subjected to those impositions might be utterly ruined; and were, on every occasion, likely to lose much more than the value of what was demanded from them. When the abuses, however, of which the crown was guilty in relation to these exactions, had risen to a certain height, they became the subject of general complaint, and attracted the notice of the legislature. Scutages, payable by the military vassals of the crown, came to be fixed by parliament, of which those vassals were members. After the soccage tenants and the burgesses had acquired a degree of opulence, the same rule was extended to the hydages, and talliages, levied from those two orders of men. The aids, demanded promiscuously from all the different <99> sorts of crown vassals, came to be regulated by the same authority.* The customs, originally of little importance, were, by the gradual extension of trade, and the increasing demands of the crown, brought likewise into public view, and acquired such magnitude as to occasion the interposition of parliament. By a statute in the reign of Edward the first, it is provided that those duties shall not be levied without the "common assent of the realm."†

With respect to the manner of convening the national council, it was not immediately varied by the Norman conquest. The parliament, from the accession of William the First, was held, like the Wittenagemote in the Saxon times, either according to ancient usage, at the three stated festivals of Christmas, Easter, and Whitsuntide, or, upon particular exigencies, by virtue of a summons from the king. By degrees, however, the occasional meetings ex-

* With regard to aids, and scutages, this provision is made in the charter of king John, § 12. The statutes 25 Edward I. c. 5, 6. and 34 Edward I. contain the same regulation with respect to aids and talliages.

† 25 Edw. I. c. 7.

3. A forced contribution levied by the kings of England on their subjects.

tended the subjects of their deliberation; while, <100> on the other hand, the regular customary assemblies were frequently prevented by the disorderly state of the country. In the war between the empress Matilda and king Stephen,[4] they met with great interruptions, and from the beginning of the convulsions in the reign of king John, were entirely discontinued. The power of calling parliaments, and consequently of putting a negative upon its meetings, was thus in all cases devolved upon the sovereign.*

From these particulars, it is evident, that the English monarchs, after the Norman conquest, were far from possessing an absolute authority; and that the constitution, notwithstanding the recent exaltation of the crown, still retained a considerable proportion of the preceding aristocracy.[5] As the national council, composed of the nobility or great proprietors of land, was invested with the legislative power, including that of imposing taxes, and with the power of distributing justice in the last resort,[6] it enjoyed, of course, the right of controlling and directing the sovereign in the most important parts of administration. <101>

From the state of the revenue, indeed, in that period, the executive power was under less restraint from the legislature than it has become in later ages. As the king had seldom occasion to solicit a supply from parliament, he was the less liable to be questioned about the disposal of his income. The people, who gave nothing to the public magistrate for defraying the expence of government, had but little incitement or pretence, either to find fault with his oeconomy, or to require a strict account of his management. He managed the revenue of the kingdom, as other individuals were accustomed to manage their own estates; and the idea of a public officer, or magistrate, was apt to be sunk in that of an ordinary proprietor, to whom the crown, and the revenues connected with it, have been transmitted like a private inheritance.

It must at the same time be admitted, that abuses in the exercise of the executive power were then extremely frequent, and were often suffered to pass without animadversion or notice. The legislature had too little experience, to provide regulations for preventing the numerous instances of malversation in office that <102> were likely to occur; judicial establishments

* Gurdon's History of Parliament.

4. The civil war continued, to a greater or lesser extent, 1139–47.

5. Millar recalls here his division of English history into three periods, the first two of which were feudal aristocracy and feudal kingship. See p. 9, note 1.

6. A tribunal having final authority; the last court to which appeal can be made.

had not yet attained such perfection as might enable them with quickness to punish the several violations of justice; nor had long usage established those equitable maxims of government, which are the common effects of polished manners, and which often supply the place of positive institutions. The conduct of the sovereign, therefore, and even that of inferior officers, in the ordinary course of administration, was in a great measure discretionary; and was no otherwise restrained, than by the fear of exciting general clamour and disturbance. But individuals might sustain much oppression before their complaints were likely to excite attention, and might be disposed, from prudential considerations, to submit to many injuries and inconveniencies, rather than contend against the whole force of the crown. In this disorderly state of society, persons who preferred any request to the king, or who had even any claim of right, in which his interest was concerned, were commonly induced to secure his favour by a present, or, if you will, by a bribe. A numerous list of those presents, which were made to the sovereign, in order to <103> procure what was barely justice, has been collected by different authors, with a view of demonstrating the despotical nature of the Anglo-Norman government. But these instances tend only to prove the frequency of abuses, from the want of a regular polity, extending to all the departments of administration. They shew that the government was rude and imperfect, and therefore in many cases arbitrary; not that it was an absolute monarchy: that the national council was negligent and unskilful in restraining disorders; not that it was destitute of authority to limit the prerogative. This is what happens in the infancy of every political system, whatever be the peculiar plan upon which it is formed. The strong find themselves often at liberty to oppress the weak; persons of inferior station are therefore obliged to shelter themselves under the wings of a superior; and are glad to obtain, by solicitation or bribery, the quiet exercise of those rights which they are unable to maintain by any other means.

What puts this observation in a clear light is, that the abuses of the executive power, which were so frequent in the early periods of <104> the English constitution, have since been removed by the gradual improvement of arts, and the correspondent progress of manners, without any considerable change in the distribution of the great powers of government. The outlines of the English constitution are not very different, at this day, from what they were in the reign of William the Conqueror; but the powers which were then universally acknowledged, have been since more minutely applied to the detail of administration; and the variations, that have occurred in the modes of living, and in the condition of individuals, have been gradually accommodated to the spirit of the old institutions. The experience of the nation has led them to fill up the picture, of which a rude sketch was delineated in that early period. <105>

CHAPTER III

Of the ordinary Courts of Justice after the Norman Conquest.

The distribution of justice, in the last resort, was not the most brilliant or conspicuous, though it was, undoubtedly, one of the most useful departments belonging to the national council. During the latter part of the Anglo-Saxon government, this branch of business was commonly devolved upon occasional meetings of the Wittenagemote; which being called for discussing matters of inferior concern, were seldom attended by any other members than such as happened, at the time, to be retained about the king's person. But, after the Norman conquest, the changes which have been mentioned in the state of the country, contributed to produce farther alterations in the judicial establishments; and particularly, to divest more entirely the public assembly of the ordinary cognizance of lawsuits. By the completion of the feudal system in France, the administration of justice in that <106> country attained a degree of regularity which was formerly unknown; and upon the accession of William the First, to the English throne, the improvements in this branch of policy, which had been extended to Normandy, at that time a part of the French dominions, were gradually introduced into Britain. As the several districts of the kingdom, which had formerly been distracted by the feuds of their independent leaders, came now to be united under the feudal superiority of the crown, the decision of private quarrels by the sword was more effectually restrained; while the vigour and influence, possessed by the two first princes of the Norman race, co-operated with the natural progress of society in bringing the differences among all the inhabitants under the determination of the magistrate. From the consequent multiplication of appeals to parliament, the members of that assembly became daily less disposed to execute this part of their duty; at the same time that, from the increasing authority of the crown, their attendance was rendered proportionably less necessary. The number of crown-vassals, convened on such occasions, was therefore gradually diminished; <107> the absence of others was more and more overlooked; and at length there was formed, out of parliament, a regular tribunal, for the sole purpose of deciding law-suits, and composed of an arbitrary number of those persons who sat in the greater assembly. The great officers of the crown, being always upon the spot, whenever a meeting of this kind was called, became its ordinary constituent members; and to these were added by the king particular persons, who, from their knowledge of law, or experience in business, were thought qualified to assist in the inferior departments of office.* <108>

This court, from the place in which it was commonly held, received the appellation of the *aula regis.*[1] In its constitution and origin, it corresponded

* Account of this tribunal in Madox's History of Exchequer. The great officers of the king's court are made by this author to be seven in number. 1. The chief justicier. 2. The constable. 3. The mareschall. 4. The seneschall or dapifer. 5. The chamberlain. 6. The chancellor. 7. The treasurer. Of these the chief justicier was originally the seneschal or high-steward. But when the primitive high-steward, who had been the chief officer of the family, came to be possessed of great ministerial powers over the whole kingdom, a deputy was appointed to manage the affairs of the household, who acquiring high rank and authority, received the appellation of seneschall, or *steward of the household,* as the other was called the *steward of the kingdom.* The subordinate appointment of a steward of the household, or *comes palatii,* [[count palatine]] is also to be found in France, Germany, and other feudal countries. [[Thomas Madox, *The History and Antiquities of the Exchequer* (London, 1711). See especially chap. 3 (56–104), which outlines the origins of the King's Court as a place to hear pleas. Sec. 6 (65–67) outlines the kinds of complaints which would have been heard in this court.]]

The office of constable, or chief groom, had come in England, as well as upon the continent, to be divided into two branches, that of the constable and marshal; or of the groom and the smith, or farrier.

The seneschal and dapifer ought, in all probability, to have been distinguished; as in France, and of course in Normandy, the offices of steward, and butler, or cup-bearer, had been long separated.

The treasurer is supposed to have been originally the deputy of the high-steward.—But in later times was more probably that of the chamberlain, who came to have the principal charge of the revenue.

See an account of the rank and employment of these officers, in that branch of the king's court which had the management of the revenue, in the *Dialogus de Scacario,* published by Madox, from the *black* and the *red books of Exchequer.*

1. See p. 190, note 3.

exactly with the *cour de roy,* which, after the accession of Hugh Capet, was gradually formed out of the ancient parliament of France; and with the *aulic council,* which, after the time of Otho the Great, arose, in like manner, out of the diet of the German <109> empire. In Scotland we meet with a court of the same nature; and there is reason to believe that, in every European kingdom of considerable extent, the progress of the feudal system gave rise to a similar institution. In all these countries, as well as in England, it appears probable, that this tribunal was detached from the national council by connivance rather than by any positive appointment; from a disposition in the people to consult their own ease and conveniency, more than from any design upon the part of the crown to limit their privileges; in short, from no preconceived plan of altering the constitution, but from a natural and obvious accommodation to the circumstances of the community; and from an immediate prospect of advantage, by facilitating the distribution of justice. As this tribunal, therefore, has been formed in a slow and gradual manner, it seems difficult, in any of the countries above-mentioned, to ascertain the precise date of its formation. In England, the institution of the *aula regis* is commonly ascribed to William the Conqueror; but this must be understood with relation to the first appearance of that court, as distinct from the <110> greater meeting of parliament, and not with respect to the subsequent variations and improvements which preceded its complete establishment.

This court was held by the English monarchs, not only in their most usual place of residence, but wherever they happened to be, when there was found occasion for its interposition. It had the same extent of jurisdiction with parliament, out of which it had grown; and therefore obtained the cognizance of all ordinary law-suits, whether civil, criminal, or fiscal.

The king himself presided in the *aula regis,* whenever he thought proper to sit there as a judge; but the ordinary president of this court was the lord high steward,[2] the principal officer of the crown; who, in rank and authority, had risen to be the second person in the kingdom; and upon whom the king,

2. The lord high steward of England ranks as the first of the great officers of state. The household of the Norman and Plantagenet kings of England included certain persons of secondary rank who were entrusted with domestic and state duties. At coronations and festivals, however, it became the custom in England and elsewhere to appoint magnates of the first rank to discharge for the occasion the domestic functions of the ordinary officials.

when absent from parliament, had likewise devolved the right of presiding in that assembly.* <111>

For some time after this tribunal had been separated from the meetings of parliament, it still consisted of all the great officers of the crown; but according as, by the gradual extension of its authority, it had occasion to sit more frequently, the attendance even of the greater part of these members was rendered more useless, as well as inconvenient; and therefore became the less regular. The king, at the same time, acquiring higher notions of his own dignity, or finding himself more engaged in the other departments of government, ceased also to exercise the ordinary functions of a judge; so that the high steward became in a manner the sole magistrate of the *aula regis;* and, from this most conspicuous branch of power annexed to his office, was denominated the *grand justiciary.*† <112>

While the judicial authority of parliament was thus delegated to another

* When the members of this court transacted civil and criminal pleas, they sat in the hall of the king: when they acted as a court of revenue, they sat in the Exchequer. Dial. de Scacario. Baron Gilbert's Hist. of Chancery.

† That the grand justiciary of England was originally the high steward, appears indisputable. 1. That the high steward, or *maire of the palace,* in France, was anciently the officer of the crown who acquired the highest dignity and authority over the kingdom, is universally admitted. 2. In Normandy a similar officer, appointed by the duke, appears to have been chief justiciar throughout the dutchy. See Coustumier du Normandie. 3. From the black and red books of Exchequer, there is distinct evidence that Robert earl of Leicester, who, in the reign of Henry the Second, was the high steward, had also the office of *grand justiciary. Non solum ad scacarium verum per universum regnum PRESIDENTIS dignitatem obtinuit.* [["He held the office of president not only at the Exchequer, but also throughout the whole kingdom."]] The author of this account was a cotemporary, who says he saw the great officer whom he speaks of. 4. That the high steward had by his office the right of presiding over the king's privy counsellors, and over all the officers and ministers of justice in the kingdom, appears also from an old manuscript, intitled, *Quis sit Seneschallus Angliae, et quid ejus officum* [["The identity of the Lord High Steward of England and the nature of his office."]], quoted by Sir Robert Cotton and other antiquaries, whose researches upon this subject are preserved in Hearne's Collection.—See the facts collected by these authors—also Spelm. Gloss. v. Justiciarius Capitalis.

It is true, that among the English historians and antiquaries there is some confusion in the accounts given of the persons who held the office of high steward and of justiciary. This seems to have arisen partly from the difficulty of distinguishing the old high steward from his original deputy the steward of the household; and partly from the occasional appointments made by the sovereign of persons to preside in particular trials, who have been mistaken for permanent justiciaries. This last seems to be the great source of error in Madox. 5. That the high steward was anciently the president over the king's judges, and even of the high court of parliament, is further confirmed by the privilege of that officer, when created, in later times, to preside in the house of lords.

court, the king exercised the chief parts of the executive power, by the assistance of a *privy-council,*[3] composed <113> of such barons as enjoyed his particular favour and confidence. Some institution of this nature had probably existed, at least occasionally, during the reigns of the later Saxon princes; but, after the Norman conquest, when the prerogative was considerably exalted, the privy-council, of consequence, rose in dignity, and its interpositions became proportionably more extensive. The members of this meeting, it is probable, were nearly the same persons who, from their employment about the king's person, had usually been called to sit in the *aula regis,* after it came to be separated from the greater meeting of parliament; and even when the king and his privy-counsellors had devolved the ordinary business of that court upon a single magistrate, they still retained the cognizance of such extraordinary causes, both civil and criminal, as more immediately excited their attention. Of the causes which came, in this manner, to be determined by the king and his <114> privy-council, and were at length, by custom, appropriated to that court, there were three different sorts.

1. When a crime was committed, for the punishment of which the common law had made no proper provision, it was thought expedient, that the criminal should not be permitted to escape from justice; but that he should be called before this extraordinary tribunal, and punished according to the nature of his offence. From the meetings of the privy-council, which gave a decision in such uncommon and singular cases, there was formed, in after times, a regular jurisdiction, known by the name of the *star chamber.**

From the nature of things, it was to be expected, that this jurisdiction

* Concerning the origin of the name of star-chamber, and the original nature of that court, see Sir Thomas Smith de Repub. Angl.—Lamb. Arch.—Blackstone's Comment.—The nature of the jurisdiction anciently possessed by the star chamber, may be conceived from the sort of offences concerning which that court is directed to enquire, by the statutes 3 Henry VII. c. 1. and 21 Henry VIII. c. 20. See Coke's Inst. [[The Star Chamber was the ancient meeting place of the king of England's counselors in the palace of Westminster in London, so called because of stars painted on the ceiling. The court of the Star Chamber developed from the judicial proceedings traditionally carried out by the king and his council, and was entirely separate from the common-law courts of the day. On its origin and abolition, Millar refers to Sir Thomas Smith, *De Republica Anglorum* (London, 1583), 94–97; and Sir William Blackstone, *Commentaries on the Laws of England,* 4 vols. (London, 1765–69). See, for example, 1:131, 259–60 and 4:263–64, 422–23.]]

3. The private counselors selected by the sovereign, together with certain persons who are members by usage, as the princes of the blood, the archbishops, and the chief officers of the present and past ministers of state.

would soon degenerate into tyranny and oppression. The procedure of the court, as it related to matters <115> in which no rule had been established, was, of course, discretionary and fluctuating: at the same time that the causes which might come before it, under pretence of not being properly regulated by common law, were capable of being multiplied without end: not to mention, that, as the members of this court were created and removed at pleasure by the king, so the decisions, whenever he chose to interfere, depended entirely upon his will. These objections, however, to the jurisdiction of the star-chamber, which appear so well founded, and which, in a future period, occasioned the abolition of that court, were not likely to be suggested upon its first establishment, when its interpositions, we may suppose, were few, and limited to cases of great necessity, and when the simplicity of the age was more disposed to regard the immediate benefit arising from any measure, than to consider the distant consequences of which, as a matter of precedent, it might possibly be productive.

2. In civil questions, the rules of common law, which had been gradually established by judges in order to avoid reflections, and to prevent inconsistency of conduct, were sometimes <116> found so extremely defective as to lay the court under the disagreeable necessity, either of refusing justice to individuals, or of pronouncing an improper decision. The king and his privy-council, upon the same principle which led them to interfere in extraordinary crimes, were induced to hear the complaints of persons who had suffered injustice from the rude and imperfect system of jurisprudence adopted by the grand justiciary; and to afford them relief by a decision according to conscience or natural equity. The interpositions derived from this source, becoming numerous, and being often attended with some difficulty, were put more immediately under the direction of the chancellor; who, as the king's secretary, was usually a man of some literature; and who, having become the clerk, or keeper of the records of the *aula regis,* was particularly conversant in matters of law, and qualified to decide in such nice and intricate cases. In what manner the decisions of this officer, who acted at first with the assistance of a committee of privy-counsellors, gave rise to the jurisdiction of the *court of chancery,* will fall more properly to be considered hereafter. <117>

3. When the Christian clergy had acquired an extensive authority and jurisdiction in the western part of Europe, we find that, whatever censure they may deserve for the interested policy which they practised in other respects, they had the singular merit of endeavouring every where to repress

the disorder and injustice arising from the anarchy of the feudal times. The weak and defenceless, who met with insult and oppression from every other quarter, found protection from the church; and the causes of widows and orphans, and of all persons in circumstances of distress,* which had been banished from the barbarous tribunal of the lay-judges, procured a welcome reception in the spiritual court; where they were commonly examined with candour, and determined with impartiality.

In imitation, as it should seem, of this ecclesiastical interposition, the king of England took under his immediate protection the causes of such as, by reason of their poverty, were unable to bear the expense of an ordinary law-suit; and, since no other court in the country <118> could give the proper redress, he encouraged those persons to bring a petition or supplication to the privy-council; which decided their claims in a summary manner, and without the forms observed in the ordinary tribunals. Hence particular persons being entrusted with this branch of business, composed at length a *court of requests,* as it was called; which, for a long time, had no warrant of ordinary jurisdiction; but which, as the complaints that came before it could not be accurately defined, assumed at length so great powers as to render it unpopular, and, in the reign of Charles the first,[4] to occasion its abolition.†

The influence of that humanity, displayed by the church, was not confined to England; but appears to have produced a similar interposition in the government of other European countries. In France it was anciently the custom to present petitions or complaints to the king at the gate of his palace; and, for the purpose of receiving and examining these, the king was early led to appoint certain persons belonging to his houshold. If any petition <119> was of too great consequence to be answered immediately by these commissioners, they were directed to make a report of it to the king, and to require the attendance of the parties, in order that the cause might be heard and determined. The persons appointed for the determination of such causes, who seem to have been members of the king's privy-council, were called *maistres des requestes de l'hostel du roy.*[5] Their number was increased to six, of which the one half were ecclesiastics; and they seem at length to

* *Personae miserabiles.* [[Wretched persons.]]

† Sir Tho. Smith de Repub. Anglor.—Blackstone's Comment.

4. Charles I (r. 1625–49).

5. Masters of requests of the royal household.

have been formed into a separate court, under the name of the *chamber of requests.**

The institution of the *aula regis,* or court of the grand justiciary, was a natural, and a very great improvement in the system of judicial policy. The great national council could not be very frequently convened, and its decisions, therefore, especially in matters of private property, were not easily procured. But the smaller tribunal of the *aula regis* was easily kept in readiness, to determine every controversy whether civil or criminal. As the king, amid the disorders of the feudal government, was under the necessity of making frequent <120> journies over the kingdom, in order to maintain his authority, and to suppress or prevent insurrections, he was enabled to receive, in every quarter, the complaints of his people, and found no difficulty in calling this court to give such redress as the occasion might require. Justice was made, in this manner, to pervade the country; reparation of injuries was rendered more certain, while the expence of litigation was diminished; and, by punishing crimes in the neighbourhood of those places where they had been committed, the axe and the halter became an immediate and powerful antidote to the poison of bad example.

From the decisions of this tribunal, there always lay an appeal to the high court of parliament. This was a consequence of the manner in which the *aula regis* was formed; by the mere disuse of attendance in the greater part of the members of parliament; who thence were understood to have delegated the ordinary judicial power to such of their number as continued in the exercise of it. But as this delegation was intended merely to save trouble to the members of parliament, it was not conceived to exclude a full meeting of that council from reviewing, in extraordinary cases the proce-<121>dure of the committee upon whom this ordinary jurisdiction had been devolved. Though parliament might wish to be disengaged from the labour attending the decision of law-suits, it was probably not willing to resign the authority connected with that employment; and, while it acquiesced in the substitution of a court for exercising the whole parliamentary jurisdiction in the first instance, it still reserved the power, which might be exerted on singular occasions, of superintending the proceedings of that court, and of controlling its decisions.

* Recherches de la France. D'Estienne Pasquier.

The *aula regis,* being a sort of deputation from the national council, or king's baron-court, had, on the other hand, a power of reviewing the sentences of the several tribunals erected in different parts of the kingdom; and became an intermediate court between them and the high court of parliament. There was the same reason for committing to the court of the grand justiciary, the province of hearing and discussing appeals from inferior tribunals, as for devolving upon it an original jurisdiction in parliamentary actions. The full establishment of this tribunal, however, together with the changes in the state of property after <122> the Norman conquest, contributed to limit the authority of these inferior courts, and to render their interposition of little importance.

When the great lords of a county had become vassals of the crown, they claimed the privilege of bringing their law-suits, in the first instance, before the baron-court of the sovereign, their immediate superior. To the same court were brought immediately, appeals from the sentences pronounced by these great lords in their own baron-courts. The sheriff, now converted into a crown vassal, beside the jurisdiction over his own feudal barony, appears to have still retained the power of deciding controversies between the *rear-vassals* or tenants belonging to different baronies within his county.

But the authority possessed by the *aula regis,* which was daily extended, from the increasing power of the crown, enabled that court even to make continual encroachments upon the subordinate jurisdiction of the sheriff and of the different barons. It could be of little advantage to the inhabitants, that their law-suits were brought in the first instance before the court of the baron or of the sheriff, since the <123> decision of those judges might, with the utmost facility, be reviewed by the court of the grand justiciary; and, as this great tribunal appeared occasionally in all parts of the kingdom, and distributed justice with superior efficacy and splendor, men were frequently disposed to pass over the inferior courts, and took encouragement to bring their disputes immediately before the court of appeal. Thus, by the gradual operation of the same circumstances, the judicatories of each barony, and county, dwindled into a state of insignificance; their jurisdiction was at length restricted to matters of small value; and the greater part of causes, civil and criminal, as well as fiscal, were appropriated to the ordinary baron-court of the sovereign.

Mr. Hume imagines, that none of the other feudal governments in Europe had such institutions as the county-courts; and seems to be of opinion, that as these courts, by requiring the frequent attendance of the barons, contributed to remind them of their dependence upon the king, they must have had remarkable effects in reducing those great personages under the authority of the chief magistrate. <124>

But the county-courts were so far from being peculiar to England, that they appear, in the early periods of the feudal system, to have existed throughout all the western parts of Europe. In France, and in several other countries upon the continent, those courts began sooner to lose their authority than in England; because the sovereign had sooner acquired a feudal superiority over the great lords: by which they were reduced under the immediate jurisdiction of the king's baron-court, and withdrawn from that of the chief officer of a county. In Scotland, on the other hand, where the influence of the crown over the nobles advanced more slowly than in England, the county-courts were enabled much longer to preserve their primitive jurisdiction; so that a considerable share of it has been transmitted to the present time, and become a permanent branch of the judicial polity.

It seems difficult, therefore, to suppose that the long continuance of the courts of the sheriff in England had any tendency to increase or maintain the authority of the king over the barons. The decay of those judicial <125> establishments appears, on the contrary, to have been a necessary consequence of a correspondent exaltation of the crown; and we shall find that, in every country, they remained longer in power and splendor, according as particular circumstances contributed to thwart the ambitious views of the monarch, and to prevent the extension of his prerogative.

In the dominions belonging to France the judicial power of the *cour de roy* advanced very quickly from the reign of Hugh Capet, by the disuse of the county courts, and by receiving appeals from the courts of the barons. These appeals, agreeable to the general custom of the feudal governments, contained at first a complaint that injustice had been committed by the inferior judge, who, therefore, was obliged to appear as a party, before the superior tribunal. But according as the practice of appealing became more frequent, the petitions of appeal were admitted upon slighter grounds; the charge of wilful injustice against the inferior courts was more and more overlooked; the magistrates who had presided in these courts, were no longer sufficiently interested to appear for the justification of their conduct; <126> and the controversy was examined in the court of review, for the sole purpose of determining the propriety or impropriety of the former decision.

It is true, that from the disorders which prevailed in France, under the later princes of the Carlovingian race,[6] one or two of the great lords had acquired such independence, as, for some time after the reign of Hugh Capet, prevented the king from reviewing their sentences; but this is mentioned by all the historians as a remarkable singularity. It also merits attention, that the French monarchs, about this period, were not content with the power of receiving appeals from the several courts of their barons. An expedient was devised of sending royal bailiffs into different parts of the kingdom, with a commission to take cognizance of all those causes in which the sovereign was interested, and in reality for the purpose of abridging and limiting the subordinate jurisdiction of the neighbouring feudal superiors. By an edict of Philip Augustus, in the year 1190, those bailiffs were appointed in all the principal towns of the kingdom.* <127>

* Hainault's Abridgment of Hist. of France.

6. The Carolingian dynasty. See p. 66, note 12.

CHAPTER IV

Progress of Ecclesiastical Jurisdiction and Authority.

The hierarchy of the western church grew up and extended itself over the kingdoms of Europe, independent of the boundaries which had been set to the dominion of secular princes, and of the revolutions which took place in the state of any civil government. The Roman pontiff, having found the means of uniting under his protection the clergy of each particular kingdom, was equally interested in promoting their influence, as they were in maintaining the authority of their spiritual leader. By taking advantage, therefore, of the various and successive contentions among opposite and rival powers, he was enabled to extort concessions from those whom he had supported, to levy impositions, and to exalt the dignity and prerogatives of the holy see.

The Norman conquest, in England, was followed by a complete separation of the <128> ecclesiastical from the temporal courts. By a regulation of William the Conqueror, the bishop was no longer permitted to sit as a judge in the court of the county, nor the rural dean in that of the hundred.* This alteration had undoubtedly a tendency to promote that exclusive jurisdiction which the clergy were desirous of establishing; and to build up that system of church power which the wisdom of after ages found it so necessary, and at the same time so difficult, to pull down. Under the dominion of the Anglo-Saxon princes, while the spiritual judges were associated with the civil magistrate, many causes of an ecclesiastical nature were brought under the cognizance of the temporal courts; and though, from the superior knowledge and address of churchmen, the decisions given by those tribunals might be apt, in some cases, to savour of a clerical spirit, there was little danger,

* William the Conqueror's charter, with advice of the national council. Spelman.

from this arrangement, that the church would become totally independent of the state. But from the moment that the clergy were excluded from a voice in the courts of the <129> hundred and of the county, ecclesiastical controversies were appropriated, in all cases, to the judicatories of the church; and the ambition of churchmen immediately excited them to extend their own peculiar jurisdiction, by invading that of the civil magistrate.

The encroachments made by the spiritual, upon the province of the temporal courts, were of a similar nature in England, and in all the other countries belonging to the Western church. The pretence for these encroachments was, the privilege of the clergy to inflict censure upon every irregularity, which could be considered as a *sin,* or an offence in the sight of God. Under this description every act of injustice, every violation of the laws of the land, was manifestly included; but the offences which in this view attracted more particularly the attention of churchmen were such, it may easily be conceived, as had an immediate connexion with their own interest, or with those religious observances from which their own dignity and importance were in some measure derived.

One of the first interpositions of the church, in a matter of civil jurisdiction, appears to <130> have been made with relation to *tythes,*[1] and other ecclesiastical revenues. Even after the rights of the clergy, in this particular, had received the sanction of public authority, they were not likely to meet with a vigorous and hearty support from the civil magistrate; and it was therefore considered by the church, as a matter of general concern, to render them effectual in the spiritual court.

The performance of testamentary bequests was viewed in a similar light. As in the exercise of their profession, the clergy were frequently employed about dying persons, and had almost the exclusive possession of all the literature of that ignorant age, they were usually consulted upon the making of testaments, and became the common witnesses to those deeds. It would be doing them injustice to say, that they neglected to avail themselves of that situation, for increasing the revenue of the respective corporations to which they belonged. With so great diligence and success did they perform this part of their duty, that few persons adventured to take a near prospect of a future state, without making considerable donations for *pious uses;* and the effect of in-<131>culcating the same doctrine, was at length rendered so universal,

1. On tithes, see p. 83, note 8.

that, in many countries of Europe, a great proportion of every personal estate was, without any testament, and in virtue of a tacit or presumed will of the proprietor, transferred, by the ordinary course of succession, to the church. Thus the clergy were not only the best qualified for explaining the will of the testator, but had besides a peculiar interest in the execution of it; and therefore, by their activity and vigilance, joined to the indifference and remissness of the civil tribunals, they found it not difficult, in questions of this nature, to acquire an exclusive jurisdiction.

From the same principle which recommended penances and mortifications as highly meritorious, the ministers of religion thought it incumbent upon them to censure and discourage all excesses in sensual pleasure; and in a particular manner to restrain every irregularity with respect to the intercourse of the sexes. The contract of marriage was therefore brought under their immediate inspection; and, as it came to be celebrated by a clergyman, and to be accompanied with religious forms and solemnities, was regarded as <132> a species of sacrament. Upon this account, every breach of the duties of marriage, every question with relation to its validity, or concerning the terms and conditions which were held compatible with that institution, became an object of ecclesiastical cognizance.

This branch of jurisdiction afforded, by degrees, a pecuniary revenue, which the clergy did not fail to improve. By the Roman law, which was at first adopted in ecclesiastical courts, marriage was prohibited between collateral relations in the second degree; that is, between brothers and sisters. This prohibition, comprehending those persons who usually were brought up in the same family, and who, unless their union had been entirely prevented, might be frequently exposed to the hazard of seduction, is founded upon manifest considerations of expediency. But no sooner was the church possessed of sufficient authority in this point, than, becoming dissatisfied with such a reasonable and salutary regulation, she thought proper to introduce a stricter discipline; and proceeded, by degrees, to prohibit the union of more distant relations; in so much that marriage between persons in the fourteenth <133> degree, according to the Roman computation, was at length declared illegal.* Not contented with preventing the intercourse of

* The fourteenth degree, according to the computation of the civilians, is equal to the seventh degree among the canonists; comprehending persons removed by seven generations from the common stock. To change the Roman method of counting kindred,

natural relations, the superstition of the age recommended, and the interested policy of the church ordained, a restraint of the same nature, in consequence of the spiritual connexion arising from baptism, between the person baptized and his godfathers and godmothers, as well as the clergyman by whom that sacrament was administered; and the marriage of those persons, together with their relations, as far as the fourteenth degree, was likewise forbidden. The number of people, thus prohibited from intermarrying, came to be so immense, that persons at liberty to form that union, at a time when relations were not, as at present, scattered over the world by the influence of <134> commerce, could seldom be found, at least among persons of rank, in the same quarter of a country, and hardly ever in the same circle of acquaintance.*

These regulations were intended merely for the purpose of levying contributions from the people; for, though marriages contracted within the forbidden degrees were null and void, the church assumed a power of dispensing with the law; and to such as were able to pay for it, with exception of parents and children, and some other very near relations, a dispensation, in most cases, was readily granted.

By this jurisdiction with relation to testaments, and with relation to the validity of marriage, the church decided the most important questions concerning the transmission <135> of property. She possessed the sole power of determining the legitimacy of children, upon which depended their capacity of inheritance; at the same time that she gave authority to the nomination of every person who succeeded to an estate by the *will* of the proprietor.

Amid the disorders which prevailed in Europe for many centuries after the downfal of the Roman Empire, and by which the inhabitants were sunk

---

was the first contrivance of the clergy in the dark ages, for extending the laws of ancient Rome with respect to the relations prohibited from contracting marriage. [[For Blackstone's calculation of the number of relations which may exist in different degrees of consanguinity, see *Commentaries on the Laws of England,* 4 vols. (London, 1765–69), 1:202–8.]]

* Blackstone in his Comment. vol. ii. calculates the number of relations which may, at an average, exist in different degrees of consanguinity; by which it appears, that every person may have at least 16,000, in the 14th degree, according to the Roman computation, not to mention such as are a step or two nearer, who may be living at the same time; and of *spiritual relations,* in consequence of baptism, he may have three or four times as many more.

in profound ignorance and barbarism, the clergy exerted themselves in restraining the perfidy and injustice of the times; and, by the influence of religious motives, endeavoured, as far as possible, to induce mankind to the observance of good faith in their various transactions. For this purpose they introduced a general practice, that contracts of every sort should be confirmed by the sanction of an oath; by which means the violation of a contract, being considered as the breach of a religious duty, fell under the cognizance of the church. From the strictness observed in the decisions of the spiritual court, the private party, at the same time, found it more adviseable to bring his complaint before this tribunal than that of the civil magistrate. <136> The extent of jurisdiction, acquired in this manner may easily be conceived.

Lastly. To the church courts were appropriated, as I formerly had occasion to observe, the causes of widows and orphans, and of all persons in circumstances of distress. Causes of this description were too apt to be neglected by those military barons invested with civil jurisdiction, who paid but little attention to the claims of any person from whose future services they could derive no benefit, or from whose resentment they had nothing to fear.

It must be remembered, to the honour of the clergy of those times, that they were the friends of order and regular government; that, if they laboured to rear a system of ecclesiastical despotism, their authority was generally employed in maintaining the rules of justice; and that they discovered a uniform inclination to protect the weak and defenceless, against that violence and oppression which was too much countenanced by such of the laity as were possessed of opulence and power. From this circumstance, the extensions of ecclesiastical jurisdiction were highly acceptable to the people; and, notwithstanding the pernicious <137> consequences which they ultimately tended to produce, were, in the mean time, of great advantage to the lower ranks of men, if not of general benefit to the community.

Having thus occasion to determine a multitude of causes, both of an ecclesiastical nature, and such as fell within the province of the civil magistrate, the church courts advanced in the knowledge and experience of judicial business. As, by their literature, the clergy could not fail to be acquainted with the ancient Roman law, they were led, in many cases, to adopt the rules of that equitable system: Their own decisions were collected, in order to serve as precedents in future questions; and from these, together with the opinions of learned fathers in the church, the decrees of councils, and regulations of popes, was at length formed that body of canon-law,[2] which obtained universal reputation in the western part of Europe.

It would have been to little purpose, however, for the church to assume a jurisdiction, had she not been able to render herself independent in the exercise of it. But the same vigour and dexterity, by which the clergy established their power in any European king-<138>dom, were exerted in order to withdraw their subjection from the sovereign, and to render them subordinate only to the Roman pontiff. In England this was, in some measure, effected so early as the reign of William the conqueror, by the expedient of appointing papal legates, or commissioners, to hear and determine ecclesiastical causes. As those appointments might be renewed at pleasure, they soon opened the way for a direct appeal from the English church-courts to that of Rome; which was first attempted in the reign of William Rufus, and finally accomplished in that of king Stephen.*

The entire exemption of churchmen, or *clerks,* from secular jurisdiction, which had been early introduced into some other European countries, and which appears to be a natural consequence of the advancement of ecclesiastical power, was, in England, made effectual about the time of Henry the second. The effects of this exemption, which have, in some measure, been retained in later ages, are universally known by what is called the *benefit of* <139> *clergy.* As the church-courts never inflicted a capital or corporal punishment, those offenders, who could be subjected to no other jurisdiction, were of course exempted from such punishment, unless in some few cases, where the church might refuse her interposition, or was pleased to deliver over the criminal to the secular arm. After the reformation, this privilege of clerks, which, by the progress of literature,[3] came to be within the reach of almost all the inhabitants, was looked upon as a convenient method for moderating the rigorous punishments of the common law; and therefore, with various modifications by statute, was then incorporated in the legal system.

* Burne's Ecclesiastical Law.

2. In the Roman Catholic Church, the body of law based on the legislation of the councils and the popes, as well as the bishops. It is the law of the church courts and is distinguished from other parts of ecclesiastical law, such as liturgical law.

3. The diffusion of literacy, by which increasing numbers of persons could claim to be clerics—regarded as having a monopoly on reading—and therefore enjoy the benefit of clergy.

In the reign of Henry the first, the monastic rule of celibacy, after long and violent struggles, was at length imposed upon the secular clergy of England; and received the sanction of ecclesiastical authority.* By this regulation, churchmen, being freed from the cares of a family, and from the burden of making a provision for posterity, were detached, in a great measure, from the rest of the community, and, by motives of interest and ambition, were more <140> uniformly and firmly united in that ecclesiastical corporation of which they were members. Though it may be true, therefore, that this absurd system of mortification was introduced from perverted notions of refinement, and by the universal influence of superstition, there can be no doubt that it was afterwards promoted and extended from the interested policy of churchmen, and more especially from that of their spiritual sovereign.

But the great circumstance which contributed to establish the independent power of the church, was the privilege of bestowing ecclesiastical preferments.[4]

Upon the first establishment of ecclesiastical benefices, by the donation of dying persons, and the consequent rise of ecclesiastical dignities, the inferior clergy of each diocese were chosen by the bishop and chapter, and the bishop himself, by the dean and chapter of the cathedral church. After the modern European kingdoms had been erected upon the ruins of the ancient Roman Empire, the sovereign, in each of those kingdoms, was tempted to interfere in ecclesiastical elections, and, by his influence over those who had the power of nomination, <141> acquired at length the privilege of bestowing the higher church livings. But when the authority of the bishop of Rome had risen to a great height in the western church, he left no measure unattempted, in order to wrest out of the hands of princes an instrument of so much importance as the nomination of the superior clergy. The dispute concerning this point, which lasted for more than a century and a half, is one of the most remarkable events in the history of modern Europe.[5] It was

* Lyttelton's Hist. of Henry II.

4. The right to appoint candidates for ecclesiastical offices.

5. Late in the eleventh century, the struggle concerning clerical investiture broke out largely due to the divergence between Pope Gregory VII (1073–85) and Emperor Henry IV (r. 1056–1106). At that time, there was no general agreement as to the powers of the papacy and the Holy Roman Emperor in installing German bishops: it was only generally

begun by the famous Gregory the seventh; a man who, by his abilities, his intrepidity, and his unbounded ambition, was qualified to draw the utmost advantage from the situation in which he was placed. This pontiff not only rejected with disdain the prerogative which the German emperors had for some time exercised, of confirming the election of the popes, but prohibited them from interfering in the election of all bishops and abbots; and proceeded so far as to issue decrees, by which he excluded the laity, of every rank or condition, from the collation to ecclesiastical benefices. Henry the fourth, who at this time wore the imperial diadem, defended his rights with vigour; and, <142> as many princes were, by various motives, induced to support the interest of the church, the contending parties had recourse to arms. During the progress of the quarrel, all Italy and Germany were thrown into convulsions; millions of people were destroyed upon the one side and the other; and it is computed that no less than sixty battles were fought in the reign of this emperor; together with eighteen more in that of his son and successor, Henry the fifth, who at length was persuaded to conclude a peace with the court of Rome, by granting an express renunciation of all his pretensions.*

The contest, with respect to the right of investitures, was not confined to Italy and Germany, but extended itself over the other countries of Europe; in which the church, for the most part, was equally successful. In France, the decrees of the pope were made effectual with less rapidity; but without violence, and even without much disturbance. In England, the right of the laity to confer ecclesiastical benefices, was first disputed in the reign of Henry the first, when Anselm,[6] the archbishop <143> of Canterbury, refused to consecrate the bishops nominated by the king. The controversy was continued under several of the succeeding princes; but no blood was spilt in the quarrel, farther than by the assassination of Becket, or than what might arise from the scourging of Henry the second.[7] In this kind of warfare, the church was properly in her own element; and managed her weapons with her usual dexterity. When king John had been weakened by an unsuccessful war, and

recognized that both had rights in the matter, touching off the controversy. Henry was succeeded as emperor by his son, Henry V (r. 1106–25).

* Father Paul's History of Benefices.

6. St. Anselm (1033–1109): archbishop of Canterbury from 1093.

7. See p. 220, note 21.

had incurred the contempt and resentment of his subjects, the pope laid hold of that opportunity to invade his prerogative; and, by thundering out against him the different orders and degrees of ecclesiastical censure, at the same time that he had the address to employ the secular arm of France to support his authority, he at length obliged the infatuated English monarch, not only to relinquish all claim to the right of investitures, but even to resign his kingdom to the church, and to hold it for the future as a feudatory of the holy see.

It could hardly be expected that the pope would engage in such long and violent struggles for the sake merely of the clergy over whom <144> he presided, and that when he had at last gained a complete victory, he would not endeavour to improve it to his own advantage. No sooner was the nomination of bishops and abbots placed in the clergy of each cathedral church or monastery, than his holiness began to interfere in elections, by recommending particular persons to vacant benefices. Considering the influence and authority which he possessed over all the members of the church, and the exertions which he had made in procuring the right of election to the clergy, such a recommendation could not, with decency, be overlooked; and, in most cases, could scarcely fail of success. The frequency, however, of these recommendations disposed the electors to anticipate them on particular occasions, by filling up the vacancy with the utmost expedition. Foreseeing the death of some particular incumbent, the pope endeavoured sometimes to prevent a precipitate supply of the vacancy, by requesting that it should be delayed for some time. Such recommendations and requests, having come at length to be frequently disregarded, were afterwards accompanied with commands; and commissioners <145> were sent to put them in execution, as well as to punish the clergy, in case of their disobedience. To all these expedients was added, at length, a more effectual interposition for preventing every disappointment. With regard to the mode of electing bishops and abbots, and the qualifications of the person to be elected, a set of regulations was made, so numerous and intricate, that the strict observance of them became impossible; while it was declared, that, upon the least failure in any point, the election should be void, and the nomination should devolve to the apostolic see. By these artifices the bishop of Rome acquired, in reality, the power of appointing all the dignified clergy, together with all that influence and revenue which could be obtained, either directly or indirectly, from the disposal of every important ecclesiastical preferment. <146>

CHAPTER V

General View of the kingly Power, from the Reign of Edward I. to that of Henry VII.

The period of the English monarchy, from Edward the First to the accession of the house of Tudor, corresponds, with great exactness, to that of the French, from Philip the Fair to Lewis the Eleventh.[1] About the beginning of these periods, the government, in each of those countries, assumed a degree of regularity unknown in former ages; and it afterwards continued, by similar steps, advancing towards maturity. The power of the king, and that of the nobles, formed, at this time, the only balance in the constitution; which came, in the natural course of things, to lean more and more to the side of the former. The nobility were too much divided among themselves, to be capable of prosecuting any regular plan for the aggrandisement of their own order. Their opulence, which, if collected in one great current, might have borne <147> down every obstacle before it, was deprived of its efficacy by being broken into many separate channels, and spent in various contrary directions. In order to make an effectual opposition to the crown, it was requisite that the greater barons should be firmly united in defence of their privileges; but such a union was not easily procured, and, for any length of time, could hardly ever be maintained. Distracted by mutual animosity, and actuated by private jealousies, or by opposite views of interest, these restless, but short-sighted chiefs, were, without much difficulty, persuaded to abandon any joint measures; and excited to employ their force in weakening and destroying one another. What they gained, therefore, upon some occasions, by a sudden and violent effort, was afterwards thrown away, from the want

1. The period from 1272 to 1485. Philip IV, the Fair (r. 1285–1314); Louis XI (r. 1461–83).

of perseverance or management; and the effect of a temporary combination was more than compensated by their usual tendency to disunion and dissension. But the crown was not capable of being divided against itself. Its property, being under the disposal of a single person, was always directed, however injudiciously, to the same end; and made subservient to <148> one political purpose; that of extending the royal prerogative. The revenue of the crown, therefore, created a degree of influence, which was continually extending itself, and which, by its uniform operation, afforded continual opportunities for increasing that revenue. While the aristocracy was thus remaining stationary, or left in a fluctuating state, according to the impulse of casual circumstances, the monarchy, by receiving regular supplies from every quarter, was gradually rising to a greater height, and overflowing its ancient boundaries.

It must, however, be admitted, that the period of English history, now under consideration, is distinguished by many powerful efforts of the nobility to support their privileges; and that the crown did not rise to the summit of dignity and splendor which it attained in the possession of the Tudor family, without surmounting a variety of obstacles, and without being frequently checked and retarded by unfavourable occurrences.

There is even good reason to believe, that, in England, the regal authority was more limited, about the time of Edward the First, <149> than it was in France, during the reign of Philip the Fair. Though the English crown was considerably exalted upon the accession of William the Conqueror, yet, under the succeeding reigns, its progress was apparently more slow and gradual. The barons, by taking advantage of particular conjunctures, and, in some cases, by proceeding to such extremities as threatened an immediate revolution, obtained from the sovereign the most important concessions; and, in little more than a century and a half, no fewer than six great charters were granted, some of them repeatedly, by six different princes. By these charters the power of the crown does not, indeed, seem to have been contracted within a narrower compass than immediately after the Norman conquest; but it was undoubtedly restrained in its advancement, and prevented from rising to that height which it would otherwise have attained. In France, on the other hand, the extension of the royal prerogative appears, from the time of Hugh Capet, to have scarcely met with any opposition. No formidable combination of the nobles, to withstand the incroachments of the kingly power! No series of charters, as <150> in England, relinquishing the supposed usurpations of the crown, and confirming the privileges of the aristocracy! The only deed of this nature, which we meet with in the French history, was near half a century posterior to the reign of Philip the Fair; and was extorted from king John in consequence of the difficulties under which he laboured from the invasion of his kingdom by the English monarch.*

To what causes may we ascribe this diffe-<151>rent spirit of the French from that of the English nobility? From what circumstances were the former disposed to look with so much tranquillity and indifference upon the exaltation of the crown, as never, but upon one occasion, to exert themselves in repressing it; while the latter discovered such a constant jealousy of the sovereign, and made so many and such vigorous attempts to restrain the progress of his authority? The importance of this question is obvious; for the efforts then made to resist the usurpations of the crown, may be regarded as the groundwork of those more precise limitations of the prerogative, which have been introduced in a later period.

1. There occurs one remarkable difference between the situation of the French and the English kings; that in France, the crown was, without interruption, transmitted directly from father to son, during a period of more than three hundred years; that is, from the time of Hugh Capet to that of Philip the Long;[2] including a series of eleven different reigns; whereas in England, during the same period, we meet with no less than five deviations from the lineal course of succession; and about one <152> half of the reigning princes, who, however their title might be recognized by parliament, or their pretensions might be supported by the prevailing party, were, according to the common notions of that age, considered in the light of usurpers. In

* "The opportunity of the states general, assembled in the year 1355," says the count de Boulainvilliers, "is favourable to my design; since, upon their remonstrances, king John gave a declaration which irrevocably established the right of those assemblies, and which, upon that account, might justly be compared to the *great charter* granted to the *English* by a prince of the same name; were it not unfortunately too true, that it has been buried in oblivion for above two hundred years past, even so far that there is no public instrument of it remaining, except one copy preserved in the king's library; from whence I took that of which I shall give you an extract in the course of this letter." [Boulainv. account of the ancient parliaments of France.] See a full account given by this noble author, of that famous *French charter,* which in reality has a great resemblance to the *English charter* above mentioned.

2. The period from 987 to 1322. For Hugh Capet, see p. 11, note 5. Philip V, "the Tall" (r. 1316–22).

France, therefore, the crown passed, with perfect tranquillity, from one sovereign to another; and each of those princes, when he mounted the throne, having no competitor to obstruct his immediate possession, no flaw in his title to weaken or disturb the general prepossession in his favour, succeeded, of consequence, to all that hereditary influence which had been accumulated by his predecessors. To render the succession still more secure, Hugh Capet introduced the precaution, which had been in some measure suggested by the Roman emperors, of crowning his heir in his own lifetime; and the same practice was uniformly observed by six of the succeeding monarchs; that is, till the reign of Philip Augustus,[3] when, from the superior stability of the throne, any ceremony of this kind was become superfluous.

In England, on the contrary, the succession of those princes, whose title was ill founded or <153> disputable, gave always occasion to dissatisfaction and complaint, if not to direct opposition, and open resistance; and, as the nobles were invited to lay hold of these opportunities for maintaining or extending their privileges, the king was obliged to compound for the possession of sovereignty, by submitting to limitations in the exercise of it. The personal authority of William the Conqueror, produced a submission to William Rufus, though in preference to his elder brother Robert, a man of popular character; but Henry the First, and Stephen, may be said to have purchased the crown, by the respective great charters which they granted to their vassals. With respect to Henry the Second, it must be acknowledged, that, though he was a foreigner, and though he had in some measure fought his way to the throne, yet in the end his accession was agreeable to the whole nation. But after having suffered a variety of disappointments, and having been exposed to much uneasiness from the unnatural behaviour of his own children, he appears to have confirmed the two preceding charters, from a disposition to guard against any future accident, by securing the good-will of his <154> people. The usurpation of John, accompanied with the murder of the lawful heir, had excited against that prince an indignation and resentment, which his future conduct, instead of removing, tended only to confirm; and the concessions which he made to his subjects, were plainly extorted from him by the accumulation of distress and embarrassment under which he laboured. Henry the Third, though there were no objections to his title, inherited, while he was yet a minor, a civil war from his father; and

3. Philip II Augustus (r. 1179–1223).

afterwards, by his imbecility and imprudence, was involved in calamities, from which nothing less than the good fortune, and the great abilities, of his son Edward the First could have extricated him. The charters granted by the former of those two princes were evidently the fruit of these difficulties.*

2. Another circumstance which, in that early period, produced a peculiar exaltation of the monarchy in France, was the forfeiture of Normandy by the king of England, and the reduction of that extensive country into an <155> immediate fief of the French crown.[4] This forfeiture, though the particular time when it happened might be accidental, was to be expected from the situation of that country, with respect to the king of England, the immediate superior, and to the king of France, the lord paramount. The effect of so great an accession of revenue and influence to the French crown was visible; and Philip Augustus, in whose reign it happened, became evidently possessed of much more authority than his predecessors.

No acquisition of equal importance was made to the crown of England at this early period; for the settlement which was effected in Ireland, by Henry the Second, and which the historians have been pleased to dignify with the splendid appellation of a conquest, was productive neither of wealth nor of authority to the English monarch; nor does it appear, for several centuries, to have yielded any advantage whatever.

3. The insular situation of Britain may be considered as a general cause of the slower advancement of the royal prerogative in Eng-<156>land, than is to be found in the greater part of the modern kingdoms upon the continent of Europe. As, in the infancy of government, the kingly office arose from the necessity of having a general to command the united forces of the state, it was to be expected, that the oftener any sovereign had occasion to act in this capacity, his authority and dignity would sooner arrive at maturity. During the time of a military enterprize, when the national forces, the great body of the people, were placed under the immediate direction of the king, they acquired habits of submitting to his orders; their admiration was excited by his high station or distinguished prowess; and they were taught by experience to look up to him as the principal source of honours and preferment. In times of peace, on the contrary, when the members of different

* It appears, that one of the charters granted by Henry III. was subscribed by his son Edward. Blackstone, History of the Great Charters.

4. King John lost Normandy to the French in 1203.

baronies, or tribes, had retired to their several places of abode, they were, in a great measure, withdrawn from the influence of the king, and were accustomed to no other jurisdiction or authority but that of the baron or chief by whom they were protected. Even after the <157> feudal governments had attained some degree of regularity, and when the sovereign had acquired numerous branches of civil power, it still was in the field that his preeminence attracted superior attention, and that he had the best means of procuring popularity.

It seems reasonable to conclude, therefore, that, upon the continent of Europe, where every sovereign found his dominions surrounded by bordering nations, whom he was frequently tempted to invade, and against whom he was obliged to be constantly upon his guard, the most ample scope was afforded him for displaying those talents, and for availing himself of those situations which were best calculated for extending his authority. In England, on the other hand; a country in which there were fewer inducements to undertake a national war, and in which the military operations of the sovereign were chiefly employed in quelling the disturbances excited by his rebellious barons, or in repelling the inroads of the Scots, which were not of much more importance than the insurrection of particular <158> barons, he had fewer opportunities of exciting a national spirit in his favour, and consequently found it more difficult to reduce the nobility into a state of dependence.

The prosperous reign of Edward the First had undoubtedly a considerable effect in confirming and exalting the prerogative. This prince was equally distinguished by his policy in the cabinet, and by his activity, courage, and conduct in the field; at the same time that he does not appear, by any scrupulous regard to the principles of honour or justice, to have been, on any occasion, prevented from directing those talents to the pursuit of his own grandeur or emolument. By the conquest of Wales he not only gained an enlargement of dominion, but freed himself from the vexatious depredations of a troublesome neighbour.[5] Had he lived somewhat longer, it is more than probable that he would also have completed the entire conquest of Scotland; in which case, there is good ground to believe, that the reduction

5. By Edward I's conquest of Wales (1276–84), the English established complete control over the region. With the Statute of Wales of 1284, Wales was brought within the government of England.

of the northern and southern parts of the island into one monarchy, would have been productive of such advantages to both <159> countries, as might in some measure have atoned for the perfidy and injustice by which it was accomplished.

The reign of Edward the Second[6] was no less adverse to the influence of the crown, than that of his father had been favourable to it. By the total deficiency of that prince, in vigour and military capacity, he soon lost all the acquisitions which his father had made in Scotland; and saw the independence of that kingdom completely re-established. For the internal administration of government he was equally disqualified. The nobility of that age were, with difficulty, reconciled to the dignity and pre-eminence of the sovereign; but they could not endure, that any person of inferior condition should, by the favour of the monarch, be exalted over them, and be invested with the exercise of the prerogative. The extreme facility of Edward subjected him, however, to the constant dominion of favourites, in supporting whom he excited the indignation of the nobles; and the queen, whose affections had been seduced by Mortimer,[7] and who seems to have thought herself better entitled than any other person to govern her husband, hav<160>ing joined the malcontents, the king was formally deposed by a meeting of parliament; was kept for some time in confinement; and at length barbarously murdered. The fate of this unhappy prince cannot fail to move compassion, as it proceeded from the weakness of his understanding, and even from the gentleness of his disposition, more than from ambition, or any passion for arbitrary power: while it afforded a salutary lesson to his successors, by exhibiting a striking example of the authority of parliament, to controul, and even to punish, the sovereign.

The same power of the nobles, which had deposed Edward the Second, advanced to the throne his son Edward the Third, while yet a minor. The early indications of genius, and of a martial disposition, discovered by this prince, dispelled very quickly the gloom which had for some time hung over the nation, and gave a total change to the aspect of public affairs. He soon

6. Edward II (r. 1307–27). The English were expelled from Scotland after the victory of Robert I, the Bruce (r. 1306–29) at Bannockburn in 1314.

7. Roger Mortimer (ca. 1287–1330), baron of Wigmore and earl of March, was the lover of Queen Isabella. In league with young Edward (III), king of England (r. 1327–77), he captured Edward II in Wales in 1326. Edward was coerced into abdicating in 1327 and was killed shortly thereafter upon Mortimer's orders.

freed himself from the direction of the queen his mother, and put to death her favourite Mortimer,[8] with little ceremony, and without much regard to the forms of justice. His first military enterprise was <161> directed to the recovery of what his father had lost in Scotland, in which, from the weak and disorderly state of that country, he met with little obstruction; but he was prevented from the execution of this plan, by another object, which was thought of much greater importance, and which, during the remainder of his reign, ingrossed his whole attention. This was his pretension, in right of his mother, to the crown of France;[9] a claim which, though founded neither in justice nor expediency, was yet sufficiently plausible to palliate that love of extensive dominion, with which not only princes, but even the people in all ages and countries, have been almost constantly intoxicated. The conduct of Edward, in asserting this claim, was probably such as every monarch of spirit, in that age, must have held, and in so doing was sure of meeting with the general approbation of his subjects. As the undertaking, therefore, was crowned with unexpected and amazing success, it is no wonder that the splendid victories obtained by this king, and by his son the Black Prince,[10] who acted so conspicuous a part in those scenes, procured them the admiration as well as the affections of the <162> whole English nation. While these two princes flattered the national vanity, by the prospect of conquering so great a kingdom as France, they displayed all the talents and virtues which, in those times, were supposed to enter into the composition of the most complete military character. Even at this day, when we contemplate the gallantry of the Black Prince, and the humanity and generosity with which he treated the king of France, his prisoner, we must acknowledge that they are surpassed by nothing either in ancient or modern story.[11] Without detracting from the merit of this distinguished personage, we are led at the same time to conceive an exalted idea of the institutions and manners of *chivalry,* which, in so rude a state of society, were capable, among people of the better

8. Edward III had Mortimer put to death in 1330.

9. Edward's maternal grandfather was Philip IV, the Fair. His aggressive pursuit of this claim initiated what is traditionally called the Hundred Years' War, beginning in the year 1338.

10. Edward, the Black Prince (1330–76): Edward III's eldest son.

11. John II, the Good, king of France (r. 1350–64) was held for ransom by the English 1356–60. The legend of the Black Prince, to which Millar refers, was popularized by Jean Froissart (b. 1337) author of the *Chroniques,* written between 1369 and 1400.

sort, of promoting so much delicacy of sentiment, and of encouraging any individual to form such a perfect model of propriety and refinement.

In the course of his long war against France, the king obtained, more and more, an ascendant over those nobles who followed his banner, and were smitten by an universal enthusiasm to distinguish themselves in that illustrious <163> field of national glory. His administration at home was equally prudent and vigorous, and calculated to restrain injustice, as well as to command respect. Though not disposed to relinquish any part of his prerogative, he appears to have had a real regard for the ancient constitution; and though he acquired greater authority than was possessed by the former kings of England, he confirmed, on many occasions, the great charters of his predecessors. He was under the necessity of making large and frequent demands of money from his subjects; but, as he endeavoured, in most cases, to procure it by the concurrence of parliament, and as the nation entered heartily into the views which gave occasion to so much expence, the supplies which he required were commonly furnished without any complaint. His numerous applications to the national assembly contributed, besides, to ascertain its powers and privileges, as well as to establish and reduce into order the forms and method of its procedure.

It merits attention, that, notwithstanding the alacrity with which the English nation supported the claim of their sovereign to the <164> crown of France, the parliament seem to have been alarmed at the idea of their falling under the government established in that country: and, to remove this apprehension, a statute was made, in which the king expressly declares, that the realm and people of England "shall not, in any time to come, be put in subjection nor in obeisance of us, nor of our heirs nor successors, as kings of France, nor be subject nor obedient, but shall be free and quit of all manner of subjection and obeisance aforesaid, as they were wont to be in the time of our progenitors, kings of England, for ever."* From this precaution, it may be inferred, that the parliament understood the French monarchy, at this time, to be more absolute than the English; and were afraid that their monarch, if he came to the possession of that kingdom, might be led to exercise over them a power inconsistent with the constitution of England.

* 14 Edw. III.

The reign of Richard the second[12] is, in many respects, a repetition of the same disgusting and melancholy scenes, which that of <165> his great grandfather, Edward the second, had exhibited. In each of them we behold a young prince ascending the throne with great advantages; regarded by the nation with a partiality and affection derived from paternal connections; incurring the general contempt and indignation, by his folly and misconduct; governed, through the whole course of his administration, by favourites; dethroned at length by parliament, imprisoned, and brought to a tragical end. But the occurrences, in the time of Richard, were accompanied with circumstances which, in a review of the English government, are more particularly worthy of observation.

This reign affords a memorable example of the interference of parliament for the removal of the king's ministers. To the address which was presented for this purpose, Richard is said to have answered, that, *at the desire of parliament, he would not remove the meanest scullion of his kitchen.* Having occasion for a subsidy, however, which could not otherwise be obtained, he was obliged to comply with their demand: the earl of Suffolk,[13] the chancellor, was not only removed from his office, but im-<166>peached, and found guilty of misdemeanours; an inquiry was ordered into the disposal of the public revenue; and a commission was granted by parliament to fourteen persons, for the space of a twelvemonth, to concur with the king in the administration of government.

To these regulations Richard submitted no longer than till he thought himself in a condition to oppose them; and it soon became evident, that he had formed a resolution of extending his prerogative beyond its ancient limits. For this purpose he consulted with the principal judges and lawyers of the kingdom, from whom he found no difficulty in procuring an unanimous opinion agreeable to his wishes. Whatever may be the virtue of individuals, it is not to be expected that a body of men, sprung very frequently from a low origin; bred up in the habits of a gainful profession; whose views must be continually directed towards preferment, and the emoluments of office; soldiers of fortune, and whose fortune depends chiefly upon the favour of

12. Richard II (r. 1377–99) was the son of Edward, the Black Prince, and the grandson of Edward III.

13. Michael de la Pole (ca. 1330–89), earl of Suffolk, was appointed chancellor in 1386.

the crown; will be disposed to stand forth in critical times, and expose themselves to much hazard in maintaining the rights of the people. <167>

This design was frustrated by the vigour and activity of the nobles, who levied a great army, and defeated that of the crown. The king's ministers made their escape; but in their absence were impeached, and their estates confiscated. Two persons of note, one of whom was the famous Tresilian, chief justice of the king's bench, who happened to be caught, were tried and executed. The rest of the judges, who had concurred in the opinions abovementioned, were banished to Ireland.[14]

The behaviour of the king in this situation was abject and mean, in proportion to his former haughtiness. At an interview with the nobles, he is said to have answered their reproaches with a flood of tears. But Richard was possessed of a high degree of obstinacy; a quality which is frequently connected with inferiority of understanding: whether it be that the same stupidity which leads men into error, puts them out of the reach of conviction by reasoning; or that, in proportion as they are incapable of examining objects on every side, they are commonly self-conceited and opinionative. <168>

The parliament being then composed of two houses, as will be mentioned more fully hereafter, it was perceived by the advisers of this infatuated prince, that the easiest method of carrying his views into execution, was by dividing that assembly, and, in particular, by procuring a majority in the house of commons. We accordingly find, that by adhering invariably to the same plan; by directing the nomination of sheriffs, and of the principal magistrates of boroughs; and by employing the interest and address of all those different officers in the election and return of representatives, this object was, in a few years, entirely accomplished. The king now ventured to avow his pretensions to absolute power; and in a meeting of parliament, in the year 1397, the opinions of the judges, which had been formerly condemned, were approved of and ratified; the chief heads of the aristocracy were put to death, or banished; the duke of Glocester, the king's uncle, was privately murdered; and, to supersede the necessity of calling the national assembly for the future, a

14. This uprising, which occurred in 1386, was raised by Thomas, duke of Gloucester, the earl of Arundel, Thomas Beauchamp, the earl of Warwick, Thomas Mowbray, the earl of Nottingham, and Henry Bolingbroke, the duke of Hereford and Richard's cousin [later Henry IV, king of England (r. 1399–1413)]. Sir Robert Tresilian and Nicholas Brembre, lord mayor of London, were executed as traitors in 1388.

committee was appointed, consisting of twelve peers and <169> six commoners, upon whom the authority of both houses was devolved.[15]

This expedient of the crown, to pack the house of commons, is the first of the kind that occurs in our history; and it must be considered as forming a remarkable aera in the British constitution. It shows, in the first place, the limited nature of our ancient government; since, notwithstanding the late advances of the regal authority, the king, in order to carry his measures, was obliged to employ such indirect means for procuring the concurrence of parliament.

It proves also, that political consideration was not, at this period, confined to the greater nobility; but that men of small property, and of inferior condition, the representatives of counties and boroughs, were possessed of so much interest as enabled them, by throwing their weight into the scale of the sovereign, to bestow upon him an entire ascendant over the national council.

From the consequences which followed this undue influence, acquired by the king over the house of commons, we may plainly perceive that a spirit of liberty, or, if you will, of <170> opposition to the tyranny of the crown, was even then diffused, in some measure, over the nation. Finding that he was now master of the resolutions of parliament, Richard supposed the dispute was at an end; was therefore lulled in perfect security; and abandoned himself to the dictates of his own arbitrary will. But the people saw with concern, that they had been betrayed by their own representatives; their indignation and resentment were excited, and they became ripe for a general insurrection. The leaders of the malcontents cast their eyes upon the duke of Hereford, the eldest son of the duke of Lancaster,[16] who, by the injustice of the king, had been sent into exile, and afterwards excluded from the inheritance of his father's large possessions. This nobleman, the most distinguished by his rank and accomplishments, was invited to put himself at the head of the conspiracy, for the purpose of redressing his own private injuries, no less than of delivering the nation from tyranny and oppression. Richard, mean while, went over to Ireland, in order to quell the disturbances of that

15. Gloucester, Arundel, and Warwick were arrested in 1397. Shortly thereafter, Gloucester and Arundel were killed, and Warwick banished to the Isle of Man. Mowbray was exiled for life and Bolingbroke for ten years, a sentence later extended to life.

16. Afterward Henry IV, king of England. See note 14.

country, and thus gave to his enemies the opportunity which they wanted <171> of executing their designs. The general sentiments of the people were made abundantly evident by the events which followed. The duke of Hereford landed at Ravenspur, in Yorkshire, with no more than eighty attendants; but in a short time found himself at the head of an army amounting to sixty thousand. The duke of York,[17] on the other hand, who had been left regent of the kingdom, assembled a body of troops to the number of forty thousand; but these, from disaffection, were unwilling to fight; and being therefore disbanded, they immediately joined the enemy. Another army having been transported by the king from Ireland, were infected with the same spirit, and the greater part of them deserted the royal standard.

Richard, abandoned by the whole nation, was forced to subscribe an instrument of *resignation,* in which he acknowledged himself unworthy to govern the kingdom. An accusation for misbehaviour, consisting of no less than thirty-five articles, was preferred against him to parliament, and universally approved of: after which, this prince was solemnly deposed by <172> the suffrages of both houses; and the crown was conferred on the duke of Hereford.

It is remarkable, according to the observation of an eminent writer, "that these extremities fell upon Richard the second, at a time when every thing seemed to contribute to his support, in the exercise of that arbitrary power which he had assumed. Those whom he had most reason to fear, were removed, either by violent death or banishment; and others were secured in his interest by places, or favours at court. The great offices of the crown, and the magistracy of the whole kingdom, were put into such hands as were fit for his designs; besides which, he had a parliament entirely at his devotion; but all these advantageous circumstances served only to prove, that a prince can have no real security against the just resentments of an injured and exasperated nation; for, in such governments as that of England, all endeavours used by the king to make himself absolute, are but so many steps towards his own downfal."* <173>

The right of Henry the fourth to the crown of England was derived from

* Remarks upon the History of England by H. Oldcastle. [[Millar quotes this passage from Henry St. John, Viscount Bolingbroke, *Remarks on the History of England, from the Minutes of Humphrey Oldcastle, Esq.* (London, 1743), 74–75.]]

17. Edmund Langley, duke of York (1341–1402).

the authority of parliament, confirmed by the voice of the whole kingdom. No transaction of the kind was ever compleated with greater unanimity. But although, in that age, the people gave way to their natural feelings in dethroning an arbitrary and tyrannical prince, they were probably little accustomed to reason upon those philosophical principles, by which, in cases of extreme necessity, the right of doing so may be vindicated. Even so late as the revolution, in the year 1688, when the necessity and propriety of the settlement, which then took place, was universally understood, the parliament were unwilling to avow, in express terms, that power which they were determined to exercise; they had recourse to childish evasions, and fictitious suppositions; and the absurd pretext of an *abdication* was employed to cover the real deposition of the sovereign. It is not surprising, therefore, that, in the days of Richard the second, the speculative opinions of men, concerning points of this nature, were loose and fluctuating. Henry appears to have been sensible of this; and <174> founds his claim to the throne upon three different circumstances; upon the mal-administration of Richard; upon the right of conquest; and upon a popular, though probably a groundless tradition, that, by his mother, he was descended from Henry the third, by an elder brother of Edward the first, who, on account of his personal deformity, had been excluded from the succession to the crown. These particulars, however, are jumbled together, in a manner calculated to avoid a minute investigation. "In the name of Fadher, Son, and Holy Ghost," says he, "I Henry of Lancaster challenge this rewme of Ynglande, and the crown, with all membres and appurtenances; als I that am descendit by right line of the blode, coming fro the gude King Henry therde, and throge that right that God of his grace hath sent me, with helpe of kyn, and of my friends, to recover it; the which rewme was in poynt to be ondone by defaut of governance, and ondoying of the gude lawes."

As no credit seems due to this connection with Henry the third; so it must be admitted, that, supposing it necessary to set aside <175> Richard the second, for *defaut of governance,* Henry the fourth was not, according to the established rules of succession, the next heir of the crown. He was the grandson of Edward the third, by the duke of Lancaster, third son of that monarch. But the duke of Clarence, Edward's second son, had left a daughter, who was married into the house of Mortimer,[18] and whose grandson, the

18. Edmund Mortimer, earl of March (1391–1425).

earl of Marche, now a boy of seven years of age, was the representative of that family.

In examining this point, however, it ought to be remembered, that by the rules of succession established among rude and warlike nations, what is called the right of *representation* is unknown, and the nearer descendants of a family are frequently preferred to the more distant; as also, that, upon similar principles, female relations are usually excluded by the males. According to the early laws of almost all Europe, the title of Henry the fourth to the crown was therefore preferable, from both of these considerations, to that of the earl of Marche. A contrary custom, indeed, in consequence of more improved manners, had undoubtedly been gaining ground, before this <176> competition became an object of attention; but we must not suppose that it had yet become universal, or had acquired such a degree of stability, as the peaceful situation, and the scientific views of a polished age, have since bestowed upon it.

But whatever might be the opinions of parliament, or of the people, upon this point, the preference of Henry to any other competitor was, at this time, a matter of the highest expediency, if not of absolute necessity. To dethrone a prince, who had for years been establishing a system of absolute power, and who had given proofs of his violent and sanguinary disposition, was a measure no less dangerous than it was difficult; and the successful execution of it could only be expected under a leader of great popularity, weight, and abilities. Henry appears to have been the only person in the kingdom qualified for conducting such an enterprise, and likely to secure the public tranquillity under the new establishment. To depose Richard, and at the same time to commit the reins of government to a person who, in that extraordinary exigence, was manifestly incapable of holding them, <177> would have been to attempt the abolition of despotism by substituting anarchy in its place; and wantonly to introduce a revolution at the hazard of much bloodshed and injustice, but with no reasonable prospect that it could be productive of any lasting advantages.

Henry the fourth enjoyed, however, but little tranquillity in the possession of that sovereign power which was thus conferred upon him. The great lords, who had taken a distinguished part in placing him on the throne, and who probably over-rated their services, became dissatisfied with that share of the royal favour and confidence which he thought proper to bestow upon them; and were disposed to believe they might easily pull down that fabric which they themselves had erected. The persevering activity, the deliberate valour, and sound policy, displayed by this monarch, through the whole of his conduct, enabled him to crush those frequent conspiracies which were formed against him; although it must be admitted, that his uncommon talents, which were uniformly exerted for this purpose, during a reign of thirteen years, were hardly sufficient to recover the prerogative <178> from the shock which it had received by the deposition of his predecessor.

The splendid character of Henry the fifth;[19] his courage and magnanimity; his clemency, moderation, and humanity; his engaging appearance and deportment; his affability, address, and popular manners; together with his renewal of the claim to the kingdom of France, and his invasion of that country, accompanied with most astonishing success; these circumstances revived the flattering and delusive prospects entertained by the English in the days of Edward the third; and, by seizing the national enthusiasm, reinstated the crown in that authority and dignity which it had formerly maintained.

But the death of that monarch produced a sad reverse in the state of the kingdom. By the long minority of Henry the sixth,[20] and his total incapacity, after he came to be of age; by the disasters which befel the English in prosecuting the war with France; and by their entire expulsion from that country, without the least hope of recovering it;[21] the people were filled with discontent; were inspired with contempt of their sovereign; and of <179> course were disposed to listen to any objections against the title by which his family had obtained the crown. In the preceding reign those objections were held to be of so little moment, that Henry the fifth discovered no jealousy or apprehension of the Earl of Marche, the lineal heir of Richard; and there even subsisted between them an intercourse of mutual confidence and friendship; a circumstance which reflects great honour both upon the king and upon that nobleman. As the right of the governing family had been confirmed by a possession of three successive reigns, it would not, in all probability, have now been called in question, had not the weakness and

19. Henry V (r. 1413–22). Chief among his victories was the rout of the French forces at Agincourt in 1415.

20. Henry VI (r. 1422–61; 1470–71) was nine months old when he inherited the English throne.

21. The English were expelled from France in 1453, ending the Hundred Years' War. Among the English defeats was the fall of Orleans to the army of Jeanne d'Arc in 1429.

misfortunes of the present administration destroyed all respect to the government, and excited uncommon dissatisfaction.

Upon the death of the earl of Marche without heirs male, the duke of York, in right of his mother, was now become the representative of that family; and from the extensive property possessed by this nobleman, together with his powerful connections, in consequence of various alliances among the principal nobility, he found himself in a condition to assert <180> that claim to the crown, which had been over-ruled by the prevailing ascendant of the house of Lancaster. It is needless to enter into particulars of the famous contention between those two branches of the royal family; which was continued through the reigns of Henry the sixth, of Edward the fourth, and of Richard the third; and which, during a period of about five-and-thirty years, filled the kingdom with disorder and with blood.[22] That this long continued civil war, in which different princes were alternately set up and dethroned by the different factions, and in which all public authority was trampled under foot, was extremely unfavourable to the prerogative, will readily be admitted. It cannot, however, escape observation, that, in the course of this violent contention, the nobles were not, as in some former disputes, leagued together in opposition to the king; but, by espousing the interest of different candidates, were led to employ their whole force against one another. Though the crown, therefore, was undoubtedly weakened, the nobility did not receive proportional strength; and the tendency of this melancholy situation was not so much to <181> increase the aristocracy, as to exhaust and impoverish the nation, and to destroy the effect of all subordination and government.

When we consider, in general, the state of the English constitution, from the accession of Edward the first, to that of Henry the seventh,[23] we must find some difficulty to ascertain the alterations produced in the extent of the regal authority. That the powers of the monarch were, upon the whole, making advances during this period, it should seem unreasonable to doubt; but this progress appears to have been slow, and frequently interrupted. If, in the vigorous and successful reigns of Edward the first, of Edward the third, and

22. Edward IV (r. 1461–70; 1471–83); Richard III (r. 1483–85). The Wars of the Roses, the conflict between the houses of York and Lancaster, lasted ca. 1450–87. The Lancastrian faction proved victorious at the Battle of Bosworth in 1485.

23. Henry VII (r. 1485–1509): the first monarch of the Tudor dynasty.

of Henry the fifth, the sceptre was remarkably exalted, it was at least equally depressed by the feeble and unfortunate administration of Edward the second, of Richard the second, and of Henry the sixth. By what circumstances the prerogative acquired additional strength, under the princes of the Tudor family, we shall afterwards have occasion to examine. <182>

CHAPTER VI

History of the Parliament in the same Period.

Among the important subjects of inquiry, which distinguish the period of English history, from the accession of Edward the first to that of Henry the seventh, our first attention is naturally directed to the changes which affected the legislative power; by the introduction of representatives into parliament; by the division of that assembly into two houses, attended with the appropriation of peculiar powers to each of them; and lastly, by the subsequent regulations, with respect to the right of electing members of the national council. These particulars appear to be of such magnitude, as to deserve a separate examination.

SECTION I

The Introduction of the Representatives of Counties and Boroughs into Parliament.

The parliament of England, from the time of William the Conqueror, was com-<183>posed, as I formerly took notice, of all the immediate vassals of the crown, the only part of the inhabitants that, according to the feudal constitution, could be admitted into the legislative assembly. As the English nobility had accumulated extensive landed property, towards the latter part of the Anglo-Saxon government; as yet larger territories were acquired by many of those Norman barons who settled in England at the time of the conquest; and as the conversion of allodial into feudal estates, under the crown, occasioned no diminution in the possessions of individuals; the original members of parliament must have been, for the most part, men of great power, and in very opulent circumstances. Of this we can have no doubt, when it is considered that, in the reign of William the first, the vassals of the crown did not amount to more than six hundred, and that, exclusive of the royal demesne, the whole land of the kingdom, in property or superiority, was divided among so small a number of persons. To these opulent barons, attendance in parliament was a duty which they were seldom unwilling to perform, as it gave them an opportunity of <184> asserting their privileges, of courting preferment, or of displaying their influence and magnificence. But in a long course of time, the members of that assembly were subjected to great revolutions; their property was frequently dismembered, and split into smaller divisions; their number was thus greatly increased; while the consideration and rank of individuals were proportionably impaired; and many of those who had appeared in eminent stations were reduced to poverty and obscurity. These changes proceeded from the concurrence chiefly of three different causes.

1. During that continual jealousy between the king and the nobles, and that unremitting struggle for power, which arose from the nature of the English constitution, it was the constant aim of the crown, from a consciousness of inferiority in force, to employ every artifice or stratagem for undermining the influence of the aristocracy. But no measure could be more effectual for this purpose, than to divide and dismember the overgrown estates of the nobles; for the same wealth, it is evident, which became formidable in the hands of one man, would be of no significance when <185> scattered among twenty. As the frequent insurrections and disorders, which prevailed in the country, were productive of numberless forfeitures, they afforded the king opportunities of seizing the property of those barons who had become obnoxious to him, and of either annexing it to the crown, or disposing of it at pleasure. In this manner a considerable part of the land in the kingdom, during the course of a century or two, passed through the hands of the sovereign, and, being distributed in such parcels as coincided with his views of policy, gave rise to a multiplicity of petty proprietors, from whose exertions he had no reason to fear much opposition to the progress of his authority.

2. Another circumstance which contributed still more effectually, though perhaps more slowly and gradually, to diminish the estates of the crown-vassals, was the advancement of arts and manufactures.

The irruption of the Gothic nations into the Roman empire; the struggles which took place during their conquest of the different provinces; the subsequent invasions carried on by new swarms of the same people, against the

<186> states erected by their predecessors; the violent convulsions which, in a great part of Europe, were thus continued through the course of many centuries, could not fail to destroy all industry, and to extinguish the mechanical as well as the liberal professions. The rude and barbarous manners of the conquerors were, at the same time, communicated to those countries which fell under their dominion, and the fruits of their former culture and civilization being gradually lost, the inhabitants were at length sunk in universal ignorance and barbarism.

When these disorders had risen to a certain pitch, the countries which had so long poured out their inhabitants to disturb the peace of Europe, put a stop to their depredations. The northern hive,[1] it has been said, was then exhausted. Those countries, however, were in reality so far from being drained of inhabitants, that they had increased in population. But they had become a little more civilized, and, consequently, had less inclination to roam in quest of distant settlements, or to procure subsistence by the plunder of nations who were now in a better condition to withstand them. <187>

The greater tranquillity which was thence-forward enjoyed in the states that had been formed upon the ruins of the Roman empire, gave the people more leisure and encouragement to introduce regulations for securing property, for preventing mutual injuries, and for promoting their internal prosperity. That original disposition to better their circumstances, implanted by nature in mankind, excited them to prosecute those different employments which procure the comforts of life, and gave rise to various and successive improvements. This progress was more or less accelerated in different countries, according as their situation was more favourable to navigation and commerce; the first attention of every people being usually turned to the arts most essential to subsistence, and, in proportion to the advancement of these, being followed by such as are subservient to conveniency, or to luxury and amusement. The eleventh and twelfth centuries have been marked by historians as presenting, in modern times, the first dawn of knowledge and literature to the western part of Europe; and from this period we begin to trace the rude footsteps <188> of manufactures in Italy, in France, and in the Netherlands.

1. A reference to the migrations of the northern or Gothic nations who eventually destroyed the Roman Empire. The phrase is used by a variety of authors, including Sir William Temple (1628–99), Montesquieu (1689–1755), and Edward Gibbon (1737–94).

The communication of the Normans with England, in the reign of Edward the Confessor, which began in 1041, and still more from that of William the Conqueror, contributed to spread, in this island, the improvements which had made a quicker progress upon the continent: the common arts of life were now more and more cultivated; tradesmen and mercantile people were gradually multiplied; foreign artificers, who had made proficiency in various branches of manufacture, came and settled in England; and particular towns upon the coasts of the sea, or of navigable rivers, or which happened to be otherwise advantageously situated, began to extend their commerce.

This alteration in the circumstances of society, which became more and more conspicuous through the reigns of the several princes of the Norman and Plantagenet race, was productive, as we may easily suppose, of a correspondent variation of manners. The proprietors of land, for whose benefit the new improvements were chiefly intended, endeavoured to render their situation more comfortable, by purchasing those <189> conveniences which were now introduced; their ancient plainness and simplicity, with respect to the accommodations of life, were more and more deserted; a mode of living more expensive, and somewhat more elegant, began to take place; and even men of smaller fortunes were tempted in this, as well as in most other particulars, to follow the example of their superiors. By an increase of their annual expence, without any addition to their annual revenue, many individuals, therefore, were laid under difficulties, found it necessary to contract debts, and being subjected to incumbrances, were at last obliged to dismember and alienate their estates.

To this general cause of alienation, we may add the epidemical madness of the crusades, by which many persons were induced to sell or mortgage their possessions, that they might put themselves in a condition for bearing a part in those unprosperous and expensive expeditions.

It may accordingly be remarked, that as, about this time, the commerce of land was rendered more frequent, it was gradually freed from those legal restraints to which it had an-<190>ciently been subjected. According to the simplicity of manners which had prevailed among the rude inhabitants of Europe, and which had kept estates invariably in the same families, no person was understood to have a right of squandering his fortune to the prejudice of his nearest relations.* The establishment of the feudal system produced

* Vide L. L. Aelfred, c. 37.

an additional bar to alienation, from the circumstance that every vassal being a military servant, and having obtained his land as a consideration for services to be performed, could not transfer the property without the consent of his master. In England, upon the dawnings of improvement after the Norman conquest, persons who had acquired an estate by purchase, were permitted to dispose of it at pleasure; and in towns, the inhabitants of which became familiar with commerce, the same privilege was probably soon extended to every tenement, however acquired. When the disposition to alienate became somewhat more general over the country, the conveyance, even of estates descending by inheritance, was executed in a manner con-<191>sistent with feudal principles, by *subinfeudation;*[2] the purchaser became the vassal of the person who sold the lands, and who still continued liable to the chief lord for all the feudal obligations. But in the reign of Edward the first a statute was made, by which an unbounded liberty was given to the alienation of landed property; and when any person sold an estate, the superior was bound to receive the purchaser as his immediate vassal.*

3. By the course of legal succession, the property of the crown vassals, or members of parliament, was also frequently broken and dismembered. The right of primogeniture,[3] indeed, which, among the feudal nations, was introduced in order to shelter the individuals of every family under the protection of their own chief or leader, prevented, so far as it went, the division of estates by inheritance. But primogeniture had no place in female succession. Besides, the improvements of society, by enlarging the ideas of mankind, with rela-<192>tion to property, contributed to extend and to multiply *devises,*[4] by which even landed possessions were bequeathed at pleasure, and, according to the situation or caprice of the owner, were liable to be split and distributed among different persons.

When the alienation of estates, together with those divisions of landed

* The famous statute *quia emptores* [[Forasmuch as purchasers. For a modern edition of the statute, see *Select Charters and Other Illustrations of English Constitutional History from the Earliest Times to the Reign of Edward the First,* ed. William Stubbs, 9th ed., rev. H. W. C. Davis (Oxford: Clarendon Press, 1921; 1960), 473–74.]], passed in the 18th of Edward I. This law was farther extended, or at least received a more liberal interpretation, in the reign of Edward III.

2. The granting of lands by a feudatory to an inferior.

3. The right of the firstborn to inherit the entire estate.

4. A gift by will of freehold land is called a devise. A gift by will of personal property is called a bequest.

property which arose from female succession, or from devise, had proceeded so far as to threaten the destruction of great families, the nobility took the alarm, and had recourse to the artifice of entails for preserving their opulence and dignity. In the reign of Edward the first, they are said to have extorted from the king a remarkable statute, by which the privilege of entailing[5] was greatly extended; from which it may be inferred that there had appeared, about this time, a strong disposition to alienate and dismember estates; since, in order to check the progress of the evil, this extraordinary remedy was thought requisite.* <193>

These changes in the state of landed property had necessarily an extensive influence upon the government, and more especially upon the interest and political views of those persons who composed the national council. Many of the crown-vassals were now, from the smallness of their fortune, unable to bear the expence of a regular attendance in parliament; at the same time that they were discouraged from appearing in that assembly; where, instead of gratifying their ambition, they were more likely to meet with situations to mortify their vanity, by exposing the insignificance into which they had fallen. They were no longer in a condition to view the extensions of the royal prerogative with an eye of jealous apprehension; but had commonly more cause of complaint against the great barons, who lived in their neighbourhood, and by whom they were frequently oppressed, than against the sovereign, whose power, being more distant, and operating in a higher sphere, gave them less disturbance.

But while, from these considerations, the small barons were disposed, in many cases, to withdraw themselves from the meetings of parliament, the king had commonly an in-<194>terest in requiring their punctual attendance; because he found it no difficult matter to attach them to his party, and by their assistance was enabled to counterbalance the weight of the aristocracy. On every occasion, therefore, where any measure of public importance was to be agitated, the king was usually solicitous that many of the poorer members of parliament should be present; and a great part of these,

* This was the statute of Westminster *de donis conditionalibus* [[Concerning gifts with conditions attached. See *Select Charters,* 463.]], 13 Edward I c. 1. By which it was provided, that an estate left to a person, and *the heirs of his body,* should in all cases go to the issue, if there was any; if not, should revert to the donor.

5. The settlement of the succession of a landed estate in a secured inheritance, so that it cannot be bequeathed at pleasure by any one possessor.

on the other hand, were continually excusing themselves from so burdensome a service. The longer the causes which I have mentioned had continued to operate, in dividing and dismembering landed estates, the number of crown-vassals, desirous of procuring an exemption from this duty, became so much the greater.

Comparing the condition of the different landholders of the kingdom, towards the latter part of the Anglo-Saxon government, and for some time after the Norman conquest, we may observe a similar distinction among them, proceeding from opposite causes. In the former period, when people of small fortune were unable to subsist without the protection of their superiors, the property of many allodial <195> proprietors was gradually accumulated in the hands of a few, and those who possessed a landed territory of a certain extent, acquiring suitable consideration and rank, were distinguished by the title of *proceres,* or chief nobility. Under the first Norman princes, when the dependence of the lower ranks had produced its full effect in the completion of the feudal system, the owners of small estates were almost entirely annihilated; and in the condition of those opulent barons among whom the kingdom came to be divided, no difference was probably acknowledged. But when the revival of arts, and the progress of the people towards independence, had begun to dismember estates, and to multiply the vassals of the crown, the disproportion between the property of individuals became, once more, conspicuous; and the former distinction between the *great* and *small* barons excited the attention of the legislature.

The prior accumulation, and the subsequent dissipation, of wealth, had in this respect a similar effect. In amassing great fortunes some of the barons were necessarily more successful than others, which rendered estates extremely <196> unequal. In that state of society which tempted men to spend, or promoted the division of their estates, some proprietors proceeded likewise in this career with greater rapidity, by which the same inequality was produced.

In the great charter of king John it is ordained, that the archbishops, bishops, earls, and *greater barons,* shall be summoned to the meetings of parliament, by particular letters from the king; and that all other persons, holding immediately of the crown, shall receive a general citation from the king's bailiffs or sheriffs. But, although the more opulent vassals of the crown are thus clearly exalted above those of inferior wealth, and dignified with particular marks of respect, it is difficult to ascertain the extent of property by which those two orders of men were separated from each other. That the statute has a reference to some known boundary between them, can hardly be doubted; but whether, in order to obtain the rank and title of a *great baron,* an estate amounting to forty hides of land was requisite, agreeable to the distinction of the *chief nobility* in the reign of Edward the Confessor, or whether the qualification in <197> point of property had been varied according to the alteration of times and circumstances, no account can be given.

The effect of a regulation for summoning the small barons to parliament, by a general citation only, was to place them in greater obscurity, and to encourage their desertion, by giving them reason to hope that it would pass without observation. In such a situation, however, where a complete and regular attendance was not to be expected, and where each individual was endeavouring to excuse himself, and to throw as much as possible the burden upon his neighbours, an agreement would naturally be suggested to the inhabitants of particular districts, that they should relieve and succeed each other by turns, in the performance of this duty, and thus contribute to their mutual ease and advantage, by sharing among them an inconvenience which they could not entirely avoid. Of these joint measures, it was an obvious improvement, that, instead of a vague and uncertain rotation, particular persons, who appeared the best qualified for the task, and were most willing to undertake it, should be regularly elected, and <198> sent, at the common expence, to represent their constituents in parliament. Nor can it be doubted that the king would be highly pleased with such an expedient, by which he secured a proportion of the small barons in the ordinary meetings of the national council, and which did not hinder him from convening a greater number on extraordinary occasions.

In this manner the knights of shires[6] appear to have been first introduced into parliament. The date of this remarkable event cannot be fixed with

6. An obsolete term for the separate class of knights which was employed in the administration of English counties and shires. Burgesses were broadly defined as residents of a borough, and toward the end of the medieval period the term was more likely to be used to distinguish one group of privileged townsmen from a less privileged group. Millar's note cites Thomas Carte, *A General History of England,* 4 vols. (London, 1747–55). More specifically, see vol. 2, bk. 7 (on Henry III), 60. On Carte, see p. 307, note 14, in the present volume.

precision; but it was undoubtedly as early as the reign of Henry the third.[*] The division of counties produced a separate association among the crown vassals, in each of <199> those districts, for electing their own representatives. The number of these appears to have been originally precarious, and probably was varied in different emergencies. On different occasions we meet with four knights called from each county; but they were gradually reduced to two, the smallest number capable of consulting together for the interest of their constituents.[†]

The same changes in the state of the nation, which contributed principally to the rise of the knights of shires, introduced likewise the burgesses[7] into parliament.

By the advancement of agriculture, the peasants, in many parts of Europe, had been gradually emancipated from slavery, and been exalted successively to the condition of farmers, of tenants for life, and of hereditary proprietors. In consequence of the freedom attained by this inferior class of men, a great proportion of them had engaged in mechanical employ<200>ments; and, being collected in towns, where the arts were most conveniently cultivated, had, in many cases, become manufacturers and merchants. The situation of these manufacturing and trading people enabled them, after the disorders which prevailed in Europe had in some measure subsided, to make a rapid progress in improving their circumstances, and in acquiring various immunities and privileges. By mutual emulation, and by the influence of example, the inhabitants of the same town were excited to greater industry, and to the continued exertion of their talents; at the same time that they were in a capacity of uniting readily for mutual defence, and

* The records of parliament, for several reigns after the Norman conquest, are in a great measure lost, having probably, during the barons wars, been destroyed alternately by each prevailing party, who found them unfavourable to their interest. [Prynne's preface to Cotton's Abridgment of Records in the Tower.] This circumstance accounts for the great obscurity in which, after all the labour of antiquaries, the origin of so great a change in the constitution of that assembly still remains. The first introduction of representatives of counties may, with some probability, be traced as far back as the reign of king John. See Carte's Hist. reign of Edward I.

† In the eleventh year of Edward I. four knights were summoned for each county. [Brady's Hist. of England.] In the reign of John, there had been a writ issued to the sheriff of Oxfordshire, to return four knights for that county. Carte, in the reign of Edward I.

7. One possessing full municipal rights as a citizen or freeman of a borough, a town possessing municipal organization.

in supporting their common interest. Being originally the tenants or dependents, either of the king or of some particular nobleman, upon whose demesne they resided, the superior exacted from them, not only a rent for the lands which they possessed, but various tolls and duties for the goods which they exchanged with their neighbours. These exactions, which had been at first precarious, were gradually ascertained and fixed, either by long custom, or by express regulations. But, as many artifices had, no <201> doubt, been frequently practised, in order to elude the payment of those duties, and as, on the other hand, the persons employed in levying them were often guilty of oppression, the inhabitants of particular towns, upon their increasing in wealth, were induced to make a bargain with the superior, by which they undertook to pay a certain yearly rent, in room of all his occasional demands: and these pecuniary compositions, being found expedient for both parties, were gradually extended to a longer period, and at last rendered perpetual.

An agreement of this kind appears to have suggested the first idea of a *borough,* considered as a *corporation.* Some of the principal inhabitants of the town undertook to pay the superior's yearly rent, in consideration of which they were permitted to levy the old duties, and became responsible for the funds committed to their care. As managers for the community, therefore, they were bound to fulfil its obligations to the superior; and, by a natural extension of the same principle, it came to be understood that they might be prosecuted for all its debts; as, on the other hand, they obtained, of course, a right of pro-<202>secuting all its debtors. The society was thus viewed in the light of a body politic, or fictitious person, capable of legal deeds, and executing every sort of transaction by means of certain trustees or guardians.

This alteration in the state of towns was accompanied with many other improvements. They were now generally in a condition to dispense with the protection of their superior; and took upon themselves the burden of keeping a guard, to defend them against a foreign enemy, and to secure their internal tranquillity. Upon this account, beside the appointment of their own administrators, they obtained the privilege of electing magistrates, for distributing justice among them. They became, in a word, a species of *soccage tenants,* with this remarkable peculiarity in their favour, that by remaining in the state of a corporation from one generation to another, they were not liable to the *incidents* belonging to a superior, upon the transmission of lands to the heirs of a vassal.

The precise period of the first incorporation of boroughs, in the different kingdoms of Europe, is not easily determined; because the <203> privileges arising from the payment of a fixed rent to the superior, in the room of his casual emoluments, and the consequences which resulted from placing the revenue of a town under permanent administrators, were slowly and gradually unfolded and brought into the view of the public. In the eleventh and twelfth centuries, we may trace the progress, if not the first formation, of those communities, in Italy and in Germany, which corresponds with the advancement of trade and manufactures in those countries.* The towns in France are said by Father Daniel[8] to have been first incorporated in the reign of Lewis the Gross; but it appears that they had then acquired considerable privileges, were intrusted with their own government, and the inhabi<204>tants were formed into a militia for the service of the crown.†

In the reign of Henry the first of England, the cotemporary of Lewis the Gross, the inhabitants of London had begun to farm their tolls and duties, and obtained a royal charter for that purpose.‡ Their example was followed by the other trading towns, and from this time forward, the existence of English boroughs becomes more and more conspicuous.

When the towns, under the immediate protection of the king had been incorporated, and, of course, exalted into the rank of crown-vassals, it was agreeable to the general system of the feudal policy, that they should have a voice in the national council; and more especially, when extraordinary aids, beside their constant yearly rent, were demanded from them, as well as from the other tenants *in capite,* that they should have an opportunity of refusing or consenting to these demands. Their attendance in that assembly was, at the same <205> time, of advantage to the sovereign, and even more so than that of the small barons; for the trading people of all the inferior part of the nation were the most liable to be insulted and oppressed by the nobles, and

* With respect to the rise of the cities of Italy, see Muratori Antiq. Ital. Med. Aevi, tom. iv. The advancement of the German free cities appears to have been rather posterior to that of the Italian; their chief privileges having been acquired under the princes of the Swabian family. They attained their highest pitch of grandeur in consequence of the famous Hanseatick confederacy, which began in the year 1241. See Abrégé de l'histoire et du droit public d'Allemagne, par M. Pfeffel.

† M. Pfeffel's History of the reign of Lewis VII.

‡ Hume's History of England.

8. Gabriel Daniel (1649–1728), French Jesuit and royal historian, author of the *Histoire de France depuis l'éstablissement de la monarchie françoise de la Gaules* (1713) and *Histoire de la milice françoise* (1721). Louis VI, the Gross (r. 1081–1137).

were of consequence proportionably attached to the monarch, who had found his account in protecting and supporting them.

It was impossible, however, that all the members of every royal borough should assemble in order to deliberate upon the business of the nation; and in this, as well as in the separate concerns of each respective community, it was natural for them to commit the administration to particular commissioners or representatives. In England, accordingly, it appears, that after the boroughs had been incorporated, and had been raised, by their trade, to a degree of consideration and independence, they began to send representatives into parliament. The records of parliament, as has been before remarked, during several reigns after the Norman conquest have not been preserved; so that it is no less uncertain at what precise time the burgesses, than at what time the knights of shires, made their first ap-<206>pearance in that assembly; but as those two events proceeded from the same cause, the advancement of commerce and manufactures, it is probable that they were nearly coeval.*

In the great charter of king John, it is expressly ordained, that aids shall not be imposed upon the boroughs without the consent of parliament; from which it may be inferred, that those communities had then acquired the rank of soccage tenants, and that matters were at last ripened and prepared for their introduction into the councils of the nation. The first instance upon record of the burgesses attending in parliament, occurs in the forty-ninth year of the reign of Henry the third; when they are said to have been called by the famous earl of Leicester, in order to support his ambitious views: but this is not mentioned by any historian as a late innovation; neither is it probable that this nobleman, at the very time when he was endeavouring to screen himself from the resentment of the nation, <207> would have ventured to open a new source of discontent, by making a sudden and violent change in the constitution. It is likely that some of the burgesses had been present in former parliaments; as we find that they afterwards were, upon two different occasions, in the early part of the reign of Edward the first: but the number of them was not fixed; nor were they accustomed to give a regular attendance.

* Sir Henry Spelman declares, that, from the most careful examination, he could find no traces of the representatives of boroughs in parliament, before the latter part of the reign of Henry III. Glossar. v. Parliamentum.

The policy of Edward the first led him to take hold of the circumstances, which have been mentioned, for promoting the interest of the crown. In the twenty-third year of his reign, directions were given to summon regularly the knights of the shires, together with the burgesses; of which, after the example of the former, two were generally sent by each borough; and from that period, both these classes of representatives continued to be constant members of the legislature.

The same circumstances, according as they existed more or less completely, in the other countries of Europe, were productive of similar changes in the constitution of their national councils. <208>

In Scotland, a country whose government and laws bore a great analogy to those of England, not only from the common circumstances which operated upon all the feudal nations, but also from that vicinity which produced an intercourse and imitation between the two countries, the parliament, as far back as we can trace the records of Scottish history, appears to have been composed of the greater thanes, or independent proprietors of land. The representatives of boroughs are supposed by historians to have been first introduced into its meetings during the reign of Robert Bruce, which corresponds to that of Edward the second; but satisfactory evidence has lately been produced, that this event must have happened at an earlier period.* From the slow progress, however, of trade in Scotland, the number of burgesses in her national council was for a long time inconsiderable; and their appearance was limited to a few extraordinary cases.

The representatives of counties became con-<209>stituent members of the Scottish parliament by the authority of a statute, which, being still preserved, affords great light with respect to the origin of this establishment both in Scotland and in England. By that statute it is provided, that the smaller vassals of the crown should be excused from personal attendance in parliament, upon condition of their sending representatives, and maintaining them at the common expence. This regulation was introduced by James the first,[9] who, as he had resided for many years in England, and was a prince of learning and discernment, had probably been induced to copy this branch

* See Dr. Stuart's acute researches into the ancient government of Scotland. [[On the introduction of borough representatives by Mary, Queen of Scots, see Gilbert Stuart, *The History of Scotland, from the Establishment of the Reformation, till the Death of Queen Mary,* 2 vols. (London, 1782), 1:66.]]

9. James I, king of Scotland (r. 1406–37).

of policy from the institutions of a people, among whom the monarchy had made greater advances than in his own country. But the Scottish barons, whose poverty had given occasion to this regulation, laid hold of the dispensation which it bestowed upon them, without fulfilling the conditions which it required; and it was not until the reign of James the sixth,[10] that their obligation to send representatives into parliament was regularly enforced.* <210>

In France, the representatives of boroughs, according to the most probable account, were first introduced into the national assembly in the reign of Philip the Fair, by whom they are said to have been called for the purpose chiefly of consenting to taxes.† It is remarkable, however, that in the French *convention of estates,*[11] no set of men, corresponding <211> to the knights of shires in England, was ever admitted. The improvement of arts, in France as well as in England, contributed not only to raise the trading people, but also to dismember the estates of many proprietors of land; but the king does not seem to have availed himself of that situation for obliging the small barons to send representatives into the national council. The greater authority possessed, about this period, by the French monarch, was probably the cause of his not resorting to the same shifts, that were practised in England, to counterbalance the power of the aristocracy. That a sovereign should court the lower part of his subjects, and raise them to consideration, with a view of deriving support from them, is none of the most agreeable expedients; and nothing, we may suppose, but some very urgent necessity, could make him think of submitting to it.

* In the reign of James the first, we meet with two statutes upon this subject. By act 1425, c. 52. it is required, that all the *freeholders* shall give personal attendance in parliament, and not by a *procurator;* unless they can prove a lawful cause of their absence. Afterwards, by a statute 1427, c. 102. it is enacted, "that the small barons and free tenants need not come to parliaments, provided that, at the head court of every sheriffdom, two or more wise men be chosen, according to the extent of the shire, who shall have power to hear, treat, and finally to determine all causes laid before parliament; and to chuse a *speaker,* who shall *propone* all and sundry needs and causes pertaining to the commons in parliament."

From these two acts of parliament, it is evident the king had first endeavoured to enforce the attendance of all the small barons; and, upon finding this impracticable, had resorted to the expedient of introducing representatives.

† This happened about the year 1300. See Pasquier Recherches de la France.

10. James VI, king of Scotland (r. 1567–1625) and England (r. 1603–25).

11. The Estates General, first summoned in Paris in 1302.

The circumstance now mentioned, created a most essential difference between the national council in France and in England; the latter comprehending the representatives of counties as well as of boroughs, and consequently a large proportion of the people; whereas the former <212> admitted no other representatives but those of boroughs, the number of which, in either country, was for a long time inconsiderable.

The free cities of Germany had, in the thirteenth century, acquired such opulence as enabled them to form that famous Hanseatick league,[12] which not only secured their independence, but rendered them formidable to all the military powers in their neighbourhood. From these circumstances they rose to political power, and obtained a seat in the diet of the empire. But in Germany, the representatives of the small barons were not admitted into that assembly, from an opposite reason, it should seem, to that which prevented their admission into the French convention of estates. At the time when the rise of commerce had led the way to such a regulation, the nobility, and the free states of the empire, had so firmly established their independence, and the emperors had so far declined in authority, that it was vain to expect, by any artifice or exertion, to stop the progress of the aristocracy. The great exaltation of the German states had indeed produced a wide difference in the power and dignity of the different nobles; and those <213> of inferior rank, instead of maintaining an equal voice with their superiors, were at length associated in different classes; each of which, having only a single vote in the diet, were, in fact, reduced to a worse condition than if they had acted by representatives.

In Flanders, in the several principalities which afterwards composed the Spanish monarchy, and, in general, in all the feudal governments of Europe, we may observe, that whenever the towns became free and opulent, and where they continued members of a larger community, they obtained a seat in the legislative assembly. But with respect to the representatives of the small barons, or inferior nobles, their introduction into the legislature is to be regarded as a more singular regulation, which, depending upon a nice balance between the crown and the nobility, has been adopted in some countries,

12. The Hanseatic League was a late medieval federation of north European, especially German, towns, including Hamburg, Bremen, and Lübeck. The Hansa facilitated trade among towns and dominated trade in the north Atlantic and the Baltic Sea. At its height, it encompassed two hundred towns.

and in others neglected, according as it happened to suit the interest and policy of the sovereign, or the peculiar circumstances of the people.* <214>

In Italy, a country which had been broken into small principalities, under princes possessed of little power, or residing at such a distance as to have little capacity of exerting it over the inhabitants, the principal towns, whose prosperity in trade, if we except the territories belonging to the Moors in Spain, was prior to that of the other parts of Europe, became separate and independent states; and fell under such modes of republican government as were agreeable to the situation of their respective societies.

From a connected view of the different countries of Europe, during the period now under examination, it seems hardly possible to entertain a doubt, that the representatives in the English parliament were introduced in the manner, and from the causes, which have been <215> specified. It appears, at the same time, surprising, and may perhaps be considered as an objection to the account which has been given, that there is a profound silence, among all cotemporary writers, concerning this important event. The historians of that age, it is true, were neither philosophers nor politicians; they were narrow-minded and bigotted ecclesiastics, who saw nothing of importance in the history of England, but what was immediately connected with those religious institutions to which they were devoted. But still it may be said, that if the commons were unknown in the early assemblies of the nation, the introduction of that order of men into parliament, would have been such a novelty, as could hardly fail to strike the imagination, and to be mentioned in some of the writings of those times.

It is necessary, however, to remark, that this alteration was produced in a gradual manner, and without any appearance of innovation. When the

* The boroughs are said to have been introduced into the *cortes* of the different petty kingdoms of Spain, about the same time as in the other nations of Europe. In each of those kingdoms the cortes came to be composed of the nobility, of the dignified ecclesiastics, and the representatives of the cities. But in none of them do we find that the representatives of the small proprietors of land were admitted into those assemblies; though, in the kingdom of Arragon, it appears that the nobility were distinguished into those of the first, and those of the second rank. See Dr. Robertson's History of Charles V. [[Millar cites William Robertson's discussion of the *cortes* in Spain. See the introduction to the *History of Charles V,* published in a modern edition: *The Progress of Society in Europe: A Historical Outline from the Subversion of the Roman Empire to the Beginning of the Sixteenth Century,* ed. Felix Gilbert (Chicago: University of Chicago Press, 1972), 114–20.]]

knights of shires began to attend the meetings of parliament, they were no other than barons formerly entitled to that privilege. Their being sent at the common expence of the small barons be-<216>longing to a district, was a circumstance that would excite little attention; as it probably arose from the private contribution of the parties concerned, not from any public regulation. The burgesses, in like manner, were not admitted into parliament all at once, or by any general law of the kingdom; but when particular towns, by their incorporation, and by the privileges bestowed upon them, had acquired the rank of crown-vassals, their obtaining a share in the legislature, by means of representatives named for that purpose, was a natural consequence of their advancement. This privilege, so far from being regarded as new or uncommon, had regularly been acquired by such of the churles, or peasantry, as were exalted to the condition of soccage tenants; and was in reality a consequence of vassalage, interwoven in the system of that feudal government, with which the people of that age were familiarly acquainted. Neither was it likely that the appearance, from time to time, of a few of these inferior persons, along with the greater lords of parliaments, would have an apparent tendency to vary the deliberations of that assembly; and the practice had, in all pro-<217>bability, been long continued, and greatly extended, before the effects of it were of such magnitude as to attract the notice of the public.

SECTION II

The Division of Parliament into two Houses, and the peculiar Privileges acquired by each House.

The members of the great council, in all the feudal governments of Europe, were divided originally into two classes or orders; the one composed of ecclesiastical, the other of lay barons. These two sets of men, from their circumstances and way of life, having a different interest, and being actuated by different views of policy, entertained a mutual jealousy, and were frequently disposed to combat and thwart the designs of each other. In the conduct of national business, they usually held separate conferences among themselves; and when they afterwards came to a joint meeting, were accustomed, instead of voting promiscuously, to deliver, upon the part of each, the result of their previous deliberations. As each of those bodies was possessed of independent authority, <218> it would have been dangerous to venture upon any measure of importance, in opposition to the inclination or judgment of either; and, therefore, in all public transactions which they had occasion to determine, the concurrence of both was held indispensable. Hence, by long custom, they became two separate *estates,* having each a negative upon the resolutions of the legislature.

When the burgesses were admitted into the national assembly, they were, by their situation and character, still more distinguished from the ecclesiastical and lay barons, than these last from each other. They acted, not in their own name, but in the name of those communities, by whom they had been appointed, and to whom they were accountable: at the same time that the chief object in requiring their attendance, was to give their consent to such peculiar aids, or taxes, as were demanded from their constituents. It was necessary, therefore, that they should consult among themselves, in matters relating to their peculiar interest; and, as the department allotted them was unconnected with that of all the other members, they naturally obtained a separate <219> voice in the assembly. We may easily conceive, that when this method of procedure had been established in the imposition of taxes, it was afterwards, upon the subsequent rise of the burgesses, extended to every branch of parliamentary business, in which they claimed the privilege of interfering. Thus, in all the feudal kingdoms which had made advances in commerce, the great council came to be composed of three estates:[13] each of whom, in the determination of public measures, enjoyed a separate negative.

Whether these different classes of men should be convened in the same, or in different places, depended, in all probability, upon accident, and in particular on the number of their members, which, at the times of their meeting, might render it more or less difficult to procure them accommodation. In England, the prelates, and the nobility, were accustomed, in ordinary cases, to meet in the same place; although it is likely that each of them, in order to settle their plan of operations, had previous consultations among themselves. When the deputies from counties and boroughs were first <220> called into parliament, they proceeded upon the same plan, and were included in the same meeting with the ancient members. It is probable, that the boroughs, then in a condition to use this privilege, were not numerous.

13. That is, the nobility, the upper clergy, and the commons.

To a parliament held in the eleventh of Edward the first, we find that no more than twenty towns were required to send representatives; of which two were summoned from each town.* But upon the regular establishment of the deputies from counties and boroughs, in the twenty-third year of that reign, the number of the latter was greatly encreased. The returning boroughs, from each of which two representatives were generally required, are said to have then amounted to about an hundred and twenty; besides thoses belonging to Wales, of which there are supposed to have been about twelve.† <221>

From the number of the burgesses at this time, from the influence and weight which they had acquired, and from their peculiar character and circumstances, as representing the commercial interest, they now found it convenient, it should seem, to have a different place of meeting from the other members of parliament, and began to form a separate body, which was called the house of commons. <222>

The knights of shires continued, for some time after, to sit in what now became the house of peers. Although the small barons were, in general, excused from personal attendance, yet, as crown-vassals, they had still a title to vote in parliament; and such of them as attended, even in consequence of an election, were at first considered in the same light with the greater nobility. By appearing frequently, however, in the capacity of mere representatives, not only elected, but having their charges borne by their constit-

* The trading towns, who sent representatives to this parliament, were London, York, Carlisle, Scarborough, Nottingham, Grimesby, Lincoln, Northampton, Lynne, Yarmouth, Colchester, Norwich, Chester, Shrewsbury, Worcester, Hereford, Bristol, Canterbury, Winchester, and Exeter. See Carte's Hist.

† Some of these boroughs, however, were omitted in the summons to future parliaments. Mr. Browne Willis, from a diligent inspection of such materials, as he could find, to afford any information upon this point, is of opinion, that from about the middle of Edward the third's reign, to the beginning of that of Edward the sixth, the parliament consisted of a pretty uniform number of boroughs: that, about this last period, it consisted of 126, and at no former time amounted to 130. See Notitia Parliam.

Mr. Hume asserts, that the sheriff of each county had anciently a discretionary power of omitting particular boroughs in his returns, and was not deprived of this power till the reign of Richard II. [Hist. 4to, vol. ii. p. 287.] In proof of this assertion, he refers to 5 Richard II. c. 4. But that statute proves the direct contrary. It declares, "That if any sheriff leaves out of his returns any cities or boroughs which be bound, and of old time were wont to come to the parliament, *he shall be punished in the manner as was accustomed to be done in the said case in times past.*" Statutes at Large.

uents, their privilege of attending in their own right was gradually lost and forgotten. In consequence of the progressive alienation and division of landed property, their personal influence was continually sinking, while that of the mercantile people was rising in the same proportion; and, as these two classes were thus brought nearer to a level, the landed gentry were often indiscriminately chosen to represent either the one or the other. In such a situation, it became at length an obvious improvement, that the deputies of the counties and boroughs, as by the circumstance of their being representatives, and responsible <223> to those who had appointed them, they were led into a similarity of procedure, should meet in the same house, and carry on their deliberations in common. It is conjectured by Carte, the historian, that this change was not effected before the latter part of the reign of Edward the third; but with respect to the precise time when it happened, there seems to be no evidence whatever.[14]

The coalition of these two orders of deputies may perhaps be regarded as the great cause of the authority acquired by the English house of commons. The members of that house were by this measure exalted to higher consideration and respect, from the increase of their numbers, as well as from the augmentation of their property. They now represented the mercantile people and the landed gentry; who, exclusive of those who remained in a state of servitude, composed the great body of the people, and who possessed a great proportion of the national wealth. Of those two classes of the free inhabitants, the landed gentry, for a long time, enjoyed the first rank; and the deputies of boroughs were therefore frequently <224> chosen among the neighbouring gentlemen, who, by reason of their independence, were more capable than their own burgesses of protecting their constituents. By joining together and confounding these different orders of representatives, the importance of either was in some degree communicated to both; at the same time that the people, under so many leaders, became attentive to their common privileges, and were taught to unite in defending them. Had all the constituents been to appear in the national council, they would have been a disorderly multitude, without aim or direction: by choosing deputies to

14. Thomas Carte (1686–1754), English Jacobite historian and author of *A General History of England* (1747–55). For his argument that counties and boroughs do not start to meet in common before the latter part of Edward III's reign, see vol. 2, bk. 10, 451; on the 1339 parliament and knights of shires pleading to not grant a tax without consent of constituents, see 433.

manage their parliamentary interest, they became an army, reduced into regular subordination, and conducted by intelligent officers.

We accordingly find, that, even so early as the reign of Richard the second, the commons, when they had been induced to take party with the crown, were able to defeat the designs of the nobility, and to raise the sovereign from the lowest extremity to the height of absolute power. The sudden revolution, produced at that time by the national representa-<225>tives, was a prelude to those greater exertions, which, at a subsequent period, they displayed in a better cause.

In the principal kingdoms upon the continent of Europe, the *third estate* was differently constituted. It comprehended, as I formerly observed, no other deputies but those of the trading towns; a set of men, who, in comparison even of the small barons, or inferior gentry, were long obscure and insignificant. In supporting their privileges, the boroughs were not aided by the joint efforts of the counties; and the family interest of the representative was not super-added to the weight of his personal wealth.

In some of those kingdoms, therefore, as in France and in Spain, the monarch was enabled to break the aristocracy, and to annihilate the national council, before the *third estate,* in consequence of the advancement of commerce, was in a condition to establish its authority: in others, as in the German empire, the great nobles, before the deputies of towns had acquired much influence in the *diet,* reduced the power both of that assembly, and of the emperor, to a mere shadow. <226>

After the members of parliament had been accustomed to meet regularly in two separate places, the three estates were gradually melted down and lost, in the division of the two houses. The ecclesiastical and lay barons, who sat in the upper house, were led, most frequently, into a promiscuous deliberation; and did not think it worth while to demand a separate voice, except in determining any nice or important question, by which the interest of either was particularly affected. But as government came to be more established upon a regular plan, those extraordinary questions occurred less frequently; at the same time that the progress of knowledge, and of the arts, diminished the influence of the clergy, and rendered them less willing to hazard a direct and avowed contest with the nobles. The custom of deliberating promiscuously, was thus more and more confirmed, and the exertions of a separate negative, being considered as indications of obstinacy or a factious disposition, were marked with disapprobation and censure, and at length entirely exploded. It appears that, in the time of Richard the second, this innovation was not entirely compleated. <227>

The two houses, on the other hand, having occasion always to deliberate apart, acquired an independent authority, and were naturally regarded as distinct branches of the legislature. The resolutions of each house constituted a separate voice; and the concurrence of both was necessary in all the determinations of parliament.

After the formation of the two houses of parliament, in the manner just mentioned, each of them came to be possessed of certain peculiar privileges; which, although probably the objects of little attention in the beginning, have since risen to great political importance.

1. The house of commons, from the nature of its original establishment, obtained the sole power of bringing in money-bills. This was not, at first, regarded as a privilege, but was introduced merely for the sake of dispatch. The primitive house of commons was composed of burgesses only, empowered to grant the king a supply, by one general agreement, in place of the separate bargains, which had formerly been made with each borough. In conducting this business, each borough seems to have directed its repre-<228>sentatives with respect to the rate of assessment to which they should consent; and by collecting these particular directions, the sum total to be granted by the whole trading interest was easily ascertained. In a matter so simple as that of determining the extent of the contribution which, on any particular occasion, they were willing to make, the constituents found no difficulty either in preparing their deputies, by expressing a previous opinion upon the subject, or by sending them clear and pointed instructions, in case, from any new exigence, after the meeting of parliament, an unexpected demand was made by the sovereign.

According to this constitution of parliament, the imposition of taxes produced no intercourse between the two houses; but each house consented to the exactions laid upon that order of men with which it was connected. This method of procedure was continued so long as the house of commons consisted only of burgesses; but when the deputies from counties came to sit and deliberate along with them, a variation was necessary. The deputies of the counties having, by this change, assumed entirely the character of representatives, came <229> naturally to be limited, in the same manner as the burgesses, by the instructions of their constituents.* But those two orders of men, who now formed the cumulative body of the commons, were connected with different parts of the nation; and, while the burgesses were interested in the taxes laid upon the boroughs, the county-members had an equal concern in such as were paid by the landed gentry. In their promiscuous deliberations, therefore, upon the subject of taxation, it was found convenient, that each of them should not confine their views to that part of the community which they represented, but should agree in the duties to be paid in common by the whole of their constituents; and, as the taxes paid by landed gentry or small barons were of the same nature with those which were laid upon the great barons or peers, this naturally suggested the idea of a general assessment upon the nation at large, to be imposed by the concurrence of both houses of parliament. Hence <230> the introduction of *tenths, fifteenths,* and *subsidies;* the two former of which were taxes upon personal property; the last, upon estates real and personal. In the imposition of such taxes, both houses of parliament were equally concerned; and the concurrence of both was therefore held requisite.

The house of commons, however, if the precise sum to be granted by them had not been previously specified, were accustomed, in cases of this nature, to consult their constituents, and to regulate their conduct by the instructions which they received.

They could have no debate, therefore, on any occasion, upon the subject of taxation; as their province extended no farther than merely to declare the determination of their constituents. Upon this account, it was to no purpose that any particular tax should first become the subject of deliberation among the peers, and afterwards be submitted to the consideration of the commons; since, after the fullest and most laborious discussion of the question by the former, no other point could be considered by the latter, but whether the intended supply was agreeable to their instructions. The <231> most expedient course, in order to save time and useless disputation, was evidently, that the commons should begin with stating the exact sum which they had been empowered to grant; and that the tax proposed by them should afterwards be examined and canvassed in the house of peers, whose conduct, in

* In a parliament held in the year 1339, that is, about the middle of the reign of Edward the third, we find the knights of shires pleading that they durst not grant a tax without the consent of their constituents. Carte.

this as well as in other particulars, was not subject to any direction or controul.

From the same circumstance which introduced the practice, that every proposal for a tax should originate in the house of commons, it became customary that every such proposal or bill, when presented to the house of peers, should receive their simple assent, or negative, without variation or amendment. It could answer no purpose, to return the bill, with amendments, to the house of commons; because the members of that house had no power of deliberating upon such matters, and, having once declared the opinion of their constituents, could not venture to deviate from it in any subsequent stage of the business.

It is probable, at the same time, that this mode of conducting the business of taxation was promoted by the king; who, finding the <232> people of inferior condition most ready to acquiesce in his demands, was willing that, by taking the lead in the imposition of taxes, they might incite the nobility to follow their example, and make them ashamed of declining a burden which they were much more able to bear.

Such appears to have been the origin of this important privilege, which is now justly regarded by Englishmen as one of the greatest pillars of their free constitution. Like many other parts of the British government, it arose from views of immediate conveniency; and its distant consequences were neither foreseen nor intended: but, after it had received the sanction of immemorial custom, it was preserved inviolable, without any consideration of the circumstances from which it had taken its rise. As the commons interfered by degrees in legislation, and in various other branches of business, their interpositions became too extensive and complicated, to permit that they should be regulated by the opinion of constituents living at a distance. In consequence of more liberal views, it came also to be considered as the duty of each representative, to pro-<233>mote the good of the nation at large, even in opposition to the interest of that particular community which he represented. The instructions, therefore, of constituents were laid aside, or regarded as producing no obligation, upon any set of deputies, to depart from the dictates of their own conscience. The expediency of this important privilege, with which the house of commons came thus accidentally to be invested, will fall more properly to be examined hereafter.

2. Upon the establishment of the two houses of parliament, the supreme judiciary power was, on the other hand, appropriated to the house of peers.

The jurisdiction belonging to the Saxon Wittenagemote was exercised promiscuously by all the members of that assembly; and in the Norman parliaments, both before and after the formation of the *aula regis,* the same rule was observed. It seems, however, to be a principle of natural law, that when a magistrate of any sort is invested with jurisdiction, he is bound to a personal discharge of the duties of his office, and has no power to commit the exercise of them to a delegate. The public, by whom he is appointed, has a <234> right to the fruit of that capacity or diligence, upon account of which he was selected to the office; and as, in the decision of law-suits, no security can be given that different individuals will act precisely in the same manner, the appointment of a delegate for the discharge of this employment, would be to impose upon the public a different rate or measure of service from that which was due. Upon this principle, the members of the house of commons, having only a delegated power, were excluded from the exercise of that jurisdiction with which the members of parliament, in general, had been anciently invested. Their disqualification, at the same time, was rendered still more apparent, by their acting in consequence of instructions from their constituents. The counties and boroughs might be in a condition, from their general information, to instruct their deputies concerning the taxes to be imposed, or even concerning any law to be enacted, but were altogether incapable of directing them how to proceed in the determination of law-suits. The decision given in any cause must depend upon a complex view of the proofs and arguments produced in court; <235> and, therefore, no person who is absent, especially in cases where the chief part of the business is transacted *viva voce,*[15] can form any proper judgment concerning it. Upon this account, the only members of parliament, qualified to act as judges, came to be those who sat in their own right, who had the liberty to form their opinions upon the spot, and, by an immediate investigation of the circumstances, were capable of deciding from the impression made upon their own minds.

From the same cause, therefore, which bestowed upon the commons the right of suggesting taxes, the house of peers became the ultimate tribunal of the nation, and obtained the power of determining, in the last resort, both civil and criminal actions. Thus, while one of these branches of the legislature enjoyed an immediate access to the purses of the people for the

15. Spoken aloud.

public service, the other was intrusted with the guardianship of their lives and fortunes. What was acquired by the commons, in one department, was fully compensated by what fell to the share of the peers in another; so that the constitution remained upon its an-<236>cient basis, and was kept in equilibrio by an equal distribution of privileges.

It may farther deserve to be remarked, that, by the exclusion of the commons from the judicial power, the supreme tribunal of the nation came to be composed of a moderate number of persons; a circumstance highly conducive to the uniformity of their decisions, as well as to the expedition and regularity of their procedure.

When law-suits before the Norman parliament had become frequent, it was found inconvenient to determine them in a full meeting, and they were brought, in the first instance, before the *aula regis.* But even as a court of review, the parliament, after the deputies of boroughs and counties were obliged to give constant attendance, was perhaps too numerous; while, by the division of its members into two houses, they were prevented, at least, according to their usual forms, from co-operating with one another in the distribution of justice. The same regulation, therefore, which was introduced from the peculiar situation of the lords and of the commons, was <237> afterwards recommended, no doubt, and supported by general considerations of utility.

3. The supreme judiciary power being limited to the house of peers, the right of *impeachment* was of course devolved upon the commons.

When the persons intrusted with great offices under the crown, or enjoying any share in the public administration, were guilty of malversation in office, or of what are called high misdemeanors, it was frequently thought necessary, that they should be tried before the highest court in the nation, whose weight alone was adequate to the task of bringing such powerful offenders to justice. In the earlier periods of the English government, the national council was accustomed to inquire into the conduct of the different executive officers, and to punish them for their offences. The king himself was not exempted from such inquiry and punishment, more than persons of inferior rank. On such great occasions, the prosecution, instead of being committed, as in ordinary crimes, to the management of an individual, was usually conducted by the assembly, who acted both in the capacity of accusers and <238> judges. This was, doubtless, a practice ill calculated for securing a fair trial to the delinquent; but it was no more than what happened in criminal trials before the ordinary courts of justice, where the king was both judge and prosecutor.

Upon the establishment of the two houses of parliament, it became a natural and obvious improvement, that, as the power of trying those offences was restricted to the house of peers, the privilege of conducting the accusation should belong to the commons; that branch of the legislative assembly, which had no share in the judicial department, though it was no less concerned than the other to prevent the abuses of administration. In this manner the two characters of a judge and a prosecutor, which, in the ordinary courts, had been placed in different hands by the custom of appointing deputies to officiate in the name of the crown, came likewise to be separated in the trial of those extraordinary crimes, where, from the danger of arbitrary measures, an amendment of the ancient method of proceeding was most especially requisite.

4. Beside the foregoing privileges, which, <239> from the influence of peculiar circumstances, were acquired by the different branches of parliament, either house was led to assume the power of ascertaining the persons of whom it was composed; a jurisdiction and authority over them, and the cognizance of the several rights and immunities belonging to their own order. Hence it came to be established, that the house of commons should determine questions concerning the election of its own members; and that every bill affecting the rights of the peerage should take its origin in the house of peers. The privileges arising from this principle, which have been acquired by the house of commons, were afterwards greatly multiplied, and variously subdivided, in consequence of the attention given by that house to the forms of its procedure, and to the rules and maxims necessary for securing its independence. <240>

SECTION III

Concerning the Manner of electing the national Representatives, and the Forms of Procedure in Parliament.

The establishment of a house of commons, consisting entirely of representatives, required a set of regulations for the election of its members. From the different situation of the counties and boroughs, the deputies of those two classes of men came to be chosen in a very different manner.

1. Upon the first incorporation of a borough, the nomination of particular persons, for distributing justice, for managing the funds, and for executing the other business of the community, would seem naturally to belong to all its members, who have a common concern in those branches of administration. In those towns, accordingly, where commerce had introduced a degree of wealth and independence among the bulk of the inhabitants, such a popular plan of government appears to have been generally adopted. But in many of the <241> boroughs, whose trade was more in its infancy, the people of inferior rank were still too poor, and in too servile a condition, to claim the privilege of electing their own administrators; and by their neglecting to intermeddle in public business, the care of every thing relating to the community was devolved upon particular citizens, distinguished by their opulence. When the boroughs were afterwards permitted to have a voice in parliament, the differences in their condition occasioned the same, or even a greater diversity in the mode of choosing their representatives; and, in a long course of time, many other varieties were added, from the operation of accidental circumstances. In some towns, therefore, the representatives were chosen by a considerable part, in others, by a very small proportion, of the inhabitants; in many, by a few individuals, and these, in particular cases, directed, perhaps, or influenced, by a single person.

Two sorts of inequality were thus produced in the representation of the mercantile and manufacturing interest: the one from the very different magnitude of the boroughs, who sent, for the most part, an equal number of representatives: the other, from the very <242> different number of voters, by whom, in each borough, those representatives were chosen. But this inequality, whatever bad consequences may have flowed from it in a later period, was originally an object of little attention, and excited no jealousy or complaint. The primitive burgesses were sent into parliament for the purpose chiefly of making a bargain with the crown, concerning the taxes to be imposed upon their own constituents; and the representatives of each borough had merely the power of consenting to the sum paid by that community which they represented, without interfering in what was paid by any other. It was of no consequence, therefore, to any one borough, that another, of inferior size or opulence, should have as many representatives in the national assembly; since those representatives, as far as taxes were concerned, could only protect their own corporation, but were incapable of injuring or hurting their neighbours. So far were the boroughs from entertaining a jealousy of one another upon this account, that some of them found it more eligible to acquiesce in whatever aids the king thought proper to demand, than to be at the expence of supporting their depu-<243>ties in parliament; and were willing to renounce the privilege, in order to be free of the burden attending it. Many instances of this occur in the English history, from the reign of Edward the first. Mr. Browne Willis has produced a large list of boroughs, which had early sent representatives into parliament, but which lost that privilege by disuse;[16] and there is no doubt that several towns, which had been incorporated, and which obtained the denomination of boroughs, exerted themselves from the beginning, and successfully, in avoiding any parliamentary representation.

Neither was it originally of much importance to any parliamentary borough, in what manner its deputies were chosen; for these, being instructed by the corporation, with respect to the precise amount of the supply to be granted, were only the messengers, who declared the will of their constituents; and as they were not intrusted with discretionary powers, their behaviour occasioned no apprehension or anxiety. The honour of being the representative of a borough was, in those times, little coveted; and the privilege of voting in his election was yet less. The rank which the <244> burgesses held in parliament was too low to become the object of much interest or solicitation; and those who voted for a burgess, were so far from gaining any thing by it, that they had scarcely an opportunity of obliging their friends.

2. The knights of the shires were at first elected, in each county, by a meeting composed of the small barons, or vassals of the crown. Of this, from the nature of the thing, it seems hardly possible to doubt. The small barons had been originally members of parliament, but were excused from personal attendance, upon condition of their sending representatives. Who could have a right to chuse those representatives, but the persons whom they represented; the persons by whom they were sent; and who bore the charges of their attendance?

But although the vassals of the crown only had, in the beginning, a right to interfere in the appointment of the knights of shires; the *rear-vassals,* or

16. Browne Willis (1682–1760): English antiquary and author of *History of the Counties, Cities, and Boroughs in England and Wales* (1715–16), among other works. Both volumes of this work detail the history of counties, boroughs, and towns, and the representatives they sent to every Parliament from Edward VI to 1715, with only the exception of the twelfth of James I.

such as held their lands of a subject-superior, were afterwards admitted to a share in the election. This, although an important change in the constitution of par-<245>liament, has passed, like many others, without any notice of cotemporary historians. Of the circumstances from which it proceeded, a probable conjecture seems to be the utmost that can be attained.

The small barons, or vassals, who, exclusive of the nobility, held their lands of the crown, and those who held them of a subject-superior, were separate orders of men, who originally, by their situation, were removed to a great distance from each other. As members of the community, they appeared to be distinguished most remarkably in two respects. The vassals of the crown sat in parliament: those of a subject-superior were members of his baron-court. The former were liable for aids, and for the other feudal incidents, to the king: the latter were bound, for similar duties, to their inferior liege lord.

But these distinctions, arising from the feudal policy, continued no longer than while that system remained in its vigour. After the reign of Edward the first, the small barons, having ceased to attend in parliament, otherwise than by representatives, were at length understood, unless when particularly called by <246> the king, to have no more a seat in that assembly than the vassals of a subject-superior.

With respect to the feudal incidents, great alterations, in the course of time, were also produced. The demesnes of the crown, together with the extraordinary aids, and other incidents, drawn from the crown-vassals, were the only original funds for supporting the expence of government. But when the charges of the public, in consequence of the gradual advancement of society, had from time to time been encreased, these funds became at length insufficient; new supplies were demanded by the king; and after stretching as far as possible the ancient duties of the crown-vassals, it was found necessary to levy an assessment upon all the proprietors of land, without considering whether they held immediately of the king, or of a subject. The greater part of the public burdens came thus to be imposed upon the nation at large; and the casual emoluments, which the crown derived from its immediate vassals, became, in proportion, of little importance.

In this situation, there was no longer any essential difference between the small pro-<247>prietors of land, who held immediately of the crown, and those who held of a subject. Neither of them had any right, in their own persons, to sit in the house of commons. Both of them, according to the later notions of property, had the same full power over the respective estates which they possessed; and the estates of both were equally subject to the taxes imposed upon the counties. Both of them, therefore, were equally beholden to the knights of the shires, by whose consent those taxes were imposed, and who had it in their power to secure either the one or the other from oppression. As those two classes of men thus reaped an equal benefit from the service of the knights of shires, it became reasonable that they should contribute jointly to the expence with which that service was attended; and if they joined in maintaining the county representatives, it was no less equitable, that they should have a voice in their election. If they submitted to the burden, they could not decently be excluded from the privilege.

By this relaxation of the feudal system, the foundation of the house of commons was en-<248>larged; and its establishment was rendered more extensively useful. The knights of the shires became properly the representatives, not of one class, but of the whole gentry of every rank and description. All the independent property in the kingdom was, according to this constitution, represented in parliament: the lords appeared in behalf of their own possessions; the inferior landed interest fell under the care of the county members; and the burgesses were entrusted with the protection of that wealth which was employed in trade.

Such, in all probability, were the circumstances, from which the rear-vassals obtained a share in the election of county-members; but at what time this change was produced is very uncertain. Mr. Hume has concluded, that it took place in consequence of an act of parliament in the reign of Henry the fourth. But when we examine that statute, it does not appear to have introduced any such regulation: on the contrary, it supposes that proprietors of land, not holding directly of the crown, had been formerly entitled to vote for the county-members; and makes a general provision for <249> securing the freedom of their election, as well as for preventing undue returns by the sheriff.*

A late respectable historian,[17] notwithstanding all the light which has been thrown upon the subject in the present age, declares it still to be his opinion,

* 7 Henry IV. c. 15. See a farther provision to the same purpose, II Henry IV. c. 1.

17. Millar is referring to Baron George Lyttelton and his *History of the Life of King Henry the Second,* 3rd ed., 4 vols. (London, 1769). See vol. 3, bk. 2, 220–25, 373–79.

not only that the knights of counties were coeval with the existence of the English parliament; but that, from the beginning, they were chosen, as at present, in a joint meeting of the rear-vassals, and those who held immediately of the crown.[*] The former part of this opinion has been already examined. With regard to the latter, it is totally inconsistent with the original plan of the feudal government. But what puts the matter beyond all possibility of doubt, is, that in Scotland, whose constitution, from a similarity of circumstances, as well as from imitation, is extremely analogous to that of England, but who, from the slow progress of arts, has retained a number of her primitive regulations; in Scotland, the original practice has been in<250>variably continued; and, from the first introduction of county-representatives to the present day, no person who does not hold his lands immediately of the crown, whatever be the extent of his property, has ever been permitted to vote in a county election.[†]

When a number of crown-vassals had been excused from personal attendance in parliament, on account of the smallness of their fortunes, it might have been expected that some rule would be established, concerning the precise extent of property which gave a title to this concession; and that an exact line of partition would thus be formed between the small barons, or *gentry,* and the great barons, or *nobility.* It appears, however, that no such regulation was ever made. The liberty of absence enjoyed by particular members of parliament, seems to have depended, at first, upon the mere will of the sovereign, who never thought of restraining himself with regard to the terms upon which he granted this indulgence. To procure this liberty was the aim <251> of by far the greater part of the crown-vassals; as to prevent the unreasonable extension of it was the great object of the king; and the exemption was, by custom, established in favour of individuals, before any precautions had been suggested for ascertaining its boundaries.[‡]

* See Lord Lyttelton's History of Henry II.

† Holding of the prince of Wales, is in Scotland viewed in the same light with holding of the king.

‡ It seems at one time to have been intended by Edward I. that personal attendance in parliament should be required from every landed proprietor, whose yearly rent was above 20l. This was the rule prescribed to the sheriffs of counties, in summoning the crown-vassals to an assembly held in the eleventh of that king's reign. This was also the extent of property in Scotland, which distinguished the *great* barons, or those who were "*constrenzied* to come to the parliament or general council." Parl. 1457, c. 75.

The want of a general rule to define the limits, in point of property, between the *small* and the *great* barons, appears to have produced an irregularity in this part of the constitution. Those crown-vassals whose attendance in parliament had been dispensed with, continued ever after to be excluded from that assembly, and their posterity remained in the same situation, however great the fortune which they might happen to acquire. On the other hand, those opulent barons who continued, in their own right, to sit in parliament, after the time <252> of Edward the first, retained for the future their seat in the house of peers, notwithstanding all the vicissitudes of their fortune, and whatever might be the degree of poverty to which they were afterwards reduced. Property, the natural source of influence and authority, was, in this manner, detached from political power; while indigence, the parent of servility and dependence, was often invested with privileges which he was not qualified to exercise. The former inconvenience might, in particular cases, be removed by the interposition of the sovereign; who could, at pleasure, create any commoner a member of the house of peers: but the latter admitted of no remedy; since a peer, who had squandered his estate, could not, unless he committed a crime, be deprived of his rank; and since by that rank he was excluded from the usual means of repairing his fortune.*

As there was no regulation concerning the <253> *greatest* extent of property, from which a baron might be excused from attending in parliament, so there was originally none, with respect to the *least,* which entitled him to vote for a county-member. All the crown-vassals whatever, whose personal attendance was dispensed with, had of course a title to choose representatives, and were bound by their joint contribution to defray the expence of maintaining them.† But when landed property had undergone so much division, that the possessions of many individuals were become extremely insignificant; more especially after the rear-vassals had been joined with those who held immediately of the crown, in voting for the county-members; the poorer sort of proprietors endeavoured to excuse themselves from contrib-

* There occurs, in the reign of Edward IV. an act of parliament, declaring, in the case of George Nevil, duke of Bedford, that his title of honour, as a duke, was void and extinguished, in respect of his poverty, by which he was incapable of supporting his dignity.

† With respect to the contribution laid upon the counties for maintaining the members, see Madox *Firma-burgi.* It was at first levied by the king's writ; and afterwards by act of parliament, from the time of Richard II. See 12 Rich. II. c. 12.

uting to the support of national representatives; and, upon being relieved from that burden, had no longer a pretence for interfering in their election. <254>

By an act of parliament, in the reign of Henry the sixth, it is provided, that the knights of shires shall be chosen by persons residing within the same county, and possessed of lands or tenements, of which the yearly rent, free from all charges, amounts to forty shillings.* By another statute, in the same reign, it is declared, that the voter shall have this estate within the county where the election is made.† Mr. Hume is of opinion, that forty shillings, at that time, making allowance for the alteration in the weight of the coin, and in the price of commodities, was equivalent to near twenty pounds of our present money.

According as parliament had occasion to determine a greater variety of questions, had attained more experience in discussing the business which came before it, the forms of parliamentary procedure became an object of greater attention, and received, as we may easily imagine, a variety of improvements. The appointment of a president, in order to prevent confusion in delivering opinions, to declare the <255> result of a debate, and even, in some measure, to direct the method of handling any question, was a step so necessary in a numerous meeting, that we meet with it as far back as there are any records of the English national council. The lord high steward, as I formerly took notice, was anciently the person who, in absence of the king, presided in that assembly; and when that officer no longer existed, the chancellor, who then rose to the chief consideration in the king's household, was commonly entrusted with this department. After the division of parliament into two houses, this officer continued in most cases to preside in the house of peers; but in that of the commons, whose deliberations were totally separate, another president became necessary.

From the primitive situation of the commons, who, in all cases, were instructed how to act, they had no opportunity of debating upon any subject; but they required a person to intimate their determinations to the king; and for this purpose they, at first, elected a *speaker.* The farther the business of that house was extended, the more they ventured to form resolutions without the advice of their con-<256>stituents; the power and privileges of

* 8 Henry VI. c. 7.
† 10 Henry VI. c. 2.

their speaker were enlarged in proportion, and he at length obtained the province of an ordinary president. The first election of this officer, upon record, occurs in the first parliament of Richard the second. From the influence and dignity acquired, in that reign, by the commons, their speaker was exalted to an eminent station; and the persons who enjoyed the office became so conspicuous, as to attract the attention of the public.

One of the principal branches of business which fell under the consideration of parliament was legislation. The first method of conducting a measure of this kind was by a petition from parliament addressed to the king, setting forth some particular grievance or inconvenience, and requesting that it should be removed. To the king belonged the direction both of the executive and judicial powers; and, agreeably to the spirit of a rude age, he was originally under no restraint in the exercise of his prerogative, farther than what might arise from his apprehension of incurring the public displeasure. By a statute it was proposed to limit the former discretionary power of the <257> king, and, out of respect to his dignity, any proposal to this effect was made in the form of a request, that he would consent to the intended regulation. As every new law was, in fact, an innovation of the ancient establishment, it required the agreement of all parties concerned; that is, of the national assembly, including virtually the whole people, and of the king, whose power was to undergo a limitation. When the petition, therefore, had passed the two houses, and had obtained the consent of the king, it became an act of the legislature.

The petitions which had thus been granted, during the course of a parliament, were afterwards digested into the form of a statute; and, as the execution of this task required a degree of legal knowledge, it was devolved upon the principal judges of the kingdom. From the observation, it is said, that mistakes and abuses were committed in a matter of such importance, it was provided, in the reign of Henry the fifth, that the statutes should be drawn up by the judges before the end of each parliament; and, in the reign of Henry the sixth, the present mode of presenting bills to parliament, <258> already digested in the form of a statute, was first introduced.*

For some time after the introduction of the commons into parliament, no notice was taken of them in the character of legislators. The burgesses who composed the first house of commons, were not regarded as the advisers

* See Blackstone's Commentaries.

of the crown; and if on any occasion they were capable of extorting a redress of grievances, it was merely by creating an apprehension that they might refuse the supply which was demanded from them. In the beginning of the reign of Edward the third, the commons are mentioned in the character of petitioners; and the statutes are said, in the preamble, to have been ordained "at the request of the commonalty of the realm, by their petition made before the king and his council in the parliament, by the assent of the prelates, earls, barons, and other great men assembled at the said parliament." The union of the knights of shires, in the same house with the burgesses, contributed quickly to bestow a deliberative voice upon the aggregate body of the commons; and in the reign <259> of Richard the second, we find them interfering in public regulations of the highest importance.* In digesting the statutes, however, the old stile was continued, until the reign of Edward the fourth; when laws are said to be established *by the advice and consent of the lords, at the request of the commons, and by the authority of the same parliament.*†

From the primitive method of conducting bills for a new law, in the form of a petition to the king, was derived the custom that they should take their origin from parliament, and that the king should give no opinion concerning them, till they had been approved of in that assembly. As the king had no inclination to limit his own discretionary powers, it was never supposed that a bill for that purpose would be suggested by the crown. All that could be expected from the sovereign, in a matter of this nature, was, that he would be graciously pleased to comply with the desires of his people, communicated to him by the national council: and when a bill had come to be agitated in parliament, it was not yet <260> considered as the request of the nation, and could not, therefore, be regularly presented to the king, for the royal assent, before the two houses had given their authority for that measure.

Such was the original foundation of a maxim, which is now regarded as one of the main pillars of the British constitution; that the king's negative upon bills shall not be interposed, until they have undergone the final discussion of the two houses of parliament; and, as a consequence of this, that he shall not take notice of any bill depending in parliament, until it shall be communicated to him in the usual and parliamentary manner. The effect of

* See Gurdon's History of Parliament.

† See the preamble to those statutes.

this maxim, in supporting the democratical part of the government, is now universally admitted; but that it was dictated by a regard to the interest of the people, or from the view of encreasing their weight in the exertions of the legislature, there is no reason to believe. It is probable, on the contrary, that the form of procedure above mentioned was thought advantageous, or at least respectful, to the sovereign; as it prevented his being troubled with solicitations to limit his power, <261> until there was an immediate necessity for it. But in reality, this method of conducting the deliberations of the legislature, was not the fruit of any pre-conceived system of policy, nor the result of any claim of right, either upon the part of the king, or of parliament; it arose merely from the nature of the business under consideration, which was most conveniently brought to an issue in that manner; and, as this gave rise to a practice, which was observed with some degree of uniformity, so, in the revolution of ages, the ancient usage, whose utility became daily more observable, was invested with complete legal authority.

It merits attention, however, that what has been observed, concerning the method of ordinary legislation, is not applicable to the imposition of taxes. As the effect of a statute was to ascertain and determine the behaviour of the king, and consequently implied a privilege gained by the people; that of taxation was to bestow some emolument upon the crown, and to lay a correspondent burden upon the nation. An opposite course, therefore, was followed in those two branches of government. The people were understood to be the <262> prime movers in the former; the king, in the latter. The proposal for a new law proceeded upon a petition from parliament to the crown. The proposal for a new tax proceeded upon a request or solicitation of the crown to parliament. Each of these parties having something to bestow which the other wanted, they both became coy and reserved in their turn, and, by their address and perseverance, were enabled to extort reciprocal advantages. When the king was in want of money, he offered his consent to beneficial regulations, upon condition that certain taxes were imposed. When parliament were about to grant supplies to the crown, they took advantage of its necessities, and, as a preliminary article, stipulated the redress of grievances.

Upon this principle, that taxes are granted by parliament, at the desire of the king, is founded a rule, at present, "that the house of commons shall receive no petition for any sum of money relating to the public service, but what is recommended from the crown." And when a money bill is offered to that house, it is necessary, that the chancellor of the exchequer, or some other <263> officer of the crown, should declare, "that his majesty having been informed of the contents of the said bill, recommends the same to the consideration of the house."* After this preliminary step, a bill for the imposition of taxes is conducted in the same course, and passes through similar stages, with every other matter which comes under the determination of the legislature. <264>

* See Hatsell's Proceedings in the House of Commons. [[Millar's source for these passages is John Hatsell, *Precedents of Proceedings in the House of Commons* (London, 1785), 3:142.]]

CHAPTER VII

Alterations in the State of the ordinary Courts of Justice.

The reign of Edward the first is no less distinguished by institutions of great importance relating to the distribution of justice, than by those which have been mentioned with regard to the legislative authority; and in both these particulars we may trace back to this period, the introduction of that regular system which we at present enjoy. The chief of those institutions respecting the exercise of the judicial power, and some of the most remarkable consequences with which they were attended, we shall proceed to examine.

SECTION I

Establishment of the Courts of Common Law, at Westminster.

The *aula regis,* which, after the Norman conquest, had risen by degrees out of the high <265> court of parliament, was productive of great advantages, by facilitating the distribution of justice. A full meeting of parliament could not be obtained, unless upon singular occasions; but this tribunal, consisting of a small number of judges, and these commonly attending the king's person, could easily be held upon any emergency, and was ready to take cognizance of every complaint.

Although the institution of the *aula regis,* however, was, at the time of its introduction, accommodated to the infant state of improvements in the country, yet, in a subsequent period, when those improvements were advanced to greater maturity, and when the authority of government was better established, its interpositions became not only defective, but liable to many inconveniencies. For some time after the Norman conquest, the investigation of law-suits, although requiring a degree of attention unknown to the preceding ages, was not so tedious as to prevent their being commonly decided in the neighbourhood of the place in which they had been commenced. But when the advancement of law and government had farther multiplied the legal dis-<266>putes among the members of society, as well as the forms of judicial procedure, such a quick dispatch of the business was no longer practicable; and, as the court had no fixed residence, but followed the king, wherever the political state of the kingdom required his presence, it was frequently necessary that causes should be decided in a part of the country very remote from that in which they had arisen. The circumstances of this ambulatory court became thus inconsistent with the leisure and deliberation requisite for judges in forming their decisions; and still more incompatible with the interest of parties, who, in many cases, were obliged to attend the court from place to place, and sometimes, before they could obtain a final sentence, to travel over a great part of the kingdom. This attendance was rendered more expensive and burdensome, from the gradual advancement of law, as a science; which tended to promote the employment of lawyers, as well as other retainers of judicial controversy; and which, by contributing to encourage the fullest and most ample discussion of every plea, laid parties frequently under the <267> necessity of calling a number of witnesses in support of their several averments.

It was to be expected, therefore, that, according to the general improvements of the country, the attention of government would be directed to the removal of these inconveniencies; by rendering the *aula regis* a stationary court, or at least by appointing, that it should hold regular meetings at particular places.

While the natural progress of improvement in the kingdom appeared to require this alteration in the state of the principal tribunal, the increase of judicial business had likewise a tendency to distinguish different branches of jurisdiction, and to place them in the hands of different judges. The prosecutions carried on against atrocious offenders, to satisfy public justice, and to prevent the future commission of crimes, came to be viewed in a different light from private controversies concerning property, and the various rights and obligations which occur among individuals. Law-suits of the former sort, or *criminal actions,* are usually much less numerous than those of the latter, which have received the appellation of *civil* <268> *actions.* The trial of a crime is apt to be terminated in a more expeditious manner, than a civil process. Those heinous offences, which are supposed to require a prosecution at the instance of the public, excite, for the most part, a general indignation in the minds of men, who are therefore disposed to call for a speedy vengeance upon the criminal. In many of those offences, besides, it is necessary, that, before a prosecution is commenced, the person suspected of the crime should be arrested and imprisoned, in order that, if guilty, he may be prevented from escaping a trial; and the hardships to which he is thus unavoidably subjected, together with the difficulty of securing his person, afford additional reasons, from expediency, as well as from justice, for bringing the action against him to a speedy conclusion. To all these peculiar circumstances, we may add, that the laws of a country, respecting the punishment of crimes, are usually plain and simple; so that, in prosecutions of this nature, the judge can seldom have any farther difficulty, than what arises from the investigation of the fact. <269>

Law-suits about private property are in a different situation. A cool spectator feels himself but little interested in such disputes; and it seems reasonable that the parties should be left, in a great measure, to their own discretion, in bringing the business to an issue. As in such differences there is no reason to suspect that either party will endeavour to escape from justice, no imprisonment of either is necessary. The laws, too, relating to the civil rights of mankind, are apt to become so numerous and intricate, as may occasion great hesitation and embarrassment in applying them to particular cases. These peculiarities, by multiplying the pleadings of parties, as well as the delays of court, and by introducing peculiar forms of procedure, have contributed to distinguish a civil from a criminal action.

To these two species of law-suits may be subjoined a third, arising from disputes between the king and the people, in matters of revenue. Such law-suits are calculated to interest the public, at least the crown, like a criminal trial; at the same time that they are strictly of a mere pecuniary nature. Though <270> the public revenue of a state is really the property of the community, yet, in a monarchical government, the sovereign, who has the immediate disposal of that revenue, and who reaps more benefit from it than any other individual, is likely to consider it as his own patrimony, and to become particularly attentive to the support and encouragement of those judges by whom it is made effectual.

Thus, in every kingdom which is advancing in improvement, the same division of labour which takes place in the arts becomes also convenient in the conduct of law-suits; and, upon the same principle which gives rise to separate trades and professions, the province of distributing justice will be divided, and appropriated to a number of distinct judicatories.

These two objects, the fixing the residence of the *aula regis* to a particular place, and the division of the powers with which it was invested, had not been entirely overlooked by the English, before the time of Edward the first. From what has been already observed, it is evident, that an ambulatory court is less qualified for discussing a civil than a criminal <271> action. From the multitude of civil, in comparison of criminal causes, such an unsettled tribunal is attended with more inconvenience to the judge; from the greater length of time required in their discussion, it is more burdensome to the parties.

We accordingly find, that, by a clause in the great charter of king John, an improvement was made with respect to the exercise of civil jurisdiction; a court of *common pleas* was detached from the ancient *aula regis,* and was appointed, for the future, to have a permanent residence.* The making this an article in that great transaction between the king and his nobles, is a proof that a regulation of this nature was thought of the utmost importance; and that the want of it, in former times, had been a ground of general complaint. The new court of common pleas, which was thus erected, and held by separate judges, appears to have been deemed inferior in rank to the criminal court, held by the grand justiciary, and in which the king continued sometimes to sit in person. <272> For this reason, the latter court was permitted, in certain cases, to review the decisions of the former.†

Even at an earlier period, the *aula regis,* when acting as a court of revenue, had been so far distinguished as to have a separate *president;* that officer who had the charge of the public treasury.‡

At last, in the reign of Edward the first, these changes were completed:

* "Communia placita non sequantur curiam regis, sed teneantur in aliquo loco certo." [["Common pleas shall not follow [the king's] court, but shall be held in some fixed place." J. C. Holt, *Magna Carta,* 2nd ed. (Cambridge: Cambridge University Press, 1992), 454.]]

† See Blackstone's Commentaries, Book III. [[For Blackstone on the criminal court being permitted to review decisions of the common pleas court, see *Commentaries on the Laws of England* (London, 1765–69), vol. 3, bk. 3, 39–40, 43, 60.]]

‡ Baron Gilbert's History of the High Court of Chancery. Dialogus de Schaccario.

the court of the grand justiciary was entirely abolished; and three permanent courts were established at Westminster;[1] a court of king's bench, to have the cognizance of crimes; a court of common pleas, to determine civil causes; and a court of exchequer, to decide in matters of revenue. As the jurisdiction committed to these three tribunals was totally different, they had, each of them, a separate place of meeting, a different president, and were composed of different judges.

There is ground to suppose, that the jealousy entertained by the king, of that great officer <273> who presided in the *aula regis,* co-operated with the natural course of things in abolishing this court, and in producing the institutions which came in its place. The office of the grand justiciary was originally an appendage of that of the lord high steward; who, in all the feudal kingdoms, was the chief officer of the king's household, and the person next in power and dignity to the sovereign. As an employment of such high importance was naturally claimed by one of the greatest of the nobility, so his remaining in the possession of it could not fail to augment his opulence and authority. It was the same officer in France, who, at an early period, found himself in a condition to dethrone the Merovingian race of kings,[2] and to establish the crown in his own family. We need not wonder, therefore, that Edward, a prince of equal policy and activity, and who had been successful in extending the regal authority, should be desirous, at the same time that he improved the judicial establishments, of putting an end to the existence of a minister, of whose designs he might be apprehensive, and whom he found it difficult to retain in subjection. The chief justice, who <274> presided in the new criminal court, was considered merely in the light of a judge, without any share of public administration.

In this, as well as in other branches of government, the history of modern Europe exhibits a remarkable uniformity; accompanied, however, with certain varieties, the effect of accidental circumstances. The *cour de roy* in France, which, like the English *aula regis,* had grown out of the national council, and which was likewise an ambulatory court, was at length productive of similar inconveniencies to those felt in England; and it was thought proper to remove them by giving a permanent residence to this tri-

1. Westminster Hall, the new home of the Court of King's Bench, Common Pleas, and Exchequer. Originally built by William Rufus by 1099.

2. See p. 66, note 12.

bunal. By an ordinance, in the reign of Philip the Fair, a branch of the *cour de roy* was fixed at Paris, and another at Thoulouse;* to both of which the name of parliaments was given. Other courts of the same nature were afterwards added in different districts, or had arisen in provinces which came to be reduced under the French monarchy; so that the whole kingdom, instead of being placed, like England, under one set of great tribunals, re-<275>maining in the capital, was divided into a number of separate territories, in each of which there was a particular court, invested with a supreme and independent jurisdiction. The multiplication of law-suits in any of those courts occasioned a subdivision of its members into different *chambers,* among which the different sorts of judicial business were distributed.

The *aulic council* in Germany, as I formerly observed, was, in like manner, an ambulatory court, which had arisen from the diet of the empire; but, from the slower improvements of that country, or perhaps from the decline of the imperial dignity, the attempts of the German legislators, to correct this inconvenient mode of distributing justice, occurred at a much later period. In the year 1495, and the reign of the emperor Maximilian,[3] was formed the *imperial chamber,* a new and stationary court, with similar powers to those of the aulic council. But, as this latter tribunal was not abolished, the German empire has come to be provided with two distinct judicatures, the one ambulatory, the other with a <276> fixed residence, which have, in the greater part of causes, a concurrent jurisdiction.

In Scotland, the *aula regis,* both in its original constitution, and in its powers, was perfectly similar to the court of the same name in England; and, from similar motives of conveniency, it was afterwards broken into the different courts, of the session, the exchequer, and the justiciary; corresponding to the distinction of civil, fiscal, and criminal causes; and these tribunals came, at length, to have a regular establishment in the capital.

In considering the policy of the judicial institutions, in modern Europe, those of England and France, the two most powerful nations, appear to merit particular notice.

In France, the establishment of a number of parliaments, or supreme tribunals, in different districts throughout the kingdom, has the manifest advantage of diminishing the expence of litigation, by bringing the distri-

* In the year 1302.

3. Maximilian I, Holy Roman Emperor (r. 1493–1519).

bution of justice near the residence of the different inhabitants: an advantage which is farther improved, by the appointment of subordinate courts, held by the *lieutenant civil* and *criminel,* within the district of every superior judicatory. <277>

The independence of these great tribunals has, on the other hand, a tendency to produce inconsistent and jarring decisions. The districts belonging to the different parliaments may, so far as the interpretation of law, and the opinion of the judges, are concerned, be considered as in the state of separate kingdoms; having, in the ordinary operation of government, no means for securing uniformity of conduct. This, no doubt, is one great cause of the diversity of laws and customs, which, notwithstanding the general influence of civilized manners, is to be found at present in different parts of the French monarchy.

To remove this inconvenience, an extraordinary measure is, in some cases, adopted. The king, who is the fountain of justice, nominates, at pleasure, any number of persons, to receive an appeal from the decision of any particular parliament: and in this way, the members of one parliament are sometimes appointed to review the sentence of another. But this is a partial remedy, which cannot be effectual to prevent all discordance in the judgment of those different courts. In a few instances of gross absurdity, or flagrant in-<278>justice, the interposition of the sovereign may be procured; but it is impossible that he should give attention to the ordinary course of decisions, through the whole extent of his dominions, and restrain the numberless varieties and inconsistencies which are introduced into the common law of the country.

The judicial establishments of England are totally free from this inconveniency. As the principal courts have a jurisdiction over the whole kingdom, the principles of law, in every department, being determined by the same set of judges, are reduced to an uniform standard. As these courts have, besides, a fixed residence in the neighbourhood of each other, it was easy for them to communicate their opinions; and hence, in order to secure the propriety of their decisions, it became customary, in matters of great difficulty, depending before any one court, to refer the decision to a meeting composed of the judges of all the three courts. With the same view, it was provided by a statute in the reign of Edward the third, that the decisions of the court of exchequer may be reviewed by a court consisting of the judges of the king's bench <279> and common pleas, with the assistance of certain officers of the crown; and by another statute, in the reign of Elizabeth,[4] that certain proceedings of the king's bench may be reviewed in a joint meeting of the justices of the common pleas and the barons of the exchequer.

The system of English jurisprudence has become what might be expected from this general plan of the English tribunals. There seems to be no country in the world where the lawyers and judges are so strongly impressed with a notion of the advantages derived from uniformity and stability in the rules of law. That a certain rule should be established, and invariably maintained, is justly esteemed of more consequence, than that the rule itself should be the most perfect imaginable. Almost any regulation whatever is preferable to fluctuation and uncertainty. To such an extreme, it should seem, has this principle been carried in England, as to have produced a maxim, that when any point has once been decided in a judicial controversy, or has even been settled by the opinion of any lawyer of good authority, it shall be regarded as not <280> liable, on any future occasion, to be altered or disputed.

But the English tribunals, according to the plan above mentioned, were calculated to render litigation expensive and troublesome, by giving to the capital a monopoly in the distribution of justice. The inferior judicatories, those of the baron in his own demesne, and of the sheriff in each county, had, upon the advancement of the *aula regis,* been so far reduced as to retain only the cognizance of petty crimes, and the determination of civil actions below the value of forty shillings. These, therefore, could be of little service in settling disputes, and restraining injustice, throughout the kingdom; and, as no intermediate courts were provided, the most part of law-suits, both in civil and criminal matters, and whether of small or of great importance, could only be decided by the courts of Westminster-hall. In a country so extensive as England, a great proportion of the inhabitants were thus removed to a great distance from the seat of justice, and laid under many disadvantages in making their rights effectual. <281>

To supply this deficiency in the ordinary establishment, the king appointed certain extraordinary judges, as auxiliaries to those of the capital, for the purpose of circulating the administration of justice through every corner of the kingdom.

Although the distant residence of individuals from the seat of justice is, in all cases, inconvenient, it is more so in criminal than in civil actions. It

4. Elizabeth I (r. 1558–1603).

seldom happens that a crime can be proved in any other manner than by parole evidence; for a criminal does not usually act with so little caution as to afford a written document of his guilt; neither is it competent to demand his oath concerning the truth of the facts with which he is charged. But of all the methods of proof, that which requires the attendance of witnesses, more especially when they must be conveyed from distant parts of a country, is necessarily the most expensive and burdensome. In the view of public utility, it is likewise expedient, that every criminal trial should be conducted, and that the punishment of the offender should be inflicted, as much as possible, in the neighbourhood of the place where the crime has <282> been committed. The chief object in the punishment of crimes is to preserve the peace and good order of society, by deterring others from following the example of the criminal; and this is most effectually obtained, when the same persons who have beheld the violation of the law, are also spectators of the terror, mortification, and misery, with which that violation is attended.

From these considerations, when the king's bench came to have its usual residence at Westminster, the sovereign was induced to grant special commissions, for trying particular crimes, in such parts of the country as were found most convenient; and this practice was gradually modelled into a regular appointment of certain commissioners, empowered, at stated seasons, to perform circuits over the kingdom, and to hold courts in particular towns, for the trial of all sorts of crimes. These judges of the circuit, however, never obtained an ordinary jurisdiction; but continued, on every occasion, to derive their authority from two special commissions; that of *oyer and terminer,*[5] by which they were appointed to hear and determine all treasons, felonies, and misdemea-<283>nors, within certain districts; and that of *gaol delivery,* by which they were directed to try every prisoner confined in the gaols of the several towns falling under their inspection. Thus, by the addition of an ambulatory court, in supplement of another which has a fixed residence, precautions are taken to prevent the various and opposite inconveniencies incident to the distribution of criminal justice; and, as far as human insti-

5. O*yer* and *terminer:* A commission formerly directed to the king's judges, serjeants, and other persons of note, empowering them to hear and determine indictments on specified offenses, such as treasons and felonies; special commissions being granted on occasions of extraordinary disturbance such as insurrections.

tutions are capable of attaining perfection, the most complete establishment seems to be made for the trial and punishment of crimes.

The appointment of the circuit judges, in order to facilitate criminal trials, naturally suggested the idea, that the same commissioners might assist the courts at Westminster in another department, and be made subservient to the more expeditious decision of civil causes. With this view the commission of *assise,* and that of *nisi prius*[6] was granted to these judges. By the former they were impowered to take the verdict of a jury in the trial of landed disputes. The latter was intended to shorten the procedure in ordinary civil actions, by directing the judges in the circuits to investigate <284> all such matters of fact, as were then under dispute before any court of Westminster-hall.*

What is commonly an article of the greatest magnitude, even in a civil process, the proof of the different averments made by the parties, came thus to be discussed within the county, and frequently in the very neighbourhood of the place where the dispute had arisen; while the mere matter of law was left to the consideration of the great court at a distance; a court, from its permanent situation, as well as from its authority and dignity, the best qualified for deciding points of such difficulty and importance.

To these regulations, of such manifest utility, there was added a further provision, for maintaining the general tranquillity. When quarrels arose among individuals, when outrage and violence were committed, and these were likely to be followed by riots and insurrections, it was in vain to expect, that, by application to the ordinary courts of justice, a timely interposition could be procured for sup-<285>pressing such disorders. It was expedient, therefore, that men of rank and character, living in the different parts of the country, and who might, of consequence, be at hand upon any emergency, should be invested with sufficient authority to seize disorderly persons, to

* See Blackstone's Commentaries. Hawkins's Pleas of the Crown.

6. In late medieval England, royal commissioners were appointed to travel the countryside and mete out justice, empowered by temporary commissions to hear certain types of cases in a particular area (usually a county) at a particular time. Commissions of assize empowered the commissioners to hold their sessions. The Statute of Nisi Prius (literally, "unless before"), passed in 1285, held that justices of assize or circuit justices were to try the issues in ordinary actions and return the verdict to the court at Westminster.

put them under confinement, and, in general, to prevent violations of the public peace.

We find accordingly, that, by the ancient law of England, *conservators of the peace,* with powers of that nature, were, in the different counties, elected by the freeholders; and the same powers were also annexed to many of the higher offices of government. It appears that those magistrates had originally no cognizance of crimes, but merely an authority to secure offenders, in order to their trial before the ordinary tribunals. We may easily conceive, however, that such an employment would lead to a species of jurisdiction. When a person has been guilty of a breach of the peace, his conduct, although deserving animadversion, may often be unworthy of the trouble and expence which would attend a trial before the ordinary courts; and if, in such a case, the <286> magistrate, who has taken the offender into custody, and who must, in some measure, have already examined the case, should proceed of himself to inflict a moderate punishment, the expediency of such a measure would afford its justification, or at least would induce the public to connive at so small an extension of authority.

In the reign of Edward the third, the appointment of those magistrates, as might be expected from the rising state of the prerogative, was transferred to the crown; at the same time that they were invested with a power of trying all offences excepting those which inferred a capital punishment.* From this period they acquired the appellation of *justices of the peace.* By subsequent regulations they came to be entrusted with various branches of civil jurisdiction; by which they were enabled, in many questions of importance, to supersede the interposition of the superior tribunals.

Although, in Scotland, the principal courts of law were established in the capital, upon <287> the same plan as in England, the inhabitants were not subjected to the same inconvenience by their distance from the place where justice was administered. To say nothing of the narrowness of the country, compared with England, the Scottish nobles maintained their authority much longer than the English; and the courts of the baron, and of the sheriff, were therefore enabled to preserve a great part of their original jurisdiction. As these tribunals had the power of determining both civil and criminal

* By 18 and by 34 Edward III. the justices of peace are empowered to determine felonies and trespasses; but in practice their jurisdiction is restricted to such felonies as are within the benefit of the clergy. See Hawkins.

actions, in their several districts, there was no necessity for bringing such matters, in the first instance, before the superior courts in the capital; and upon this account, although the judges of the court of justiciary were empowered to make circuits over the country, as in England, there was no occasion for bestowing upon them any civil jurisdiction, corresponding to what arises from the English commission of *nisi prius.*

The appointment of justices of the peace, to supply what is defective in the jurisdiction of the ordinary courts for suppressing riot and disorder, was introduced into Scotland at a later period, but in a similar manner, and upon the same footing, as in England. <288>

SECTION II

Of the Petty Jury—and the Grand Jury.

From the progressive alterations, which have been mentioned, in the English courts of justice, it is natural to conclude, that the judges were continually advancing in experience and knowledge, and that the forms of judicial procedure were daily attaining higher degrees of perfection. Of all the institutions relative to the management of judicial business, which may be considered as the effect of that improvement, those of the *petty jury,* and the *grand jury,* are most deservedly the boast of English jurisprudence; and as, in the period which we are now examining, both of them appear to have arrived at their complete establishment, a review of the circumstances from which they proceeded, and of the steps by which they were introduced, may not be improper.

1. I had formerly occasion to observe, that, under the government of the Anglo-Saxon princes, the chief magistrates of the several <289> counties and hundreds, found it unnecessary, in the determination of law-suits, to call a full meeting of the courts over which they presided; and, for the greater dispatch of the business, as well as for the ease and convenience of the people, were accustomed to select a certain number of the freemen, or allodial proprietors, in each particular cause, to assist in giving a decision. Hence the first idea of the *petty jury* was probably suggested.

In a subsequent period, a similar practice was adopted in the courts of a barony. When the vassals of a superior had acquired hereditary fiefs, they were no longer under the necessity of submitting to his arbitrary will; and in regulating their conduct, as well as in distributing justice among them, he found it expedient to act with their advice and concurrence. To have assembled the whole of his vassals, for the determination of every law-suit, would have been too great a hardship upon them; but a moderate number were convened, in order to satisfy the parties, and to give weight and authority to the sentence.

The calling, occasionally, a number of the vassals, in each case, to assist the superior, was <290> a more natural expedient, than the appointment of certain permanent assessors. It was attended with no trouble or expence; for every vassal was bound not only to fight for the superior, but also to perform such other services as might be requisite, in order to support his authority and dignity. According to the simple notions of that age, these persons were sufficiently qualified to determine the points referred to their decision; more especially as they might receive advice and direction from the magistrate. In some respects they were held even preferable to every other sort of judges; being men of the same rank and condition with the parties; and, from their situation, having frequently access to know the state of the controversy, as well as the circumstances of the facts in question.

The introduction of juries in the courts of a barony, arose from the establishment of hereditary fiefs; for, so long as vassals held their land precariously, or even were not secure of transmitting it to their posterity, they had too much dependence upon their superior, to dispute his authority, either in settling their differences or punishing their offences. We may <291> easily suppose, therefore, that, under the Anglo-Saxon government, this mode of procedure was not very common; because the custom of securing landed estates to the heirs of a vassal was then far from being general. It is from the reign of William the Conqueror, that we may date the remarkable extension of jury-trials; proceeding partly from the imitation of Norman or French customs; but still more from the completion of the feudal system, and the consequent multiplication of hereditary fiefs.

It merits attention, that this institution had been hitherto limited to the hundred and county courts, and to those of a feudal barony, but never had taken place in the judiciary proceedings of the national council. The causes which came under the cognizance of the Wittenagemote were not so numerous, as to create much trouble to its members, or to suggest the measure of devolving that branch of business upon any sort of committee, or partial meeting, in place of the full assembly.

Upon the establishment of the Anglo-Norman parliament, its ordinary judicial business <292> was, in a short time, committed to the *aula regis;* a court which at first consisted of several members, but was afterwards held by a single magistrate, the deputy judge of the sovereign. This tribunal was properly the ordinary baron-court of the king; and, being in the same circumstances with the baron-courts of the nobility, it was under the same necessity of trying causes by the intervention of a jury. As the vassals of the crown were usually more independent of the king, than the rear-vassals were of their immediate superior; it is not likely, that, while justice was administered by the *pares curiae* to the latter, the former would submit to the decisions of a single magistrate, named at pleasure by the sovereign. We find, accordingly, that, by a general law in the reign of Henry the second, either party in a law-suit was allowed to decline the customary mode of trial by single combat, and to demand that his cause should be determined by an *assize* or *jury* of twelve persons. From this time forward, there can be no doubt that jury-trials were admitted in all the courts of ordinary jurisdiction. They are expressly re-<293>cognised and established by the great charters of king John, and of Henry the third.*

When the office of the grand justiciary was abolished, in the reign of Edward the first, and when the powers of the *aula regis* were distributed to the king's bench, the common pleas, and the exchequer, it was natural for these courts to follow the same forms of procedure which had been observed by that high tribunal to which they were substituted. The former practice of determining law-suits by a jury, was doubtless viewed, at the same time, in the light of a privilege, which the nation would not have been willing to resign. The number of judges, in each of the courts of Westminster-hall, was much inferior to that of the ordinary assize; and, as they were not men of the same rank with the parties, it was not likely that the same degree of confidence would be reposed in them. To have transferred the powers of an institution so popular as that of juries, to a set of courts constituted in this manner, would, notwithstanding the late advances of prerogative, have been a <294> dangerous measure. What is called the petty jury was therefore introduced into these tribunals, as well as into their auxiliary courts employed to distribute justice in the circuits; and was thus rendered essentially necessary in determining causes of every sort, whether civil, criminal, or fiscal.

* Magna Charta reg. Johan. c. 21. M. C. reg. Hen. III. c. 32.

In the high court of parliament, however, this method of trial was never admitted: being neither found requisite for the convenience of the members, nor conducive to the interest of parties. It was not requisite for the convenience of the members; because the trials which came before parliament were few, and speedily brought to an issue. It was not conducive to the interest of parties; because they were better secured from partiality and oppression, by a judgment of the whole house, consisting of all the crown vassals, than they could expect to be from a decision given by a limited number of those vassals, arbitrarily appointed by the president.

It has been questioned, whether an institution, similar to that of the petty jury in England, had place in any of the nations of antiquity. Among the Greeks and Romans, as <295> far back as we can trace the history of their judicial establishments, it does not appear that the inhabitants of certain districts were ever invested with jurisdiction, or that a part of their number were in each trial selected by the ordinary magistrate to assist him in giving a decision. The ordinary courts of Greece and Rome were composed of a chief magistrate, and of certain assessors; but these last were permanent officers, appointed, as it should seem, from year to year, or for the same period with the magistrate himself.

The Roman *judex pedaneŭs,*[7] indeed, was nominated for each trial; but he was originally no more than a commissioner for taking a proof of the facts in question; and, although he was afterwards empowered, in many cases, to determine the law, as well as the fact, the intention of his appointment was not to give weight and authority to the decision, but merely to relieve the magistrate and his assessors from a part of their labour.

Among the Gothic nations of modern Europe, the custom of deciding law-suits by a jury seems to have prevailed universally; first in the allodial courts of the *county,* or of *the* <296> *hundred,* and afterwards in the baron-courts of every feudal superior. The same custom, however, does not appear, in any European kingdom except England, to have been extended to those great courts, which, upon the advancement of civilized manners, arose out of the national council, and were invested with the principal branches of ordinary jurisdiction.

The *cour de roy,* in France, was not, like the court of the grand justiciary in England, reduced under the direction of a single magistrate; but consisted

7. A lesser judge appointed by a magistrate to decide a legal case.

of an indefinite number of the same persons who sat in the national assembly. The parliament of Paris, formed out of the *cour de roy,* was likewise composed of as many of the nobles as chose to attend; with the addition of a body of lawyers, who, it was understood, were to direct the forms of procedure, and to take upon them the drudgery of the business.* The parliament <297> of Toulouse, which was authorised at the same time, and the other parliaments which were afterwards formed in particular districts, conducted themselves upon the same principles with the parliament of Paris; and, as all of them were composed of a numerous council of judges, the intervention of a jury, to prevent erroneous judgments, or even to secure the parties from oppression, was the less necessary.

This observation is applicable to the principal courts of the German empire. The aulic council was composed of an indefinite number of the same persons who had a right to sit in the diet. The imperial chamber was a numerous council of judges. In both of these tribunals, therefore, the assistance of a jury was probably thought unnecessary.

In Scotland, the court of the grand justiciary came to be established upon the same plan as in England; and admitted, in like manner, the form of jury-trials. But upon the division of the powers of that court into different branches, the civil tribunal, then introduced, was a committee of parliament; that is, a committee of those crown-vassals of <298> whom juries had been composed. By one or two variations of that model, was formed the present court of session, which was made to consist of fifteen ordinary judges, the usual number of jurymen in Scotland; with a view, it should seem, to supersede the use of jury-trials: and as this mode of judicial procedure was laid aside in the principal civil tribunal, the example appears to have been quickly followed in the inferior civil courts of the kingdom. In the court of justiciary, however, which consisted of a smaller number of judges, and consequently in the inferior criminal courts, the ancient practice of jury-trials was continued.

Beside the circumstance now mentioned, relating to the constitution of the principal courts of justice in several European kingdoms, the influence

* Soon after the establishment of the parliament of Paris, the king dispensed with the attendance of the dignified clergy. The ordinary lay barons afterwards absented themselves, without any express dispensation; and there remained only the princes of the blood, and peers, who retained the privilege of attending that court on solemn occasions.

of the ancient Roman law, as delivered in the compilations of the emperor Justinian, was another more general cause, which contributed to the disuse of juries through the greater part of Europe. Upon the revival of letters in Europe, that improved system of jurisprudence was recommended and propagated by the clergy; was taught, <299> under their direction, in almost all the universities; and its decisions and forms of procedure were considered by the civil magistrate as models for imitation. The Gothic institution of juries, which had been unknown to the Romans, was therefore brought more and more into discredit; and, that the whole cognizance of a law-suit should be committed to judges, who, by being set apart for that purpose, and by devoting themselves to this employment, might become peculiarly qualified for the exercise of it, was regarded as an improvement in the state of judicial policy.

In England, where, from circumstances that will be mentioned hereafter, the Roman system was less incorporated with the common law than in other countries, the custom of jury-trials has, accordingly, been most religiously maintained. But even in England, this custom has been totally excluded from ecclesiastical tribunals, from those of the two universities, and from all other courts in which, from particular causes, the maxims and principles of the civil law have been adopted.

Scotland was, in some degree, under the influence of opposite systems; and seems, upon <300> that account, to have held a middle course. Like the nations upon the continent, she was led into a close imitation of the Roman decisions and forms of procedure; while, by her vicinity to England, she was induced to borrow many regulations and customs from that more cultivated and powerful country. Thus the Scottish tribunals imitated the English, by retaining a jury-trial in criminal prosecutions; but followed the practice of the Romans, by neglecting that institution in the greater part of civil actions. In the former, it was natural to entertain a greater suspicion of the court than in the latter; because in a criminal trial, the king, who nominates the judges, and to whom they must look for preferment, is always a party; whereas in a civil action, or controversy between private individuals, the crown has no interest; and there is commonly no circumstance to influence the magistrate upon either side, or lay him under a temptation to gross partiality.

It is not likely that the institution of juries would, in any country, be very acceptable to the sovereign; since it limited the power of those judges whom he appointed, and of whom <301> he had, in some measure, the direction.

We may easily imagine, therefore, that, according as, among any people, the prerogative was exalted or depressed, its influence would be exerted, more or less effectually, in discouraging this mode of trial; and hence we may discover an additional reason for the continuance of juries in England. As the English were successful in reducing the power of the monarch within moderate bounds, and acquired proportionably higher notions of liberty; they became, of course, the more attached to that method of distributing justice, by which the disposal of their lives and fortunes was committed to their fellow citizens, rather than to officers in the nomination of the crown. They became not only the more passionately fond of this privilege, which had been handed down to them from their ancestors, but at the same time the more capable of maintaining it. There is no reason, indeed, to believe that this circumstance alone would have been sufficient to retain, in England, the practice of jury-trials; for other European states have had also the good fortune to restrain the prerogative, and to establish a popular government. <302> But this circumstance undoubtedly co-operated, with the other causes formerly mentioned, in rendering the people of England more tenacious of that ancient appendage of the feudal policy, and more jealous of every attempt, from whatever pretences, either to limit the power of juries, or to exclude them from the decision of particular causes.

2. In order to secure the regular distribution of justice, it is not enough that courts are properly constituted, and that judges are attentive to the determination of law-suits. The magistrate must also be informed of those cases which require his interposition; and measures must be taken for bringing them under his examination. A distinction, however, in this respect, may be observed between that branch of judicial business which relates to civil, and that which relates to criminal causes. In a controversy between private individuals, each party is likely to prove sufficiently attentive to his own interest; and may therefore be left to vindicate his own rights as he shall think fit. But when a crime is committed, which requires a punishment for the sake of a public example, there is danger that <303> the interest of the community will be neglected; that no information of the fact will be given to the judge; and that no person will take upon him the trouble, the odium, and the expence, of bringing an accusation. It is here that some regulation is necessary, to prevent the disorders that might be apprehended, from permitting criminals to pass with impunity.

Among the Romans, not only the person injured, but any one of the people, was allowed to prosecute a public offence. As the crime was understood to affect the whole community, any one of its members, being in some degree a sufferer, was entitled, upon that account, to come forward and claim redress.

It requires but little sagacity to discover, that this mode of prosecution was liable to great abuses. It was likely, on the one hand, to produce negligence in prosecuting crimes; and, on the other, to encourage unjust and groundless prosecutions. Few people were found so public-spirited, as to undertake the disagreeable task of convicting criminals, from the view of promoting the interest of society, while many were tempted to become public accusers, from secret motives of resentment <304> or malice, or even for the purpose of obtaining a pecuniary composition from the person whom they had found an opportunity to prosecute. To prevent this latter enormity, severe penalties were inflicted upon such as brought an unjust accusation of a public offence. In particular, it was enacted, that he who failed in proving his accusation, should suffer the same punishment to which, if he had been successful, the defendant would have been subjected: a regulation which, if strictly enforced, must have put an end to every capital prosecution: for who is there that will hazard his own life, upon the uncertainty of prevailing in any criminal trial?

In the modern feudal nations, the judge himself was originally the public prosecutor. Every feudal lord, whether a sovereign prince or a subject, was excited to punish offences within his demesne; not only from the desire of repressing disorders, but also from that of procuring fines and amerciaments. As representing the community, of which he was the leader and executive officer, he first brought an accusation against those whom he suspected of crimes: as the chief magistrate, he after-<305>wards examined the proof, and gave judgment in the cause.

The mischief attending this practice must have soon become notorious. It can hardly be supposed that the same person would acquit himself with propriety in the twofold character of an accuser and a judge. Even in the course of a speculative debate, men usually acquire a prejudice in favour of those tenets which they are endeavouring to support; and find it extremely difficult to preserve a degree of candour in judging of such as are advanced upon the opposite side. What shall we say then of a person who is engaged in preparing a public accusation; who sets out with a strong suspicion, that the defendant is guilty; who converses with informers, likely to employ every artifice to strengthen that opinion; and who, to pass over his pecuniary interest, involved in the issue of the cause, has exerted himself in collecting and arranging all the facts and arguments in confirmation of his hypothesis? How is it possible to avoid that blind zeal and prepossession, that eagerness to convict the defendant, acquired in the capacity of a prosecutor; and to behave with that impartiality, coolness, and <306> moderation, which are essentially requisite in the distribution of justice?

To prevent this dreadful enormity, and at the same time to secure a proper attention to the public interest, the prosecution of crimes was, in all the feudal countries, reduced into a separate employment by the appointment of a procurator or factor to act in the name of the sovereign. Hence the attorney-general in England, and the king's advocate in Scotland, were appointed to manage the judicial business of the crown, before the principal tribunals; and a similar institution, from the same views of expediency, was even extended to inferior courts.

But, previous to the prosecution of offences, there must be information of their existence; and frequently, too, the immediate interposition of the magistrate is necessary, to apprehend and imprison the offender. In a rude nation, however, especially if it is of considerable extent, many crimes are likely to be hid from the public eye, and to escape the examination of any court. It appears, accordingly, that, in modern Europe, this branch of police had early become an object of general attention. <307> To make inquiry concerning the commission of public offences, and to transmit an account of them to the criminal court, was one great purpose of the appointment of *coroners;*[8] a set of officers who had place not only in England and Scotland, but in the greater part, if not in all, of the feudal kingdoms upon the continent.

The office of the coroners, in England, is of so great antiquity, that the commencement of it is entirely lost in obscurity. It seems to have been an immemorial custom of the Anglo-Saxons, that several persons of distinction should be named by the freeholders in each county, with power to secure and imprison criminals of all sorts, to the end that they might be brought to a trial. From this employment, these officers, as in after times the justices

8. Officers of a county, district, or municipality (formerly also of the royal household), originally charged with maintaining the rights of the private property of the crown.

of the peace, found the means of assuming a criminal jurisdiction, which, from small beginnings, became gradually more and more extensive. Another branch of business, devolved upon the coroner, and which may be regarded as an appendage or consequence of the former, was that of ascertaining and determining the value of the fines, amerciaments, <308> and forfeitures, or of any other emoluments, which accrued to the sovereign, either from the condemnation of public offenders, or from the right of the crown to all the goods, of which no other proprietor could be found.

When the coroner had occasion to inquire into the truth of any fact, either with a view to determine those matters which fell under his own jurisdiction, or in order to transmit an account of it to some other criminal court, he proceeded, in the same manner that was customary in the courts of the hundred, and of the county, by the assistance of an *inquest* or jury; and the number of jurymen, who, in those cases, were called from the neighbouring townships, was not less than was employed in other judicial investigations.

After the Norman conquest, when the *aula regis* drew to itself the cognizance of the greater part of crimes, it became the duty of the coroner to certify to that court his inquisition concerning those offences which fell under its jurisdiction; and upon this information, the most authentic that could well be procured, a trial before the grand justiciary was commenced. <309> Upon the establishment of the king's bench, and of the commissions of oyer and terminer and gaol delivery, the like certification, and for the same purpose, was made by the coroner to those tribunals.

But in proportion to the advancement of the prerogative, the authority of the coroner, an officer elected by the county, was diminished; his jurisdiction was daily subjected to greater limitations; and his reports became gradually more narrow and defective: whether it be that, by having a fellow-feeling with the inhabitants, he endeavoured to screen them from justice, or that, from the rust and relaxation to which every old institution is liable, his operations became tardy and inaccurate; certain it is, that he came to overlook the greater part of the offences which require the interposition of the magistrate, and his inquisition was at length confined to a few of those enormous crimes, which excite universal indignation and resentment.

To supply the deficiency of the coroner's inquest, the sheriff, who had come, in a great measure, under the appointment of the crown, was directed, upon the meeting of judges in <310> the circuits, or of the other criminal courts, to call a jury, in order to procure information concerning the crimes committed in particular districts. Hence the origin of what is called the *grand jury,* by whose inquisition the judges were authorised to proceed in the trial of public offenders.

It is probable, that when the grand jury were first called, they made an inquiry at large concerning every fact which ought to become the subject of a criminal trial, and of their own proper motion delated the persons whom they found to deserve an accusation; but, by degrees, when the agent for the crown had been led to suspect any particular person, he was accustomed to lay before them the immediate question, how far that suspicion was well founded? Hence the two methods of finding the fact; by *presentment,* and by *indictment.*[9]

It seems evident, from what has been observed, that the original purpose of the inquisition by the coroner, and of a *presentment* by the grand jury, was to prevent offenders from being overlooked, and from escaping a trial. When the custom of preferring *indictments* to the grand jury was introduced, the intention <311> of that measure was, probably, to avoid the trouble and expence of a fruitless prosecution. But whatever was originally intended by this practice, the necessity of procuring the previous approbation of a jury, by one or other of the forms above mentioned, was productive of the highest advantage to the people, that of securing them from groundless or frivolous accusations. If a person is known to have committed a crime, or lies under a strong suspicion of guilt, the voice of the whole neighbourhood will probably call aloud for justice, and demand an immediate trial of the offender. But if, on the contrary, an innocent man is attacked, if he is threatened with a prosecution, from apparently malicious motives, or for the purpose of serving a political job, it is most likely that his fellow citizens will view this proceeding with indignation; that they will consider his misfortune as, in some measure, their own; and that, from a principle of humanity and justice, as well as from a regard to their own interest, they will be excited to stand forth as the protectors of innocence.

This is a new instance, perhaps more conspicuous than any that we have had occasion <312> to observe in the history of the English government, of

9. A presentment is a report or return made by a jury, after holding an inquisition, or from some other knowledge. An indictment is a written accusation against a person, charging him with serious crime triable by jury.

a regulation whose consequences were not foreseen at the time when it was introduced. The great benefit arising to society from the interposition of the grand jury is not only totally different, but even diametrically opposite to that which was originally intended by it. The original purpose of that institution was to assist the crown in the discovery of crimes, and by that means to encrease the number of prosecutions. But when an accurate police had been established in the country, there was little danger that any crime of importance would be concealed from the public; and it became the chief end of the grand jury to guard against the abuses of the discretionary power with which the officers of the crown are invested, that of prosecuting public offences.

The employment of the coroner in Scotland was the same as in England; and he appears to have used the same forms in the exercise of his jurisdiction. With the assistance of a jury, he inquired into the commission of crimes, and either punished them by his own authority, or transmitted information concerning them <313> to the competent court. The negligence of this officer seems, in that country, to have likewise produced the interposition of the sheriff, or chief magistrate of particular districts, by calling a jury for the same purpose. By a statute in the reign of Alexander the second,[10] it is enacted, that no prosecution, at the instance of the crown, shall proceed against any person, unless by an accusation, upon the inquisition of a jury, consisting of the chief magistrate of the place, and three respectable persons in the neighbourhood. This rule continued till near the end of the sixteenth century; when, in consequence of the establishment of the court of session, and from other causes, the investigation of judicial matters, by a jury, came to be much more limited than it had formerly been. By an act of the Scottish parliament, in 1587, certain commissioners, instead of the inquest formerly called, were appointed in the several counties, for inquiring into public offences; and indictments, framed upon the report of these commissioners, were put into a list, which got the name of the *porteous roll.** <314>

The same statute empowered the king's advocate to prosecute crimes of his own proper motion;† and, as he was the person employed to raise indictments, upon the information transmitted by the commissioners, he nat-

* See act of Parliament, 1587. ch. 82.

† Ch. 77.

10. Alexander II, the Peaceful, king of Scotland (r. 1214–49).

urally assumed the privilege of determining whether the facts laid before him ought to be the ground of a prosecution or not. Thus in Scotland the ancient grand jury was abolished; and criminal actions, at the instance of the public, came, in all cases, to be directed at the discretion of a crown officer.

The attorney-general, in England, and the master of the crown-office, have acquired, in like manner, a power of prosecuting by *information,* without any previous authority of a grand jury; but this mode of prosecution is confined to misdemeanours tending to disturb the government, or the peace and good order of society, and is never extended to crimes of a capital nature.

How far the nations upon the continent were possessed of a similar provision, to secure the people from unjust and groundless prosecutions, it is not easy to determine. That in <315> the greater part of them the coroner's inquest was employed for bringing to light those disorders which required the interposition of a criminal court, there is no room to doubt. But when, from the circumstances which have already been pointed out, the method of trial by the petty jury had fallen into disuse, it is not likely that a previous inquest would still be employed to judge of the necessity or expediency of commencing a criminal accusation. From the rapid advancement of the prerogative in these nations, the sovereign was freed from any restraint in this branch of administration, and an unbounded liberty of trying public offences was committed to the officers of the crown. To whatever causes it may be ascribed, the English grand jury is now the only institution of the kind that remains in Europe; and perhaps, as it is modelled at present, there cannot be found, in the annals of the world, a regulation so well calculated for preventing abuses in that part of the executive power which relates to the prosecution of crimes. <316>

SECTION III

Circumstances which prevented the Civil Law from being so much incorporated in the System of English Jurisprudence, as in that of other European Countries.

To those who survey the common law of England, in its progress towards maturity, there is one peculiarity which must appear extremely remarkable; the little assistance it has borrowed from the ancient Roman jurisprudence; that system of equity, which has been so highly esteemed, and which, in the other countries of Europe, has excited such universal imitation. Why the English have deviated, in this particular, from the practice of all the neighbouring nations, and have disdained to draw supplies from those plentiful sources of legal knowledge, by which many systems of modern law have been so amply enriched, it seems a matter of curiosity to inquire: at the same time that, by examining the causes of a proceeding so singular, and apparently so unreasonable, we shall, perhaps, be enabled to <317> discover the advantages or disadvantages which have resulted from it; and likewise to form an opinion, how far expediency may, in the present state of things, recommend the same, or a different line of conduct.

The Gothic nations who subdued the provinces of the Roman empire, and settled in the countries which they had over-run, were by degrees incorporated with the ancient inhabitants; and from the communication and mixture of these two races of men, there was formed a composition of laws, manners, and customs, as well as of language; in which, upon different occasions, and from a variety of circumstances, the proportions contributed by the one people, or by the other, were accidentally more prevalent. Although the ancient inhabitants were, every where, the vanquished party, they possessed that superiority which knowledge and civilization have usually bestowed over ignorance and barbarism; and hence we find a multitude of Roman institutions inserted in the codes of law, which, at an early period, were published by many kings or leaders of those barbarous nations.

Soon after the settlement of those barbarians, <318> or rather before it was completed, they embraced Christianity, and fell under the direction of the Christian clergy; who, having been firmly established in the Roman empire, were enabled to preserve their footing in those new states that were formed. These ecclesiastics were attached to the Roman law, in opposition to the barbarous customs of the new settlers; both as it was the system with which they were acquainted, and as it was calculated to maintain that peace and tranquillity, which their profession and manner of life disposed them to promote.

The doctrines of Christianity, unlike the fables which constituted the mythology of the Greeks and Romans, contained philosophical truths, which the teachers of that religion were under the necessity of knowing, and by the knowledge and propagation of which they supported their credit among the people. Those teachers, therefore, became conversant in several branches of literature; and, as their theological system afforded them great scope for speculation and reasoning, and consequently for difference of opinion, they soon arranged themselves in different sects; disputed eagerly <319> with one another; and, in proportion to their zeal in making proselytes, acquired a degree of acuteness and skill in defending their several tenets.

The learning and abilities which came, in this manner, to be possessed by the clergy, together with the general ignorance and superstition of the people, bestowed upon the former an influence and authority over the latter, and produced, as I formerly took notice, an extensive jurisdiction both in ecclesiastical and secular matters. It is sufficient here to observe, that in the exercise of this jurisdiction, ecclesiastical judges were guided, as far as the difference of circumstances would permit, by the rules and principles of the Roman jurisprudence; which had been transmitted from the ancient inhabitants of the provinces, and were delivered in the collections made by different Roman emperors, by Theodosius the younger,[11] by Justinian, and by many of his successors. The Roman system became, in a great measure, the law of the church; and was therefore propagated by her, with the same zeal, and from the same views and motives, by which she was actuated in supporting and extending her influence and authority. The disorders which, for some cen-<320>turies, were continued, by the successive invasions of new barbarous tribes, retarded, no doubt, the progress of every regular establishment. But when Europe began to recover from these convulsions, and when the restoration of public tranquillity was followed, as there was reason to expect, by the revival of letters, the efforts of the clergy, to extend the credit and authority of the Roman law, became highly conspicuous and successful. Innumerable schools were founded in cathedrals and monasteries, many of which, under the patronage of the church, obtaining large endowments, and being invested with jurisdiction and various privileges, became what are now called universities. Both the *canon law,* which was the rule of decision in ecclesiastical courts, and the *civil law,* properly so called, the original fund from which a great part of the former had been gathered, were taught in these different seminaries, and thus rendered familiar, not only to those who had views of entering into holy orders, but to all who received the benefit of a liberal education.

11. Theodosius II, Eastern Roman emperor (r. 408–50), issued the Theodosian Code in 438 as an effort to systematize the complex mass of laws that had been issued since the reign of Constantine. See p. 58, note 6.

About the end of the eleventh century, Ivo de Chartres[12] published a collection of canon-<321>law, much more complete than any that had been formerly made; though it was much inferior to the subsequent compilation of Gratian, a Benedictine monk, known by the title of the *Decretum.*

In the year 1137, the Pisans, at the taking of the town of Amalphi, found a copy of Justinian's Pandects; and to this accident, the rapid cultivation of the civil law, from that period, has been commonly ascribed. But we may be allowed to entertain some doubt, whether an event of that magnitude could have proceeded from a circumstance apparently so frivolous.

There is no reason to believe that this book had been entirely lost in the western part of Europe, although, for a long time, it had been less in request than other compilations upon the same subject. Ivo de Chartres, in the preceding century, quotes the laws of the Pandects; and Irnerius,[13] professor of law at Bologna, as early as the year 1128, prelected upon some part at least of Justinian's compositions.

Even supposing the Pandects to have been lost, there were many other writings upon the Roman law still remaining, from which the <322> knowledge of it might, in some degree, have been preserved; the Institutes, the Codex; and the Novellae of Justinian; the Theodosian Code; and the compilations, published after the time of Justinian, by different emperors of Constantinople.

Neither is it likely that, if men had possessed no previous disposition to that study, it would have been inspired by finding an old book upon the subject. Few people will be at the pains to peruse a long book, upon any abstract science, unless they already feel a strong inclination to acquire the knowledge contained in it. But, in the twelfth century, when, from different circumstances, a spirit of improvement began to diffuse itself in Italy and France, it is probable that men of learning were excited to the discovery of ancient books upon every subject; and, as the civil law became then a principal object of attention, the Pandects, containing the fullest collection of legal opinions and decisions, was considered as the most instructive work of the kind, and copies of it were greedily sought for. As Amalphi was, at

12. St. Ivo de Chartres (ca. 1040–ca. 1116): French churchman and bishop of Chartres known for his collections of canon law. Gratian was a twelfth-century Italian jurist and monk who compiled the *Decretum Gratiani* (1139–50), the basic text for all later studies of canon law.

13. Irnerius (d. before 1140), Italian jurist, scholar, and teacher of law at Bologna.

this time, the chief trading state of Italy, an Amalphitan merchant, ob-<323>serving the demand for books of that nature, is said to have brought from Constantinople this copy of the Pandects, which was found by the Pisans. Some authors mention another copy of the same book, that had been discovered in the year 1128, at Ravenna.*

However this be, the Roman law was, upon the revival of letters in Europe, universally held up and admired as the great system, from an imitation of which the laws of each particular country might receive the highest improvement. This the modern lawyers were, by their education, accustomed to consider as the standard of reason and equity; and, wherever their own municipal customs were defective, they had recourse to it, in order to supply what was wanting, or to correct what was amiss. Even such of the modern writers as endeavoured to delineate the principles of natural justice,[14] independent of all positive institutions, made use of the Roman system, almost exclusively of every other, in order to illustrate their doctrines.

Although the Roman law was, in this man-<324>ner, generally incorporated in that of the modern European nations, it acquired more authority in some of these nations than in others. The German emperors appear to have considered themselves as the successors to the Roman empire in the west, and their dominions as therefore subject to that system of law, by which the Romans were governed. Hence, in Germany, properly so called, in the Southern part of France, or what are called the *Pays de droit ecrit,* and in several parts of Italy, which, at the time when the German emperors enjoyed the highest prosperity, were included under their dominion, the Roman law is understood to be the common law of the country, to which the inhabitants, upon the failure of their own municipal customs and regulations, are bound to submit. In other European countries it is viewed in the light of a foreign system; which, however, from its intrinsic merit, is entitled to great attention and regard; and of which many particulars have been, in a manner, naturalized by long usage, or adopted by the positive will of the legislature. This is the case in Spain, in Portugal, in the northern parts, or what are called

* Giannone, History of Naples.

14. Millar here refers to the Natural Law theorists, most prominently Hugo Grotius (1583–1645), Dutch jurist and humanist, and Samuel Pufendorf (1632–94), German jurist and historian. See p. 794, note 7.

the <325> *Pays de coutumes,* in France, in Sweden, in Denmark, and in Scotland.*

Upon the revival of letters, the same regard to the Roman law was discovered in England as in the other countries of Europe. It was propagated with equal zeal by the clergy, and, in the twelfth century, became the subject of public lectures in both the universities. The decisions and principles delivered in the writings of Justinian, were borrowed, and even the expression was frequently copied, by Bracton, by the author of Fleta, and by other English lawyers of that period.[15] The work attributed to Glanville, the grand justiciary of Henry the second, and a Scotch law book, known by the name of *Regiam Magistatem,*[16] both set out with a passage which is almost literally the same; whence, as well as for other reasons, it is concluded, that the latter of these productions has been copied from the former. Upon examination, however, the passage in question is <326> found in the preface to the Institutes of Justinian.

The settlement of the chief courts of common law in the neighbourhood of the capital, which was begun in consequence of the great charter of king John, and completed in the reign of Edward the first, made it necessary that the lawyers, and other practitioners in those courts, should reside there also. Hence arose the *inns of court,* and *of chancery,*[17] which were lodging-places in the neighbourhood of London, intended for the accommodation of the retainers about the courts of Westminster. Seminaries of common law were

* Duck de Auctoritate Jur. Civil.—It should seem, that, since the time when this author wrote, the ideas of the inhabitants, in some of those countries, have undergone a considerable change upon that subject.

15. Henry de Bracton (d. 1268?), English writer on law and until recently considered the author of *De Legibus et Consuetudinibus Angliae,* written before 1259 and one of the most important early English legal texts; *Fleta,* a treatise of unknown authorship on the English common law, was written in the late thirteenth century.

16. Ranulf de Glanvill (d. 1190), English jurist; the *Regiam Majestatem* (1609), covering "the auld lavves and constitutions of Scotland" of 1004–1400, was compiled and translated by Sir John Skene (d. 1617), lord clerk register to James VI and lord of session.

17. The Inns of Court is the collective name of the four legal societies in London that have the exclusive right of admission to the bar (Lincoln's Inn, Gray's Inn, the Inner Temple, and the Middle Temple). These societies date from before the fourteenth century and take their name from the buildings where the original law schools were established. The Inns of Chancery were lesser societies that depended on the former: their importance waned in the eighteenth century, and they disappeared entirely in the nineteenth century.

soon formed in those places of resort; and lectures upon that subject were given to the elder students, in the inns of court, and to the younger students, in the inns of chancery. The king gave encouragement to these institutions, by forming the members of each lodging-place into a sort of corporation, and by establishing a set of rules for their conduct. We find that Henry the third bestowed upon them an exclusive privilege, by prohibiting any other school for teaching law within the city of London. <327>

The universities of Oxford and of Cambridge were the only other institutions in the kingdom, in which law was taught with public encouragement. But in those learned societies, the only systems which had reputation, and which were thought worthy of public lectures, were those of the civil and the canon law. The municipal law, from its tendency, in many particulars, to encourage violence and disorder, from the barbarous jargon in which it was involved, and from the want of literature among its practitioners, was treated with contempt. These practitioners, we may easily imagine, were disposed to retaliate those unfavourable sentiments. Upon this account, and from the distance between the seats of instruction, in civil and municipal law, the former contributed no assistance to the latter. Those two branches of education were carried on apart, and became entirely distinct, and separate. The teachers of each, instead of co-operating in order to form a complete lawyer, were actuated by mutual jealousy and opposition; and the one science being treated as despicable in the universities, the other was probably represented as useless by the practitioners of the common law. <328>

For some time the civil law, under the patronage of the clergy, and of the universities, was in the highest esteem throughout the nation; and the study of the municipal law was confined to mere lawyers by profession; but at length, from the natural course of things, the comparative value of those two branches of science was of necessity altered. The latter, being that system by which the property and the conduct of individuals were chiefly regulated, could not fail to rise in consideration and importance; at the same time that, by the progress of judges in experience and refinement, its defects were gradually supplied; while the laws of Rome, which were unconnected with the ordinary courts of justice, and therefore of no practical utility, became an object of little attention.

We accordingly find, that, in the reign of Edward the fourth, and even before that time, the inns of court and chancery had become the fashionable places of education for men of rank and fortune, and were frequented by a great multitude of students. There were four inns of court, and no less than ten of chancery: in each of the former, the number of students <329> amounted to about two hundred, in each of the latter, to about an hundred. Neither was the system of education, in this great seminary, confined entirely to law: it comprehended all exercises, and every sort of accomplishment becoming a gentleman of the king's court; such as dancing and music. Sir John Fortescue[18] informs us, that it was likewise customary to study divinity *on festival days;* I suppose, by way of relaxation.*

Justice Shallow is introduced by Shakespear,[19] boasting, that he had been a student of *Clement's Inn,* and that he had often heard the chimes at midnight; as a proof that he was a young man of fashion and spirit.—In the same manner as he boasted of his acquaintance with John of Gaunt.

When those teachers of the common law had begun to feel their own consequence, they assumed the privilege of bestowing rank upon their students of a certain standing; and conferred the degrees of *serjeant,* and *apprentice,* corresponding to those of *doctor* and *bachelour* in the universities. <330>

As the separation of the civil and the municipal law produced an aversion to the former in the inns of court and chancery, we may easily conceive, that the same prejudice would be communicated to their numerous pupils, and thus become prevalent among the nobility and gentry of the kingdom. Hence the jealousy discovered, on several occasions, by the English parliament, lest, by the influence of the clergy, the laws of ancient Rome should be introduced into England; of which a remarkable instance is mentioned in the reign of Richard the second; when the nobility, in parliament, declare, "that the realm of England hath never been unto this hour, neither by the consent of our lord the king, and the lords of parliament, shall it ever be ruled or governed by the civil law."† As the laws of ancient Rome had not been incorporated in the municipal system, they seem to have been viewed,

* Fortescue de laudibus Leg. Ang.—Also the discourses on this subject preserved in Hearne's collection of antiquities.

† Blackstone's Commentaries. [[Millar quotes Blackstone's *Commentaries on the Laws of England,* 4 vols. (London, 1765–69), vol. 1, sec. 1 ("On the Study of the Law"), 19–20. Blackstone, in turn, cites Selden.]]

18. Sir John Fortescue (ca. 1385–1476): English jurist, chief justice of the Court of King's Bench, and author of *De Laudibus Legum Angliae* (ca. 1470), an important work on the history of English law.

19. "Justice Shallow" appears in Shakespeare's *Henry IV, Part II.*

by the partizans of the latter, in the same light with the doctrines of a rival sect, which has with difficulty been prevented from acquiring the superiority in the national establishment. <331>

It has been alleged by authors of note, that the opposition of the English nobility to the civil law, arose from its being the law of a despotic government, and therefore inconsistent with their notions of English liberty. But whoever has examined the compilations of Justinian with any attention, must be sensible that there is no foundation for this remark. Those collections relate almost entirely to the private, and touch very slightly upon the public law of the empire. But with respect to property, and the rights of private persons, the opinions and decisions of the Roman lawyers do not seem to have been at all perverted by the nature of their government. Perhaps it will be difficult to point out any modern system of law, in which the rules of justice among individuals appear to be so little warped by the interest of the crown, and in which the natural rights of mankind are investigated and enforced with greater impartiality. In one or two cases, you meet with an observation, "that the prince is above the laws." These, however, are detached, and, as it were, insulated expressions, delivered in general terms, and without any visible effect upon the body <332> of the work; which relates, not to disputes between the emperor and his subjects, but to such as may arise among the people.

After the free government of Rome was overturned, the emperors found it expedient for a long time to conceal the extent of their usurpation, and to leave the ordinary judges, in a great measure, undisturbed in the exercise of that jurisdiction which had been founded in the more fortunate times of the republic. Augustus first set the example of this prudent dissimulation, which was copied by a great number of his successors. Beside the apprehension that the old republican spirit was not entirely extinguished, and the circumstance that the throne continued elective, the emperors were kept in awe by those powerful armies, under particular officers of distinction, which were maintained in the provinces. These were much superior to that praetorian guard, which, for the immediate support of the imperial dignity, was established in the neighbourhood of Rome. In this manner a sort of balance, however precarious, was for some time held, by the military forces dispersed over the empire, and by the jealousy between the emperor and the <333> leader of each considerable army; in consequence of which, the former was deterred from invading and destroying the internal structure of the constitution.

Some of the first emperors, indeed, were guilty of enormous crimes and disorders; but the effect of these appears to have been limited, in a great measure, to persons high in office, or in such rank or station as to be involved in the intrigues of the court. In the succeeding period the Romans were more fortunate, and the throne was filled by a series of princes who are an honour to human nature; Nerva, Trajan, Adrian, Antoninus Pius, and Marcus Aurelius.[20] Under these emperors no interference of the crown prevented the equal distribution of justice; the experience of an empire, which included the whole civilized world, was accumulated in one mass; and the system of private law was thus brought to much greater perfection than it had attained in the preceding ages.

In the reign of Adrian was composed the *perpetual edict,*[21] the first great compilation of the rules of decision; and this became the ground-work of most of the writings published <334> by succeeding lawyers. It was about this time that the law began to be regularly cultivated as a science; that it became the object of a lucrative profession; and that it was taught at Rome with public encouragement.*

Severus new modelled the praetorian guard, by appointing that it should consist of above fifty thousand men; about four times the ancient number; and that it should be recruited, not, as formerly, from the effeminate inhabitants of Italy, but from the hardy and well-disciplined legions upon the frontiers. With the command of this army the emperor possessed a force which nothing in the whole empire was able to oppose; and the government of course degenerated into an absolute military despotism. From this time, therefore, the law could not fail to decline. From the influence of long usage, however, it appears to have declined very slowly; and, notwithstanding the <335> ignorance and barbarism in which the people were sunk, together with the heavy yoke of tyranny to which they were subjected, the ancient system was treated with respect.

It merits attention, that the opinions and decisions contained in the *Pan-*

* The practice of lawyers taking an *honorarium* [[fee]], had been introduced before the end of the commonwealth, but was prohibited by statute. Complaints of the violation of this law were made in the reign of Claudius; when it was enacted, that no lawyer should receive, in one cause, more than 100 *aurei* [[gold coins]], or about 80l. sterling.

20. Roman emperors Nerva (r. 96–98), Trajan (r. 98–117), Hadrian (r. 117–38), Antoninus Pius (r. 138–61), and Marcus Aurelius (r. 161–80).

21. The perpetual edict was commissioned by Hadrian ca. 130 and was a substantial revision of earlier edicts.

dects of Justinian, were delivered by authors, who either lived entirely, or at least received their education, before this great revolution was introduced; and probably a considerable time before its effects, in subverting the private law of the country, had been very sensibly felt. Modestinus, the latest of those authors, wrote in the reign, I think, of the younger Gordian, and only about thirty years below that of Severus.[22]

The *Institutes,* an elementary book upon the science of law, intended as an introduction to the perusal of the *Pandects,* was likewise composed, with a very few additions of Justinian, by an old lawyer, who lived within the period above mentioned.

As the proscription of civil law from the courts of Westminster-hall proceeded entirely from the animosity and opposition between the universities and the inns of court and chancery; it may be supposed that this would con<336>tinue no longer than while the latter preserved their consideration and popularity. For a long time, however, these institutions have not only ceased to be the great seminaries for educating the nobility and gentry; but have become of little use for conveying instruction to practical lawyers. No lectures are now given in the inns of court or chancery; no exercises are performed; no measures are taken for directing the application of those who, of their own accord, may be disposed to study. The whole care of education seems to be devolved upon the cook; and the only remaining part of the ancient regulations is, that the student shall eat his commons for a certain number of terms.

The causes of this alteration it is not difficult to discover. Beside the luxury of a great metropolis, which is calculated to produce idleness and dissipation both in teachers and scholars, the profits arising from the practice of the law, together with the prospect of preferment in the state, have allured men of spirit and abilities to desert the more speculative and less distinguished employment of communicating the principles of the science to a set of pupils. <337> To counteract this natural tendency, and to maintain the vigour of teaching law, notwithstanding the superior advantages derived from the practical profession of a lawyer, public encouragement, as well as the strictest regulation, would have been requisite; but this object appears to have been

22. Herennius Modestinus, a Roman jurist of the third century A.D. whose work is represented in Justinian's *Corpus Juris Civilis;* Roman emperors Gordian II (r. 238); Gordian III (r. 238–44); and Lucius Septimus Severus (r. 193–211).

overlooked by government; and, upon the advancement of national wealth and prosperity, the old institutions were left to their natural course.

But the decay of the inns of court and chancery did not immediately change the ideas which, in their more flourishing condition, they had impressed upon the nation. The movement continued, and its direction was little varied, for a long time after the hand that gave it was withdrawn. It is but of late years that the prejudices, which had so long prevailed, have begun to disappear, and that the same liberal spirit with which the nation is animated in the prosecution of other sciences, has been extended to the interpretation of the rules of justice. In ecclesiastical courts, indeed, and in those of the universities, the civil law has been long followed; but this proceeded in some measure from prepossession; <338> as the rejection of that system, in the courts of Westminster-hall, was the effect of prejudice. Upon the rise of the court of chancery, its decisions were commonly directed by a clergyman; who naturally possessed an attachment to that system of equity, the propagation of which was the great aim of the whole ecclesiastical order. In the court of the admiral, which acquired a jurisdiction in maritime causes, the principles adopted were such as had been suggested, not by the peculiar customs of England, but by the common intercourse of commercial nations, and in which a great proportion of the civil law was introduced. A similar system was embraced in the courts of the constable and marshal; who, from having the command of armies, more especially when engaged in foreign expeditions, were permitted to assume a military jurisdiction. These officers, as might be expected, were led to imitate the general practice of Europe, or what may be called the law of nations.

It was reserved for the enlightened judges of the present age to estimate the system of Roman jurisprudence, according to its intrinsic merit; and without being influenced by ad-<339>ventitious circumstances, to derive from it, in the courts of common law, such assistance as it was capable of bestowing. Of all the sciences, law seems to be that which depends the most upon experience, and in which mere speculative reasoning is of the least consequence. As the Roman system contains the accumulated experience and observation of ages, and of the most extensive empire that ever existed in a civilized form; the advantages resulting from it, as an example to the lawyers and judges of any modern country, must be proportionably great. It presents the largest collection of equitable decisions, and rules, that is any where to be found. These are calculated to enlarge the compass of legal knowledge, without having the influence to mislead; they have all the benefit of precedents, without any authority to impose; and, therefore, may render the system of English law more full and comprehensive, without any danger of corrupting it. <340>

SECTION IV

The Rise of the Court of Chancery.

In attempting a general outline of the principal English courts, the judicial authority of the chancellor now remains to be considered. The jurisdiction of this officer was plainly derived from the nature of his employment in the king's household, and from the ministerial powers over the kingdom, with which he thence came to be invested. By being the king's secretary and chaplain, he enjoyed the peculiar confidence of his master; and had the sole charge of writing his letters; and afterwards of issuing *writs* in the name of the crown. As it became customary that every vassal should hold his fief by a charter from the superior, the power of granting those deeds, throughout the royal demesne, became the source of great influence, and, after the Norman conquest, when the nobility were all reduced into the state of crown-vassals, raised the chancellor to be a principal officer of state. <341>

When the deeds issuing from the crown became numerous, the care of expediting many of them was devolved upon inferior persons; and, to ascertain their authenticity, the subscription of the chancellor, and afterwards a public seal, of which he obtained the custody, was adhibited.*

At what time signatures became customary, in England, to deeds proceeding from the crown, appears uncertain. It is probable that they were known to the Anglo-Saxons; but that they did not become frequent until the settlement of the Norman princes. From this period the chancellor was

* The subscription of the *referendarius* [[referendary]], who was probably the chancellor, occurs as far back, in the Anglo-Saxon period, as the reign of Ethelbert, the first Christian king. In the reign of Edward the Confessor we meet with a charter subscribed by the chancellor, under that express appellation: "Ego Rembaldus cancellarius subscripsi." Selden on the office of lord chancellor in England. [["I, Rembald the chancellor, have subscribed my name." John Selden, *A Brief Discourse Touching the Office of Lord Chancellor of England* (London, 1672), 2.]]

In France, and probably in all the kingdoms in the western part of Europe, the chancellor came to be the ordinary keeper of the king's seal.

considered as having a title to the keeping of the great seal; but as, from the caprice of the monarch, there occurred some instances in which it was en-<342>trusted to a different person, a statute was made in the reign of Henry the third, requiring that the employments of lord-keeper and chancellor should always be conjoined; a regulation which, having sometimes been overlooked, was afterwards renewed in the reign of Elizabeth.*

In this manner all important writings, issued by the king, either came through the medium of the chancellor, or were subjected to his inspection. Before he affixed the great seal to any deed, he was bound to examine its nature, and, if it proceeded upon a false representation, or contained any thing erroneous or illegal, to repeal and cancel it. So early were laid the foundations of a maxim, which in after days has been gradually extended; that the servants of the crown are justly responsible for measures which cannot be executed without their concurrence. As the exercise of these powers required a previous examination and cognizance, it gave rise to an ordinary jurisdiction, which, although of great importance, has occasioned no controversy, and appears to have excited little attention. <343>

The extraordinary jurisdiction of the chancellor arose more indirectly, from his character and situation. The origin of his interposition, to correct the decisions of the ordinary tribunals, was formerly suggested. When the king's baron-court, confining itself within the rules of common law, had been laid under the necessity of giving a decision, which, in its application to particular cases, was found hard and oppressive, the party aggrieved was accustomed to petition the king for relief. Applications of this nature were brought before the privy-council; and the consideration of them was naturally referred to the chancellor; who, as the secretary of the king, being employed to register the decrees, and to keep the records of his baron-court, was rendered peculiarly conversant and intelligent in all judicial discussions.

A jurisdiction of this nature appears to have been acquired by the same officer, in several, if not in the greater part, of the kingdoms of Europe. Such, in particular, was that of the chancellor in France; who, under the kings of the first and second race,[23] had the custody <344> of their seal, and was distinguished by the appellation of the *grand referendaire.*†

* Selden on the office of chancellor, 5 Eliz. c. 18.

† See Pasquier's Recherches de la France, and the authorities to which he refers.

23. The Merovingian and Carolingian dynasties, respectively. See p. 66, note 12.

In England, it should seem that, before the end of the Saxon government, the chancellor was employed in giving redress against the hard sentences pronounced by the judges of the king's demesne. As those judges, however, had then a very limited authority, his interpositions were proportionably of little importance. But, after the accession of William the Conqueror, when the *aula regis* became the king's ordinary baron-court, and drew to itself almost the whole judicial business of the nation, the exercise of such extraordinary jurisdiction began to appear in a more conspicuous light. From this period, the multiplication of law-suits before the grand justiciary, produced more various instances of imperfection in the rules of common law; and, from greater experience and refinement, the necessity of relaxing in the observance of these rules, by the admission of numerous exceptions, was more sensibly felt. <345>

As applications for this purpose became frequent, provision was made in order to facilitate their progress; and the tribunal to which they were directed grew up into a regular form. A committee of the privy council had, in each case, been originally appointed along with the chancellor to determine the points in question. But, as these counsellors paid little or no attention to business of this nature; of which they had seldom any knowledge; their number, which had been arbitrary, was therefore gradually diminished; and at last their appointment having come to be regarded as a mere ceremony, was entirely discontinued. Subordinate officers were, on the other hand, found requisite in various departments, to assist the chancellor in preparing his decisions, and in discharging the other branches of his duty.

The authority, however, which was thus exercised by this great magistrate, in order to correct and to supply the most remarkable errors and defects in the ancient rules of law, appears to have still proceeded upon references from the king or from the privy council. His interpositions depended upon the decisions given by other courts, and were of too singu-<346>lar a nature to be easily reduced into a system, or to be viewed in the light of a common remedy. It was at a later period, that the chancery became an *original* court,[24] for determining causes beyond the reach of the ordinary tribunals. This institution, arising from circumstances more accidental than those which produced the jurisdiction above-mentioned, does not seem to have pervaded the other European countries, but is in a great measure peculiar to England.

24. A court of first instance, as against a court of appeal.

According to the feudal policy in the western part of Europe, all jurisdiction was inseparably connected with landed property; and actions of every sort proceeded upon a mandate, or commission, from that particular superior within whose territory the cause was to be tried. If an action was intended before a court deriving its jurisdiction from the king, the plaintiff made application to the crown, stating the injustice of which he complained; in answer to which, the sovereign ordered the adverse party to appear before a particular court, in order that the cause might be heard and determined. The *writ* or *brief*, issued for this purpose by the king, served not only to <347> summon the defendant into court, but also, in that particular question, to authorize the investigation of the magistrate. The different barons, in their respective demesnes, issued briefs in like manner, for bringing any law-suit under the cognizance of their several courts.

In England this mode of litigation was uniformly observed, in proceedings before the *aula regis;* and was afterwards adopted in the three courts of common law, among which the powers of the grand justiciary were divided.

The primitive writs, upon which any action was commenced, being accommodated to the few simple claims that were anciently enforced in a court of justice, were probably conceived in such terms as might occur without much reflection. But complaints upon the same principle of law being frequently repeated, the same terms naturally continued; so that, by long usage, a particular form of writ was rendered invariable and permanent in every species of action. This preservation of uniformity, although perhaps the effect of that propensity, so observable in all mankind, to be governed <348> on every occasion by analogy, proved, at the same time, of great advantage, by ascertaining and limiting the authority of the judge. From the advancement of property, however, and from the multiplied connections of society, there arose new claims, which had never been the subject of discussion. These required a new form of writ; the invention of which, in consistency with the established rules of law, and so calculated as to maintain good order and regularity in the system of judicial procedure, became daily a matter of greater nicety and importance.

Application, in such cases, was made to the chancellor; who, from a scrupulous regard to precedents, was frequently unwilling to interpose, but referred the parties to the next meeting of parliament. These references, however, as might be expected, soon became burdensome to that assembly; and, by a statute in the reign of Edward the first, it was provided, that, "Whensoever, from thenceforth, it shall fortune in chancery that, in one case a writ is found, and in like case, falling under like law, and requiring like remedy, is found none, the clerks in chancery shall <349> agree in making the writ, or shall adjourn the plaintiffs to the next parliament, where a writ shall be framed, by consent of the learned in the law; lest it might happen for the future, that the court of our lord the king should long fail in doing justice to the suitors."*

The new writs, devised in consequence of this law, were, for some time, directed to such of the ordinary courts as, from the nature of the case, appeared to have the most proper jurisdiction. At length, however, there occurred certain claims, in which, though seeming to require the interposition of a judge, it was thought the courts of common law would not interfere. In these, the chancellor, willing to grant a remedy, and, perhaps, not averse to the extension of his own authority, adventured to call the parties before himself, and to determine their difference.† This innovation is said to have been introduced about the time of Richard the second, and for the purpose of supporting a contrivance to elude the statute <350> of *mortmain,*[25] by the appointment of trustees to hold a landed estate, for the benefit of those religious corporations to which it could not be directly bequeathed. The courts of common law could give no countenance to a stratagem so palpably intended to disappoint the will of the legislature. But the chancellor, as a clergyman, was led, by a fellow-feeling with his own order, to support this evasion; and, pretending to consider it as a matter of conscience, that the trustees should be bound to a faithful discharge of their trust, took upon him to enforce the will of a testator, in opposition to the law of the land.

Having successfully assumed the cognizance of one case, in which he was particularly interested, the chancellor found little difficulty in extending his jurisdiction to others. In these, he appears to have acted more from a general regard to justice; and, in consequence of the limited views entertained by the ordinary courts, his interposition seemed immediately necessary. His authority thus grew up imperceptibly: what was begun in usurpation, by acquiring the sanction of long usage, became a legal establishment; and, when

* Statutes at Large, 13 Edward I. c. 24.

† This was done by the writ of *subpoena.*

25. Mortmain denoted the condition of lands held inalienably by an ecclesiastical order or other corporation.

it afterwards <351> excited the jealousy of the courts of common law, its abolition was regarded as impolitic and dangerous. After the direction of chancery had long been possessed by clergymen, who, from their situation, were intent upon the increase of its jurisdiction, it was, upon some occasions, committed to lawyers by profession; by whom its procedure was more digested into a regular system.

From what has been observed, concerning the extraordinary jurisdiction of the court of chancery, there can be no doubt that it was originally distinguished from that of the other courts of Westminster-hall, by the same limits which mark the distinction between *common,* or *strict law,* and *equity.*[26] Its primitive interpositions were intended to decide according to conscience, upon those occasions when the decisions of other courts, from an adherence to ancient rules, were found hard and oppressive. It was afterwards led to interpose in original actions, in order to make effectual those new claims which the ordinary courts accounted beyond the limits of their jurisdiction. The first branch of this authority in the court of chancery was therefore designed to correct the <352> *injustice,* the other to supply the *defects,* of the other tribunals.

This accordingly seems to have been the universally received idea of that court; which is called a *court of equity,* by every author who has occasion to mention it. In this view it is considered by Lord Bacon,[27] who himself held the office of chancellor, and who, among all his cotemporaries, appears to have been the best qualified to understand its nature. The same opinion of this court was entertained by the learned Selden. "Equity," says that author, "is a roguish thing; for law we have a measure; know what to trust to. Equity is according to the conscience of him that is chancellor; and, as that is larger or narrower, so is equity. It is all one as if they should make the standard for measure a chancellor's foot. What an uncertain measure would this be! One

26. *Strict law* denotes the rigid adherence to the literal requirements of law as distinct from more liberal compliance with the substance. *Equity* denotes what seems naturally just and right in given circumstances.

27. Francis Bacon (1561–1626): English philosopher, statesman, and, after 1618, lord chancellor. A prolific author and polymath, he wrote several legal texts, including *Maxims of the Law* (1630), *Reading on the Stature of Uses* (1642), and *Elements of the Common Laws of England* (1630).

chancellor has a long foot; another a short foot; a third, an indifferent foot. 'Tis the same thing in the chancellor's conscience."*

The ingenious and acute author of "The Principles of Equity"[28] has adopted this no-<353>tion concerning the nature of the court of chancery; and disputes with Lord Bacon, whether it is more expedient, that the equitable jurisdiction, and the jurisdiction according to strict law, should be united in the same court, as in ancient Rome; or divided between different courts, as in England?

In opposition to these authorities, Justice Blackstone,[29] a writer whom, in a practical point of this nature, we can hardly suppose to be mistaken, affirms† that there is no such distinction between the chancery and the other courts of Westminster; and maintains that the latter are possessed of an equitable jurisdiction; while the former, to which, however, like other writers, he gives the appellation of a *court of equity,* is accustomed to decide according to the rules of strict law.

To reconcile these different opinions, it seems necessary to suppose that they refer to different periods; and that both the chancery, and the other courts in question, have, since their first establishment, been subjected to great alterations. This is what, from the nature of things, might reasonably be expected. Lord Bacon <354> and Mr. Selden speak of the court of chancery as it stood in a remote period: and, in a matter relating to the history, or even the philosophy of law, Justice Blackstone might easily be deceived.

* Selden's Table-talk. [[John Selden (1584–1654): English antiquary, jurist, and politician. His historical texts include *Jani Anglorum,* a treatise on the ancient constitution, *Titles of Honour* (1614), and *The History of Tithes* (1618). The quotation from Selden is a paraphrase: see *Table Talk of John Selden,* ed. Sir Frederick Pollock (London: Quaritch, 1927), under the alphabetical heading "Equity."]]

† See his Commentaries, Book III. chap. 4 and 7.

28. *Principles of Equity* (1760), by the Scottish jurist and philosopher Henry Home, Lord Kames (1696–1782). In his introduction, Kames disagrees with Bacon that common law and equity should have separate courts: "may it not be argued, that dividing among different courts things intimately connected, bears hard upon every man who has a claim to prosecute? . . . Weighing these different arguments with some attention, the preponderancy seems to be on the side of an united jurisdiction." 2nd ed. (Edinburgh, 1767), 49–50.

29. Sir William Blackstone (1723–80): English judge and jurist, the first professor of English law at Oxford. Blackstone is most widely known as the author of *Commentaries on the Laws of England,* 4 vols. (London, 1765–69; facsimile repr., 4 vols., Chicago: University of Chicago Press, 1979), a highly influential work on the English constitution.

The distinction between strict law and equity is never, in any country, a permanent distinction. It varies according to the state of property, the improvement of arts, the experience of judges, the refinement of a people.

In a rude age the observation of mankind is directed to particular objects; and seldom leads to the formation of general conclusions. The first decisions of judges, agreeable to the state of their knowledge, were such as arose, in each case, from immediate feelings; that is, from considerations of equity. These judges, however, in the course of their employment, had afterwards occasion to meet with many similar cases; upon which, from the same impressions of justice, as well as in order to avoid the appearance of partiality, they were led to pronounce a similar decision. A number of precedents were thus introduced, and, from the force of custom, acquired respect and authority. Different cases were decided, from the view of <355> certain great and leading circumstances in which they resembled each other; and the various decisions, pronounced by the courts of law, were gradually reduced into order, and distributed into certain classes, according to the several grounds and principles upon which they proceeded. The utility of establishing general rules for the determination of every law became also an object of attention. By limiting and circumscribing the power of a judge, they contributed to prevent his partiality in particular situations; and by marking out the precise line of conduct required from every individual, they bestowed upon the people at large, the security and satisfaction arising from the knowledge of their several duties and rights.

But although the simplification of decisions, by reducing them to general principles, was attended with manifest advantage, it was, in some cases, productive of inconvenience and hardship. It is difficult, upon any subject, to establish a rule which is not liable to exceptions. But the primitive rules of law, introduced by unexperienced and ignorant judges, were even far from attaining that perfection <356> which was practicable. They were frequently too narrow; and frequently too broad. They gave rise to decisions, which, in many instances fell extremely short of the mark; and which, in many others, went far beyond it. In cases of this nature, it became a question; whether it was more expedient, by a scrupulous observance of rules, to avoid the possibility of arbitrary practice, or by a particular deviation from them, to prevent an unjust determination? In order to prevent gross injustice under the sanction of legal authority; an evil of the most alarming nature; it was thought adviseable, upon extraordinary occasions, to depart from established maxims, and, from a complex view of every circumstance, to decide according to the feelings of justice. The distinction between *strict law* and *equity* was thus introduced; the former comprehending the established rules; the latter, the exceptions made to those rules in particular cases.

But when questions of equity became numerous, they too, were often found to resemble one another; and, requiring a similar decision, were by degrees arranged and classed according to their principles. After a contract, for ex-<357>ample, had been enforced by a general rule, it might happen, on different occasions, that an individual had given a promise, from the undue influence of threats and violence, from his being cheated by the other party, or from advantage being taken of his ignorance and incapacity. On every occasion of this nature an equitable decision was given; and, by an exception to the common rule of law, the promiser was relieved from performance. But, the remedy given in such cases being reduced into a regular system, could no longer be viewed in the light of a singular interposition; and, by the ordinary operation of law, every contract extorted by force, elicited by fraud, or procured in consequence of error and incapacity, was rendered ineffectual. Every primitive rule of justice was productive of numerous exceptions; and each of these was afterwards reduced under general principles; to which, in a subsequent period, new exceptions became necessary: as from the trunk of a spreading tree there issue large branches; each of which gives rise to others, that are lost in various divisions. <358>

Law and equity are thus in continual progression; and the former is constantly gaining ground upon the latter. Every new and extraordinary interposition is, by length of time, converted into an old rule. A great part of what is now strict law was formerly considered as equity; and the equitable decisions of this age will unavoidably be ranked under the strict law of the next.

Although the chancellor, therefore, was originally entrusted with the mere province of equity, the revolutions of time have unavoidably changed the nature of his jurisdiction. He continues to exert an authority in all such claims as were anciently taken under his protection; but his interpositions concerning them are now directed by general principles, to which various exceptions, according to equity, have since been introduced. He continues, likewise, those modes of procedure which were suitable to his primitive situation, and adapted to such investigations as the purpose of his establishment required.

The ordinary courts of Westminster-hall have, on the other hand, extended their jurisdiction beyond its ancient limits. Though <359> they originally did not venture to deviate from the rules of strict law, the improvements of a later age have inspired them with a more liberal spirit; and have rendered their decisions more agreeable to the natural dictates of justice.

Thus the court of chancery has been gradually divesting itself of its original character, and assuming that of the courts of common law; while those matters have been, in the same proportion, enlarging their powers, and advancing within the precincts of equity.

According to Justice Blackstone, the essential difference at present, between the chancery and the courts of common law, consists in the modes of administering justice peculiar to each. It may deserve to be remarked, that these differences are such as would naturally arise between courts originally distinguished, by having the separate departments of strict law and equity.[30]

1. From the mode of proof adopted by chancery, all questions which require a reference to the oath of a party are appropriated to that court. This peculiarity arose from an opinion, entertained by early judges, that it was a hard-<360>ship to compel any person to furnish evidence against himself. But the view suggested by equity was more liberal and refined. It appeared unjust that a defendant should refuse to satisfy a claim which he knew to be well founded; and, unless he was conscious of having fraudulently withheld performance, he could suffer no damage by his judicial declaration.

2. The chancery alone is competent for taking proofs by commission, when witnesses are abroad, or shortly to leave the kingdom, or hindered by age or infirmity from attending. In the courts of common law, the method of trial by a jury was universally established; and as this form required that the witnesses should be examined in court, the interposition of equity was indispensable, to authorize their examination in absence.

3. Instead of awarding damages for neglecting to fulfil a contract, the court of chancery has power to order specific performance. From the narrow principles embraced, in early times, by the courts of strict law, no complaint was regarded unless the plaintiff had suffered in his pecuniary interest; and, consequently, <361> upon the breach of contract, nothing farther could be

30. Blackstone notes that "the extraordinary court, or court of equity, is now become the court of the greatest judicial consequence. This distinction between law and equity, as administered in different courts, is not at present known, nor seems to have ever been known, in any other country at any time." See *Commentaries,* 3:49–50.

claimed than reparation of the damage incurred. In a more equitable view, it appeared that every innocent and reasonable purpose of the contractors ought to be enforced; although, perhaps, the loss arising from the failure of performance could not be estimated in money. A court of equity, therefore, was accustomed to enjoin, that a contract should be expressly fulfilled.

4. Two other branches of power are mentioned as peculiar to the court of chancery: the one to interpret securities for money lent. This arose from the prohibition, introduced by the canon law, of taking interest for the loan of money; which occasioned an evasion, by means of what is called a *double bond.* The true construction of this deed, according to the intention of the parties, and in opposition to the words, was beyond the jurisdiction of the ordinary courts. The other branch of power alluded to was that of enforcing a *trust.* This, as I formerly observed, was intended to evade the statute of *mortmain;* and afforded the chancellor the first ground for assuming his extraordinary authority in original actions. <362>

Considering the origin of the court of chancery, there was no reason to expect that its jurisdiction would be separated from that of the ordinary courts by any scientific mode of arrangement. It was the offspring of accidental emergency; being merely a temporary expedient for granting an immediate relief to those who had suffered from legal injustice. Supposing that, after it became a permanent and regular tribunal, it had remained upon its original footing, the advantages likely to have resulted from it may reasonably be called in question. That one court should have a jurisdiction according to strict law, and another according to equity; that the former should be obliged, with eyes open, to pronounce an unjust sentence, in conformity to an old rule, leaving parties to procure relief by application to the latter; that, in a word, the common-law tribunal should be empowered to view the lawsuit only upon one side, and the court of equity upon a different one; such a regulation appears in itself no less absurd and ridiculous, than its consequences would be hurtful, by producing a waste of time, and an accumulation of expences: not to mention the <363> uncertainty and fluctuation of conduct arising from the inaccurate and variable boundaries by which equity and strict law must ever be distinguished. Even according to the later form which the chancery has assumed, and by which it has appropriated causes of a very peculiar description, or such as require a singular mode of procedure, its line of partition from the ordinary civil courts may be thought rather arbitrary and whimsical. But, however the present distribution of the judicial powers may be deficient in speculative propriety, it seems in practice to be attended with no inconvenience. The province belonging to each of the courts of Westminster-hall appears now to be settled with an exactness which prevents all interference or embarrassment; and there is, perhaps, no country in the world where equity and strict law are more properly tempered with each other, or where the administration of justice, both in civil and criminal matters, has a freer and more uniform course. <364>

CHAPTER VIII

Of the Circumstances which promoted Commerce, Manufactures, and the Arts, in modern Europe, and particularly in England.

The commerce of the ancient world was confined, in a great measure, to the coasts of the Mediterranean and of the Red Sea. Before the invention of the mariner's compass, navigators were afraid of venturing to a great distance from land, and in those narrow seas, found it easy, by small coasting expeditions, to carry on an extensive traffic. Not to mention what is related concerning the fleets of Sesostris and of Solomon, which are said to have been built upon the Red Sea, we may ascribe to this cause the commerce of the Phenicians, the Carthaginians, the Athenians, the Rhodians, and many other states, in the islands and upon the coast of the Mediterranean.[1] <365>

From the time of Alexander the Great, when Greece had become one extensive kingdom, and had formed connections with Asia, the two narrow seas above-mentioned became the channel of a more distant commerce along the Indian ocean, by which the valuable productions of the East were imported into Europe. It was in order to facilitate this traffic, that the city of Alexandria is said to have been built.

The same commerce was carried on, and probably much extended, in the flourishing periods of the Roman empire, when the numerous articles of

1. Sesostris was a legendary Egyptian ruler who is mentioned in the writings of the Greek historians Herodotus (fifth century B.C.) and Diodorus (first century B.C.) as a great conqueror of Africa and Asia. The reign of Solomon, king of the ancient Hebrews (ca. 970–930 B.C.), marked the greatest extension of Israel's territory in biblical times. Rhodes is an Aegean island and important port. Carthage, on the northern coast of Africa near present-day Tunis, was founded by the Phoenicians and grew into a great seagoing power that rivaled Rome.

Asiatic luxury were in such universal request among that opulent people. The decline of the Roman power tended gradually to diminish that branch of trade; but did not entirely destroy it. Even after the downfall of Rome, when Italy had been often ravaged, and a great part of it subdued, by the barbarous nations, there arose upon the sea-coast some considerable towns, the inhabitants of which continued the ancient course of navigation, and still maintained a degree of traffic with India. The road, however, to that country was a good deal changed by the revolutions and disorders which happened in Egypt, and <366> by the rise of the Saracen empire; so that the Indian trade was carried on less frequently by Alexandria, and most commonly by the Black Sea and part of Tartary, or by a middle way through the city of Bagdat.[2]

During the barbarous period that succeeded the destruction of the Roman empire, the same cause which had formerly promoted the commerce of the Mediterranean, gave rise, in the northern part of Europe, to a small degree of traffic upon the narrow sea of the Baltic. The inhabitants of the southern coast of Scandinavia, and the northern parts of Germany, being necessitated, in that inhospitable climate, to fish for their subsistence, became early acquainted with navigation, and were thereby encouraged not only to undertake piratical expeditions, but also to exchange with each other the rude produce of the country. From the conveniency of that situation, numbers of people were drawn, by degrees, to reside in the neighbourhood, and trading towns were formed upon the coast, or in the mouths of the adjoining rivers. For several centuries, the commerce of the northern part of Europe was ingrossed by those towns, in the same manner as that of the <367> southern was ingrossed by some of the Italian states. As the laws relating to commerce are usually established by the general custom of merchants, it commonly happens, that the practice of nations who have gained a remarkable superiority in trade, becomes a model for imitation to their neighbours, or such as come after them in the same employment. Thus, as the Rhodian laws at one period regulated the commerce of the ancient world, the statutes of Wisby,[3] the famous capital of Gothland, in the Baltic, ob-

2. Baghdad was founded in 762, and its fortunate situation enabled it to become a center of commerce.

3. Visby, a city on Gotland Island off the southeast coast of present-day Sweden in the Baltic Sea. An important center of trade in the Hanseatic League, Visby produced a widely used international maritime code.

tained a similar authority, and have since been considered, by many European states, as the basis of all their mercantile regulations.

In modern Italy, the maritime laws of Amalphi[4] were, in like manner, respected and observed by the merchants in that part of Europe.* Nothing can shew more decisively the early advances in trade which were made by those towns.

While the inhabitants of those different parts of Europe were thus advancing in navigation and in commerce, they could hardly <368> fail to make some progress also in manufactures. By having a vent for the rude produce of the country, they must have had frequent opportunities of observing that, by bestowing a little labour upon their native commodities, they could draw a much greater profit upon the exchange of them. In this manner they were encouraged to occupy themselves in working up the raw materials; to acquire habits of industry; and to make proficiency in mechanical employments. If we examine the history of commercial nations, those especially of the ancient world, we shall find that this has been the usual course of their advancement; and their trade and manufactures have been commonly derived from a convenient maritime situation; which, by affording them the benefit of water-carriage, opened a distant market for their goods, and tempted them to engage in foreign commerce.

The commerce of Italy seems accordingly to have been followed by a rapid improvement of the mechanical arts. In the twelfth and thirteenth centuries, many of the Italian towns had arrived at great perfection in manufactures; among which we may take notice of <369> Venice, Genoa, Bologna, Pisa, Sienna, and Florence. It was from Italy that the art of making clocks and watches, as well as many other of the finer branches of manufacture, together with the most accurate method of keeping mercantile accompts, was afterwards communicated to the other nations of Europe.

The advancement of the common arts of life was naturally succeeded by that of the fine arts, and of the sciences; and Florence, which had led the way in the former, was likewise the first that made considerable advances in the latter. That city, after having been aggrandized by trade, banking, and

* Giannone's Hist. of Naples.

4. Amalfi, located in southern Italy, was an early center of commerce. The *Tavole Amalifitane,* Amalfi's maritime code, was widely influential. In the 1130s, Amalfi was sacked by the Normans and the Pisans, after which it declined rapidly as a center of commerce.

manufactures, began, about the middle of the thirteenth century, to discover a taste of elegance and refinement, and to promote the cultivation of letters. Charles of Anjou,[5] who then obtained the kingdom of Naples as a donation from the Pope, and who was, at the same time, the feudal sovereign of Florence, is said to have been a zealous encourager of these liberal pursuits. The example of the Florentines was soon followed by the other states of Italy, in proportion as trades and manufactures had raised them to ease and opulence. <370>

The intercourse of those Italian states with some of the opulent nations of the east, in consequence of the crusades, or of other casual events, may have contributed something towards the revival of letters in Europe. But the operation of this accidental circumstance must have entirely been subordinate to the great natural cause of improvement already suggested. While the inhabitants of Europe continued rude and barbarous, they were not likely to procure much knowledge by their transient or hostile communication with Asia; but after they had acquired a taste for the cultivation of arts and sciences, they, doubtless, found instructors in that part of the world.

As the people upon the coast of the Baltic inhabited a poorer country, the produce of which was not so easily wrought up into valuable manufactures, they made a proportionably slower progress in the mechanical arts; though, by continuing to export their native commodities, they acquired a degree of wealth, and many of their towns became large and powerful. Having been much oppressed, and obstructed in their trade, by the barons and military people in their neighbourhood, they were led by <371> degrees into joint measures for their own defence; and, about the twelfth century, entered into that famous Hanseatic league, which, being found of great advantage to the commercial interest, was at length rendered so extensive as to include many cities in other parts of Europe.

As the situation of towns, upon the coast of a narrow sea, was favourable to foreign commerce, a country intersected by many navigable rivers gave a similar encouragement to inland trade, and thence likewise to manufactures. An inland trade, however, cannot be rendered very extensive, without greater expence than is necessary to the trade of a maritime town. That all the inhabitants may have the benefit of a market, canals become requisite, where the river-navigation is cut off; roads must be made, where water-carriage is

5. Charles of Anjou, king of Naples and Sicily (r. 1265–85).

impracticable; machinery must be constructed; and cattle, fit for draught, must be procured and maintained. It may be expected, therefore, that inland trade will be improved more slowly than the commerce which is carried on along the sea-coast; but, as the former hold out a market to the inhabitants of a wider coun-<372>try, it is apt, at length, to produce a more extensive improvement of manufactures.

We accordingly find, that, after the towns of Italy, and those upon the coast of the Baltic, the part of Europe which made the quickest advances in trade was the Netherlands; where the great number of navigable rivers, which divide themselves into many different branches, and the general flatness of the country, which made it easy to extend the navigation by canals, encouraged the inhabitants to employ themselves in the manufacture of their natural productions.

Beside the facility of water-carriage, the inhabitants of the Netherlands appear to have derived another advantage from the nature of their soil. The two most considerable branches of manufacture, which contribute to supply the conveniencies or luxuries of any people, are the making of linen and of woollen cloth. With regard to the former of these branches, that country seems fitted to produce the rude materials in the greatest perfection. As early as the tenth century, we accordingly find that the people had, by this peculiar circumstance, been excited to attempt the manufacture of <373> linens; and that, in order to promote an inland trade of this kind, which supposes that the commodity must often be carried to a considerable distance, Baldwin the young,[6] the hereditary count of Flanders, established fairs and markets in particular towns, as the most convenient places of rendezvous between the merchants and their customers.

After the Flemings had made some progress in this trade, and when, of consequence, individuals among them had acquired some stock, as well as habits of industry, they also endeavoured to supply the demand for *woollen* manufactures, which required no very different species of skill and dexterity from what they had already attained. In this employment, however, they were subjected to greater inconveniency; as, after pushing it to any considerable extent, they were under the necessity of purchasing the rude materials from foreign nations. This obliged them to carry on a regular trade with Spain, and with Britain, the two countries of Europe in which wool was

6. Baldwin IX, the Young, count of Flanders (d. 1205).

produced in greatest abundance. The union, however, of the sovereignty of Spain, with that of the Netherlands, which happened <374> in the person of the emperor Charles the fifth,[7] contributed in part to remove that inconveniency, by securing to the latter country the wool produced by the former; and the Spanish monarch, who saw the rude materials manufactured within his own dominions, had an opportunity of protecting and encouraging every branch of the labour connected with that employment. From this time the woollen and linen manufactures of the Netherlands came to be in the same flourishing condition.

But while this part of Europe enjoyed such advantages for inland trade, it was not entirely excluded from a share in foreign commerce, by means of Antwerp,[8] and of some other maritime towns in the neighbourhood. The inhabitants of Italy, and of the countries upon the coast of the Baltic, having reciprocally a demand for the commodities produced in such different climates, were led by degrees into a regular traffic. As the ships, employed in this extensive navigation, found a convenient middle station in the ports of the Netherlands, the merchants of this country were furnished with opportunities of transporting their <375> linen or woollen cloths, both to the southern and northern parts of Europe; and a sure market was thus opened for those valuable commodities. It merits attention, that the opulence, thus acquired by Flanders, and the neighbouring provinces of the Low Countries, had the same effect as in Italy, of giving encouragement to literature, and to the cultivation of the fine arts. The rise of the Flemish painters was later than that of the Italian, because the trade of the Netherlands was of a posterior date; and their not attaining the same perfection may, among other causes, be ascribed to this circumstance, that the flourishing trade of that country was of shorter duration.

The encouragement given, in the Netherlands, to painting, was extended also to music, and was productive of a similar proficiency in that art. It is observed, that the Flemings were accustomed, in this period, to supply the rest of Europe with musicians, as is done in our days by the Italians.*

Towards the end of the sixteenth, and the <376> beginning of the sev-

* See Reflections on Poetry, Painting, and Music, by the Abbé du Bos.

7. Charles V, Holy Roman Emperor (r. 1519–58). The Netherlands came to Charles upon the death of his father in 1506.

8. In the mid-sixteenth century, Antwerp was northern Europe's chief commercial and financial center.

enteenth century, three great events concurred to produce a remarkable revolution upon the state of trade and manufactures in general, and that of Europe in particular.

1. The first of these was the invention of the mariner's compass; which changed the whole system of navigation, by enabling navigators to find their way with certainty in the wide ocean, to undertake more distant expeditions, and to complete them with much greater quickness. When this discovery had been properly ascertained, and reduced to practice, those who inhabited the coast of a narrow sea had no longer that superiority, with respect to commerce, which they formerly possessed; for, whatever advantages they might have in a small coasting navigation, these were overbalanced by the inconveniencies of their situation, whenever they had occasion to sail beyond those adjacent capes or promontories by which they were limited and circumscribed. The harbours, which became then most favourable to commerce, were such as had formerly been least so; those which were the farthest removed from streights, or dangerous <377> shores, and, by their distance from opposite lands, admitted the freest passage to every quarter of the globe.

2. The discovery of America, and the opening of a passage to the East-Indies by the Cape of Good Hope,[9] which may be regarded as a consequence of the preceding improvement in navigation, contributed still farther to change the course of European trade. By these discoveries a set of new and magnificent objects of commerce was presented, and Europe began to entertain the prospect of forming settlements in distant countries; of trading with nations in various climates, producing a proportional variety of commodities; and of maintaining an easy correspondence between the remotest parts of the world. The merchants of Italy, and of the northern parts of Germany, were naturally left behind, in the prosecution of these magnificent views. Their situation, hemmed in by the coast of the Baltic, or of the Mediterranean, was particularly unfavourable for that new species of trade. They had, besides, a reluctance, we may suppose, to abandon their old habits, and to relinquish that settled traffic in which they <378> had been long engaged, for the new and hazardous adventures which were then pointed out to them. Adhering, therefore, to their former course, they found their profits decrease

9. Bartholomeu Diaz rounded the Cape of Good Hope in 1488; Vasco Da Gama reached India by that route in 1498.

according as the new commerce became considerable; and their commercial importance was at length, in a great measure, sunk and annihilated.

3. The violent shock given, by the Spanish government, to the trading towns of the Netherlands, occasioned, about this period, a change in the manufactures of Europe, no less remarkable than the two foregoing circumstances produced in its commerce. Philip the second of Spain[10] embraced the narrow and cruel policy of his father Charles the fifth, in attempting to extirpate the doctrines of Luther[11] throughout his dominions; at the same time that he added a bigotry, peculiar to himself, which led him to seek the accomplishment of his purpose by measures yet more imprudent and sanguinary. The doctrines of the reformation had been spread very universally in the Netherlands; and had been adopted with a zeal not inferior to that which appeared in any other part of Europe. Philip employed <379> the whole force of the Spanish monarchy in order to subdue that spirit of religious innovation; and, after a long and obstinate struggle, he at last prevailed; but it was by extirpating a great part of the inhabitants, and ruining the manufactures of the country. The most independent and spirited, that is, the most active and skilful part of the manufacturers, disdaining to submit to a tyranny by which they were oppressed in their most valuable rights, fled from their native country; and, finding a refuge in other European nations, carried along with them that knowledge and dexterity in manufactures, and those habits of industry, which they possessed in so eminent a degree.

Of all the European nations, Great Britain was in a condition to reap the most immediate profit from these important changes in the state of commerce and manufactures.

England has long enjoyed the peculiar advantage of rearing a greater number of sheep, and producing larger quantities of wool, fit for manufacture, than most other parts of the world. This is probably derived from the flatness of the country, by which a great part <380> of it is plentifully supplied with moisture, and from the moderate temperature of its climate; both

10. Philip II, king of Spain, Naples, and Sicily (r. 1556–98): Philip was troubled in the latter half of his reign by the revolt of the Netherlands (1566–1609), which proved successful in expelling the Spanish from a large part of the country, despite a bloody and destructive attempt by Philip to reclaim these lands for Hapsburg rule and the Roman Catholic Church.

11. Martin Luther (1483–1546): German religious reformer whose famous protest against the abuses of the Catholic Church sparked the Protestant Reformation.

of which circumstances appear favourable to the production of pasture, and to the proper cultivation of sheep. But, whatever be the causes of it, the fact is certain, that, Spain excepted, no other country can, in this particular, be brought in competition with England. Particular mention is made of the English wool, even when Britain was a Roman province; and, in the early periods of our history, the exportation of that commodity was a considerable article of commerce. What is remarkable, the English wool of former times appears to have been of a finer quality than the present; and there is even reason to believe that it was held superior to the Spanish.* Of this extraordinary fact it seems difficult to give any satisfactory account. I am credibly informed, that the improvements, made of late years, in the pasture-grounds of England, have greatly debased the quality of the wool; though, by the increase <381> of the quantity, they have sufficiently indemnified the proprietors.

By possessing the raw material in great plenty, the English appear to have been incited, at an early period, to make some attempts toward the fabrication of it. The woollen cloth of England is taken notice of while the country was under the dominion of the Romans. The disorders which followed while the Saxons were subduing the country, and during the subsequent ravages of the Danes, gave great interruption to manufactures; but, soon after the Norman conquest, and particularly in the reigns of Henry the third and Edward the first, that of woollen cloth appears to have become an object of attention.

The flourishing reign of Edward the third was extremely favourable to improvements; and that enterprising monarch, notwithstanding his ardour in the pursuit of military glory, was attentive to reform the internal policy of the kingdom, and gave particular encouragement to the woollen manufacture. He invited and protected foreign manufacturers; and, in his reign, a number of Walloon[12] weavers, with their families, came and settled in Eng-<382>land. An act of parliament was made, which prohibited the wearing of foreign cloth; and another, by which the exportation of wool was declared to be felony. These regulations, however narrow the principles upon which

* See Observations upon National Industry, by James Anderson, and the authorities to which he refers.

12. *Walloons* denotes a group of peoples with a shared language, residing in the present-day Belgian regions of Hainaut, Liege, Namur, and Luxembourg.

they were built, were certainly framed with the best intentions; but they could have little or no effect, as the English, at that time, were neither capable of manufacturing the whole of their wool, nor even of supplying their own demand for woollen cloth. The crown, therefore, in virtue of its dispensing power, was accustomed to relieve the raisers of wool, by granting occasionally, to individuals, a licence for exportation; and, as a dispensation in this case was absolutely necessary to procure a market for the commodity, it became the source of a revenue to the sovereign, who obtained a price for every licence which he bestowed.

The woollen trade of England made considerable advances in the reign of Henry the seventh, when, after a long course of civil dissension, the people began to enjoy tranquillity under a prince who favoured and protected the arts of peace. About this time were set on foot the coarse woollen manufactures of York-<383>shire; particularly at Wakefield, Leeds, and Halifax; places remarkably well adapted to that species of work, from the plenty of coal, and the numerous springs of water with which they are supplied.

The extension of manufactures, about this period, became so considerable as to produce an alteration in the whole face of the country; and, in particular, gave rise to improvements in husbandry, and in the different arts connected with it. The enlargement of towns and villages, composed of tradesmen and merchants, could not fail to encrease the demand for provisions in the neighbourhood, and, by enhancing the value of every article raised by the farmers, to advance the profits of their employment. From this improvement of their circumstances, the tenants were soon enabled, by offering an additional rent, to procure leases for a term of years; and the master, whose daily expences were encreased by the progress of trade and luxury, was content to receive a pecuniary compensation, for the loss of that authority over his dependants, which he was obliged to relinquish. Thus the freedom and independence, which the mercantile <384> and manufacturing people derived from the nature of their employment, was, in some measure, communicated to the peasantry; who, instead of remaining tenants at will, were secured for a limited term in the possession of their farms.

In consequence of these changes, the number of villeins in England was greatly diminished, in the reign of Henry the seventh; and before the accession of James the first, that class of men had entirely disappeared. Without any public law upon the subject, their condition was gradually improved by particular bargains with their master; and, according as their opulence enabled them to purchase higher privileges, they acquired longer leases, or were converted into *copyholders,* or *freeholders.*

As, from this time, the English continued, with unremitting ardour, to prosecute their improvements, and were continually advancing in opulence, as well as in skill and dexterity, and in the habits of industry, it was to be expected that, in the long run, the possession of the rude material of the woollen manufacture would give them a manifest superiority <385> in that branch of business, and put it in their power to undersell other nations who had not the same advantage.

In the reign of queen Elizabeth, that severe blow, which I formerly mentioned, was given to the trade of the Low Countries; by which every branch of manufacture was greatly impaired, and that of woollen cloth was totally destroyed. Thus the destruction of the woollen trade of the Netherlands happened at the very critical period, when the English were come to be in a condition of turning that event to their own emolument. The manufacturers who had been driven from their native land found a welcome refuge from queen Elizabeth; and the greater part of them took up their residence in England; so that the inhabitants of the former country became, in the highest degree, instrumental in promoting the trade of the latter; instead of retarding or depressing it, by that superiority of industry and skill, and that uninterrupted possession of the market which they had long maintained.

In Spain, the only other country of Europe enjoying similar advantages to those of Eng-<386>land, the improvement of the woollen manufacture was prevented by a variety of concurring circumstances. The rooted animosity between the professors of the Christian and Mahometan religions, herished by the remembrance of many acts of cruelty and oppression, had excited Ferdinand of Arragon, when he became master of the country, to persecute the Moors, the only industrious part of the inhabitants. In a subsequent reign, they were entirely extirpated.[13] The same imprudent and barbarous policy interrupted and discouraged the trade of the Netherlands; and, after these two fatal events, the sudden importation of gold and silver into Spain, in consequence of the possession of America, completed the destruction of industry among the people, by raising individuals to sudden

13. Ferdinand II, king of Aragon (r. 1479–1516), and, after his marriage to Isabella I, joint ruler of Castile and Leon (r. 1474–1516). Ferdinand and Isabella, fervently Catholic, set out to expel or convert all Jews and Moors from the newly united Spain.

wealth, and making them despise the slow and distant returns of trade and manufactures.[14]

Upon the ruin of the Spanish Netherlands, were established the fine woollen manufactures of Wiltshire, and some of the neighbouring counties; those parts of England which produced the greatest number of sheep, <387> and in which the superior quality of the wool was most remarkable. The rapid improvements in that great branch of manufacture, which became conspicuous in England, had a natural tendency to introduce other branches, more or less connected with it; and, when a great body of the people had acquired industry and skill in one sort of employment, it was not very difficult, as occasion required, to extend their application to other trades and professions.

While these circumstances bestowed upon England, a superiority in manufactures, she began to enjoy advantages no less conspicuous, with regard to navigation and commerce. When the people of Europe had become qualified for extensive naval undertakings, the distance of Britain from the continent, and her situation as an island, afforded her a superiority to most other countries in the number of such harbours as have a free communication with all parts of the globe. Her insular situation was, at the same time, no less advantageous with respect to inland trade, from the numerous bays and rivers, which, by intersecting <388> the country in different places, extended the benefit of water-carriage to the greater part of the inhabitants. As the bulk of the people became thus familiar with the dangers and vicissitudes incident to those who live upon water, they acquired habits which fitted them for a seafaring life, and rendered them dextrous in those arts which are subservient to navigation, the great instrument of commerce. In these circumstances, there has been formed a numerous body of sailors, equally prepared for commercial and for military enterprises. As, in the early state of the feudal nations, the great body of the people were, without labour or expence, qualified for all the services of the field; so, in Britain, a great proportion of the inhabitants, after the advancement of commerce, became a sort of naval militia, ready, upon all occasions, for the equipment of her

14. Spain's American territories proved to be immensely lucrative, providing Spain's rulers with vast amounts of gold and silver from their colonies in Mexico and Peru. The economic and cultural effects of this influx of wealth—and of the inflation that followed—has long been a matter of debate.

fleets, and, without the assistance of *navigation acts,* or other precautions of the legislature,[15] fully sufficient for the defence of the country.

These advantages, however, were rendered more stable and permanent by the great extent of this island, superior to that of most others <389> upon the globe. This, as it united the inhabitants in one great state, made them capable of exerting a force adequate to the protection of its commerce and manufactures. To the extent of her dominions Great Britain is indebted for her long-continued prosperity. The commercial states, both in ancient and modern times, which were formed in islands of small extent, have been frequently overturned in a short time, either by the jealousy of neighbours, or by an accidental collision with more powerful nations. The present combination of European powers against Great Britain, demonstrates the jealousy which a national superiority in trade is likely to excite, and the force which is necessary to maintain that dangerous pre-eminence.*

That the government of England, in that period, had also a peculiar tendency to promote her trade and manufactures, it is impossible to doubt. As the inhabitants were better secured in their property, and protected from oppressive taxes, than in any other European kingdom, it is natural to suppose that their in-<390>dustry was excited by the certain prospect of enjoying whatever they should acquire. Though the English constitution was then destitute of many improvements which it has now happily received, yet, compared with the other extensive governments of Europe in that age, it may be regarded as a system of liberty. <391>

* This was written before the peace in 1782. [[The entry of the French and the Spanish was decisive to the English defeat in the American War of Independence (1776–83).]]

15. The sense of Millar's argument is that the population of England developed its seagoing skills as a natural response to the advancement of commerce and did not need the encouragement of legislation to form a ready reserve of naval skills.

CHAPTER IX

Of Henry the Seventh.— Circumstances which, in his Reign, contributed to the Exaltation of the Crown.— Review of the Government of this Period.

In the reign of Henry the seventh, the power of the crown, which had been gradually advancing from the Norman conquest, was exalted to a greater height than it had formerly attained. The circumstances which produced this alteration, either arose from the general state of the country, and the natural tendency of its government; or were the consequence of singular events, and occasional conjunctures.

1. The improvements in agriculture, and in trade and manufactures, which appeared so conspicuously from the accession of the Tudor family, contributed, more than any other circumstance, to increase the influence and authority of the crown.[1] By these improvements, persons of the lower class were led to the ac-<392>quisition of different privileges and immunities: instead of remaining in the idle state of retainers, they found employment either as farmers, who paying a fixed rent, were exempted from the arbitrary will of a master, or as tradesmen and merchants, who, at a distance from any superior, were enriched by the profits of their industry. These circumstances naturally produced that spirit of independence which is so favourable to civil liberty, and which, in after times, exerted itself in opposition to the power of the crown. But such was the situation of the

1. In Millar's view, material changes in the economy and in the condition of the people were decisive in reshaping relations between the authority of the Crown and the power of the nobility. Similar arguments had been important to both Hume and Smith. For Hume, see *HE,* 4:383–85; for Smith, see *WN,* 1:418–22, and *LJ,* 59–60, 261–65.

great body of the people, upon their first exaltation, that, instead of attempting to depress, they were led to support the political influence of the monarch. His protection they had formerly experienced, in opposition to those great proprietors of land in their neighbourhood, by whom they had been oppressed, and who still were endeavouring to retain them in subjection. Notwithstanding the change of their condition, their power was not so established as to enable them, alone and unprotected, to withstand these ancient oppressors; and from their former habits, as well as from the dan-<393>gers and difficulties which were not yet entirely removed, they still adhered to the sovereign as their natural protector. In this peculiar state of things, the interest of the crown coincided with that of the great body of the people; while the ambition of the nobles appeared equally inconsistent with both. To humble the aristocracy was therefore the first aim of the lower order of the inhabitants; but, in their attempts to destroy two or three hundred petty tyrants, they incurred the hazard of raising up a single one more powerful than them all.

This union of the crown with the great body of the people, at the same time that it primarily encreased the authority of the monarch, contributed indirectly to preserve the ancient privileges of parliament. As the house of commons, which daily rose to higher consideration, was in the interest of the king, and usually supported his measures if not extremely odious and oppressive, he found it expedient to call frequent meetings of that assembly. Thus the very power, which the interpositions of parliament were calculated to restrain, invited and prompted this national <394> council to exercise its rights; because, in the exercise of them, it was disposed to gratify the inclination or humour of the sovereign, who regarded present convenience more than the future effects of example.

The same views of interest, which led the king to call frequent meetings of parliament, induced him to bestow additional weight upon the house of commons, by encreasing the number of its members. For this purpose, many small towns, upon the demesne of the crown, were incorporated, and invested with all the privileges of royal boroughs; in consequence of which they became entitled to send the usual number of burgesses to parliament. In other towns, which had anciently been incorporated, but which had long neglected to send representatives, that obligation was renewed and inforced. The poorer and more insignificant these boroughs were, they promoted more effectually the design with which they were created; being so much the more dependant upon the sovereign, and the more likely to choose representatives willing to follow his direction.

During the reigns of the Tudor princes, <395> after that of Henry the seventh, and even upon the accession of the Stewart family, this expedient was put in practice to a great extent, and apparently with great success. Henry the eighth[2] restored, or gave, to twelve counties, and to as many boroughs in Wales, the right of sending, each of them one representative. In other parts of his domain he also created eight new boroughs, requiring two delegates from each. Edward the sixth created thirteen boroughs; and restored ten of those which had given up the right of representation. Mary created ten, and renewed the ancient privilege in two. In the reign of Elizabeth, no fewer than twenty-four parliamentary boroughs were created; and seven were restored. James the first created six, and restored eight. Charles the first restored nine.[3] From each of these boroughs two representatives appear to have been admitted.*

The circumstances now mentioned will, in a great measure, account for that very unequal representation in parliament, which has been so often and so justly complained of. No view of national utility could ever have pro<396>duced so gross an absurdity. But, as the king had an interest in augmenting the house of commons, in order, with their assistance, to counteract the influence of the peers; so by multiplying the small and insignificant boroughs, he secured a more numerous party in that house, and was enabled, with greater facility, to over-rule its determinations.

2. The occurrences which had preceded the accession of Henry the seventh, and the general disposition which these had produced in the nation, were likewise highly favourable to the interest of the monarch. During the long and bloody civil war between the houses of York and Lancaster, every person of distinction had been engaged in supporting one or other of the competitors; and, from the various turns of fortune exhibited in the progress of the contest, had alternately fallen under the power of the adverse party. At the final termination of the dispute, many of the great families were totally ruined; all of them were much exhausted and weakened. The dignity

* See Notitia Parliamentaria, by Browne Willis.

2. Henry VIII (r. 1509–47).

3. Edward VI (r. 1547–53); Mary I (r. 1553–58); Elizabeth I (r. 1558–1603); James I (r. 1603–25); Charles I (r. 1625–49).

of the crown had, indeed, from the same causes, been also greatly impaired. But the royal demesnes were not so liable to be dis-<397>membered as those of the nobility; and, upon the restoration of public tranquillity, the numerous resources of the monarch, which were all directed to the same object, afforded him great advantages, in extending his authority over a broken and disjointed aristocracy. During the alternate government of the two contending branches of the royal family, the partizans of both had probably occasion to think their services undervalued; and to be disgusted with the system of administration which prevailed. Henry the sixth, in whom the line of Lancaster forfeited the crown, had, by his incapacity, excited universal contempt. The crimes of Richard the third, the last monarch of the house of York, had rendered him the object of horror and detestation. Time and experience had gradually abated the zeal of party; and the nation, tired in wasting its blood and treasure in so unprofitable a quarrel, was become willing to adopt any system that promised a removal of the present disorders. Henry the seventh, accordingly, obtained the crown by a sort of compromise between the two parties; being the acknowledged head of the house of Lan-<398>caster; and having come under a solemn engagement to marry Elizabeth, the daughter of Edward the fourth, and now heiress of the house of York.[4] In that conjuncture a better bargain for the Yorkists, or one more likely to promote the general interest of the nation, could hardly be expected. Henry was the deliverer of his country from the tyranny of Richard; and appears to have been the only person possessed of such credit and influence, as were necessary to hold the sceptre with steadiness, and to create the expectation of a quiet and permanent reign. The same views and dispositions which had established this prince upon the throne, were likely to produce a general submission to his authority, and aversion to every measure which might occasion fresh disturbance, or threaten once more to plunge the nation into the former calamities.

3. The personal character of Henry was calculated for improving, to the utmost, the advantages which he derived from his peculiar situation. Less remarkable for the brilliancy of his talents, or the extent of his genius, than for the solidity of his judgment, he discovered uncommon sagacity in discerning his own in-<399>terest, and unremitting assiduity and vigour in

4. Henry's marriage to Elizabeth of York (1466–1503) united the houses of Lancaster and York in the new Tudor dynasty.

promoting it. His great objects were, to maintain the possession of the throne, to depress the nobility, and to exalt the prerogative; and these he appears to have invariably pursued, without being ever blinded by passion, relaxed by indolence, or misled by vanity. Cautious in forming no visionary or distant schemes, he was resolute in executing his measures, and dextrous in extricating himself from difficulties. In war he displayed activity, valour, and conduct, and was fortunate in all his undertakings; but he seems to have engaged in them from necessity, or from the prospect of emolument, more than from the desire of procuring military reputation. Full of suspicion, he admitted no person to his confidence; but assumed the entire direction of every public department; and was even attentive to the most minute and trivial concerns. His ministers were generally ecclesiastics, or men of low rank; and were employed as the mere instruments of his government.

The jealousy which Henry discovered of all the friends of the York family, and the severity with which he treated them, have been <400> usually censured as illiberal and impolitic. To the praise of liberal views and sentiments, this monarch had certainly no claim. But that this plan of conduct was contrary to the maxims of sound policy, may perhaps be doubted. When a political junto is so much broken and reduced as to be no longer formidable, prudence seems to require that its members should not be pointed out by invidious distinctions; but that, by gentle treatment, they should be induced to lay aside their peculiar principles and opinions. But when the individuals of an unsuccessful party are still possessed of so much power, as to afford the prospect of rising to superiority in the state, it is vain to expect that their attachment will be secured by marks of confidence and favour. Hope cooperates with resentment, to keep alive the spirit of opposition; and the participation of honours and emoluments is only furnishing them with weapons for the destruction of their political enemies. Such was the situation of the numerous adherents of the house of York. They had, indeed, yielded to the exigency of the times; but they were still possessed of much influence, and were far <401> from being thoroughly reconciled to the advancement of a family which they had so long opposed.

From the imputation of avarice the character of Henry cannot so easily be vindicated. That vice, it should seem, was equally promoted by those habits of minute attention for which he was noted, and by the circumstances of the crown during the period in which he lived. In the present age, when the chief support of government is derived from taxes, and when it is regarded as a duty upon the people to supply all the deficiencies of the public revenue, the disposition of the king to accumulate wealth would be a most extravagant and ridiculous propensity. But in those times, when the private estate of the sovereign was the principal fund for defraying his expences, and when every new exaction from his subjects was deemed a general grievance, he had the same interest with every other individual to practise oeconomy; and his love of money might be in reality the love of independence and of power. In all countries, accordingly, in which commerce and the arts have made little progress, it becomes <402> the aim of every wise prince, by frugality in time of peace, to prepare for war by amassing a treasure. "Whereunto," says my Lord Bacon, in his character of Henry the seventh, "I should add, that having every day occasion to take notice of the necessities and shifts for money, of other great princes abroad, it did the better, by comparison, set off to him the felicity of full coffers."[5]

The use that might be made of the advancement of the commons, in raising the power of the crown in opposition to that of the nobility, seems not to have escaped the penetration of Henry; and in the statutes which passed in his reign, we discover the policy of the monarch, co-operating with the natural improvements of society, in diminishing the influence of the aristocracy.

The artifice of entails, rendered effectual by a statute, in the reign of Edward the first, had for a long time prevented the barons from dismembering their estates. But the general propensity to alienation, arising from the advancement of commerce and manufactures, became at length so strong, that it could no longer be withstood by such unnatural re-<403>straints. When a law is directly contrary to the bent of a whole people, it must either be repealed or evaded. In the reign of Edward the fourth, the device of a *common recovery,* that is, a collusive judgment by a court of justice, was accord-

5. Francis Bacon's *History of the Reign of King Henry VII* (1622), a classic of English Renaissance historiography, is the implicit target of much of Millar's discussion of the shift of power toward the crown, in which impersonal and especially economic factors take priority over matters of character emphasized by Bacon. For the quoted passage, see *The History of the Reign of King Henry VII and Selected Works,* ed. Brian Vickers (Cambridge: Cambridge University Press, 1998), 199.

ingly held sufficient to defeat an entail. For the same purpose, the ingenuity of lawyers had suggested the expedient of a *fine,* or collusive agreement, entered upon the records of a court; to which Henry the seventh, by an act of parliament, in the fourth year of his reign, procured the sanction of the legislature. Thus, by the dissolution of entails, an unbounded liberty was given to the alienation of land; and by the growing luxury of the times, a great part of the wealth, which had been artificially accumulated, in the possession of the nobility, was gradually dissipated and transferred to the commons. Whatever might be the ultimate consequences of this alteration, its immediate effects were undoubtedly advantageous to the monarch.

The wealth of the barons being lessened, while their manner of living was becoming more expensive, they were laid under the ne-<404>cessity of reducing the number of their military servants. This change in the situation of the nobility, so conducive to the good order of the kingdom, parliament had repeatedly endeavoured to promote, by prohibiting their keeping retainers in liveries, for the purpose of assisting them in their quarrels; a regulation which Henry is said to have exerted the utmost vigilance and activity to enforce.

Many other regulations were introduced in this reign, by tending to improve the police, and to promote the industry and the importance of the lower orders of the people, contributed more indirectly to the same political changes.

From these concurring circumstances, the prerogative was, no doubt, considerably advanced, after the accession of Henry the seventh. Its advancement, however, appears not so much in the assumption of new powers by the monarch, as in the different spirit with which the ancient powers began to be exercised. This will be evident from an examination of those different branches of government which custom had then appropriated to the king, and to the national assembly. <405>

The legislative power, in conformity to the ancient constitution, was, without all question, exclusively vested in parliament; as the executive power, that of declaring peace and war, of levying troops, of commanding the armies, and, in general, that of providing for the national defence, was committed to the king. There were two methods, however, by which, upon some occasions, the king evaded or encroached upon this power of parliament.

When a statute prohibited any action, or enjoined any rule of conduct, the king, as representing the community, might remit the penalties incurred by the transgression of it. From a step of this nature it was thought no considerable stretch, that he should previously give to individuals a dispensation from the observance of the law; since the latter seemed to be nothing more than a different mode of exercising a power which he was universally allowed to possess. To pardon a criminal, after he has been guilty, is indeed less dangerous to society than to give a previous indulgence to the commission of crimes; but in a rude age, this difference was likely to be overlooked. Hence the origin of the *dispensing power;*[6] <406> which was early exercised by the sovereign; and which, as long as it was kept within a narrow compass, appears to have excited little attention. By degrees, however, these extraordinary interpositions of the crown were multiplied, and extended to things of greater importance; and in some cases, instead of granting a mere exemption to particular persons, were at length carried so far as at once, by a general dispensation, to suspend all the effects of a statute. This last exertion of the regal power, which was of much greater magnitude, appears to have been, in some measure, concealed under the mask of the former; and had never been avowed as a distinct branch of the prerogative.* It was indeed impossible that the parliament could admit such a claim of the sovereign, without surrendering to him its legislative authority. <407> The general suspension of a law is equal to a temporary abrogation; and therefore can only proceed from the same power by which the law was made.

But the dispensing power of the crown, even in favour of particular persons, had been virtually disallowed and reprobated in parliament. In the reign of Richard the second, a power was granted to the king of *making such sufferance, touching the statute of provisors as should seem to him reasonable and profitable.* But this statute, at the same time that it implies his having, of himself, no such authority, allows this power only until the next parliament;

* See the trial of the Bishops in the reign of James II. In the course of that trial, in which all the lawyers of eminence were engaged, and contended every point with great eagerness, it is asserted by the counsel for the bishops, and not contradicted on the other side, that from the Norman conquest, until the accession of the house of Stewart, a general power of suspending or dispensing with the laws had never been directly claimed by the crown.

6. The power of the monarch to suspend specific statutes on behalf of particular individuals or groups.

and contains a protestation, that it is a *novelty,* and that it shall not be drawn into example for the time to come.* <408>

As the king attempted, in some cases, to interrupt the course of the statutes already <409> made, so he endeavoured, sometimes, by his commands, to supply the place of new regulations. In the character of chief magistrate, he assumed the care of maintaining the police of the kingdom; and, in order to put his subjects upon their guard, so that none might pretend ignorance of the duties required of them, he frequently issued proclamations, with respect to those rules of conduct which he had occasion to enforce. But as these commands of the sovereign were not always confined to the mere execution of the laws already in being, it was not easy for the people at large to distinguish in what cases they exceeded that boundary, or to determine the degree of obedience to which they were strictly entitled. As, however, few would be willing to incur the king's displeasure by calling their validity

* The statute, which passed in the fifteenth of Richard the second, is as follows: "Be it remembered, touching the statute of *Provisors,* that the commons (for the great confidence which they have in the person of our lord the king, and in his most excellent knowledge, and in the great tenderness which he hath for his crown, and the rights thereof, and also in the noble and high discretion of the lords) have assented in full parliament, that our said lord the king, by advice and assent of the said lords, *may make such sufferance, touching the said statute, as shall seem to him reasonable and profitable, until the next parliament,* so as the said statute be not repealed in no article thereof: and that all those who have any benefices by force of the said statute, before this present parliament; and also that all those, to whom any aid, tranquillity or advantage is accrued by virtue of the said statute, of the benefices of holy church (of which they were heretofore in possession) as well by presentation or collation of our lord the king, as of the ordinaries or religious persons whatsoever, or by any other manner or way whatsoever; may freely have and enjoy them, and peaceably continue their possession thereof, without being ousted thereof, or any ways challenged, hindered, molested, disquieted, or grieved hereafter, by any provisors or others, against the form and effect of the statute aforesaid, by reason of the said sufferance, in any time to come. And moreover, that the said commons may disagree, at the next parliament, to this sufferance, and fully resort to the said statute, if it shall seem good to them to do it: with *protestation,* this assent, which is a *novelty,* and has not been done before this time, *be not drawn into example or consequence,* for time to come. And they prayed our lord the king, that the protestation might be entered of record in the roll of parliament: and the king granted and commanded to do it."

The statute of *Provisors* had prohibited, under severe penalties, the procuring or accepting ecclesiastical benefices from the pope; and it is evident that, by the present act of parliament, it was intended that the king should dispense with that statute in favour of particular persons only, not that he should all at once suspend the effect of it. Even this dispensation to individuals is termed a *novelty.*

in question, the royal proclamations were allowed to advance in authority, according to the increasing influence and dignity of the crown. In the reign of Henry the seventh, <410> they rose to higher consideration than they had possessed in any former period. But even in this reign, it is not pretended that they had the force of laws; nor does it appear that they were made effectual by the ordinary courts of justice.

2. Under the legislative power was included that of determining the rules by which the people should contribute to defray the expence of government. The right of imposing taxes had therefore been invariably claimed and exercised by parliament. But, in order to procure money, without the authority of that assembly, the king had recourse to a variety of expedients.

The first, and most obvious, was that of soliciting a *benevolence.* This was originally a contribution made by the king's immediate vassals; but, from a relaxation of the ancient feudal principles, had afterwards, in the reign, it should seem, of Edward the fourth, been extended over the whole kingdom.* It was always, except in three singular cases, consi-<411>dered as a free gift; and could not be levied, by force, from such as persisted in refusing it. But although the people were not bound, in law, to contribute; they had every inducement from expediency; since a refusal was likely to be attended with greater inconveniency than the payment of the money which was demanded. From the discretionary power of executing the law, the crown had many opportunities of harassing those who shewed themselves unwilling to relieve its necessities; and seldom could fail to make them heartily repent of their obstinacy. In particular, from the direction of the army, the king had the power of quartering troops in any part of the kingdom; by which means he was enabled, however unjustly, to create expence and vexation to such of the inhabitants as had not complied with his demands. The very solicitation of a benevolence upon the part of the crown, was therefore justly regarded in the light of hardship; and, in the preceding reign, appears to have been, in every shape, condemned and prohibited by parliament: which provides, "that the king's subjects shall from henceforth, in no wise, be charged by such charge, <412> exaction, or imposition called a *benevolence,* nor by such like charge; and that such exactions called *benevolences,* before this time

* This extension of a *benevolence* is probably what is meant by Lord Bacon, when he says, "This tax was devised by Edward the fourth, for which he sustained much envy."

taken, be taken for no example, to make any such, or any like charge of any of the king's subjects hereafter, but shall be *damned and annulled for ever.*"[*]

Notwithstanding the violence with which the legislature had thus testified its disapprobation of this practice, we find that in the seventh year of Henry the seventh, the parliament, upon occasion of a war with France, expressly permitted the king to levy a *benevolence.* That this, however, was intended as a mere voluntary contribution, appears from the account of it given by Lord Bacon, who says, it was to be levied *from the more able sort,* and mentions a tradition concerning the arguments which the commissioners for gathering the benevolence were instructed to employ; "that, if they met with any that were sparing, they should tell them, that they must needs have, because they laid up; and if they were spenders, they must needs have, because it was seen in their port, and manner of living: so <413> neither kind came amiss." This was called by some bishop Morton's *fork,* by others his *crutch.*[†]

In a few years after, parliament made what my Lord Bacon calls *an underpropping act of the benevolence,* by ordaining that the sums, which any person had agreed to pay, might be levied by the ordinary course of law. This act, however, still supposes that, independent of the consent of the party, no contribution of this nature could ever be made effectual.

Beside the benevolence formerly mentioned, which was obtained by the permission of the legislature, there was only one more levied by Henry the seventh. On all other occasions, the general assessments procured by this monarch were supported by the authority of parliament, and imposed in the direct form of a tax.

When the kings of England had reason to suspect that the benevolence of their subjects might be exhausted, they had sometimes recourse to another expedient, that of requesting a *loan.* This mode of relief, as it strongly <414> marked the necessities of the crown, and its reluctance to burden the people, and required no more than the temporary use of their money, could with less decency be withheld. But, in reality, a loan, when granted to the sovereign, come to be nearly of the same amount with a benevolence. From the condition of the debtor, he could never be compelled to do justice to his

* 1 Richard III. c. 2.

† Hist. of the reign of Henry the seventh. [[For this passage in Bacon that Millar both paraphrases and quotes, see *History of the Reign of King Henry VII,* 85–86.]]

creditors; and his circumstances were such as always afforded plausible pretences for delaying and evading re-payment. Although the nature of a loan, implying a mutual transaction, appeared to exclude any idea of right in demanding it, yet the same indirect methods might easily be practised by the crown for procuring a supply in this manner, as under the form of a benevolence. We accordingly find, that in a parliament, as early as the reign of Edward the third, the commons pray the king, "that the loans which were granted to the king by many of that body may be released; and none compelled to make such loans for the future against his will, for that it was against reason and the franchise of the land; and that restitution might be given to those <415> who had made the loans." The king's answer was, "that it should be done."* It does not appear that Henry the seventh ever practised this mode of exaction.

Purveyance[7] was another species of exaction, by which the people were exposed to great vexation from the crown. It was requisite that the king and his followers, who in early times were frequently moving over different parts of the country, should, wherever they came, be speedily supplied with provisions. Instead of making, therefore a previous bargain with the inhabitants, the officers of the crown were accustomed to lay hold of such commodities as were wanted, leaving commonly the indemnification of the proprietors to some future occasion. It may easily be supposed, that this practice was liable to much abuse, and that those whom the king employed in this department would endeavour to make profit at the expence of the people. The number of statutes, that, from the reign of Edward the first, were made for preventing the fraud and oppression of the king's purveyors, afford suffi-<416>cient evidence of the great enormities with which that set of people had been charged, and of which they probably were guilty.†

It must not be overlooked, that, from the exclusive power of making laws, with which parliament was invested, that assembly had the privilege of restraining these, and all other arbitrary proceedings of the crown. Its exertions

* 26th of Edward III. See Parliamentary History in that year.

† See 28 Edw. I. c. 2.—4 Edw. III. c. 4.—5 Edw. III. c. 2.—10 Edw. III. stat. 2.—25 Edw. III. stat. 5.—36 Edw. III.—1 Rich. II. c. 3.—6 Rich. II. stat. 2. c. 2.—23 Hen. VI.

7. The requisition of provisions as a right or prerogative, particularly the right formerly appertaining to the crown of buying whatever was needed for the royal household at a fixed price and of exacting the use of horses and vehicles for the king's journeys.

for this purpose, however, were frequently interrupted or prevented by the want of a fixed rule with respect to the times of its meeting.

Upon the disuse of the ancient practice, by which parliaments had been regularly held at the three stated festivals of Easter, Whitsuntide, and Christmas, the power of convening those assemblies devolved entirely upon the king. The magistrate, entrusted with the supreme execution of the laws already existing, was the best qualified to discover, in what cases these were defective, and upon what occasions a new interposition of the legislature was requisite. In that simple age it was perhaps not apprehended that, with a view of extending the <417> prerogative, he would be disposed to avoid the meetings of parliament; or rather, the barons trusted, that, whenever they had a mind, they could compel him to summon those meetings. But when experience had shewn the abuses in this particular, which were likely to arise, it was thought proper that the discretionary power of the crown should be limited; and accordingly, by a statute in the fourth year of Edward the third, it was expressly provided, that "a parliament shall be held every year once, and oftener if need be." By another statute, in the thirty-sixth year of the same reign, this regulation is confirmed.* In a subsequent period, when the house of commons had begun to throw considerable weight into the scale of the crown, it became the interest of the king to summon frequent meetings of parliament; and the nobility were, of consequence, less anxious to enforce this branch of his duty. Henry the seventh, during a reign of twenty-three years, had occasion to convene seven different parliaments.

To dissolve a parliament was originally no-<418>thing more than to put an end to the attendance of its members; with which, as it saved them from farther expences, they were commonly well satisfied. Before the introduction of representatives into that assembly, every new meeting of the barons was properly a new parliament; and there could be no distinction between a *dissolution* of parliament and a *prorogation.*[8] But, after the establishment of the house of commons, which consisted of members whose election was attended with trouble and expence, it became convenient that the same parliament should, in some cases, be prolonged, and that there should be intervals in its meeting. When the meetings of parliament came thus to be

* Statutes at large.

8. Prorogation is the termination of a session of Parliament, as opposed to the actual dissolution of Parliament.

divided into different sessions, the power of proroguing a parliament from one session to another, like that of dissolving it, was devolved upon the crown; and, for a long time, this branch of the prerogative was exercised within such narrow limits as to excite no apprehension or jealousy. The danger of allowing too great an interval between one parliament and another, as well as that of permitting the king to reign entirely without a parliament, was always manifest; but the mischiefs arising <419> from the long continuance of the same parliament; the reducing the members of the house of commons, more immediately, under the influence of the crown, and rendering them less dependent upon their constituents; in a word, the erection of the national assembly into a standing senate, and destroying, or at least greatly impairing, its representative character; these evils had never been felt, and, in that early age, were not likely to be foreseen.

3. With respect to the judicial power, it must be acknowledged, that the extent of the prerogative was, in several respects, incompatible with an equal and proper distribution of justice.

The nature and origin of the *star-chamber*[9] have been formerly considered. This court consisted of the king and his privy-council, together with the judges of the principal courts, and such other persons as, in each particular case, he thought proper to nominate; and was intended for the determination of such criminal actions as were beyond the jurisdiction of the ordinary tribunals. Being calculated to supply the deficiency of the common rules of penal law, like the chancery in those relating <420> to civil rights, it was regarded, in early times, as an institution of great utility. But, as the limits of its jurisdiction could not be ascertained with accuracy; as the actions of which it took cognizance related principally to crimes affecting the state, in which the crown was immediately interested; and as the king, by sitting in this tribunal, was enabled to controul and direct its decisions; we have every reason to believe that its proceedings were partial and arbitrary, and that it might easily be employed as an engine of ministerial oppression. According as the crown rose in authority, the jurisdiction of this court was enlarged; and being, in certain cases, confirmed by act of parliament, in the reign of Henry the seventh, was, by the subsequent princes of the Tudor line, rendered yet more instrumental in promoting the incroachments of the monarch.

9. On the Star Chamber, see p. 254, asterisked note.

When a military enterprize had occasioned the levying of troops, it was necessary that among these a stricter and more severe discipline should be enforced, than among the rest of the people. Hence the origin of the *martial law,*[10] as distinguished from the common law of the kingdom. As, according to the policy <421> of the feudal governments, the king had the power of calling out into the field all his military vassals, with their followers, it seemed a natural consequence, that he might, at pleasure, extend to the whole of his subjects that arbitrary system of law, which was held suitable to men living in camps. In that period of the English history, when family feuds and civil wars were frequent and universal, this extension might often prove salutary, as the means of quelling and preventing disorders. It was, at the same time, a measure from which great abuses might be expected; as it superseded, at once, that mild and equitable system of regulations, by which the rights and liberties of the nation were secured.

But the chief handle for the oppression of individuals, arose from the influence of the crown in the direction and conduct of public prosecutions. As every public prosecution proceeded in the name of the king, and was carried on by an officer whom he appointed during pleasure, he possessed, of course, a discretionary power in bringing the trial to an issue. Thus, by directing the prosecution of individuals for any atrocious crime, it was in the <422> power of the sovereign to deprive them of their liberty, and subject them to an indefinite imprisonment. Early attempts had been made to prevent this abuse of the prerogative; and in the great charter of king John, as well as in that of Henry the third, it is provided, that there shall be no unreasonable delay of justice.

This regulation was conceived in terms too vague and general, to be of much advantage; although its meaning and spirit are sufficiently obvious. Henry the seventh carried the abuse to such a height, as, upon pretence of crimes, to make a trade of imprisoning persons of great opulence, and of extorting from them sums of money as the price of their liberty. The names

10. Originally, measures taken within the country for the defeat of rebels or invaders or (more generally) for the maintenance of public order. Subsequently, it denoted the government of the country or district by military authority, with ordinary civil law suspended.

of Empson and Dudley,[11] as the common agents of the crown in that infamous traffic, have been handed down to posterity; and it is remarkable that the house of commons, instead of discovering a resentment of such notorious oppression, made choice of Dudley for their speaker. The house of commons were at this period attached to the crown; and probably took little concern in the fate of the great barons, against whom, upon account of their opulence, and their opposition to the king, this kind of <423> extortion was most likely to be committed. But although these minions, for some time, escaped the vengeance due to their iniquitous practices, it overtook them in the beginning of the next reign; when, in consequence both of the sentence of a court, and of a bill of attainder in parliament, they were condemned to death and executed.

Upon the whole, it is a gross error to suppose, that the English government was rendered absolute in the reign of Henry the seventh.[12] There is, on the contrary, no reason to believe, that any material variation was produced in the former constitution. Although the influence of the crown was increased, the prerogative remained upon its former basis. The king's authority was entirely subordinate to that of the national assembly; and if, in some cases, precautions had not been taken to prevent his arbitrary and oppressive measures, this was owing to the want of experience, which prevented the legislature from suggesting a remedy. Such abuses of prerogative, although they might have excited occasional discontent and clamour, had not yet attained so great magnitude, or been so long continued, as <424> to demonstrate that a general limitation was necessary.

The period of Henry the seventh in England, corresponded, in some measure, to that of Lewis the eleventh in France.[13] Charles the seventh, the father of this prince, had recovered the kingdom from the English; and, after long convulsions and disorders, had re-established the public tranquillity. The nature of the struggle in which he was engaged, had excited a national spirit in favour of the crown, while the success of his undertaking rendered him

11. Sir Richard Empson (d. 1510) and Edmund Dudley (d. 1510), members of Henry VII's council, were regarded by contemporaries as the chief agents of his arbitrary financial exactions. They were executed by Henry VIII on a charge of treason.

12. This is leveled against Hume, who claimed that the power of the Crown "was scarcely ever so absolute during any former reign." See *HE,* 4:74.

13. Louis XI (r. 1461–83): the son of Charles VII (r. 1422–61), whose reign saw the expulsion of the English from French territory at the end of the Hundred Years' War.

highly popular, and disposed his subjects to promote and support all his measures. By the seizure of those lands which had been in the possession of the enemy, it is probable that the royal demesnes were also augmented. Lewis came to the throne at a time when these favourable circumstances had begun to operate, and by his abilities and political character was capable of improving them to the utmost. The sudden annexation of many great fiefs to the crown contributed likewise to extend its influence. Upon the decease of the duke of Burgundy,[14] without male descendants, the monarch found himself in a <425> condition to seize that dutchy, as not being transmissible to females. He acquired Provence by a legacy; and, in a little time after, his son Charles the Long, by marrying the heiress of Brittany, became the master of that territory.[15]

The authority of the sovereign, however, which had formerly been advancing with greater rapidity in France than in England, became now much more absolute and unlimited. Lewis the eleventh new-modelled, and afterwards laid aside, the convention of estates, having united in his own person the legislative and executive powers. The same line of conduct was in general pursued by his successors; although, in one or two extraordinary cases, the temporary exigence of the prince might induce him to summon that ancient assembly. In several other governments upon the continent, we may also observe, that, nearly about the same period, the circumstances of the monarch were such as produced a similar exaltation of the prerogative. <426>

14. Charles the Bold, duke of Burgundy (1433–77).
15. Charles VIII, the Long (r. 1483–98), married Anne of Brittany in 1491.

CHAPTER X

Of Henry the Eighth.—The Reformation.—Its Causes.—The Effects of it upon the Influence of the Crown.

Henry the eighth reaped the full benefit of those favourable circumstances which began to operate, and of that uniform policy which had been exerted, in the reign of his father. By uniting, at the same time, in the right of his father and mother, the titles of the two houses of York and Lancaster, he put an end to the remains of that political animosity which had so long divided the nation, and was universally acknowledged by his subjects as the lawful heir of the kingdom. The personal character of this monarch was better suited to the possession and enjoyment of power, than to the employment of the slow and gradual means by which it is to be acquired. Vain, arrogant, headstrong, and inflexible, he shewed little dexterity in the management of his affairs; was unable to brook opposition or con-<427>troul; and, instead of shunning every appearance of usurpation, was rather solicitous to let slip no opportunity for the display of his authority.

The most remarkable event, in the reign of Henry the eighth, was the sudden downfal of that great system of ecclesiastical tyranny, which, during the course of many centuries, the policy of the Roman pontiff had been continually extending. To this religious reformation, the minds of men, in other European countries as well as in England, were predisposed and excited by the changes which had lately occurred in the general state of society.

1. The christian religion, by teaching mankind to believe in the unity of the Deity, presented to their minds the contemplation of the astonishing attributes displayed in the government of the universe. While the professors of christianity thus agreed in the main article of their belief, their disposition to speculate upon other points was promoted by their differences of opinion,

by the controversies with one another in which they were unavoidably engaged, and by the variety of sects into which they were at length divided. The church, however, assumed the <428> power of determining the orthodox faith; and by degrees availed herself of the prevailing superstition, in order to propagate such opinions as were most subservient to her interest. Hence the doctrines relating to purgatory, to the imposition of penances, to auricular confession, to the power of granting a remission of sins, or a dispensation from particular observances, with such other tenets and practices as contributed to encrease the influence of the clergy, were introduced and established. Not contented with requiring an implicit belief in those particular opinions, the church proceeded so far as to exclude entirely the exercise of private judgment in matters of religion; and, in order to prevent all dispute or enquiry upon that subject, even denied to the people the perusal of the sacred scriptures, which had been intended to direct the faith and manners of christians. A system of such unnatural restraint, which nothing but extreme ignorance and superstition could have supported, it was to be expected that the first advances of literature would be sufficient to overturn. Upon the revival of letters, accordingly, in the fourteenth and fifteenth centuries, it was no longer pos-<429>sible to prevent mankind from indulging their natural propensity in the pursuit of knowledge, and from examining those fundamental tenets of christianity which had been so anxiously withheld from their view. They were even prompted, so much the more, to pry into the mysteries of religion, because it was prohibited. To discover the absurdity of many of those doctrines, to which an implicit assent had been required, was not difficult. But the mere examination of them was to reject the decrees of the church, and to merit the censure of contumacy.

2. While the advancement of knowledge disposed men to exert their own judgment in matters of religion, the progress of arts, and of luxury, contributed to diminish the personal influence of the clergy. "In the produce of arts, manufactures, and commerce," says the ingenious and profound author of the Inquiry into the Nature and Causes of the Wealth of Nations,*

* I am happy to acknowledge the obligations I feel myself under to this illustrious philosopher, by having, at an early period of life, had the benefit of hearing his lectures on the History of Civil Society, and of enjoying his unreserved conversation on the same subject.—The great Montesquieu pointed out the road. He was the Lord Bacon in this branch of philosophy. Dr. Smith is the Newton. [[Adam Smith (1723–90): Millar's teacher and mentor at the University of Glasgow and author of the *Theory of Moral*

"the clergy, like the great barons, <430> found something for which they could exchange their rude produce, and thereby discovered the means of spending their whole revenue upon their own persons, without giving any considerable share of them to other people. Their charity became gradually less extensive, their hospitality less liberal, or less profuse. Their retainers became consequently less numerous, and by degrees dwindled away altogether. The clergy, too, like the great barons, wished to get a better rent from their landed estates, in order to spend it in the same manner, upon the gratification of their own private vanity and folly. But this increase of rent could be got only by granting leases to their tenants, who thereby became, in a great measure, independent of them. The ties of interest, which bound the inferior ranks of people to the clergy, were, in this manner, gradually broken and dissolved.—The inferior ranks of people no longer looked upon that order, as they had done before, as the comforters of their distress, and the re-<431>lievers of their indigence. On the contrary, they were provoked and disgusted by the vanity, luxury, and expence of the richer clergy, who appeared to spend upon their own pleasures what had always before been regarded as the patrimony of the poor."

3. The improvement of arts, which obliged the dignified clergy, as well as the great barons, to dismiss their retainers, enabled this inferior class of men to procure subsistence in a different manner, by the exercise of particular trades and professions. By this way of life, they were placed in a condition which rendered them less dependent upon their superiors, and by which they were disposed to resist every species of tyranny, whether ecclesiastical or civil. That spirit of liberty, however, which, from these circumstances, was gradually infused into the great body of the people, began sooner to appear in opposing the usurpations of the church, than in restraining the encroachments of the king's prerogative. In pulling down the fabric of ecclesiastical power, and in stripping the clergy of their wealth, all who had any prospect of sharing in the spoil might be expected to give their

---

Sentiments (1759) and *An Inquiry into the Nature and Causes of the Wealth of Nations* (1776). Millar's footnote to this section is an often-quoted tribute to his teacher, and it expresses the view that, while Montesquieu was the pioneer of the Enlightenment's naturalistic approach to the study of human society, Smith was its true founder. For the influence of Smith's teaching, see the introduction. For the quoted passage, see *WN*, bk. 5, 1, 3, 3. Smith's argument about the effects of luxury encompassed the nobility as well as the clergy, but Millar makes most use of it in relation to the Church.]]

concurrence. But in <432> limiting the power of the crown, the efforts of the people were counteracted by the whole weight of the civil authority. Thus, in England, the reformation was introduced more than a century before the commencement of the struggle between Charles the first and his parliament; although the same principle which produced the latter of these events, was evidently the chief cause of the former.

But whence has it happened, that the circumstances above-mentioned have operated more effectually in some parts of Europe than in others? What has enabled the pope to retain in obedience one half of his dominions, while the other has rejected his authority? That this was owing, in some measure, to accident, it seems impossible to deny. The existence of such a person as Luther in Germany, the dispute that arose in England between Henry the eighth and his wife, the policy of particular princes, which led them to promote or to oppose the interest of his holiness; these, and other such casual occurrences, during the course of this great religious controversy, had undoubtedly a considerable influence in determining its fate. We may take notice, how-<433>ever, of certain fixed causes, which contributed more to the progress of the reformation in some of the European countries than in others.

1. The Roman pontiff found it easier to maintain his authority in the neighbourhood of his capital than in countries at a greater distance. The superstition of the people was not, indeed, greater in the neighbourhood of Rome than in the distant parts of Europe. The contrary is well known to have been the case. But Rome was the centre of ecclesiastical preferment, and the residence, as well as the occasional resort, of great numbers of the most opulent churchmen, whose influence over the people was proportionably extensive. Here the pope was a temporal, as well as an ecclesiastical sovereign; and could employ the arm of flesh, as well as the arm of the spirit. Besides, he had here a better opportunity, than in remoter countries, of observing and managing the dispositions and humours of the inhabitants; and, being at hand to discover the seeds of any disorder, was enabled to crush a rebellion in the bud. This circumstance tended to prevent, or to check, the reformation in <434> Italy, or in France, more than in Sweden, in Denmark, in Germany, in England, or in Scotland.

2. Independent of accidental circumstances, it was to be expected that those countries, which made the quickest progress in trade and manufactures, would be the first to dispute and reject the papal authority. The im-

provement of arts, and the consequent diffusion of knowledge, contributed, on the one hand, to dispel the mist of superstition, and, on the other, to place the bulk of a people in situations which inspired them with sentiments of liberty. That principle, in short, which is to be regarded as the general cause of the reformation, produced the most powerful effects in those countries where it existed the soonest, and met with the greatest encouragement.

This alone will account for the banishment of the Romish religion from the independent towns of Germany, from the Dutch provinces, and from England; those parts of Europe which were soon possessed of an extensive commerce. In the ten provinces of the Netherlands, the advancement of trade and manufactures was productive of similar effects. The <435> inhabitants acquired an attachment to the doctrines of the reformation; and maintained them with a degree of courage and firmness which nothing less than the whole power of the Spanish monarchy was able to subdue. In France too the same spirit became early conspicuous, in that part of the inhabitants which had made the greatest improvement in arts; and, had it not been for the most vigorous efforts of the crown, accompanied with the most infamous perfidy and barbarity,[1] and assisted by the celebrated league of the Catholic powers, it is probable that Calvinism would have obtained the dominion of the Gallican church. The tendency of mercantile improvements to introduce an abhorrence of the Catholic superstition, and of papal domination, is thus equally illustrated from the history of those kingdoms where the reformation prevailed, as of those where, by the concurrence of casual events, it was obstructed and counteracted.

3. In those countries where the smallness of a state had given rise to a republican constitution, the same notions of liberty were easily extended from civil to ecclesiastical government. The people, in those governments, were <436> not only disposed to reject the authority of the pope, as they did that of a temporal sovereign; but were even disgusted with the hierarchy, no less than with that subordination which is required in a monarchy. Hence that high-toned species of reformation, which began in Geneva, and in some of the Swiss cantons; and which, from the weakness and imprudent opposition of the crown, was introduced by the populace into Scotland.

1. Thousands of Huguenots were killed in the St. Bartholomew's Day Massacre of 1572. The League, headed by the Guise family, was formed in 1576 to stamp out Protestantism in France. See p. 471, note 27.

The small states of Italy, indeed, although they fell under a republican government, and some of them were distinguished by their early advancement in commerce, have remained in the Catholic church. In some of the cantons of Switzerland, notwithstanding their very limited extent, and their popular government, the reformation has likewise been unsuccessful. The vicinity of the pope's residence, and of his temporal dominions, appear, in spite of the circumstances which had so plainly an opposite tendency, to have retained them under his jurisdiction. It may deserve, however, to be remarked, that the Venetians, the principal traders of Italy, and who formed the most eminent republic, though they did not establish <437> the doctrines of any sect of the reformers, effected what is perhaps more difficult, and had more the appearance of moderation: they diminished the authority of the pope, without rejecting it altogether; and, though they did not attempt to root out the ancient system, they lopped off such parts of it as they deemed inconsistent with their civil constitution.

After the controversy between the Catholics and Protestants had proceeded so far, in England, as to divide the whole nation, Henry the eighth became possessed of additional influence, by holding a sort of balance between the two parties.[2] Although that prince had quarrelled with the papal authority, and was willing to enrich himself by the plunder of the church, he adhered religiously to many of those tenets which had given the greatest offence to the reformers. While he took the lead in the reformation, he assumed the power of directing and controuling its progress; and, as he still kept measures with both parties, he was at the same time feared and courted by both. In the end, however, he established a system which was agreeable to neither. <438>

The reformation, as it was modelled in this reign, opened a new source of influence and authority to the sovereign. The dissolution of the monasteries, whose revenues were immediately annexed to the crown, bestowed upon him a large accession of riches. These funds, indeed, in consequence of the improvements in trade and manufactures, which tended to augment the expences of the king, as well as of the great barons, were afterwards

2. Henry clashed with the papacy not only over his proposed annulment of his marriage to Catherine of Aragon, but also over the perceived ecclesiastical abuses of the English clergy. Henry's "reforms" were largely political rather than doctrinal. The Six Articles in 1539 reasserted the fundamentally Catholic doctrines of the new English Church.

dissipated, and, in the end, transferred to that lower order of people, who, by their industry, were enabled to accumulate wealth.

As the pope was stripped of all that authority which he had possessed in England,[3] the king became the head of the church; and as the English hierarchy was, without any variation, permitted to remain, he acquired, by the disposal of all the higher benefices, the entire direction of the clergy, and consequently the command of that influence which they still maintained over the people. By claiming, at the same time, the supremacy of the Roman pontiff, the sovereign was furnished with a new pretext for assuming the power to dispense with the law. <439>

But, notwithstanding all the circumstances which contributed to extend the influence of the crown, the prerogative, during the greatest part of this king's reign, appears to have remained upon the same footing as in that of his predecessor. Through the whole of it, the power of imposing taxes was uniformly exercised by parliament. Upon one occasion, a loan was demanded by the king; but so little money was raised by it, that an immediate application to parliament became necessary for procuring a subsidy.

Cardinal Wolsey,[4] in the plenitude of his power, seems to have projected an encroachment upon this branch of the constitution. He began by interfering in the debates of the commons, in relation to a money-bill, and insisted upon the liberty of reasoning with them upon the subject. But this demand was peremptorily refused; and he was unable to procure the supply, in the terms which he had proposed. Not long after, he attempted to levy a *tax* by the authority of the crown; but this measure excited such universal commotion, and resentment, that Henry thought fit <440> to disavow the whole proceeding, and sent letters all over England, declaring, *that he would ask nothing but by way of benevolence.**

From this time no money was levied by the king without the consent of parliament; except in the thirty-fifth year of his reign, when a benevolence

* This attempt was made in the year 1526, and the 17th of this king. See Parl. History, vol. III.

3. After the Act of Annates (1532), Act of Appeals (1533), Act of Supremacy (1534), First Act of Succession (1534), and the Treasons Act (1534) effectively replaced papal supremacy with regal supremacy, Henry enriched the Crown by the dissolution of the monasteries (1535).

4. Thomas Wolsey (ca. 1473–1530), cardinal of the Roman Catholic Church and lord chancellor of England from 1515.

was again solicited. It is further to be observed, that the parliamentary grants of supply to the king, were sometimes preceded by an inquiry into the propriety of the wars which he had undertaken, or of the other measures of government by which his demand of money had been occasioned.

The legislative authority of the national council was no less regularly exerted. It was by act of parliament that the monasteries were suppressed; that the king became the head of the church; that the authority of the pope in England, together with all the revenues which he drew from that kingdom, was abolished; in short, that the ancient system of ecclesiastical government was overturned. In the numerous divorces procured by the sovereign, in <441> the regulations that were made concerning the legitimacy of the children by his different wives, in the various and contradictory settlements of the crown, Henry never pretended to act by virtue of his own prerogative, but continually sheltered himself under the sanction of parliamentary establishment.

Nothing, indeed, could exceed the servility with which the parliaments, especially in the latter part of this reign, complied with the most eccentric inclinations of the monarch. Pleased with the general tendency of his measures, by which the nation was delivered from the yoke of papal dominion, they seem to have resolved not to quarrel with his ridiculous humours, nor even with particular acts of tyranny and oppression. In a dangerous distemper, they were unwilling to reject a violent medicine, on account of the uneasiness and trouble with which its operation was attended. Their complaisance, however, was at length carried so far as to make them abandon their own privileges. In the thirty-first year of Henry the eighth, it was enacted, "That the king, with the advice of his council, might issue pro<442>clamations, under such penalties as he should think necessary, and that these should be observed, as though they were made by act of parliament," with this limitation, "that they should not be prejudicial to any person's inheritance, offices, liberties, goods, chattels, or life."* What are the particular subjects of proclamation, which do not fall within the restrictions mentioned in this act, is not very clear. But there can be no doubt that it contains a delegation, from parliament, of its legislative authority; which, in practice, might soon have been extended beyond the original purpose for which it was granted. By another statute, about the same time, the king was

* 31 Henry VIII. ch. 8.

impowered, with the assistance of a committee, or even by his own authority alone, to regulate the religious tenets, as well as the external observances, of the kingdom.

If these powers had been ascertained, and confirmed by usage, the government of England would have become as absolute as that of France was rendered by Lewis the eleventh. <443> Fortunately, the English monarch, from the obsequiousness of parliament, had little occasion to exercise this new branch of prerogative; and, as he did not live to reduce it into a system, the constitution, in the reign of his successor, returned into its former channel.[5] The last years of Henry the eighth exhibited the greatest elevation, which the crown ever attained, under the princes of the Tudor family. <444>

5. Millar stresses that although the final years of Henry VIII's reign brought England as close to absolutism as it ever came, the power of Parliament was retained. This is aimed at Hume's view that the Tudor monarchs "drew the constitution so near to despotism, as diminished extremely the authority of parliament." *HE,* 5:557.

CHAPTER XI

Of Edward the Sixth—Mary—and Elizabeth.—General Review of the Government.—Conclusion of the Period from the Norman Conquest to the Accession of the House of Stewart.

By the minority of Edward the sixth,[1] the ambitious designs of his father became entirely abortive. The administration was committed to a council of the nobles; who, from want of authority, from disagreement among themselves, or from the desire of popularity, were induced to retrench all the late extensions of the prerogative. The very first year of this reign produced a repeal of that offensive statute, by which royal proclamations had, in any case, obtained the force of laws. Other innovations, which had proceeded from the extraordinary influence of Henry the eighth, were likewise abolished; and, in a short time, the former constitution was completely restored. The reformation, although it continued the direction which had been <445> given to it by Henry the eighth, was carried, in this reign, to an extent, and acquired a form, somewhat more agreeable to the general sentiments of the party by whom it was embraced.

The reign of Mary is chiefly distinguished by the violent struggle which it produced, in order to re-establish the Roman catholic superstition.[2] Although the reformation was, at this time, acceptable to the majority of the

1. Edward was only nine at the death of his father, Henry VIII. He was raised a Protestant, and during his reign England was pushed decisively in a Protestant direction.

2. Mary I (r. 1553–58): the eldest daughter of Henry VIII and Catherine of Aragon. In Protestant mythology, her attempts to restore the Catholic faith earned her the epithet "Bloody Mary."

nation, there still remained a numerous body, zealously attached to the ancient religion, and highly exasperated by the late innovations. With this powerful support, and by the most vigorous exertion of crown-influence upon the elections of the commons, Mary was able to procure a parliament entirely devoted to her interest, and willing to execute her designs.* The restitution of the revenues, of which the monasteries had been plundered, and in which a great part of the nobility and gentry had been sharers, was the only measure at which they seemed to feel any scruple of conscience. But the reign of Mary, though it occasioned a violent shock to the reformation, was too short <446> for extirpating those religious opinions, which had taken a deep root through the kingdom; and which, upon the accession of her successor, were prudently cultivated and brought to maturity.

In the English annals, we meet with no reign so uniformly splendid and fortunate as that of Elizabeth.[3] Never did any sovereign, since the days of Alfred, enjoy such high and such deserved popularity, or procure such extensive advantages to the nation. To her the nation was indebted for the security of religious, the great forerunner of civil liberty. Her own religion coincided with that of the greater part of her subjects; who looked up to her as their deliverer from a superstition which they abhorred. Nor did she appear in this light to her own subjects only: she was the great support and protector of the protestant interest in Europe; and, while this drew upon her the enmity of all the Catholic powers, she was endeared to her own people by the reflection, that her zeal in defending them from the tyranny of Rome, was continually exposing her to machinations, which threatened to bereave her of her crown and her life. Her magnanimity and <447> public spirit, her penetration and dexterity, her activity and vigour of mind, her undaunted resolution, and command of a temper naturally violent and impetuous, were equally conspicuous in her domestic and foreign transactions; and, in the whole course of her administration, it will be hard to point out an instance where she mistook her political interest, or was guilty of any error or neglect in promoting it. Notwithstanding the number and power of her enemies, and in spite of all the combinations that were formed against

* Burnet's History of the Reformation.

3. Elizabeth I (r. 1558–1603): daughter of Henry VIII and Anne Boleyn. The most successful of the Tudor monarchs, Elizabeth succeeded in establishing religious peace under a national church, while stirring English patriotism to resist both Spain and France.

her, she maintained invariably the peace and tranquillity of her own dominions; and her subjects, during a reign of five and forty years, enjoyed a course of uninterrupted prosperity and happiness.

Whether Elizabeth entertained a just idea of the English constitution, has been called in question.[4] But such as her idea was, her behaviour seems to have been strictly conformable to it. Between the prerogative, and the privileges of the parliament, she appears to have drawn a fixed line; and, as in her greatest prosperity she never exceeded this boundary, so <448> in the utmost distress and perplexity she never permitted the least encroachment upon it.

With the legislative power of parliament she never interfered. The exclusive privilege of that assembly, in imposing taxes, was neither controverted by her, nor impaired. There is no vestige of her either attempting, or desiring, to violate these important branches of parliamentary authority.* Mention is made of her having, in one or two cases, obtained a loan from her subjects: but there is no appearance that any compulsion was employed in making it effectual; and her conduct is, in this particular, illustriously distinguished from that of most other princes, by her punctual repayment of the money.

Instead of asking a benevolence, she even refused it, when offered by parliament. Such expedients, indeed, for procuring supplies, were in a great measure superfluous. So rigid was her oeconomy, so great and so apparent were <449> the occasions upon which she ever demanded a supply, such was the confidence reposed in her by parliament, and so intimately did they conceive her enterprizes to be connected with the public welfare, that they never discovered any reluctance to grant whatever sums of money she thought proper to require.

There was one point invariably maintained by Elizabeth, in which, to those who form their notions of the English government from what is at present established, she appears to have been guilty of an encroachment. An act of parliament originally proceeded upon a petition to the sovereign for

* In the 13th of Elizabeth, we find parliament strongly asserting its power to settle and limit the succession to the crown, by declaring it high treason for any person to call this power in question.

4. As elsewhere, Hume is alluded to, rather than named, in Millar's defense of the limited and constitutional character of Elizabeth's rule. For Hume's contrary view, see, for instance, *HE,* 4:363.

the redress of a grievance, or the removal of some inconvenience; and when this petition had obtained the king's consent, it acquired the force of a law. According to this method of conducting the business of legislation, the king had no occasion to declare his resolution concerning any bill, until it was discussed, and finally approved of, by both houses of parliament. Before this was done, it could not be considered as a national request, to which an answer from the throne was demanded.

From the nature of this transaction, and <450> from the view of saving trouble to the sovereign, a regular course of procedure was thus introduced, by which any new law received the assent of the crown, after the sanction of the other two branches of the legislature had been given to its enactment. This practice, deriving authority from custom, was at length followed independent of the circumstances from which it had been originally suggested; and was confirmed by the experience of a later age, which discovered, that any deviation from it would be attended with dangerous consequences. When the proposal of a new law, after being fully debated in parliament, has excited the public attention, and its utility has become apparent to the nation, the crown is, in most cases, unwilling to counteract the inclinations of the people, by refusing its consent to the measure. But if the sovereign were permitted to smother any bill, the moment it was proposed in parliament, there could scarcely exist a possibility, that any new law, disagreeable to the crown, or adverse to the views of a ministry, should ever be enacted. It has therefore become a fundamental principle of the constitution, that, with a few exceptions, the <451> king shall not take notice of any bill depending in parliament; and that, before it has passed the two houses, the royal assent or negative shall not be declared.

But that this rule was completely and invariably established in the reign of Elizabeth, there is no reason to believe. The political expediency of such a regulation was, in that age, not likely to become an object of general attention. Neither was it inconsistent with the nature of the business, however contrary to the usual practice, that the king, upon the introduction of a bill into parliament, should prevent the labour of a fruitless discussion by an immediate interposition of his negative.*

* We find, however, that even so early as the second of Henry the fourth, the commons petitioned the king, that he would not suffer any report to be made to him of matters debated amongst them, till they should be concluded: to which the king assented.

Of this interposition Elizabeth exhibited some remarkable instances. The first improvement of arts, manufactures, and commerce, by raising the lower class of the inhabitants to a better condition, disposed them to free themselves from the tyranny of the <452> great barons, and for that purpose to court the protection of the crown. But when this improvement was farther extended, the great body of the people became still more independent, and found themselves capable of defending their privileges, whether in opposition to the crown or to the nobles. This gave rise to a new spirit, which became conspicuous after the accession of James the first, but of which the dawn began to appear in the reign of his predecessor; a spirit of liberty in the commons, by which they were incited to regulate and to restrain such branches of the prerogative as appeared the most liable to abuse, and most inconsistent with the enjoyment of those rights which they were disposed to assert.

Whenever a bill of this tendency was brought into parliament; such as that for limiting the crown as head of the church, or for the diminution of its power in granting monopolies; the queen made no scruple to declare immediately her opposition to the measure, and even to prohibit any farther debate upon the subject. In doing this, she seems to have considered herself as merely defending those rights of the crown which had been <453> transmitted by her ancestors. Is not the sovereign, said the ministry in those cases, a branch of the legislature? Has she not a voice in the passing of laws? When her negative has once been interposed, all farther deliberation upon the subject must be entirely excluded; and the bill must be laid aside, in the same manner as if it had been rejected by either house of parliament.

This view of the prerogative suggested another exertion of authority, which, in the present age, has been thought still more illegal and arbitrary than the former. If, at any stage of a bill in parliament, the crown was entitled to interpose its negative, it seemed to be a consequence, that, upon the exercise of this right, any farther debate or deliberation upon the subject was precluded. The attempt to prosecute the bill, after such intimation was given upon the part of the crown, was to reject the determination of the legislature, to condemn the authority of the sovereign, and, by faction and clamour, to stir up disorder and discontent. A behaviour of this kind was thought liable to punishment; and Elizabeth, upon several occasions, adventured to imprison those members <454> of parliament who persisted in pushing forward those bills which had been refused by the crown.

It is proper to remark, that these exertions of her power were limited to cases of that nature. She never prevented the discussion of any bill in parliament, except in cases where her ancient prerogative was invaded; nor did she ever pretend to punish the liberty of speech, unless when indulged in continuing to push those bills which she had declared her final resolution to reject.

That such proceedings, however, by intimidating members of parliament, are calculated to prevent the proper discharge of their duty, is indisputable. The liberal ideas upon this point, which are now happily reduced into practice, may be regarded as one of the greatest improvements in the British constitution. That a senator may be encouraged to perform his duty to the public with steadiness and confidence, he ought to enjoy an unbounded liberty of speech, and to be guarded against the resentment either of the sovereign, or of any other persons in power, whom that liberty may offend. From the controul of that house, of <455> which he is a member, he is likely to be prevented from any great indecency and licentiousness in the exercise of this privilege; and his parliamentary conduct should not be impeached, or called in question, in any other court, or from any other quarter. This principle is now sufficiently understood, and universally acknowledged. Its establishment, however, marks a degree of refinement, and of experience in political speculation, which, under the government of the Tudor princes, the nation could hardly be supposed to attain; and the liberty of speech, then belonging to the members of parliament, was probably limited to subjects which that assembly had a right to discuss.

The situation of religious controversy, in the reign of Elizabeth, gave rise to a new ecclesiastical tribunal, which, in after times, was likewise held inconsistent with free government, the *court of high commission.*[5] It must be acknowledged, that the primitive reformers, in any country of Europe, though they zealously opposed the papal tyranny, were far from adopting the liberal principle of religious toleration. Such a principle would, perhaps, have <456> been unsuitable to their circumstances, which required that they should combat the most inveterate prejudices, and overturn a system, which

5. Ecclesiastical court instituted by the Crown in the sixteenth century as a means to enforce the laws of the Reformation settlement and exercise control over the church. In its time it became a controversial instrument of repression, used against those who refused to acknowledge the authority of the Church of England.

for ages had been advancing in respect and authority. As, in England, the king succeeded to the supremacy, which had been vested in the Roman pontiff, he became the judge of orthodoxy in matters of religion; and assumed the power of directing the modes and forms of religious worship. This authority was, by Henry the eighth, delegated to a single person, with the title of *Lord vicegerent.* In the reign of Elizabeth, parliament thinking it safer that such jurisdiction should be entrusted to a numerous meeting, empowered the queen to appoint a commission for the exercise of it.* This alteration was a manifest improvement, yet the court of high commission was so little fettered by the rules of law, and was so much calculated to indulge the rancour and animosity inspired by theological disputes, that we may easily suppose the complaints, which it excited, were not without foundation. Its abolition, in a subsequent reign, was farther recommended <457> from this consideration, that, after the full establishment of the reformation, the same necessity of inculcating uniformity of religious tenets could no longer be pretended.

The great historian of England, to whom the reader is indebted for the complete union of history with philosophy, appears very strongly impressed with a notion of the despotical government in the reign of Elizabeth, and of the arbitrary and tyrannical conduct displayed by that princess.[6]

1. He observes, that "she suspended the laws, so far as to order a great part of the service, the litany, the Lord's prayer, the creed, and the gospels, to be read in English. And, having first published injunctions, that all the churches should conform themselves to the practice of her own chapel, she forbade the hoste to be any more elevated in her presence; an innovation, which, however frivolous it may appear, implied the most material consequences."

But we must not forget, that, in this case, the dispensing power was exercised under great limitations, and in very singular circumstances. Upon the accession of Elizabeth, the Protes-<458>tants, who now formed the greatest part of her subjects, exasperated by the late persecution, and in full confidence of protection, began to make violent changes; to revive the service authorized by Edward the sixth, to pull down images, and to affront the priests of the Roman catholic persuasion. The queen had called a parliament

* Burnet, Hist. Reform.

6. The reference is to David Hume and his *History of England.* For the quoted passage, see *HE,* 4:8. For Millar's relationship to Hume's historiography, see the introduction.

to settle the national religion; but, in order to stop the progress of these disorders, an immediate interposition of the crown was necessary. It was even pretended by some, that the parliaments, in the late reign, had not been legally held, and that of consequence the laws of Edward the sixth, relating to the government of the church, were still in force.* But, whatever regard might be due to this, a temporary indulgence to the protestants, with respect to the external forms of religious worship, was highly expedient for quieting their minds, and for preventing the commission of greater enormities. This indulgence was followed by a proclamation prohibiting all innovations, until the matters in dispute should be finally determined by <459> parliament; and, considering the circumstances of the case, ought to be regarded rather as a measure calculated for the present security of the established religion and its professors, than as a violent exertion of the prerogative, in opposition to the laws of the land.

2. But this author, not contented with ascribing to the crown a power of suspending the laws, has gone so far as to assert, that it was entitled, at pleasure, to introduce new statutes.[7] "In reality," says he, "the crown possessed the full legislative power, by means of proclamations, which might affect any matter, even of the greatest importance, and which the star-chamber took care to see more rigorously executed than the laws themselves."†

In answer to this, it will perhaps be thought sufficient to observe, that anciently the crown possessed no legislative power; that royal proclamations were first declared to have the force of laws, in the latter part of the reign of Henry the eighth; that even then, this force was given them under great restric-<460>tions, and in singular cases; and that in the beginning of the subsequent reign, it was entirely abolished by the same authority from which it had proceeded.

If the star-chamber, therefore, supported this power in the reign of Elizabeth, it must have been in direct violation of the constitution; and it is not likely, that stretches of this kind would often be attempted. But let us consider what were the proclamations issued in this reign, which the star-chamber had an opportunity to enforce. In virtue of the papal supremacy, with which she was invested, Elizabeth prohibited *prophecyings* or particular

* Burnet.

† Hist. of Eng. vol. V. Appendix 3.

7. See *HE,* 4:363.

assemblies instituted for fanatical purposes, and not authorized by the church.* Having the regulation of trade and manufactures, she also <461> prohibited the culture of *woad,* a plant used for the purpose of dying. And, as a director of ceremonies, prescribing rules for the dress of those who appeared at court, or in public places, she gave orders that the length of the swords, and the height of the ruffs then in fashion, should be diminished. These are the important instances adduced in order to prove that Elizabeth superseded the authority of acts of parliament, and assumed the legislative power in her own person.

3. The same historian appears to conceive, that, among other branches of prerogative exercised by Elizabeth, was that of imposing taxes.[8] "There was," he remarks, "a species of *ship-money* imposed at the time of the Spanish invasion: the several ports were required to equip a certain number of vessels at their own charge; and such was the alacrity of the people for the public defence, that some of the ports, particularly London, sent double the number demanded of them."† And in a subsequent period of the English history, having mentioned a requisition made by Charles <462> the first, that the maritime towns, *together with the adjacent counties,* should arm a certain number of vessels, he adds; "This is the first appearance, in Charles's reign, of ship-money; a taxation which had once been imposed by Elizabeth, but which afterwards, when carried some steps farther by Charles, occasioned such violent discontents."‡

Ship-money was originally a contribution by the maritime towns, for the support of the fleet, corresponding, in some measure, to the scutages which were paid by the military people in room of personal service in the field. When it came, therefore, to be a regular assessment, exacted by public authority, it fell of course under the regulation of parliament; and, like other taxes, being gradually pushed beyond its original boundaries, was extended to the counties in the neighbourhood of the sea, and at length to the most

* In the fifth of Elizabeth there was passed an act, conformable to a preceding one in the reign of Edward the sixth, against *fond and fantastical prophecies concerning the queen and divers honourable persons,* which, it seems, had a tendency to stir up sedition. From the name, it is not unlikely that the assemblies, alluded to in the proclamation above-mentioned, were supposed guilty of the like practices, and that Elizabeth was merely following out the intention of an act of parliament.

† Vol. V. Appendix 3.

‡ Vol. VI.

8. Millar continues his critique of Hume, citing *HE,* 4:361, 5:176.

inland parts of the kingdom. To oppose an invasion which threatened the immediate destruction of her empire, Elizabeth had recourse to the customary assistance of the sea-port towns; and, so <463> far from using compulsion to procure it, was freely supplied with a much greater force than she required. How can this measure be considered as analogous to the conduct of Charles the first, in levying that *ship-money,* which gave rise to such violent complaints? The contribution obtained by Elizabeth was altogether voluntary: that which was levied by Charles was keenly disputed by the people, and enforced by the whole power of the crown. The supply granted to Elizabeth was furnished by the maritime towns only; who, by their employment and situation, were connected with the equipment of vessels: that which was extorted by Charles, had been converted into a regular tax; and was imposed upon the nation at large. The ship-money of Elizabeth was procured in a single case, and one of such extraordinary necessity, as would have excused a deviation from the common rules of government. But the ship-money of Charles was not palliated by any pretence of necessity: it was introduced, and, notwithstanding the clamours of the people, continued for a considerable period, with the avowed intention of enabling the king to rule without a parliament. <464>

4. But the chief ground of this opinion, concerning the tyrannical behaviour of Elizabeth, and the despotical nature of her government, appears to be her interference in the debates of parliament; her imprisonment of members for presuming to urge the prosecution of bills, after she had put a negative upon them; and the tameness with which parliament submitted to those exertions of prerogative.

It must be confessed, that if, in the present age, a British monarch should act in the same manner, and should meet with the same acquiescence from parliament, we might reasonably conclude that our freedom was entirely destroyed. But the submission of that assembly, at a period when the order, in which the king's negative should be interposed, was not invariably determined, does not argue the same corruption; and therefore will not warrant the same conclusion. Whatever might be the view entertained by some members of parliament in that age, the greater part of them were probably not aware of the consequences with which those exertions of the crown might be attended; and as, with reason, they placed <465> great confidence in the queen's intentions, their jealousy was not roused by a measure which did not seem to violate any fixed rule of the government.

Neither have we any good reason to infer, that, because this point had hitherto been left undetermined, the constitution was of no value or efficacy to maintain the rights of the people. It was, no doubt, a great defect in the political system, that the king might put a stop to any bill depending in parliament, and prevent any farther debate with relation to it. But even this power of the sovereign was far from rendering the government despotical. By means of it, he might the more effectually defend his own prerogative, but it could not enable him to encroach upon the liberty of the subject. The parliament, without whose authority no innovation could be made, was the less capable of introducing any new regulation; but not the less qualified to maintain the government as it stood. The power of taxation, at the same time, threw a prodigious weight into the scale of parliamentary influence. By the increasing expence of government, a consequence of the improvement of arts, and the <466> advancement of luxury, the old revenues of the crown became daily more inadequate to the demands of the sovereign; which laid him under the necessity of making frequent applications to parliament for extraordinary supplies. This, as it reduced him to a dependence upon that assembly, enabled it to take advantage of his necessities, and to extort from him such concessions as experience had shown to be requisite for securing the rights and privileges of the people.

5. According to Mr. Hume, "the government of England, during that age, however different in other particulars, bore, in this respect, some resemblance to that of Turkey[9] at present: the sovereign possessed every power, except that of imposing taxes: and in both countries this limitation, unsupported by other privileges, appears rather prejudicial to the people. In Turkey, it obliges the Sultan to permit the extortion of the bashaws and governors of provinces, from whom he afterwards squeezes presents, or takes forfeitures. In England, it engaged the queen to erect monopolies, and grant patents for exclusive trade: an inven-<467>tion so pernicious, that had she gone on, during a tract of years, at her own rate, England, the seat of riches, and arts, and commerce, would have contained, at present, as little industry as Morocco, or the coast of Barbary."*

But surely, in England, the sovereign was not possessed of every power,

* History of England, vol. V. Appendix 3.

9. Millar continues his debate with Hume over the nature of the English constitution in Elizabeth's reign, responding to Hume's flamboyant assertion that English government resembled that of Turkey or (a little earlier) that of Muscovy. See Hume, *HE,* 4:360.

except that of imposing taxes. The power of legislation was vested in the king, lords, and commons. The judicial power was not, in ordinary cases, exercised by the crown, but was distributed among various courts of justice; and though, in these, the judges, from the manner of their appointment, might be supposed to favour the prerogative, yet the modes of their procedure, and the general rules of law, were in most cases too invariably determined, to permit very gross partiality. The institution of *juries,* besides, which had long been completely established in England, was calculated to counterbalance this natural bias of judges, and to secure the rights of the people. Is it possible that, in such a government, the power <468> of the monarch can be seriously compared to that which prevails in Turkey?

The sovereign, indeed, was entitled to erect monopolies, and to grant exclusive privileges; which, in that period, were thought necessary for the encouragement of trade and manufactures.[10] That these grants were often bestowed for the purpose merely of deriving a pecuniary advantage to the crown, it is impossible to deny. But who can believe that the perquisites, arising from this branch of the prerogative, or from such of the feudal incidents as were still of an arbitrary nature, were ever likely to defray the extraordinary expences of the crown, and to supersede the necessity of soliciting taxes from parliament?

The star-chamber, and the court of high commission, were doubtless arbitrary and oppressive tribunals; and were in a great measure under the direction of the sovereign. But their interposition, though justly the subject of complaint, was limited to singular and peculiar cases; and, had it been pushed so far as to give great interruption to the known and established course of justice, it would have occasioned such odium and clamour, as no <469> prince of common understanding would be willing to incur.

To be satisfied, upon the whole, that the English constitution, at this period, contained the essential principles of liberty, we need only attend to its operation, when the question was brought to a trial, in the reigns of the two succeeding princes. At the commencement of the disputes between the house of commons and the two first princes of the Stewart family, the government stood precisely upon the same foundation as in the time of Elizabeth. Neither the powers of parliament had been encreased, nor those of

10. Like other rulers of the time, Elizabeth favored some of her subjects by granting exclusive rights for the manufacture or sale of particular classes of goods.

the sovereign diminished. Yet, in the course of that struggle, it soon became evident, that parliament, without going beyond its undisputed privileges, was possessed of sufficient authority, not only to resist the encroachments of prerogative, but even to explain and define its extent, and to establish a more compleat and regular system of liberty. It was merely by withholding supplies, that the parliament was able to introduce these important and salutary regulations. Is the power of taxation, therefore, to be considered as prejudicial to the people? <470> Ought it not rather to be regarded as the foundation of all their privileges, and the great means of establishing that happy mixture of monarchy and democracy which we at present enjoy?

Conclusion of the Period, from the Norman Conquest.

When we review the English constitution, under the princes of the Norman, the Plantagenet, and the Tudor line, it appears to illustrate the natural progress of that policy which obtained in the western part of Europe, with such peculiar modifications, as might be expected, in Britain, from the situation of the country, and from the character and manners of the inhabitants. By the completion of the feudal system, at the Norman conquest, the authority of the sovereign was considerably encreased; at the same time that his powers, in conformity to the practice of every rude kingdom, were, in many respects, discretionary and uncertain. The subsequent progress of government produced a gradual exaltation of the <471> crown; but the long continued struggle between the king and his barons, and the several great charters which they extorted from him, contributed to ascertain and define the extent of his prerogative. While the monarchy was thus gaining ground upon the ancient aristocracy, the constitution was acquiring something of a regular form, and, by the multiplication of fixed laws, provision was made against the future exertions of arbitrary power.

By the insular situation of Britain, the English were little exposed to any foreign invasion, except from the Scots, whose attacks were seldom very formidable: and hence the king, being prevented from engaging in extensive national enterprizes, was deprived of those numerous opportunities for signalizing his military talents, and for securing the admiration and attachment of his subjects, which were enjoyed by the princes upon the neighbouring continent. Thus the government of England, though it proceeded in a similar course to that of the other monarchies in Europe, became less absolute than the greater part of them; <472> and gave admittance to many peculiar institutions in favour of liberty.

The same insular situation, together with the climate and natural produce of the country, by encouraging trade and manufactures, gave an early consequence to the lower order of the inhabitants; and, by uniting their interest with that of the king, in opposing the great barons, disposed him to encrease their weight and importance in the community. Upon this account, when the crown had attained its greatest elevation, under the princes of the Tudor family, the privileges of the commons were not regarded as hostile to the sovereign, but were cherished and supported as the means of extending his authority.

In consequence of these peculiar circumstances, the government of England, before the accession of James the first, had come to be distinguished from that of every other kingdom in Europe: the prerogative was more limited; the national assembly was constituted upon a more popular plan, and possessed more extensive powers; and, by the intervention of <473> juries, the administration of justice, in a manner consistent with the rights of the people, was better secured.

These peculiarities, it is natural to suppose, could hardly escape the attention of any person, even in that period, who had employed himself in writing upon the government of his country. And yet the historian, whom I formerly quoted,[11] imagines that, before the reign of James the first, the English had never discovered any difference between their own constitution and that of Spain or France; and declares "that he has not met with any writer in that age, who speaks of England as a limited monarchy, but as an absolute one, where the people have many privileges."* This appears the more extraordinary, as foreigners, he acknowledges, were sufficiently sensible of the distinction. "Philip de Comines[12] remarked the English constitution to be more popular, in his time, than that of France. And Cardinal Bentivoglio[13] mentions the English government as similar to that of the Low

* See note Q, at the end of vol. VI.

11. See *HE,* 5:562.

12. Philip de Comines (ca. 1447–ca. 1511): French historian, courtier, and diplomat, author of *Mémoires sur les règnes de Louis XI et de Charles VIII* (1464–98).

13. Guido Bentivoglio (1579–1644), Italian cardinal and author of *Historia della guerra di Fiandra* (1668).

Countries under their <474> princes, rather than to that of France or Spain."*

To prove that English authors did not conceive their government to be a limited monarchy, it is farther observed, that Sir Walter Raleigh,[14] a writer suspected of leaning towards the puritanical party, divides monarchies into such as are *entire,* and such as are *limited* or *restrained;* and that he classes the English government among the former. It must be observed, however, that by a limited monarchy, in this passage, is meant that in which the king has not the sovereignty in time of peace, as in Poland. This is the explanation which the author himself gives of his doctrine.

But not to insist upon the expressions of Sir Walter Raleigh, a courtier, who thought it incumbent upon him to write of queen Elizabeth in a style of romantic love; an adventurer, continually engaged in projects which required the countenance and support of the prince; I shall mention two English writers, whose authority upon this point will perhaps be thought superior, and whose opinion is much more direct and explicit. <475>

The first is Sir John Fortescue,[15] the lord chief justice, and afterwards the chancellor to Henry the sixth, who has written a treatise upon the excellence of the English laws, and who, from his profession, as well as from the distinguished offices which he held by the appointment of the sovereign, will not readily be suspected of prejudices against the prerogative.† This author, instead of conceiving the English government to be an absolute monarchy, describes it in language that seems, in every respect, suitable to the state of our present constitution. After distinguishing governments into *regal* and *political,* that is, into absolute and limited, he is at pains, through the whole of his work, to inculcate, that the English government is of the latter kind, in opposition to the former. "The second point, most worthy prince, whereof you stand in <476> fear," (I make use of the old translation, to

* See note Q, at the end of vol. VI.

† This book was translated into English, and published in the reign of Elizabeth, by Robert Mulcaster, a student of law, and dedicated to one of her justices of the Common Pleas. From the dedication, it should seem that the doctrines contained in this publication, were not understood to be, in any degree, offensive to administration, or contrary to the ideas, of the English constitution, entertained by the lawyers of that reign.

14. Sir Walter Raleigh (1552–1618): English courtier, navigator, and author. Raleigh wrote an unfinished *History of the World* (1614), as well as *The Prerogative of Parliaments* (1628), and *The Cabinet Council* (1658).

15. On Fortescue, see p. 356, note 18.

avoid the possibility of straining the expression) “shall in like manner, and as easily as the other, be confuted. For you stand in doubt whether it be better for you to give your mind to the study of the laws of England, or of the civil laws; because they, throughout the whole world, are advanced in glory and renown above all men’s laws. Let not this scruple of mind trouble you, O most noble prince: for the king of England cannot alter nor change the laws of his realm, at his pleasure. For why, he governeth his people by power, not only *regal* but *political.* If his power over them were regal only, then he might change the laws of his realm, and charge his subjects with tallage and other burdens without their consent.”[*]—<477> The aim of a limited monarchy he afterwards explains more fully. “Now you understand,” says he, “most noble prince, the form of institution of a kingdom *political;* whereby you may measure the power, which the king thereof may exercise over the law, and subjects of the same. For such a king is made and ordained for the defence of the law of his subjects, and of their bodies, and goods, whereunto he receiveth power of his people, so that he cannot govern his people by any other power.”[†]—Then follows a more particular application of this doctrine to the constitution of England. “Now whether the statutes of England be good or not, that only remaineth to be discussed. For they proceed not only from the prince’s pleasure, as do the laws of those kingdoms <478> that are ruled only by *regal* government, where sometimes the statutes do so procure the singular commodity of the maker, that they redound to the hinderance and damage of his subjects.—But statutes cannot thus pass in England, for

* “Secundum vero, princeps, quod tu formidas, consimili nec majori opera elidetur. Dubitas nempe, an Anglorum legum, vel civilium studio te conferas, dum civiles supra humanas cunctas leges alias, fama per orbem extollat gloriosa. No te conturbet, fili regis, hae mentis evagatio: nam non potest rex Angliae ad libitum suum, leges mutare regni sui. Principatu namque, nedum *regali,* sed et *politico,* ipse suo populo dominatur. Si *regali,* tantum ipse praeesset iis, leges regni sui mutare ille posset, *tallagium* quoque at caetera onera eis imponere ipsis inconsultis.”—*Fortescue, de Laudibus Legum Angliae,* c. 9. [[Millar includes the Latin in his note, and in the text uses the Robert Mulcaster translation. For a modern translation, see Sir John Fortescue, *On the Laws and Governance of England,* ed. Shelley Lockwood (Cambridge: Cambridge University Press, 1997), 17.]]

† “Habes in hoc jam, princeps, *instituti* omnis *politici* regni formam, ex qua metire poteris potestatem quam rex ejus in leges ipsius, aut subditos valeat exercere. Ad tutelam namque legis subditorum, ac eorum corporum, et bonorum, rex hujusmodi erectus est; et ad hanc potestatem a populo effluxam ipse habet, quo ei non licet potestate alia suo populo dominari.”—Cap. 13. [[See Fortescue, *Laws and Governance,* 21–22.]]

so much as they are made, not only by the prince's pleasure, but also by the assent of the whole realm: so that of necessity they must procure the wealth of the people, and in no wise tend to their hinderance."*—After stating some objections, in the name of the prince, he goes on; "Do you not now see, most noble prince, that the more you object against the laws of England, the more worthy they appear?—I see plainly, quoth the prince, that in the case wherein you have now travailed, they have the pre-eminence above all other laws <479> of the world; yet we have heard that some of my progenitors, kings of England, have not been pleased with their own laws, and have therefore gone about to bring in the civil laws to the government of England, and to abolish their own country laws. For what purpose and intent they so did I much marvel.—You would nothing marvel thereat, quoth the chancellor, if you did deeply consider with yourself the cause of this intent. For you have heard before, how that among the civil laws, that maxim or rule is a sentence most notable, which thus singeth, *The prince's pleasure standeth in force of a law;* quite contrary to the decrees of the laws of England, whereby the king thereof ruleth his people, not only by *regal* but also by *political* government; insomuch that, at the time of his coronation, he is bound by an oath to the observance of his own law: which thing some kings of England, not well brooking, as thinking that thereby they should not freely govern their subjects as other kings do, whose rule is only regal, governing their people by the civil law, and chiefly by that foresaid maxim of the <480> same law, whereby they, at their pleasure, change laws, make new laws, execute punishments, burden their subjects with charges; and also, when they list, do determine controversies of suitors, as pleaseth them. Wherefore these your progenitors went about to cast off the yoke *political,* that they also might rule, or rather rage over the people their subjects in *regal* wise only: not considering that the power of both kings is equal, as in the foresaid treatise of the law of nature is declared; and that to rule the people by government *political* is no yoke, but liberty, and great security, not only to the subjects, but also to the king himself, and further no small lightening

* "Statuta tunc Anglorum, bona sint necne, solum restat explorandum. Non enim emanant illa a principis solum voluntate, ut leges in regnis quae tantum *regaliter* gubernantur, ubi quandoque statuta ita constitutentis procurant commodum singulare, quod in ejus subditorum ipsa redundant dispendium.—Sed non sic Angliae statuta oriri possunt, dum *nedum principis voluntate, sed et totius regni assensu,* ipsa conduntur, quo populi laesuram illa efficere nequeunt, vel non eorum commodum procurare."—Cap. 18. [[See Fortescue, *Laws and Governance,* 27.]]

or easement to his charge. And that this may appear more evident unto you, ponder and weigh the experience of both regiments; and begin with the king of France, perusing after what sort he ruleth his subjects, by *regal government alone:* and then come to the effect of the joint governance, *regal* and *political,* examining by experience how and in what manner the king of England governeth his <481> subjects."* After these observations, the author, in two separate chapters, contrasts the <482> misery produced by the absolute government in France with the happiness resulting from the limited monarchy in England. The whole treatise is well worth an attentive perusal; as it contains the judgment of a celebrated lawyer, concerning the mixed form of the English constitution, at a period when some have conceived it be no less arbitrary and despotical than that which was established in France or in any other kingdom of Europe.

It will occur to the reader, that the opinion of Sir John Fortescue, in the passages above quoted, is widely different from that of Mr. Hume, who maintains that the legislative power of the English parliament was a mere *fallacy.*

The other English writer, from whose authority it appears that the gov-

* "Nonne vides jam, princeps clarissime, leges Angliae tanto magis clarescere, quanto eisdem tu amplius reluctaris? *Princeps,* video, inquit, et eas inter totius orbis jura (in casu quo tu jam sudasti) praefulgere considero; tamen progenitorum, meorum Angliae regnum quosdam audivimus, in legibus suis minime delectatos, satagentes proinde leges civiles ad Angliae regimen inducere, et patrias leges repudiare conatos: horum revera consilium vehementer admiror. *Cancellarius.* Non admirareris, Princeps, si causam hujus conaminis mente solicita pertractares. Audisti namque superius quomodo inter leges civiles praecipua sententia est, maxima sive regula illa quae sic canit, *quod principi placuit legis habet vigorem:* qualiter non sanciunt leges Angliae, dum nedum *regaliter,* sed et *politice* rex ejusdem dominatur in populum suum, quo ipse in *coronatione* sua ad legis suae observantiam astringitur sacramento; quod reges Angliae aegre ferentes, putantes proinde se non libere dominari in subditos, ut facient reges *regaliter* tantum principantes, qui lege civili, et potissime predicta legis illius maxima, regulant plebem suam, quo ipsi, ad eorum libitum, jura mutant, nova condunt, poenas infligunt, et onera imponunt subditis suis, propriis quoque arbitriis, contendentium, cum velint dirimunt lites. Quare moliti sunt ipsi progenitores tui hoc jugum *politicum* abjicere, ut consimiliter et ipsi in subjectum populum *regaliter* tantum dominari, sed potuis debacchari queant: non attendentes quod aequalis est utriusque regis potentia; ut in predicto tractatu *de natura legis naturae* docetur; et quod non jugum sed libertas est *politice* regere populum, securitas quoque maxima nedum plebi, sed et ipsi regi, allevatio etiam non minima solicitudinis suae. Quae ut tibi apertius pateant, utriusque regiminis experientiam percunctare, et a regimine *tantum regali,* qualiter rex Franciae principatur in subditos suos, exordium sumito: deinde a *regalis* et *politici* regiminis effectu, qualiter rex Angliae dominatur in sibi subditos populos, experientiam quaere." Vide cap. 32, 33, 34. [[See Fortescue, *Laws and Governance,* 47–49.]]

ernment of Eng-<483>land was, at this time, understood to be a limited monarchy, is Sir Thomas Smith,[16] a distinguished lawyer, and principal secretary both to Edward the sixth and to Elizabeth. In his *Commonwealth of England;* a work which unites liberality of sentiment with some philosophy; this author, after explaining the origin and progress of government, has occasion to consider more particularly the nature of the English constitution. "The most high and absolute power," says he, "of the realm of England, consisteth in the parliament.—The parliament abrogateth old laws, maketh new, giveth order for things past, and for things hereafter to be followed, changeth rights and possessions of private men, legitimateth bastards, establisheth forms of religion, altereth weights and measures, giveth form of succession to the crown, defineth of doubtful rights, whereof no law is already made, appointeth subsidies, tailles, taxes, and impositions, giveth most free pardons and absolutions, restoreth in blood and name, as the highest court, condemneth or absolveth them whom the prince will <484> put to that trial. And, to be short, all that ever the people of Rome might do, either in *centuriatis, comitiis,* or *tributis,* the same may be done by the parliament of England, which representeth, and hath the power of the whole realm, both the head and the body. For every Englishman is intended to be there present, either in person or by procuration and attorney, of what preeminence, state, dignity, or quality soever he be, from the prince to the lowest person of England. And the consent of the parliament is taken to be every man's consent."*—Among the privileges of parliament, mentioned by this well-informed writer, one is, that the members "may frankly and freely say their minds, in disputing of such matters as may come in question, and that without offence to his majesty."†—He also enumerates the several branches of the prerogative; such as that of making peace and war, of coining money, of appointing the higher officers and magistrates of the realm, <485> of drawing the tenths and first fruits of ecclesiastical benefices, of issuing writs and executions, of levying the wardship, and first marriage, of all those

* Commonwealth of England, b. ii. ch. 2.

† Ibid. ch. 3.

16. Sir Thomas Smith (1513–77): English classical scholar, professor of civil law at Cambridge, and author of *De Republica Anglorum* (*The Commonwealth of England*), London, 1583. A prominent Protestant, his fortunes rose and fell with the reigns of Henry VIII, Edward VI, Mary, and Elizabeth. These passages are from *The Commonwealth of England* (London, 1612), 36–37, 40, 48.

who hold of the king in chief. What he says concerning the *dispensing power* of the sovereign deserves particular notice, as he mentions the foundation of that power, and the limitations under which it was understood to be exercised.

"The prince," he observes, "useth also to dispense with laws made, whereas equity requireth a moderation to be had, and with pains for transgressing of laws, where the pain of the law is applied only to the prince. But where the forfeit, (as in popular actions chanceth many times) is part to the prince, the other part to the declarator, detector, or informer, there the prince doth dispense for his own part only. Where the criminal is intended by inquisition (that manner is called with us at the prince's suit) the prince giveth absolution or pardon, yet with a clause *modo stet rectus in curia,* that is to say, that no man object against the offender. Whereby, notwithstanding that he hath the <486> prince's pardon, if the person offended will take upon him the accusation (which in our language is called the appeal) in cases where it lieth, the prince's pardon doth not serve the offender."* With what reason, therefore, or plausibility, can it be asserted, that no lawyer, in the reign of Elizabeth, conceived the English constitution to be a limited monarchy?

In perusing these accounts of the English government, we cannot fail to remark, that they are so little enforced by argument, and delivered with such plainness and simplicity, as makes it probable that they contained the doctrines universally received in that age, and which had never been the subject of any doubt or controversy.

The views of this important question, which have been suggested by other writers, it is not my intention to examine. But the opinions of this eminent historian are entitled to so much regard, and appear, in this case, to have so little foundation, that I could not help thinking it improper to pass them over in <487> silence. The improvements made in the English government, from the accession of the house of Stewart to the present time, with the present state of the British constitution in all its principal branches, are intended for the subject of a future inquiry.

END OF THE SECOND VOLUME.

* Commonwealth of England, b. ii. ch. 4.

AN

HISTORICAL VIEW

OF THE

ENGLISH GOVERNMENT

FROM THE

SETTLEMENT OF THE SAXONS IN BRITAIN

TO

THE REVOLUTION IN 1688.

To which are subjoined,

SOME DISSERTATIONS CONNECTED WITH THE

HISTORY OF THE GOVERNMENT,

From the Revolution to the Present Time.

BY JOHN MILLAR ESQ.

Professor of Law in the University of Glasgow

IN FOUR VOLUMES

VOL. III.

London:

PRINTED FOR J. MAWMAN, NO 22 IN THE POULTRY.

1803.

By T. Gillet, Salisbury-Square

CONTENTS[1]
OF THE THIRD VOLUME

1. The page numbers in the Contents are those of the 1803 edition.

AN HISTORICAL VIEW OF THE ENGLISH GOVERNMENT

FROM THE ACCESSION OF THE HOUSE OF STUART, TO THE PRESENT TIME.

Introduction

From the accession of James the First to the English throne, we may date the commencement of what, in a former part of this inquiry, I have called the Commercial Government of England.[1] The progress of commerce and manufactures had now begun to change the manners and political state of the inhabitants. Different arrangements of property had contributed to emancipate the people of <2> inferior condition, and to undermine the authority of the superior ranks. A new order of things was introduced; the feudal institutions natural to a rude nation, were, in great measure, abolished and forgotten; and, upon the venerable stock of our ancient constitution, were engrafted other customs and regulations more consistent with the genius and circumstances of a civilized and opulent kingdom. The commercial improvements which about the same time took place in other parts of Europe, were also attended with great political changes. These, however, were, in each country, accommodated to the peculiar state of society, and therefore

1. Here Millar refers back to his periodization of English history as falling in three parts: "feudal aristocracy," "feudal monarchy," and "commercial government."

exhibited very different combinations and modes of government. According as mankind have been more successful in cultivating the arts of life, their political systems are likely to be more diversified, and to afford a more interesting picture. The attention of a rude people is confined to few objects; and the precautions which occur to them for preventing injustice, and for maintaining good order and tranquillity, are simple and uniform. By experience and observation, by the gradual expansion of the <3> human understanding,[2] new measures are discovered for the removal of particular inconveniences: while, from the various pursuits in which men are engaged, and the wealth of different kinds which they accumulate, a variety of regulations are suggested for the security and enjoyment of their several acquisitions. Their systems of policy are thus rendered more comprehensive, and, to the eye of the philosopher, present a richer field of instruction and entertainment.

The historical aera from which the present inquiry sets out, is further distinguished by an accidental event of great importance; the union of the crowns of England and of Scotland.[3] By the accession of the house of Stuart to the English throne, the whole island of Great Britain, which had long been divided into two separate kingdoms, independent of each other, and frequently engaged in mutual depredations, was reduced under one sovereign, by whose authority their future animosities were effectually restrained, and their military force invariably directed against their common enemies. That this federal union was highly beneficial to both nations, <4> by exalting their power and consideration among foreign states, as well as by promoting their security, together with their trade and opulence at home, appears abundantly manifest. How far it affected their political circumstances, and contributed to improve the form of their government, I shall afterwards endeavour to explain.

The whole period of English history from the accession of James the First to the present time, may be divided into two branches: the one compre-

2. The theme of growing complexity in human society is also a concern throughout Millar's *Distinction of Ranks.*

3. The crowns were joined on the accession of James VI of Scotland as James I in 1603.

hending the occurrences prior to the revolution in 1688;[4] the other the occurrences posterior to that great event. The former contains the rise and progress of the long contest between the king and parliament concerning the extent of prerogative;[5] a contest which, after involving the nation in a civil war, and after producing various political changes and turns of fortune, was at last happily terminated by a judicious and moderate correction of the ancient limited monarchy. We have here an opportunity of considering the condition of England and of Scotland, after the union of the two crowns; the circumstances in the state of society, which <5> encouraged the king to claim a despotical power, and which, on the other hand, prompted the people to demand an extension of privileges; the views of the two great parties, into which the whole kingdom was naturally divided; and the several events, whether proceeding from local and temporary, or from general and permanent causes, which promoted or obstructed the success of either party.

In the latter branch of this period, the political horizon assumed a different aspect.[6] By the revolution in 1688, the extent of the prerogative was understood to be fixed in such a manner as to preclude any future disputes. The modes of arbitrary power, with which the nation had formerly been threatened or oppressed, were now completely restrained. The eminent advantages of a constitution, which appeared effectually to secure the most important rights of mankind, and which England enjoyed without a rival, promoted, in a wonderful degree, her commerce and manufactures, exalted her power as a maritime nation, and enabled her to plant colonies as well as to <6> establish her dominion in distant parts of the globe.

The accumulation of wealth, arising, in these prosperous circumstances, from a long course of industry and activity, could not fail to increase the expence of living to every individual, and, of consequence, the expences incurred in the management of public affairs. Hence the necessity for a proportional increase of taxes, and augmentation of the public revenue under the disposal of the sovereign. The patronage and correspondent influence of the crown, which were thus rendered more and more extensive, began to

4. The Glorious Revolution of 1688–89 displaced the Stuart monarch, James II (r. 1685–89), who was replaced by his son-in-law, William of Orange, as William III (r. 1689–1702), and his daughter as Mary II (r. 1689–99).

5. See p. 235, note 45.

6. Here, and in the paragraph that follows, Millar outlines the essence of the Whig view of the change in the British constitution following 1688.

excite apprehension, that, if permitted to advance without controul, they might undermine and subvert the pillars of the ancient constitution. Thus the two great political parties were not extinguished at the revolution; though, according to the change of times and circumstances, their object was considerably varied. The Whigs,[7] who had formerly opposed the extension of the prerogative, now opposed the secret influence of the crown; and the Tories, upon a similar variation of the ground, still adhered to the interest of the monarch. <7>

The operation of this influence was, indeed, retarded, for some time, by that warm attachment to the exiled royal family[8] which prevailed through a part of the nation. While a powerful faction in Britain supported the claim of a pretender to the crown,[9] those who exercised the executive power were laid under the necessity of acting with extreme circumspection, and of keeping at a distance from every measure which might occasion suspicion or alarm. The greater diffusion of knowledge, however, contributed, by degrees, to discredit and dissolve this foreign connection, and, of course, to remove those restraints which it had created; but, in the mean time, the progress of liberal opinions, and the growing spirit of independence, disposed the people to examine more narrowly the corruptions of government,

7. The Whig party took its name from *whiggamore,* a term applied to the Scots Covenanters who opposed the Catholic duke of York (the future James II) as the heir to the British throne. The Glorious Revolution of 1688–89 brought the Whigs, with their ideology of limiting the royal prerogative, into favor as the consistent supporters of the Hanoverian settlement. In common with other "radical Whigs," Millar feared that "secret influence" had replaced authority in giving the Crown sway over the Parliament and people. *Tory,* derived from an Irish word for bandit or cattle thief, was originally a pejorative term for the supporters of the duke of York (James II), and then became a more general term for those loyal to king and church over the issue of the sovereignty of Parliament. In the early part of the eighteenth century, the party suffered from internal divisions and was excluded from office under the first two Hanoverian monarchs (1714–60). The reaction to the French Revolution in the 1790s helped to legitimate Tory values, and the name became voluntarily applied.

8. The Stewart dynasty was established in Scotland with the ascension of Robert the Steward as Robert II (r. 1371–90). The Scottish spelling was anglicized to Stuart after the union of the English and Scottish crowns in 1603.

9. The term *Jacobite,* derived from the Latin form of James, was applied to those who continued to support the Stuart claim to the British throne via the exiled James Edward Stuart, the "Old Pretender" (1688–1766), son of the deposed James II. Major Jacobite uprisings occurred in 1715 and in 1745–46 under the "Young Pretender," Charles Edward Stuart (1720–88).

and to reform the abuses of administration. In this manner the popular and monarchical parts of our constitution have been again set at variance; a struggle between them has proceeded with some degree of animosity; and express regulations have been thought requisite for limiting that ascendant which the latter has gained, and is farther <8> likely to gain, over the former. The latter branch of our history will exhibit the conduct of political parties, in this critical situation, and the various events and circumstances which have tended to prevent, or delay, an amicable conclusion of their differences. <9>

Book I

OF THE ENGLISH GOVERNMENT, FROM THE ACCESSION OF JAMES THE FIRST, TO THE REIGN OF WILLIAM THE THIRD.

CHAPTER I

Review of the Government of Scotland.

As the union of the two crowns placed the administration of England and of Scotland in the same hands, we shall here turn our attention to the history of the latter country, and examine the leading features of its government. In this review, without entering into a long detail, it will be sufficient to point out the principal circumstances, from which we may discover the general analogy,[1] and the most remarkable differences in the constitution and political state of the two countries.

The armies of Rome never penetrated far into Scotland, nor did they long maintain a dominion over that part of the country which <10> they had subdued.[2] While the inhabitants in the southern part of Britain were disarmed, and gradually civilised by that mighty power, the Caledonians[3] of the north retaining their primitive independence, and warlike dispositions, were little affected by the vicinity, either of Roman arts, or of Roman man-

1. Millar frequently draws on Scottish developments for comparative purposes, as he does here.

2. Scotland cannot be considered as having been part of the Roman Empire. There were, however, a number of Roman incursions from the north of England, following which parts of the country were briefly retained under Roman military rule.

3. Caledonia was the ancient Roman name for Scotland. Tacitus used this term to comprehend all the country north of the Forth-Clyde isthmus.

ners. Those high-spirited barbarians, therefore, when the Romans were under the necessity of withdrawing their forces from Britain, found no enemy capable of resisting them, and threatened to overrun and subdue the whole of the island. They were afterwards repulsed, however, by the Saxons, whom the Britons called to their assistance; and, after various turns of fortune, were obliged to contract the limits of their dominion within that southern wall which in later times had formed the boundary of the Roman province.[4] Even within the territories of what was called Scotland, the Saxons made frequent inroads, more especially upon the eastern side of the country; where many Saxon families were enabled to form a settlement, and to acquire landed possessions.

Notwithstanding the original similarity ob-<11>servable in all the governments of modern Europe, they exhibit certain shades of difference, from which they may be divided into two classes; the first, comprehending such as were founded upon the ruins of the Roman provinces; the second, such as arose in the countries which had never been subject to the Roman empire. In both of these, what is called the feudal system was introduced; but it was more completely and rapidly established in the former than in the latter. In those modern states which grew up from the ruins of the western empire, the inhabitants of so large a territory as that which composed an ancient Roman province, were naturally attracted to a kind of centre, and formed a political union under one sovereign. But the authority of this monarch, over a people so barbarous, and so little accustomed to subordination, was, in proportion to the extent of his dominions, feeble and precarious: and the less capable he was of restraining animosities and quarrels among his subjects, or of protecting them from oppression, it became the more necessary that they should take measures for defending themselves. For this <12> purpose, every chief, or proprietor of a landed estate, was induced to maintain an intimate connection with all his kindred and retainers, and to distribute among them a great part of his lands, upon condition of their being ready to fight for him against all his enemies. It was thus that Spain, France, England, and a great part of Italy, soon after they had been conquered by the Gothic nations, became extensive rude kingdoms, in which the free people

4. The emperor Hadrian (r. 117–38) ordered the construction of "Hadrian's Wall" in 122 A.D. It runs between the River Tyne and the Solway Firth.

were all united in separate feudal dependencies, each under its own military leader and protector.

The European countries which had never been subjected to the Roman yoke, such as Denmark, Sweden, and a great part of Germany, were in circumstances a little different. The inhabitants, originally no less rude and barbarous than the conquerors of the western empire, were not incorporated with any people more civilized than themselves, nor induced by any prior union subsisting, through an extensive territory, to associate in very large communities. Their different tribes, or families, accordingly, following the natural course of improvement, advanced very slowly in their <13> political associations; and were collected in small principalities, before they rose to considerable kingdoms. But in proportion as the boundaries of any particular state were narrow, the prince was more powerful, and his administration more vigorous; in consequence of which, the people, depending more upon him for protection, resorted less to private combinations for mutual defence. The connection between the head of a tribe and its members, between the proprietor of a landed estate and his retainers, between a superior and his vassals, could not fail to subsist in all those nations, after they had acquired a fixed residence; but this connection was less extended in proportion to the narrowness of each political community; and the services, or duties, to which it gave occasion, were less multiplied, and reduced into a regular system. Afterwards, however, the feudal institutions and customs were promoted in those countries, from an intercourse with such neighbouring states as, by settling in the Roman provinces, had made greater progress in that system of policy.

Scotland appears to have been in a middle <14> situation between these different countries. A part of it had fallen within the limits of a Roman province, like the other countries in the west of Europe. A part of it, likewise, had received a number of Anglo-Saxon inhabitants, who contributed to propagate those institutions and customs which prevailed in England. The remainder was in the condition of those European countries, where the dominion of the ancient Romans afforded the people no peculiar motive to extensive combination, or, of consequence, to feudal subordination.

In tracing the history of the Scottish government, there are three great periods which fall to be distinguished.[5] The first reaches from the time when

5. The first period stretches from approximately the beginning of the fifth century

Britain was abandoned by the Romans to the reign of Malcolm the Second. This comprehends the primitive aristocracy; and is analogous to the period of the Anglo-Saxon government in the southern part of the island. The second extends from that reign to the time when James the Sixth of Scotland mounted the English throne. This corresponds to the reigns of the Norman, Plantagenet, and Tudor princes in England, <15> and exhibits the circumstances which, from the nature of the feudal policy, contributed to exalt the power of the monarch. The third contains the interval between the union of the crowns of England and Scotland, to the union of the two kingdoms. In this last period, the Scottish nation had not made such advances in commerce as could produce any great alteration in their political system; but the administration of their government was then rendered subordinate to that of England, a manufacturing and commercial country.

SECTION I

Of the Government of Scotland, from the Time when Britain was abandoned by the Romans, to the Reign of Malcolm the Second.

During this early period, little is known with certainty; and we must be satisfied with a delineation, from probable conjecture,[6] of the bare outlines and prevailing character of <16> the Scottish government. The appropriation of land gave rise in Scotland, as well as in the other countries of Europe, to several distinctions in the condition and rank of the people. The owner of a landed estate obtained universally an authority over all those persons whom he maintained upon his property. Those who acquired considerable estates were led to distribute a part of them among their kindred and followers, under conditions of military service, and to put the remainder under the management of servants employed in the several branches of agriculture. The people subsisting upon any estate came thus to be composed of the

---

until early in the eleventh century: the Roman abandonment of Britain was complete by 410, and Malcolm II reigned 1005–34. James VI (r. 1567–1603) became James I upon the union of the crowns in 1603, and the Act of Union was passed in 1707.

6. Millar refers here to the "conjectural" method that was a prominent feature of Scottish historical thought in the eighteenth century. In addition to Millar's own work *The Origin of the Distinction of Ranks,* the outstanding examples of conjectural history were Adam Ferguson's *Essay on the History of Civil Society* (1767) and Lord Kames's *Sketches of the History of Man* (1774).

master, or proprietor, of the vassals who attended him in war, and of the peasants by whose labour his household was supported. As the whole kingdom comprehended a number of landed estates, disposed and regulated in the same manner, and differing only in the degrees of their magnitude, the whole people, exclusive of the clergy, were divided into these three orders of men.

It is probable, however, that in Scotland the peasantry, in proportion to the collective body of the nation, were less numerous than <17> in England; and that their condition was less abject and servile. They were less numerous; because agriculture was in a lower state, and a great proportion of the country was employed merely in pasturage. Their condition was less abject and servile; because, as the country had never been conquered, like the provinces of the western empire, there had been no opportunity, by captivity in war, of reducing a great part of the inhabitants into a state of absolute slavery.

In all rude countries, those who earn subsistence by their labour are apt to feel much dependence upon the person who employs them; and there can be no doubt that in Scotland, as well as in the neighbouring feudal kingdoms, the peasants were considered as inferior in rank to the military tenants. But they appear to have been less distinguished by peculiar marks of inferiority; less disqualified from serving their master in war; and more capable, by their industry and good behaviour, of bettering their circumstances. It should seem, accordingly, that the distinction between the villeins and the military tenants was earlier abolished in Scotland than in England. In the latter country, the <18> *copy-holders,* the remains of the ancient villeins, are still considered as inferiour in rank to the *free-holders,* or military tenants; and are not, even at this day, admitted to a full participation of the same political rights: whereas in Scotland, no such class of men as the *copy-holders* have any existence; nor in the present laws and customs of that country are any vestiges of the primeval villanage to be found.

As the state of property in Scotland was very similar to that which took place in the other countries of modern Europe, the form of government resulting from it was in all probability nearly the same. The proprietor of every landed estate was the natural governour of the district which it comprehended. He was the military leader, and the civil magistrate, of all the people who lived upon it. These proprietors, originally independent of each other, were led by degrees into a confederacy, or political union, more or less extensive according to circumstances.

In England the proprietors in the same neighbourhood were united in a town or village, commonly called a *tything.* Ten of these villages are said to have been associated in form-<19>ing an *hundred* or *centenary;* and an arbitrary number of these hundreds formed a *shire* or *county.* These districts were subordinate one to another: and in each of them there was appointed a military leader; by whom, with concurrence of the several free proprietors, all its political concerns were transacted. The proprietors of the different shires were united under a king, their great military leader; by whom they were occasionally called to deliberate, in the last resort, upon the legislative, executive, or judicial business of the nation.

It is highly probable that this political arrangement, so natural and simple, took place in Scotland, as well as in England, and in other kingdoms upon the neighbouring continent; though, from the deficiency and imperfection of the Scottish records, a complete proof of it can hardly be adduced. The name of *tything* is scarcely to be found in the ancient monuments or histories of Scotland; but there are clear vestiges of the most important regulations connected with that institution. A tything in England, as well as upon the continent of Europe, was in reality a town or village divided into ten parts; and in the towns or villages of <20> Scotland, as I had occasion to observe in a former part of this inquiry, the whole of the inhabitants were liable to make a pecuniary compensation for the crimes committed by any individual. This affords a distinct evidence of the intimate union subsisting among the members of those little societies, which were the basis of the more extensive combinations.

The institution of *hundreds* can scarcely be traced in Scotland; but the division of the whole kingdom into shires, or counties, each under its own governour, the alderman or earl, and afterwards his deputy the sheriff, seems to be fully ascertained; nor can there be any reason to doubt, that the political business of the nation was ultimately determined by a great council, corresponding to the Wittenagemote in England. This council was in all probability composed of the free or allodial proprietors of land; was called by the king in any important emergency; and exercised an authority which pervaded all the different branches of government.

The aristocratical nature of this constitution, which placed the supreme power in the independent proprietors of land, is abundantly <21> manifest. It is probable that, in the course of time, it became gradually more aristocratical than it had originally been. Upon the first appropriation of land, it is natural to suppose that the occupiers were numerous, and the estates of individuals proportionably moderate. But in the turbulent and disorderly state of the country, men of small property were unable to defend their possessions; and therefore found it necessary to resign their estates into the hands of some powerful neighbour, and to hold them for the future as his vassals upon conditions of military service. In this manner the number of independent proprietors was gradually diminished; the foundation of political influence was more and more contracted; and the right of sitting in the national assembly was at length limited to a few individuals who had accumulated great estates. <22>

SECTION II

Of the government of Scotland, from the Reign of Malcolm the Second, to the union of its crown with that of England.

The same darkness which involves the first period of the Scottish history, and which renders it, in great measure, a field of mere conjecture, hangs over a considerable part of the second. The commencement of the second period, however, is distinguished, according to the testimony of all the historians, by the reduction of the great lords, the remaining allodial proprietors of land, into a state of feudal dependence upon the king; an event similar to that which took place in England at the Norman Conquest; and in France, during the reign of Hugh Capet and his immediate successors. This fact is confirmed by a collection of antient laws, ascribed to king Malcolm the Second, in which it seems to be stated, though in vague and general terms, that this <23> monarch, by a course of transactions with his subjects, became the feudal superior of all the lands in the kingdom.

As the account there given is contrary to the opinion of many British antiquaries concerning the origin of the feudal system, they have generally disputed the authenticity, or at least the date of that antient record. We must acknowledge, that the information which it contains, with respect to an event of such importance, is very lame and unsatisfactory; and that, in many other particulars, it seems to be replete with blunders and inaccuracies. A conjecture has thence been suggested, which is highly probable, that the compilation in question was not made by public authority, in the reign to which it refers; but has been the work of a private individual, in a later age: and contains the ideas of the writer concerning the regulations introduced in the reign of Malcolm the Second. In this view, with all its inaccuracies and defects, it appears entitled to some regard. It may be considered in the light of a very antient and universal tradition, and, when supported by the general testimony of historians, may be held of sufficient weight to counterbalance any slender <24> evidence which can, at this day, be thrown into the opposite scale.*

* Lord Hales, an author whose acute researches concerning antient facts, and whose extreme caution in advancing any conjecture with respect to their causes, are equally conspicuous, asserts that the collection of old laws ascribed to Malcolm the Second, is a plain and palpable forgery. In proof of this assertion he seems to depend chiefly upon two arguments, 1. The improbability of the fact stated in the collection, viz. That the king gave away the whole land in Scotland to his men. "Dedit, et distribuit totam terram de Scotia hominibus suis, et nihil sibi retinuit in proprietate, nisi regiam dignitatem, et montem Placiti in villa de Scona." [["He gave and distributed the whole land of Scotland among his followers, and he kept nothing back for himself as his property except the royal dignity and Moot Hill in the town of Scone." The quotation is taken from the Laws of King Malcolm the Second, of which the text is in John Skene, *Regiam Majestatem Scotiae. Veteres Leges et Constitutiones, ex Archivis Publicis, et Antiquis Libris Manuscriptis Collectae, etc.* (Edinburgh, 1609), 1.]] But it seems evident that the expression here made use of, is not meant to be literally understood. The *royal dignity* cannot be considered as a piece of land; and yet it is said, that the king gave *the whole land, except the royal dignity.* By the *royal dignity* seems in this passage to be meant those *royal demesnes* by which the dignity of the crown was supported; and probably the lands distributed to his subjects, under the conditions of feudal tenure, were these only which they had previously resigned to the king for that purpose, or which had fallen to him by forfeiture. The *moot hill of Scone,* the place where the national council held its meetings, is mentioned as distinct from the ordinary demesnes of the crown. 2. The other argument against the authenticity of this antient record is taken from the *fees* or *salaries* mentioned as given to certain officers. These the author thinks are in certain cases immoderately high; in others, inconsistent with the respective ranks of those officers. But before any argument from topicks of this kind can have much weight, it will be necessary to show distinctly the rate of money used in Scotland, both during the reign of Malcolm the Second, and of Malcolm the Third, which this learned author appears unable to do. In addition to this remark, it may be proper to subjoin a note, which lord Hales has the candour to insert at the end of his dissertation, and by which it should seem, that his labours upon that subject are in some degree superseded. "A friend of mine," says he, "distinguished in the literary world, observes, that the *Leges Malcolmi* are the composition of some private man who meant to describe the great outlines of the laws and customs of his country, which he supposed, or had been told by tradition, were first introduced by some ancient and famous king of the name of Malcolm, either Malcolm Mackenneth, or Malcolm Canmore; the former just as probably as the latter. It does not appear that the author himself ever meant that they should pass for the original statutes of that king. The whole book is a narrative or history of the regulations which he sup-

Concerning the introduction of the feudal tenures into Scotland, there occur two particulars which merit attention. In the first place, it is the uniform doctrine of the antient lawyers and antiquaries who have written upon the subject,[7] that the feudal system in Europe arose from the immediate act of the king, who, upon subduing any country, laid hold of the land, and <25> reserving so much of it as he found requisite for his own subsistence, distributed the remainder among his great officers, to be enjoyed by them upon condition of military service. A part of what had thus been bestowed upon these leading persons, was by them distributed, upon similar terms, among their dependants; so that, from one great stock, different orders of vassals, in subordination one to another, sprung up in various ramifications. To this account, when <26> applied to the history of Scotland, it occurs as an insuperable objection, that no such considerable conquest ever took place in the country, as could enable the sovereign to seize and distribute the lands in the manner supposed. There seems, therefore, to be a necessity for admitting, that, in Scotland at least, the feudal system was propagated in a different course; that it began by the occupiers of land bestowing fiefs upon <27> their kindred and followers; that it was extended by the poorer allodial proprietors purchasing the protection, and becoming the vassals of the more opulent; and that it was at length completed by these opulent proprietors falling, in consequence of the numerous quarrels and difficulties in which they were involved, under the immediate vassalage of the crown.

The other circumstance to which I alluded is, that the passage, in this old collection of laws concerning the introduction of the feudal tenures, mentions the vassals of the crown only. We are told that, in the reign of king Malcolm, the great lords became the vassals of the crown; but we have no information as to the period when the inferior military people became the vassals of the great lords. It is natural to conclude, therefore, that the feudal subordination of the inferior people had immemorially existed in the country: for otherwise, had it either immediately preceded or followed the infeu-

---

posed had been made in times that were ancient in comparison of his own. The style is every where not statutary, but historical. He called them the *Laws of King Malcolm;* because he supposed they had originally been instituted by some king of that name. The supposition of their being the statutes of any king is a blunder, and a very gross one, of later writers, for which the author is not answerable." [See Lord Hales' Dissertation on the LL. Malcolmi.]

7. For a list of Millar's principal sources, see appendix 1.

dation of the great lords, it would probably have been mentioned in stating that event, with which it was so evidently connected.

It is the opinion of Sir Henry Spelman,[8] and has been followed by several respectable authors, <28> that the collection of laws above-mentioned is, by a mistake of the publisher, ascribed to the reign of Malcolm the Second, and belongs in reality to that of Malcolm the Third, about fifty years posterior to the former. According to this conjecture, the feudal system was completed in Scotland about the time of the Norman Conquest, that is about the same time as in England; whereas, by the common account, that event was produced about fifty years earlier. The completion of the feudal structure, by exalting a king to be the feudal superior of all the lands in his dominions, was, in all the countries in Europe, a regular step in the progress of society and government; and that the Scottish nation had become ripe for so great a political change, at an earlier period than the English, is what we should not naturally have supposed. But we seem scarcely entitled, from conjecture alone with respect to a fact of this nature, to set aside the evidence of tradition; more especially when it is considered, that accidental circumstances frequently concur, in particular countries, to retard or accelerate the operation of general causes.[9]

Malcolm the Second, though the lineal heir <29> of the crown, was obliged to enforce his right by the sword. He was afterwards engaged in fierce and bloody wars with the Danes, at that time masters of England; and, after various success, was at length so fortunate as to drive those formidable invaders out of the kingdom. It is not improbable, therefore, that the losses sustained by the nobility, in this long and obstinate contest, had considerably weakened their power, while the continued military operations in which the people were engaged, together with the splendid victories and complete triumph of the monarch, in a quarrel so national and popular, had, on the

8. Sir Henry Spelman (ca. 1564–1641): English historian and antiquarian who argued that both feudal law and parliament in England date from after the Norman Conquest in 1066. His ideas became influential through Robert Brady (see pp. 212–13, note 12). In *Feuds and Tenure by Knight-Service,* Spelman discusses the matter of the *Leges Malcolmi* as belonging to the reign of Malcolm III, not Malcolm II. See *The English Works of Sir Henry Spelman* (London, 1723), 2:26–28.

9. For Millar's distinction between accidental and general causes, see for example, Hume's "Of the Rise and Progress of the Arts and Sciences," in *Essays, Moral, Political, and Literary,* ed. Eugene F. Miller (Indianapolis: Liberty Fund, 1985), 111–37.

other hand, increased the influence of the crown, so as to produce, in the chief proprietors of land, a disposition to purchase the king's protection by submitting to his feudal authority.

At any rate the alteration contended for does not seem very material. To those who imagine that the feudal tenures were introduced into Scotland merely from an imitation of the practice in England, it must appear necessary to overthrow every monument, or account, which tends to shew their complete establishment in the former country at an earlier period than <30> in the latter. But if we suppose, what is now generally admitted, that those institutions, both in the southern and northern parts of Britain, were derived from the general state of society and manners, though afterwards, perhaps, promoted and modified by imitation, the precise date of their introduction will seem of little moment; and their occurring half a century sooner or later will make no considerable difference in the political history of the country.

It is of importance, however, to observe, that even after the sovereign had thus reduced the great lords of the kingdom into a state of military subordination, his authority was not thence greatly augmented. Although, when exposed to imminent danger, and eager to take vengeance upon their enemies, the barons had sheltered themselves under the protection of the crown, and promised to support its authority; yet no sooner were they relieved from their difficulties, than they naturally forgot their promises, and resumed that independent spirit which was habitual to them. The feudal superiority of the king came, therefore, in many respects, to be more nominal than real; and he <31> often found it extremely difficult, if not impossible, to enforce that submission and obedience which the tenure of a military vassal required. The assistance and protection which he afforded his vassals were understood, in all cases, to be fully compensated by the regular services, and by the incidental emoluments which he drew from them, and the reluctance with which they often performed their ordinary duties, left no room to expect that they would acquiesce in any additional demands. They had not only the right of enjoying their estates during their own life, but that of transmitting them to their heirs; and it was not more their interest to obtain the favour of their superiour, than it was his interest to secure their fidelity and attachment. They were servants, in a word, who punctually obeyed their master when his orders were suited to their own inclinations; but who frequently acquired an extraordinary premium, or inducement, if he wished they should serve him with spirit and alacrity.

From the slightest attention to the political history of England and of Scotland, it will appear that the progress of the regal power was much more slow and gradual in the latter country <32> than in the former, and that the primitive aristocracy gained a more absolute and lasting ascendant. For the slow advancement of monarchy in Scotland, so far as it has not proceeded from accidental occurrences, two great causes may be assigned.

1. The nature of the country, rugged, mountainous, and in many parts hardly accessible, produced a number of separate districts, in which particular barons were enabled to establish and maintain an independent authority.[10] Within those natural barriers which divided one territory from another, a great lord easily reduced all the small proprietors into subjection: and, at the same time, residing in the midst of his retainers and followers, was in a good measure secured from any foreign invasion. Landed property was thus quickly accumulated by a few great nobles, whose power over their inferiours, and whose influence in the government, became proportionably extensive. While they lived at home in rustick state and magnificence, they had little temptation to court the favour of the crown, and still less to purchase it by a surrender of their privileges; nor did the sovereign often find it adviseable, however they might <33> incur his displeasure, to run the hazard of marching against them in their fastnesses, and of endeavouring by force to subdue them. In this situation they continued for many centuries to suffer little degradation, either from the immediate power of the most warlike, or from the secret intrigues of the most artful and politic princes.

2. The other cause which operated in retarding the advancement of the crown, though, perhaps, it may be considered as partly arising from the former, was the slow progress of arts and manufactures. From the state of society in most of the countries of modern Europe, the king had usually an interest in protecting the peasantry, as well as the trading part of the nation, and in promoting the extension of their privileges; for in that manner he infallibly weakened their dependence upon their immediate superiors, and of consequence undermined the power of his rivals, the nobility. It was to be expected, also, that when the inferiour orders of the community had, by

10. The most famous eighteenth-century advocate of the influence of geography on political development was Montesquieu. See *Spirit of the Laws,* ed. and trans. Anne Cohler, B. C. Miller, and H. S. Stone (Cambridge: Cambridge University Press, 1989), 285–92.

the encouragement given to their industry, been emancipated from their primitive bondage, and had attained a degree of opulence and considera-<34>tion, they would naturally be prompted to a return of good offices, and induced, by motives of interest, as well as by habitual attachment, to support the dignity of the crown, and to throw their whole weight in opposition to the aristocracy.

But in Scotland the barrenness of the soil and coldness of the climate obstructed the progress of agriculture, and of course chilled the growth of manufactures. The necessaries of life must be had in plenty, before there can be a general demand for its conveniencies. Accordingly, though villages and towns employed in some branches of traffick, arose in different parts of the country, and though these, in conformity to the practice of other European kingdoms, were incorporated by the king, and endowed with various exclusive privileges, yet, in spite of every encouragement, they continued poor and despicable, and were for a long time unable, as political auxiliaries of the crown, to perform any important service.

The Scottish parliament from the time of Malcolm the Second, like that of England from the Norman Conquest, appears to have been composed of all the immediate vassals of the <35> crown; and these were divided into two estates, the one comprehending the ecclesiastical, the other the lay-barons; each of which claimed, at least on some occasions, a separate voice in the assembly. But after the creation of royal boroughs[11] the king was induced, from similar circumstances in the northern as in the southern part of the island, to require that these corporations should send deputies for making a general bargain with regard to the taxes or duties demanded from them; and hence those deputies, whose consent was requisite for procuring a part of the national supplies, were by degrees admitted into the national council.

Concerning the time when this change in the government was effected, as it proceeded apparently from no public regulation, but merely from the private interpositions of the sovereign, we have no decisive information. It seems to be admitted, that the representatives of the boroughs were introduced into the national assembly as early as the reign of Robert the First;[12] though some authors, with no small degree of probability, have placed this event at an earlier period. But as the number of these representatives was,

11. The granting of borough status began in the twelfth century.
12. Robert I (r. 1306–29).

for a long time, inconsiderable, and as they <36> took little share in the public transactions, their political existence appears to have been in a great measure overlooked.

It is remarkable, however, that notwithstanding the insignificance of the Scottish boroughs, they formed, at an early period, a peculiar court, composed of their own deputies, to which nothing similar occurs in the southern part of the island. Four of those communities, probably the most opulent and flourishing; namely, Edinburgh, Stirling, Berwick, and Roxburgh, were accustomed, by their delegates, to hold meetings for the purposes of reviewing the judicial sentences passed by the magistrates of particular boroughs, and of deliberating upon the concerns of the whole order. A meeting of this kind received the appellation of the *Parliament of Boroughs.*[13] When Berwick and Roxburgh had fallen into the hands of the English, Linlithgow and Lanark were substituted in their place; and we find that, afterwards, all the royal boroughs, to the southward of the Spey, were invited to send representatives to this commercial council.* <37>

Of the circumstances which gave rise to this institution, or the period of its commencement, no account is given by historians. It was natural that the manufacturing and mercantile people, like the clergy, or any other class of men distinguished by their peculiar situation from the rest of the community, should hold consultations for promoting their common interest; but it is difficult to conceive that the towns in Scotland were, at a very remote

* See the treatise intitled *curia quatuor burgorum* [[the court of the four burghs. Translated from John Skene, *Regiam Majestatem Scotiae. Veteres Leges et Constitutiones* (Edinburgh, 1609), 154]], in the collection of old laws published by Skene. At what time the meeting, called the *Parliament of boroughs,* was first introduced, it seems impossible to ascertain. That part of the collection above mentioned, intitled *consuetudines burgorum* [[the constitution of burghs. Translated from Skene, *Regiam Majestatem Scotiae,* 132]], and supposed by Skene to have been established in the reign of David the First, is conjectured to have arisen from the interpositions of this ancient court. The act of the legislature substituting the boroughs of Lanark and Linlithgow to those of Berwick and Roxburgh, which had fallen into the hands of the English, was passed in the year 1368, in the reign of David the Second.

13. The Convention of Royal Burghs was known to have existed in the thirteenth century. It drew up the laws of the Four Burghs (Edinburgh, Stirling, Lanark, and Linlithgow [the latter two replaced Berwick and Roxburgh in 1368]), which applied to all royal burghs throughout the realm. Its formal records began in the middle of the sixteenth century.

period, possessed of such weight as could enable them, by their joint meetings, to assume any considerable jurisdiction or privileges. As the ancient parliament of boroughs was called and held by the king's chamberlain, the officer employed in superintending the royal revenue drawn from that class of the people; it is probable that the authority <38> acquired by this meeting had proceeded from the policy of the sovereign; and that it was calculated to answer the same purpose which he had afterwards in view, by introducing the burgesses into the national assembly. By subjecting the decisions and deliberations of the inhabitants of the towns to a representative court of their own order, he secured a degree of uniformity in their measures; was enabled, with greater facility, to overrule their determinations, more especially with regard to the contributions and duties which he levied from them; and taught them, by the habit of acting in their collective capacity, to discern their common interest in opposing the nobles, by whom they were frequently oppressed, and in supporting the king, by whom they were usually protected.

From the original parliament of boroughs, augmented and modified by the attendance of the delegates from other boroughs throughout the kingdom, was at last suggested the idea of a general meeting, composed of representatives from all the towns under the immediate patronage of the crown, and invested with powers to regulate the concerns of all <39> those trading societies. Such was the *convention of the royal boroughs,* authorised by an act of the legislature in the reign of James the Third, and confirmed by another statute in the reign of James the Sixth.[14] The records of its annual meetings have been preserved from the year 1552; though its constitution and forms of procedure have been somewhat varied by subsequent regulations.

From the spirit and facility with which the individuals who compose the trading part of a nation are apt to unite in maintaining and extending their privileges, it might be expected that this early institution would have bestowed upon them an extensive influence in the government. But while Scotland remained an independent kingdom, the low state of her commerce prevented any combination whatever from raising her merchants to political importance; and in the present century, since, by her union with England, and by our own exertions, her circumstances in this respect have been greatly improved, her opulent mercantile towns no longer think it an object to as-

14. See note 25 in this chapter. James VI/I reigned 1567–1625.

sociate with those inconsiderable corporations which chiefly compose the con-<40>vention of royal boroughs; but rather endeavour, by a voluntary association with the larger commercial societies of Great Britain, and by the formation of numerous committees, or *chambers of commerce,*[15] to inforce their demands, and advance their common interests.

In the English parliament the knights of the shires were introduced about the same time with the burgesses; but in Scotland the greater poverty of the lower classes of the gentry prevented them from aspiring to political importance, and therefore obstructed a similar improvement. It has been mentioned in a former part of this treatise, that James the First,[16] about an hundred years after the time of Robert Bruce, having been long detained a prisoner in England, was disposed to imitate the institutions of a country more advanced in regular government than his own: and finding, upon his return home, that many vassals of the crown, from a variety of circumstances which had contributed to dismember their estates, were averse from the expence of attending in parliament; and at the same time observing that these men of <41> narrow fortunes, and of inferior rank, were commonly, from their jealousy of the greater barons, inclined to support the prerogative, he endeavoured, first of all, by an act of the legislature, to enforce their attendance. As this injunction, however, was disregarded, he soon after procured another statute, excusing the small vassals from that duty, but requiring that, in the same manner as in England, they should send representatives. The small vassals of the crown in Scotland, probably less able to bear the expence than the people of the same description in England, laid hold of the dispensation, but neglected to fulfil the conditions; so that before the reign of James the Sixth, that is, a full century after this period, the attendance of the knights of shires[17] had not been made effectual.

Thus, during a period of two centuries at least, the national council in Scotland was composed of the barons who sat in their own right, of the dignified clergy, and of a small number of burgesses. In the forms of its

15. All major cities and most large towns formed chambers of commerce in the eighteenth and nineteenth centuries to give the business community a forum in which common interests could be identified and strategies pursued. The two most significant for Scotland were those of Glasgow and Edinburgh.

16. On James I and his successors on the Scottish throne, see note 25 in this chapter.

17. See p. 295, note 6.

procedure it was further distinguished from the correspondent council in England by two remarkable peculiarities. <42>

1. The Scottish parliament was never divided, like that of England, into two houses. In the parliament of England, the knights of shires, and the burgesses, were, each of them, a numerous body, not easily accommodated in one apartment, and deriving suitable consideration and importance from that large proportion of the community which they represented. United, however, by their common character of representatives, they, instead of claiming distinct suffrages in the assembly, were led naturally to act in concert with each other; and, for the convenience of their joint deliberations, were collected in a separate place from the other members. But in the parliament of Scotland there were no knights of shires, and the few burgesses, the only other species of representatives, were too inconsiderable to claim such marks of distinction; and their pretension to sit and vote in a separate house would have been held ridiculous. Thrown into the common mass, they rather found it comfortable to escape observation, and to cover their insignificance; serving only, like the rubbish of a building, to fill a corner unoccupied with more solid materials. <43>

This union of all the different members of parliament in one house had a visible effect upon the government. Though that assembly consisted of three different estates, or orders, who had each a separate interest, yet, in their promiscuous deliberations, it was to be expected that the influence of the nobility would greatly predominate. The ecclesiastical and mercantile orders became unavoidably subordinate to that more powerful body; and their measures were deeply tainted with the prevailing leaven of aristocracy. The delegates of the boroughs were more especially affected by this mode of deliberation. It was in vain to expect that a set of tradesmen, but lately emerged from a servile condition, would lay aside their native habits, and speak or act with firmness and intrepidity. Voting under the immediate eye of the great barons, men whom they had been accustomed to treat with respect and reverence, or whom they still wished to serve in the exercise of their professions, they were not likely to stand forward in maintaining their own opinions, or in pursuing any line of conduct that might expose them to the resentment or displeasure of those eminent personages. To <44> concur in silence with whatever should be proposed by their superiors, or to avoid those meetings which threatened a violent contest, was more agreeable to their circumstances, and to fall in with every prevailing party became naturally their temporizing system of policy. The introduction of those delegates into the legislature was therefore an event of little importance, and, for a long time, unproductive of any interference upon the part of the *commons,* either for exalting the prerogative, or establishing the rights of the people.

2. Another peculiarity in the procedure of the Scottish parliament consisted in the appointment of a committee, under the name of the *Lords of the Articles,* for the purpose of preparing and digesting the bills to be laid before that assembly. This institution appears to have arisen from the small number of members who sat in the national council, and their impatience under the delays of business, the consequence of their inexperience, which made it commonly difficult to procure a decently full meeting during the time requisite for the regular discussion of public affairs. To relieve themselves from a tedious and disagreeable at-<45>tendance, they devolved upon a few of their members the burden of putting the business into such a form, that nothing more than the mere assent or dissent of the meeting should be requisite; and that thus, in a day or two at the most, its deliberations might be completely ended.[18]

This practice, which can be traced no higher than to the reign of David the Second,[*] and which did not acquire a regular establishment for some time after,[†] was indirectly favourable to the prerogative; and therefore was, no doubt, secretly promoted by the sovereign, though the lords of the articles appear to have been originally nominated by parliament itself,[‡] the nomination was likely, in most cases, to fall upon those members, who, by their experience in such matters, and by residing about court, were the best qualified for executing the business. Such persons, however, were the usual ministers of the crown, and most commonly devoted to its interest; so that, by their means, the king was <46> frequently enabled to keep out of view all those topics of discussion which he wished to avoid, and to seize a convenient opportunity for introducing those measures which he was eager to carry. It appears, indeed, that the lords of the articles had not an absolute negative upon the deliberations of parliament, but that the members of that assembly

* See Annals of Scotland by Sir David Dalrymple. [[David II reigned 1329–71.]]

† See Wight's Inquiry into the Rise of Parliament.

‡ Wight's Inquiry. Ibid.

18. First recorded in the fifteenth century, this was a committee of elected members to draft legislation. Articles were legislative proposals which had to pass through this committee.

were at liberty, of their own proper motion, to suggest whatever subjects they might think proper. But such a mode of proceeding was a deviation from the usual course of business, uniformly discouraged and reprobated by the king and his ministers, and was not likely to be often proposed, or insisted on, by a set of rude barons, more distinguished for valour in the field, than for address and penetration in the senate.

Notwithstanding this expedient, however, which bestowed upon the sovereign such a manifest advantage in managing the deliberations of parliament, the super-eminent power of the nobility is every where discernable in the proceedings of that assembly, and in all the departments of government.

It was the practice in England, as I had for-<47>merly occasion to observe, that an act of parliament should proceed upon a petition from the two houses to the sovereign, requesting that some grievance might be redressed, or some branch of the public administration altered. This humble and respectful mode of proceeding never had place in Scotland, where we see the national council holding a very different language. They assume a dictatorial tone; avow the enactment of laws by their own authority; and even frequently ordain, without ceremony, that the king shall carry their measures into execution.

Thus, in a statute made in the reign of James the First, it is said, "the parliament has determined and ordained, that our lord the king shall *gar* (cause to) mend his money, and *gar* strike it in like weight and fineness to the money of England."*

In another statute, the *parliament ordains,* that the king shall command the judges to distribute justice impartially between the poor and the rich, and that he shall rigorously punish those who do otherwise.† <48>

In the reign of James the Second,[19] *the three estates order,* that courts shall be held at certain seasons throughout the kingdom; and that the *king himself* shall be in each town when the court is held, or near it, where his council thinks fit.—The *three estates have* also *concluded,* that the king shall ride through the realm when information is received that rebellion, slaughter, or

* Parl. 1. ch. 25. *Black Acts.*

† Ibid. ch. 49.

19. See note 25 in this chapter.

other atrocious crimes, have been committed, and shall cause immediate cognizance thereof to be taken.[*]

In the reign of James the Third,[20] the *lords,* understanding that there has been great *sloth* in the execution of the laws relative to bringing in and keeping the bullion, so as to occasion great scarcity thereof, they require, that the king shall put the statutes on that subject *sharply* in execution, and shall appoint true and able *searchers* for the time to come.[†]

The style of the legislature was gradually softened and varied in later times; but the custom of passing statutes in the name of the three estates of parliament is continued occa-<49>sionally through the reigns of James the Third, of James the Fourth, and of James the Fifth.[‡]

The course of parliamentary business in England, by which every bill passed through both houses in the form of a petition to the sovereign, produced, of necessity, a negative in the crown; for a petition would have no force unless when granted by the person to whom it was addressed. But in Scotland, where statutes were enacted by the general authority of parliament, there was no foundation for this controuling power of the monarch. As parliament in that country was not divided into two houses, the king does not appear to have constituted a separate branch of the legislature. He seems to have been originally regarded as the president of that assembly, and his voice to have been included in its general determinations. In the early history of the Scottish parliament, we meet with no traces of the interposition of the royal negative upon bills; the style and tenure of those transactions is, at the same time, utterly repugnant to any such idea; and there occur <50> instances of statutes which are known to have been enacted in direct opposition to the will of the crown. The religious reformation which took place in the reign of Mary,[21] derived its authority from an act of the legislature, to which the assent of the queen, or of her husband, the king of France, was never obtained, but which does not appear, either at that time or afterwards, to have been considered, on that account, as defective.[§]

* Ja. II. ch. 5. and ch. 6. *Black Acts.*

† Ja. III. ch. 80.

‡ See instances of this, Ja. III. ch. 130. ch. 131. ch. 132. Ja. IV. ch. 37. ch. 82. Ja. V. ch. 4. ch. 102.

§ See the political publications about the time of the Union.

20. See note 25 in this chapter.

21. See ibid.

The Scottish house of parliament had thus the uncontrouled power of legislation. It exercised also the exclusive privilege of imposing taxes, together with that of directing their application to the particular purpose, and of superintending the expenditure of the money. It was accustomed to determine peace and war; to regulate the forces; to appoint governors of the fortresses in the kingdom; and to make provisions for arming the people, and for training them up to the use of arms.* <51>

In most of the European governments the national council was held regularly at particu-<52>lar seasons. It came afterwards to meet more frequently, according to the increase of its business; and the power of calling, or of dismissing their occasional meetings, which were at length substituted altogether in place of the former, was generally assumed by the king. In England this power was uniformly exercised by the crown; and the legislature interfered no farther in that matter than by ordaining that the king should

* See particularly a discourse on the Union of Scotland and England, published 1702; also an historical account of the ancient rights of the parliament of Scotland, published 1703.

In the parliament held 1481, during the reign of Ja. III. the three estates, considering the design of the *ricfar,* (robber) Edward, to invade Scotland, *of their own free will,* grant and promise to remain in defence of the king's person and realm, according to the practice of their ancestors. And they appoint a certain number of armed men to be employed at their expence, as a garrison in the town of Berwick, and as guards in different parts of the borders. It is also ordained in the same act, that an ambassador shall be sent to solicit aid from the king of France. Ja. III. ch. 100. *Black Acts.*

In the statutes of William, the people are required, according to their wealth, to provide themselves with arms of a certain description, and to appear with these at the stated times of rendezvous. See Stat. Will. regis. c. 23. *Black Acts.*

That parliament took upon itself the care of causing the people to be provided with arms, and to be instructed in the use of them, appears from a multiplicity of statutes. See Statutes, Ja. I. ch. 20. ch. 48. ch. 67. Ja. II. ch. 71. Ja. III. ch. 106. Ja. IV. ch. 53. Ja. V. ch. 61. *Black Acts.*

By act of parliament, in the reign of James the Fourth, orders are given for renewing the alliance of Scotland with France, with Spain, and with Denmark; and for sending, on that account, an embassy to Denmark. See Ja. IV. ch. 22. ch 23. *Black Acts.*

Even the naval force of Scotland, however inconsiderable, seems to have fallen under the immediate regulation of parliament. See act Ja. I. ch. 140. *Black Acts.*

By an act in the reign of James IV. the parliament appoints a governor to the castle of Edinburgh, and orders the castle of Dunbar to be demolished. By another act, in the reign of James VI. the order for the demolition of the castle of Dunbar is repeated, with an additional injunction for demolishing the castle of Inch-kieth, ch. 25. *Black Acts.*

By an act, James VI. parl. 9. ch. 8. money is assigned for keeping the castles of Edinburgh, Dumbarton, Stirling, and Blackness, not to be applied to any other purposes.

call meetings of parliament once a year, or oftener if the business of the nation should require it. But in Scotland this branch of the prerogative seems to have been treated with little ceremony; and we find the parliament, by its own authority, putting an end to its meetings, and appoint-<53>ing others to be held at particular times and places, either for the determination of particular points, or for the discussion of its ordinary business.*

Even the domestic arrangements of the royal family were not, in Scotland, exempted from the interference of parliament; and the marriages of the sovereign were dictated by such political considerations as had occurred to that assembly. How far it is the duty of a prince to sacrifice his own inclination, in a matter of this kind, to artificial reasons of state, and to convert the most important and agreeable bond of private society into a prostituted and disgusting connection; and how far the alliances derived from such political <54> considerations are likely to be of much national benefit, and worthy the attention of a spirited people, it may, perhaps, be difficult to determine. By the old feudal system, the vassals were obliged to marry with consent of their liege lord; but that the sovereign should be forced in this point to comply with the will of the nobles, the superior to take a wife by the direction of his vassals, may be thought an unusual strain of aristocracy. We find that in England, Queen Elizabeth treated such interpositions of parliament with disdain, and considered them as manifest encroachments upon the prerogative. It must at the same time be acknowledged, that the fetters thus imposed on the sovereign, were probably more vexatious, in those times of simplicity, than they would be in ages of luxury and dissipation, when, from different modes of living, the felicity of persons in high rank is less governed by those principles which affect the condition of their inferiors.

The authority assumed by the Scottish parliament, with relation to the distribution of justice, which was no less extensive than in the other branches

* Thus by act James I. ch. 125, the parliament which met April 1429, is, *by its own consent,* adjourned to the Martinmas following. A similar adjournment ch. 145.

By act James II. ch. 22, it is ordered that a parliament shall, at a certain day, be held at Perth, for the discussion of business particularly specified.

By act James II. ch. 38, passed in August 1442, a parliament is appointed to be held at Edinburgh in the March following.

See other acts to the same purpose—James II. ch. 42. ch. 52. James III. ch. 61. ch. 75. *Black Acts.*

of administration, will fall <55> more properly to be considered, in taking a connected view of the judicial establishments of Scotland.

The particulars above-mentioned, concerning the aristocratic nature of the government in Scotland, are proved by the most authentic evidence, that of the statutes, collected from the records, and published by authority. It is remarkable, however, that a great part of the statutes referred to, are to be found in the first edition only of that collection, published in the reign of Queen Mary, and, from its being printed in the Saxon character, known by the name of the *Black Acts.*[22] In the reign of James the Sixth, when the prerogative had been greatly extended, a design was formed of concealing, as far as possible, the ancient state of the government; for which purpose an attempt was made to suppress this edition: and another was published, in which those acts which appeared to demonstrate the high powers of parliament were carefully omitted. This mutilated collection is copied in the last edition of the statutes published in the reign of Charles the Second, which is now commonly used. The copies <56> of the Black Acts which remain at present are not numerous, and the peculiar knowledge to be derived from that ancient compilation is, in some degree, limited to those who are conversant in the legal antiquities of Scotland. The glaring imposition upon the public, thus attempted by the authority and direction of the crown, affords a noted example of the unprincipled measures of that reign, and conveys a strong presumption, that the old constitution of Scotland was diametrically opposite to the political views entertained by the sovereign, and to that system of regal power which he was labouring to realize.

Through the whole history of the period now under consideration, we discover numberless events which mark the rivalship between the king and the nobility, as well as the exorbitant power in the hands of the latter. In that famous manifesto drawn up by parliament in 1320, and addressed to the pope,[23] they plainly intimate, that by their authority Robert Bruce had been advanced to the throne; and they expressly declare, that if ever he should

22. The name given to an edition, printed in black letter, of Acts of the Scottish Parliament for the period 1535–94.

23. The Declaration of Arbroath, a response to Pope John XXII's threat of excommunication and supposedly written on 6 April 1320 by the Scottish nobility but in reality expertly drafted by a cleric on their behalf. It was intended to justify Scotland's struggle for independence.

abandon their cause, and be-<57>tray their privileges, they would expel him as an enemy, and choose another king to rule and protect them.

When the same Robert Bruce had, by his persevering valour and prudence, delivered the country from subjection to the English monarch, and by a train of brilliant exploits, attained universal admiration and popularity, he ventured in parliament, a little inconsiderately, to question some of the nobility, by what title they held their estates? The tendency of this question was immediately perceived; and the memorable answer given unanimously by the barons is known to all the readers of Scottish history. They drew their swords: "By these," said they, "we have acquired our possessions, and with these we will maintain them."

A late elegant writer,[24] who, in his history of Scotland, unites to the facts collected by former historians such philosophical views and discussions as the diffusion of knowledge in the present age was able to supply, has observed, that the disorders which prevailed in the country, and the disasters which befel so many of its monarchs, from the reign of <58> James the First, to that of James the Fifth, proceeded, in great measure, from the eagerness of those princes to undermine and destroy the exorbitant power of the ancient aristocracy.

James the First,[25] a prince of great abilities, and of elegant accomplish-

24. William Robertson (1721–93): Scottish clergyman and historian, leader of the Moderate faction in the Church of Scotland. His reputation as a historian rests on the *History of Scotland* (1759), the *History of the Reign of Charles V* (1769), and his unfinished *History of America* (1777). Millar is here referring to a leading theme in book 1 of the *History of Scotland.*

25. Millar's narrative in this section refers to the following events. In 1424, James I (r. 1406–37) returned to Scotland after eighteen years of captivity in England and attempted to reform the Scottish parliament along English lines. In 1437 an aristocratic conspiracy resulted in his murder at Perth. James II (r. 1437–60) killed the leader of the rebellious Douglas family (the eighth earl of Douglas) in 1452, but died himself during the siege of Roxburgh in 1460. James III (r. 1460–88) was betrayed by his own nobility, whose discontent focused on the low-born favorites and courtiers with whom he consorted, many of whom were hanged at Lauder Bridge. He was killed at Sauchieburn near Bannockburn, where his forces were defeated by an opposition led by his son and heir, James, duke of Rothesay, who ascended as James IV (r. 1488–1513). Anglo-Scottish relations deteriorated in 1511, and James IV renewed the "auld alliance" with the French, who were at war with England. James and a good deal of the Scottish nobility were killed fighting the English at Flodden (Northumberland) in 1513. The English tried to woo James V (r. 1513–42) away from French and Catholic influence, but the Scottish clergy prevented this. By 1542 Scotland was again at war with England, and James fell into a state of

ments, was led, not only to aim at the introduction of the superior good order and policy which he had observed in England, but also to promote a similar aggrandizement of the crown. For this purpose he endeavoured gradually to weaken the nobility, by seizing the estates of particular barons upon pretence of defects in their titles, and by procuring the condemnation and forfeiture of others, upon a prosecution for crimes. His measures, however, at length produced a general combination against him, and gave rise to an insurrection, in which he was cruelly murdered.

His son, James the Second, prosecuted the same plan of humbling the nobles, but with a brutal impetuosity and fierceness, and with a perfidy which paid no regard to the most sacred engagements. His behaviour soon excited a formidable rebellion; from which he <59> found means to extricate himself by the treachery of some of the rebels, and by the irresolution and weakness of their leader. He had proceeded, for some time, in improving the advantages arising from the discomfiture of his enemies, when a sudden death, by a splinter from the bursting of a cannon, put a stop to his career, and delivered the nobles from so formidable an adversary.

He was succeeded by James the Third, a prince totally destitute of the capacity and vigour requisite for the government of a rude and turbulent people; but who paid some attention to the fine arts, and to frivolous exhibitions of mechanical dexterity. He endeavoured to mortify and depress the nobles by neglect, by excluding them from his councils, and by depriving them of the offices and privileges with which they had formerly been invested; while he suffered himself to be governed by persons of mean birth, and passed his whole time in the company of those favourites, whose petty talents and accomplishments afforded him amusement. The indignation of the nobility was inflamed by finding the favour and confidence of the so-<60>vereign, to which they aspired, and which they considered as their due, bestowed upon such unworthy and contemptible objects. Taking advantage, therefore, of an invasion from England, which required that they should

depression until his death late in the year. Mary, Queen of Scots (1542–87), spent her minority rule in France 1542–61. After the death of her husband, François II (king of France 1559–60), she returned to Scotland in 1561. But in 1559–60, during the regency of her mother, Marie de Guise, the Calvinist reformation under the ideological leadership of John Knox (ca. 1514–72) and his followers succeeded in overthrowing the Catholic establishment in Scotland. This was confirmed by the "Reformation Parliament" of 1560.

assemble their vassals, they formed a conspiracy to rid themselves of these despicable rivals, broke into the king's apartment, seized his principal minions, and, without any form of law, hanged them over a bridge near the town of Lauder. The infatuated monarch was not rendered wiser by this humiliating check. Persevering in the same system of favoritism, he afterwards established a body guard, and debarred the nobility from all access to his person. This at length produced a rebellion, in which he was slain at the battle of Bannockburn, and which by its fortunate issue, augmented, for a time, the power of the aristocracy.* <61>

The character of James the Fourth was very different from that of his father; and he experienced a very different fortune. Full of the ideas of chivalry, his great object was military glory; and, instead of entertaining a jealousy of his nobles, he regarded their fidelity and attachment as indispensably necessary for promoting his own greatness, and admited them to that degree of intimacy which the spirit of the feudal system introduced between a military leader and his vassals. Their gratitude and affection corresponded to his open and generous dispositions; and their utmost exertions and services were at his devotion. It is observed, however, in the history of this reign, that they suffered more from attachment to the king, than they had ever suffered, on former occasions, from the jealousy and ma-<62>chinations of the crown. In the fatal field of Flowden, the Scottish nobility, unwilling to desert or to survive their beloved sovereign, received a blow which greatly impaired their strength, and from which, for a long time, they did not perfectly recover.

Of the three estates in parliament, the great superiority of the nobles created in the two others a disposition, so far as they acted from political considerations, to form a league in their own defence, and even to unite their influence with that of the crown. The boroughs were too insignificant to render their aid of much consequence; but the clergy were possessed of great

* Concerning this prince, there is mentioned an occurrence, which may appear too ludicrous for the gravity of history, and which is too inconsistent with royal dignity to be recorded by later historians. It is said that James, having torn to pieces a charter of the Earl of Morton, on account of the privileges which it contained, the nobility insisted that he should make satisfaction for the outrage, and obliged his majesty, while sitting on the throne, with a needle and thread, to sew together, carefully, the several fragments of the manuscript. There may be some ground to question the authenticity of this anecdote; but it must be evident, that the authority of the monarch could not be very exalted in a country where such a report was believed or circulated. (See a Discourse of the Union, published 1702.)

wealth, and many individuals among them, from their education and professional habits, were distinguished by learning, abilities, and political talents. The higher benefices, at the same time, both of the secular and regular clergy, were in the gift of the crown, a circumstance which could hardly fail to conciliate the favour of the church, and to warm and enliven her zeal in supporting the prerogative. James the Fifth, who is represented as a prince of some abilities, but of a gloomy and sullen temper, appears to have <63> been fully sensible of this natural connection, and aware of the advantages to be derived from it. He bestowed his confidence almost exclusively upon ecclesiastics, appointed them to fill the most lucrative offices in the state, and employed them in the chief branches of administration. By their dexterity, prudence, and vigour, the public tranquillity was maintained, and the business of the nation, for some time, prosperously conducted; while the nobles were kept at a distance, and carefully excluded from every situation either of power or emolument. The whole order of the nobility was thus depressed and weakened; at the same time that no opportunity was neglected, by accusations and punishments, to accomplish the ruin of individuals.

These plans of the monarch had for some time been prosecuted with success, when, from the very system of policy to which he had resorted, he was involved in difficulties which could not easily be surmounted. Henry the Eighth, in his attempts to deliver his dominions from the authority of the Roman pontiff, was naturally desirous of procuring the co-operation and countenance of neighbouring states; <64> and, in particular, had proposed a treaty of alliance with his nephew, the king of Scotland. By this proposal, the bigoted ministers of James, foreseeing that, from an intimate correspondence between the two countries, the spirit of religious innovation was likely to be propagated from the one to the other, were thrown into the utmost consternation. They exerted all their influence to defeat the projected alliance; employed every artifice to prevent a communication with the heretics of England; and were even so far successful as to persuade their master to reject a conference with Henry, to which he had been invited. The consequence of this measure, so contrary to the interest of James and of the nation, but so conformable to the views of the churchmen, whose advice he implicitly followed, was an immediate war with England, which made it necessary to convene the nobles for the purpose of procuring a military force.

James had now the mortification to discover that his prospects were totally blasted, and to find himself without hopes of relief, under the power of those haughty barons, whose jealousy he had excited, and whose indigna-<65>tion and resentment he had incurred. Unable to bear the disappointment, he died of a sort of pet, into which he was thrown by the repeated disobedience of his orders, the contempt shown to his authority, and the insults that were offered to his dignity.

The most important event in the reign of the unfortunate Mary, an event which affected the whole train of her public and private transactions, was the religious reformation. The new system which then took place in Scotland was more democratical than, from the state and circumstances of the country, could, perhaps, be expected. It arose, no doubt, from a variety of causes, among which the great power and influence of the nobles was probably not the least remarkable.

1. The diffusion of knowledge over the countries of modern Europe, and the consequent disposition which appeared in many of them to deliver themselves from the tyranny of the church of Rome, were gradual and progressive. To pass over those theological opinions, which, from their absurdity and pernicious tendency, had given scandal to Christians, and to consider the reformation merely <66> in a political view, it is to be remarked, that the first reformers were content with a total emancipation from the papal power, and with an entire abolition of those monastic orders, the great nurseries of superstition, by which that papal power had been chiefly supported. But, in the course of inquiries, and in the heat of controversy upon that subject, the number and variety of abuses in the old church became gradually more apparent, and the breach between the disputants was widened. The rottenness of the ancient fabrick being more and more laid open, alterations of greater extent and importance were thought necessary for the security of the new edifice. To strike at the root of superstition, and to prevent mankind from being enslaved by their spiritual guides, it appeared proper to many, that the number even of the secular clergy should be reduced; that their opulence ought to be diminished; and that their subordination in rank and authority, by which they were closely combined, and brought under the direction of one, or a few, leaders, should be abolished.

In most of those countries, therefore, in <67> which the people began to think of renouncing the errors of the church of Rome, after they had long been the subject of examination and censure, the ancient hierarchy came to be entirely destroyed, a perfect purity among the clergy introduced, and provision made by the moderation of the livings bestowed upon them, for preventing their future power and grandeur. As the reformation made its way, at a later period, into Scotland than into most other parts of Europe, it was likely to be adopted by the Scottish nation in that higher state, which a long continued ferment in the minds of men had produced, and which coincided with the ardent and exalted spirit of the times. The doctrines and the model of church-government which had been established at Geneva by Calvin,[26] the latest apostle of the reformers, were thus imported into Scotland by John Knox and his followers; and being received by the people with a warmth of approbation suitable to the enthusiastic ardour with which they were inculcated, produced an abhorrence of the hierarchy, and of the pompous worship retained in England, scarcely inferior to that which was ex-<68>cited by the gross errors and abuses exhibited by the church of Rome.

2. The manner in which the reformation was effected in Scotland, contributed also to the peculiar modification which it received in that country. As in England, the king was the leading reformer; he, of course, modelled the new system in conformity to the interest of the crown, and carefully preserved that ancient hierarchy which was calculated for supporting the power of the monarch. But in Scotland, the mother of Mary, and her uncles, of the powerful house of Guise,[27] were bigoted Roman Catholicks; and, by their authority in the administration, together with their influence over the young queen, gave such a direction and bias to the course of public affairs as produced an uniform and vigorous opposition to every step of the reformation. As the people, therefore, became the reformers, in open defiance of those who conducted the machine of government, they were led to establish a popular system; and, as they had many and great obstacles to surmount before they could accomplish their ultimate object, their enthusiastic notions of religious purity swelled in <69> proportion, and prompted them,

26. Jean Calvin (1509–64): French theologian and Protestant reformer. After fleeing to Switzerland, he wrote his *Christianae Religionis Institutio* in 1536. Calvinism exerted a profound influence throughout western Europe from the 1550s. On Knox, see note 25.

27. A ducal family of Lorraine, and the head of the Catholic party in France that sternly repressed Calvinism. Marie de Guise (1515–60) married James V and was the mother of Mary, Queen of Scots. Marie de Guise's brothers were François, duc de Guise (1519–63), and Charles de Guise (1525–74), who became a cardinal in 1547. The power of the Guise family reached its height during the brief reign of Mary's husband, François II, as King of France 1559–60. See p. 407, note 1.

by the common animosity which attends every violent contest, to recede so much the farther from the ancient establishment.

3. But the prevalence of aristocracy in Scotland contributed, perhaps, more than any other circumstance, to the destruction of the hierarchy, and to the very limited provision that was made for the ministers of the protestant church.[28] As the ignorance and superstition of the Scottish nation was probably not inferior to that of most other European countries, it appears that the property accumulated in the hands of the church, considering the general state of wealth in the country, was not less extensive. It is computed that, immediately before the reformation, the collective body of the secular and regular clergy possessed, in tythes and landed estates, a yearly revenue amounting to a full half of the landed rent in the kingdom.* This opulence presented a rich field of plunder to the nobles, who, at the same time that their political resentment was excited against an order of men which had of late been the great pillar of the crown, had the <70> prospect of stripping the church of her large benefices; and, by their great influence and authority, converting to their own use the greater part of that immense revenue. They united, therefore, most cordially with the populace in promoting the presbyterian system of church government;[29] and, from strong motives of interest, adopted the same line of conduct which the latter eagerly pursued from principle.

Thus we find that the nobility took a very active share in the reformation; and having obtained from the crown a great proportion of what was called the *spirituality,* as well as the *temporality,* of ecclesiastical benefices, continued afterwards to interest themselves in the new establishment, and particularly to guard against the future designs of the crown for increasing the power and revenue of the church. For this purpose they became members of the *general assembly,*[30] or chief ecclesiastical council; and continued to sit in it for near thirty years after its first institution. When James the Sixth afterwards introduced a sort of episcopal government, they took care to prevent

* See Forbes on Tythes.

28. As a "son of the manse," Millar understood the relatively poor material conditions of the Scottish clergy, which he attributes here to the power of the aristocracy.

29. A system of church governance based on the presbytery rather than the authority of a bishop (i.e., episcopacy). The model was Calvin's Geneva.

30. The governing body of the Scottish Church; since 1560 it has convened annually in Edinburgh.

the restitution of any part of those church-revenues <71> which they had appropriated; and when, at a subsequent period, the measures of Charles the First threatened the more complete establishment of the hierarchy in Scotland, they became active in forming with the people that *solemn league and covenant,*[31] by which the whole power of the nation was exerted with the most decisive effect in defeating the measures of that ill-advised and infatuated monarch.

It may here be remarked, that, from a difference of circumstances, the presbyterian religion came to be more deeply rooted, and sprung up with more vigour in some parts of Scotland than in others. In the north, the slower advancement of knowledge and the arts disposed the inhabitants to retain the old superstition, and produced a reluctance to those innovations which were so generally adopted in the other parts of the kingdom. In the neighbourhood of the capital, the influence of the crown was more immediately felt, and counteracted, in some measure, the natural bent of the people, not only towards the reformation in general, but also towards the destruction of the hierarchy in particular. It was in the western coun-<72>ties, at some distance from the seat of government, though not so remote as to preclude a strong tendency to improvement, that the presbyterian religion was embraced with a degree of ardour and enthusiasm which nothing could withstand, and which the most violent persecution, in the reign of Charles the Second, served only to augment. The puritanical principles, and the fanaticism of those counties, became a source of distinction; and the peculiarity of aspect and manners observable in the zealots from this quarter, is said to have procured from the courtly inhabitants of the east the nick-name of *whigs,*[32] a religious appellation, which being afterwards applied to the political opponents of the crown, has had the fortune to spread over the whole island, but which in its original acceptation is still sometimes used in the western parts of Scotland. <73>

31. After Charles I attempted to impose the 1637 Prayer Book, most Scottish nobles signed a national covenant to defend the Scottish Church against episcopacy (1638). Its objectives were incorporated in the English Parliament's alliance with the Scots, the Solemn League and Covenant, in 1643.

32. See p. 440, note 7.

SECTION III

Of the Government of Scotland, from the Union of the Scottish and English Crowns, to that of the two kingdoms.

From the beginning of this third period,[33] the political history of Scotland is so interwoven with that of England, that it would be inconvenient to enter into a full examination of the former, before we have also an opportunity of considering the latter. At present, therefore, a few preliminary observations concerning what was peculiar in the state of Scotland, will be sufficient.

The government of Scotland, by the accession of her sovereign to the English throne, experienced a very sudden and important revolution. The monarch, from the sovereignty of a petty state, was at once exalted to the head of an opulent and powerful monarchy, in which the greater part of the feudal institutions had fallen into disuse; and in which, upon the ruins of the aristocracy, the prerogative of the crown, on the one hand, had <74> risen to a considerable height; while, on the other, the people were beginning to lay the foundation of their privileges. In these circumstances, the king of England found little difficulty in extending to the northern part of the island that authority which he possessed in the southern part.

But while the nobles in Scotland were thus easily reduced under subjection to the crown, the people at large were not raised to suitable independence. In England, as well as in many other European governments, where the prerogative advanced gradually and slowly, in consequence of the gradual advancement of society, the king was under the necessity of courting the lower orders of the community, and of promoting their freedom, from the view of undermining the power of the nobility, his immediate rivals. But in Scotland, after James the Sixth had mounted the English throne, neither he, nor his immediate successors, had any occasion to employ so disagreeable an expedient. They were above the level of rivalship or opposition from the Scottish vassals of the crown; and had therefore no temptation to free the vassals of the nobility <75> from their ancient bondage. A great part of the old feudal institutions, in that country, were accordingly permitted to remain, without undergoing any considerable alteration; and the troublesome

33. In Millar's three-part division of Scottish history, the third period is the interval from the union of the crowns to the Act of Union: that is, 1603–1707.

forms and ceremonies, formerly used in the transmission or conveyance of landed property, continue, even at this day, to load and disfigure the system of Scottish jurisprudence.

The political changes, introduced by James the Sixth, were such as contributed to depress the aristocracy, without exalting the lower classes of the people.

1. This prince enforced the regulation of his predecessor, James the First, by requiring that the representatives of counties should give a regular attendance in parliament. In Scotland, however, this measure, though professedly in imitation of the practice in England, was adopted with peculiar modifications agreeable to the views of the monarch. By the practice in England, all who held lands of a certain value, whether as vassals of the crown or of a subject, and all who enjoyed leases for life of lands to the same amount, were entitled to vote for the knights of shires; <76> whereas in Scotland, none but the immediate vassals of the crown, how extensive soever their landed property might be, obtained a right of suffrage. In England their elective franchise had been brought so low as a yearly rent of forty shillings; and the same rule appears by the regulation of James the First, to have been introduced into Scotland. By the debasement, however, of the money in Scotland, the qualification for voting, according to this nominal rent, would have fallen a great deal lower; but it suited the purposes of James the Sixth to explain this regulation, as if it had required the voters to possess, not merely a real rent of forty shillings, but a rent amounting to that sum, according to an old valuation of all the lands in Scotland, which had long been the rule to the vassals of the crown for the payment of their taxes. This valuation, from the low state of agriculture when it was made, bearing no proportion to the real value of estates, the right of electing the representatives of counties, instead of being communicated, as in England, to people of small property, was confined to a few <77> of the gentry, who might easily be secured in the interest of the crown.

2. The number of burgesses who sat in the Scottish parliament had, from the time of their first introduction, been gradually increasing by the incorporation of additional boroughs. The nobility, at the same time, living in the neighbourhood of particular towns, had often found means to gain an influence over the inhabitants, and to obtain the direction of such incorporated bodies. In all the royal boroughs of Scotland, the distribution of justice, and the management of their public affairs, were committed to a set of magistrates, and a town council, who, according to the primitive regu-

lations, appear to have been annually chosen, in each borough, by the collective body of the burgesses.*

By degrees, however, such individuals as had obtained the patronage of particular bo<78>roughs, whether the king or any of the great barons, endeavoured to establish a permanent influence, by substituting other modes of election more favourable to their interest. Thus, by a statute in the reign of James the Third, it is provided, "that the old council shall annually elect the new; and that the old and new council jointly shall elect the officers of the boroughs."†

It is probable that this regulation was dictated by the nobility, who had procured an entire ascendant in many of the boroughs, and frequently held the principal offices in those communities. It is, accordingly, further provided in the same statute, "that no captain, nor constable of the king's castles, shall bear any office in the town where he resides."‡

For securing still more effectually the interest which had been already established in a borough, it was afterwards enacted by the legislature, "that *four persons only* of the old council should be changed each year"; a regulation plainly intended to relieve the patron from the embarrassment he might be under, in <79> substituting, all at once, an entire new set of adherents to those who had been displaced.

We meet also with other statutes, apparently calculated to limit the effects of the former, and probably suggested by the crown, ordaining that the officers of boroughs should be *real inhabitants,* and *traders of the community;* but the frequent repetition of these acts affords undoubted evidence that little regard had been paid to them.

After James the Sixth was invested with the authority of king of England, he found that many of the regulations, introduced by the nobility for the management of the boroughs, were become highly subservient to the maintenance of that influence over them which had then been transferred to the crown; and therefore, instead of abolishing that system of policy, he was

* See Leges Burgorum, c. 77. Statuta Gildae, c. 33. c. 34.

This mode of electing the magistrates and town-council was probably continued for a long time in all the boroughs, as may be concluded from a great number of their charters. See state of the evidence contained in the returns to the house of commons 1791.

† 1469. c. 30.

‡ Ibid.

disposed to encourage and make improvements upon it. From this time forward, the members of those communities were, by various alterations, more and more stript of the administration and government of their own affairs; while their nominal administrators and governors became, in reality, the agents and tools of the crown. This observation will ex-<80>plain a passage in the *claim of rights,* presented by the estates of Scotland soon after the revolution of 1688; in which it is said, "That the abdicated family had subverted the rights of the royal boroughs, by imposing upon them the *magistrates,* the *town-council,* and the *clerks and other officers,* contrary to their liberties, and their express charters."[34]

3. Notwithstanding the introduction of the presbyterian church-government into Scotland, the king contrived to continue an appearance of the ecclesiastical order in parliament. The prelates, whom James retained in that assembly, were a sort of bishops possessed of small revenue, destitute of all authority, and loaded with the contempt and censures of the church. But after he became king of England, he found means to increase their powers and emoluments, and to lay the foundation of that episcopal government which was completed by his son and his grandsons, but which was finally abolished at the revolution.* <81>

4. The parliament of Scotland was thus, after the union of the crowns, composed of the same orders with that of England; the nobility, the bishops, the knights of shires, and the burgesses. To these different members, however, were added the great officers of state, who sat in parliament, not as in England by representing particular counties or boroughs, but merely in consequence of holding their several offices. It is probable that their admission into that assembly had proceeded, not from any formal regulation, but from the ordinary course of business, which required that, as ministers of the crown, they should make frequent propositions to the legislature concerning those measures which called for its direction. In England, where an act of parliament was passed in the form of a petition to the crown, the king had no occasion to interfere in the business before it was presented to him for his consent. But in Scotland, where the three estates enacted laws by their

* Before the reformation, there were in Scotland two archbishoprics, 12 bishoprics, 27 abbacies, and 13 priories. Balfour's Pract. p. 34.

34. Millar's quotation is a paraphrase of the original text. See *The Declaration of the Estates of the Kingdom of Scotland* (Edinburgh, 1689), 4.

own authority, and where the crown had no negative, it was necessary that his majesty, if he was to give his opinion at all, should mix in the deliberations of parliament, and take some share in its debates. The <82> dignity of the crown, however, seemed to require that this communication with the national assembly should be made, not by the sovereign in person, but through those great officers to whom the ordinary administration of government was delegated. At what time these officers were first considered as invested with this privilege, is unknown; but in the reign of James the Sixth, if not at an earlier period, it appears to have been completely established.*

5. The appointment of the *lords of the articles*[35] underwent a number of successive alterations, all of them calculated to render it a more effectual engine of parliamentary management. When those commissioners were in the nomination of parliament, it became a natural practice that a certain number of them should be named by each particular estate as its own representatives. At the reformation the suspi-<83>cion entertained of the bishops seems to have introduced a regulation that the spiritual commissioners, though chosen from the dignified clergy, should be nominated, not by their own order, but by the nobles.†

James the Sixth obtained an act of the legislature, ordaining, that, before the meeting of parliament, four persons should be named out of each estate as a committee previously to consider and determine the business to be laid before the lords of the articles; and, as the king appears to have assumed the nomination of this committee, he was thus invested with a previous negative upon those commissioners themselves who prepared matters for the deliberation of parliament. Charles the First superseded this regulation by bringing the appointment of the lords of the articles directly under the guidance of the crown. He procured an act of parliament empowering the peers to choose eight bishops, the bishops eight peers; and those sixteen persons to elect <84> eight knights of shires and eight burgesses; to all of whom were

* By parl. 1617, the number of these officers who should, *ex officio* enjoy a seat in parliament, was limited to the eight following: 1. The high treasurer. 2. The deputy treasurer. 3. The secretary. 4. The privy seal. 5. The master of requests. 6. The clerk register. 7. The justice clerk. 8. The advocate.

† Some writers think that the same act which made this regulation, provided also that the commissioners of the peerage should be named by the bishops; but this appears doubtful. See Wight on the Scottish parliament.

35. See note 18 in this chapter.

added the eight great officers of state. It is observed by an acute author,* that as at this time the bishops, from the manner in which they were upheld in parliament, were uniformly in the interest of the crown, and as, from the ordinary state of the peerage, the bishops might easily find one or two commissioners of that class in the same interest, a majority of the sixteen, and consequently of the whole committee, would infallibly be the adherents of the prerogative. Upon this footing, unless during the usurpation of Cromwell, the lords of the articles continued until the revolution, when they were finally abolished.

By the union of the crowns of England and Scotland, the capital city of the former became the usual residence of the monarch; and the latter country was reduced into the situation of a distant province. The baneful effects of this change upon the administration of the government in Scotland will be the subject of a future examination. We may at present take notice of its immediate consequences <85> with respect to the character and manners of the inhabitants, and with respect to their progressive improvements in arts and literature.

The removal of the king and of the court to the southern part of the island, was followed by a correspondent migration of the Scottish nobility and gentry, who naturally resorted to the new seat of government in quest of amusement, or in hopes of sharing the favour of the prince. Deserted by these men of rank and fortune, Scotland lost unavoidably that market which formerly arose from supplying them with the necessaries and conveniencies of life, and consequently that industry which it had put in motion. She lost, in like manner, some of the principal sources of emulation and of exertion in the liberal arts; while the standard of taste and fashion being transferred to a foreign kingdom, her candidates for fame were consequently withdrawn from the day-light of honour and distinction. Her language, I mean that used in the lower parts of the country, originally a branch of the Anglo-Saxon, ceased to be considered as an independent dialect, and was regarded merely as a corruption of English. Her writers, of course, labouring <86> to express themselves in a tongue no longer native to them, and struggling

* See Essays on British Antiquities by Lord Kames. [[Henry Home, Lord Kames, *Essays upon Several Subjects Concerning British Antiquities,* 2nd ed. (London, 1749), 52–53.]]

to become acquainted with its idioms, were no more the competitors, but reduced to be the humble imitators of their southern neighbours.

From this change of circumstances, the inhabitants of Scotland were greatly discouraged and retarded in the improvement of manufactures; and remained for a long time in that simple state of society which precedes the minute division of labour among the different kinds of artificers. They were also prevented from cultivating those elegant arts which are the natural offspring of luxury and refinement, more especially those branches of literary composition whose object is merely entertainment.

But though the Scots were left far behind their neighbours of England, in the accumulation of wealth, in the habits of industry, and in those inventions which contribute to shorten and facilitate labour, they had already made some advances in knowledge, and they were surrounded by other civilized nations, from whom they could hardly fail to catch a degree of science and literature. The revival of letters in modern Europe, was attended by <87> a spirit of activity and exertion, which diffused itself, more or less, over the whole; and by imitation or emulation, by a correspondence among persons of genius and enterprize, by the patronage of princes and men of wealth, pushed on the people of every country to a variety of useful and liberal pursuits. The inhabitants of Scotland were affected by the same general causes of improvement which operated upon the surrounding nations; though, in comparison with the English, they lay under disadvantages; but as their objects were varied, so their path was a good deal different. The people of Scotland, so far as they cultivated letters, were directed into the road of general science. Despairing of reputation, either as poets, or fine writers, they advanced by degrees in those branches of learning and philosophy, which had diffused themselves over the rest of Europe.

The peculiar spirit with which the Scots had overturned the Roman Catholic superstition, gave a particular modification to their intellectual pursuits.[36] The great ferment excited over the whole nation, the rooted anti-<88>pathy to the former ecclesiastical doctrines, produced a disposition to inquire, and to embrace no tenets without examination. The energy requisite for the accomplishment of the reformation, and the impulse which that event gave to the minds of men, continued after the new system was estab-

36. The edge of national pride in Millar's description of the Scottish intellect is reminiscent of Francis Jeffrey's description of Millar himself, as quoted in the introduction.

lished; and produced a boldness and activity, not only in examining religious opinions, which were of great extent, but in the general investigation of truth. Even the common mass of the people took an interest in the various points of theological controversy; became conversant in many abstract disquisitions connected with them; and were led to acquire a sort of literary curiosity.

The activity and vigour of mind which had thus been excited, produced a general attention to the propagation of knowledge, by a liberal education. In the reign of James the Sixth, public schools were established in every parish, to teach reading in the vulgar tongue, writing, and accounting; and in those places where it was found requisite, the Latin, or even the Greek language. This institution has been frequently regarded as the cause of the <89> diffusion of knowledge among the lower classes in Scotland; but it seems, in reality, to be the effect of a general demand for instruction, without which, any regulation of this nature would have soon fallen into disuse.

The same circumstances which tended in Scotland to multiply seminaries of education, contributed also to model those institutions according to utility and the conveniency of the inhabitants. While the principal schools and universities of England, from the remains of antient prejudice, confined their attention, in a great measure, to the teaching of what are called the learned languages, those of Scotland extended their views in proportion to the changes which took place in the state of society, and comprehended, more or less, in their plan of instruction, the principles of those different sciences which came to be of use in the world.

While the Scottish nation in general received an intellectual stimulus by the violent impulse given at the reformation, the lower and middling ranks of the people were peculiarly affected by the slow progress of manufactures. In England, a great proportion of <90> the inhabitants, engaging in active employments, and having their attention fixed upon minute objects, acquired, by their situation and habits, great professional skill and dexterity; but in every thing beyond their own trade or profession, remained proportionably destitute of experience and observation. In Scotland, on the contrary, the great body of the people were either idle, or slightly occupied by a coarse trade or manufacture, in which various branches of labour were united; so that the same persons, though less dexterous or skilful in any one department, were not prevented from attending successively to a variety of objects, from applying themselves to different pursuits, and consequently from attaining different kinds of information. From such a difference of circumstances, knowledge, as well as labour, came, in the one country, to be minutely divided; and, though a great quantity of this mental treasure was contained in the whole aggregate, yet from the manner of its distribution, a very small portion commonly fell to the lot of an individual: whereas in the other country, though the sum total of improvement was inconsiderable, yet that little <91> was not appropriated in such diminutive parcels, but remained, in some measure, as a common stock, which every member of the community might bring at pleasure to market.

In all parts of the world it is accordingly observable, that the great body of the people, while they remain in a state of rudeness and simplicity, are distinguished by their intelligence, acuteness, and sagacity; and that in proportion to their advancement in commerce and manufactures, they become ignorant, narrow-minded, and stupid. But in the period of the Scottish history now under consideration, the lower and middling classes of the people were placed in the former situation; at the same time that, from the causes already mentioned, the more enlightened part of the nation was not altogether destitute of literature and philosophy. While a great number of all ranks were neither immersed in business nor engrossed by the early pursuit of gain, they were at leisure to procure instruction, to go through a regular course of education at schools and universities, and to spread over the community a relish for such parts of learning as was then fashionable. A strong pre-<92>dilection for what are called the learned professions became thus very prevalent in Scotland; and men of an active disposition, little accustomed to an ordinary routine of employments, were easily induced to change their professional objects, or even to migrate into foreign countries for the purpose of advancing their fortune.*

The intelligence, sagacity, and disposition to learning, in the common people of Scotland, were inseparably connected with that modesty and re-

* Of all the common trades, in the hands of the vulgar, that of gardening approaches the nearest to a liberal profession. A gardener, by the cultivation of fruits and vegetables, acquires a considerable branch of the knowledge in the department of a farmer; by collecting a number of plants, by observing their analogies and differences, and by arranging and assorting them, he becomes a proficient in botany; by studying their medical virtues, and by taking advantage of the credulity of his neighbours, he is exalted into a species of physician.

These advantages produced a powerful attraction to this employment; the same bias remains even to the present times; and Scotland, it is well known, has the merit of furnishing a large proportion of the gardeners over Great Britain.

serve which makes a distinguishing feature in the manners of all rude and simple na-<93>tions. These qualities proceed from the necessitous condition of mankind antecedent to the improvements of society, when, from the difficulty of supplying their own wants, they have little opportunity or disposition for exercising a mutual sympathy or fellow-feeling with each other; and, consequently, are ashamed and unwilling to disclose the secret emotions and sentiments which they know will meet with little attention or regard. That style of distance and reserve which the Scots possessed in common with all rude nations, was confirmed, we may suppose, and peculiarly modified by the nature of their government and political circumstances. As the common people were extremely dependent upon the higher classes, they became necessarily cautious of giving offence, and desirous of recommending themselves to their superiors by an obliging deportment, by obsequious attention, and by a studied expression of zeal and affection. The habits produced by such a situation are, doubtless, not very favourable to plain-dealing and sincerity; however, they may fit the possessor for the intercourse of the world, and render him expert in smoothing <94> the frowns or improving the smiles of fortune.

The national characters bestowed upon the inhabitants of different countries, must be received with large allowances for exaggeration and prejudice; though, as they proceed upon general observation, they have usually a foundation in truth. In this light we may view the character of the Scottish nation delineated by her English neighbours; and so far as the picture is genuine, it will, perhaps, be in some measure explained by the foregoing remarks.

The shrewdness, cunning, and selfishness, imputed to the people of Scotland, are merely the unfavourable aspect of that intelligence and sagacity by which they are distinguished above the mere mechanical drudges in the southern part of the island, and by which they are more able to discover their own interest, to extricate themselves from difficulties, and to act, upon every occurrence, with decision and prudence.

They are accused of not being over-scrupulous with respect to the dignity of those methods by which they endeavour to better their circumstances. It is to be feared that this ac-<95>cusation has no very peculiar application to the inhabitants of the north. If it has any real foundation, it must undoubtedly be imputed to the debasing effects of the old Scottish government, and to the long continuance of that poverty and dependence, from which the people, in our days, are but beginning to emerge.

The national spirit of Scotchmen has been much taken notice of; insomuch that they are supposed to be all in a confederacy to commend and extol one another. We may remark, that, as candidates, either for fame or profit, in the London market, they are greatly the minority; and it is not surprising, that in such a situation they should feel a common bond of union, like that of strangers in a hostile country.* <96>

The deficiency of Scottish authors, in every department connected with wit and humour, has been universally admitted. This we may ascribe to the sly and cautious temper of the people, which is calculated to repress every exertion of mirth and pleasantry. It may also have proceeded, in some measure, from the difficulty they meet with in attaining such a command of the English language as must be requisite for the forcible and humorous delineation of ordinary life and manners.† <97>

* It is said that the common people in Scotland never give a direct answer. This may proceed, no doubt, from habits of caution, concealment, and dissimulation; but it may also be derived from a habit of reflection, which leads them to discern not only what you directly inquire, but what farther information you may wish to obtain. "Pray, friend, am I in the right road to such a place?" "What place did you come from, Sir?" "What business have you, friend, with the place I came from?" "None at all, Sir; but I have as little with the place to which you are going."

† A noted literary character has waggishly observed, in speaking of the learning of Scotland, "That every one has a mouthful, but nobody a bellyful." The amount of this criticism seems to be, that instead of consuming their whole life by a vain endeavour to become adepts in two dead languages, they have divested themselves of a superstitious reverence for antiquity, and are content to cultivate each branch of knowledge so far only as they find it useful or agreeable. The mouthful of the Scot may be somewhat scanty, but it is fresh and wholesome food; to him the English bellyful seems *offal.* [[Millar is referring to a passage from Hester Thrale Piozzi's *Anecdotes of the Late Samuel Johnson* (London, 1786).]]

CHAPTER II

Changes in the Political State of England from the Accession of the House of Stuart—the Advancement of Commerce and Manufactures—Institutions for National Defence—Different Effect of these in Britain, and upon the Neighbouring Continent.

The accession of James the First to the English throne, while it gave rise to such remarkable changes in the state of his ancient hereditary dominions, became the source of great advantages, in common to both countries; from which, however, England, as the ruling power, derived the principal benefit. As far back as we can clearly trace the history of the two kingdoms, we find them engaged in a course of mutual depredation and hostilities, during which, indeed, England was commonly in the end victorious; though, at the same time, from her superior wealth, <98> she was usually the principal sufferer. Upon the Norman conquest, when England was involved in connections with the continent of Europe, her enemies were of course incited to cultivate the friendship of Scotland; and after the pretensions of the king of England to the sovereignty of France had produced a rooted animosity between the two countries, the monarchs of the latter became the constant allies of the Scottish princes.[1] In this situation, Scotland was commonly the

1. The "auld alliance" between France and Scotland took formal shape in the thirteenth century, and served Scotland well during its Wars of Independence against England in the fourteenth century. Later, the success of the English Reformation prompted France to strengthen the traditional alliance with dynastic marriages. The high point of French influence came soon after, during the regency of Marie de Guise just prior to the Scottish Reformation.

dupe of French politics; and was found a convenient instrument for creating a powerful diversion of the forces in the southern part of the island. The invasions of England by her Scottish neighbours, being thus directed and assisted by a foreign power, became in many cases alarming and formidable. In the reign of Elizabeth, France had an opportunity of retaliating the vexation and embarrassment she had felt from her ancient enemy, by supporting the claim of Mary, Queen of Scots, to the crown of England. The artful policy of the English queen, in order to counteract and disappoint the machinations practised against her, has been supposed by many to throw an indelible <99> stain upon her character; and even when regarded in the most favourable point of view, can be justified only by its necessity. The intrigues of this wise princess, the expense incurred by her on that account, the extreme vigour, not to say injustice, with which she treated her unfortunate rival, a measure which, she foresaw, was likely to draw upon her the public censure and resentment: all these are sufficient proofs of the danger to which she found herself exposed, and of the mischief which her dominions were liable to suffer through the medium of Scotland.[2]

By the union of the two crowns in the person of James the First, England was completely delivered from every hazard of that nature. The two kingdoms, having the same sovereign, possessed of the power of declaring war and peace, were reduced under the same administration, and consequently destined for the future to live in perpetual amity. As their whole military force acted under one head, and against their common enemies, they were enabled to assume a superior rank in the scale of Europe; while the insular situation of Britain gave her little ground to apprehend <100> any foreign invasion, and little reason to interfere in the politics of the continent.

The peace and security which England derived from these favourable circumstances contributed to the encouragement of industry, and to the improvement of those commercial advantages which the peculiar situation of the country had bestowed upon her. After the accession of the house of Stuart, therefore, the advancement of trade and manufactures became still more conspicuous than it had been under the princes of the Tudor family; and its consequences, in diffusing opulence and independence, were proportionably more extensive. Towards the latter part of the reign of Elizabeth, the woollen manufacture, which, from the tyranny of Spain in the Neth-

2. See *HE,* 4:354–60.

erlands, had been transported into England, gave employment to a number of industrious hands, and put in motion a correspondent amount of capitals, which, upon the extension or variation of the demand for commodities, could easily be diverted into other channels. Various branches of manufacture sprung up, one after another; and found a market for their productions. The prosperity of inland <101> trade produced an inclination, as well as a capacity, for greater commercial enterprizes; and occasioned the formation of colonies in distant parts of the world. To promote such undertakings, the assistance of government was given to the private adventurers; and a number of trading companies, with various exclusive privileges, which at that time proved of general utility, were established.

By the progress of these improvements, a greater proportion of the inhabitants, instead of living as retainers or servants of the rich, became engaged in various mechanical employments, or in different branches of traffick, from which they could earn a livelihood without the necessity of courting the favour of their superiors. An artificer, whose labour is enhanced by the general demand for it, or a tradesman who sells his goods in a common market, considers himself as his own master. He says that he is obliged to his employers, or his customers; and he treats them with civility; but he does not feel himself greatly dependent upon them. His subsistence, and his profits, are derived not from one, but from a number of persons; he knows, besides, that <102> their employment, or their custom, proceeds not commonly from personal favour, but from a regard to their own interest; and consequently that, while he serves them equally well, he has no reason to apprehend the decline of his business. Rising more and more to this independent situation, artificers and tradesmen were led by degrees to shake off their ancient slavish habits, to gratify their own inclinations or humours, and to indulge that love of liberty, so congenial to the mind of man, which nothing but imperious necessity is able to subdue.

The independence and the influence of this order of people was farther promoted by the circumstance of their being collected in towns, whence they derived an extreme facility in communicating their sentiments and opinions. In a populous city, not only the discoveries and knowledge, but the feelings and passions of each individual are quickly and readily propagated over the whole. If an injury is committed, if an act of oppression is complained of, it immediately spreads an alarm, becomes the subject of clamour and censure, and excites the general indignation and resentment.

<103> Every one roused by the example of those around him, loses the sense of his own danger in the ardour and impetuosity of his companions. Some bold and enterprizing leader acquires an ascendancy over their common movements; and while their first impressions are yet warm, finds no difficulty in uniting them to defend their privileges, or to demand redress for their wrongs.

While the tradesmen, manufacturers, and merchants of England, were thus rapidly increasing in number, and advancing to such comfortable situations, many individuals in those classes were, by successful industry in the more lucrative branches of trade, and by a rigid and persevering economy, the natural effect of their habits, enabled to acquire splendid fortunes, and to reflect a degree of lustre upon the profession to which they belonged. In this, as in all other cases, property became the source of consideration and respect; and, in proportion as the trading part of the nation became opulent, they obtained more weight in the community.

The progressive advancement of the freedom and independence of the manufacturing <104> and mercantile people was followed, in the natural course of things, by that of the peasantry or farmers, the other great class of the commonalty. From the multiplication of the trading towns, and their increasing population and riches, the consumption of all the necessaries of life was promoted, and the market for every species of provisions proportionably extended. The price of every article produced by the land was therefore enhanced by a greater competition of purchasers; and the labour of those persons employed in agriculture was called forth and rewarded by an augmentation of profits; not to mention, that the activity and enterprizing genius of merchants, arising from their large capitals, their extensive dealings, and their mutual intercourse, were naturally communicated to the neighbouring farmers; who, from the limited nature of their undertakings, and from their dispersed and solitary residence, trusting to the slow experience and detached observations of each individual, were likely, independent of this additional excitement, to proceed with great caution and timidity, and therefore to advance very slowly in the knowledge of their <105> profession. In proportion to the general improvement of agriculture, it was expected that farmers should undertake more expensive operations in manuring and meliorating their grounds; and to encourage these undertakings, the master found it necessary to give them a reasonable prospect of indemnity, by securing them for an adequate length of time in the possession of their farms. By the extension of leases of land, which became more and more universal, the farmers of England not only were emancipated from their primitive dependence, but acquired a degree of rank and importance unknown in most other countries.

The same causes which exalted the common people, diminished the influence of the nobility, or of such as were born to great fortunes. The improvement of arts, the diffusion of all those accommodations which are the natural consequence of that improvement, were accompanied with a change of manners; the ancient plainness and simplicity giving place by degrees to a relish for pleasure and to a taste of luxury and refinement, which were productive of greater expence in all the articles of living.[3] Men of high rank, who found <106> themselves, without any exertion of their own, possessed of great wealth, were not prompted by their situation to acquire habits either of industry or of economy. To live upon their estates, to pass their time in idleness, or to follow their amusement, was regarded as their birth-right. Gaining nothing, therefore, by their industry, and exposed by the growing luxury of the times to the daily temptation of increasing their expences, they were, of course, involved in difficulties, were obliged to devise expedients for raising money, and reduced to the necessity of purchasing an additional rent, by granting long leases, or even more permanent rights to their tenants. The ancient retainers, whom every feudal baron had been accustomed to maintain upon his estate for the purpose of defending him against all his enemies, were unavoidably dismissed; and the military services, which had been formerly exacted from the vassals, were converted into stated pecuniary payments. These conversions, indeed, were at the same time recommended from the change of manners and the alterations in the state of the country; as, by the suppression of private feuds among the <107> great lords, and the general establishment of peace and tranquillity, the maintenance of such retainers, on account of personal defence, was become superfluous.

The nobility, or great barons, were thus deprived of that armed force, and of that multitude of adherents and dependents by which they had formerly supported their authority and dignity. Many individuals among them, from the progress of dissipation and extravagance, were at length obliged, upon

3. Millar here takes up an explanation of aristocratic luxury and its role in changing the balance of social and political power that was earlier articulated by both Hume and Smith.

the failure of other resources, to contract debts, to mortgage, and to squander away their estates. The frugal and industrious merchant, who had acquired a fortune by trade, was enabled, in such a case, to purchase what the idle and extravagant proprietor found it necessary to sell. Property in land, originally the great source of influence, was in this manner transferred from the higher to the lower classes; the character of the trader and that of the landed gentleman were in some measure confounded; and the consideration and rank of the latter were, by a change of circumstances, communicated to the former.

These gradual changes in the state of the <108> country could not fail to affect the condition of the monarch, as well as the authority of parliament, and, in particular, the relative weight of the two houses.

The improvement of arts, and the progress of luxury and refinement, which increased the rate of living to every nobleman, or private gentleman, had necessarily the same effect upon that of the sovereign. The additional accommodations and pleasures, the various modes of elegance or ostentation, which the fashion of the times was daily introducing, occasioned a proportional addition to the expence requisite for supporting the king's household, and maintaining the dignity of the crown. The different officers and servants employed in all the branches of public business, finding their subsistence more expensive than formerly, required of course an augmentation of salaries or emoluments. From the advancement of society in civilization, from the greater accumulation of property in the hands of individuals, and from a correspondent extension of the connections and pursuits of mankind, a more complicated set of regulations became necessary for main-<109>taining good order and tranquillity; and the number of different officers and servants in the various departments of administration was unavoidably augmented. Upon all these accounts, the king, who found his ancient revenue more and more inadequate to his expences, was laid under greater difficulties in supporting the machine of government, and obliged more frequently to solicit the aid of parliament for obtaining additional supplies.

These effects of the increasing trade and opulence of the country had begun to be felt in the reign of Elizabeth; who, at the same time, from her peculiar situation, from the number and power of her enemies, and from the intricate and artful policy to which she resorted in order to frustrate their designs, was involved in extraordinary expences. Wishing, however, to preserve her popularity, and having probably little regard to her apparent successor, she was willing to alienate the crown-lands, rather than impose new burdens upon her subjects; insomuch that, upon the accession of James, when the state of the monarchy demanded an augmentation of revenue, the ancient patrimony of the crown had been <110> greatly reduced. From particular accidents, therefore, as well as from the operation of general causes, there was opened at this period a new source of influence, tending, in some degree, to reverse the former channels of authority, and to render the monarch dependent upon the national council. As the king had no ordinary funds for the execution of any important measure, either house of parliament, by withholding its assent to the taxes proposed, might with the utmost facility arrest his most favourite enterprizes, and even put a stop to all the movements of administration.[4]

It is manifest, however, that the circumstances which had thus contributed to extend the authority of parliament, must have tended in a peculiar manner to exalt the house of commons. In consequence of the growing wealth and independence of the people, the house of commons, composed of the representatives of the people, rose to superior eminence, and assumed more extensive privileges. Its dignity and power were, at the same time, promoted by the king, who, in the long continued struggle with the nobles, had endeavoured to undermine their influence by exalting the lower orders of <111> the community. For this purpose the interest of the crown had been employed in bringing the knights of shires into parliament, in separating them from the great barons, and uniting them in one house with the burgesses. With the same view the kings of England, more especially those of the Tudor family, not only encouraged the frequent meetings of parliament, but promoted the interference of the house of commons in all the branches of parliamentary business, and connived at those forms of proceeding by which it acquired the exclusive right of introducing all bills intended to impose any tax or pecuniary burden upon the people. Wherever the monarch was afraid of hazarding the direct exertion of his prerogative, he had commonly recourse to the lower house of parliament, of whose aid, in opposing the nobility, he seldom had any reason to doubt.

4. Millar's account of the rise of parliamentary authority should be compared with Hume's insistence that the initial effect of opulence and the loss of feudal dependency was to give the crown "an authority almost absolute." See *HE,* 4:384.

But the time was now come when this union of interest between the crown and the house of commons could no longer subsist. The inferior ranks having attained a certain pitch of independence, had no longer occasion for the protection of the sovereign; while the nobili-<112>ty, fallen from their ancient power and grandeur, had ceased to be the objects of terror. The commons were now in a condition to defend those privileges which they had invariably exercised, and which immemorial custom had sanctioned. They represented by far the greatest part of the landed property, and almost the whole personal wealth of the kingdom; and in their measures for promoting their own interest and that of their constituents, they were likely to be supported by the great body of the people. Their apprehension and jealousy, instead of being excited by the peers, was now more properly directed to the monarch, whose power had of late become so exorbitant, and of whom the peers, no longer the rivals, were become, a great part of them, the dependents and subordinate agents.

In the reign of queen Elizabeth this independent spirit of the commons had begun to appear; but, from the accession of James the First, becoming much more conspicuous, it was productive of uniform and repeated exertions for limiting the encroachments of the prerogative, and for maintaining and extending the popular part of the constitution. <113>

Of all the innovations arising from the progress of the arts, and the advancement of civilized manners, that which related to the national defence was the most remarkable. The dismission of the ancient retainers belonging to the proprietors of land, and the employment of a great proportion of the lower people in arts and manufactures, made it no longer possible, in those emergencies when a military force was required, to call out the feudal militia into the field. The vassals of the crown, therefore, unable to fulfil the engagements implied in their original tenures, were obliged, in place of military service, to offer a pecuniary composition, from which a general contribution or tax was at length introduced; and with the money collected in this manner, the king, upon whom was devolved the care of defending the country, was put in a condition to hire soldiers for the purpose. This alteration in the system of national defence, which began upon the dawn of improvement in the kingdom, was gradually making advances till the reign of James the First, when the attendance of the vassals was totally relinquished; and the <114> armies levied for the future came to be composed entirely of mercenaries.

The introduction of mercenary forces was, in different respects, attended with very different, and even opposite consequences.[5] It occasioned an immense addition to the former expences of government; and, in proportion, rendered the king more dependent upon that power which had the disposal of the public money. As he could execute no enterprize of importance without obtaining from parliament an adequate supply, he was under the necessity of procuring the concurrence of that assembly in almost all his measures; and when money was wanted, he could seldom find a decent pretence for refusing a redress of grievances, or any other compliance which either house might require as the condition of the grant. The house of commons, in which it was understood that all money-bills must originate, stood forward on such occasions, and availed itself of this privilege for guarding those avenues of the constitution which the inexperience or negligence of the former times had left open to the attacks of the crown.

The changes in the military system had, in <115> another view, a tendency to aggrandize the monarch. An army levied and maintained by the crown, separated by their employment from the rest of the community, and alienated from the interest and pursuits of their fellow-citizens, deriving not only their present subsistence, but all their hopes of preferment from the sovereign, accustomed to obey his orders, and, by the peculiar spirit of their profession, taught to place their punctilio of honour and duty in the implicit strictness of that obedience: a body of men so circumstanced became a powerful instrument in the hands of a master, ready to be moved at pleasure in the execution of his designs. The employment of mercenary troops, in place of the ancient feudal militia, had thus a tendency to exalt the crown in two different ways. In the first place, by affording a beneficial and reputable profession to a multitude of people, it held up to a great proportion of the inhabitants, in particular to the nobility and gentry, who consider themselves as excluded from many other professions, the prospect of attaining a provision, and even rank and distinction, to themselves and their families. It instilled in-<116>to all these persons the habit of looking invariably to the sovereign as the dispenser of those advantages, and consequently disposed them to adhere to his party in all political disputes, and to distinguish themselves by their exertions in support of the prerogative.

5. The importance of mercenary forces or "standing armies" was a major theme in the republican tradition of English political thought and carried considerable influence on the framers of American independence.

But, secondly, this new system of national defence furnished the king with an armed force, which he might commonly govern at his discretion, and which, therefore, if raised to a certain magnitude, might be capable of bearing down and crushing all resistance or opposition to his will. The introduction of mercenaries, which, from similar causes, took place over a great part of Europe, was the more likely to be attended with this fatal consequence; because, in the natural course of things, they were soon converted into regular standing armies. When a body of troops had been enlisted, and properly disciplined for war, it was thought a prudent measure to retain, if not the whole, at least a part of them even in time of peace, that the country might not be left totally defenceless; and that, with the assistance of those veterans, the new levies might the sooner be fitted for service. The farther the <117> improvements of military discipline had been pushed, the more difficult it became, from the progress of trade, to recruit the army upon any sudden emergency; and the more that princes, from their situation, found an interest in being constantly prepared for war, the number of standing forces, in particular countries, was increased; the trade of a soldier was more separated from every other, and rendered more permanent; and the great body of the people, unarmed and unwarlike, were consequently reduced under the power of that formidable class who had come to be constantly and exclusively paid for fighting.

In England, therefore, as well as in the other European countries which had made considerable progress in arts and manufactures, we may discover the operation of two principles which had an opposite political tendency; the independence and opulence acquired by the lower classes of the people, which tended to produce a popular government; and the introduction of mercenary armies for the purpose of national defence, which contributed to extend and support the power of the crown. This gave rise, unavoidably, to a contest be-<118>tween the king and the people; while the former was endeavouring to extend his prerogative, and the latter to maintain or augment their privileges. In tracing the commencement and progress of this contest, which forms an interesting and critical period in the history of those countries, it will be found that the success of either party has frequently depended upon peculiar and accidental circumstances.*

* This point I had formerly occasion to consider in a treatise upon "The Origin of the Distinction of Ranks."

In most of the countries of Europe, the practice of hiring troops was begun at an earlier period than in England, and was pushed to a much greater extent. The kingdoms upon the continent were greatly exposed to the attacks of neighbouring powers; and in those disorderly times, when every ambitious prince aimed at foreign conquest, were obliged to be constantly in a posture of defence; so that when the vassals of the crown began to decline the military service, there was an absolute necessity to surmount every difficulty in procuring a great body of mercenaries. Thus, before the spirit of liberty had risen to a high pitch, <119> the king had obtained an army devoted to his interest, and easily diverted from its original destination, to that of supporting and enlarging his power.

We accordingly find, that, upon the continent of Europe, the disuse of the feudal militia, and the formation of mercenary armies, enabled the sovereign, in most cases, to establish a despotical government. This happened in France during the reign of Louis the Thirteenth, and in Spain during that of Philip the Second. In Germany, indeed, the independence of the different states of the empire had, long before this period, been settled upon so firm a basis, that every attempt of the crown to reduce them to subjection proved ineffectual. But the vigorous efforts which were made for this purpose by the emperor Ferdinand the Second,[6] sufficiently demonstrate that the new system of military arrangements, introduced about this time by the monarch, had the same tendency here as in the other European kingdoms.

The circumstances of Britain, however, at this critical period, were a good deal different from those of the countries upon the neigh-<120>bouring continent. By the union of the crowns of England and Scotland, an entire stop was put to the inroads and hostilities between the two countries; which, at the same time, from their insular situation, were little exposed to the attacks of any foreign potentate. When the vassals of the crown, therefore, had withdrawn their ancient military service, there was no immediate necessity for employing any considerable body of mercenary soldiers. The defence of the country was devolved, in a great measure, upon its navy; which, without much difficulty, could be rendered fully sufficient for the purpose. By the maritime situation, and the commercial improvements of Britain, a great part of its inhabitants, becoming acquainted with the navigation and

6. Louis XIII (r. 1610–43); Philip II (r. 1556–98); Ferdinand II, Holy Roman Emperor (r. 1619–37).

the arts depending upon it, formed a body of sailors capable of manning such fleets as might be necessary to repel any foreign invasion, and requiring little additional discipline or instruction to fit them for that species of military service.

The sea and the land forces may, both of them, no doubt, be properly ranked in the class of mercenaries; yet, when we consider <121> their tendency to support the authority of the crown, they must be viewed in a different light. The soldiers of a land army have usually no other employment, or at least none which, upon being disbanded, they can exercise with equal advantage. But the sailors of the royal navy are usually drawn, and often dragged by force, from the merchant service; to which, being less hazardous, and commonly more lucrative, a great part of them are desirous of returning. The officers, indeed, in the sea and in the land service, are nearly in the same situation, depending entirely upon the crown for their professional advancement; and having no other employment from which they can expect either distinction or emolument. But the great body of the sailors, in the pay of government, are somewhat in the condition of common mechanics; deriving subsistence from their labour and skill; and secure, that whenever they shall be dismissed from their present service, their proficiency in a collateral branch will afford them a comfortable livelihood.

Though sea-faring people, by being peculiarly distinguished from the rest of the com-<122>munity, are usually animated with an uncommon degree of the *esprit du corps,*[7] they are not fitted, either by their situation or dispositions, to act as the tools of a court in supporting the encroachments of the prerogative. From their precarious way of life, exposing them to great and unexpected vicissitudes; exempting them at some times from all care for their own provision, and at others producing such affluence as tempts them to extraordinary dissipation, they become thoughtless about futurity, and little impressed by motives of interest. Their disinterested character, joined to their want of reflection, and habitual contempt of danger, creates a spirit of independence, bordering upon licentiousness, from which they are with difficulty recalled to the obedience and submission consistent with their duty. The fleets in the service of the crown are, besides, at too great a distance, and their operations of too peculiar a nature, to admit of their being employed occasionally in quelling insurrections at home, or in checking the

7. Spirit of solidarity (usually *esprit de corps*).

efforts of the people to maintain their privileges. They are confined to a different element. <123>

From these observations it will not appear surprising that the fate of the English government was different from that of most of the other feudal governments upon the continent. At the period when the commons had imbibed a higher spirit of liberty, and acquired an increase of power and influence from the increasing opulence and independence of the people, the sovereign was not provided with an army sufficient to maintain his pretensions. James the First, and Charles the First, appear to have embraced the same political principles with most of the other princes of Europe. They saw the absolute power of the crown exercised in the neighbouring kingdoms, and were not willing to be left behind by their neighbours. But the secure and peaceable state of their dominions afforded no plausible pretence for the imposition of such taxes as would have been requisite for keeping on foot a great body of mercenary troops; and parliament, alarmed at the unusual demands of money, upon the part of the crown, became proportionably circumspect in granting even the most moderate supplies. To accomplish their purpose, those monarchs, in the <124> extreme perplexity arising from their circumstances, were induced to practise a variety of shifts, and to carry on a train of dissimulation very unbecoming their station; but having no sufficient military force to support their claims, they were laid under the necessity of making such concessions, and of permitting the erection of such barriers against oppression, as the awakened suspicion and jealousy of the nation thought indispensable for securing the ancient constitution, and restraining the future abuses of the prerogative.

The ocean with which Britain is encompassed, had thus, at two different periods, a powerful and happy influence upon the course of the English government. During the highest exultation of the feudal monarchy in modern Europe, the safety which England derived from its insular situation, and its remote connection with the disputes and quarrels upon the continent, gave the sovereign, as was observed upon the early part of our History, few opportunities of acting as the general of the national forces; and, consequently, of acquiring the popularity and authority which result from that eminent station. As the great feu-<125>dal superior in the kingdom, he became, therefore, less absolute than the sovereign in any of the great nations upon the continent. When, in a later age, the improvements of commerce and manufactures dried up the ancient sources of the feudal dominion, and turned the course of authority into different channels, the same line of separation between Britain and the neighbouring countries withheld, from the sovereign of the former, that new system of military arrangement which was then introduced into the latter, and which in them became the great instrument of despotism. The *feudal king* of England saw no other path to greatness than by undermining the aristocracy; and was willing to barter the exaltation of the lower, for the depression of the higher classes. Her *commercial sovereign* found that he was unable to set bounds to those liberties, which his predecessors had endeavoured to promote, and was thence induced, though with infinite reluctance, to compound the disputes with his people, and to relinquish a part of his prerogative in order to retain the rest. <126>

CHAPTER III

In what Manner the Political System was Affected by the State of Religious Opinions.

In those European countries which embraced the doctrines of the reformation, religious disputes continued for some time to agitate the minds of men; and the different sects which became prevalent, or obtained consideration, were allied with different parties in the state. The latter, in such cases, derived a prodigious advantage from the former, being supported by that zeal which religion is wont to inspire, and by that animosity which is often the bitter fruit of religious contention.

With those who endeavoured to pull down the fabric of superstition and ecclesiastical tyranny, erected in the dark ages, it was one of the first objects to withdraw that exorbitant power which the Roman pontiff, as the head of the western church, had found the means of usurping. It required but little reflection to <127> discover the inconvenience and absurdity of a foreign prince being permitted to obtain the superintendence and government of religion, in a country whose interest was not only different, but frequently opposite to that of his own dominions; that he should be allowed to interfere in the distribution of justice, as well as in the disposal of the most lucrative offices; and that he should exercise these privileges without limitation or controul, and by virtue of an authority paramount and superior to that of the civil magistrate. In England, the private controversy in which Henry the Eighth was engaged with the court of Rome, led him to view this point in a strong light; and the delivery of himself and his kingdom from the dominion of the holy see, together with the gratification of his avarice, by acquiring possession of the monastic revenues, may be regarded as the sole purpose for which he prosecuted the reformation. So great was the authority possessed by this monarch, and so much afraid was either religious party of pushing him to extremities, that the new system came, in a great measure, to be modelled by his direction; and, upon this account, it retained a <128> greater affinity to the ancient establishment than could otherwise have been expected. The papal supremacy was not extinguished, but only transferred to the king; and in other respects, the hierarchy suffered no material variation.

This plan of church government, which Henry had laboured with all his might to establish, was far from being disagreeable to the temper of Elizabeth; and though not perfectly suitable to the inclination of all that part of her subjects who favoured the reformation, yet, being patronised by the sovereign, and having obtained the sanction of two preceding reigns, it was considered as the system most likely to prevail over the ancient establishment, and was therefore admitted without opposition by every denomination of protestants.

Two great religious parties, at this time, divided the whole nation; the Protestants and the Roman Catholics: the former, who, by undaunted resolution and fortitude, and with various success encountering severe trials and bloody persecutions, had at length obtained a decided superiority. The latter, who, though defeated, were not broken; and who, though <129> they had quitted the open field, were still powerful in number, connections, and resources, and were only lying in wait for the first favourable opportunity to retrieve their fortune. These two parties were animated by mutual hatred and resentments. The oppression to which the Protestants had been subjected, and the barbarities which at the instigation of the church, they had suffered from the secular arm, were still fresh in their memory; while they dreaded the machinations of a party, with whose unrelenting dispositions they were well acquainted, and whose activity and power, seconded by the papal influence and authority over a great part of Europe, were still very formidable. The Roman Catholics, on the other hand, could not easily forget the mortifying degradation which they had suffered; the complete overthrow of their faith and worship; the loss of their splendid and lucrative establishment; the insolence and contempt of heretics, irritated by former bad usage; and the hardships which they had reason to expect from adversaries, now triumphant, and supported by the civil magistrate. <130>

After the accession of the house of Stuart, when the terror of popery began to subside, the subordinate distinctions among Protestants were brought more into notice, and their chief differences of opinion gave rise to different sects. According as the terms of the established religion had been limited and circumscribed by the influence of the crown, the sectaries became numerous and powerful. The tide of religious faith and worship, being turned from its natural course, and forced into an artificial channel, was the more likely to overflow its banks, and to find a passage in various collateral streams and currents.

The presbyterians, who had gained the ascendancy in Scotland, were in England, about this period, the most numerous body of sectaries. Their system appears to have arisen from a natural progression of the same views and opinions by which the religious reformation had been originally suggested. They proposed to correct the abuses of the Roman Catholic church, and to guard against the undue influence and domination of the clergy, by the abolition of ecclesiastical dignities, by establishing a perfect parity among churchmen, <131> by restricting them to very moderate livings, and by rejecting that pomp and pageantry of worship which is manifestly calculated to promote superstition, and to create in the people a blind veneration for their spiritual directors.

While the presbyterians disapproved of the ancient hierarchy, there arose another great sect, who considered all ecclesiastical establishments as incompatible with religious freedom. To this description of religionists, the interference of government in favour of any one sect, by maintaining its clergy at the public expence, appeared a kind of persecution of every other, and an encroachment upon the rights of private judgment. As every man employs and pays his own physician or lawyer, it seemed to them equally proper and expedient that every one should be left to choose his own religious instructor, and to bestow upon him such a reward for his labour as might be settled by an agreement between them. In this manner the clergy, it was thought, instead of acquiring an undue influence over the people, would become dependent upon them; and, like men in other professions, prompted to exertion by a regard to their own interest, would commonly be successful in pro-<132>portion to their abilities and good behaviour. The different modes of faith, as well as the forms of public worship, would thus be placed upon an equal and liberal footing; and the community at large being freed, in matters of religion, from the bias either of interest or of authority, would be encouraged to follow the dictates of reason and conscience. The political advantages of such a regulation were supposed to be not less conspicuous. By the simple expedient of leaving the people at liberty to conduct their own religious concerns, the charge of levying taxes, or providing any permanent fund for the support of the national religion, together with the hardship of obliging any part of the inhabitants to pay for maintaining the clergy of a different communion; not to mention the loss that must be sustained, in that case, if the established pastors are deserted by their flock, and remain an useless load upon the public; all these inconveniences would be entirely avoided.

Such was the general system of the *independents;*[1] which, by a natural progress of reasoning, seems to have grown up from that of the presbyterians, as the latter was an obvious <133> extension of the doctrines embraced by those primitive reformers who continued the hierarchy. The Christian religion had been reduced into a monopoly, under the authority of a governor,[2] with extensive territories and numerous forts commanded by regular officers to defend the trade and prevent interlopers. For correcting the evils which had arisen from such an oppressive establishment, the first remedy went no farther than to cashier the governor, to dismiss a number of useless and expensive servants, and to cut off a multitude of pernicious exclusive privileges. To demolish the forts, to disband their opulent and powerful commanding officers, and to strip the corporation of its overgrown territorial possessions, appeared, upon further experience and reflection, an additional improvement. To dissolve the company altogether, and to lay the trade entirely open, was at length suggested as the most effectual means for promoting laudable industry, for discouraging unfair practices, and for communicating an equal benefit to a whole people.

These four religious parties, the Roman Catholic, the Church of England, the Presby-<134>terian, the Independent, which comprehended nearly the whole nation, were led to embrace different political systems, and became allied to different parties in the State. The two first, in a political view, exhibited characters diametrically opposite to those of the two last; and though differing in some respects from each other, their leading features were similar.

1. A term first used in the 1640s, and employed in two different senses—religious and political—to describe groups that overlapped but were not identical. Millar goes on to explain the differences between the Presbyterians and the Independents.

2. In this extraordinary passage, Millar implicitly compares the Christian church to the East India Company, the reform of which had been a major political issue, especially during the impeachment trial of its governor, Warren Hastings (1732–1818), which commenced in 1788.

The Roman catholic religion may be regarded as a deep-laid system of superstition, which took a firmer hold of the human mind than any other that has appeared in the world.[3] It was founded upon a more complicated and national theology than the rude systems of a former period; and gave rise to a multiplicity of interesting opinions and tenets, which exercised and frequently perplexed the pious believer, so as to lay him under the necessity of resorting to the aid of a religious instructor for the regulation and direction of his faith. It represented the Deity as an omnipotent, but an austere and vindictive being, capable of anger and resentment against those who transgress his laws, and intending this world, not for the present comfort and satisfaction of his <135> creatures, but as a place of preparation for a future state of eternal happiness or misery. As all men must be conscious of great weakness and frailty, of not only deviating from the standard of perfect virtue, but of being frequently stained with numberless vices, and even atrocious crimes, which excites self-condemnation and remorse, they could not fail, upon conceiving themselves in the all-seeing eye of this impartial and severe Judge, to be covered with shame and confusion, and overwhelmed with consternation and terror. Under the impression of these feelings, it was natural that they should endeavour to procure consolation from the intercourse of some ghostly father whom they should call upon to supplicate the offended Deity in their behalf, and whose advice and direction they should eagerly solicit in attempting to atone for their transgressions, by submitting to voluntary penances or mortifications, and by every expression or demonstration of humility and abasement, of sorrow and repentance. These dispositions and circumstances of the people had produced a clergy, opulent and powerful beyond example, who had laboured to promote and regulate <136> that superstition which was the original foundation of their authority; and who, in their advancement to riches and dominion, had, like the officers of a regular army, fallen into a subordination of power and rank. The doctrines and the practical conduct inculcated by this clergy, were such as might

3. Millar's description of Catholicism as a "deep-laid system of superstition" might be compared to Hume's discussion of the typology of religious behavior in volume 1 of the first edition of his *History,* in which he speaks of the Reformation as a contest between "two species of religion, the superstitious and the fanatical." See *History of Great Britain* (Edinburgh, 1754), 8. Hume was sharply criticized by Daniel McQueen (d. 1777) in his *Letters on Hume's History of Great Britain* (1756), and the passage was excised from later editions.

contribute most effectually to their own aggrandizement. The people were taught to believe in mysteries which their pastors alone pretended to explain, to approach and worship the Supreme Being by superstitious rites and ceremonies, in which the clergy presided, to discover to their spiritual instructor all their secret thoughts and actions, and, upon submitting to the discipline prescribed by the church in such cases, to receive from him absolution and pardon for their sins. In a word, the clergy were understood to have in their possession the keys of heaven; in consequence of which, the treasures of the earth, and the hearts of mankind, were laid open to them.

In the exercise and extension of their power, they were supported, not only by their ecclesiastical leader, the Roman pontiff, but also by their temporal sovereign, who, though on some oc-<137>casions he might quarrel with them for their encroachments upon his prerogative, had commonly an interest to promote their influence over the people; as they, on the other hand, from his having a great share in the disposal of their livings, were induced to employ that influence in promoting and maintaining his authority. Thus, between the great power of the crown and that of the church, both of which were the offspring of ignorance and prejudice, there arose a sort of family compact, which being consolidated by length of time and by mutual habits, proved no less advantageous to either party than it was inimical to the interest of the whole community.

Of all the systems of religion established at the time of the reformation, the church of England approached the nearest to that Roman catholick stock upon which it was engrafted. It rejected, indeed, many absurd opinions adopted by the church of Rome, and, from the greater diffusion of knowledge, it acquired a more limited influence over the minds of the people. But so far as its authority extended, its character and tendency were the same. Though its features were a little softened, it <138> presented the same aspect of superstition, the same pomp and parade of worship, the same dignitaries invested with jurisdiction and authority, the same opulence and splendour in the higher clergy, which tended to procure them consideration and respect, the same train of subordination in the ranks and orders of churchmen, which united them in one compact body, and enabled them, in promoting their common interest, to act with unanimity and vigour.

The constitution of the church of England had even a stronger tendency than that of Rome to render its clergy devoted to the interest of the crown. They were more uniformly dependent upon the sovereign; who, by the annihilation of the papal supremacy, became, without a rival, the acknowledged head of the church, and obtained the entire disposal of the higher ecclesiastical dignities.

The presbyterian and independent systems were of a different spirit and complexion. The adherents of the former, in correcting the errors and abuses of the church of Rome, had acquired a degree of ardour and enthusiasm, which led them, in their acts of pub-<139>lic worship, to reject with indignation all forms and ceremonious observances, and to consider their approaches to the Deity, by prayer and supplication, as a mere sentimental intercourse, calculated to demonstrate and improve those feelings of the heart which were due to their Creator. They regarded the functions of a clergyman, therefore, as of no further importance than to preserve good order in the public exercise of religious worship, to inspect the behaviour of the people under his care, and to instruct them in the great duties of morality and religion. It was consistent with this moderate and rational estimation of the clerical character, that the clergy should be moderately provided in livings, that they should not be exalted one above another by any scale of dignities or jurisdiction, and that their authority, upon the whole, should be inconsiderable. By their activity, indeed, and by their attention to the duties of their profession, they were capable of gaining great influence and respect; but in order to do this, it was necessary that they should recommend themselves to the people rather than cultivate the patronage of men in power. They <140> could, therefore, be of little service to the sovereign in supporting his prerogative, and, of consequence, had little to expect from his favour. On the contrary, as their interest and habits connected them with the populace, they entered with alacrity into the popular feelings and views, beheld with jealousy and apprehension the lofty pretensions of the crown, and sounded throughout the kingdom the alarm of regal usurpation.

As the system of the independents proceeded a step further than that of the presbyterians, by declaring against all ecclesiastical establishments, and rendering the provision of every religious instructor perfectly precarious, their clergy becoming still more dependent upon their employers, were proportionably more interested in courting popular favour, and in struggling for the extension of popular privileges.

The presbyterians, as they approved of a permanent clergy, appointed and paid by the public, and possessed of a certain jurisdiction, so, in their political system, they had no aversion to a hereditary monarch, invested with permanent civil powers, and superintending all the <141> ordinary branches of executive government. But the independents, who held that the appointment of the clergy should be left to the discretion of those who thought proper to employ them, were led, in consistency with this doctrine, to maintain that every civil officer, whether supreme or subordinate, should likewise be elected by the community. The presbyterians, therefore, were the friends of limited monarchy. The independents preferred a democratical constitution. The connection, however, between these religious and civil plans of government, though sufficiently obvious, was not acknowledged, nor perhaps discovered all at once; but was gradually developed and brought to light, during the course of the long contest between the king and the commons. For some time after the establishment of the reformation, the Roman catholics continued to be the object of hatred and resentment to all denominations of protestants; but their disposition to support the prerogative did not escape the two first princes of the house of Stuart, who secretly favoured their interest, as much as they hated the presbyterians and independents. Upon pretence of lenity to tender <142> consciences, these two princes assumed the power of dispensing with the penal statutes against *nonconformists;*[4] but the real purpose of those dispensations was apparent to all, and the nation felt equal alarm and indignation from considering those exertions of the prerogative as no less direct and palpable violations of the constitution, than they were decided marks of predilection for a party, the apprehension of whose return into power still continued to fill the nation with terror.

Of the two succeeding monarchs, Charles the Second,[5] it is now known, was a concealed, as his brother, James the Second,[6] was an avowed and bigoted Roman Catholic. The constant favour shewn by the four princes of the house of Stuart to the people of this persuasion, could not fail to procure for them returns of gratitude and affection, and to render them zealous defenders of the prerogative; as, on the other hand, the dislike which those princes invariably manifested to the presbyterians and independents, contributed to strengthen the political bias acquired by those dissenters, and to confirm the original principles by which they were attached to the popular cause. <143>

4. Dissenting Protestant sects that did not conform to the Church of England.
5. On Charles II, see chapter 6, p. 609.
6. James II (r. 1685–89).

But although the different religious parties in England were thus disposed to embrace those opposite political systems, their natural dispositions, in this respect, were sometimes warped and counteracted by peculiar circumstances. For some time after the accession of the house of Stuart, the terror of the restoration of popery, which had been inspired into every description of protestants, produced an extreme jealousy of the king, on account of his marked and uniform partiality to the Roman catholics; and united the church of England with the dissenters in opposing the designs of the crown. This was visible through the whole reign of James the First, and a considerable part of the reign of Charles the First, during which the nation, exclusive of the Roman catholics, and a few interested courtiers, acted with wonderful unanimity in restraining the encroachments of the prerogative.

To form a proper notion of the effects arising from this union, we must consider the state of religious differences in those times. How inconsistent soever it may seem with the genuine principles of religious reformation, the primitive reformers, of every denomination, <144> were no less destitute than the Roman catholics, of that liberality of sentiment which teaches men to indulge their neighbours in the same freedom of opinion which they claim to themselves. They were, all of them, so highly impregnated with a spirit of bigotry and fanaticism as to regard any remarkable deviation from their own tenets in the light of a damnable error, which ought, by every possible means, to be corrected or suppressed; and for the attainment of this object, they were easily excited to brave every danger, and to submit to any inconvenience or hardship. Their interference, therefore, was always formidable to the civil power, and became frequently the chief cause of revolutions in government. At a subsequent period, the harshness and asperity attending the first exuberant growth of religious differences, have been gradually mellowed and softened in their progress to maturity; and the prejudices contracted in the dawn of philosophy, have been dissipated by the fuller light of science and literature, and by that cool and dispassionate inquiry which is the natural fruit of leisure, tranquillity and affluence. It may, perhaps, be considered as the strongest proof of <145> those intellectual improvements which mankind have attained in the present age, that we have beheld the most astonishing political changes, to which religion has in no respect contributed, and which have been regarded by the ministers of the altar in no other light but that of pecuniary interest.

In the latter part of the reign of Charles the First, the disputes between the king and the commons began to assume a different aspect. The apprehensions which were so long entertained of the Romish religion, had then, in a good measure, subsided; and the public attention was engrossed by the arbitrary measures of the crown, which produced a very general opinion, that certain precautions were necessary for guarding against the future encroachments of the prerogative. Here the church of England appeared to follow her natural propensity, and her clergy almost universally deserted the popular standard. The presbyterians and the independents, on the other hand, stood forward as the supporters of the national privileges; and while they became powerful auxiliaries to the <146> cause of liberty, they derived a great accession of strength and reputation from the general tide of political opinions.

Of those two sects, the presbyterians were, for some time, the most powerful, and by their exertions, in conformity to their views of government, many regulations, calculated for securing a limited monarchy, were successively introduced. But the progress of the contest, by holding the minds of men in continual agitation, contributed to push the people to greater extremities, both in religion and politics; in religion, by overthrowing all religious establishments; and in politics, by the entire abolition of regal authority. Such was the aim of the independents, who at length became the ruling party, but who, falling under the direction of an extraordinary genius, utterly devoid of all principle, were made, in his hands, an instrument for the destruction of the monarchy, for the purpose of introducing an odious species of despotism. Had Cromwell[7] possessed less enterprize and abilities, the crown would have been preserved: had his <147> ambition been better directed, England, which under his authority assumed the name of a commonwealth, might have, in reality, obtained a popular government.

The restoration of Charles the Second,[8] gave rise to new religious combinations. The church of England, having now recovered her former establishment, could not fail to entertain a violent jealousy of those dissenters by whom her power had been overturned; and she was led, of course, to cooperate with the Roman catholics, in promoting the arbitrary designs of the monarch. The cry of *church and king,* and the alarm, that *the church was in danger,* were now sounded throughout the nation, and were employed on

7. On Cromwell, see p. 575, note 39.
8. The restoration of the monarchy occurred in 1660.

every critical emergency, to discredit all endeavours for securing the rights of the people.

The barefaced attempt of the infatuated James the Second, to re-establish the Roman catholic religion in England, tended once more to break down these arrangements, and to produce a concert, between the leading men in the church and the protestant dissenters, for the purpose of <148> resisting the unconstitutional measures of the king. As this concert, however, had arisen from the immediate fear of popery, it remained no longer than while that fear was kept alive; and accordingly the revolution in 1688 was hardly completed, before these loyal ecclesiastics began to disclaim the part they had acted, and returned with fresh ardour to their congenial doctrines of passive obedience and non-resistance. <149>

ꙮ CHAPTER IV ꙮ

Progress of the Disputes between the King and Parliament, during the Reigns of James the First, and of Charles the First.

The long contest between the king and parliament, under the two first princes of the Stewart family, forms a very interesting part of the English history; and its origin and consequences deserve the most attentive examination. The object in dispute was no less than to determine and establish the political constitution of a great nation; and the agitation produced by so important a controversy could not fail to rouse the passions of men, to call forth and display their most eminent characters, and to develop those combinations and occurrences which tended to facilitate or to obstruct the improvement of civil society. We are not, however, to imagine that, from the beginning to the end of this contest, the same line of conduct was invariably pursued by <150> either of the parties. They were sometimes actuated by the feelings of the moment; changed their ground, according to the alteration of times and circumstances; and varied their measures, according to the character and views of those individuals by whom they were occasionally directed. To distinguish the most remarkable of these variations, the whole period under consideration may be divided into three branches: the first extending from the accession of James to the meeting of the long parliament, as it is called, in the year 1640; the second, from the meeting of the long parliament to the commencement of the civil war; the third, from thence to the death of Charles the First.[1] <151>

1. These three periods are 1603–40, 1640–42, and 1642–49.

SECTION I

The Reign of James the First; and that of Charles the First, from his Accession to the Meeting of the Long Parliament.

The behaviour of James the First, after he obtained the crown of England, might seem surprising to those who remembered his former circumstances, and who beheld the sudden and remarkable change of his fortune.[2] Born and brought up amid civil dissentions; surrounded by nobles, many of whom possessed a power little inferior to his own; exposed to numerous plots, by which his life was endangered, or which tended to lay a restraint upon his person, and under his name, to convey the exercise of government to his rebellious subjects; in such a situation he received his political education, and his early habits were formed. But no sooner was he seated upon the Eng-<152>lish throne, than he began to hold a language, and to discover pretensions, that would have suited the most absolute monarch upon the face of the globe. There is, however, in reality, nothing uncommon or singular in this appearance. None are so likely to abuse their power as those who have recently obtained it; none so apt to be guilty of extravagant profusion, as those who have suddenly been raised from poverty to great riches; whether it be, that they are intoxicated by the novelty of their situation; or, from a consciousness of their former inferiority, are jealous, lest they should not appear with sufficient dignity in their new station.

Though, in his private deportment, James had no tincture of arrogance or superciliousness, he set no bounds to his authority as a king. He found that the aristocracy, by which he had been so much harassed in Scotland, was reduced in England from a state of rivalship to that of subordination and dependence; but he overlooked the influence and rank which had at the same time been acquired by the great <153> body of the people. He saw that the sovereigns in the principal European kingdoms, exercised an arbitrary and despotical power; and, without examining the means by which it had been acquired, or the circumstances by which it was maintained, he seems to have thought that, from the extent and opulence of his own dominions, he was entitled to follow their example. In public as well as in private, in his

2. For Hume's discussion of the character and behavior of James I, see *HE,* 5:121–23.

letters and speeches to parliament, and in his ordinary conversation, the divine, hereditary, indefeasible right of kings to govern their subjects without controul, was always a favourite topic. This was the fundamental principle of that *kingcraft,* to which, as he frequently declared, he had served so long an apprenticeship, and which therefore he pretended fully to understand. That his prerogative was absolute and unlimited; that the concurrence of parliament was not necessary in any of the acts of government; and that all the privileges of the people, were mere voluntary concessions made by his ancestors, which he might revoke at pleasure; these were propositions which <154> he not only maintained, but which he would not suffer to be questioned. "As to dispute," said he, "what God may do, is blasphemy; so it is sedition to dispute what a king may do in the height of his power."[3] Even the judges, when called upon, in the execution of their duty, to decide between the king and the people, were prohibited from canvassing the rights of the crown. "Deal not," says his majesty, "in difficult questions, before you consult with the king and council, for fear of wounding the king through the sides of a private person. The absolute prerogative of the crown is no subject for the tongue of a lawyer, nor is it lawful to be disputed."*

We may easily suppose, that the same principles and doctrines which were thus openly avowed by the sovereign, were propagated at court, and embraced by all who wished to procure the royal favour and patronage. "When Waller,[4] the poet, was young, he had the curiosity to go to court; and he stood in the circle and <155> saw James dine; where, among other company, there sat at table two bishops, Neile and Andrews.[5] The king proposed aloud this question, whether he might not take his subjects' money, when he needed it, without all this formality of parliament? Neile replied, *God forbid you should not; for you are the breath of our nostrils.* Andrews declined answering, and said he was not skilled in parliamentary cases; but upon the king's urging him, and saying he would admit of no evasion, the bishop

* King James's Works.

3. For a modern edition of Millar's quotations from James I, see *King James VI and I: Political Writings,* ed. J. P. Sommerville (Cambridge: Cambridge University Press, 1995), 184 and 214.

4. Edmund Waller (1606–87): English poet and royalist politician.

5. Richard Neile (1562–1640) held many important bishoprics, including Rochester, Durham, and York. Lancelot Andrewes (1555–1626), bishop of Winchester 1619–26, assisted with the King James translation of the Bible in 1604.

replied pleasantly; why then I think your majesty may lawfully take my brother Neile's money, for he offers it."*

That writers were easily found to inculcate similar doctrines, cannot be doubted. In the books published by Cowel and Blackwood,[6] it was roundly asserted, that from the Norman conquest, the English government had been an absolute monarchy; that the king was not bound by the laws, or by his coronation oath; and that, independent <156> of parliament, he possessed the power of legislation, and that of imposing taxes.

Widely different from this was the idea of the constitution entertained by the house of commons. They considered it as a mixed form of government, in which the king was merely the chief executive officer, and in which the legislative power, together with that of taxation, was vested in parliament. So far from admitting the king to be above the laws, or his being entitled to change the form of government at pleasure, they looked upon him as only the guardian and protector of the constitution; placed in that high station, not for his own benefit, but in order to promote the happiness and prosperity of his people. They well knew, that at no period of the English history was the sovereign ever possessed of an unlimited authority; that, in the latter part of the Anglo-Saxon government, and under the princes of the Norman and Plantagenet race, the chief power was in the hands of the nobility, or great proprietors of land; and that, when the advancement of manufactures and of agri-<157>culture, in the reigns of the Tudor princes, had contributed to dismember the estates, and to diminish the influence of the nobles, the same change of circumstances tended to advance the middling and lower classes of the people, and to bestow proportional weight and authority upon that branch of parliament composed of the national representatives. Between the decline of the nobility and the exaltation of the people, there had indeed occurred an interval, during which the monarch had endeavoured to extend his prerogative; but his endeavours had met with constant opposition, and had proved ineffectual for destroying the fundamental

* Hume's History of England. [[For Millar's quotation from Hume, see *HE,* 5:60.]]

6. John Cowell (1554–1611): English jurist and regius professor of civil law at Cambridge. His *Interpreter* (1607) was a glossary of legal terms that was censured for its absolutist opinions. Adam Blackwood (1539–1613) was a Scottish Catholic legal philosopher trained in France and best known for his *De Vinculo Religionis et Imperii* (1575) and *Apologia pro Regibus* (1581), both intended as defenses of divinely instituted monarchical authority.

privileges of parliament, or subverting, in any degree, the ancient fabric of the constitution.[7] Nothing could betray more gross ignorance and misinformation, than to believe that the crown of England was enjoyed by a divine, indefeasible, hereditary right; for nothing is more certain than that, had it been transmitted upon that principle, it never could have devolved upon the house of Stewart; and that the lineal succession of the English royal family was <158> frequently broken, in some cases by occasional usurpation, in others by the interposition of the national council. By an act of the legislature, in the reign of queen Elizabeth, it is declared to be high treason for any person to assert that parliament has no right to vary and settle the succession to the crown.

Fortunately the talents of James were ill-suited to the task of subverting the ancient government. Whatever might be his abilities as a scholar, or his proficiency in the literature of the times, his understanding and discernment in the conduct of life were greatly below mediocrity. Nature had formed him for a pedagogue, and intended he should wield no better instrument than a birch. Possessed with the lofty idea of absolute monarchy in church and state, he seems to have thought that, by mere dint of argument, he could persuade the English nation to become slaves; and he provided no ultimate resources for carrying his design into execution. Mean and contemptible in his amusements and pleasures, weak and childish in his affections, his <159> behaviour, upon ordinary occasions, was not only unbecoming the dignity of a king, but inconsistent with common decorum and propriety. Though obstinate and conceited, he was highly susceptible of flattery; and though not exempted from avarice, he was profuse in his expences, and extravagantly liberal to his favourites. These were commonly chosen from a regard to their beauty of person; and as they gained an entire ascendancy over him, their incapacity and profligacy, joined to his own folly and arbitrary views, rendered his government equally odious and ridiculous.

One of the chief sources of dispute, after the accession of James the First, was the money required for supplying the exigencies of the sovereign. Many circumstances, independent of the bad economy of the prince, contributed to render this an object of much greater magnitude than it had formerly

7. In recounting the views of the Commons on the constitution, Millar is tacitly disputing Hume's view that under the Tudors, the monarchy exercised a complete authority over government, not one that "met constant opposition." See *HE,* 4:383–85.

been. The difficulties in which Elizabeth, from her peculiar situation, was involved, had obliged her to alienate a great proportion of the ancient revenue of <160> the crown. The increase, on the other hand, of the quantity of the precious metals, since the discovery of America, had debased that part of the ancient crown revenue which was payable in money; while the influx of national wealth, from the advancement of trade and manufactures, by increasing the expence of living to each individual, had also augmented charges attending the administration of government. The demands of the crown were thus daily increasing, at such a rate as to render its old patrimony more and more insignificant, and to give room for expecting that the chief part of the public revenue was for the future to be derived from the taxes imposed on the people. So new, and so disagreeable a prospect, excited alarm and discontent throughout the nation. As the public supplies granted in former periods were inconsiderable, and took place only in extraordinary cases, it was of little consequence how the money was bestowed; but now, when the ordinary funds of the crown were shrunk almost to nothing, and when the <161> executive power was, in a great measure, to be maintained by extraordinary contributions, creating a permanent burden upon the nation, it behoved the parliament, and in particular it was the duty of the lower house, entrusted with the guardianship of the people, to watch over the rising demands of the sovereign, and to be cautious of introducing such precedents of taxation as might be hurtful to the community.

The religious divisions of the kingdom became another source of alarm and jealousy, and the occasion of many disputes between the king and parliament. The adherents of the Romish religion, who still were numerous and opulent, regarded the protestants, not only with the abhorrence produced by the most violent opposition of theological tenets, but with the rage and resentment of a losing party against those who had stript them of their ancient power, dignity, and emoluments. Of this the gunpowder conspiracy,[8] formed by persons of some rank, and who had formerly borne respectable characters, affords a shocking, and a singular proof. <162>

Had the Roman catholics in England been merely a branch of the sec-

8. On November 5, 1605, a group of Catholics led by Robert Catesby attempted to blow up James I, the Lords, and the Commons at the opening of Parliament. Their agent was Guy Fawkes. The anniversary merged with earlier Protestant November celebrations to become a permanent commemoration.

taries, depending upon their own efforts for procuring influence and popularity, it must be admitted, that from the spirit now diffused over the kingdom, the terrors of the growth of popery would have been entirely groundless. But the influence and power of that party were, at this time, regarded in a different light. The Roman catholics in England were zealously supported by those of the same persuasion in all the countries of Europe; and the restoration of popery in this kingdom was one of the great objects, not only of the Roman pontiff, but of all the princes who acknowledged his jurisdiction. For this end, no pains nor expence had been spared. Seminaries for the education of the English youth in the principles of that religion were established in different parts of Europe; secret emissaries were spread over England, and insinuated themselves among the religionists of every sect and description; and pecuniary, as well as other advantages, were held out in order to make proselytes, or to <163> confirm and encourage the friends of the party. In such a situation, it is not surprising that, from the remembrance of their former power, and the experience of their tyranny and virulence, they should have excited a national apprehension, and that it should have been deemed a salutary regulation to exclude them from offices of trust and consequence.

The king, however, from causes which have already been explained, discovered a disposition to favour and indulge the Roman catholics, declaring, that if they would renounce their peculiar subjection to the authority of the Pope, they ought to be admitted to the same privileges with the members of the church of England; but he was far from holding the same liberal opinion with respect to the protestant dissenters, who, about this time, on account of their pretensions to austerity of manners, came to be distinguished by the name of puritans.*

These two articles, therefore, the obtain-<164>ing supplies, and the enforcing the penal laws against the Roman catholics, were, during the reign of James the First, continual subjects of contention between the king and parliament.

In calling his first parliament, an attempt was made by James to over-rule the elections of the commons, which, had it proved successful, would have rendered that house entirely subservient to the will of the king. He issued a proclamation, declaring what particular descriptions of persons were inca-

* See Rapin's History of England.

pable of being elected, and denouncing severe penalties upon such as transgressed the rules which he had prescribed. Sir Francis Goodwin having been elected member for the county of Buckingham, it was pretended that his election was void according to that proclamation; and the question being brought before the court of chancery, his seat was vacated. The county, upon this, proceeded to choose another representative; but the commons paid no regard to that sentence, and declared Sir Francis the member duly elected. They justly considered themselves as having the <165> sole right to determine the validity of the elections of their own members; a privilege essentially requisite to secure the independence of their house. Sensible of its importance, they resolutely maintained this constitutional point, and James, having urged them to a conference with the peers, and afterwards demanded in a peremptory tone that they would consult his judges, it was at last agreed, by a species of compromise, that both competitors should be set aside, and a writ issued for a new election.* <166>

In this parliament, which first met in the year 1604, and was continued through five different sessions to the year 1610, the sums demanded by the king were several times refused by the commons; who repeatedly, but in vain, petitioned the throne to execute the penal statutes against popish recusants, and endeavoured to procure a relaxation of such as had been enacted against the protestant dissenters. As the monarch found so much difficulty in obtaining money from the national assembly, he employed other expedients for augmenting his revenue. The advancement of trade suggested the *customs,* as a growing fund, the profits of which, without exciting much attention, and without any application to parliament, might be gradually enlarged. By his own authority, therefore, he ventured to alter the rate of those burdens, and to impose higher duties upon various branches of merchandize

* In a remonstrance to the king, the commons assert, "That, until the reign of Henry the Fourth, all parliament writs were returnable into parliament; and that though chancery was directed to receive returns, this was only to keep them for parliament, but not to judge in them." They conclude with observing, "that the inconvenience would be great, if the chancery might, upon *suggestions* or *sheriff's returns,* send writs for new elections, and those not subject to examination in parliament. For so, when fit men were chosen by the counties and boroughs, the Lord Chancellor, or the sheriffs, might displace them, and send out new writs until some were chosen to their liking; a thing dangerous in precedent for the time to come. Howsoever," say they, "we rest securely from it at present, by the now Lord Chancellor's integrity." Parliamentary History, vol. v. [[The Goodwin versus Sir John Fortescue contest took place in 1604.]]

than had been formerly exacted. The illegality of these exactions was indisputable; at the same time they <167> created an apprehension the more universal, because, from the necessities of the crown, they were likely to be pushed to a far greater extent, and because they were plainly calculated to lay a foundation for claiming the general power of taxation as a branch of the prerogative. They gave rise, therefore, to violent debates in the house of commons, which, however, were cut short by a sudden dissolution of parliament.

There followed an interval of three years, in which the king endeavoured to supply his wants by the regal authority, and in which, among other contrivances for obtaining money, loans and benevolences were indirectly extorted from the people. But these expedients having proved insufficient, James, by the advice of his ministers, who undertook to manage the elections, was persuaded, in the year 1614, to make trial of a new parliament. The experiment was without success. In this house of commons there appeared such a spirit, as made it evident that no supplies could be obtained until the late abuses of the prerogative <168> should be corrected. With these terms the king was not willing to comply; upon which account this parliament, after sitting a few weeks, and without having finished any business whatever, was, like the former, suddenly dissolved, with strong marks of his anger and resentment; and several members of the house of commons, who had been the most active in opposing the measures of the court, were committed to prison.*

James had now resolved, it should seem, to call no more meetings of parliament; and in this resolution he persisted about seven years. But the loss of the Palatinate,[9] from which his son-in-law, the elector, the great supporter of the protestant interest in Germany, was expelled, afforded him a plausible pretence for demanding parliamentary aid; and he again had recourse to that assembly in the year 1621. The measure proposed was highly popular throughout the nation; and parliament gave him two subsidies with the utmost alacrity; but finding, soon after, that the <169> money was diverted to other purposes, and most ineffectually and foolishly squandered

* Wilson.—Hume.

9. The Palatinate was one of the electorates of the Holy Roman Empire. The Elector Palatine, Frederick V (1596–1632), married Elizabeth, the daughter of James I, and was elected king of Bohemia in 1619 in the early phase of the Thirty Years' War.

away, they refused to give any more. The commons, in the mean time, proceeded, as formerly, to an examination of grievances; among which the favour shewn to the Roman catholics was the principal. The terrors of the nation on this head had been increased by two circumstances.

The first was the avowed intention of James to marry his son, the prince of Wales, to the Infanta of Spain; a measure which gave rise to universal apprehensions that it would be productive of dangerous concessions in favour of the Romish religion. The other was the apparent backwardness of the king to make any vigorous exertion for the recovery of the Palatinate, which was considered by the nation as the common cause of protestants. Upon these topics the house of commons took the liberty of presenting to the king a petition and remonstrance, which he regarded as an insult to the royal dignity. Enraged at their presumption, he commanded them not to interfere in these mysteries of go-<170>vernment; threatened them with punishment in case of disobedience, and reminded them that all their privileges were derived from the mere grace and permission of him and his ancestors. The commons were neither intimidated by those threats, nor disposed to acquiesce in such arrogant pretensions. They protested, "that the liberties, franchises, privileges, and jurisdictions of parliament are the ancient and undoubted birth-right and inheritance of the subjects of England; and that the defence of the realm, and of the Church of England, the maintenance and making of laws, and the redress of mischiefs and grievances, which daily happen within this realm, are proper subjects and matter of debate in parliament."* With this protestation the king was so incensed, that, at a meeting of the privy council, he tore it, with his own hands, from the journals of the commons; and having soon after dissolved the parliament, he threw into prison several members of the lower, and some also of the <171> upper house. Among the former, Sir Edward Coke, and Sir Robert Philips, were committed to the Tower; Mr. Selden, Mr. Pym, and Mr. Mallory, to other prisons.[10] Some, as a lighter punishment, were sent out of the

* Parliamentary History. [[See *Cobbett's Parliamentary History of England,* vol. 1 (London, 1806).]]

10. Sir Edward Coke (1552–1634), English jurist and politician, author of the *Institutes of the Laws of England* (1628–44); Sir Robert Philips (d. 1650?) was confessor to Queen Henrietta Maria; John Pym (ca. 1584–1643) was a leading militant politician in opposition to Charles I; on Selden see p. 367, asterisked note.

kingdom, upon pretence of executing public business, which employments they were not permitted to refuse.*

In the fourth and last parliament of James, which was called in the year 1623, there occurred no dispute with the crown. The treaty with Spain, to which neither the influence of the national assembly, nor the voice of the people, could produce the least interruption, was at length broken off by the caprice of his favourite, Buckingham;[11] and as this occasioned a war with which the nation was highly satisfied until the real ground of the quarrel was discovered, the king found no difficulty in procuring the necessary supplies.

Besides the two leading articles above-mentioned, there were other subjects of importance which attracted the notice of par-<172>liament, and became the ground of controversy.

The king, as the superior of trading towns, and the patron of their commerce and manufactures, had early assumed the power of creating royal boroughs, and of erecting, in each of those communities, inferior corporations of particular trades. By an easy transition, he had thence been led to grant, in particular branches of trade, exclusive privileges to individuals, or to trading companies. These monopolies, in the infancy of trade, had been accounted necessary, or at least beneficial, for carrying on extensive and hazardous undertakings; but, in proportion to the advancement of commerce, such extraordinary encouragements, from the increase of mercantile capitals, became less needful; at the same time that they were found more inconvenient, by narrowing the field of free competition among traders. The king was, besides, under the temptation of abusing his power of granting these monopolies, by bestowing them for money, or obtaining a share in the profit of the trade which they <173> were intended to encourage. Complaints of such abuses had been made in the reign of queen Elizabeth; they became still more frequent in that of James, when the wants of the crown had left no expedient unattempted for procuring money; but at length, by the vigorous interposition of parliament, the sovereign was prevailed upon to limit the disposal of those grants, and several important regulations upon this point were introduced.†

* Parliamentary History.

† Parliamentary History, vol. v. and vi.

11. George Villiers, fourth duke of Buckingham (1592–1628), courtier and favorite of James I.

From the manner in which the legislative business was conducted, a bill, being originally conceived in the form of a petition to the king, required the approbation of parliament before it could be presented to his majesty for the royal assent. Hence it became unusual, and was at length regarded as irregular, that the king should take notice of any bill, while it was depending before either house. At what time the uniformity of practice, in this respect, may be considered as having established an invariable rule in the constitution, it is <174> difficult to determine; though it is clear that queen Elizabeth did not conceive herself to be precluded from stopping bills in parliament at any stage of their progress. In the year 1607, James objected to a petition laid before parliament concerning popish recusants; and it was insisted that the petition should not be read: to which it was answered, "that this would be a great wound to the gravity and liberty of the house." The speaker replied, "that there may be many precedents in the late queen's time, where she restrained the house from meddling in petitions of divers kinds." Upon this a committee was appointed, "to search and consider of such precedents, as well of ancient as of later times, which do concern any messages from the sovereign magistrate, king or queen of this realm, during the time of parliament, touching petitions offered to the house of commons." Two days thereafter, the petition, by the king's consent, was read; and the following declaration appears on the record: *"that his majesty hath no meaning to infringe our* <175> *privileges by any message; but that his desire is, we should enjoy them with all freedom."** It should seem that hence-forward no monarch of England has ventured to dispute this privilege of parliament.

During the whole reign of James, the behaviour of the commons was calm, steady, and judicious, and does great honour to the integrity and abilities of those eminent patriots by whom the determinations of that assembly were chiefly directed. Their apprehensions concerning the prevalence of popery were, perhaps, greater than there was any good reason to entertain; but this proceeded from the prejudice of the times; and to judge fairly of the spirit with which, in this particular, the members of parliament were animated, we must make allowance for the age and country in which they lived, and for the occurrences which were still fresh in their memory. Though placed in circumstances that were new and criti-<176>cal, though heated by

* See the journals of the house of commons, on the 16th and 18th of June, 1607. [[See *Cobbett's Parliamentary History of England,* vol. 1 (London, 1806).]]

a contest in which their dearest rights were at stake, and doubtless alarmed by the danger to which, from their perseverance in their duty, they were exposed, they seem to have kept at an equal distance from invading the prerogatives of the crown, and betraying the liberties of the people. They defended the ancient government with vigour; but they acted merely upon the defensive; and it will be difficult to shew that they advanced any one claim which was either illegal or unreasonable. The conduct of James, on the other hand, was an uniform system of tyranny, prosecuted according to the scale of his talents. In particular, his levying money without consent of parliament, his dispensing with the laws against popish recusants, and his imprisoning and punishing the members of parliament for declaring their opinions in the house, were manifest and atrocious violations of the constitution.

This last exertion of arbitrary power some authors have endeavoured to excuse, or palliate, by alleging that it was con-<177>formable to the practice of queen Elizabeth. But the apology, such as it is, must be received with some limitations in point of fact; though in both cases the measure was arbitrary and violent, the grounds upon which it was adopted, by James and by Elizabeth, were widely different. Elizabeth imprisoned the members of the house of commons, because they proposed to abridge those powers which the crown indisputably possessed. If the crown was at liberty to interpose a negative upon bills before they had finished their progress in either house of parliament (and perhaps, in the days of Elizabeth, the contrary had not become an established rule) the behaviour of those members who, after the interposition of such negative, endeavoured to revive the debate, and to push on the business, might be considered as irregular, and as an invasion of the prerogative. The ultimate aim of Elizabeth was to prevent innovation, and to maintain the form of government transmitted by her ancestors, though the measures employed for that purpose could not be defended. But the <178> imprisonment of the members by James, was in support of a fixed resolution to overturn the constitution. This violent step was taken in the year 1614, because the commons refused to grant the supply which he demanded; and in the year 1621, because they had asserted that their privileges were their birth-right, and had remonstrated against the dispensing power exercised by the crown in favour of popish recusants. As they had an undoubted right to act in that manner, the king, when he punished them upon that account, cannot be regarded as defending his prerogative; his object was to deprive the commons of their most important privileges, and to convert the mixed government of England into a pure despotism.

The first fifteen years of the reign of Charles presented nearly the same view of political parties which had occurred in the reign of his father, and particularly the same objects of contention between the house of commons and the sovereign. Charles had thoroughly imbibed his father's arbitrary principles; at the same time that, <179> by greater steadiness and capacity, and by the superior gravity and decorum of his deportment, he was better qualified to effect his purposes. During the controversy in the former reign, both parties had become gradually more keen and determined; and, from greater experience, their measures had been rendered more systematic. They looked farther beyond the points in agitation, and were less actuated by their immediate feelings and passions, than by the consideration of distant consequences. In the original state of the controversy it appears that parliament, in demanding a rigorous execution of the laws against popish recusants, had been stimulated by the general apprehension concerning the growth of popery; and that the reluctance expressed by the king to comply with these demands, had proceeded from his belief of that religion being favourable to the exaltation of the crown, together with the views he had formed of marrying his son, the prince of Wales, to a Roman catholic princess. But in the reign of Charles, the parliament complained of <180> abuses committed by the crown, not so much from their own magnitude, as because they seemed parts of a regular system, and might afterwards become precedents of despotical power; and the king refused to reform these abuses, chiefly because he was unwilling to admit, that the redress of grievances might be extorted by parliament as the condition of granting supplies.

Money was wanted by Charles to carry on the war with Spain; and as this war had been a popular measure, and undertaken with consent of parliament, the king flattered himself that a liberal supply would readily be obtained. But several circumstances concurred to change, in this respect, the sentiments of the people, and to render them now averse from an undertaking which they had formerly embraced with general satisfaction. The rupture with Spain was at first beheld in England with universal joy and exultation, because it prevented the heir of the crown from marrying a Roman catholic princess; and because it produced an expectation that the <181> king would be induced to join the protestant league in Germany. But the marriage of Charles to a daughter of the house of Bourbon, which happened soon after, demonstrated that, though James had varied his measures, his object was invariably the same; and that no regard to the religious apprehensions of his people, or to the preservation of public tranquillity, could divert him from his purpose of uniting the prince of Wales with a Roman catholic consort.[12]

The marriage treaty with France contained even higher concessions to the English Roman catholics than had been proposed in the former stipulations with Spain. In particular, it provided that the children should be under the care and direction of their mother, and consequently might be educated in the Popish religion till the age of thirteen; though by the projected Spanish treaty, that maternal direction was limited to the age of ten. Whatever dangers, therefore, had been foreseen from the marriage with the infanta, these were <182> increased rather than diminished by the French alliance.

The blunders, too, which had been committed, the ignorance and incapacity displayed in the management of the war, contributed to cool the ardour of the people, and to disgust them with a measure which, under such directors, had so little the appearance of producing any good effect. They had even the mortification to observe, that one of the first fruits of the treaty with France was, the lending the ships of England to the French monarch, for the purpose of reducing his protestant subjects;* and that the English forces were thus employed in ruining that very cause which parliament, in advising the war, had intended to support.

The secret transactions which had occasioned the rupture with Spain, and which had now transpired, could not fail to co-operate with the foregoing circumstances, and to become a separate ground of dissatisfaction and distrust. The war <183> with Spain was undertaken upon pretence of the insincerity and double-dealing of that court with relation to the marriage-treaty; and parliament had consented to this war in consequence of the strong and solemn representation to that purpose, given by Charles and the duke of Buckingham. But the real ground of the dispute was a private quarrel between that favourite and the count Olivarez, the Spanish minister;[13] and the account which had been laid before parliament was an artful system of falsehood, calculated at once to take advantage of the national aversion from the Spanish alliance, and to rouse the public indignation and resent-

* Rushworth, i. 174.

12. In 1625, Charles I married Henrietta Maria, the daughter of Henri IV, king of France (r. 1589–1610), and Maria de Medici.

13. Gaspar de Guzman, Count Olivares (1587–1645). Appointed chief minister on the accession of Philip IV (1621), he attempted to reassert Spanish strength throughout Europe.

ment for the unworthy treatment which their prince was understood to have suffered.

In a matter of this kind, however, the truth could not long be concealed. The arrogant and supercilious behaviour of Buckingham while in Spain, and the menaces which he had been vain enough to throw out against the Spanish minister, were not unknown to Bristol, the English ambassador,[14] and to many other persons <184> who had an interest that the people of England should be undeceived. It appears from lord Clarendon,[15] that king James knew the real state of the fact, at the very time when his son and the duke were imposing their fictitious narrative upon parliament;* and in the first year of the reign of Charles, we find hints thrown out in the house of commons, *that Buckingham had broken the Spanish match from spleen and malice to the count Olivarez.*†

It must have been highly mortifying to an English parliament, to find that they were made the dupes of a profligate minister, and had involved the nation in a war to gratify his vanity and resentment. They could, at the same time, have but little confidence in their present sovereign, who was implicitly governed by that minion, and who had shewn himself so unprincipled as to sacrifice his own honour to the wicked designs of his favourite.

Some authors have alleged as an apology <185> for Charles, that he himself might be deceived, and that he might really believe the story told by his minister. But this it seems hardly possible to conceive. That prince must be supposed a perfect changling, not to have discovered the particulars of a quarrel which was known to the whole court of Spain, which by his peculiar situation he had so many opportunities of observing, and which Buckingham, under the immediate impressions of resentment, had been at no pains either to cover or disguise.

In these particular circumstances, it is not surprising that, upon the first meeting of parliament, in the reign of Charles, that assembly, though strongly urged to support a war undertaken by its own recommendation, should testify no great zeal in prosecuting the views of the monarch. After

* History of the Rebellion, vol. i. p. 22.

† Rushworth's Collections.—Whitelock's Memorials.

14. John Digby, first earl of Bristol (1580–1653).

15. Edward Hyde, first earl of Clarendon (1609–74), English statesman and historian. Clarendon wrote the royalist *History of the Rebellion and Civil Wars in England,* which was not published until 1702–4.

the house of commons had granted two subsidies, which Charles regarded as very inadequate to his necessities, they proceeded to examine the mismanagement of the revenue, and the unseasonable indulgence and <186> favour shewn by the crown to popish recusants.*

The principal transactions in the two first parliaments of Charles, present nearly the same general aspect of the controversy between the crown and the people, which had occurred in the reign of his father; the king eagerly demanding supplies; threatening that, unless his demands are complied with, he must have recourse to other methods of procuring money; and declaring that, as the existence of parliaments depends entirely upon his will, they must expect, according to their behaviour, either to be continued or laid aside. Parliament, on the other hand, with inflexible resolution, insisting upon the previous redress of grievances; its members imprisoned, and called to account for their behaviour in that assembly; repeated dissolutions of parliament for its perseverance in refusing to grant the sums demanded; and each dissolution followed by the arbitrary <187> exaction of loans and benevolences, and by such other expedients as the crown could put in practice for procuring money.†

The third parliament in this reign was called on account of the extraordinary expences and difficulties in which the king was involved by the war with France; a war occasioned partly by a misunderstanding between Charles and his queen, which had produced the dismission of all her French servants, and partly by the levity, the insolence, and the precipitate rashness of Buckingham.‡ The accumulation of abuses, in every department of regal authority, now filled the kingdom with indignation. To the same spirit which had animated the two preceding houses of commons, the members of this parliament joined an experience of the measures which the king had hitherto pursued; and as, from these, they could not fail to discern his deliberate purpose to establish an unlimited power in the crown, so they were determined, with firmness and unanimity, <188> to stand forward in defence of their privileges. Through the whole of their proceedings we may observe a regular system, planned with consummate wisdom, and executed with equal steadiness and moderation. No menaces could shake them; no artifice could de-

* See Parliamentary History—Rushworth's Collections—Whitelock's Memorials.

† See Parliamentary History—Rushworth's Collections—Whitelock's Memorials.

‡ Whitelock—Hume.

ceive their vigilance; no provocation could ruffle their temper, or make them forget either the dignity of their station, or the decency of expression which became subjects in addressing their sovereign.

The language held by the king, at the opening of this assembly, was lofty and imperious. He informed them, in direct terms, that "unless they did their duty in contributing what the state required, he would be obliged to use the other means which God had put into his hands. He desired they would not construe this into a threatening, *as he scorned to threaten any but his equals.* He promised, at the same time, to forgive what was past, if they would leave their former distractions, and follow the counsel which he had given them."* <189>

The commons entered immediately upon the consideration of grievances. These had become so numerous, and had acquired such magnitude, that, for procuring redress in the most effectual manner, it was thought proper to collect them in one view, and to bring them under the consideration of the legislature. This was done by the famous *petition of right,*[16] which, in the form of a bill, was laid before parliament, and after a full discussion, having passed through both houses, and obtained the royal assent, became a declaratory statute, ascertaining, in some of the most essential points, the acknowledged limitations of the prerogative, and the indisputable rights of the people.

This petition began with stating the ancient and most fundamental laws of the kingdom, from the great charter downwards, by which it is provided, that no tallage, aid, or other charge, shall be levied by the king, without consent of parliament; that no money shall be extorted from the subject, by way of loan or bene-<190>volence; and that no person shall be imprisoned, without being brought to answer by due process of law, or be deprived of his freehold, or otherwise suffer in his person or goods, but by the judgment of his peers, or by the law of the land. It afterwards enumerated the many gross violations of these privileges upon the part of the crown, by compelling the subjects to lend, or to contribute money to the king; by imprisoning individuals without any cause being specified, and by detaining them in prison without any charge being made, to which they might answer accord-

* Parliamentary History, v. vii.

16. Sir Edward Coke resurrected this formal appeal to the monarch in 1628. After grudgingly accepting it, Charles I ignored its provisions.

ing to law; by quartering soldiers upon the inhabitants, against the laws and customs of the realm; and by appointing commissioners to proceed in the trial of crimes according to the summary course of martial law. And lastly, it humbly prayed the king's most excellent majesty, that, for the future, all these abuses might be removed and prevented.

From the time when this petition was understood to be in agitation, Charles em-<191>ployed every artifice that could be devised for defeating its purpose. He procured numerous conferences between the two houses of parliament, and proposed many different schemes of accommodation. He acknowledged the faults of his administration, and promised of his own accord to remove all grounds of complaint. He represented the absurdity of making a new law to confirm an old one; and he prevailed upon the house of lords to move the addition of a clause, that by this deed the sovereign power of the king should be left unimpaired. But this ambiguous limitation was rejected by the commons.

When the petition had passed the house of lords, and was presented to the king for his concurrence, his presence of mind seemed entirely to forsake him, and instead of the simple expression used on such occasions, he returned an evasive answer, importing merely his will that the statutes of the realm should be put in due execution. So unprecedented a mode of speech, in that critical juncture, was more likely to create fresh jealousy than to afford satis-<192>faction; and he found it necessary, soon after, though with a bad grace, to give the royal assent in common form.*

It is remarkable, however, that to all the copies of this deed which, by the king's order, were dispersed over the kingdom, the first answer, and not the second, was annexed.† To such pitiful shifts was this monarch reduced, and so strongly did he evince his reluctance to acquiesce in this important transaction. When he could no longer evade, he endeavoured to conceal and to deceive.[17]

The legislature, by declaring the essential parts of the constitution, precluded, in appearance, all future disputes upon that subject. A bill for five subsidies was now passed through both houses of parliament, and carried

* Hume.

† Parliamentary Hist. vol. viii. anno 1628.

17. For Hume's account of Charles's evasive manner surrounding the petition of right, see *HE,* 5:197–200.

into effect. So large a supply had, in the beginning of the session, been held out to the king as the reward of his consenting to the *petition of right.* The commons, however, were not diverted by their late success, from the further consideration <193> of such grievances and abuses of administration as appeared still to require animadversion and redress: the dissipation of the revenue, the frequent dissolution of parliaments, the sale of indulgences to popish recusants, and the unlimited influence and power of the duke of Buckingham, to whom the public disgrace and mismanagement were chiefly imputed, became successively the objects of complaint and censure.

During a period when practical despotism continued to be the avowed object of the king, it is not surprising that a multitude of speculative reasoners were found willing to second his pretensions, and that the labours of the press, for that purpose, were openly employed and encouraged. Wherever men of letters form a numerous class, their ambition, the narrowness of their funds compared with their ideas of elegance, and their capacity of exercising many offices in the gift of the crown, are likely to produce a powerful body of mercenary writers, ready to enlist under the banner of prerogative, and possessed of <194> ingenuity to palliate, even to their own minds, the mean prostitution of their talents. Among these literary, or rather political auxiliaries, the first rank seems due to the clergy, on account of that peculiar zeal and good discipline which their professional education and circumstances are wont to create. Two ecclesiastics, Sibthorpe and Manwaring,[18] distinguished themselves by the preaching and publication of sermons, in which they inculcated doctrines entirely subversive of civil liberty; maintaining that the king is not bound to observe the laws; that the authority of parliament is not requisite in raising subsidies; that the sovereign has a right to demand loans and contributions at pleasure; that those who refuse payment of the taxes imposed by him, incur eternal damnation; in fine, that an implicit and unlimited obedience to his will is an indispensable religious duty. Archbishop Abbot,[19] whose political principles happened, it seems, not to coincide with those of the court, refused a license to Sibthorpe's publication; for which he was suspended from the exercise of <195> his ecclesiastical functions, and confined to one of his country seats. Manwaring's ser-

18. Roger Manwaring (1590–1653), chaplain to Charles I; Robert Sibthorp[e] (d. 1662), chaplain to Charles I.

19. George Abbot (1562–1633), archbishop of Canterbury, was suspended in 1627.

mon, upon inquiry, was found to have been printed by the special command of the king. The author was impeached by the commons, and condemned by the lords to a high fine. But he soon after received a pardon from the king, and afterwards was made a bishop.

Charles having felt the want of a standing army to enforce his measures, his attention had been directed to the methods of removing that inconvenience. Part of the troops employed in the war abroad had now returned home, and were kept in pay, for the purpose of rendering his exactions effectual. He had also remitted money to levy a thousand German horse, and had transported those foreign troops into England. This body was doubtless too small to perform any great service; but the precedent of introducing foreign mercenaries being once established, their number might easily be increased. Such a measure could not fail to alarm the <196> nation, and to call for the interposition of parliament.

After the *petition of right* had passed into a law, there was ground to expect that all disputes concerning the extent of the prerogative would, at least for some time, be completely removed. But a misunderstanding, with respect to the meaning of that declaratory statute, soon involved the king and the commons in fresh contention, and threatened to frustrate all the former labour for composing their differences.

Tonnage and *poundage* were duties on the importation and exportation of commodities, derived in early times from the protection and assistance which the merchant received from the public, and which, from the nature of his trade, was of the utmost advantage, if not indispensably necessary to him. When the amount of these duties became so considerable as to appear worthy of notice, they fell, of course, under the direction of parliament, and, like all other taxes, were imposed and regulated by that assembly. The grant was renewed from time to time, sometimes for a shorter, and <197> sometimes for a longer period; and as the burden fell, at least in the first instance, upon mercantile and sea-faring people, it was generally allotted for the purpose of guarding the seas, or of carrying on a foreign war. Towards the end of the Plantagenate race, a custom was introduced of granting these duties during the king's life; and under the princes of the Tudor family the same custom was continued. None of those princes, however, appear to have imagined that they had a right to levy this tax by virtue of their prerogative. The authority of parliament had always been esteemed necessary to the imposition of this, as well as of all other branches of taxation; and upon obtaining a grant for *tonnage* and *poundage,* the form of words used by the sovereign was the same as in all other subsidies: *The king heartily thanketh the subjects for their good wills.*

It is true, that in the beginning of several reigns, the crown officers were accustomed to levy tonnage and poundage before the first meeting of parliament, or before it <198> was convenient for that assembly to take the matter under their consideration. This irregularity, in that rude age, was overlooked, more especially as no claim of right in the king had ever been founded upon the practice, and as the subsequent application for an act of parliament to authorize the tax, was a clear acknowledgment of his own defect of power to levy it by virtue of his prerogative.

James was the first English monarch who directly and openly claimed a right to impose these duties, and who, by his regal authority, ventured to advance the rates of the customs upon merchandize, and to establish these burdens as a permanent revenue of the crown.* This measure had not failed in that reign to be brought, among other grievances, under the cognizance of the commons, who had unanimously determined that the king had no such right. Charles, however, had fol-<199>lowed his father's footsteps, and continued to levy the customs according to the advanced rates which he found already introduced. To ascertain this point, and put a stop to such arbitrary and illegal exactions, the commons, in the first parliament of this reign, had brought in a bill for granting tonnage and poundage for the very limited period of one year. But this limitation was not approved by the upper house. It was not to be expected that a matter of so great importance would be soon forgotten; and in the second parliament of Charles, we find that the levying tonnage and poundage, by virtue of the prerogative, made a principal grievance in the offensive remonstrance, for which that assembly was dissolved.

It is not a little surprising that, notwithstanding the proceedings in these two parliaments, the king, after he had, in the next parliament, given his assent to the petition of right, should still affect to consider tonnage and poundage, as in a different situation from other taxes, and as not comprehended under those regulations, <200> with respect to every species of taxation or public burden, which had, with so great anxiety, been provided by

* See the remonstrances on this subject, and the pleadings in the case of ship-money, preserved in Rushworth's Collections, vol. ii.

that fundamental transaction. Could it be supposed that, when parliament had prohibited the levying of any tax whatever, by the mere authority of the crown, they tacitly meant an exception of one branch of public revenue, in its consequences to national prosperity the most important, and the most liable to produce oppression and injustice? If such a supposition were possible, the behaviour of the commons in the two former parliaments must have been sufficient to remove it, by shewing that this branch of taxation had been so recently under their view, and that they invariably regarded it in the same light with other taxes.

It is probable that Charles, having obtained a supply of money, and being freed from those difficulties which had induced him to consent to the petition of right, had now begun to repent of his acceding to that deed, and was willing, by any, the most frivolous pretences, to evade the restrictions <201> which it imposed. However this may be, he continued to levy tonnage and poundage without the authority of parliament; and when the house of commons complained of this measure, considering it as a violation of the petition of right, he was highly displeased, and put a stop to their proceedings by a sudden prorogation.

In the beginning of the next session, he thought fit to assume a more moderate tone, and to relinquish his former pretensions. He declared that he had not taken these duties "as appertaining to his hereditary prerogative; but that it ever was, and still is, his meaning to enjoy them as a gift of his people; and that if he had hitherto levied tonnage and poundage, he pretended to justify himself only by the necessity of so doing, not by any right which he assumed."[20] As the parties were now agreed in their principle, the only question that could remain, related to the mode of granting this tax. The commons, considering the former claims both of the king and his father, and the powers which they had exercised in relation to <202> these duties, thought it necessary, for the future security of the people, that there should be an immediate interruption to the assessment before the new grant was bestowed. They were willing that the king should enjoy the tax to the same amount as formerly, but they insisted that he should receive it in such a manner as clearly to ascertain that it proceeded from the gift of parliament. But the king obstinately refused to accept it upon those terms; and he suddenly took the resolution of dissolving that assembly, rather than admit of

20. See *Cobbett's Parliamentary History of England,* vol. 1 (London, 1806).

a compromise apparently so unexceptionable. The alarm spread in the house of commons, upon receiving intelligence of this resolution, may easily be conceived. They immediately framed a remonstrance for the occasion. But the speaker refused to put the question upon it; and being urged by several members, declared, *that he had express orders from the king to adjourn, and to put no question.* Indignation, anxiety, and resentment, gave rise to unusual vehemence of speech and behaviour, and suggested a measure suited to the exigency. The <203> speaker was forcibly held in the chair until a protest was read, and approved by the general acclamation of the house.

The dissolution of parliament, in these unusual circumstances, was a plain intimation that Charles intended to keep no measures with his people. He immediately gave orders to prosecute those members of the house of commons who had distinguished themselves in the late violent proceedings. Sir John Elliot,[21] who had framed and read the last remonstrance; Mr. Selden, who had taken a great share in conducting the petition of right, as well as in the measures concerning tonnage and poundage, and whose learning and abilities gave him great weight with the party; Hollis and Valentine,[22] who had by force detained the speaker in his seat, with several others, whose conduct upon that occasion had rendered them obnoxious, were imprisoned, and examined before the privy council; but they refused to answer the interrogatories of any person, or to give to any court whatever an account of their behaviour in parliament. <204> After an imprisonment of thirty weeks, an offer was made that they should be admitted to bail, upon finding sureties for their good behaviour; but they declined accepting their liberty upon terms which they considered as inconsistent with their duty to their country. Sir John Elliot, Mr. Hollis, and Mr. Valentine, were brought to a trial in the King's-bench, and subjected to a high fine, and to imprisonment during the king's pleasure. The first of these gentlemen, who had distinguished himself as a leader in the cause, died in prison. Several of the members remained in confinement until the meeting of the next parliament in the year 1640.*

* See Pym's speech, Parliam. Hist. vol. viii. p. 427.

21. Sir John Elliot [Eliot] (1592–1632) was fined £2,000 and imprisoned until his death.

22. Denzil Holles, first Baron Holles (1599–1680), a political opponent of Buckingham; Benjamin Valentine (d. 1652?), a parliamentarian who joined in forcing Speaker Finch to allow Eliot to read his resolutions against Charles I in 1629.

From the dissolution of parliament in the beginning of the year 1629, Charles avowed his purpose of ruling without a parliament, and of raising the whole of the public supplies by his own authority.* From this period we are no longer to look upon the monarch as endeavouring secretly to undermine the <205> constitution, but as acting in open defiance of all those maxims upon which it had been established.

In the prosecution of this plan, however, he did not neglect those arts of corruption, which the experience of a later age has brought to greater maturity, but which, even at that time, were far from being unsuccessful. A few of the leading members of the last house of commons were now gained over to the interest of the crown, and obtained a distinguished rank in administration. Among these, the most noted was Sir Thomas Wentworth,[23] who, from being one of the most able and violent opposers of the prerogative, was prevailed upon to desert his former principles, and soon after became the confidant and prime minister of Charles.

It would be superfluous to enumerate the instances of tyranny and oppression exhibited in a period of more than eleven years, during which this arbitrary system was pursued. All the abuses which had formerly been complained of, and of which <206> redress had so often, and with so great solemnity been promised, were now repeated, and digested into a regular plan. All the powers of government were now centered in the monarch, and the rights and privileges formerly claimed by either house, were sunk in the prerogative.

Two of the measures which during this period excited universal attention, and contributed most remarkably to inflame the popular discontents, may be worthy of particular notice. The first was the imposition of ship-money;[24] an exaction which, from the time of its first introduction, had been greatly extended, and almost entirely altered in its nature. According to the English constitution, as well as that of the other feudal governments, all the military people were bound to assist in the defence of the kingdom, and might be required by the sovereign to attend him in the field with arms and provisions,

* See his proclamation, 1629. Parliam. Hist. vol. viii. p. 389.

23. Wentworth (1593–1641): created the first earl of Strafford, he was privy council and the most trusted member of Charles's entourage. He was executed in 1641.

24. A tax levied for naval defenses, initially only on coastal cities but later a more general form of taxation.

agreeable to the nature of their service. Upon the same principle, the maritime towns were liable to a peculiar <207> burden, corresponding to their circumstances; that of furnishing ships, with sailors and naval stores, which, upon any foreign invasion, or extraordinary exigence, might be demanded by the king, and employed under his direction. The mercantile part of the nation were thus put upon an equal footing with the rest of the community; being subjected to a duty corresponding to that kind of protection which they received from government, and to the nature of that support and defence which they were best qualified to afford.

The mercantile towns, however, were not obliged to build and prepare new ships, but only to furnish those of which they were already possessed; for this obvious reason, that if the extraordinary emergency which had created the demand, admitted such a delay as would be requisite for the building of new ships, it might afford unquestionably sufficient leisure for calling a parliament, and procuring its concurrence; a measure held, by the common law of England, and by the uniform tenor of the <208> statutes, to be indispensably necessary in the imposition of taxes.*

But the requisition made by Charles, under the appellation of ship-money, now assumed a very different form. It was not limited to the maritime towns; but extended also to the counties; and to those at a distance, as well as to those in the neighbourhood of the sea. He demanded, <209> not a number of ships; for of every thing relative to shipping, the inland counties were totally destitute; but a sum of money, to be employed at the discretion of the crown, for the purpose of procuring a naval armament. And, to crown

* See the proceedings in the case of ship-money, particularly the argument of Sir George Crooke, one of the justices of the King's-bench.—State Trials.

It appears, that though the ships were commonly furnished at the king's charge, yet, in some few cases, the expence was laid upon the towns. Of this complaints were made to parliament, and redress was given by a statute, 25 Edw. I. During the war with France, in the reign of Edward III. the king renewed the practice of requiring the maritime towns to prepare ships at their own expence; but this was again prohibited by a statute in the 14th of that reign. By an act of parliament [I Rich. II.] it was provided that such ancient cities, boroughs, or towns, as chose to fit out a single ship for the defence of the kingdom, should, without any fine or charge, obtain a confirmation of their charters; and, with exception of the voluntary armaments referred to in that statute, it became an established rule, that the maritime towns should not be burdened with the expence of the shipping which, by the king's orders, they were bound to furnish.

the whole, he made this demand, not on account of any foreign invasion, or of any public calamity, or danger requiring a sudden exertion of national force; but in times of profound peace and tranquillity, when he could find no other pretence, but that the sea had been infested with pirates; an enemy too insignificant, surely, to create any disturbance, and whose depredations might have easily been suppressed by the ordinary vigilance of the royal navy, and the ordinary supplies to be obtained by the interposition of parliament. In this form, ship-money became a general tax, imposed, in direct terms, by virtue of the prerogative, and subject to no controul from parliament; a tax which might be extended at pleasure, and of which the profits might be applied to any purpose whatever.

To smooth and prepare the way for this <210> imposition, Charles took the precaution of consulting the judges upon a fictitious case: whether ship-money could be demanded by the king when the necessities of the state should require it; and whether the king alone was the judge of such necessities? To the everlasting disgrace of the English courts of justice, those corrupt and pusillanimous guardians of the law returned an answer in the affirmative. Fortified by that opinion, the monarch was emboldened to pursue a measure which seemed to promise inexhaustible resources; and he ventured to employ the same methods for enforcing the payment of this duty, as if it had been levied by act of parliament.*

About four years after ship-money had begun to be enforced, Mr. Hampden[25] had the courage to refuse payment; and for the sum of twenty shillings, in which he had been assessed, brought the cause to a judicial determination. Of the abuses which, at this time, contributed to alarm the nation, it was not the least, that the arbitrary <211> spirit of the sovereign had perverted the streams, and poisoned the sources of justice. Upon a full hearing of all the judges, a very great majority concurred in pronouncing a sentence in favour of the crown; "which judgment," says my lord Clarendon,[26] "proved

* Rushworth's Collections.

25. John Hampden (1594–1643): English parliamentarian. He was prosecuted before the Court of Exchequer in 1637 for refusing to pay his share of ship-money, an event which made him extremely popular.

26. Edward Hyde, earl of Clarendon, *The History of the Rebellion and Civil Wars in England* (Oxford: Clarendon Press, 1888), 6:86.

of more advantage and credit to the gentleman condemned, than to the king's service."*

The innovations introduced by Charles in the forms of religious worship, and in the government of the church, though, perhaps, less directly subversive of the <212> constitution, were still more calculated to rouse and alarm the people; and had, in reality, an obvious and powerful tendency to increase the authority of the crown. From the behaviour and character of this monarch, some doubts have arisen with respect to his religious opinions. The gravity of his deportment, the sobriety and regularity of his private life, together with his apparent zeal in support of ecclesiastical dignity, procured him the reputation of piety and devotion; while his prepossession in favour of ridiculous ceremonies, and superstitious observances, in consequence of the good sense attributed to him, created a suspicion of artifice and hypocrisy. His friends have asserted his invariable attachment to the church of England: his enemies insinuate that he was a secret abettor of popery. That both he and his father were less adverse to the latter system of religion than to that of the puritans, cannot reasonably be denied. The fact seems to be, that in religious matters, these two princes were much guided by their political interest. As the hierarchy in <213> England was highly favourable to the regal authority, they endeavoured to extend and fortify it with all their might. By the abolition of the papal power in this country, the king, becoming the head of the church, and possessing the gift of the higher church livings, acquired a very absolute ascendancy over the superior members of that great incorporation. The spirit of inquiry introduced at the reformation, and the diffusion of knowledge which followed it, contributed, on the other hand, to relax the bands of ecclesiastical authority, and greatly to diminish that influence over the laity which churchmen had formerly maintained. It appears to have been the great object of Charles to repair, in these two re-

* Two judges, Crooke and Hutton, gave their opinion in favour of Mr. Hampden, upon the general merits of the question. The argument of the former, as delivered in the state trials, exhibits a clear view of the English constitution with respect to the ancient power of the crown in levying ship-money. Two other judges, Davenport and Denham, spoke also upon the same side. The former supported the right of the crown to levy ship-money, but thought the action void upon a point of form; the latter, at first gave his opinion for the crown, upon mistaking the plaintiff for the defendant, but afterwards corrected his mistake. He had from sickness been absent during part of the pleadings, and seems to enter very little into the matter.

spects, the ruins which time had produced; to renew and invigorate the ecclesiastical machine, so as to create a proper union and subordination of its different wheels and springs, and to render its movements more effectual in directing and governing the people. For this purpose, in conjunction with archbishop Laud,[27] his great spiritual minister, he ventured to <214> new model the liturgy; and, in the public services of religion, introduced a multitude of decorations and ceremonious observances, in imitation of those employed by the Roman catholics. Some authors appear to consider these as insignificant and ridiculous mummery, the offspring of mere folly and superstitious weakness; but there is no room to doubt that this pomp and pageantry of religious worship was intended to promote superstition among the populace; to exalt the clerical character, to create a high veneration for the sacerdotal functions, and a belief, with respect to the happiness of men in a future state, of the efficacy and indispensable necessity of the interposition and good offices of the church. He also established a new set of ecclesiastical canons, by which a stricter discipline, and a more absolute authority in the superior orders of churchmen was introduced; and these regulations were enforced with unremitting vigilance and with inflexible rigour. It is not impossible, that by these innovations Laud gratified that vanity and love of power which his rank and situation <215> contributed to inspire; while the king viewed them in a political light, as promoting his designs of managing the church, and, through her, of governing the nation. The court of star-chamber, and that of high-commission, were employed in punishing both laity and clergy who neglected, in the smallest article, to comply with these rules; and the bishops administered an oath to the churchwardens, that they would, without fear or affection, inform against all offenders.*

It was impossible entirely to suppress the indignation and clamour excited by these proceedings; but such as ventured openly to censure them, were sure to encounter the implacable resentment of an incensed and bigotted churchman, armed with the whole power of the state.

Some men of austere character, or of intemperate zeal, being found hardy enough to venture upon the publication of books, inveighing with great

* Rushworth.

27. William Laud (1573–1645): archbishop of Canterbury and the first minister of Charles I after the assassination of Buckingham in 1628. He was executed at the Tower of London.

acrimony against the usurpations of churchmen, and against the <216> levities and vices of the age, or supposed to contain insinuations against the measures of government, were treated with a degree of barbarity repugnant to the manners of a civilized nation. These authors, though of liberal professions, and in the rank of gentlemen, were condemned not only to an immoderate fine, but to the pillory, and to whipping in the severest manner, accompanied with the loss of their ears, and the slitting of their noses; and this outrageous and shocking punishment was, without the least mitigation, actually carried into execution.*

To prevent such publications as tended to inflame the minds of the people, it was ordained, by a decree of the star-chamber, in the year 1637, that the printers in the kingdom should be limited to a certain number, and that no book should be printed without a licence, or imported for sale without the inspection of persons appointed <217> for the purpose. This regulation was enforced with similar punishments.† What is called the liberty of the press was, doubtless, totally incompatible with the designs of administration.

From the same views which led to the exaltation of the hierarchy in England, Charles was equally solicitous of extending that favourite system of church policy to Scotland. By a variety of steps, many of which were highly arbitrary and illegal, James had already established a species of episcopal government in that country; but from the influence of the nobles, and other very opulent proprietors of land, who had obtained a great part of the ancient ecclesiastical revenues, he found it impossible to restore the bishops to that wealth and dignity which they enjoyed in times of popery, or which they still held in England. The <218> enthusiasm of the Scottish nation in favour of that mode of worship which they had established at the reformation, and their prejudices against the forms used in the English, as well as in the Roman catholic church, were well known to Charles; notwithstanding which he was not deterred from the attempt of compelling them to receive the new English canons and liturgy. The obstinacy with which he pur-

* See, in particular, the account given by historians, of the punishment inflicted upon Dr. Leighton, a Scotch presbyterian; on Prinne, a lawyer; on Burton, a divine; and on Bastwick, a physician.

† For printing and publishing without a licence, John Warton and John Lilburne were brought into the star-chamber, and upon refusing to answer interrogatories, were sentenced to a fine and the pillory. The latter, though a man of family, was likewise whipped through the streets, and otherwise treated with great barbarity.—Rushworth.

sued this object, even after the people had risen up in arms to oppose it, and had formed that solemn association known by the appellation of the *national covenant,* can hardly be imputed to the pretended motives, the mere love of order and uniformity in the external worship of the two kingdoms; but, in all probability arose from the desire of subjecting the people in Scotland as well as in England, to an order of men who, from their dependence upon the crown, were likely to be the zealous and constant supporters of the prerogative.

The Scottish army having reduced the king to great difficulties, he again found it expedient, after an interval of more than <219> eleven years, to call a parliament. But this meeting, which was held in April 1640, having, like the three former parliaments, insisted upon a redress of grievances previous to the granting of supplies, was quickly dissolved by the king; who, immediately after, imprisoned two of the commons, for refusing to answer interrogatories concerning their behaviour in the house.

Such, during the first fifteen years of the reign of Charles, were the chief matters in dispute between the king and parliament; and such were the chief circumstances in the conduct of either party.

From the whole behaviour of the king during this period; from numberless instances in which he publicly declared his political sentiments; from the countenance and favour which he shewed to the authors of doctrines entirely subversive of civil liberty; from his peremptory demands of supply, accompanied with menaces in case they should not be complied with; from his repeated dissolutions of parliament, for persisting to inquire into national grievances; and from his continuing, in <220> consequence of an avowed resolution, for so long a period as that of eleven years, to rule without the aid of any national council, and to levy money, both directly and indirectly, by his own authority; from all these circumstances it is manifest, that he considered himself as an absolute monarch, and that, although he made repeated applications to parliament for supplies, he was far from admitting the necessity of such an expedient, but claimed the power of imposing taxes as an inherent right of the crown.

It appears, at the same time, indisputable, that such doctrines and claims were inconsistent with the original constitution and fundamental laws of the kingdom. By the uniform series of statutes, from the reign of William the Conqueror, and according to the principles and maxims recognized and admitted in all public transactions, the legislative power, and that of imposing taxes, were exclusively vested in parliament. These laws, indeed, had been sometimes violated by particular princes, who had not always been called to account <221> for such violations. But these illegal measures of the crown were neither so numerous, so uniform, nor so long continued, as to make the nation forget that they were usurpations, or lose sight of those important privileges which had thus been invaded. The king was no more understood to have acquired a right to such powers, from his having occasionally exercised them, than individuals become entitled to commit rapine or theft, merely because they have sometimes been guilty of those crimes, and have had the good fortune to escape with impunity.

It is worthy of notice, that although several kings of England exacted money from their subjects without the authority of parliament, they never pretended to vindicate those proceedings, nor alleged that, by virtue of the prerogative, they had the right of imposing taxes. Henry VIII. the most powerful and arbitrary of all the Tudor princes, disclaimed any power of this nature; and upon one occasion, when cardinal Wolsey had set on foot a project for levying a tax by the regal authority, found <222> it necessary to quiet the minds of the people by an express declaration, that he asked nothing more than a benevolence or voluntary contribution.

When we examine, on the other hand, the conduct of the four first parliaments of Charles, there appears no good reason for suspecting them of any design to alter the constitution. The circumstances of the crown were such, at this time, as required particular attention to every proposal for new taxes, and rendered an extreme jealousy upon this point not only natural, but proper. From the alterations which had gradually and almost insensibly taken place in the state of society, the circumstances of the people with respect to taxation had been totally changed. The old revenue of the crown was become very inadequate to the expence of government; and as the estates of individuals were liable to supply the deficiency, the nation was deeply concerned, not only to prevent arbitrary impositions, but also to limit those burdens which every member of administration had continually an interest in accu-<223>mulating. Like sureties for a person in hazard of bankruptcy, it was incumbent on them to watch over the principal debtor, and to prevent his extravagance. As from the charges attending the civil and military establishments, the king could never be at a loss for pretences to demand money from his subjects, it was from this quarter that they were most in danger of oppression, and had most reason to guard against the encroachments of prerogative.

The alterations, at the same time, in the military state of the kingdom, were such as rendered unusual care and vigilance necessary to preserve the ancient constitution. While the feudal vassals continued to perform the military service, the people had the sword in their own hands; and, consequently, the means of defending themselves from oppression. But after the substitution of mercenary troops to the ancient feudal militia, the nation became an unarmed and timorous multitude, without discipline or capacity for any sudden exertion, and seemed to be entirely at the mercy of the king, who levied at pleasure, and <224> directed the whole military force. Had no new circumstance occurred upon the side of the people, to counterbalance the additional weight thus bestowed upon the crown, their liberties could not have been maintained. But the necessities of the king requiring continual grants of money from parliament, afforded this countervailing circumstance, by rendering him dependent upon the national representatives, and obliging him to listen to the complaints of his people. It was in this manner only that the prerogative could be retained within its ancient limits.

If parliament, however, had always been ready to supply the wants of the king; if they had never stood upon terms, and demanded a rectification of abuses as the condition of their consenting to taxes; their power would soon have dwindled into a shadow, and their consent would have become a mere matter of form. They would have soon found themselves in the same state with those ghosts of national councils, who continued to hover about the courts of some European monarchies, <225> and were still called to give an imaginary sanction to that will of the prince which they had no longer the capacity of opposing. By good fortune the imprudence of Charles, and still more that of his father, by discovering too plainly the lofty ideas they entertained of the regal authority, alarmed the fears of parliament; and the house of commons, by having the courage to *refuse,* preserved their privilege of bestowing the public money at a time when they had lost all other means of compulsion.

In the history of the world, we shall perhaps discover few instances of pure and genuine patriotism equal to that which, during the reign of James, and during the first fifteen years of the reign of Charles, was displayed by those leading members of parliament, who persevered, with no less temper than steadiness, in opposing the violent measures of the court. The higher exertions of public spirit are often so contrary to common feelings, and to the ordinary maxims of conduct in private life, that we are, in many cases, at a loss whether to condemn or to admire them. It may also be remarked, that in the most brillant examples <226> of heroism, the splendour of the achievement, at the same time that it dazzles the beholder, elevates and supports the mind of the actor, and enables him to despise the difficulties and dangers with which he is surrounded. When Brutus took away the life of Caesar, he ran counter to those ordinary rules which bind society together; but, according to the notions of his own age, he secured the applause and veneration of the worthier part of his countrymen. To perform a great service to our country by means that are altogether unexceptionable, merits a purer approbation; and if the action, while it is equally pregnant with danger, procures less admiration and renown, it affords a more unequivocal and convincing proof of true magnanimity and virtue. When Hampden, by an appeal to the laws of his country, exposed himself to the fury of Charles and his ministry, he violated no friendship, he transgressed no duty, public or private; and while he stood forth to defend the cause of liberty, he must have been sensible that his efforts, if ineffectual, would soon be neglected and forgotten; and that even if successful, they were less calculated to procure the ap-<227>plause of his contemporaries, than to excite the admiration and esteem of a grateful posterity.

To the illustrious patriots who remained unshaken during this period, we are indebted, in a good measure, for the preservation of that freedom which was banished from most of the other countries of Europe. They set the example of a constitutional resistance to the encroachments of prerogative; accommodated their mode of defence to the variations in the state of society which the times had produced; and taught the house of commons, by a judicious exercise of their exclusive right of taxation, to maintain and secure the rights of their constituents.

SECTION II

Of the Reign of Charles the First, from the Meeting of the Long Parliament to the Commencement of the Civil War.

The meeting of what is called the Long Parliament, towards the end of the year 1640, presented a new aspect of public affairs, and <228> seemed to require that the patriotic leaders of that assembly should embrace a new system of conduct. The designs of Charles had now been prosecuted for such a length of time, and displayed in such a variety of lights, as to become perfectly notorious. From his behaviour during his three first parliaments, it appeared, that though he condescended to procure money by parliamentary authority as the smoothest and safest course, he was far from acknowledging the necessity of this mode of procedure, but claimed, and whenever his occasions might require, was determined to exercise the prerogative of imposing taxes. In his intercourse, at the same time, with those assemblies, he had made no scruple to practise every artifice in his power, to intimidate them by threats, to work upon their hopes by temporising professions, and even to deceive them by direct promises. Of this there occurred a remarkable proof in the circumstances relating to the *petition of right,* a bill to which, after many evasions, he at length solemnly consented, but which he afterwards no less openly violated; a bill in which he plainly had renounced the errors of his former conduct, and <229> had in particular admitted, by an express and positive declaration, that the power of imposing taxes, or of levying from the people any sort of contribution or duty, was exclusively vested in parliament.

After the dismission of his third parliament, he had thrown off the mask, had avowed the resolution of reigning without the aid of those national councils; and for more than eleven years, had continued to usurp all the supreme powers of government, levying money, not only by the indirect means formerly practised, but also by the direct imposition of taxes, and issuing royal proclamations, to which he required the same obedience as to acts of parliament. During this period he altered, both in England and in Scotland, the established forms of religious worship and the system of church government; and by the interposition of the star-chamber, or by his corrupt influence over the ordinary tribunals, he often inflicted the most arbitrary and illegal, as well as barbarous punishments upon those individuals who had the courage to thwart, or in any shape to oppose his measures.

His behaviour to his fourth parliament <230> served only to show, that, while he remained immoveable in his plans of despotism, he had not relinquished his disposition to artifice and duplicity.

Such had been the conduct of Charles, and such was the character of that monarch, which had been deeply impressed upon the great body of the people, when the defeat of his forces by the Scottish army obliged him to call another parliament within a few months after his angry and contemptuous dissolution of the former. The indignation and resentment of the nation were now raised to such a pitch as to overbear the court influence in the greater part of elections, and to produce in this assembly a prodigious majority, resolutely determined to restrain the arbitrary measures of the sovereign.

From the transactions of this and of the preceding reign, it was now become evident, that the preservation of public freedom required more effectual measures than had been pursued by former parliaments. By refusing supplies, the house of commons might occasionally extort from the king a promise to correct the abuses of administration; but experience had <231> shown that no practical benefit could result from promises to which he paid so little regard, and which he might so easily violate with impunity. Those difficult situations, in which the king was obliged to solicit the parliament for money, were now likely to occur but seldom, since he had found that, by other methods less disagreeable to himself, he was capable, in ordinary cases, of supplying his wants. These methods, indeed, were illegal and unpopular, but they had been frequently repeated with success, and had for a considerable period been continued without interruption. The danger of such precedents had now risen to an alarming height; and as, on the one hand, it was hardly to be expected that the monarch would stop short in that career which he had hitherto maintained, so on the other, it was to be feared that the people, whose feelings are but little affected by evils which do not strike their senses, would be gradually reconciled to these innovations, and that the sanction of custom would at length be pleaded in support of measures totally subversive of the constitution.

Though the English government had im-<232>memorially exhibited the plan of a limited monarchy, and had so distributed the chief powers of the state as mutually to check and controul one another; yet, from want of experience and foresight, the workmanship was, in several of its minuter parts, far from being so complete and perfect as to preclude every kind of irregularity or disorder. By commiting the powers of legislation and taxation to parliament, and the supreme judicial power to the house of lords, it seems to have been thought that the ministerial or executive power of the king would be kept in proper subordination; and probably no suspicion was entertained of the numerous artifices by which he might elude the superintendance of his great council, or of the different expedients to which he might resort for establishing an independent authority. But after the decline of the aristocracy under the reign of the Tudor princes, it was found that the precarious appointment of the inferior judges gave him an absolute sway over the courts of justice; and upon the disuse of the ancient feudal service, after the accession of the house of Stuart, the direction of the mercenary forces, the number <233> of which was likely to be continually increasing, afforded him an engine which was becoming daily more effectual for enforcing his measures, and for controuling all opposition to his will.

At this alarming crisis, therefore, when the king had made such formidable advances towards the introduction of despotism, it was the indispensable duty of parliament to redouble its efforts, and to study more effectual measures for opposing his designs. It was no longer sufficient, for this purpose, to repel the encroachments made by the crown, and to re-instate the government in the situation which it had maintained before the late innovations. The parliaments had hitherto stood entirely upon the defensive; it seemed now high time that they should attack in their turn, and endeavour to disarm an adversary so persevering, so watchful, and so powerful. It was not enough that they should fill up the breaches which had been made, and repair the fortifications which had been demolished; but in providing for future security, it was necessary to fortify the constitution in those avenues and passes which had formerly been <234> left most open and defenceless; and at the same time to dispossess the prerogative of those particular stations, from which there appeared the most imminent danger of invasion.

Such appear to have been the leading views of that celebrated parliament, which met in the latter part of the year 1640, and of whose conduct political writers, according to their different inclinations and *systems,* have given such opposite representations.

Their first measure was to attack those ministers who had been chiefly instrumental in the late proceedings of the crown. That these might with propriety be called to account for the part they had acted in the course of their administration, was indisputable; and that they, rather than the sovereign, should suffer punishment for the abuses or misdemeanors which had been committed, was an acknowledged maxim of the English government. It was accordingly resolved, that Strafford and Laud, the two persons who had enjoyed the principal share of the king's confidence, the one in civil, the other in ecclesiastical matters, should be impeached; and, <235> for this purpose, they were immediately taken into custody.

Many circumstances contributed to render Strafford the general object of popular odium and resentment. He had been a distinguished leader of the patriotic party; and had been seduced by the court to abandon his principles, and join the standard of prerogative. In those times, when the spirit of patriotism had risen to so high a pitch, and when the minds of men were so heated with an enthusiastic love of liberty, a political renegado, who had betrayed the cause of his country, and had descended to become a vile instrument of that oppression, against which he had declaimed and struggled with so much vehemence, could not fail to draw upon himself a double portion of that indignation which the measures of the crown had excited; and as this apostacy happened soon after the dissolution of Charles's third parliament, that is, at the very period when the arbitrary and despotical views of the monarch had been, in the most unequivocal manner, proclaimed to the whole nation, and when attempts, by the court, for gaining other eminent members in opposition, had been <236> repulsed with disdain, it was beheld in circumstances of peculiar aggravation, and marked with indelible characters of infamy. The haughty and insolent temper of Strafford contributed, at the same time, to procure him many personal enemies: not to mention, that his known abilities and vigour, which had raised him to the head of administration, gave real apprehension to all such as were anxious to guard against the encroachments of prerogative.

Against the condemnation of this minister, much has been said and written, which, in the present age, will hardly be thought worthy of a serious refutation. That *the king can do no wrong* was, even at this time, understood, in the ordinary course of administration, to be a constitutional maxim: From which it follows, as a necessary consequence, that his ministers must be responsible for all the abuses committed by the executive power. No person, according to this rule, could suffer more justly than the Earl of Strafford, who had been confessedly the king's principal and confidential minister, and whose administration demonstrated a deep-laid and regular sys-<237>tem to subvert the constitution. It may be asked, what crime deserves a capital punishment, if this does not?

The clamour, therefore, which was raised against the punishment of that nobleman could have no foundation in the principles of material justice. It could only relate to the forms of procedure by which he was tried and condemned. And here it is remarkable, that the chief handle for objection was afforded by the extreme anxiety of the commons to proceed with great circumspection, and to conduct the trial in such a manner as would avoid any ground of complaint.

With respect to the facts upon which the accusation was founded, instead of resting upon a general statement of the arbitrary measures pursued by the crown during the period when Strafford was a principal and confidential minister, about which there could be no dispute, the commons thought proper, for the satisfaction of the public, to bring a specific charge of particular violations of the constitution, to which he had been accessary, either as an adviser, or as an immediate actor; and the proof <238> which they afterwards adduced in support of one of the chief of those articles, was alleged to be defective. Strafford was charged with having said, in council, that the king was now *absolved from all rule of government, and to do whatever power would admit;* and with having advised his majesty *to go on vigorously in levying ship-money,* and to employ the forces in Ireland for *reducing this kingdom to obedience.* Other expressions of a similar import were imputed to other members of council. Sir Henry Vane,[28] the secretary, had taken short notes of this debate; and from these, which were accidentally discovered by his son, a copy was produced on the trial. It appears from Lord Clarendon, that some of the words alluded to, *of a high nature,* according to his expression, were remembered by the Earl of Northumberland, another member of council; but the rest were not recollected by any person present, except Sir Henry Vane; nor by him, till after repeated examinations. It was contended, however, that the notes added to this verbal testimony should be held equivalent to two witnesses, which, by the <239> law of England, are necessary in proofs of high treason.* <240>

28. After serving as governor of Massachusetts, Vane (1613–62) returned to England and entered the commons in 1640, later playing a major part in securing Strafford's execution. From 1643 to 1653 he was, in effect, the civilian head of the parliamentary government.

* See Clarendon's Hist. Vol. I.—Whitlock's Memorials—Parliamentary History, Vol. IX.

The title of the notes was, *No danger of a war with Scotland, if offensive, not defensive.* Then followed the opinions marked as below.

K. C. How can we undertake an offensive war, if we have no more money?

L. L. Ir. Borrow of the city 100,000l. Go on vigorously to levy ship-money; your majesty having tried the affection of your people, you are absolved and loose from all rule of government, and to do what power will admit. Your majesty having tried all ways, and being refused, shall be acquitted before God and man: and you have an army in Ireland that you may employ to reduce this kingdom to obedience; for I am confident the Scots cannot hold out five months.

L. Arch. You have tried all ways, and have always been denied; it is now lawful to take it by force.

L. Col. Leagues abroad there may be made for the defence of the kingdom: the lower

In prosecuting the impeachment of Strafford, some doubts came to be suggested, whether the facts imputed to him, though cer-<241>tainly deserving the highest punishment, amounted, by the common or statute law of England, to the specific crime of high treason with which he was charged. According to the rude conceptions introduced into all the feudal monarchies of Europe, the crime of high treason could only be committed *against the king;* and it was alleged, that a charge of this nature was not applicable to the conduct of Strafford, who had, indeed, invaded the constitution, and subverted the fundamental laws of the kingdom, but who had acted, all along, with the perfect concurrence of the sovereign, and in direct obedience to his will. These doubts were, surely, very ill founded; since it is obvious

---

house are weary of the king and church: all ways shall be just to raise money by, in this inevitable necessity, and are to be used, being lawful.

L. Arch. For an offensive, not any defensive war.

L. L. Ir. The town is full of lords. Put the commission of array on foot; and if any of them stir, we will make them smart.

The evidence arising from these notes, however informal, can hardly fail to produce conviction. They were apparently taken when the debate happened, immediately after the dissolution of the preceding parliament, and some months before there could be any view of trying the Earl of Strafford. Their authenticity is supported by the parole testimony of Sir Henry Vane, the secretary, by whom they were taken, and who, being present, as a member of council, was an accomplice in the conspiracy, and had therefore an interest to conceal the fact. This circumstance, together with his oath, as a privy counsellor, to secrecy, accounts for his reluctance to reveal the truth. His testimony, at the same time, with respect to some expressions *of a high nature,* in the foregoing dialogue, appears, by the admission of Clarendon, to have been confirmed by that of the Earl of Northumberland, another privy counsellor, and an unexceptionable witness. Thus a full proof being brought of some important parts of the dialogue, though it is not ascertained which these are, the credulity of the notes must be strongly established as to other parts where we have only one witness.

But what must contribute, above all, to remove any doubt concerning the authenticity of the notes, is the probability of their contents, from the situation and past behaviour of the king and his ministers. The expressions used by the different speakers tally exactly with their former conduct. The measures proposed are nothing but the continuation, and the natural consequence of those which had been pursued by administration for eleven years past; and the embarrassment produced, immediately upon the dissolution of the fourth parliament of Charles, was likely to occasion a consultation of the nature that is reported.

It is unnecessary to add, that the interlocutors referred to are clearly King Charles, the Lord Lieutenant of Ireland, the Archbishop of Canterbury, and Lord Collington, and that the designs which they express are subversive of the constitution.

that, by the presumption of <242> law, the king, in pursuance of his duty, must be supposed at all times ready to defend the constitution, and consequently exposed to the hazard of losing his life in its defence. Whoever, therefore, attempts to overthrow the constitution, may be held, in the construction of the law of Edward the Third, to *compass or imagine the death of the king;* and this although in any particular case the king should betray his trust, and, instead of defending the government, should combine with its enemies in promoting its destruction. But how ill founded soever the opinions of those may be who opposed the impeachment upon this ground, it was thought adviseable to comply with their pretended scruples, and to carry on the prosecution by a *bill of attainder.*[29] This mode of trial is, doubtless, very liable to abuse, and ought never to be admitted, unless in cases of extraordinary necessity. It does not appear, however, that Strafford was, in consequence of it, subjected to any peculiar hardship. The proof of the facts was investigated, not only by the commons, but also by the lords, the same judges by whom it would have been determined in the case of an <243> impeachment; and before passing the bill, the judges delivered their unanimous opinion, *that upon all which their lordships have voted to be proved, the Earl of Strafford doth deserve to undergo the pain and forfeitures of high treason by law.*[*]

The consent given by Charles to this bill, and his yielding to the execution of his favorite, could not fail to strike all his adherents with consternation and astonishment, and have been considered, even by those who view his conduct with the most extreme partiality, as the great blot upon his character. If we suppose that Charles was now a real convert from his former principles; and that, weary of so disagreeable a contest, he had relinquished the system of establishing an absolute government; it is natural to think that he would have met with no difficulty in giving complete satisfaction, both to parliament and the nation, without abandoning the life of a minister whom he had seduced into his service, and whose fidelity to him was his only crime. But if this monarch still persisted in his ambitious designs; if his present concessions to <244> parliament were no more than temporary expedients for procuring the supplies which he wanted; and if the death of Lord Strafford was merely a sacrifice, to avert the national resentment, and, by a seem-

* Parliamentary History, Vol. IX. p. 2.

29. An act of parliament used to convict political opponents of treason without benefit of a trial. The procedure was abolished in 1870.

ing atonement for past offences, to deliver the king from his present embarrassment; if this, as there is good reason to believe, was the real state of the fact, it is hardly possible for imagination to figure a more glaring instance of meanness, of perfidy, and of barbarity.

It will throw light upon the feelings of this monarch to recollect the terms of a letter which, after he had given his consent to the bill of attainder, he wrote, with his own hand, to the house of peers, expressing a strong desire that Strafford's life might be spared. The letter concludes with this extraordinary postscript: "If he must die, it were charity to reprieve him till Saturday."[30] The only apology that has been invented for this brutal indifference is, that the postscript was probably dictated by the queen, who, it seems, bore no good-will to Strafford.* <245>

The condemnation and execution of archbishop Laud were delayed for some years; and in perusing the history of those times, the rigorous punishment of this old and infirm ecclesiastic, when the contest had come to be decided by force, is apt to be regarded as an unnecessary strain of severity. He had not the same abilities with Strafford, to render him formidable; nor had his character been in the same manner rendered odious by political apostacy. He was, however, the firm associate and coadjutor of that nobleman, and was equally guilty of a deliberate attempt to subvert the constitution; nor can it escape observation, that, from the department in which he acted, the superintendance of the great machine of the hierarchy, he was capable of doing more mischief, by poisoning the minds of the people, and sowing the seeds of a tyranny more luxuriant, more extensive, and more deeply rooted. The vigour, the activity, and the high sentiments of liberty which, from the beginning of this parliament, had been displayed by a great majority of its members, were at the same time warmly and uniformly supported by the general spirit which prevailed throughout the <246> nation. Petitions against the arbitrary measures of the court pouring in from every quarter, contributed to animate the commons in their endeavours to reform abuses. The other ministers and instruments of Charles were either forced, by flight, to save themselves from the terrors of an impeachment, or, if their

* See Life of Charles I. by William Harris.—King Charles's Works, p. 138; Burnet's Hist. Vol. I.

30. For Hume's similar account of the excessive punishment of Laud, see *HE,* 5:457. For the quotation from Charles's letter, see *Basilika: The Works of King Charles the Martyr* (London, 1687).

obscurity rendered them less obnoxious, they remained in silent apprehension, lest, by opposing the popular current, they might provoke their destiny.

The lower house proceeded unanimously to declare, that the imposition of ship-money by the king was contrary to the fundamental laws of the kingdom; and that the sheriffs, who had issued the writs on that occasion, as well as the persons who had been employed in levying the tax, were liable to punishment. In this declaration they were joined by the unanimous voice of the peers, who farther ordained that the judgment given in Mr. Hambden's case should be cancelled in their presence. A similar judgment was passed upon the levying of tonnage and poundage, without consent of parliament, and upon the late collectors of this duty, and, in order to ascertain, for the future, <247> the exclusive power of that assembly, in this respect the tax was now voted for two months only, and afterwards renewed for very short periods. The enlargement of the forests, the revival of monopolies, which had been lately abolished by the legislature; every illegal method of raising money, or unwarrantable exertion of prerogative; the arbitrary interposition of the star-chamber, and high commission, and the corrupt and oppressive decisions of the ordinary judges, were subjected to severe scrutiny, and stigmatised with strong marks of disapprobation and censure.*

These resolutions and declarations were sufficient to demonstrate the sentiments of parliament, and of the nation; but hitherto no provision had been made against the future encroachments of prerogative. The government was not in a better condition than at the time when the petition of right had passed into a law; and the public had no security against the monarch, after being freed from his present embarrassment, renewing his former pretensions, and resuming that system of conduct which he had been compelled to abandon. <248>

From the time when the great body of the people had acquired a degree of opulence and independence, the frequent meetings of the national council had been deemed essential to the preservation of liberty. During the sitting of parliament the attention of the community was awakened to political discussions; the proceedings of the executive power were scrutinized, and held up to public notice; and the nation was possessed of a great organ, by which its grievances and its demands could be communicated to the monarch, with a force and energy often irresistible. But, in the intervals between

* See Hume.

those great councils, the voice of the legislature was not heard; there existed no superior power to controul the abuses of administration; no monitor to warn and rouse the people in defence of their privileges; and the usurpations of the crown, if cautiously conducted, and artfully disguised, were likely in many cases to pass unobserved. If the country was maintained in peace and tranquillity; if arts and manufactures were protected, and continued in a flourishing condition; if the inhabitants did not feel themselves grossly oppressed or injured in their private rights; they were not <249> apt to testify much uneasiness from the illegal measures of government, or to complain even of clear and palpable violations of the constitution.

To avoid the meetings of parliament, therefore, became the great object of the crown; in the prosecution of which, Charles had been so successful, as for a period of more than eleven years to have avoided the necessity of calling that assembly. The very mention of parliaments, during this period, was regarded as a kind of sedition, and upon that account strictly prohibited. It is not surprising that, in the present emergency, when the king had been obliged to renounce those heretical doctrines, and to solicit once more the assistance of his national council, it should have been thought indispensably necessary to prevent the recurrence of measures so completely despotical, and effectually to secure this great palladium of the constitution.

While the feudal aristocracy remained in its vigour, the barons, who were the principal part of this council, were not very anxious about the regularity or frequency of its meetings. Relying upon the number and fidelity <250> of their vassals, they trusted more to their prowess in the field, than to their eloquence or address in the cabinet. We find, however, so early as the reign of Edward the Third, a provision by two several statutes, that parliaments shall be held *once every year, or oftener, if need be.** This law had never been repealed, though, from the state of the kingdom, for several centuries, it had excited but little attention. When the commons had acquired some weight in the constitution, they generally threw themselves into the scale of the prerogative; and it became as much the interest of the king to call frequent meetings of parliament, as it was that of the barons to avoid them. This was the case during the latter part of the Plantagenet line, and under the whole government of the Tudor princes; during which, it should seem that this point had never become the subject either of discussion or controversy. But

* 4 Edw. III. c. 14. 36 Edw. III. c. 10.

after the accession of the House of Stuart, when the interest and views of the different branches of the legislature underwent a total revolution, it <251> was natural for the house of commons to look back to those ancient statutes by which the annual meetings of parliament were secured. They did not, indeed, think proper to insist upon a literal observance of that regulation; but making allowance for the difference of times and circumstances, they were willing to admit such variations as might render it consistent with the ease and convenience of the crown. Instead of calling parliaments annually, it was thought reasonable that the king should, at least once in three years, be obliged to convene those assemblies; and a bill for that purpose was introduced by the commons, and passed through both houses. To secure the observance of this regulation, it was provided, that if the chancellor failed to issue writs every third year, any twelve peers might exercise that power; that, in their default, the sheriffs and other returning officers might summon the electors; and, lastly, that the voters, if not summoned, might assemble of their own accord and elect representatives. It was further provided, that after the two houses of parliament had met, they should not, without their <252> own consent, be either prorogued or dissolved within the space of fifty days.

While this and other salutary regulations were under the consideration of parliament, there was good reason to apprehend, what had happened on so many former occasions, that their deliberations, however important, might be cut short by a sudden dissolution. Unless they could guard against this fatal interruption, it was needless to propose a reformation of abuses; and while their members exposed themselves to great personal danger from the resentment of the crown, there was nearly a certainty that their labours would be rendered abortive. The necessity of the case, therefore, appeared to justify an extraordinary precaution, and a bill was carried through both houses, importing, that until the present grievances were redressed, they should not, without their own concurrence, be dissolved.*

Among the various tools employed by Charles for the execution of his measures, the readiest, and the most subservient to his pur-<253>poses, were the courts of star-chamber and high-commission.

The former of these tribunals arose from an idea entertained by the lawyers of an early age, that the rules of criminal justice could not be extended

* Whitlock's Memorials, page 45.

to the numberless instances of delinquency which occur in society; and that, of consequence, a discretionary power was necessary for taking cognizance of extraordinary offences. This jurisdiction was naturally assumed by the king and privy council, with the assistance of his ordinary judges, or of such individuals as he thought proper to call in particular cases.

It is probable that, in the infancy of judicial procedure, when the ordinary courts, from their narrow experience, were extremely cautious and timid in explaining the rules of justice, or when, from a suspicion of their partiality, it appeared expedient to limit and circumscribe their decisions within the strict letter of the law, this ultimate remedy, to supply the defect of every other jurisdiction; a remedy which probably was applied very sparingly, and with great moderation, proved of signal advantage to the public. It is remark-<254>able that, even in the days of Lord Bacon, the interpositions of the star-chamber, which had then been rendered more extensive than formerly, are highly extolled by that eminent lawyer and philosopher.

In the progress of society, however, the rules of law were gradually enlarged and extended to a much greater diversity of cases; and courts of an undefined and arbitrary jurisdiction, as they were found highly inconvenient and dangerous, became, at the same time, superfluous and useless. But of all the tribunals invested with discretionary powers, that of the star chamber appeared the most liable to abuses. The particular crimes, or offences, which chiefly fell under its cognizance, were such as immediately affected the interest of the crown; so that while the court was confessedly tied to no rule, the judges were either parties, or, what amounts to the same thing, under the direction of a party. It happened, therefore, as might be expected, that whenever the king adventured to stretch his prerogative beyond the bounds of law; when he wished to levy money under the pretence of a loan or benevolence; when he wanted to enforce the <255> royal proclamations, and put them upon a level with acts of parliament; or when he was disposed to punish any person who, by opposing his measures, or by sounding an alarm to the people, had incurred his displeasure; in all such cases this was the court to which he applied, and in which he never failed to procure a decision according to his wishes. A tribunal of this nature was a sort of excrescence, whose polluted and cancerous fibres were likely to contaminate the whole constitution, and which, independently of the distempers of the present reign, there was an urgent necessity to lop off and eradicate.

The high commission, as was mentioned in a former part of this discourse, had obtained a similar province in spiritual, to that of the star-chamber in temporal matters. During the first fervour of religious reformation, it had been thought expedient that government should controul and direct the faith of individuals; and that a court should be appointed for the sole purpose of restraining heresies, as well as for punishing all offences against the order and dignity of the church. This tribunal was at first levelled principally <256> against the Roman catholics; but came afterwards to be a weapon, in the hands of the clergy, and consequently of the sovereign, for the support of the hierarchy, and for depressing those branches of the sectaries which had become eminent or obnoxious. Being in reality a court of inquisition, unconfined by rules, and actuated by the love of clerical domination, as well as by that rancorous hatred which is the offspring of religious controversy, its proceedings in the department belonging to it, were, if possible, still more oppressive and arbitrary than those of the star-chamber; at the same time, having assumed the power of enforcing its decrees by fine and imprisonment, it was enabled to acquire a most extensive authority. The same observation, which already has been made with respect to the star-chamber, is also applicable to the court of high commission; that it proceeded from conjunctures which had now ceased to exist. Whatever might be the pretences, during the heat of controversy, at the beginning of the reformation, for establishing such an extraordinary jurisdiction, these could have no place after the new system of <257> religion had obtained a complete victory, and gained a full and peaceable establishment. Amid the disorders which are apt to accompany a violent revolution, there may be some excuse for the exercise of such irregular and arbitrary powers as would be altogether inadmissible and intolerable in times of peace and tranquillity.

It was thought proper, therefore, by the unanimous voice of both houses of parliament, to abolish those courts; a measure, which the changes in the state of society would have recommended even at a time when no danger was apprehended from the encroachments of prerogative; but which, in the present circumstances of the nation, and under the impression made by the conduct and temper of the monarch, appeared immediately and indispensably necessary.

To all these important bills the king was prevailed upon to give the royal assent; and if he had done nothing, in the mean time, to call in question the sincerity of his compliances, it is probable that parliament, and the nation, would have been satisfied with the redress which they had procured, and with <258> the amendments on the constitution which had been introduced. But they soon found reason to believe, that, in these concessions, the monarch was far from being sincere. When Charles called this parliament, he must have expected a good deal of clamour; that grievances would echo from every quarter; and that liberal promises of redress and amendment, as a previous step to obtaining supplies, would be unavoidable. For all this, it is not unlikely, he was prepared; and had made a virtue of necessity. But when he saw that the regulations proposed by parliament struck at the root of all his projects; carried their defensive operations into all the departments of the state; and would effectually prevent his recurring to those expedients which he had formerly employed in the extension of his prerogative, he was thrown into the utmost consternation and perplexity. Parliament had now shewn that they would grant no money except upon their own terms; and such was the tide of popular opinion, that, without their consent, no considerable supplies could be expected. There seemed only to remain, therefore, in his present situation, the alterna-<259>tive of abandoning altogether his design to change the constitution, or of endeavouring, by some desperate enterprize, to extricate himself from the surrounding difficulties.

The Scottish army, which, after its success, had penetrated into England, and still remained in the country, had not only been the cause of summoning the present parliament; but also, by its well known disposition to support the popular party, had contributed to promote the vigorous and spirited resolutions of that assembly. The English forces, on the other hand, were not yet disbanded; and though their late discomfiture had been chiefly imputed to their not being hearty in the quarrel, it was believed that, by sowing a national jealousy between the two armies, and by representing parliament as partial to the Scots, the English might be gained over to the interest of the king. To this end a conspiracy was formed by several military officers of distinction,[31] together with certain agents employed by the queen; and it was concerted, as there is good reason to believe, that the English army should be brought up to London, in order to take possession of the tower, to overawe the <260> parliament, and to procure a permanent settlement of the king's revenue. As the plan was never carried into execution, some doubts

31. The so-called first army plot in 1641. The conspirators included Sir Henry Percy of Alnwick (d. 1659), brother of the earl of Northumberland, and Baron George Goring (1608–57), a key royalist military leader.

have arisen concerning the precise view and intention of the conspirators. But that they intended, in some shape or other, to employ the army for the purpose of preventing the two houses of parliament from prosecuting the measures in which they were engaged; that they meant to controul the deliberations of the legislature, by the terrors, or by the actual interference of a military force, there can be no room to doubt. It appears also to be proved beyond the shadow of controversy, notwithstanding the awkward attempts of some authors to conceal or disguise the fact, that this project was communicated to the king, and carried on with his approbation and concurrence.* <261>

The discovery of this plot, which happened while the king was apparently pursuing a system of conciliation with his great council, and was pretending heartily to agree in the schemes proposed for the redress of grievances, opened a scene of dissimulation and perfidy, which could not fail to excite the most alarming apprehensions. What confidence could be reposed in the professions of a prince who solicited, in secret, the assistance of the military power, to deliver him from those regulations and measures with which he publicly expressed his entire satisfaction?

This incident was followed immediately by the insurrection of the Roman catholics <262> in Ireland, and the massacre of their protestant fellow subjects. Whether Charles had promoted and instigated this insurrection, as was pretended by the insurgents, appears not very easy to determine. That he had any share in the bloody tragedy which was acted upon that occasion, his bitterest enemies have never alleged. But, considering the views of this monarch, it was natural to suspect, that he secretly wished the Roman cath-

* The greater part of the conspirators made their escape. Percy, one of the chief of them, wrote to his brother, the Earl of Northumberland, a letter dated 14th June 1641, in which he confessed the principal facts alleged. Goring, another conspirator, was laid hold of, and repeatedly examined by the commons. His deposition, though he endeavours to palliate his own conduct in the transaction, tallies in good measure with Percy's letter. The draught of a petition, from the army to the king and parliament, had been privately communicated to Charles, and countersigned by him, with the letters C. R. in token of his approbation. See the whole of the depositions relative to this transaction, in Rush. Col. vol. IV.

It has been observed, upon this subject, that neither Goring, upon his examination, nor Percy in his letter, were thought by Charles to have said too much. Since the former was continued in his government of Portsmouth, and the latter afterwards made a lord, and master of horse to the Prince of Wales. See Harris's life of Charles I.

olics, to whom he had shewn so much favour, should take up arms in defence of his prerogative; or even that he might propose to reap some advantage, by having a pretence for setting himself at the head of an English army to march against the insurgents. The transactions which he afterwards concluded with the Irish rebels, or which were concluded in his name, have rather a tendency to confirm this unfavourable suspicion.* But whatever opinion, upon this point, we may at present be disposed to entertain, it is not surprising, that, <263> from the character of Charles, and his equivocal behaviour, such reports to his prejudice, which were then universally, and perhaps maliciously circulated, should have made a strong impression upon the public, and increased the general anxiety and terror respecting the danger to which the constitution was exposed.

In their efforts to restrain the encroachments of prerogative, the parliament had been constantly opposed and obstructed by the votes of the bishops in the upper house, and by the interest of the clergy throughout the nation. The puritans, on the other hand, had been uniformly distinguished by their zeal in opposing the measures of the court, and in supporting the claims of parliament. It is no wonder, therefore, that the real friends of the constitution were irritated and provoked by the former, and warmed with sentiments of gratitude and affection towards the latter. The presbyterians and independents in the house of commons formed, at the same time, a numerous party, whose political principles were unavoidably warped by their religious tenets, and who, doubtless, were glad of any pretence for invading the hierarchy. <264>

But, independent of all party connections, and party prejudices, the circumstances of that critical period might naturally give rise to a question, how far the secular power of the bishops was consistent with sound policy; and whether, considering their strong propensity to support the arbitrary measures of the king, their interposition, as members of the house of peers, was not likely to prevent the establishment of any permanent system of liberty.

According to the principles of the ancient feudal system, the dignified clergy, being possessed of large estates, enjoyed an extensive jurisdiction over

* See the facts respecting the accession of Charles to the Irish insurrection—Rapin's history of England—Macauley's history of England—Harris's life of Charles I.—On the other hand, the vindication of Charles in Hume's history of England.

their tenants and vassals, and were, equally with the lay-barons, entitled to vote in the great assembly of the nation. By their situation they were, at the same time, independent, in a great measure, of the civil power; and having a separate interest from that of the king or of the nobles, they claimed a distinct voice in the legislature, and formed one of the three estates of the kingdom.

But the revival of letters, and the religious reformation which followed the improvement of arts and manufactures, produced a great revolution in the circumstances of churchmen, <265> and in the rank and dignity which they held, either as members of parliament, or of the nation at large. The dissipation of the clouds of superstition which formerly hung over the minds of men had greatly diminished the spiritual influence of those ghostly fathers. The dignified clergy were now in the appointment of the crown, and the whole order looked up to the sovereign as the great source of their preferment. So far were the bishops from constituting a separate estate and maintaining a distinct negative in the national council, that they were become subordinate to another branch of the legislature; and their weight was now uniformly thrown into that scale which it had been formerly employed to counterbalance. Whatever was the original purpose, therefore, of bringing the bishops into parliament, this could no longer be served; but, on the contrary, was likely to be counteracted and frustrated by their continuance in that assembly. If they had formerly maintained a proper balance between the different powers of the state, it was evident that, by a reverse of situation, their exertions were now calculated <266> to produce the opposite effect, and to destroy this equilibrium.

With equal reason it might be contended, that the higher officers of the army and revenue, as that the dignified clergy should, in virtue of their places, have a seat in parliament; since both of those classes depend equally upon the crown for their emolument and rank; and since the former are not in more hazard than the latter of being influenced by those motives of private interest which govern the greater part of mankind.

There is, at the same time, no pretence for allowing the church, considered as a great corporation, to send representatives to the national council. Supposing the ecclesiastical to be distinct from the temporal interest, and to require a separate management, an effectual provision was made in its favour by the right of holding *convocations;* which, at the period now under consideration, exercised, as will be observed more fully hereafter, the exclusive privilege of taxing the clergy. But in reality there is no ground for bestowing upon the church, or any other societies, in their collective capacity, any peculiar share in the legisla-<267>ture farther than is enjoyed by the individuals of which they are composed. If the inhabitants of a country are singly possessed of a due proportion of political power in the election of representatives, this will enable them to take sufficient care of their interest, even so far as they happen to be united in corporate bodies; and it should seem that such corporations have no just claim to any additional representation.

Had the bishops, on this great emergency, behaved with common discretion; had they shewn, in the numerous important questions which occurred, a decent regard to the public interest; had they not, in fact, shewn themselves to be the mere tools of the monarch, determined to persist, without shame or scruple, in promoting his designs; it is highly probable that their privileges, however inconsistent with the present state of ecclesiastical livings, would never have been invaded, and that no attempt would have been made to deprive them of their seats in parliament. But, as they had inlisted under the banner of despotism, their political power became a sacrifice to that limited monarchy which parliament had resolved to establish. <268>

In this particular, however, the opinions entertained by the real friends of the constitution being more various, the attempts to diminish the power of the bishops were prosecuted with less unanimity than had appeared in relation to the other measures for setting bounds to the prerogative. A bill was first passed in the house of commons to restrain persons in holy orders from intermeddling in secular affairs; but this was rejected in the upper house. Another bill was introduced for abolishing entirely the power of bishops, and of all other ecclesiastical dignitaries: this was unsuccessful among the commons themselves.

These attacks were followed by an accusation of high crimes and misdemeanours against the bishops who had been concerned in the establishment of the late ecclesiastical canons, and in other innovations with respect to the discipline of the church; and this charge was accompanied by a demand on the part of the commons, that those prelates, during the dependence of the trial, should be excluded from the privilege of voting in parliament. The resentment of the populace, in the mean time, occasioned such tumults, that the bishops, <269> finding it unsafe to appear in public, had the imprudence to present to the king and to the peers a protestation that all proceedings in parliament, during their absence, should be held null and void. This was considered by both houses as a violent attempt to subvert the fundamental laws of parliament; and was made the subject of an impeachment for high treason, upon which those prelates were taken into custody.

By the progressive measures which had already been executed, or which were manifestly in contemplation of the patriotic party, it should seem that the patience of Charles was entirely exhausted, and that he was no longer able to maintain the temporising system of dissimulation which he had hitherto practised. In spite of every prudential consideration, and throwing aside all regard to consistency of conduct, he now appears to have taken a resolution of yielding to the violence of his temper, and attempting by force to subdue all opposition. Having suddenly given orders that Lord Kimbolton,[32] among the peers, and five members of the house of commons, should be accused of high treason, and having sent to the <270> commons to demand that these five members should be delivered up to him, to which message no positive answer was returned, he came next day with an armed retinue into the lower house; and having occupied the chair of the speaker, he demanded to know whether any of these members were present, declaring, "that he must have them wheresoever he could find them."*

The warmest friends of Charles have condemned this measure as the height of rashness and folly; but they would gladly overlook the chief point of view in which it deserves to be considered, as affording complete evidence of the arbitrary principles by which he was governed, and of the secret motives by which, in all his transactions with parliament, he had hitherto been actuated. The guilt imputed to these individuals, it was well known, consisted of the share they had taken in the deliberations and resolutions of that assembly; and with equal reason the same charge might have been brought against the majority of both houses. So far was he, therefore, from regarding the <271> late acts of parliament, which he had confirmed by the sanction of royal authority, as binding either upon him or upon the nation, that he held those regulations to be the most atrocious offences, and looked upon

* See Whitlocke's Rushworth.

32. Lord Kimbolton: Edward Montagu, second earl of Manchester (1602–71). The leader of the Puritan faction in the House of Lords, he was among those arrested for treason in 1642.

every person who had been accessary to their introduction as liable to a capital punishment.

The views and principles of Charles were not more apparent from the nature of this accusation, than from the manner in which it was conducted. That the king should not, in any shape, interfere in the deliberations of parliament, was a maxim understood in the former reign to be fully settled. But that, with an armed force, he should come in person into the house of commons to intimidate its members, and, without farther ceremony, to seize and imprison those individuals who, by their conduct in parliament, had incurred his displeasure, was an exertion of despotic power and violence of which no precedent occurred in the annals of parliament, and which plainly intimated that the king, by his prerogative, might at pleasure dispense with all the privileges of that assembly. <272>

That the members of parliament were not exempted from prosecutions, either for high treason, or for other great crimes, was universally admitted; but when an accusation was brought against them upon points relating to their conduct in that assembly, it was thought requisite, as a preliminary step, that the house of parliament to which they belonged, should be satisfied concerning the grounds of the charge, and should deliver up its respective members to justice. If this form were not held indispensably necessary, the freedom and independence of parliament must be destroyed; as, in critical questions, it would always be in the power of administration, by sudden and groundless accusations, to deprive the legislature of such members as had rendered themselves obnoxious, and were most likely to frustrate the measures of the crown. No danger, on the other hand, could with reason be apprehended from this privilege of parliament; for it never could be supposed that, when a crime of an atrocious nature had really been committed, the majority of either house would be so corrupt, or so foolish, as to oppose the trial of its members. <273>

By the alarm and commotion which this extraordinary measure excited in the city, and through the nation, Charles was at length convinced of its imprudence; but he found that the impression which it had made was not to be erased by appearances of repentance, nor even by professions of future amendment. The bill for depriving the bishops of their seats in parliament now passed the house of peers; and to this the royal assent was given without delay. According as the behaviour of the king had created a stronger suspicion of his designs, it seemed necessary to lay a greater restraint upon his actions; and the commons accordingly rose in their demands. Nothing less than the obtaining some influence over the military force of the kingdom was now capable of yielding them satisfaction; and as, notwithstanding the disuse of the feudal services in the field, there still remained a shadow of the ancient militia, under the command of the lieutenants of counties, a bill was carried through both houses, containing a nomination of those officers, and rendering them accountable for their conduct to parliament. The authority <274> acquired by this regulation was intended to counterbalance, in some degree, the direction of the mercenary troops with which the sovereign was invested. But though Charles was desirous, by his concessions, to regain the confidence of the nation, he could not be prevailed upon to relinquish a branch of prerogative so essential to his darling schemes; and he rather chose to hazard a new rupture than give his assent to the bill.

Both parties now began to despair of settling their differences in an amicable manner; and looking forward to another, and what seemed a more effectual method of decision, endeavoured to collect a military force. The king retired to York, where he was attended by such of the nobility and gentry as were disposed to support his pretensions. The parliament, wishing to secure a magazine of arms, took possession, for that purpose, of Hull, by appointing a governor of the place under their own direction. The subsequent remonstrances, or proposals of accommodation, which passed upon either side, are of little moment; as no other benefit seems to have been expected from them than merely to <275> procure delays, or to create an impression throughout the nation, which might be favourable to the warlike preparations either of the king or parliament.

Whoever examines with attention the proceedings of this parliament, from their first meeting to the commencement of the civil war, will easily perceive that their views were somewhat different from those of the four preceding parliaments; and perhaps will find reason to conclude, that they did not continue, throughout the whole of this period, invariably the same. It was the object of this parliament to reform such parts of the constitution as were grossly defective; but their plan of reformation was necessarily varied and extended according to the pressure of circumstances; and in proportion to their discoveries of the hazard to which they were exposed from the temper and disposition of the king, they were led to insist upon a greater limitation of his powers. How far they were justified in all their demands, has been the subject of much controversy. To judge candidly of their behaviour, we must enter into the situation in which they were placed, and make <276> allowance for the difficulties with which they were surrounded; we must also make allowance for the passions under which they were obliged to form sudden resolutions; for the jarring opinions, the irregular influence, and the accidental humours of individuals; for the slippery ground of popular favour upon which they stood, and for the errors and prepossessions from which, in an age when philosophy was far from its meridian height, they could not be exempted. With these allowances they will not only be acquitted of any bad intention, but will appear entitled to a high degree of approbation, even to the warmest gratitude of posterity. However much they might be tinctured by enthusiasm and religious prejudices, they seem to have acted from pure and disinterested motives; and were neither seduced nor intimidated, upon any occasion, to swerve from those patriotic principles by which they professed to be guided. It would perhaps be difficult, even at this day, to point out a line of conduct more eligible than that which they pursued; and which, with no greater deviation from the former practice, would be better calculated to frustrate the am-<277>bitious designs of Charles, or to guard against the attempts of any future monarch for subverting the constitution.

That the parliament had, at this time, any intention to overturn the monarchy, and to establish a republican form of government, there is no good reason to suppose. After all the regulations which this parliament introduced, the sovereign still remained in the possession of very ample powers. He still would have enjoyed a voice in the legislature. He would still have exercised the power of collecting and disposing of the public revenue at his discretion. He would still have remained the fountain of honour; would have nominated all the judges during pleasure; and have had the sole privilege of declaring peace and war, with that of levying and commanding all the mercenary forces of the kingdom. In a word, his direct authority would have been more absolute than that of the British monarch at present. The patriots of that day overlooked a variety of limitations upon the crown, which the more enlarged experience of a later period has taught the English nation to establish. They had no thought of a permanent <278> provision, to prevent extravagance and bad economy in the expenditure of public money. They suggested no restriction with respect to the number of standing forces maintained in time of peace. Though they prohibited the king from extending martial law to the whole community, they put no restraint upon him in the application of that system to the army. They made no attempt to secure the independence of judges, by fixing their nomination for life. Having no suspicion of any undue influence which the king might obtain over parliaments, they permitted him to continue the same parliament as long as he pleased. In all these particulars, it was found necessary to make additional regulations upon the accession of William the Third; from which it may with reason be inferred, that the parliament which met in the latter part of the year 1640, instead of being liable to the censure of doing too much, was rather exposed to that of having done too little, for preventing the encroachments of prerogative.

With respect to the conduct of Charles during this period, we meet with no important variation: The same arbitrary system in-<279>variably pursued, and by the same unscrupulous means of dissimulation and duplicity. To those, indeed, who look no further than the immediate transactions, and who are unable to trace the intention and motives of the parties, it may seem that the ground of the dispute had been changed; while parliament was labouring to introduce a set of palpable innovations; and the king, who certainly consented to these with reluctance, is presented to us in the light of a secret friend to the old constitution. This is the aspect of the controversy, which those authors who attempt to excuse or justify the monarch,[33] are at great pains to exhibit, and to which they would willingly confine the attention of the reader. They endeavour to conceal, or to keep out of view, the former measures of the sovereign, by which he had subverted the fundamental laws of the kingdom, and the evidence which had occurred of his obstinate resolution to persist in the same designs. Thus they impute to parliament the offences, in reality, committed by the king; and represent as violations of the constitution the regulations which had become absolutely necessary for its preservation; <280> that is, they consider as a poison the antidote given to prevent its baneful effects.

SECTION III

Of the Reign of Charles the First, from the Commencement of the Civil War to his Death.

The progress of the civil war was productive of many and great alterations, both in the state of the contending parties, and in the temper and disposition

33. Millar's allusion is principally to Hume, who emphasized that Parliament took the initiative against the Crown.

of the nation. After the king and parliament had appealed to the sword, as the sole arbiter of their differences, they were no longer capable of retreating; and it was vain to shrink from a decision which must render the one or the other party completely triumphant. Both became sensible that their all was at stake; and that nothing but a decisive victory could either support their respective claims, or ensure their personal safety. From their mutual exertions in prosecuting the quarrel, and from the dangers and bad treatment to which they were continually exposed, <281> their passions were daily inflamed and rendered more furious; while every new advantage, upon either side, becoming the source of exultation and oppression in the one party, and of provocation and resentment to the other, contributed to widen the breach between them, and afforded fresh fuel to their mutual animosities.

The progressive measures which, during the whole reign of James, and in the former part of that of Charles, were gradually adopted by parliaments, have already been pointed out. Before the year 1640, those great councils appear to have stood altogether upon the defensive, and to have aimed at nothing further than barely to defend the ancient modes of government. From the meeting of what is called the Long Parliament, the abuses committed by the king had given rise to different views, and were thought to require more effectual precautions for securing the liberties of the people. The various wheels and springs of the constitution having, from negligence, gone into disorder, or being, from the inexperience of the original artificers, left, in some particulars, inaccurate and imperfect, the opportunity <282> which then offered was accounted highly favourable, for repairing the state machine, and for removing its defects or imperfections. Men who entertained this opinion were friends to the monarchy, while they attempted to impose new limitations upon the monarch; and were anxious to preserve the spirit and principles of the constitution, though they contended that, in several of its parts, a reformation was indispensably necessary.

How far the pruning hand of a reformer should be permitted was a difficult question; about which even speculative reasoners might easily differ; and upon which men who had opposite interests were by no means likely to agree. When all hopes of accommodation, upon this point, were completely blasted, when both king and parliament had recourse to arms, the popular party were pushed on to greater extremities, and embraced a bolder system of reformation. The opposition to the crown had proved so ineffectual; the power, the influence, and the resources of the king were so extensive; and the artifices by which he might elude the controul of the legislature, and undermine the privileges of the people, <283> had been found so numerous and so various, that every attempt to confine the prerogative within due bounds, was in danger of being regarded as desperate. To many it appeared that the old constitution was no longer tenable, and that the only method of preventing the abuses of regal power was to abolish it altogether. The exaltation, it was observed, of an individual to the rank of a sovereign prince proves commonly such an incentive to ambition, as renders him impatient of restraint, and dissatisfied with any thing less than absolute dominion. Accustomed to the high station in which he is placed, and having received it through a long line of ancestors, he is apt to look upon it as his birthright; and instead of conceiving it to be an office derived ultimately from the consent of the people, or bestowed upon him for their benefit, he is disposed to consider it in the light of a private estate, intended for his own use, and to be enjoyed at his discretion. By the natural order of things; that is, by the disposition of Providence, it appears to be his province to command, as it is that of his subjects to obey; and every effort, upon their part, to limit his <284> authority, is regarded by him as an act of rebellion, which, in duty to himself and his posterity, and in the capacity of the vice-gerent of heaven, he is bound to elude by artifice or repel by force.

To avoid these dangers to liberty, with which recent events had strongly impressed men's minds, it was by some thought requisite to abolish the kingly office altogether, and these republican doctrines came to be propagated especially by men of knowledge and speculation, who reasoned upon the general principles of government, and compared the different political systems which have taken place in different ages and countries. Those who consider the usual incitements to genius will not be surprised to find, that, amidst all the disorders of that period, the number of speculative reasoners upon government was far from being inconsiderable. The important disputes, and violent struggle in which a great part of the nation was engaged, by awakening a spirit of activity and enterprise, contributed to accelerate, instead of retarding the pursuits of science and literature; and by opening to men of letters a wide field of am-<285>bition, excited them to cultivate their talents, and to bring forward their learning to the public. To the operation of such causes we may, in part at least, refer the political treatises of Milton,[34] which breathe that ardent love of liberty, and that vehement spirit

34. John Milton (1608–74) became Latin secretary to the Council of State after the

of invective, to be expected from the sublime author of Paradise Lost; at the same time that they are apt, on some occasions, to disgust the reader by an appearance of prejudice and prepossession, and by an air of confidence and arrogance which runs throughout those performances.

During the horrors of the civil war, a number of philosophers, men totally free from the religious enthusiasm and party prejudices of the times, are said to have employed themselves in conversing and reasoning upon political subjects. After the death of the king, these persons were formed into a regular society, for examining and discussing the most important questions concerning the best form of a commonwealth, and the advantages or disadvantages of such forms as had, in different periods of the world, been reduced into practice. The Oceana, and other discourses, <286> published by Mr. Harrington;[35] appear to have been, partly, the fruit of those lucubrations. These writings discover an extensive knowledge of history, the most liberal views with respect to government, a thorough acquaintance with the true principles of democracy, and great skill and discernment in accommodating those principles to the peculiar circumstances of the English nation.

The chief instances of popular government, which had fallen under the experience of that age, were the celebrated republics of Greece and Rome; which, for the most part, were established among a handful of people inhabiting a narrow district; in most cases, a single town with its dependencies. In these very limited states, there was little inconvenience or difficulty in convening the whole people to deliberate on public affairs, and to exercise the supreme powers of government. The legislative power, therefore, together with a considerable part of the executive, was commonly lodged in the great body of the people; though the privilege of proposing the subjects of deliberation to the legislative assembly was often committed, exclusively, to a smaller <287> council, or senate, composed of the higher order of citizens, or elected by the legislative body itself. A constitution of this nature was evidently impracticable in a large community, the members of which were spread over an extensive country. In a great nation, like that of England,

execution of Charles I in 1649. Briefly imprisoned at the Restoration, he used his years of political disgrace to write *Paradise Lost* (1667), *Paradise Regained* (1671), and *Samson Agonistes* (1671). His chief politico-historical works were the *Tenure of Kings and Magistrates* (1649) and the *History of Britain* (1669).

35. James Harrington (1611–77): political theorist and author of *The Commonwealth of Oceana* (1656). He formed the Rota Club for political discussion in 1659–60.

the assembling of the whole people to make laws, or to deliberate upon the national business, would produce a meeting so numerous and disorderly, as must be incapable of any regular procedure, and liable to endless disorders. But, fortunately, in Britain, the custom of convening the representatives of the people, as a constituent part of the legislature, had been long established; and upon this principle Harrington, and the other speculative politicians of that time, laid the foundation of that commonwealth which they recommended to their fellow citizens. They proposed that the supreme powers of government should be committed to a body of representatives, chosen by the nation at large, in the manner which appeared the best calculated to prevent the effects of bribery and undue influence upon the electors; and in such a moderate number as might enable them to main-<288>tain the utmost regularity in their proceedings, and to extend their care and superintendence to every department of administration. By this expedient it was thought, that the evils incident to kingly government on the one hand, and to pure democracy on the other, at least in the shape in which it had been exhibited in the ancient republics, might be equally avoided. The dangers arising from the ignorance, the prejudices, the violence, and confusion, of a large tumultuary assembly were effectually precluded; while the interest of the people at large was understood to be sufficiently guarded by that controul and influence over their commissioners, which, from the frequency of elections, they might be expected to retain.

The commencement and progress of the civil war had an effect, no less remarkable, with respect to the religious, than with respect to the political sentiments of the nation. From the increasing heat of controversy, and according as the adversaries of the king had been more successful, the opposition to the hierarchy became, of course, more violent. For some time after the accession of James, the <289> Puritans, under which denomination were comprehended all the protestant dissenters, who were, for the most part, distributed into the two great branches of presbyterians and independents, were contented with liberty of conscience, and with an indulgence in their peculiar modes of worship. But the continuance of the controversy suggested other views to those two orders of sectaries, and inspired them with higher pretensions. After the meeting of the long parliament, the presbyterians, whose doctrines were supported by many leading members in that assembly, and particularly by a great majority in the house of commons, were encouraged to attempt the subversion of the established religion, by destroying all subordination in the rank and authority of churchmen. But when the king and parliament had come to decide their differences by force, even this religious reformation was held by many to be insufficient: the opinions of men deviated still farther from the old establishment; and the independents, who rejected all interposition of the public, either in the appointment of the clergy, or in the care and direction of religion, <290> advanced, with rapid strides, in consideration and popularity.

The different principles of those two branches of the sectaries produced a natural conjunction, as was formerly mentioned, with the respective systems of the two great political parties now in opposition to the king. The presbyterians, who, by abolishing the several ranks and dignities of the church, proposed to emancipate the clergy from their dependence upon the crown, as well as to diminish their influence over the laity, were disposed to support the system of those political reformers, whose object it was to check the abuses of prerogative, and circumscribe without subverting the authority of the sovereign. The independents, who advanced a step further in relation to the church, pushed also their political tenets to a proportional height, disapproved of all ecclesiastical establishments, and holding that every voluntary association of christians ought to have the liberty of choosing their own religious teachers, they were, in like manner, averse from every modification of monarchy, and were led to join those republicans who contended that all the <291> executive officers of the state should be under the appointment of the people.

As these republican doctrines were thus gaining ground in the nation, they made also considerable advances, though with less rapidity, in parliament. The leading members of that assembly, who had long acted in consequence of their professed opinions in favour of limited monarchy, were likely, the greater part of them, to retain their former sentiments. If some, during the violence of the struggle, were induced to aim at greater innovations, and to seek the total abolition of kingly power, there were others, corrupted by motives of interest, or alarmed by the ungovernable spirit of reformation which now discovered itself, who either seized the opportunity of joining the court, or thought proper to retire from public business. In a situation so new and hazardous, we need not wonder that several persons, who had hitherto withstood the encroachments of the prerogative, should now shrink from a contest which threatened to involve the kingdom in anarchy and blood; and should thus leave the field to men of keener tempers, and of more persevering re-<292>solution. Lord Falkland, and Mr. Hide,[36] whose abilities and personal character entitled them to great consideration, and who, at the beginning of the long parliament, had stood forth in censuring the measures of the king, and concurred in the important regulations then introduced, deserted their former political friends; but though they were now enlisted upon the side of the crown, they still professed a regard to the ancient constitution, and a disposition to moderate the violent councils of Charles.

The proceedings of parliament were still more affected by the death of some of its principal members. Soon after the parties had recourse to arms, Mr. Hampden,[37] whose inflexible integrity, and sound understanding, joined to his great modesty and vigour of mind, had procured him almost equal influence in war and in peace, and, without the appearance, had rendered him the real leader of the whole party, was killed in an action, while he conducted the troops under his command to repel a sudden attack of the enemy. The loss of such a man in that cloudy and tempestuous season, may justly be regarded as a <293> national calamity. He was, in religion, a presbyterian; and, in politics, a steady adherent of the old constitution. His death was followed, soon after, by that of Mr. Pym,[38] whose talents for public speaking, and whose great experience in the business of parliament, had raised him to a principal share in all the important transactions of that period. His eloquence distinguished him above all his cotemporaries, and is said to have been productive of extraordinary effects. So far as we can form a judgment from the specimens that have come down to us, he seems to speak like a man who labours to convince and to persuade, more than to entertain; and though liable, perhaps, to the imputation of some formality and prolixity, he discovers great ability in bringing many arguments to centre in one point; and presenting such views of a subject as are calculated to lay hold of the prejudices, and to overpower the reason of his hearers.

Notwithstanding the extreme simplicity of manners and frugality for which Mr. Pym was noted; though, beside his private fortune, he enjoyed a

36. Lucius Cary, second Viscount Falkland (1610?–1643): served in the Long Parliament (1640) and spoke against Laud and Strafford in 1641. After 1642 he supported Charles I. On Edward Hyde, Lord Clarendon, see note 15 in this chapter.

37. Hampden died 18 June 1643 at Chalgrove Field, fighting royalist forces led by Prince Rupert, the nephew of Charles I.

38. On Pym, see note 10 in this chapter.

salary as master of the ordnance; <294> and though he acted in a high department, at a time when parliament, in open war with the king, had occasion to manage considerable funds levied on that account; he died in great poverty, a satisfactory proof that he had served the cause with disinterested fidelity. So sensible were the commons of his faithful services, that they not only ordered a monument to be erected to his memory, and his corpse to be interred in Westminster-abbey, but also voted a considerable sum of money for the payment of his debts.

While time and accidents were thus producing great changes in the leading characters who had hitherto appeared upon the stage, the war opened a new scene of action, and gave birth to a new set of talents and accomplishments, by which individuals, formerly obscure and unknown, rose to consideration and importance. Eloquence, and dexterity in managing parliamentary business, were now degraded into a secondary rank; and, in a great measure, eclipsed by that courage and conduct in the field, and by those peculiar virtues and qualities displayed in the military profession. Men who, by serving in a foreign country, had <295> already acquired experience and reputation in war, were immediately placed in the higher military departments; while others, whose disposition and genius peculiarly fitted them for the service, found opportunities of signalising their activity, valour, or capacity, and were soon brought into notice.

The adherents of the king were chiefly composed of the nobility and higher gentry, men who, by their wealth and station, had much to lose; and who, in the annihilation of monarchy, and in the anarchy that was likely to follow, foresaw the ruin of their fortunes, and the extinction of their consideration and influence. The middling and inferior gentry, together with the inhabitants of towns; those who entertained a jealousy of the nobles, and of the king, or who, by the changes in the state of society, had lately been raised to independence, became, on the other hand, the great supporters of parliament, and formed the chief part of the armies levied by that assembly. The differences in the character and situation of the troops, which came, in this manner, to be arranged upon the opposite sides, were very remarkable. The forces of the king were <296> commanded by officers whose rank in life had led them frequently to serve in the wars upon the continent, and who possessed a degree of influence over their followers, which, in some measure, supplied the want of military discipline. The armies of parliament, on the contrary, were composed of an unruly and disorderly multitude, under the direction of persons, who, for the most part, had no natural authority corresponding to their stations, and who, unless in a few instances, appear, at the beginning of the war, to have been destitute of military knowledge. Mr. Hume has, with his usual discernment, pointed out the consequences of these different situations, which are such as might be expected. For some time after the war broke out, the king was generally successful, and in every struggle the forces of parliament were either worsted or rendered incapable of improving those advantages which fortune threw in their way.

It might easily be foreseen, however, that if the operations of the war should be protracted for any considerable period, the fortune and circumstances of the parties would be reversed. The nobility, who supported the cause of the <297> monarch, were too independent and too jealous of each other to be reduced under proper subordination, and were fitter to act in separate pillaging parties, at the head of their respective followers, than to unite and co-operate in such a large body as the execution of a great enterprise might require. The parliamentary troops were in a different situation. Without any previous attachment to particular leaders, they acquired habits of submission to those officers under whom they had fought; men who derived their preferment, not from their birth or their opulence, but from their military services; and whom different degrees of experience, of capacity, and of success, had established in their several stations. As the forces of parliament comprehended the great mass of the people, we need not wonder that when they came to surpass those of the king in subordination and discipline, as well as in numbers, they should immediately obtain a decided superiority.

Among all those who took party against the king, it is natural to suppose that such as had taken up arms in the cause, and had, through the whole course of the contest, been retained <298> in the service, would be distinguished by their zeal, and by the extremities to which they pushed their system of reformation. The greatest part of these troops were, accordingly, independents in religion, and in the state, republicans. That original ardour which led them to take so active a part in the controversy, joined to the circumstances which, during the progress of it, could not fail to inflame their passions, had confirmed their aversion to all regal power, and to all ecclesiastical establishments, and had riveted their affections to an opposite system, both of civil government and of religious worship.

By a singular concurrence of accidents, the command of the chief parliamentary army, towards the conclusion of the war, was devolved upon an officer* of great integrity and worth, distinguished by his military talents, but otherwise (which daily experience proves to be no inconsistency) of slender capacity; while the real direction and management of those forces, together with their commander, was acquired by a leader of the most extraordinary abilities which that, or perhaps any age, has produced. <299> This was the famous Oliver Cromwell,[39] whose character is universally known.

During those parliamentary disputes which preceded the commencement of hostilities, Cromwell, though a member of parliament as early as the year 1628, appears to have remained in obscurity. It should seem that, although the ardent enthusiastic spirit by which he was possessed, could hardly fail to be remarked, and to gain him credit with the party to which he was devoted, the inelegance and rudeness of his manners, and his total deficiency in public speaking, prevented his acquiring much reputation or influence. But no sooner had the war opened a new scene of action, than he began to display that uncommon genius with which he was endowed, and to assume that consideration and importance to which he was entitled. The troop which he commanded was immediately distinguished by superior discipline, and by good behaviour in every engagement. The intrepidity, vigour, and enterprizing disposition of its leader were no less conspicuous.† By his decisive <300> judgment in forming resolutions, and by his rapidity and steadiness in the execution of them; by his penetration in discovering, and his dexterity in managing the characters of his adherents and associates, he quickly rose to eminence, both as a partizan, and as a military officer. That he was originally sincere in his religious professions is extremely probable; though he

* Fairfax.

† It must excite amazement to find, in opposition to every other account, that Oliver Cromwell is taxed with cowardice, in the most pointed terms, by no less a personage than Denzil Hollis, a zealous presbyterian, and eminent leader of the commons. If any credit could be given to this charge, it would rather increase than diminish our admiration of this extraordinary man; since it would lay us under the necessity of supposing that Cromwell, by his dexterity, judgment, and political firmness, was capable of concealing and counteracting the effect of a personal weakness, apparently, of all others, the most adverse to a military reputation. See Hollis's Memoirs, pub. 1699.

39. Oliver Cromwell (1599–1658): English statesman who superintended the trial and execution of Charles I in 1649. From late 1653 he was Lord Protector, a title that gave him supreme legislative and executive power in association with Parliament and the Council of State.

afterwards employed the mask of piety to cover and promote his ambitious designs. How far the characters of a hypocrite and a fanatic are capable of being reconciled; or whether inconsistency be not frequently a prominent feature of the human mind, I shall not pretend to determine;[40] but certain it is, that the consummate hypocrisy of Cromwell <301> was the great engine by which he procured the confidence of his whole party, and obtained an ascendancy over all their movements.

One of the first and most masterly of all the stratagems employed by this arch politician, after he had risen to a high situation, was the new modelling of the army, by which he secured to himself and his party the entire direction of all the forces of parliament. Towards the conclusion of the war, although a great proportion of those troops were of the independent party, there were still among them a number of presbyterians. The Earl of Essex, Sir William Waller, the Earl of Manchester, (formerly Lord Kimbolton,)[41] with many other distinguished officers, had shewn an uniform attachment to the principles of that sect; and, however they might think that, in the present emergency, it was proper to limit the prerogative, were still the friends of monarchical government. While such persons remained in the army, they could not fail to be possessed of considerable influence; and Cromwell saw that it was necessary to get rid of them, in order to accomplish his designs.

For this purpose his friends suggested a re-<302>formation in point of military discipline; the neglect of which became a topic of universal complaint, and was considered as the immediate cause of many important miscarriages. A measure of this kind, so popular in itself, was warmly supported by Fairfax,[42] the general, and by those who, not entertaining any suspicion of the secret motives by which it was dictated, had been the most active and zealous in the cause of the people. In the prosecution of this plan, it was

40. Eighteenth-century accounts, such as Hume's, generally agree in considering Cromwell a fanatic and a hypocrite. It was only later in the nineteenth century that a new, more heroic image emerged, principally in the works of Thomas Carlyle.

41. Robert Devereux, third earl of Essex (1591–1646), commanded the parliamentary forces at Edgehill (1642) and took Reading (1643) before he was forced to relinquish his command in 1645; Sir William Waller (1597?–1668), a parliamentary general who held joint commands with Essex and Cromwell, and was also forced to step down by the Self-Denying Ordinance (see note 43 in this chapter).

42. Thomas Fairfax, third baron (1612–71): English soldier and statesman, was given command of the New Model Army in 1645 and crushed the royalist forces at Naseby. Later he was instrumental in restoring Charles II in 1660.

artfully represented, that those who had a voice in parliament were possessed of authority and rank incompatible with military subordination, and, by the attendance in that assembly which their duty required, were disqualified for the exercise of other employments. A *self-denying ordinance*[43] was therefore proposed, by which members of parliament were declared incapable of civil and military offices; and this regulation, by means of the popular clamour which had been excited, was carried through both houses. In this manner the leaders of the presbyterian party, who had long enjoyed seats in parliament, and had been the chief conductors of parliamentary business, were excluded from all share in the <303> direction of the forces. The army was immediately new-modelled, and formed into different regiments and companies, under a new set of officers; with which measure many of the presbyterian party, whom the late regulation did not affect, were so disgusted as to throw up their commissions. Cromwell himself, though a member of parliament, found means, by the solicitation of the general, to delay, for some time, and afterwards entirely to evade the resignation of his command. The decisive battle of Naseby, which was fought soon after the self-denying ordinance was carried into execution, reflected no less credit upon that measure than upon the personal abilities of its contriver.

After the king's troops had been completely defeated, and when his Majesty found it no longer practicable to face his enemies in the field, he seems to have placed his last refuge in the opposition and discord between those different parties into which the nation was divided. He appears to have thought that, by availing himself of their political animosities, he might hold a balance among them, and still, in some measure, maintain his authority. <304> With this view, he threw himself upon the protection of the Scottish army, then at Newark; thinking, perhaps, that the Scots, from the concessions which he had made to them, from their ancient hereditary connection with his family, and from their being of late under some discontent with the behaviour of the English parliament, were most likely to afford him a favourable reception. It must be admitted, however, that whether we consider the principles of the Scotch covenanters, or the strength which they could muster in opposition to the English forces, there was no ground to expect

43. A bill passed by the Commons on 19 December 1644 stipulating that no member of the House of Commons or Lords could hold any military command. Only Cromwell was exempt.

that, either from inclination or from prudential motives, they would undertake the defence of Charles, or attempt to rescue him from the hands of his enemies: Nor can it enter into the wildest imagination to conceive that such an attempt would have been either just or proper; they were the most violent religious adversaries of the king; they were the allies of parliament; they had hitherto struggled with all their might, and had been very instrumental in obliging the former to submit to the demands of the latter. Would it not have been the height of <305> absurdity, and even of bad faith, now that their object was nearly accomplished, to change sides all at once, and, by a vain effort in behalf of the king, to assist or countenance him in refusing or delaying that submission? They were, no doubt, highly censurable in delivering him up to parliament.[44] It was incumbent on them to take no advantage of the circumstance by which they had obtained a power over his person. From a punctilio of delicacy, they should rather have connived at the escape than have agreed to the surrender of their prince, who had fled to them for shelter. But to make that surrender an expedient for extorting the arrears of pay, which they could not otherwise have procured, was unquestionably a disgraceful transaction.

The leaders of parliament, meanwhile, had penetrated the ambitious designs of Cromwell and his associates; and, upon the termination of the war, thought it high time to free themselves from such unruly and turbulent servants. They had accordingly taken measures for that purpose. It was proposed that a part of the troops should be sent to Ireland, to assist in quelling the disorders in that coun-<306>try; and that the remainder should be dismissed from the service. These proceedings did not escape the notice of that powerful body against which they were directed; and their tendency was too manifest not to excite universal commotion, and suggest precautions for guarding against the danger. A petition was drawn up by the army to their general, to be laid before parliament, complaining of grievances, requiring payment of arrears, relief of widows and maimed soldiers, and an indemnity for past irregularities committed in the course of the war. To watch over their interest, and to secure unanimity in their future operations, they appointed a sort of military parliament, composed of the superior officers, corresponding to the house of peers, and of representatives from each troop or company, under the name of *agitators,* in imitation of the house of com-

44. Charles I was given over to Parliament on 30 January 1647.

mons. To this body all disputes with parliament, and the management of all common concerns, was committed. The parliament afterwards voted that a considerable part of the army should be disbanded; and, to avoid the tumult apprehended on that occasion, gave orders that different <307> regiments or bodies of men should be separated, and receive their dismission at different times and places. But the military council were too sharp-sighted to obey such orders; and too conscious of their power to pay any regard to this resolution of parliament.

Upon the delivery of the king to the commissioners of the English parliament, a treaty was immediately set on foot between his majesty and that assembly for composing the public disorders, and settling the future exercise of the government. The schemes of the republican party required that, without loss of time, this agreement should be prevented; and therefore, by the contrivance of Cromwell, with concurrence of the military council, but without the knowledge, it is said, of Fairfax, an officer, with a party of soldiers, was dispatched to seize the king, and bring him a prisoner to the army. With this violence Charles was not displeased; as it coincided with his plans of managing the different parties, and afforded the prospect of another power, capable of controuling or counter-balancing that of parliament.

The seizure of the king, in this manner, <308> was an open declaration of war against the two houses, and was followed, in a short time, by the march of the army to London. Upon their approach it appeared that all expectation of resistance was vain. The city, after having taken a decided part against the mutinous spirit of the troops, was struck with a panic, and surrendered without attempting any defence.—The speakers of each house, attended by a number of members, deserting their functions, came to meet the army at Hounslow-heath, and to solicit their protection. The remains of parliament, confounded and dispirited by so general a defection of their friends and partizans, were, after a few fruitless attempts to maintain their authority, obliged to surrender at discretion, to repeal all their former offensive resolutions, and to yield an implicit submission to the military force.

Charles was highly satisfied with these transactions, and did every thing in his power to promote them. He had hitherto been treated with the utmost respect by the military leaders, and he believed that the exaltation and triumph of the army over parliament would, in the end, produce the reestablishment of regal <309> authority. He was, in fact, courted at this time by all parties, which had such an effect upon his spirits that he was heard frequently to declare, "You cannot do without me; you will fall to ruin if I do not sustain you." Misled by this idea, he held a correspondence with every party, while, expecting to procure still better terms from their adversaries, he was withheld from concluding an agreement with any. But these delusive appearances did not long remain. As soon as Cromwell and his associates had completely answered the purpose for which they got possession of the king's person, they began to think of delivering themselves from that incumbrance; and this they accomplished without much difficulty, by treating him with less indulgence, and instilling apprehensions that he was in danger from the soldiery. Charles, now intimidated, and disgusted with the behaviour of those whom he had so lately regarded as favourable to his interest, took the first opportunity of making his escape, and fled to the Isle of Wight,[45] by the governor of which he was detained a prisoner.

The late violent measures of the army had, <310> in the mean time, stirred up a flame in the nation, and by shewing, at once, the extent of the military power, and the immediate purpose of establishing a republican government, had roused the presbyterians both in England and Scotland, and induced them even to unite with the royalists in opposing such violent innovations. The commencement of a new civil war interrupted, for some time, the operations of the republicans in modelling the constitution, and gave leisure for new efforts to conclude a treaty between the king and parliament. But the sanguine expectations of Charles, which had been raised by this exertion in his favour, prevented his acceptance of the terms proposed, and retarded a final agreement till the opportunity was lost. The raw troops collected upon the part of the king were soon defeated by Cromwell and Fairfax, who, at the head of their veteran forces, found nothing in the kingdom capable of resistance.

It now appeared that the republican party were determined to lose no time in executing their designs. The leaders of the army presented to parliament a remonstrance, in which they painted the crimes of Charles in strong <311> colours, and demanded that he should be immediately brought to trial. They, at the same time, gave orders to lay hold of his person, and to keep him under confinement. The establishment of a common-wealth required that the king's life should be made a sacrifice; for carrying which into execution it was necessary that parliament should be laid under compulsion. By a mili-

45. Charles I fled to the Isle of Wight on 11 November 1647.

tary force, therefore, under the command of a Colonel Pride, forty commoners on one day, and on the day following ninety-one more of the presbyterian persuasion were violently secluded from the house.[46] After this operation a clear majority remained in the republican interest, and there was no longer any difficulty in procuring from them a resolution to authorise the trial of Charles. This measure was, with disdain, rejected by the upper house; upon which the commons declared that the peers were no essential part of the legislature, and proceeded to execute their own resolution. It was in virtue of a commission, appointed by this junto of the commons, that Charles was tried, condemned and executed.[47]

The character of this prince,[48] as there was <312> reason to expect, has been represented in such opposite colours, by the writers of different parties, that we can pay little regard, either to the panegyric of the one set, or the invectives of the other; and if our object be the discovery of truth, we must fix our attention solely upon that series of actions by which the eventful history of his reign is distinguished. At the distance from which we now survey the conduct of Charles, his misfortunes can hardly fail to move our compassion, and to soften that resentment which the whole tenor of his conduct is apt to excite. It is impossible, however, to overlook this glaring circumstance, that his misfortunes were, in a great measure, owing to his crimes. Disregarding the ancient constitution of the kingdom, he formed the design of establishing an absolute power in the crown; and this design he incessantly prosecuted, in spite of numberless obstacles and disappointments; notwithstanding the determined resolution, displayed by his subjects, to maintain their natural rights; and without being deterred by the immediate prospect of involving his dominions in all the calamities and horrors of a civil war. Nei-<313>ther can it be forgotten, that in the execution of his plan for exalting the regal authority, Charles was ready to practise every artifice, every species of dissimulation; that he paid little regard to good faith;

46. On 6 December 1648, troops commanded by Colonel Thomas Pride arrested 45 members of Parliament and prevented another 186 from taking their seats in the House of Commons. The excluded members were mostly Presbyterians who were regarded as antagonistic to the army and favored a settlement with Charles I. The event became known as Pride's Purge.

47. The trial opened on 20 January 1649, and Charles was executed 30 January.

48. To compare Millar and Hume on the character of Charles I, see Hume's assessment in *HE,* 5:542–46.

and even scrupled not to violate the most express and solemn engagements. From the beginning of the dispute with his parliaments, to the commencement of the war, every concession to his people seems to have been made with the view of retracting it, whenever he should find a convenient opportunity; the same duplicity is equally observable in those transactions which, after his forces had been finally subdued, he attempted to conclude with different parties; and through the whole of his life, we often discover, in his public declarations, a mean system of equivocation and mental reservation, peculiarly unsuitable to the characteristical gravity and loftiness of his deportment.

It has been the fortune of Charles to have the history of his reign transmitted to posterity by one of the first philosophers of the present age;[49] whose favorite object seems to have been to pull down the prevailing doctrines of the whigs, and to represent the peculiar opinions <314> of the two great political parties into which the nation is divided, as equally erroneous, and equally founded upon a narrow and partial examination of human society. This has given rise to a strong bias in favour of the house of Stuart, which had formerly been borne down by the tide of popular clamour, and has produced, in particular, a laboured apology for the misconduct of Charles; in which, it must be confessed, that the facts are, for the most part, fairly stated, and the general principles apparently just; but the particulars agreeable to the author's hypothesis are so amplified and brought forward, and those in opposition to it are so contracted and disguised, as to present, upon the whole, a very artful picture, calculated to mislead an incautious and superficial observer.

In vindication of Charles, it has been suggested, that his misconduct proceeded from the notions which he had imbibed of the English constitution: that he followed merely the footsteps of his father, by whom he was taught to look upon himself as an absolute prince, invested by heaven with an indefeasible hereditary dominion: that he found this <315> opinion supported by the example of many of his predecessors, those especially of the Tudor-family; and that he was farther confirmed in it, by observing the absolute authority exercised by most of the cotemporary princes upon the continent

49. The reference here is to Hume, who lies in the background of this entire account. Millar represents Hume as producing a narrative favorable to the king by seeming to stand at a distance from both the views of the Whigs and Tories.

of Europe. That the dissimulation which he employed, in the pursuit of his plans, must be imputed to the extreme difficulties and embarrassments of his situation. Conscious of the rectitude of his aim, and unable to accomplish it by direct means, he was reduced to the necessity of pursuing it by crooked artifices and expedients. In maintaining the sacred rights which, he understood, were committed to him, as the vice-gerent of God Almighty, he seems to have thought that the temporising measures, which he adopted, were imputable to his enemies, by whom he was driven into those indirect and fraudulent courses.

These observations, though delivered with such address and eloquence as mark the ingenuity and abilities of the author, are far from appearing satisfactory. Who, that acknowledges the happiness of society to be the great end of all government, can enter so far into the feelings of a tyrant as to listen to his <316> justification? when he says, "I mistook the nature of my office. I thought the people were created solely for my benefit, not I for theirs. I believed that they had no rights independent of my arbitrary will; and that their lives and fortunes might be sacrificed at pleasure to my humour and caprice. I supposed that I was entitled to maintain, either by foul or by fair means, by dissimulation and treachery, or by direct force, and by shedding the blood of my subjects, all those powers which have been assumed and possessed by my forefathers."[50]

This apology, such as it is, appears more applicable to the leader of a band of Arabs, or of Tartar freebooters, who subsist by robbery and murder, than to the king of a civilized nation, in which a regular system of law and government has been long established. The barbarous chief is probably unacquainted with any other mode of living, but Charles must have known better. He had cultivated his understanding by acquired knowledge, was no stranger to the different forms of government which had existed in different countries, nor probably to the professed purpose for which they were introduced, or to the respec-<317>tive advantages which have resulted from them. He was no stranger to the history of his own country, and could not fail to know that it never was, at any period, subjected to a despotical government. He could not overlook those *great charters* which his predecessors had so frequently granted to their subjects, and which expressly ascertained the privileges of the people and the limitations of the prerogative. If usurpations

50. See *Cobbett's Parliamentary History of England,* vol. 2 (London, 1806).

were occasionally committed by particular sovereigns, or their ministers, these were always complained of; were generally followed by a redress of grievances, and sometimes by an exemplary punishment of the offenders. Though some of the Tudor princes exercised many arbitrary powers, and stretched the prerogative beyond the pitch which it had attained at any former period; yet even their example could give no countenance to the principal usurpations of Charles; and there still were certain limits in the constitution which those tyrants did not venture to transgress. They never ventured to assume the direct power of taxation, without the concurrence of parliament, nor to carry on, for any long period, the various branches of administration without the advice of that national council. <318>

With respect to the governments upon the continent of Europe, they were originally limited like that of England, and had of late been rendered absolute from circumstances peculiar to themselves, which could never be supposed to authorise an English monarch to introduce a similar change in his own dominions. If Charles, therefore, was misled from the circumstances of the times, we cannot suppose that this proceeded from an error in judgment, but must believe that the deception was produced, as is usual in such cases, by the false lights arising from the irregularity of his passions. It is unfortunate for the memory of this monarch, that his ambition was not of that brilliant kind which is fitted to excite admiration. It was not connected with any great view, either of public or of private aggrandizement, or accompanied with the display of great military talents, or of any splendid abilities. By overturning the constitution, he neither proposed to acquire the *eclat* of a conqueror, nor to extend the empire of his country, nor to raise her importance in the scale of nations. Stately and forbidding in his deportment, obstinate in his opinions, and inflexible in his measures, he seems to have had no other object than to establish that po-<319>litical system which co-incided with his temper and disposition; to have aimed at nothing farther than to obviate the hazard of contradiction, and supersede the necessity of recommending himself to his people by affability and popular manners.

To estimate the degree of understanding or abilities possessed by Charles is not very easy. The talents and capacity ascribed to him by his friends are supposed to have been chiefly displayed in conversation and in his literary compositions. But the authenticity of the latter, which has been much questioned, can hardly be ascertained in a satisfactory manner; and the opinion entertained of the former is liable to the suspicion of being tinctured by an admiration of his high rank, and by compassion for his misfortunes. During his conferences with the commissioners of parliament in the Isle of Wight, he is said to have acquitted himself in a manner that impressed his hearers with respect and veneration. That he understood those topics, which had been the study of his whole life, may easily be conceived; and that his abilities were of a cast which qualified him for speculation more than for action, there is good ground to believe. <320> Let it also be remembered that he was a king whose crown "had not yet lost all its original brightness," and we may account for this veneration without supposing any thing extraordinary. It is at least certain that the whole course of his public conduct exhibits one continued scene of arrogance, meanness, inconsistency, and imprudence. His extravagant claims were advanced with heat and precipitation, and supported with eagerness and violence, until the nation was alarmed and thrown into a ferment; after which he had recourse to apparent submission, to humiliating compliances, and to hypocritical professions. Those who endeavour to palliate the errors of his government, observe that he suffered himself to be guided by persons of much inferior capacity to his own. But this, in a temper so little influenced by the warmth of affection, affords a certain proof of the want of discernment. There is no doubt that his measures were frequently directed by ministers, whose views he ought to have distrusted; and by the queen, whose religious principles both excited the jealousy of the English nation, and subjected her to an influence of which he had reason to be apprehensive. <321>

The private virtues of Charles have been justly the subject of commendation. Sober and temperate, he set before his people an important example of decency and regularity of manners; while, by his taste in the fine arts, and by his attention to reward the exertions of genius, he was of signal service in promoting useful improvements. Though incessantly actuated by the love of power, and much irritated by opposition, he was not violent in his resentments, nor in his temper, unforgiving and revengeful. Had he been able quietly to obtain an unlimited authority, it is not likely that he would have been guilty of great excesses in the exercise of it. Neither does he seem, on the other hand, to have been animated with much generosity towards his friends, or to have felt a strong attachment to any of those favourites, who suffered in his cause, and in whose judgment he had placed an implicit confidence. From his lofty ideas of the sacred character with which he was invested, he probably thought that his subjects in sacrificing their lives and fortunes to his conveniency, did no more than their duty; <322> and that of consequence no returns of gratitude, upon that account, were due to them.

The enthusiasm inspired by an opinion of his own dignity and self-importance, enabled him to support with becoming decency, and even with magnanimity, the sad reverse of fortune which he experienced in the latter part of his reign; and contributed to the display of that patience, resignation, and meekness, with which he bore the insults and indignities of his unfeeling enemies.

The death of Charles appears to have struck all Europe with terror and astonishment. The execution of a king upon a public scaffold, and with all the forms of judicial procedure, at a period when the state of society had begun to mitigate the severity of penal laws, and had also very generally introduced a despotical government, was a measure which ran counter to the ordinary course of political events. It was beheld like that phenomenon, which

———Disastrous twilight sheds
On half the nation, and with fear of change
Perplexes monarchs.[51] <323>

With regard to the justice of this measure, it should seem, that at this distance of time, when the animosities and prejudices of that age have in a great measure subsided, there is little room, among such as are qualified to judge, for any considerable difference of opinion; but we consider this prince merely in the light of a private individual, and compare his conduct with that of other criminals, there can, I should think, be no doubt that he merited the highest punishment. If rapine and murder are accounted capital crimes, what shall we say of that ambition, which breaks down, at once, all the barriers of personal security; overturns the whole fabric of the constitution; establishes the dominion of arbitrary will in place of legal restraint; and, in seeking to attain this object, destroys the lives and fortunes of thousands!

But the situation of a sovereign is so different from that of private individuals, and an attempt to punish him is attended with such complicated

51. The lines are from John Milton, *Paradise Lost* (1667), I, ii, 595ff.

disorders, that the only circumstance which ought to regulate the interference of government, in such cases, <324> must be the consideration of public utility. Was the trial and condemnation of Charles regulated by this consideration? Was it a measure of public expediency? Was it calculated to remove disorders; to improve the constitution; to restore tranquillity? That it was not absolutely necessary for the preservation of the liberties of the people, must, I think, be admitted; for the spirit of the king was so reduced by his misfortunes, that he would, probably, have submitted to any restrictions; he would even have consented, it is said, that the crown should be directly transmitted to the prince of Wales, under the management of a regency. By rejecting such terms, it was manifest, that the leaders of the prevailing party had abandoned every idea of improving the old government, and had resolved, that *monarchy,* in every shape, and under any limitations whatever, should be entirely exploded. The trial and execution of Charles was doubtless intended for the purpose of introducing a republican form of government; and according as we hold such a revolution to have been expedient <325> or the contrary, we shall be led to condemn, or approve of that measure.

Concerning the general question, whether a government of this nature was, at that period, accommodated to the circumstances of the English nation, it may be difficult to form a decisive opinion. Many politicians have asserted, that a republican constitution is peculiarly adapted to a small state, and cannot be maintained in a large community. This doctrine seems to have arisen from a view of the ancient republics, in which the whole people composed the legislative assembly; and is evidently inapplicable to those modern systems of democracy, in which the legislative power is committed to national representatives. Nothing is more common than for philosophers to be imposed upon by the different acceptation of words. The nations of antiquity having no notion of a representative government, countries of large extent were subjected universally to an arbitrary and slovenly despotism; and it was only in a few small states that it was thought practicable for the mass of the people to retain, in their own <326> hands, the supreme powers of public administration. The expedient, employed first in modern times, of substituting representatives, in place of the whole people, to exercise the supreme powers in the state, has removed the difficulty of communicating a popular constitution to countries of a great extent; as it may prevent the legislative assembly from being too numerous, either for maintaining good order in its deliberations, or for superintending the conduct of the chief executive officers.

If, by a republic, is meant a government in which there is no king, or hereditary chief magistrate, it should seem, that this political system is peculiarly adapted to the two extremes, of a very small and a very great nation. In a very small state, no other form of government can subsist. Suppose a territory, containing no more than 30,000 inhabitants, and these paying taxes, one with another, at the rate of thirty shillings yearly; this would produce a public revenue, at the disposal of the crown, amounting annually to 450,000 l. a sum totally insufficient for supporting the dignity and autho-<327>rity of the crown, and for bestowing on the king an influence superior to that which might be possessed by casual combinations of a few of his richest subjects.

Suppose, on the other hand, a territory so extensive and populous as to contain thirty millions of inhabitants, paying taxes in the same proportion; this, at the free disposal of a king, would bestow upon him an annual revenue, so enormous as to create a degree of patronage and influence which no regulations could effectually restrain, and would render every attempt to limit the powers of the crown in a great measure vain and insignificant. In such a state, therefore, it seems extremely difficult to maintain the natural rights of mankind otherwise than by abolishing monarchy altogether. Thus, in a very small state, a democratical government is necessary, because the king would have too little authority; in a very great one, because he would have too much. In a state of moderate size, lying in a certain medium between the two extremes, it should seem, that monarchy may be established with advantage, and that the crown may be <328> expected to possess a sufficient share of authority for its own preservation, without endangering the people from the encroachments of prerogative. How far England was in these circumstances at the period in question, I shall not pretend to determine.

But, even supposing a republic to have been in itself, at that period, a preferable form of government, it could not, in England, be expected to produce beneficial consequences; because it was not supported by the general voice of the community. The death of the king, the preliminary steps to the establishment of that system, was neither authorized by the nation at large, nor by its representatives. It had no other authority than the determination of a house of commons, from which a great proportion of the members had been expelled by a military force. The peers refused their concurrence with indignation. Cromwell, and his associates, the leaders of the army, who had obtained the direction of the Independents, were in reality the authors of this transaction, which, we may safely affirm, was diametrically opposite to the opinions <329> and sentiments of by far the greater part of the nation.

In these peculiar circumstances, the execution of Charles cannot be approved of even by the warmest admirers of a republican constitution. The authority of every government is founded in *opinion;*[52] and no system, be it ever so perfect in itself, can be expected to acquire stability, or to produce good order and submission, unless it coincides with the general voice of the community. He who frames a political constitution upon a model of ideal perfection, and attempts to introduce it into any country, without consulting the inclinations of the inhabitants, is a most pernicious projector, who, instead of being applauded as a Lycurgus, ought to be chained and confined as a madman.

Though, from these considerations, an impartial and candid observer will be disposed, upon the whole, to disapprove of the rigorous punishment of Charles, it seems impossible to deny, that it was productive of some incidental advantages. As a conspicuous example of the resentment incurred <330> by the exertions of arbitrary power, it contributed to intimidate the succeeding princes, and to render them less resolute in their violent measures. It was, probably, the memory of this event, which made James II. shrink from his attempts, and facilitated the accession of William III.

It is no less evident, however, that the unfortunate issue of the contest between the king and parliament, brought for some time a discredit upon the laudable efforts of that assembly to support the constitution, and supplied the partizans of despotism with an argument in favour of their doctrine of *passive obedience,* by shewing the disorders which may arise from all resistance to the will of the monarch. <331>

52. See Hume's remarks in "Whether the British Government Inclines More to Absolute Monarchy or to a Republic": "It may farther be said, that, though men be much governed by interest; yet even interest itself, and all human affairs, are entirely governed by *opinion.*" *Essays, Moral, Political, and Literary,* ed. Eugene F. Miller (Indianapolis: Liberty Fund, 1985), 51.

CHAPTER V

Of Oliver Cromwell, and the Protectorate.

The boldness, the dexterity, and the dissimulation of Cromwell, had been eminently successful in conducting those measures which had ended in the death of the king, and in bringing the whole kingdom under the power of the independents. But the talents of this profound politician, his enterprising spirit, and the extent of his designs, were yet far from being completely unfolded. He had hitherto only set himself at the head of his own party; and, by their assistance, at the head of the military force of the nation. But a more difficult and hazardous task yet remained—to deceive this party; to render them subservient to his private ambition; and, after they had flattered themselves with the near prospect of that political establishment with which they were so much intoxicated, to employ a great <332> part of them, together with the army which was devoted to their interest, in seating him on the throne of England, with greater power than had ever been enjoyed either by James or by Charles.

To have a proper conception of the means by which he was enabled to execute this master-piece of dexterity and villainy, we must, in the first place, consider his popularity in the army, whose power at that time, was unbounded. The weakness and the undesigning integrity of Fairfax, rendered him a mere tool in the hands of Cromwell, who made use of the name and credit of that general to accomplish his own views, while he avoided the odium and suspicion which their avowal must have drawn upon himself. The great body of the troops were devoted to Fairfax, with a blind veneration produced by an opinion of his military talents, and by a confidence in the sincerity of his professions. Possessed of little capacity or inclination, to scrutinize the conduct and motives of those who acted the chief parts on the political theatre, they were jealous of the interest and rights of the <333>

soldiery, and gratified by every event which contributed to the exaltation of their favourite leaders. A few of the principal officers appear to have seconded the designs of Cromwell, either from personal attachment or considerations of private interest. The rest were for the most part men of low education, equally destitute of penetration to discover the tendency of his measures, and of capacity to prosecute any vigorous plan of opposition.

The diversity of opinion among the independents themselves, concerning the nature of that constitution which they had it in view to establish, created at the same time innumerable difficulties, and occasioned such delays as afforded ample scope to Cromwell, for preparing and ripening that peculiar system which he meant to introduce.

A great part of those who concurred in putting the late king to death, were men of principle. Whatever fanaticism in religion, or whatever prejudices in politics they had imbibed, they appear to have been animated with fervent zeal, and with sincere dispositions, to promote the good of the public. <334> They looked upon the tyranny of Charles as inseparably connected with monarchy; and, while the kingly office was permitted to remain, they regarded the punishment of the king as a mere palliative, incapable of producing a radical cure. But the idea of a republic was vague and general, admitting a great diversity of modifications. The celebrated republics of antiquity, supplied on this occasion, no models proper for imitation; for, as those governments were all established in very small communities, the people at large were in a capacity to exercise the legislative power; while in a large and populous country like England, it was evidently necessary that it should be committed to an assembly of representatives. From this radical difference many others must follow of course; and thus, in a matter not ascertained by experience, there was opened a boundless field to political projectors, in which they might range at pleasure, and declaim without end or measure, upon their different speculative improvements.

While the zealous and disinterested friends of republicanism continued in a state <335> of uncertainty, with respect to the precise object which was to terminate their labours, the old house of commons, that meeting which remained from the wreck of the long parliament, after the violent expulsion of those members who had disapproved of the trial of Charles, and after the house of peers had been declared no part of the legislature; this garbled house of commons endeavoured to hold itself up to the public, as forming the basis of the government in question. It was composed of about ninety persons, deriving their authority, not from the voice of the people, but from the direct interposition of that military force, by which they had been encouraged and supported in all their usurpations.[1] They took upon them to abolish the upper house, but reserved to the peers the privilege of electing or being elected knights of shires, or burgesses. They ventured to declare, "that the office of a king is unnecessary, burdensome, and dangerous to the interest, liberty, and safety of the nation." Assuming the title of *the parliament of the Commonwealth of England,* they exercised the legislative and executive <336> powers; and as an auxiliary for executing the business of the latter department, they appointed a *council of state,* composed of thirty-nine persons. Not satisfied with the supreme authority of England, they did not hesitate to effect an union with Scotland and Ireland, and to determine that from each of those countries thirty representatives should be admitted.

While this remnant of a national council maintained a good understanding with the army, its commands were easily enforced throughout the nation. But things did not long remain in this fortunate situation. Although its members owed their present establishment to the violent interference of a military force, they had no intention to continue in a state of dependence upon the power which had raised them. They had already, as was formerly observed, taken direct measures, however ineffectual, for disbanding the army, and had thus incurred the strong resentment of every person connected with that department. Their continuing to exercise all the functions of government, and their claiming even the <337> power in that extraordinary emergency of reforming and new-modelling the constitution, could not fail at the same time to shock all the feelings and principles of the real friends of liberty. It had, indeed, been enacted that the parliament called in 1640, should not be dissolved without its own consent; but it surely was a wide interpretation of that statute, to contend that this enactment should operate in favour of that mere shadow of national representation, which had been so recently made use of as a cover to the tyranny of the military power. The death of the king, according to the views of all those who wished to effectuate a thorough reformation of abuses, had produced an extinction of the old government; and it would be ridiculous to devolve the formation of

1. Traditionally called the Rump Parliament or Purged Parliament, after the 1648 purging of (mostly Presbyterian) members who favored further negotiations with Charles. The remaining members were almost exclusively Independents.

the new system upon that handful of obscure individuals, who, by a train of accidents, had been left in the possession of the political machine. A transaction so important and extraordinary, seemed to require the concurrence of the whole nation; but, undoubtedly, could not with propriety be concluded, unless in a full and comprehen-<338>sive meeting of the national representatives. The existing members of this house of commons were probably not ignorant of what the public in this particular might expect from them. They had, accordingly, sometimes talked of dissolving themselves; but on these occasions found they had always pretences for delaying so disagreeable a measure; and at length they came to a resolution of superseding it altogether, by electing a set of new members to fill up their number.

These two circumstances, the resentment of the whole military order against that assembly, and the vague uncertain notions concerning that political system which the sincere republicans had in contemplation, were the main springs which Cromwell put in motion for effecting his ambitious designs.

His first object was to get rid of the old house of commons; a measure not altogether free from hazard; for that house contained the leaders of the independent and republican party, who had been embarked in the same cause with the army, in bringing the sovereign to the block; and however <339> these confederates were now embroiled by a difference of private interest, a reconciliation, from the recollection of their common sentiments, was far from being impossible. Cromwell employed every artifice to inflame this difference, and when the jealousy and resentment of the army had been raised to a sufficient pitch, he ventured, in concert with the principal officers, by a military force to turn that assembly out of doors.[2] The circumstances with which he executed this bold measure are well known. With a mixture of rage, of religious cant, and of insolent jocularity, he called upon a party of soldiers whom he had provided for the occasion, and ordered them to lay hold of those members who appeared refractory; declaring "that they were no longer a parliament, and must give place to better men."—"I have been wrestling," says he, "with God, to excuse me from this, but in vain."[3] His purpose, no doubt, was to intimidate; but it is not improbable that he fol-

2. Cromwell, at the head of the New Model Army, forcibly dissolved the Rump Parliament in 1653.

3. See *Cobbett's Parliamentary History of England,* vol. 3 (London, 1806).

lowed, at the same time, the natural bent of his temper. We may easily suppose that, however destitute of sensibility; how resolute soever in prosecut<340>ing his plans; yet, in this emergency, when he was on a sudden to shift his ground, and to abandon his old friends and associates, all was not quiet within; and that he could not prevent unusual perturbation. To stifle reflection, a vigorous effort became necessary; and he was obliged to work himself up to a degree of passion and violence.

In whatever light this measure might be viewed by the army, it was of too decided a nature not to open the eyes of the nation, and to discover his real designs. Such of the republicans as were capable of discernment, must now have been fully convinced of the treachery of their leader, and have seen with shame and indignation, the total overthrow of a fabric which they had long been endeavouring to rear. They had the additional mortification to find that they were too insignificant to procure any attention to their complaints; and that the loss of their power was beheld by the people at large with exultation and triumph. The presbyterians, as well as the adherents of the late king, must have regarded this event with cordial satisfaction; the former, pleased <341> with the ruin of a party by whom they themselves had been supplanted; the latter, deducing a complete vindication of their political tenets from the unfortunate issue of the late attempts to limit the prerogative, and rejoicing in the prospect, that the present disorders would induce men of all parties to seek the restoration of public tranquillity by recalling the royal family.

Even some of the military officers penetrated the sinister designs of Cromwell, and immediately withdrew their support from him; but they possessed neither influence nor dexterity to produce a desertion of the forces under their command. The rest were pleased with any arrangement which exalted the military power, and were easily satisfied with the dissolution of the late house of commons, as a preliminary step to the calling of a more suitable representation of the whole community. The common herd of the troops, viewing this crafty politician, either in the light of a patron and protector, to whom they were indebted for their situations, and from whom they expected preferment; or in that of a saint, whose religious charac<342>ter and professions inspired them with full confidence in his integrity, adhered invariably to his interest, and were disposed, without examination or suspicion, to promote and execute all his measures.

The army, having in this manner swept away the old government, became entirely masters of the field, and possessed an unlimited power. They had obtained a clear canvass upon which they might amuse themselves in designing future constitutions. As, in their former disputes with parliament, they had formed their several delegates into a deliberative council, under such regulations as enabled them, without confusion, to collect their general determinations, they now proceeded, in the capacity of legislators, to make trial of their political talents. One of their first attempts of this nature was to call a *convention,* the members of which, amounting to about an hundred and twenty, were elected by counties and towns in England, Scotland, and Ireland. But as this meeting, which is known by the name of *Barebone's parliament,*[4] did not, it seems, answer the views of Cromwell, he soon prevailed upon them, <343> notwithstanding a protestation by several members, to resign their authority.

This crude experiment was followed by the delineation of a system more full and complete in all its parts. In a military council, there was produced, and received with approbation, what was called *an instrument of government,* containing the outlines of the system proposed.[5] It provided that the chief powers of government should be committed to a protector, a council of state, and a parliament.

To the office of protector, bestowed, as we might easily suppose, upon Cromwell himself, were annexed the greatest part of those prerogatives formerly belonging to the monarchs of England.

The council of state was to consist of not more than twenty-one, nor of less than thirteen persons. The first members were named by the instrument itself; they were to enjoy their office during life or good behaviour; and every vacancy was to be supplied by the council naming a list of three persons, out of which the protector was empowered to choose the member. In the determina-<344>tion of peace and war, and in the exercise of the executive power, the protector was to act with the advice and consent of the council.

The parliament consisted of 400 representatives for the whole of England and Wales; of whom 270 were to be elected by the counties, the right of election belonging to such as possessed a landed estate, amounting to the

4. The Barebone's Parliament, comprising members selected by Cromwell, was called in 1653, only to be dissolved later that same year.

5. Cromwell's written constitution, the Instrument of Government, was issued in late 1653. Under it, Cromwell took the title of Protector.

value of 200*l.* The small towns, known by the denomination of the *rotten boroughs,* were excluded from the privilege of sending representatives. To the English members were added thirty for Scotland, and the same number for Ireland.

That this national assembly might resemble the ancient parliaments of England, provision was made, though at a subsequent period, for a house of lords, to be composed not of the old hereditary nobility, but of members nominated by the protector, whose privilege of sitting in that house should remain during life. Their number was limited to seventy.* <345>

The protector was empowered to summon meetings of parliament; he was required to call them every three years, at least; and to allow their deliberations to continue for five months without interruption. He had no absolute negative upon such bills as passed through parliament; unless they were contrary to those fundamental laws contained in the *instrument of government.* But by this original deed he had secured a standing army of 20,000 foot, and 10,000 horse; for the maintenance of which regular funds were provided.

Such was the famous plan of government, by the establishment of which Cromwell appears to have attained the summit of power and grandeur. It is necessary to examine minutely the particulars of this new system; which, by not admitting its chief magistrate to assume the title of king, has commonly been considered as a species of republic. In this respect, and by its extending, and in some degree equalizing the national representation in the public assembly, it may seem, from a superficial view, to favour the great body of the people. But in reality it <346> had an opposite tendency; and subjected all the branches of administration, all the exertions of government, to the arbitrary will of a single person. It established a standing army of 30,000 men, under the direction of the protector, and which could not be disbanded without his consent. Such a force, in the state of military discipline which he had produced, was fully sufficient to overcome all resistance, and to govern the nation at pleasure. By such a body of mercenaries entirely at his devotion, he could easily sweep away those cob-web laws which were spread out to decoy and ensnare others, not to restrain his own conduct. We accordingly find that the first parliament which was called, in consequence of this new

* Of those who actually sat in consequence of such nomination sixty-five are specified in *Memoirs of Cromwell,* vol. I.—The greater part collected from Thurlowe's list.

constitution, having proved refractory by disputing the title of the protector, he placed a guard at the door of the house, and refused admittance to the members, until they had subscribed an engagement to acknowledge his authority. In a future parliament, he employed a similar violence to subdue the opposition of its members. <347>

To facilitate, however, the interposition of that absolute authority which he intended to exercise, he found it convenient to make variations in the constitution which he had introduced; and in particular to enlarge the department of the army, by allowing its officers to interfere in the civil administration. An insurrection of the partizans of the royal family, which had been early discovered, and easily quelled, afforded a pretence for treating the whole party with extraordinary severity.[6] By a regulation of a most arbitrary and oppressive nature, they were subjected to a contribution amounting to a tenth of their estates; and for levying this imposition, Cromwell divided the whole kingdom into twelve military jurisdictions; each of which was put under the government of a major-general with exorbitant powers, and from his determination there lay no appeal but to Cromwell himself.

From the slightest attention it must be obvious that this political system was not framed for duration. It was such a mixture of opposite elements, such a combination of discordant and jarring principles, as could not fail to counteract one another, and to <348> produce disorder and commotion. The protectorate of Cromwell was apparently a democracy, but in reality a military despotism; the most arbitrary and oppressive species of absolute monarchy. It held out to the people the show of liberty and of privileges, by inviting them to choose their own representatives, to exert themselves in acquiring political interest, in a word, to consider themselves as legislators, and to act accordingly; while in reality, their efforts were always to end in disappointment; their ideas of self-importance and dignity to produce only mortification; their pretended interference in the administration of public affairs to be in perfect subordination to the will of a single person, by whose hand, like puppets, all their movements were guided and directed.

To render an absolute government palatable to a whole nation, it must

6. In March 1655, Colonel John Penruddock raised a royalist insurrection in Wiltshire which led to severe repression.

be confirmed by inveterate usage.[7] The attention of the people must be turned away from the conduct of their governors, and diverted into other channels. Occupied with their private pursuits, they must be taught to look <349> upon the business of the magistrate as no business of theirs, and to esteem it his province to command, as it is their duty to yield implicit submission: they must be habitually convinced that they have nothing to do with the laws but to obey them. The forms of the constitution must be calculated to keep out of view the rights of subjects, to present continually the image of unbounded authority in the prince, and to inspire a veneration for his person and dignity. The grandeur of the monarch, the rank which he holds in the scale of sovereigns, the facility with which he collects an armed force, and provides resources for supporting it, the secresy and expedition with which he enters upon a war, attacks the neighbouring states, or procures information with respect to their designs, the tranquillity which he maintains through the whole of his dominions, by repressing the animosities, the turbulence and faction so prevalent in popular governments; these advantages must be constantly held up to the nation as the peculiar blessings of despotism, which, in the opinion of some, render that political establishment upon the whole <350> superior to every other. The people, in short, must be made to exult in that power by which they are kept in subjection, to regard their own glory as involved in that of their *grand monarque,* and their own debasement and servitude, as compensated by the splendor of his prerogative, and the extent of his dominion. Experience has shewn that by long custom, and by the influence of example, such a national spirit is not unattainable; nay, that sentiments of loyalty and affection to a despot, have, in the history of the world, and even of civilized nations been more prevalent than a sense of liberty and independence. But the union of the former and the latter, in one mass, is a mixture of heterogeneous particles, which incessantly repelling each other, must be frequently shaken, and kept in continual ferment, to prevent their separation. To introduce a despotism

7. Compare Hume's remark that the first principle of "the right of magistracy, is that which gives authority to almost all the establish'd governments of the world: I mean, *long possession* in any one form of government, or succession of princes. 'Tis certain, that if we remount to the first origin of every nation, we shall find, that there scarce is a race of kings, or form of a commonwealth, that is not primarily founded on usurpation and rebellion. . . . Time alone gives solidity to their right." *A Treatise of Human Nature,* ed. David Fate Norton and Mary J. Norton (Oxford: Oxford University Press, 2000), 356.

under the guise of a popular government is to dress an avowed and bitter enemy in the garments of a friend and benefactor: it is to tantalize the people with a prospect of pleasures which they are never to enjoy; to require that they should banish from their thoughts a set of rights and pri-<351>vileges which are constantly placed before their eyes.

To the native inconsistencies and contradictions which tended to overthrow the system of usurpation introduced by Cromwell, we must add a circumstance of still greater moment, that from the beginning it had, in every shape, been opposed by a prodigious majority of the nation. Exclusive of the army, every class or description of men, whether political or religious; the episcopal party, the presbyterian, and the independent; the friends of the royal family, the supporters of limited monarchy, and of a commonwealth; all united in their aversion to the present constitution, and in their detestation of the means by which it has been established.

These dispositions of the public mind had not escaped the penetrating eye of Cromwell. He knew that his government, as an innovation, which ran counter to all the former ideas and habits of the great body of the nation, was highly unpopular; he was willing, as far as possible, to remove this prepossession; and, in the latter part of his ad-<352>ministration, he seems to have had a serious intention to restore the monarchy. After the powers which he had already assumed, he probably thought that the army would have no objection to his obtaining the title of *king;* and by the restoration of the *kingly office,* provided it were settled in his family, together with the re-establishment of the ancient house of peers, there was reason to expect, that a great part of the nation, weary of the past disorders, and less adverse to the new government, than to the dominion of the imprudent and infatuated house of Stewart, might be at length reconciled to his authority.

With this view he secretly promoted an address, intituled the humble petition and advice of the parliament of England, Scotland, and Ireland, to his highness; by which he was entreated to accept the title of king, and to revive the practice of parliaments consisting of two houses.[8] A committee was appointed to hold a conference with him upon the subject, and to urge the expediency of the measure proposed. The farce of persuading Cromwell to accept of the royal <353> dignity was carried on for some time; but the real difficulty lay in procuring the consent of the army, who hated the name

8. This was drawn up by Parliament and issued in 1657.

of king; and more especially in procuring the consent of the principal officers, who entertained the hope of succeeding to the protectorship.

Many persons of moderate opinions, throughout the nation, seem to have approved of this project, as most likely to produce a permanent settlement.* The <354> protector himself treated the proposal with the utmost indifference; delivering his public declarations in a jargon wholly unintelligible; and speaking of it in private as a trifle, which he might comply with merely to gratify the humour of others. "He had tried all possible means," says Ludlow,[9] to prevail with the officers of the army to approve his design, and knowing that lieutenant-general Fleetwood,[10] and colonel Desbrowe were particularly averse to it, he invited himself to dine personally with the colonel, and carried the lieutenant-general with him, where he began to droll with them about monarchy, and speaking slightly of it, said it was but a feather in a man's cap, and therefore wondered that <355> men would not please children, and permit them to enjoy their rattle. But he received from them, as Col. Desbrowe since told me, such an answer as was not at all suitable to

* "The Protector," says Thurloe, in a letter to Henry Cromwell, "has great difficulties in his mind, although he hath had the clearest call that ever man had; and for ought I see, the parliament will not be persuaded, that there can be any settlement any other way. The title is not in the question; but is the office that is known to the laws and this people. They know their duty to the king, and his to them. Whatever else there is will be wholly new, and will be nothing else but a probationer, and upon the next occasion will be changed again. Besides, they say, the name Protector came in by the sword, out of parliament, and will never be the ground of any settlement; nor will there be a free parliament so long as that continues; and as it favours of the sword now, so it will at last bring all things to be military. These, and other considerations, make men, who are for settlement, steady in their resolutions as to this government now in hand; not that they lust after a king, or are peevish upon any account of opposition; but they would lay foundations of liberty and freedom, which they judge this the next way to. My Lord Deputy [Fleetwood] and General Desbrowe, oppose themselves with all earnestness against this title, but think the other things in the *petition and advice* very honest."

9. Edmund Ludlow (ca. 1617–92), English republican politician and member of Parliament. Ludlow's *Memoirs,* first published in 1698–99, were a major source for Whig historiography of the Civil War. Recently, the *Memoirs* have been revealed to be a "semi-forgery." Though based on a text by Ludlow, the work was "fundamentally rewritten" to support a radical Whig point of view. See Blair Worden, *Roundhead Reputations* (London: Penguin, 2002), 12.

10. Charles Fleetwood (d. 1692), politician and major-general of the eastern district after 1655, later appointed to Cromwell's House of Lords; John Desborough (1608–80) was an officer in Cromwell's army, attaining the rank of colonel in 1648 and major-general in 1651.

his expectations or desires. For they assured him there was more in this matter than he perceived; that those who put him upon it were no enemies to Charles Stuart; and that if he accepted of it, he would infallibly draw ruin on himself and his friends. Having thus sounded their inclinations, that he might conclude in the manner he had begun, he told them they were a couple of scrupulous fellows, and so departed."*

His endeavours, however, were fruitless. A petition from the officers of the army was presented to parliament, requesting "that the protector might not be pressed to take upon him the title and government of a king";[11] and Cromwell, with great ostentation of humility, and much profession of declining a load of cares and difficulties, took the merit of refusing the crown.† But the office of protector <356> was confirmed to him, with the privilege of naming a successor.

It is probable that this attempt of Cromwell to restore the regal title and dignity, which discovered an effrontery beyond example, did not entirely proceed from the mere vanity of wishing to possess the pageantry of a crown. To think otherwise would be to suppose that he betrayed a weakness not of a piece with the rest of his character. The effect of this measure, had it been carried into execution, is extremely doubtful: but there is ground to believe that it occurred to this bold and impudent usurper as a stratagem to be hazarded, perhaps the only expedient by which he had any chance to extricate himself from the surrounding difficulties.

The time now evidently drew near, which, in spite of all his efforts, was to annihilate the ill-gotten authority of this extraordinary personage. During the four years in which he held the protectorate, he was exposed to desperate attempts from all quarters; from cavaliers,[12] from presbyterians, from independents and republicans; and he seems to <357> have never enjoyed a moment, either of quiet or security. That he escaped assassination, considering the continued ferment of the nation, and the enthusiastic zeal of the parties whom he had so highly irritated, is wonderful. By his extraordinary vigilance, by the uncommon intelligence which he procured, by a judicious mixture of lenity and of severity towards those who conspired against him, he broke

* Ludlow's Memoirs.

† On the 12th of May, 1657.

11. See Edmund Ludlow, *Memoirs,* ed. C. H. Firth (Oxford: Clarendon Press, 1894), 2:24.

12. *Cavaliers* was the name given to the royalist forces loyal to Charles I.

and disconcerted the schemes of his enemies, and reduced them to the necessity of temporising and acting with great circumspection. The obstacles, however, to a final and permanent settlement were daily encreasing. Deserted by every man of principle, unless perhaps, a few low-bred fanatics in the army, whose weakness rendered them unable to penetrate his designs, he found himself destitute of a friend in whose counsel he could repose any confidence, or from whose credit or influence he could expect any assistance. Concerning the desperate posture of his affairs, Thurloe,[13] with great simplicity exclaims, "Truely, I think nothing but an unex-<358>pected providence, can remove the present difficulties."

Towards the close of his life, he appears to have become sensible of the folly and vanity of those ambitious projects in which he had been engaged; and to have felt a conviction, that the power which he had attained was a mere shadow, likely upon the first gathering of a cloud, to vanish in a moment. If not touched with remorse, for his crimes, he was at least terrified by the prospect of that vengeance which they had provoked. He became dejected, and melancholy. The face of a stranger gave him uneasiness. He was haunted incessantly by gloomy apprehensions, and never thought himself secure in any situation. By concealing, and frequently changing the chamber which he slept, by the constant attendance of a strong guard, by wearing a coat of mail under his cloaths, by seeking indirect roads when he performed a journey, and pursuing a different way in his return home; by these, and such unavailing precautions, he endeavoured to prevent those attacks which his <359> anxious and tortured mind was continually foreboding.

The load of cares and vexation with which he was oppressed, at length affected his constitution, and produced a distemper which carried him off, in the forty-ninth year of his age. The thoughts of a future state had, for some time, suggested to him uneasy reflections; and the particulars which historians have transmitted upon that point, present the curious but disgusting spectacle of a violent enthusiast; conscious of having deserted all those principles with which he set out in life, and now covered with guilt, and with infamy, endeavouring by the illusions of fanaticism, to find religious consolation in his last moments. He is said to have asked Godwin, one

13. John Thurloe (1616–68): secretary to the Council of State of the Commonwealth. His correspondence (1742), cited here, is preserved in the Bodleian Library, Oxford, and in the British Museum. Part of it was published in 1742 by Thomas Birch.

of his preachers, whether the doctrine was true, that the *elect* could never fall, or suffer final reprobation? "Nothing more certain," replied the preacher. "Then I am safe," said the protector, "for I am sure that once I was in a state of grace." So much of the original leaven remained, that he still was capable of being wrought up to his former <360> fervors. He believed that an answer had been given to his prayers, and to those of his chaplains, promising that he should not die of the present distemper.

Few characters have united more extraordinary qualities, or afford more subject for speculation, than that of Oliver Cromwell. The ardour of his disposition should naturally, it might be supposed, have rendered him tenacious of any opinion or system of conduct which he happened to embrace; and he seems from his infancy, to have acquired a strong predilection for the peculiar tenets both religious and political, embraced at that period, by the independents. His attachments, in this respect, were fortified by early habits, and by the intercourse and example of many kindred spirits, with whom he lived in the strictest intimacy and friendship. Yet this system he afterwards abandoned; those friends he betrayed; and all those principles by which he had been distinguished, and upon which he appeared to build his reputation, he scrupled not, for the sake of a temporary and precarious power or emolument, openly to renounce. The <361> man who in the company of Pym and Hambden, and other assertors of public liberty, had formed the resolution of leaving his native country[14] rather than submit to the usurpations of the crown, was not ashamed to give the lie to all his professions; and after having put the king to death for tyranny, to hold himself up to public view as one of the most notorious tyrants and usurpers that the world ever beheld.

To his original and genuine fanaticism he was probably indebted for the success of his projects. Had he not been at first sincere in his professions, it is not to be supposed that he could have gained the confidence of his companions and associates, or that he would have risen to much consideration with the public. But being a real fanatic, and a real republican, he became distinguished among those of the same way of thinking; and in the subsequent progress of his mind towards a full and complete apostacy, it was prob-

14. The attempted emigration of the Puritan leaders is treated with considerable irony by Hume, who writes that they "had resolved for ever to abandon their native country, and fly to the other extremity of the globe, where they might enjoy lectures and discourses of any length or form which pleased them. The king had afterwards full leisure to repent this exercise of his authority." *HE,* 5:241–42.

ably a long time before they, or even before he himself, perceived the alteration. His hypocrisy and dissimulation might easily be considered as useful and excusable arts which <362> he employed in a good cause; and his own aggrandizement might be regarded as a mere collateral object, which was not incompatible with the interest of the public. The moment when he began, directly, and without any subterfuge, to sacrifice the latter to the former, when his irregular passions were no longer able to justify themselves, and when his conscience first avowed the naked truth of his detestable villainy, was doubtless a point scarcely visible, which he would have no pleasure in examining, but which, as soon as discovered, he would most carefully conceal.

It is at the same time observable, that though Cromwell was tempted by his ambition to abandon those patriotic views, to which his temper and early habits had strongly inclined him, his natural disposition still appeared conspicuously in all cases where it was not counteracted by the consideration of his own interest. Though he had set himself above the laws, and in the exercise of those illegal powers which he had assumed, was guilty of the most arbitrary proceedings, yet in maintaining the police <363> of the country, and in the ordinary administration of government, he displayed great vigour and public spirit. "Westminster hall," by the confession of Lord Clarendon, "was never replenished with more learned and upright judges than by him; nor was justice either in law or in equity, in civil cases, more equally distributed where he was not a party." He is admitted, even by his enemies, to have eagerly selected persons of ability and reputation to fill the various departments of public business; to have been a zealous promoter of science, and a munificent patron of genius and learning.

With whatever disgust or indignation every ingenuous mind will contemplate the successful villainy of this extraordinary person, it is impossible to withhold a degree of admiration from his uncommon abilities; the boldness with which he planned, and the steady resolution with which he executed his measures; the dexterity with which he availed himself of the animosity, and the jealousies prevailing among the different parties; the penetration with which he dis-<364>covered the foibles of his own partizans and the artful policy by which he rendered them the dupes of their own interested views. His situation admitted of no regular system of operations, but required such immediate exertions as were instantaneously suggested by the occasion; and in these he seldom was guilty of any oversight, or let slip any opportunity to forward his designs. The characteristical and prominent feature of his conduct was decision. Placed on a new ground, and frequently on the brink of a precipice, without any beaten path to direct him, he never hesitated in choosing his course and the pursuit of his object, seldom committed any false step, or met with any considerable disappointment.

His uncommon deficiency in elocution must appear surprising to those who consider the clearness of his judgment, and the quickness of determination which he exhibited in all his actions. This might arise from a variety of causes; from slowness of imagination, a quality not incompatible with sound understanding; from his early neglect to cultivate this useful talent; from the un-<365>intelligible jargon which his fanatical habits had rendered familiar to him; and lastly, from the necessity he frequently was under of disguising and concealing his real intentions and sentiments. Perspicuity is the foundation of eloquence; but those persons can never be perspicuous who are afraid of being understood.

A strong propensity to sarcastic mirth, and bufoonery, has been taken notice of as a remarkable ingredient in the composition of this wonderful character. The amusement he found in putting burning coals in the boots of his officers, or inviting them to a feast, while the common soldiers were directed at a certain signal, to rush in and run away with the dishes; his flinging a cushion at the head of Ludlow, when they were engaged in a conference upon a subject of no less importance than the settlement of the constitution; his taking the pen to sign the warrant for the execution of Charles, and bedaubing with ink the face of Martin, who sat next him; his indecent suggestion, that a person who saw him and his companions on their knees round the table, might <366> imagine they were *seeking the Lord,* while they were only *seeking a bottle-screw;* these and other instances of caurse and unseasonable mirth are collected by his biographers, as forming a manifest inconsistency in the character of so great a man. In that violent measure, when he dissolved the house of commons, we find him indulging a most absurd and whimsical vein of raillery and sarcasm, and insulting the members, while he put an end to their authority: "Thou art a whoremaster—thou art an adulterer—thou art a drunkard, and a glutton.—Take away this bauble (the mace.) O! Sir Harry Vane! Sir Harry Vane! The Lord deliver me from Sir Harry Vane!"[15]

When things which appear important and solemn to the rest of the world,

15. For the incidents mentioned here, see *HE,* 6:53, 6:90.

are from a singular disposition, beheld by any individual with indifference or contempt, they are apt from the contrast of his own emotions and sentiments with those of others, to excite laughter and ridicule. Thus a melancholy man who derives no pleasure from the common enjoyments of life, is dis-<367>posed to make a jest of the bustle created by avarice or ambition, and of the idle pursuits in which the bulk of mankind are engaged. The hardened villain, whose mind has become callous to the impressions of humanity and virtue, is in the same situation with regard to the sacred ties of honour and conscience; and is apt to hold in derision those kind and generous feelings, those principles of right and wrong, by which men are bound together in society, and by which they are determined in many cases to sacrifice their interest to their duty. He not only beholds from the state of his own heart, every appearance of generosity and virtue under this ridiculous aspect, but is disposed, in defence of his own conduct, and as a kind of antidote to the censure and execration of mankind, to cherish and hold up this view of things, both to himself and to others. The great painter of the human heart[16] has, in the character of Hamlet, exhibited a man of sensibility, and of a melancholy cast, indulging himself in the fancy, that the conqueror of the world might be employed to stop a beer barrel; and in such ludicrous views of <368> mankind as tend to demonstrate the vanity and folly of their boasted accomplishments, their eager desires, and their unwearied pursuits. In the character of Richard the Third, the same author has displayed the sarcastic humour of a villain, who makes a jest, not only of the follies and weaknesses, but of the virtuous dispositions and conscientious scruples of mankind. The piety of Saint Harry, the holy laws of Gray-beards, the credulity of Lady Anne, in believing his promises, the affection of his mother, and her tender concern for his welfare, with every quality that is commonly regarded as valuable and praise-worthy, are the standing objects of his derision and merriment. Somewhat akin to this disposition, in the dramatic character of Richard, is the rustic jocularity of Cromwell which appears to aim at laughing all virtue out of doors, at the same time that it seems to convey the expression of exultation and triumph in the success of

16. William Shakespeare (1564–1616), English dramatist and poet. Millar compares Cromwell to Shakespeare's study of a tyrant and "machiavel," Richard III. The play was first performed 1592–93, and printed 1597. Below, he extends the comparison to the contemporary French Revolutionary leader, Robespierre.

his hypocrisy. Upon reading the treatise of Harrington, in which that author thought proper to express a confident expectation that the protector would establish <369> a commonwealth, this facetious usurper is reported to have said—"The gentleman had like to have trepanned me out of my power; but what I have got by the sword, I will not quit for a little paper shot."*

When we examine the conduct of Cromwell in all its parts, it may seem surprising that his memory has been treated with more lenity and indulgence than it certainly deserves. This may be explained from the influence of popular feelings; and still more from the character and sentiments of political parties. His great abilities, the success of all his undertakings, and the respect which he commanded from all the powers <370> of Europe† seized the imagination of Englishmen, and were calculated to gratify national vanity. The partizans of the house of Stewart were, at the same time, induced to hold up the favourable side of the policy of Cromwell in order to blacken the memory of those patriots who were not less the enemies of that usurper than of the absolute power of the crown. They affected to consider the usurpation of the protector as a necessary consequence of the attempts to restrain the prerogative, were better pleased with the protectorate than with a republican system, and seem to have felt towards him a sort of gratitude for overthrowing that form of government to which they were most adverse.

The death of Cromwell put an end to that authority which, probably, even if he had lived, he would not have upheld much longer. His son Richard,[17] whom he had nominated to the office of protector, had <371> neither the ambition or desire, nor the capacity to maintain it. The leaders of the army, whose influence encouraged them to aim at the supreme power, could not be retained in subjection. Richard was deposed. The remains of the *long*

* The same disposition to sarcastic humour has been exhibited in our day, in a political character, resembling that of Cromwell in many respects; I mean the famous Robespiere; an enthusiast, though of a different species; of a temper more gloomy, and marked with deeper lines of cruelty; not more scrupulous in betraying his friends; but steady in supporting that system which he originally professed to adopt, and as far as appears, uncorrupted by motives of pecuniary interest.—*Dr. Moore's Journal.*

† While all the neighbouring potentates to you,
Like Joseph's sheaves pay reverence and bow.
Waller's Verses to the Protector.

[[These are the final lines of Edmund Waller's *Panegyric,* addressed to Cromwell (1656).]]

17. Richard Cromwell (1626–1712), Lord Protector (1658–59).

parliament were recalled. Fleetwood and Lambert,[18] who were at the head of the English forces, attempted to give law to this assembly; but they wanted the transcendant genius of Cromwell to effect their purposes. General Monk,[19] who commanded a smaller but probably a better disciplined army in Scotland, was immediately summoned to the assistance of parliament. Having marched up to London, he proceeded so far in obedience to the commons as to carry military execution into the city, for refusing to pay the taxes imposed by parliamentary authority.

This attempt shews pretty clearly that he intended to tread in the paths of Oliver Cromwell; but finding by the general voice of the public, that the plot was not likely to succeed, he seems to have quickly changed his ground; and endeavoured without loss of time to repair this unlucky step; he <372> exerted all his interest in recalling the royal family. In this design he was seconded by a great part of the nation; by all who had been shocked and disgusted with the late violent measures, and who saw no end to the disorders and calamities arising from the ambition and sinister views of the military leaders. <373>

18. John Lambert (1619–83): parliamentarian soldier and, after 1655, one of Cromwell's major-generals.

19. George Monk (1608–70), a professional soldier, was initially a royalist during the Civil War, but was on the parliamentary side later in Ireland, Scotland, and during the Dutch Wars. He played a decisive role in the restoration of Charles II by marching on London in 1660, forming the Convention Parliament, and advising Parliament to invite Charles to return.

CHAPTER VI

Of the Reigns of Charles the Second, and James the Second.

The restoration of Charles II.[1] to the throne of his ancestors, was produced in such hurry and agitation of spirits as precluded every attention and precaution which prudence and deliberation would have suggested. The different parties who united in this precipitate measure, were too heterogeneous in their principles, and too jealous of one another, as well as too much afraid of the partisans of the protectorate, or the supporters of a republican system, to form any regular concert, and thus to hazard the delay which an attempt to limit the powers, and to regulate the conduct of the sovereign, would have required. Having no leisure for entering into particulars, they were satisfied with the professions of Charles, conceived in vague and general terms; that, in matters of religion, he would shew indul-<374>gence to differences of opinion; that he would grant a free pardon to all offences committed against him by his subjects, reserving to the consideration of parliament the exceptions that ought to be made; and that, in relation to the changes lately introduced in the state of property, he would refer all future claims to the determination of that assembly. None of those political points, therefore, which, after the accession of James I. had been the subject of controversy, were, on this occasion, settled or explained; and the monarch, assuming the reins of government, without any limitations or conditions, was understood to recover all that extent of prerogative which, before the commencement of the civil war, had been vested in the crown.

The principal events in this reign exhibit a disgusting repetition of similar struggles to those which had occurred under the two first princes of the

1. Charles II (r. 1660–85).

House of Stewart, and afford no prospect of that splendid success with which, in a short time after, the cause of liberty was fully crowned. The great unanimity with which the nation had concurred in restoring the royal family was <375> represented as an experimental proof of the futility and imprudence of those pretended improvements in the government, which had of late been attempted; but which had ended in a new and most arbitrary species of despotism, or rather in total anarchy and confusion. The tide was now turned in favour of the monarch; and his old adherents became the governing party in the state. The shame and disgrace attending the late measures were, in some degree, communicated to all who had any share in their accomplishment, and became the subject of exultation and triumph to those who had followed the opposite course. Men strove, by their services, to compensate their former disaffection; and, in proportion to the severity with which they had treated the father, they were warm in their professions of attachment and loyalty to the son.

The agreeable qualities and accomplishments of the king, joined to the memory of the hardships which he had suffered, contributed to improve those favourable dispositions. Equally removed from the pedantic vulgarity of his grandfather, and from the haughty reserve and formality of his father, <376> Charles II. possessed an affability and ease of deportment, a fund of wit and pleasantry in conversation, a knowledge of the world, and discernment of the weaknesses of mankind, which qualified him to win the hearts of his subjects, and to procure their indulgence even to the blemishes and vices of his character. The popularity of the prince was, in some measure, extended to all that party who, having been his fellow-sufferers, had acquired, by their fidelity and attachment, a strong claim to his favour and confidence. As they now filled the principal offices of trust and emolument, the influence and power, the consideration and rank, which they now enjoyed, gave reputation and consequence to their peculiar ways of thinking and modes of behaviour. Those who had followed the fortunes of Charles were chiefly among the higher class of gentry, who, by their situation in life, had acquired that relish of pleasure and dissipation which affluence naturally bestows; and this original disposition was confirmed by their long residence in France, where gaiety <377> and elegance had made greater advances than in any other part of Europe. Upon returning to England, they propagated all their own habits and prepossessions. The sour and rigid sobriety of the puritans was now laughed out of doors. All extraordinary pretensions to devotion, all inward illuminations of the spirit, were treated as knavery and hypocrisy. Loyalty to the king; generosity, frankness, and hospitality; a taste for conversation, and for the enjoyments of society and good fellowship, were looked upon as the characteristics of a gentleman, and the distinguishing marks of a liberal education. Charles himself, from his indolence, and the easiness of his temper, had an utter aversion to business, and a strong propensity to pleasure. Careless about religion and government, and studying only to gratify his own inclinations, he was little attracted by objects of ambition, or by the pomp and pageantry of a crown; and set no value upon any talents and accomplishments but such as were subservient to his amusement, or conducive to mirth and <378> festivity. The obsequiousness of the court in adopting the manners of the sovereign, and the effect of its influence and example throughout the nation, may easily be conceived. Thus the fashion of the times passed suddenly from one extreme to another; from fanaticism, and a cynical contempt of the innocent enjoyments of life, to irreligion and libertinism, to voluptuousness and debauchery.

Upon the restoration of Charles, the first national object was the procuring an act of general indemnity and oblivion; which the king passed with great alacrity.[2] The exceptions, in exclusion of such as had been accounted notorious offenders, were not numerous; and even among those who had sat upon the trial of his father, only ten were put to death. To do justice to this prince, it must be acknowledged, that a revengeful temper was not in the number of his vices. He had, besides, every reason to court popularity; and it was necessary, for conciliating the affection and future loyalty of his subjects, to convince them that their past offences were forgotten. <379>

To procure a revenue, which might render him in some degree independent, was, on the other hand, the immediate object of the king. In this he was not unsuccessful; having obtained from parliament not only 1,200,000 l. as an ordinary peace establishment, a revenue much larger than had been enjoyed by his predecessors; but also a variety of large sums for occasional purposes; in particular, for enabling him to pay off and disband the army,

2. Under the Act of Indemnity and Oblivion (1660), a free pardon was granted to everyone who had supported the Commonwealth and Protectorate, except for those who had directly participated in the trial and execution of Charles I.

that army which had been the basis of the late usurpation, and from which the nation, we may suppose, was now anxious to be delivered.*

The disputes and disturbances which began early, and which continually clouded and disgraced this unpropitious reign, may be traced to two sources, which, however, were intimately connected; to the jealousy and bigotry produced by religious differences; and to the designs of the crown, partly through the medium of those differences, to establish a despotism. <380>

When Charles was recalled from poverty and exile to the throne of his ancestors, it is probable that, humbled in the school of adversity, he had formed the resolution to avoid any such contest as might endanger, a second time, the loss of his crown. But after he had been seated, with apparent firmness, in the full possession of regal authority, his thoughtless temper, easily subdued by the counsel of friends and favourites, disposed him to forget the salutary lesson inculcated by his misfortunes, and betrayed him into measures no less arbitrary and unconstitutional than those which had brought his father to the block. Though not ambitious of power, he was rapacious of money for the support of his pleasures; and, from his extravagant dissipation, feeling constantly the vexatious pressure of wants, he was never contented with those moderate supplies which he occasionally obtained from parliament. Weary, therefore, of continual, and often vain applications to that assembly, and impatient of the mortifications to which he was frequently subjected, he listened with avidity <381> to every proposal for delivering him from such restraints, and for enabling him to supply his necessities by virtue of his own prerogative.

With respect to religion, the jealousy, the partialities, and prejudices of the court, and of the people, operated in various directions. It is now sufficiently known, though it was then only suspected, that the king, while abroad, had been reconciled to the church of Rome;† a measure not, in all probability, dictated by any religious impressions, of which he was not very susceptible; but proceeding from political motives, or from the facility of his nature, which rendered him incapable of resisting the importunity of his friends. His brother the Duke of York,[3] the presumptive heir of the crown, was a bigoted Roman Catholic, and with inferior abilities, but more obsti-

* See Life of Charles II. by Wm. Harris.

† Dalrymples Memoirs.

3. James II, king of England (1685–88).

nacy and more talents for business, had gained a complete ascendant over the mind of Charles. But whatever desire these two princes might feel to establish the Popish religion, it was necessary to conceal their <382> sentiments, and to accommodate their behaviour to the popular opinion. The partisans of the church of England, who had been the great supporters of the crown in the reign of Charles I. and who formed the most numerous and powerful body in promoting the restoration, were justly entitled, according to the views entertained in that period, to claim the re-establishment of that authority, and of those modes of worship which they had formerly possessed. The restoration of episcopacy, therefore, went hand in hand with that of monarchical government; the bishops resumed their seats in parliament; and the lands of the church, together with those of the crown, which had been alienated under the protectorate, were immediately restored to those public uses for which they had anciently been appropriated. That no compensation was made, in this case, to the purchasers, whose titles had originated in an usurpation, now execrated by all ranks of men, will not appear surprising.* <383>

In this peculiar state of things, there prevailed universally, among the protestants of every denomination, an apprehension of the designs of the crown to promote the establishment of the Romish religion; as there existed, in the members of the church of England, a strong resentment against the puritans, and a violent suspicion of their future machinations. It may be observed, at the same time, that these two branches of Protestants felt reciprocally more jealousy and hatred of each other, than they entertained against their common enemy, the Roman Catholics; in proportion as their systems were more akin, and as their mutual animosities had been excited by more recent hostilities, as the church of England had been so lately overturned by the dissenters, it was natural to look for similar attempts from the same quarter, and to guard against them with the utmost anxiety. Unhappily, the means adopted for this purpose, were equally illiberal and imprudent. By requiring a strict uniformity in matters of religion, and by inflicting severe penalties against all non-conformists, it was proposed <384> to defend the church from the attacks of the sectaries, and to secure her establishment from the hazard of religious innovation. To say nothing of the tyranny of domineering over the rights of conscience, by compelling mankind to embrace,

* See Harris's Life of Charles II.

or profess opinions which their understandings have rejected; the experience of all ages has demonstrated that persecution, instead of exterminating, is the most effectual instrument for propagating systems of religion; and that the courage and resolution almost universally displayed by those who are martyrs to their faith, enflames the enthusiastic ardour of their adherents, and excites a general admiration, which becomes the natural source of reputation and proselytism.[4] By a statute, it was declared unlawful for more than five persons, beside those of the same family, to assemble for any species of worship different from that established by law;[5] and every transgressor was, for the first offence, subjected to the payment of five pounds, or three months imprisonment; for the second, to the payment of ten pounds, or six months imprisonment; and <385> for the third, to the payment of an hundred pounds, or transportation for seven years. Not content with these immoderate severities, the church procured a prohibition against every dissenting teacher from coming within five miles of any corporation, or of any place where he had formerly preached; and this under the penalty of fifty pounds, and six months imprisonment.*

Episcopal church government was introduced also into Scotland; and, being known in that country to be extremely adverse to the inclination of a great part of the inhabitants, was enforced by regulations yet more severe and oppressive. Meetings of the sectaries for public worship, or, as they were called, *conventicles,* were prohibited, under similar penalties as in England; but those who frequented *field conventicles,* were punished with death and confiscation of goods; a large pecuniary reward was offered to any who should apprehend those offenders; and high penalties were inflicted <386> upon such as, being called upon oath, refused to give information against them. A military force was employed to kill or disperse the people discovered in those illegal assemblies; and the execution of these barbarous measures was entrusted by the administration to men of unfeeling and brutal tempers, who, endeavouring to recommend themselves by their activity, were guilty

* Hume's Hist. of England.

4. The Corporations Act (1661) excluded Nonconformists from holding municipal office. The Act of Uniformity (1662) imposed the use of the Book of Common Prayer and insisted that clergy subscribe to Anglican doctrine.

5. Millar is referring to two parts of the so-called Clarendon Code passed by Parliament during the early years of Charles's reign: the Conventicle Act (1664) and the Five Mile Act (1665).

of the most horrible enormities.* Even those who absented themselves from church, were, upon the mere report of the clergy, and without any trial, subjected to arbitrary fines; the payment of which was enforced by quartering soldiers upon the supposed delinquents.†

The oppressive treatment of the Presbyterians, which, in consequence of these laws, was continued in Scotland for a long period, has not been sufficiently held up to the public by historians of credit, nor marked with that indignation and abhorrence which it ought to inspire. The sufferers, indeed, <387> were a set of poor fanatics, whose tenets and manners have become, in this age, the objects of ridicule: but this consideration will, surely, afford no apology for such acts of cruelty and injustice. Charles appears to have conceived a peculiar dislike to the Scottish covenanters, by whom he had been much harrassed and disgusted when under the necessity, in Scotland, of hearing their long prayers and sermons, whose enthusiastic spirit had involved his father in those difficulties which gave rise to the civil war, and whose treachery had finally delivered that unfortunate monarch into the hands of his enemies.

But though the king had, probably, little fellow-feeling with that obnoxious class of Presbyterians, he was desirous of alleviating the hardships to which the unreasonable jealousy of the church had subjected the Catholics, as well as the other sects of non-conformists; and he seems to have been pleased with an opportunity, upon plausible pretences, of granting such relief by means of the *dispensing power* of the crown. It soon became evident, that this monarch enter-<388>tained the same notions of the English government which had been inculcated by his father and grandfather; and though cautious, at first, of exciting any disgust in the nation, he was emboldened by successful experiments, and ventured more and more to shake off those restraints which had been imposed upon him by his fears. The convention which restored the monarchy, and was afterwards turned into a parliament, had contained a great proportion of Presbyterians, and of such as entertained very limited ideas of monarchy. It was, therefore, dissolved in a few months after the new settlement had been effected; and gave place to a new parliament, which, agreeably to the prevailing spirit of the times, ex-

* Hume's Hist. of England. [[A rebellion in 1679, culminating at Bothwell Bridge, was harshly suppressed.]]

† Hume.

hibited opinions and sentiments, both in church and state, more conformable to those of the king.

In the year 1664, the *triennial act,* which had passed in the reign of Charles I. and which had effectually provided that there should be no greater interval than three years between one meeting of parliament and another, was repealed; and the regular <389> calling of those assemblies was again trusted to the discretion, or rather to the occasional necessities of the king. This parliament was continued for about eighteen years; and, during a considerable part of that long period, shewed a pretty strong and uniform disposition to humour the inclinations of the sovereign; but it seemed to imbibe a different spirit, in proportion as the terror occasioned by the late civil war had abated, and as the arbitrary maxims of the crown were more clearly discovered.

So early as the year 1662, Charles declared his intention of dispensing with the penalties contained in the *act of uniformity;* at the same time that he requested the concurrence of parliament for enabling him, with more universal satisfaction, to exercise a power which he conceived to be inherent in the prerogative.* But this purpose, however cautiously expressed, and artfully recommended, was far from being agreeable to the nation. It was touching an old string which had formerly sounded an alarm to <390> the people, and reviving those apprehensions of popery and arbitrary power, which had given rise to the civil war. It produced, therefore, a remonstrance from the two houses of parliament; and was, for the present, laid aside.

In the year 1670, Charles, with concurrence of his brother, concluded a treaty with France, by which Lewis XIV.[6] undertook to assist the King of England in establishing popery and absolute monarchy; and, for that purpose, to pay him a yearly pension of 200,000 l. and to supply him with an army of 6000 men.† This scandalous transaction was kept, as we may easily believe, a profound secret from all but a few persons, whose religion and political profligacy disposed them to promote its accomplishment. The king, at this time, professed to be his own minister; but, in reality, was commonly

* Hume.

† See Dalrymple's Appendix to his Memoirs.—Hume's Hist. of England.

6. Louis XIV: "The Sun King" (1643–1715). The secret Treaty of Dover was reached in 1670.

directed by a secret council, or *cabal;*[7] while the great officers of state, who held the ostensible administration, <391> were left without influence or confidence. The nation was in this manner deprived of that security which, by the constitution, they were entitled to expect from the responsibility of those individuals who filled the higher departments of government, and who might with justice, and without endangering the public tranquillity, be called to account for the measures committed to their direction. Even of this cabal, it is said, that none were made acquainted with the French treaty but those who had embraced the popish religion.

Having thus obtained the support of a monarch so powerful, and so warmly interested in the success of his measures, Charles thought himself in a condition to act with more vigour, and ventured, by his own authority, to grant an indulgence to all non-conformists, whether of the protestant or catholic persuasion.[8] He issued, therefore, a proclamation, suspending all the penal laws against those two branches of the sectaries; and allowing to the former in public, to the latter in private, the free <392> exercise of their religion.* By this exertion of prerogative, the national suspicion was awakened; the jealousy among different sects of protestants was overwhelmed by the terror of their common adversary; and parliament, which had long connived at the designs of the crown, was roused in defence of its own privileges. The feeble mind of Charles was overcome by the violent opposition of that assembly, together with the clamour excited throughout the nation; and he retracted the measure with much profession of regard to the constitution, and of willingness to remove the grievances of the people.† By this unsteadiness of conduct, he encreased the confidence of his opposers, without removing the suspicions by which they were actuated.

From the animosity, hatred, and mutual jealousy which, during the course of this reign, prevailed among different sects and parties, men were easily disposed to credit the reports of plots and conspiracies propa-<393>gated to the prejudice of one another; and hence encouragement had been given to

* Hume's Hist. of England.

† Hume.

7. The Cabal was named for the initials of its members, Lords Clifford, Arlington, Buckingham, Ashley, and Lauderdale, of whom Henry Bennett, earl of Arlington, emerged as the most important of Charles's advisors.

8. Charles issued the Second Declaration of Indulgence in 1672, then repealed it the next year.

numerous criminal prosecutions, followed by the condemnation of the supposed offenders upon insufficient evidence. Thus in 1662, six persons of low rank were charged with a design to restore the commonwealth, and, being condemned upon the testimony of two infamous witnesses, four of them were executed.[9] In the following year, a similar charge was brought against no less than twenty-one persons, who, upon the evidence of one pretended accomplice, were all convicted and put to death. Such fictitious conspiracies, the fruit of groundless apprehension and terror, were at first imputed most frequently to the protestant sectaries and friends of republican government; but, when the immediate fear for popery and of arbitrary power had become prevalent, imputations of a similar nature were circulated, and readily believed against the Roman Catholics.

That the King, and his brother the Duke of York, had resolved to subvert the established government, in church and state, <394> and had entered into a treaty with France for this purpose, is now universally admitted. That many Roman Catholics were looking eagerly towards the same object; that they had suggested particular schemes, and held consultations for promoting and accelerating its accomplishment; or that, impatient of delays, they had even expressed, occasionally, their wishes for the King's death, which might raise to the throne his brother, their zealous patron, who now openly professed the Romish religion, is highly probable. From a few scraps of intelligence concerning such vague intentions or expressions, Oates and Bedloe, two profligates, no less ignorant than shameless and unprincipled, with other associates who became willing to participate in the same harvest, appear to have reared the structure of the *Popish Plot;*[10] by which they asserted, that a regular plan was laid, not only for the establishment of popery and despotism, but also for the murder of the King; and several persons, at different times, had been hired to carry this latter purpose into execution. The accusation was at first limited to men <395> of obscure and doubtful characters; but afterwards, noblemen professing the popish religion, and even the Queen, were involved as accomplices.[11]

9. The reference is to Blood's Plot of 1663.

10. The "Popish Plot" to establish a papist Catholic autocracy under Charles's brother James was a false rumor spread by Titus Oates (1649–1705) and William Bedloe (1650–80). Though the plot was a complete fabrication, the backlash was swift, and more than thirty-five English Catholics were executed for treason.

11. Catherine of Braganza (1638–1705).

Though the story told by these witnesses was, in many respects, full of contradiction and absurdity, though it was varied materially in the course of the different trials, and was not supported by any person of good reputation, there occurred some remarkable incidents, which contributed to bestow upon it, at least in the main articles, an air of credibility.

Godfrey,[12] an active justice of peace, before whom Oates had made oath of the narrative which he afterwards delivered to the privy council, was, in a few days thereafter, found lying dead in a ditch, with his own sword run through his body, but with evident marks of his having been previously strangled. As he had not been robbed of his money, his death was imputed to the resentment of the catholics, or considered as an attempt to intimidate the discoverers of their practices. <396>

When Coleman, secretary to the Duke of York, one of the supposed accomplices in this conspiracy, was apprehended, letters were found in his possession, containing part of a correspondence with Father La Chaise, in the years 1674, 1675, and 1676, which mentioned a design of the Roman Catholics, in conjunction with France, to overturn the established religion in England. It was conjectured that, if the subsequent parts of this correspondence had been found, they would have discovered also the later measures relating to the murder of the King, with which Coleman was charged.[13]

After the popish lords had been imprisoned, one Reading, their agent, or solicitor, was clearly detected in tampering with the witnesses, and endeavouring, by an offer of money, to make them soften their evidence. There was no proof that he had any commission for that purpose from his clients; but the transaction could not fail to throw upon them a suspicion of guilt.

These different circumstances were far from being conclusive as to the reality of the plot in question; but, concurring with the panic <397> which had seized the nation, they created a general belief of its existence. The verdicts of jurymen were found in this, as in other cases, to echo the national prejudice; and many persons apparently innocent, at least of any attempt to murder the King, were condemned and executed. The Viscount of Stafford[14]

12. Sir Edmund Berry Godfrey (1621–78).

13. Edward Coleman (d. 1678), secretary to Mary of Modena, duchess of York; Father François d'Aix LaChaise (1624–1709), confessor to King Louis XIV.

14. William Howard Stafford, first Viscount Stafford (1614–80).

was, upon the same account, found guilty by a majority of the peers, and suffered a capital punishment.

That the *Popish Plot* was a gross imposture, can hardly, it should seem, at this day, be disputed: but that it was entirely a fabrication of the party in opposition to the court, for the purpose of promoting their political interest, as has been alleged by some authors, there is no room to imagine. Had it been invented by a set of artful politicians, it would have exhibited a more plausible appearance, and have been less liable to detection from its numerous inconsistencies. It was the offspring of alarm and credulity, propagated, in all probability, from a small ground-work of truth; and, when it had grown to maturity, employed by an interested policy, as a convenient <398> engine for counteracting the pernicious measures of the crown.*

During the ferment which had thus been excited in the minds of the people, it is not surprising that the Roman Catholics had recourse to a similar expedient, and endeavoured by a counter-plot, not only to retaliate the sufferings they had met with, but also to turn the tide in their own favour. This undertaking was conducted by one Dangerfield, a man in low circumstances, and of infamous character, who offered to make discoveries of a conspiracy, for new-modelling the government, and for driving the King and the royal family out of the kingdom. He was well received by the Duke of York and the King; but the imposture was quickly detected, and even acknowledged; so as to recoil upon the inventors, and produce consequences directly opposite <399> to those which were intended.† This pretended conspiracy was, from the place where Dangerfield's papers were found, called the *Meal Tub Plot.*[15]

The alarm which, from the belief of a popish plot, had thus been excited and spread over the nation, was now pointed more immediately to the prospect, that, upon the demise of Charles, the crown would devolve upon the

* See the State Trials relating to this subject.—Also Burnet's History of his own Time; in which there is an impartial account of the particulars in this remarkable event, with a candid picture of the impression which they made upon the author and some of his friends.

† Burnet.

15. Thomas Dangerfield (ca. 1650–85): The "Meal Tub Plot" of 1679 was a supposed Presbyterian plot to assassinate both Charles II and James. When the ruse was discovered and Dangerfield claimed that he was in service to one of the Catholics implicated in the Popish Plot, anti-Catholic opinion was revived.

Duke of York, a professed Roman Catholic, totally under the dominion of the priests of that persuasion, and who, in the present reign, had, according to the general opinion, influenced and directed all the violent measures of the crown. Under such a prince, conducting with his own hands the machine of government, supported and assisted by all the catholic powers of Europe, and believing it highly meritorious to employ either fraud or force to accomplish his purposes, there was reason to apprehend that neither civil nor religious liberty could be maintained. For securing, therefore, the most important <400> rights of the community, for guarding the constitution and the protestant religion, it was thought necessary that the ordinary rules of government should, in this emergency, be superseded, and that, by an act of the legislature, the lineal heir should, in such particular circumstances, be excluded from the throne.[16] That the crown of England was commonly transmissible by inheritance, like a private estate, could not be disputed; but that this regulation, intended for the good of the people, by avoiding the inconveniences of an elective monarchy, might be set aside in extraordinary cases, was equally certain; and, if ever there occurred a case of extreme necessity, demanding imperiously a measure of that sort, the present emergency, in which the nation was threatened with the loss of every thing dear and valuable, was, doubtless, a remarkable instance.* <401>

A bill for excluding the Duke of York from the succession to the crown was accordingly introduced into the house of commons, and pushed with great violence in three several parliaments. The King, instead of yielding to the desires of the people with that facility which he had shewn on former occasions, remained inflexible in opposing the measure, and at length, when every other expedient had failed, put a stop to it by a dissolution of parliament. The bill, however, was finally permitted to pass through the commons, but was rejected in the house of peers. To explain this, it may be observed, that, beside the general influence of the crown in the upper house, there had occurred a change in the current of political opinions, which had, probably, an effect upon the sentiments of the nobility, and more especially of the bishops. In the course of the investigations concerning the popish plot, the

* See Coleman's Papers; from which the designs of the Duke of York, and of the Roman Catholic powers, to establish popery and despotism in England are sufficiently manifest.

16. The Exclusion Bill effort ultimately failed in 1681 when Charles dissolved Parliament.

numerous falsehoods and absurdities reported by the witnesses could not fail, by degrees, to shake the credit which had been at first given to their testimony, and even to create in many a total <402> disbelief of that supposed conspiracy. In proportion as the terror of popery subsided, the jealousy which the church of England had long entertained of the dissenters was revived; and gave rise to an apprehension that the hierarchy would be endangered by such limitations upon the right of the crown. This jealousy the King had the address to promote, by representing the *exclusioners* as a combination of sectaries, who meant now to overturn the government, both in church and state, as they had done in the reign of his father.

The entire defeat of the exclusion bill was followed by the complete triumph of the royalists, who, supported by the zealous friends of the hierarchy, were now become the popular party. The church and the King were now understood to be linked together by the ties of mutual interest; and they went hand in hand, exalting and confirming the powers of each other. In Scotland, great severities were committed against the Presbyterians. In England, the late behaviour of parliament afforded the Monarch a pretence for neglecting to call <403> those assemblies; and his conducting every branch of administration without their concurrence, occasioned less complaint or uneasiness than might have been expected.

To new-model the government of the city of London, Charles issued a writ of *quo warranto,*[17] by which a forfeiture of the corporation, upon some frivolous pretence of delinquency, was alleged; and the city, to preserve its privileges, was under the necessity of submitting to such conditions as the King thought proper to impose. By the terror of a similar process, most of the other boroughs in the kingdom were induced to surrender their charters, and to accept of such new constitutions as the court thought proper to grant. The direction and management of those corporations was thus brought entirely into the hands of the crown; and preparation was made for establishing an unlimited authority over the commons, if ever the calling of a future parliament should be found expedient.

While the King was thus advancing with rapid strides in the extension of his prerogative, we may easily conceive the disap-<404>pointment, indignation, and despair, of those patriots who had struggled to maintain the ancient constitution. That they should complain loudly of these proceed-

17. The writ of *quo warranto* ("by which warrant") was issued in 1684.

ings; that they should vent their discontent and resentment in menacing expressions; and that, as other methods had failed, they should even think of resorting to violent measures in defence of their natural rights, is not surprising. It was likewise to be expected, that government would have a watchful eye over the conduct of these malcontents, and would listen with avidity to every information which might give a handle for bringing them to punishment. In this irritable state of the public mind, what is called the Ryehouse Plot was discovered, and became the subject of judicial investigation.[18] It seems now to be understood, that the persons engaged in this conspiracy had formed various plans of insurrection, and had even proposed the killing of the King; but that none of their measures had ever been carried into execution.* Such of them as <405> could be convicted were punished with the utmost rigour. Every one knows that Lord Russel, and the famous Algernon Sidney suffered upon the same account. It seems, however, to be now universally admitted, that the proof brought against them was not legal.† There is no reason to suspect, that they had any accession to the Ryehouse Plot, or that they had ever intended the King's death. Though it is not improbable that they had held discourses concerning insurrections, they do not appear to have taken any specific resolution upon that subject; far less to have been guilty of any overt act of rebellion: but they were the leaders of the party in opposition to the crown; the great patrons and promoters of the exclusion bill; the irreconcileable enemies to the exaltation of the Duke of York, and to those political and religious projects which he was determined to pursue.‡ <406>

The public has of late been amused, and several well-meaning persons have been disturbed by the discovery of some particulars, from which it is alleged that both Lord Russel and Mr. Sidney, with other distinguished

* Hume—Burnet—The State Trials.

† See Hume.

‡ See the Trials of Russel and Sidney—Burnet's Hist. of his own Time—Harris's Life of Charles II.—See also, Secret History of Ryehouse Plot. With respect to the narrative of Lord Gray, contained in this publication, it can have little weight, if we consider the bad character of the author, and that it was written under a sentence of condemnation, with a view to justify the illegal measures of the court.

18. The Rye House Plot of 1683 was a plan to assassinate both Charles II and James. Implicated in the plot were several parliamentary opposition Whigs involved in the exclusion effort, including William Russell (1639–83) and Algernon Sidney (1622–83), the author of *Discourses on Government* (1698), a justification for tyrannicide.

members of parliament, were engaged by the intrigues of the French court to oppose the English ministry, and that Mr. Sidney received money from Lewis XIV. for the part which he acted on that occasion.*

Though the merits of the great political questions which were agitated at that period, or since, have no dependence upon the degree of integrity or public spirit displayed by the adherents of different parties, it is not only a piece of justice, but a matter of some importance in the political history of England, to vindicate from such disagreeable aspersions those highly celebrated charac-<407>ters, who have hitherto possessed the esteem and admiration of their countrymen.

With respect to their co-operation with the court of France, in opposing the designs of Charles and his ministry, which is all that is alleged against Lord Russel and some others of the party, we must form our opinion from the peculiar circumstances of the times. About the year 1678, when the designs of the English court to establish an absolute government had become very apparent, England, by the marriage of the Prince of Orange to the daughter of the Duke of York,[19] had been driven into a temporary connection with the States of Holland, and, in that view, had raised a considerable army to be employed against France. The interest of the French court, therefore, who dreaded the operations of this hostile armament, coincided, at this time, with the views of the Whig party in England, who, from a jealousy of the crown, were eager that the troops might be speedily disbanded; and the latter could incur no blame in making use of the incidental, and, perhaps, unexpected assistance of the former, for <408> promoting their great object, the defence of their liberties. It seems to be acknowledged, that by doing so, this party reposed no confidence in the French councils, and followed no other line of conduct than would have been adopted, if no such agreement had taken place. They forfeited no advantage, they sacrificed no duty to their own country, but merely availed themselves of the temporary policy of the French monarch, and, whatever might be his motives, employed him as an instrument to prop that constitution which he had long been endeavouring to undermine.

With respect to the allegation, that Mr. Sidney was a pensioner of France,

* See the histories of Dalrymple and M'Pherson, with the papers referred to.

19. The future William III, king of England and Scotland, and Mary II (r. 1689–1702).

the proof of this fact depends upon the letters and memorials of Barillon,[20] the French agent, and the accounts laid before his own court, in which he states two several sums, of 500 l. each, advanced to Mr. Sidney.*

The authenticity of these accounts, examined, it should seem, and transcribed with little precaution, and produced, for the <409> first time, at the distance of near one hundred years, has been thought liable to suspicion; more especially when it is considered, that the odium occasioned by the illegal condemnation of Sidney, which fell unavoidably on Charles and the Duke of York, would have been in some measure alleviated by the immediate publication of this mysterious transaction with France. But, even supposing the accounts to be genuine, there may be some reason to doubt, how far the representation of this money-jobber, in a matter where his own pecuniary interest, and his reputation and consequence with his constituents, were so nearly concerned, is worthy of credit. Barillon himself acknowledges, that "Sidney always appeared to him to have the same sentiments, and not to have changed his maxims."†—"That he is a man of great views, and very high designs, which tend to the establishment of a republic."‡ That Sidney was known, on that occasion, to be the steady friend of <410> those measures which Barillon was employed to promote, is not disputed. How, then, came this French agent to be so lavish of his master's money, as to throw it away upon a person who had already embarked in the same cause, and who, from this bribe, was induced to do nothing which he would not have done without it? There seems to be but one explanation which this will admit of; that, if the money was actually given to this eminent leader; it must have been intended merely to pass through his hands, for gaining those inferior persons, whose assistance, in the present emergency, it might be convenient to purchase. But that either Lord Russel or Mr. Sidney betrayed the interest of their own country to that of France, or deviated in any particular, from their avowed political principles, has never been alleged, nor does there seem to be any colour for supposing it.§

The death of Charles II. which happened in the beginning of the year 1685, prevented his completing that system of absolute go-<411>vernment,

* See Dalrymple.

† Dalrymple's Appendix, p. 262.

‡ Ibid. p. 287.

§ See Lady Russel's Letters.

20. Paul Barillon, marquis de Branges (ca. 1630–91), French ambassador to England.

in which he had made such considerable progress. Towards the end of his reign he found himself involved in great difficulties from want of money; and is said to have been filled with apprehension, that his late arbitrary measures would be attended with fatal consequences. It is reported that, in a conversation with the Duke, he was overheard to say: "Brother, I am too old to go again to my travels; you may, if you chuse it."[21] And it was believed, that he had formed a resolution to give up all further contest with his people, to change his counsellors, to call a parliament, and to govern for the future according to the principles of the ancient constitution.*

The character of this prince is too obvious to require any full discussion. He possessed a sociable temper, with such an eminent portion of the talents and accomplishments connected with this disposition, as rarely falls to the lot of a king. Here we must finish his eulogy. In every other view we can discover nothing commendable; and it is <412> well if we can apologize for foibles by the mere absence of criminal intention. His open licentiousness and profligacy in the pursuit of his pleasures, not only tended, by example, to corrupt the national manners, but occasioned an extravagance and profusion in his expences, which drove him to unwarrantable methods of procuring money from his subjects. He had little ambition to render himself absolute. He had no attachment to any plan of despotic government. The divine indefeasible right of kings was a doctrine to which he was willing to sacrifice neither his ease nor his amusement. But, on the other hand, he was totally destitute of that public spirit which excites an active and superior mind to admire, and to promote, at the expence of his own safety or interest, the nice adjustment of parts in the great machine of government. He was no less negligent of the national honour and dignity, than indifferent about his own. His extreme indolence, and aversion to business, leading him to devolve the weight of public affairs upon others, and particularly upon the Duke of York, who gained <413> an absolute ascendant over him, and pursued a regular system of tyranny. Upon the whole, when we consider how far the misconduct of this careless monarch was imputable to his ministers, we shall, perhaps, be disposed to admit that, with all his infirmities and vices, he had less personal demerit than any other king of the Stewart family.

* Burnet.

21. See Gilbert Burnet, *History of His Own Time* (London, 1724), 1:604–5.

The accession of James II.[22] afforded a complete justification of those who had contended, that his exclusion from the throne was necessary for securing the liberties of the people. No sooner did he assume the reins of government, than his fixed resolution to overturn the constitution, both in church and state, became perfectly evident. It was happy for the rights of mankind, that he was actuated no less by the principle of superstition than of civil tyranny; as the former contributed much more powerfully than the latter, to alarm the apprehensions, and to rouse the spirit of the nation. It was yet more fortunate that he proved to be a prince of narrow capacity, of unpo-<414>pular and forbidding manners, blinded and misled by his prejudices, and though, to the last degree, obstinate and inflexible, totally destitute of steadiness and resolution.

One of the first acts of the administration of James, after declaring in the privy council his determined purpose to maintain the rights and liberties of the nation, was to issue a proclamation, ordering that the customs and excise should be paid as in the preceding reign. By this arbitrary measure he assumed the most important province of the legislature; and though, for saving appearances, an expedient had been suggested, that the order of payment should be suspended until the meeting of parliament, he rejected this proposal, because it might seem to imply that the authority of the national council was requisite for giving validity to this exertion of the prerogative.

From the power over the city of London, and over the other boroughs in the kingdom, which had been acquired in the late reign, James had no reason to fear opposition from parliament, and was, therefore, willing to make an early trial of the disposi-<415>tions of that assembly. At their first meeting, he demanded, in a high tone of authority, that the revenue which had been enjoyed by his brother should be settled upon him during life; and this demand he accompanied with a plain intimation, that their implicit compliance was the only way to secure their frequent meetings, and to prevent his resorting to other methods for procuring a revenue.* Instead of being alarmed by such a declaration, the two houses appeared to vie with each other in their alacrity and readiness to gratify the monarch.

But, though James had good reason to rely upon the uniform support of parliament, he was not negligent of other precautions for promoting his

* Hume.

22. James II (r. 1685–89).

designs. It is impossible to withhold our indignation when we discover that this king, like his brother, had so far degraded himself and the nation, as to become the abject pensioner of France, and to render the national forces subservient to the ambition of the French monarch, <416> upon receiving from him a regular subsidy, with a promise of assistance in subverting the English government. Soon after his accession to the throne, we find him apologizing to Barillon, the French ambassador, for summoning a parliament. "You may, perhaps, be surprised," says he, "but I hope you will be of my opinion when I have told you my reasons. I have resolved to call a parliament immediately, and to assemble it in the month of May. I shall publish, at the same time, that I am to maintain myself in the enjoyment of the same revenues the king my brother had. Without this proclamation for a parliament, I should hazard too much, by taking possession directly of the revenue which was established during the life-time of my deceased brother. It is a decisive stroke for me to enter into possession and enjoyment; for, hereafter, it will be much more easy for me, either to put off the assembling of parliament, or to maintain myself by other means which may appear more convenient for me."* Upon re-<417>ceiving from Lewis XIV. the sum of 500,000 livres, this magnanimous prince said to Barillon, with tears in his eyes: "It is the part of the king your master alone, to act in a manner so noble, and so full of goodness to me."† From the subsequent dispatches of this ambassador, it is clearly proved, that James was determined to render himself independent of parliament, and was totally engrossed by those two objects, the establishment of the popish religion, and that of his own absolute power. With these views, he thought it necessary to court the protection of Lewis, from whom he was constantly begging money with unwearied and shameless importunity.‡ Barillon, in writing to his master, mentions the expressions used by James in a conversation upon that subject: "That he had been brought up in France, and had eat your majesty's bread; and that his heart was French."§

In pursuance of the plan which he had laid, his immediate design was, according <418> to the same testimony, to make the parliament revoke the

* Dalrymple's Appendix.

† Dalrymple's Appendix.

‡ Dalrymple's Appendix, p. 147, &c.

§ Ibid.

test act and the *habeas corpus act;*[23] "one of which," as he told Barillon, "was the destruction of the catholic religion, and the other of the royal authority."*

The precipitate and ill-conducted attempts of the Duke of Monmouth in England, and of the Earl of Argyle in Scotland,[24] which met with little encouragement, and were easily crushed by the king's forces, contributed to render this infatuated monarch more sanguine with respect to the success of his projects, and, by inspiring him with greater confidence, prompted him to act with less moderation and caution. The shocking cruelty exhibited on that occasion by the military, and the gross injustice committed, under the form of law, by the civil courts, which could not have happened without the approbation and countenance of the king, convey a still more unfavourable idea of his disposition as a man, than of his abilities as a politician. Bishop Burnet[25] <419> affirms, that regular accounts of those judicial proceedings were transmitted to James, who was accustomed to repeat the several particulars with marks of triumph and satisfaction. It is certain, that this king mentions, in a letter to the Prince of Orange, the hundreds who had been condemned in what he jocularly distinguishes by the appellation of *Jeffery's campaign;*[26] and that, for his services, this infamous tool was rewarded with a peerage, and with the office of lord high chancellor.†

Both Charles and James had been taught by the example of their father and by their own experience, that without an army it was in vain to think of subjecting the English nation to an absolute government. The king, therefore, after the late insurrections had been suppressed, informed the parliament, that he meant to keep up all the forces which the state of the country had obliged him to levy; and he demanded an additional supply for that

* Dalrymple's Appendix.

† See Dalrymple's Appendix.

23. *Habeas corpus* ("you shall have the body"): a writ requiring the body of a person accused to be brought before a judge or into court for the purpose of the writ.

24. James Scott, duke of Monmouth (1649–85) and nephew of James II, was executed shortly after the battle of Sedgemoor in 1685; Archibald Campbell, ninth earl of Argyle (d. 1685), led an unsuccessful insurrection in support of Monmouth in the Scottish highlands.

25. Bishop Gilbert Burnet (1643–1715): Scottish theologian and historian, the author of the *History of His Own Time* (1724–34; 1733–34) and the *History of the Reformation of the Church of England* (1679–1715).

26. George "Judge" Jeffreys (1648–89) was used by Charles II, and more extensively by James II, in pressing the crown's legal interests. Jeffreys is notorious for presiding over the "Bloody Assizes" after Monmouth's rebellion.

purpose. Not satisfied with as large an army in England, in Scotland, <420> and in Ireland, as his own revenue was capable of supporting; he entered into a treaty with the French king, who took into his pay three English regiments, and, besides, agreed to furnish James with whatever troops might be necessary in the prosecution of his designs.*

But the grand and favourite object of James, which contributed more than any other to alarm the people, was the dispensing power which he assumed in favour of popery. So far from concealing his intention in this particular, he thought proper, near the beginning of his reign, to make an open avowal of it in parliament; which produced an address from the house of commons, and a motion to the same effect in that of the peers. These measures, being regarded by the king as inconsistent with his dignity, were followed by several prorogations of that assembly, and at length by a dissolution.

In examining the earlier part of our history, I had formerly occasion to consider <421> the origin of the *dispensing power;* which arose from the interest of the sovereign, as chief magistrate, in the condemnation and punishment of crimes. As the king was the public prosecutor, against whom all transgressions of the law were understood to be chiefly directed, and who, besides, drew the pecuniary emolument from all fines and forfeitures, which were anciently the most common species of punishments, he came by degrees to exercise, not only the privilege of pardoning the offences which were actually committed, but even that of previously excusing individuals from such penalties as might be incurred by a future misdemeanor. It is commonly said, that this power was borrowed by our kings from the practice of the Roman Pontiff, who claimed the right of granting indulgences for every sort of religious transgression; but in reality, a privilege of this nature seems to have resulted from the situation of the chief civil, as well as of the chief ecclesiastical magistrate; though, in Europe, it was for obvious reasons carried to a greater extent by the latter than by the former. In <422> England, however, the king having upon the reformation, succeeded to the supremacy of the bishop of Rome, he, of course, united in his own person these different sources of power.

As the dispensing power of the crown was originally exerted in extraordinary cases only, it probably was of advantage to the community, by providing relief to such persons as were in danger of suffering oppression from

* Dalrymple.

a rigid observance of the common rules of law. But the occasions for soliciting this relief were gradually multiplied; people who found it their interest, as in evading the restrictions upon some branches of trade, were led to purchase dispensations from the crown; and the exercise of this extraordinary privilege degenerated more and more into abuse. It can hardly be doubted, that such dispensations as were granted for money would be confined to individuals, and not extended to classes or general descriptions of people; for the crown, we may suppose, receiving a profit from this branch of the prerogative, would seldom bestow an indulgence upon any but <423> those who had paid for it. But even in this limited shape, the *dispensing power,* which might lead to a shameful traffick upon the part of administration, and interrupt the due execution of the most salutary laws, was regarded as incompatible with the principles of the English constitution, and was reprobated in direct terms by the legislature. In the reign of Richard II. there was passed an act of parliament permitting the king, in particular cases, and for a limited time, to dispense with the *statute of provisors,*[27] but declaring such dispensations, in all other cases, to be illegal and unwarrantable. It must be acknowledged, however, that even after this act the dispensing power was not abandoned; and that lawyers, under the influence of the crown, were sufficiently ready in their judicial capacity, to support all such exertions of the prerogative.

The differences between the two great religious parties which took place at the reformation, afforded a new inducement for this extraordinary interposition of the crown, and in a different form from what <424> had hitherto been thought of. In particular, the princes of the house of Stewart, from their favour to the Roman catholicks, were disposed to free them from the penalties to which, by various statutes, they had been subjected; and to do this effectually, it was necessary that the dispensation should be granted not to single individuals; but, at one and the same time, to all persons of that persuasion; that is, to all those who fell under the penalties imposed by the statutes in question.[28] When the dispensing power of the crown was exhibited in this new and more extended form, it must have been universally re-

27. The Statute of Provisors (1390) reinforced the earlier Statute of Provisors (1351), which claimed the right of English monarchs to exclude papal provisions to English benefices.

28. James II's Declaration of Indulgence (1687) restored rights to Catholic and Protestant Nonconformists, in effect repealing the Test Acts of 1677.

garded as a repeal of the acts of parliament, and as a direct assumption of legislative authority.

In the petition of right,[29] the dispensing power is expressly enumerated among those remarkable grievances, of which redress was claimed from Charles I. and which, on that occasion, were declared to be violations of the English constitution. As the petition of right had passed into a law before the commencement of the civil war, and had never <425> been repealed, it continued in force during the reigns of Charles II. and of his brother.

In these circumstances, we cannot wonder that the revival of the dispensing power by James, a bigotted papist, with the avowed purpose of admitting the Roman catholics to all offices, both civil and military, should be regarded as an unequivocal declaration of his firm resolution to subvert the religion and liberties of the nation.

As in the late reign, the exclusion bill was defeated by exciting the jealousy of the church against the puritans, an attempt was now made to unite the Roman catholics in one common cause with the protestant non-conformists, by granting to both of them the same relief from the hardships under which they laboured. The artifice had in the beginning, some degree of success; but was in a short time detected by the dissenters, who had too much penetration and foresight, to sacrifice their ultimate safety to a mere temporary advantage.

To reconcile the nation to the doctrine of the *dispensing power,* a judicial determination was thought necessary, but could not <426> be procured without displacing several of the judges, and appointing others over whom the king had more influence. This produced a mock-trial, the issue of which might easily be foreseen; but so far from removing objections, it gave rise to new apprehension and disgust, by shewing, in strong colours, the inclination, as well as the ability of the crown, to poison the fountains of justice.

For this exertion of the prerogative, James alledged the most plausible motive: that of securing liberty of conscience, and preventing any person from suffering hardships on account of his religious principles. This was the reason which he gave to the prince of Orange; at the very time, that, with unparalleled effrontery, he was dispatching an ambassador to Lewis XIV. expressing his approbation of the barbarity inflicted on the protestants by

29. See p. 527, note 16.

the revocation of the edict of Nantes.[30] By this dissimulation of James, no person could be deceived; for that he was the real author of all the persecution committed against the presbyterians in Scotland was universally known. <427>

But that none might mistake his meaning, he took care that it should be illustrated by his immediate conduct. The single purpose for which he dispensed with the *test,* and with the penal laws against non-conformists and recusants, was evidently the introduction of Roman catholics into all offices of trust. To accomplish this end he was indefatigable, and had, in a short time, made far greater advances than could have been expected. Those who had no religion of their own were easily persuaded to embrace that of his majesty; while many, whose consciences did not permit them to take an active share in the present measures were unwilling, by their opposition, to incur his resentment, and endeavoured by keeping themselves out of public view, to avoid the impending storm.

In Ireland, the protestants were disarmed; the army was new modelled; and a multitude, both of private soldiers and officers of that persuasion were dismissed. The public administration, as well as the distribution of justice, was placed in the hands of Roman catholics. A plan was formed of <428> revoking what was called the *act of settlement,* by which, at the restoration of the late king, the protestants, in that country, had been secured in the possession of certain estates; and as for this purpose it was necessary to summon the Irish parliament, similar expedients to those which had formerly taken place in England, for securing elections in favour of the crown, were upon this occasion adopted. The charters of Dublin, and of other boroughs were annulled; and those communities, by a new set of regulations,[31] were brought entirely under the management of Roman catholics.*

The government of Scotland was committed to men of the same principles. In England, the king was not contented with pushing the catholics into offices in the army, and in the civil department; he had even formed the resolution of introducing them into the church and the universities. The violence with which he endeavoured to force a popish president upon the

* Hume. Rapin.

30. The Edict of Nantes (1598) provided freedom of conscience and private worship for Huguenots. The edict was revoked by Louis XIV in 1685.

31. The Irish Act of Settlement was passed in 1662.

fellows of Magdalen college, Oxford, the public conse-<429>cration of four bishops in the King's chapel, with authority to exercise episcopal functions in different districts; the royal permission which was given them to print and circulate their pastoral letters to the Roman catholics of England; the sending an ambassador to Rome, to acknowledge the authority of the Pope, and to make preparations for reconciling the kingdom to the holy see; these events which followed one another in rapid succession, plainly demonstrated that James was not satisfied with giving liberty of conscience to the professors of the Romish religion, but that he meant to invest them with a legal jurisdiction. The church of England, who from opposition to the sectaries, had supported the crown in the late usurpations of prerogative, was now roused by the dangers which threatened her establishment; and those pulpits which formerly resounded with the doctrines of passive obedience,[32] were employed in exciting the people to the defence of their religious and civil rights.* <430>

Among those who utter inflammatory discourses against the measures of the court, Dr. Sharpe, a clergyman of London, distinguished himself by the severity of his reflections upon the late proselytes to popery. The king enraged at this boldness, gave orders to the bishop of London, that Sharpe should be immediately suspended from his clerical functions; but that prelate, who seems to have entertained higher notions of liberty than most of his brethren, excused him from proceeding in that summary manner, which he alledged was inconsistent with the forms of church discipline. James was determined, not only to prevent Sharpe from escaping, but even to punish this disobedience of the bishop. With this view, and for procuring an absolute authority over the conduct of churchmen, he ventured to revive the court of high-commission, which, in the reign of Charles I. had been abolished by the legislature, with an express prohibition that this or any similar tribunal, should ever be erected. Upon this new ecclesiastical commission, the king, in open defiance of the statute, bestowed the same <431> inquistorial powers which that court had formerly possessed; and here he found no difficulty in suspending both the delinquents.†

* See Dalrymple. Appendix.

† Hume. Rapin.

32. An oath of passive obedience, or nonresistance, was required for members of the Church of England by the Corporation Act of 1661.

Armed with the powers of this tyrannical jurisdiction, James was determined, not only to overturn the church of England, but to render her the instrument of her own destruction. He now issued a new *proclamation,*[33] suspending all the penal laws against non-conformists, accompanied with orders that it should be read by the clergy in all their churches. The primate, and six of the bishops, who, God knows, were not guilty of carrying their principles of resistance to any extravagant pitch, ventured, in the most humble and private manner, to petition the king, that he would excuse them from reading this proclamation. This was followed by a resolution of the king, which nothing but an infatuation, without example, could have dictated, to prosecute those prelates for a *seditious libel.* Had this measure been successful, the fate of English liberty would <432> have been decided. It was vain to seek relief from oppression, if even to complain of hardships, and to petition for redress, though in terms the most respectful and submissive was to be regarded as an atrocious crime. This trial, the deep concern about the issue of which appeared among all ranks, the final acquittal of the prisoners in opposition to the utmost exertions of the crown, and the violent demonstrations of joy and triumph which followed that event, afforded a decisive proof of the national spirit, and served as a watch-word to communicate that indignation and terror which filled the breasts of the people.*

The situation and character of the prince of Orange made the nation look up to him as the person whom heaven had pointed out for their deliverer. Applications accordingly were made to him from every description of protestants, containing a warm and pressing solicitation, to assist with an armed force, in the re-establishment of our religion and liberties; an enterprise which was doubtless flattering <433> to his ambition; while it coincided with those patriotic views which he had uniformly discovered, and which had produced the noblest exertions in behalf of the independence of his own country, and of all Europe.[34]

When James had received information concerning the invasion intended by that prince, he was thrown into the utmost consternation; and endeavoured to avert the resentment of his subjects by pretending to relinquish the

* Dalrymple. State Trials.

33. Presumably the Second Declaration of Indulgence in 1688.

34. William's effort to drive the French from the Netherlands resulted in the formation of the League of Augsburg in 1688 to combat Louis XIV.

most unpopular of his measures. But the accident of a storm which dispersed the prince's fleet, and was believed to have defeated the whole undertaking, destroyed at once this temporising system of concession, and exposed the insincerity of his repentance.* A variety of circumstances now co-operated in producing a revolution of greater importance, and with less hurt or inconvenience to the nation, than perhaps any other that occurs in the history of the world. It is observable, that the standing army, overlooking the ordinary punctilios and objects of their profession, deserted the <434> sovereign when he became the declared enemy of the constitution. The pusillanimity of James, in forsaking his friends, and in quitting the kingdom, gave rise to an easy settlement where much difficulty was apprehended. He had the weakness to imagine that his throwing the great seal into the river would create some embarrassment to the new administration.

As the character of this prince procured no esteem, his misfortunes appear to have excited little compassion. He possessed no amiable or respectable qualities to compensate or alleviate his great public vices. His ambition was not connected with magnanimity; his obstinacy and zeal were not supported by steadiness and resolution; though, as it frequently happens, they appear to have been deeply tinctured with cruelty. The gravity of his deportment, and his high professions of religion, were disgraced by narrow prejudices, and by a course of dissimulation and falsehood. His fate was not more severe than he deserved; for, certainly, the sovereign of a limited monarchy cannot complain of injustice, when he is expelled from that <435> kingdom whose government he has attempted to subvert, and deprived of that power which he has grossly and manifestly abused. Impartial justice, perhaps, would determine that he was far from suffering according to his demerits; that he was guilty of crimes, which, in the nature and consequences, infer the highest enormity; and that, instead of forfeiting his crown, he well deserved the highest punishment which the law can inflict.

There have lately been published several extracts from the life of this prince, written by himself, from which it is supposed that the mistakes of former historians may be corrected and much light thrown upon the history of that period. What has already been published is a meagre detail, destitute of such particulars as might enable the reader to form a judgment concerning

* Hume. Rapin.

the credibility of the narration.[35] From the character, besides, and circumstances of the writer, it should seem, that even if the whole work was laid before the public, it would be intitled to little authority. The writers of memoirs concerning their own conduct are, in all <436> cases, to be perused with caution, and allowances for such embellishment, and such perversion of facts, as may proceed from motives of private interest or vanity. But of all men, James, who appears to have written his life with a view to publication, or at least of its being produced in his own vindication, was under great temptation to exaggerate or extenuate those particulars which might affect the reputation, either of himself and his friends, or of his numerous enemies. How is it possible to trust the private anecdotes of a writer, who, in a letter to the prince of Orange, could deny that he had any accession to a treaty with France, after he had been for some months eagerly engaged in promoting it; or who gravely professed to the same person his principles of universal toleration, while he was congratulating Lewis XIV. on the most intolerant act of his reign, and expressing his great satisfaction with the violent measure of that monarch for the extirpation of heresy?* As James must have been sensible that he <437> was hated by a great part of the nation, and that his views and conduct were severely censured, the relation which he gives of his transactions must be considered as, in some measure, the representation of a culprit placed at the bar of the public; and which, though affording good evidence against himself, yet when adduced in his own favour, is worthy of belief only according to its internal probability, and to the degree of confirmation which it may receive from collateral evidence. <438>

* See his Letters. Dalrymple's Appendix.

35. Millar is referring to James Macpherson's *Original Papers; containing the secret history of Great Britain, from the Restoration, to the accession of the House of Hanover; to which are prefixed, extracts from the life of James II, as written by himself* (London, 1775).

ꕥ CHAPTER VII ꕥ

Of the Revolution-Settlement; and the Reign of William and Mary.

Of all the great revolutions recorded in the history of ancient or of modern times, that which happened in England, in the year 1688, appears to have been productive of the least disorder, and to have been conducted in a manner the most rational, and consistent with the leading principles of civil society. When a sovereign has violated the fundamental laws of the constitution, and shewn a deliberate purpose of persevering in acts of tyranny and oppression, there cannot be a doubt but that the people are entitled to resist his encroachments, and to adopt such precautions as are found requisite for the preservation of their liberty. To deny this, would be to maintain that government is intended for the benefit of those who govern, not of the whole community; and, that the general happiness of <439> the human race, ought to be sacrificed to the private interest, or caprice, of a few individuals. It cannot, however, be supposed, that such resistance will ever be effected without some disturbance, and without a deviation from those forms and rules which are observed in the ordinary course of administration.[1] When the machine is out of order, it must be taken to pieces; and in the repairing and cleaning of the wheels and springs, there must be some interruption and derangement of its movements. When a general reformation of government

1. Compare Millar's judgment with Hume's: "By deciding many important questions in favour of liberty, and still more, by that great precedent of deposing one king, and establishing a new family, it gave such an ascendant to popular principles, as has put the nature of the English constitution beyond all controversy. And it may justly be affirmed, without any danger of exaggeration, that we, in this island, have ever since enjoyed, if not the best system of government, at least the most entire system of liberty, that ever was known amongst mankind." *HE,* 6:531.

has become indispensable, it must be conducted according to the exigency of times and circumstances; and few situations will occur, in which it is practicable without many temporary inconveniencies, or even without violence and bloodshed. It is the part of prudence and of justice, in those cases, to adopt such measures as are likely to produce the end in view with the least possible hardship; so that, although violent and irregular, they may be justified by the great law of necessity. <440>

In consequence of a very general and pressing invitation from the English nobility and gentry, the prince of Orange, about the end of the year 1688, landed, with an armed force, in England; and immediately published a declaration,[2] that the sole purpose of his undertaking, was to obtain the dismission of Roman catholics from those offices of trust which they held contrary to law, and the calling of a free parliament for the redress of grievances. Though the nation was in some measure apprised of this event, yet, intimidated by the unusual situation, they remained, for a short time, irresolute and in suspense; but soon after, an universal approbation of the enterprise was manifest from the conduct of the people in all quarters, who resorted to the prince, and formed an association to support his measures. The king found himself deserted by those upon whose fidelity he had most reason to rely; even by his own family, the prince and princess of Denmark, and by a great part of that army which he had provided to enforce his authority. <441>

In this alarming conjuncture, it might have been expected that James, to extricate himself from the difficulties in which he was involved, would have embraced one or other of two different plans. By encountering the present danger with firmness and resolution, by collecting the forces that were still faithful to him, and by endeavouring to scatter dissention among his enemies, who, notwithstanding their union in demanding a free parliament, were far from coinciding in their political opinions, he might perhaps have been successful, in defending his crown, at least, in protracting the war, till he might obtain assistance from France. By conciliatory measures, on the other hand, by giving way to the complaints of the people, by assembling a new parliament, and submitting to certain restraints upon the prerogative,

2. The Declaration of Rights was a condition of William and Mary's ascent to the throne. It contained an indictment of James II and his transgressions, a declaration of the rights of the people of Britain, and a declaration of the accession of William and Mary.

he might have endeavoured to lull the nation in security, trusting to some future opportunity of retracting or evading those concessions. If either of these plans, however liable to censure, had been pursued, it is likely that the consequences to the public would have been fatal. But, happily, James was <442> thrown into such consternation as to be incapable of persisting in any settled resolution. Yielding to the impressions of fear and despondency, he quitted entirely the field of action, and withdrew, for the present, into a foreign country.[3] By this imprudent step, the remains of his party became quite disheartened, and were no longer in a condition to oppose the new settlement.

The prince of Orange, having thus no enemy to cope with, proceeded to execute the task he had undertaken, by referring to the people themselves, the redress of their own grievances, and by employing the power which he possessed, for no other purpose than that of securing to them the privilege of settling their own government. As, in the absence of the King, the ordinary powers of the constitution could not be exerted, the most rational and proper expedients were adopted to supply the deficiency. The prince invited all those who had been members of any of the three last parliaments, to hold a meeting for the purpose of giving their advice in the present conjuncture. By their direction, he called a convention, <443> composed of the usual members of the house of peers, and of the representatives of the counties and boroughs, elected in the same manner as in a regular parliament.[4] This meeting assembling at a time when the whole nation was in a ferment, and when the people, having arms in their hands, were capable of making an effectual opposition, its determinations, which passed, not only without censure, but with strong marks of public approbation and satisfaction, must be considered as the voice of the community at large, delivered with as much formality, and in a manner as unexceptionable as the nature of things would permit. In this convention the main articles of the revolution-settlement were adjusted; though to remove, as far as possible, every appearance of objection, they were afterwards confirmed by the sanction of a regular parliament.

That the King, who had shewn such a determined resolution to overturn

3. James escaped to arrive in France in late December 1688.

4. The Convention met in January 1689. In February of that year, the Parliament Act transformed the convention into a regular Parliament.

the religion and government of the kingdom, and that his son,[5] then an infant, who, it was foreseen, would be educated in the same principles, and until he should arrive at the age of man-<444>hood, would be under the direction of his father, and of his father's counsellors; that those two persons, whatever might be the reverence paid to their title, should be excluded from the throne, was, in the present state of the nation, rendered indispensibly necessary. In the convention, however, this point was not settled without much hesitation and controversy. The two great parties who, since the reign of Charles the First, in a great measure divided the kingdom, had shewn themselves almost equally disposed to resist the arbitrary measures of James for introducing the popish religion. But though a great part of the tories had, from the terror of popery, joined in the application to the prince of Orange, that he would assist them with a foreign army, to procure the redress of grievances; no sooner were they delivered from their immediate apprehensions, than they seemed to repent of their boldness, relapsed into their old political principles, and resumed their former doctrines of passive obedience. They at least carried those doctrines so far as to maintain, that the people had no right, upon any <445> abuse of the regal power, or upon any pretence whatever, to punish the sovereign, or deprive him of the sovereignty; and that even supposing the King to have resigned or abandoned his royal dignity, the throne could not upon that account, be rendered vacant, but must immediately be filled by the prince of Wales, to whom, upon the death of his father, the crown must be instantly transferred. According to this view, it was contended, that, in the present emergency, the administration should be committed to a regency; either in the name of James, if he was to be considered merely as absent; or in the name of his son, if the father had actually abandoned the sovereignty.

The whigs, though they entertained more liberal notions of government, were unwilling to fall out with their present confederates, and endeavoured by a temporising system, to avoid unnecessary disputes upon abstract political questions, and to render the new-settlement, as much as possible, unanimous and permanent.

It is a matter of curiosity to observe the public debates on this important occasion; <446> in which the natural spirit and feelings of men, made up for the narrowness of their philosophical principles; and in which a feigned

5. James Francis Edward Stuart (1688–1766).

and ridiculous pretence was employed to justify a measure which they did not scruple to execute. They supposed that, by leaving the kingdom, James had abdicated the government; instead of boldly asserting that, by his gross misbehaviour, he had forfeited his right to the crown. That James made his escape rather than comply with the desires of his people, or assemble a parliament to deliberate upon the redress of grievances, was the real state of the fact.—But that he meant by this to yield up, or relinquish his authority, there certainly was no ground to imagine. His flight was the effect of his obstinacy and his fear; and was calculated to procure the protection of a foreign power, by whose aid he entertained the prospect of being soon re-instated in his dominion. We cannot help pitying the most enlightened friends of liberty, when we see them reduced, on that occasion, to the necessity of softening the retreat of James, and his attempt to overturn the government, by <447> regarding them as a virtual renunciation of his trust, or voluntary *abdication* of his crown; instead of holding them up in their true colours, of crimes deserving the highest punishment, and for which the welfare of society required, that he should at least be deprived of his office.

In Scotland, where a majority of the people were presbyterians, and felt an utter abhorrence, not only of popery, but of that episcopal hierarchy to which they had been forcibly subjected, and where the reformation, as I formerly took notice, had diffused among all ranks, a more literary and inquiring spirit than was known in England; the convention, which was likewise called by the prince of Orange for the same purpose as in the latter country, discovered, or at least uttered, without any subterfuge, more manly and liberal sentiments. "The estates of the kingdom found and declared, that James VII. had invaded the fundamental laws of this kingdom, and altered it from a legal and limited monarchy, to an arbitrary despotic power; and had governed the same to the subversion of the protestant <448> religion, and violation of the laws and liberties of the nation, inverting all the ends of government; whereby he had *forfeited* the crown, and the throne was become *vacant.*"*

But though the language employed by the leaders in the English conven-

* See continuation of Rapin, by Tindal, vol. 16. [[Nicholas Tindal, *The Continuation of Mr. Rapin de Thoyras's History of England, from the Revolution to the Accession of King George II,* 2nd ed. (London, 1787).]] This declaration was made with only twelve dissentient voices; a great number of the party in opposition having previously retired from the meeting. [[Declaration of the Scottish Convention, 11 April 1689.]]

tion, was accommodated to the narrow prejudices of the times, their measures were dictated by sound and liberal policy. Setting aside the king, and the prince of Wales, in consequence of the declaration already made, the right of succession to the crown devolved upon the princess of Orange, the king's eldest daughter, who had been educated in the protestant religion, and was thought to be under no disqualification from holding the reins of government. There was no intention of converting the constitution into an elective monarchy, or of deviating further from the lineal course of inheritance than the present <449> exigence required. The same circumstances, however, which demanded the advancement of the princess of Orange to the throne, made it also necessary that the regal authority should be communicated to her husband. It would have been absurd to banish an arbitrary and despotical prince, to break the line of descent, by which the crown was commonly transmitted, and for promoting the great ends of society, to run the hazards always attendant on the correcting former abuses, without making, at the same time, a suitable provision for maintaining the new settlement. But the state of Britain, and of Europe, rendered this a difficult matter. From the efforts of the popish party at home, from the power of Lewis XIV. and the machinations of the whole Roman catholic interest abroad; not to mention the prepossessions of the populace in favour of that hereditary succession to the crown which old usage had rendered venerable, there was every reason to fear a second *restoration,* with consequences more fatal than those which had attended the former. Against those impending calamities, nothing less than the <450> abilities, and the authority of the prince of Orange, the head of the protestant interest in Europe, could be deemed a sufficient guard; and it was happy for the liberties of mankind, that the matrimonial connection of Mary with a person so eminent, and so circumstanced, had, by suggesting his participation of her throne, provided a barrier so natural, and so effectual.

From these considerations, the prince and princess of Orange were declared, by the convention, to be king and queen of England; but the administration of the government, was committed solely to the prince.* After determining this great point, the convention, in imitation of the mode of

* Tindal. By a subsequent act in 1690, the crown, failing the king and queen, and their issue, and failing the issue of Ann, and of the king, was settled upon the family of Hanover.—BURN.

procedure at the restoration, was, by a bill passing through the two houses, and obtaining the royal assent, converted into a parliament; and that assembly proceeded immediately to a redress of grievances. <451>

Considering the disputes which, from the accession of the house of Stewart, had been the source of continual disturbance, and the extravagant claims which had been repeatedly advanced by the princes of that family, it was highly proper to lay hold of the present occasion, for ascertaining the boundaries of the prerogative, and for preventing, as much as possible, all future controversy upon the subject. The omission of this necessary and obvious precaution, at the restoration of Charles II. was an unpardonable neglect. The parliament, therefore, after the example of the *petition of right,* which had been intended for a similar purpose in the reign of Charles I. now prepared the famous *bill of rights;* which, in the year 1689, was passed into a law; and by which the constitution, in several important articles, where it had lately been invaded, was expressly declared and established.

Of the violations of the constitution, which had been the subject of complaint, the most flagrant, perhaps, was the power assumed by the crown of dispensing with statutes, and of issuing proclamations in place of laws. <452> Other encroachments might contribute to impair or disfigure our government; this was calculated to destroy the whole structure, by completely undermining its foundations. Had such a power been admitted, the king would in reality have become a legislator; the authority of parliament would have been annihilated; and the government changed into an absolute monarchy. Though all such exertions of the prerogative had been expressly reprobated and condemned in the *petition of right,* they had not been abandoned by the two succeeding monarchs; but were more especially renewed, and prosecuted with great vehemence by James II. In the *bill of rights,* therefore, it was thought necessary, once more, to mark this procedure with the express condemnation of the legislature; and to declare, "that the pretended power of suspending laws, or the execution of laws, by regal authority, without consent of parliament, is illegal."[6]

A similar declaration was made with respect to another grievance; that of levying money by virtue of the prerogative, and without the authority of parliament. That <453> the national council had the sole right of imposing

6. See Carl Stephenson and Frederick George Marcham, eds., *Sources of English Constitutional History* (London: Harper and Row, 1972), 2:601.

taxes, was an undoubted principle of the constitution, and reaching as far back as the records of parliament. But as the crown, when pressed for money, had invented a variety of shifts for procuring supplies in a clandestine and irregular manner, the legislature again interposed its authority to prohibit, in all cases, those evasive and unwarrantable practices. No part of the constitution had oftener than this attracted the eye of the public, or, by repeated decisions, been rendered more clear and indisputable. No branch of parliamentary authority, we may also observe, tends more effectually to secure the liberties of the nation, by rendering the king dependent upon the liberality of parliament, and laying him under the necessity of calling frequent meetings of the national representatives.

But little advantage could be expected from the meetings of that assembly, unless its members, when called to deliberate on the business of the nation, possessed an unbounded freedom of expressing their sentiments. Parliaments, originally, were composed of a few great barons, who maintained this free-<454>dom by their own opulence and power. Those distinguished personages were often in a condition, singly, to defy their sovereign in the field, and would have laughed at his pretensions to hinder them from speaking their minds in council. But when the splitting of large estates, and the introduction of representatives from counties and boroughs, had extended the right of sitting in parliament to many small proprietors, their authority and weight came to depend more upon their collective, than their separate power; and the greater weakness of individuals obliged them to unite more in a body for the defence of their parliamentary privileges. The increase of their members, as well as the greater extent of their business, introduced, at the same time, the practice of arguing and debating, at more length upon the different subjects before them, and rendered the eloquence, and the popular talents of particular members, an engine of greater importance in the determinations of every meeting. Their speeches, calculated to make a strong impression upon their hearers, became frequently, as we may easily suppose, offensive to the sovereign, and provoked <455> him, in some cases, to interrupt their proceedings, and even to harrass with imprisonment, and criminal prosecution, those individuals who, by their resolute opposition, or intemperance of language, had incurred his resentment.

Such measures were, no doubt, arbitrary and illegal. The English parliament, composed of the immediate vassals of the crown, formed originally the supreme court of justice in the kingdom; and its members could not, on account of any alledged irregularity in delivering their opinions, be prosecuted before an inferior judicatory. If they were guilty of any indecorum in their speeches, or of any misdemeanor in their senatorial capacity, they were liable to the correction and censure of their own tribunal, the members of which had been witnesses of the offence, and were the best judges of its demerit. But the prosecution of the offender before any other court, or magistrate, was reversing the order of judicial establishments, by authorising a subordinate jurisdiction to review the conduct of a superior, and <456> rendering the lower officers of justice, in some degree, paramount to the highest.

As the members of the ancient parliament, in questions relating to their behaviour in their own court, were not amenable to any other jurisdiction; this privilege, which had been established when that assembly consisted of one house only, was not abolished or altered when it came to be divided into two houses: For though the judicial power was, in general, appropriated to the peers; the case now under consideration was excepted. The commons becoming sharers in the rank and dignity of the national council, were led to assume the same authority with the peers, over the conduct of their own members, to judge of their misbehaviour in the character of national representatives, and to establish the same exemption from every extraneous enquiry or challenge.

It is manifest, at the same time, that an unbounded freedom of debate is necessary for enabling the members of either house to perform their duty. If they have a right to determine any measure, they must, of course, <457> be entitled to argue and reason upon it, to examine its nature and consequences, and, by placing it in a variety of lights, to prepare and ripen their minds for a proper decision. Unless they are permitted to do this, it surely is impossible for them to exercise, with national benefit, those important powers with which they are intrusted. The super-eminent authority of parliament is intended to controul and limit the executive and judicial powers; to prevent those abuses which may be expected from the ambition of the crown, or from the rapacity and dishonesty of its ministers. But how can we believe, that members of parliament will take effectual measures for this purpose, if they deliver their opinions under the terrors of the rod, and are sensible of being at the mercy of those powerful delinquents whom they ought to censure and expose, or whose illegal proceedings it is their duty to condemn and to restrain?

Towards the latter part of the Tudor line, and after the accession of the house of Stewart, when the circumstances of the nation had instilled a new spirit into the commons, and disposed them to animadvert with greater <458> freedom and severity upon the measures of the crown, the encroachments of the prerogative upon this parliamentary privilege, by imprisoning members of parliament, and subjecting them to heavy fines in the Star-chamber, were carried to such a height as threatened to destroy the independence of that assembly. This, therefore, was a grievance which, in the *petition of right,* the legislature had endeavoured to redress; and the *bill of rights* contained a declaration, "that the freedom of speech, and debates, or proceedings in parliament, ought not to be impeached, or questioned in any court or place out of parliament."[7]

Another great object which excited the attention of parliament, in this famous bill, was the power of the king to levy and maintain a mercenary army. In all the feudal governments the king had a right to summon at pleasure his vassals into the field; where they were obliged, for a limited time, to serve him at their own expence. When the stated period of their service, which was generally forty days, had elapsed, they were entitled to demand their dismission; though <459> they sometimes were induced to remain longer, upon the king promising to bear the charges of this additional attendance. But after mercenary troops had come to be substituted in place of the feudal militia, they were engaged for an indefinite time; and as fighting became their profession, from which they drew a regular subsistence, they were commonly willing to continue it as long as they could find employment. The king, who, upon the immediate pressure of a war, had been obliged to levy these troops, found it commonly expedient, even after the conclusion of a peace, to be prepared for any new enterprise, by retaining a part of them in his pay; and thus, in most of the countries upon the western continent of Europe, standing armies were introduced and increased. In Britain, however, from its insular situation, there was little danger from any foreign invasion, and as mercenary and standing armies, being less requisite for defence than in other countries, the king had less inducement to be at the expence of maintaining them. Neither James I. nor Charles I. before the commencement of <460> hostilities with his parliament, had any considerable body of mercenaries. At the conclusion of the civil war, indeed, the ruling party found itself at the head of a large and well-disciplined army;

7. Ibid.

and a great part of these troops were afterwards maintained by Cromwell for the support of his government. The disbanding of Cromwell's army was one of the first acts of the reign of Charles II.; though this monarch, when he avowed the purpose of governing without a parliament, had also recourse to the expedient of providing a military force; which his immediate successor endeavoured with all his might, to increase. But exclusive of those two instances, the English were hitherto unacquainted with mercenary standing armies, and were not accustomed to consider a discretionary power of raising and maintaining a military force, in that shape, as a branch of the prerogative. The few instances, besides, in which the sovereign or chief magistrate, had exercised this power, were such, as clearly to demonstrate its pernicious tendency, and to point out the utility of subjecting in this particular, the authority of the crown, <461> at least in times of public tranquillity, to the controul of the legislature. With great propriety, therefore, and in perfect conformity to the spirit of the ancient constitution, it was declared in the bill of rights, "that the raising or keeping a standing army within the kingdom in time of peace, unless it be with consent of parliament, is against law."[8]

By another regulation, the maintenance of a military force, whether in peace or war, was rendered entirely dependent upon the authority of parliament.

The successful operations of an army require that all its members should be under the command of a single person, that they should be compelled in the strictest manner to obey his orders, and that they should be subjected one to another in regular subordination. For attaining these ends, it is found necessary, that all disobedience in the troops, and every transgression of military duty, should be punished with greater severity and with more dispatch, than would be expedient in delinquencies committed by the rest of the inhabitants: As the king, the <462> great feudal superior, was the supreme general of the national forces, he was led, in that capacity, to introduce a military discipline, by inflicting such extraordinary penalties; and as, upon calling out his vassals into the field, with their dependents and followers, he might, at pleasure, convert all the free people of the kingdom into an army, a foundation was laid for the application of what was called, *martial law,* to all the inhabitants. In early times, this exertion of prerogative was probably

8. Ibid.

little felt, and therefore overlooked; but when it had acquired such magnitude as to become vexatious and oppressive, it excited the attention of the public, and was considered as a grievance. The genius of the English constitution demanded that any deviation from the common rules of punishment should be subjected to the inspection and controul of the legislature; and there could be no good reason, at any time, for extending this peculiar system of penal law further than to the forces actually in the service of government.

Another grievance, connected with the former, arose from the power of the crown <463> in marching and distributing the armies over the country. As the inhabitants at large were bound to supply the troops, in passing from place to place, with lodgings and with various articles of entertainment; they were apt to be more or less burdened with this duty, according as by their compliance or opposition, they merited the favour or incurred the resentment of the Sovereign. Those who had refused him a loan or a benevolence, were frequently harrassed by the quartering of soldiers upon them, until they found it expedient to acquiesce in the demand.

By the petition of right, both these grievances were completely redressed, the exercise of *martial law* by virtue of the prerogative, and the quartering of soldiers on the inhabitants without their consent, having been totally prohibited. But as without some extraordinary powers of this kind, the order and discipline requisite for conducting and regulating a military force can hardly subsist, the king, ever since the revolution, has, by special acts of parliament, been empowered to authorise *courts martial* for punishing mutiny and desertion, and to distribute the <464> troops among the innkeepers and victuallers of the kingdom. The powers, however, conferred upon the sovereign by these acts, have always been regarded with a jealous eye, and have therefore been granted only from year to year.

To these articles were subjoined several others, of manifest utility, respecting the illegality of the court of ecclesiastical commission; the right of the people to petition the king, and the free election of their representatives; together with some other immunities and privileges, which were considered as the birth-right of Englishmen, but which, in the late reigns, had been either violated or disputed. Upon the whole, the bill of rights contained no new limitations of the prerogative. It is merely a declaratory statute, exhibiting the judgment of the legislature with regard to some of the principal branches of the English constitution; and it accordingly bears this express clause, "that all and singular, the rights and liberties asserted and claimed in the declaration, are the true, ancient, and indubitable rights and liberties of the people of this kingdom."[9] <465>

After the revolution-settlement was compleated, the same spirit which had given rise to that great event was kept alive, and during the reign of William III. became productive of several regulations, tending to improve the police of the kingdom, to secure the proper distribution of justice, to guard against the corruption of ministers, and to restrain the abuses of prerogative.

In the bill of rights there was inserted a general clause; "that, for the redress of grievances, and for the amending, strengthening, and preserving of the laws, parliaments ought to be held frequently."[10] During the long controversy between the people and the princes of the house of Stewart, the regular meetings of that assembly became the object of national concern; and in the reign of Charles I. it was provided, that the interval between one meeting of parliament and another, should not exceed the period of three years; but no sooner had the frequency of parliamentary assemblies been secured at the revolution, by the impossibility of conducting the machine of government without their concurrence, than <466> there started up a new ground of suspicion, which began to occupy the public attention. As parliaments were now, of necessity, consulted by the crown in all business of importance, they became less afraid of its encroachments, and consented more freely and readily to its demands. No longer engrossed by the defence of their political rights, it was apprehended that their members would be more attentive to their private interest, would endeavour to render themselves independent of their constituents, or might be improperly influenced by the executive power. Before the revolution, the nation was jealous of the crown only; after it, they became jealous of parliament. They became apprehensive of the long continuance of the same parliament, by which its members might have leisure to form a regular connection with ministry; and were eager to establish the frequency of elections, by which the representatives might be retained under the authority and controul of the electors. This gave rise to the *triennial bill;* by which it was provided that the same parliament should not be continued for more <467> than three years; a regu-

9. Ibid., 2:602–3.
10. Ibid., 2:601.

lation to which, as it contained a new limitation of the prerogative, the king was, not without some hesitation and reluctance, prevailed upon to give the royal assent.*

Among the different subjects of parliamentary enquiry, the disposal of the revenues which fell under the administration of the crown was none of the least important. In early times, when the ordinary expence of government was defrayed out of the private estate of the king, the nation seems to have taken little concern in the administration of the royal demesnes, but to have entrusted the management of them to the prudence and discretion of the person whom they regarded as the proprietor; but, when the advancement of national wealth had increased the expence of administration much beyond what the ancient patrimony of the crown was able to discharge; and when, of course, every new enterprise was unavoidably the occasion of new impositions upon the people, it was considered more and more as the <468> duty of the national representatives to examine the expenditure of public money, and to refuse their consent to taxes, unless they were satisfied, both of the frugality with which the former funds had been managed, and of the expediency and propriety of the purposes for which the new demand was made. This, however, it may easily be conceived, was likely to be the source of endless disputes; it was difficult, in every case, to point out the exact line by which the scrutiny of parliament should be directed, or to determine the degree of latitude which, in this respect, the sovereign ought to enjoy. Though the examination of the public expenditure was highly necessary, it might undoubtedly be pushed to such a degree of minuteness as would retard the movements of government, and be equally inconsistent with the dignity of the crown than with that secrecy in the conduct of national business, which is often indispensible. To remove these inconveniencies, it was thought proper, that there should be an allowance of a certain sum, for the support of the king's household, and for the private exigencies <469> of the crown; and that, concerning the disposal of this, no account should, at least in ordinary cases, be required. The remainder of the public revenue, being more immediately regarded as the estate of the nation, was brought under the annual and regular inspection of parliament. This regulation was not a new limitation, but rather an extension of the prerogative; since it restricted to a part of the national funds, that parliamentary enquiry, which might

* See Burnet.

formerly have been extended to the whole. It appeared, at the same time, to steer in a due medium between the interest of both parties, and was calculated to avoid contention, by placing in the crown a reasonable pecuniary trust, while it secured the nation from the effects of gross mismanagement and extravagance. About the end of the reign of James II. the whole public revenue amounted, at an average, to near two millions; and the *civil list,* settled upon William and Mary, including the hereditary rents and duties, still drawn by the crown, was fixed at about 700,000 l. a year. <470>

With respect to the internal government of the kingdom, no circumstance appeared more immediately to call for a reformation than the distribution of justice. In all the principal tribunals, the judges had been hitherto appointed by the king during pleasure. In such a situation, chosen from the mercenary profession of the bar, where a servile dependence upon the crown must open the great road to preferment, and being indebted to the sovereign for the continuance of those offices from which they derived their livelihood and rank, it was not to be expected that they should often be willing to distinguish themselves by supporting the rights of the people, in opposition to the encroachments of prerogative. Wherever the king was warmly interested in a cause, or a political job was to be served, they were laid under so great a temptation to shrink from their duty, that they had seldom the resolution to withhold any decision which he wished to procure. This observation may be extended from the days of Tresilian down to those of Scroggs and Jeffries;[11] and is applicable to the ordi-<471>nary courts of law, as well as to the star-chamber and high commission, which were confessedly under the direction of the crown. Witness the opinion of the judges, in the case of ship-money, and in the question concerning the king's dispensing power, in which those grave interpreters of the law were not ashamed to betray their trust, and to become the mean tools of arbitrary power. In the trial of the bishops, indeed, there were found two justices of the king's bench who spoke in favour of the defendants; for which they were immediately deprived of their seats; but this was a question in which the basis of religion, as well as that of the constitution, was now perceived to be at stake; and in which the popular ferment had excited uncommon zeal and spirit.

In the reign of William III. it was enacted, that the judges in the three

11. Sir William Scroggs (ca. 1623–83), lord chief justice of England, was instrumental in the trials of the alleged Popish Plot conspirators. On Jeffreys see p. 629, note 26.

great courts of common law, should hold their offices during their own life and that of the king; a regulation by which they became nearly as independent as their professional character <472> and their appointment by the crown will admit.

A provision for liberty of conscience in matters of religion was another object of great importance, which the king, much to his honour, endeavoured, however unsuccessfully, to accomplish.[12]

The long contest between the church and the dissenters, had been productive of narrow prejudices, and of mutual antipathy, inconsistent with that liberality and candour which might have been expected from the rational system of religion professed, at that time, by either of the parties. When roused by the common danger of popery, to which, immediately before the revolution, they were both equally exposed, they had cordially united in defence of the protestant interest; but no sooner had that danger been removed, than their former jealousy recurred, and their mutual dissentions broke out afresh. The apprehension which the church entertained of the dissenters, was encreased by the reflection, that the king had been educated in their principles, and regarded them as that part of the nation <473> which had been the most active in placing him on the throne. But William had too much prudence, and too strong a sense of justice, to make any attempt against the national religion, which had received the sanction of public authority, and was agreeable to the sentiments of a great majority, both in parliament and throughout the nation. In conformity, however, to his enlarged views of religious freedom, he was disposed to remove those hardships to which the protestant sectaries were subjected. His first object was the repeal of the test act, by which the non-conformists were excluded from civil and military offices. Upon the supposition that the dissenters are equally good subjects as those who profess the established religion, it will be difficult to assign a plausible reason for excluding them from the service of their country, or from a share of her public honours and emoluments. The national church has, doubtless, a title to protection from every attack, whether open or concealed, by which her establishment may be endangered; but why should it be feared that the ecclesiastical establish-<474>ment is in danger from the attacks of dissenters, while these last have no assistance from the magistrate,

12. The Act of Settlement of 1701 was intended to secure Protestant succession to the throne and to entrench parliamentary supremacy and constitutionalism.

and are allowed to wield no other weapons but those of argument and persuasion? In gaining proselytes, every advantage is on the side of the church, whose doctrines and forms of worship are confirmed by ancient usage, and whose clergy are maintained at the public expence. Those who are indifferent about religion, or who look upon modes of faith as of little consequence, will generally adhere to that system which is already established, and which costs them nothing. The Roman catholics, however, were, at that time, considered, with reason, as in a different situation from protestant dissenters, having adopted political prejudices which rendered them enemies to the civil government.

The puritans, it is true, had, in the reign of Charles I. overthrown the religious establishment; but this was owing to the injudicious interference of the latter in supporting the arbitrary measures of the monarch: while the former zealously defended the rights of the people. The church having <475> embarked in the same cause with despotism, she was overwhelmed, and justly shared the same fate with her ally; whence arose the triumph and exultation of her religious with that of her political enemies.

But however groundless, at this time, the terrors of the high-church party undoubtedly were, they prevailed in parliament; and the measure of repealing the test act was rejected. William afterwards attempted a plan of comprehension; proposing to form, with mutual concessions, a religious establishment, which might include a considerable part at least of the dissenters; but in this he was not more successful. The two parties were too heterogeneous to admit of such a coalition; and, like ingredients of opposite qualities, discovered no less repugnance to a partial, than to a total union. Having failed in these liberal schemes, he suggested a bill of *toleration,*[13] by which the protestant non-conformists, if not admitted to the same political privileges with their brethren of the church, might yet be exempted from all penalties, and authorised by law in the open profession and <476> exercise of their religion. Even this indulgence, which was obtained without opposition, marks, at that period, a considerable enlargement of religious opinions; and may be regarded as forming a conspicuous era in the history of ecclesiastical government.

Notwithstanding the invaluable blessings which this prince had procured to the nation, his administration was never very popular, nor free from dis-

13. The Act of Toleration of 1689.

turbance. The two great political factions, which, before he mounted the throne, had almost entirely disappeared, were in a little time revived; and by their intrigues, and party views, he was, in some cases, provoked or deceived.

As the principles of the tories had led them early to retard and oppose the revolution-settlement, so their bad humour and disappointment excited them afterwards to practice every expedient for interrupting and preventing that success and prosperity which might otherwise have resulted from it. The situation of William, upon his first advancement to the English throne, must have naturally disposed him to place his chief confidence in the whigs, by whom <477> his undertaking had been most warmly and heartily promoted. But the subsequent views and measures of this party contributed by degrees to alienate his affections. They betrayed a constant jealousy of the crown. Their parsimony in granting supplies was pushed to an extreme, altogether incompatible with those patriotic, but expensive enterprises, in which he was engaged.[14] Their aversion to a standing army, which was carried so far as to require the dismission of his Dutch guards, the old and favourite companions of all his military operations, appears to have been regarded by him as an indication of personal enmity and distrust. Though this prince discovered an invariable attachment to the form of a limited monarchy, it must not thence be concluded, that he willingly submitted to all such restrictions of the prerogative, and to all such extensions of popular privilege, as were aimed at by many of the whigs. He probably entertained higher notions of the regal authority than were found, even in that age, to prevail among this description of the inhabitants. It is not surprising, <478> besides, that a monarch, however moderate in his general principles, should, in the ordinary course of business, be sometimes betrayed, like other men, into an impatience of opposition, that he should be ruffled with contradiction, or vent his displeasure against those who had thwarted his measures. The whigs becoming, on this account, obnoxious to the king, the tories endeavoured to conciliate his favour by their apparent assiduity and solicitude to humour his inclinations. Though it is probable that the sagacity of William penetrated the views of this party, he took advantage of their professed intentions,

14. The War of the Grand Alliance (1688–97), between France and a coalition of European powers (in which William was a major participant), was concluded with the Treaty of Ryswick, whereby William was recognized by Europe as the rightful king of England and Scotland.

and made use of their assistance in executing that great system of European policy which he had long meditated. He adopted the hazardous plan of balancing the two parties, either by promoting them jointly to offices, or by alternately employing the one and the other. In pursuing this line of conduct, so far from gaining the friendship of either, he incurred the resentment of both. The whigs, over-rating their merit in accomplishing the revolution, were highly dissatisfied with the <479> return made to their services; while the tories considered the favours bestowed upon them as the effects of interested and temporising politics, which afforded no proof of any real confidence or affection; and both parties being thus, by turns, thrown into opposition, were actuated by the animosity and rancour arising from disappointed ambition, sharpened by the acrimony and agitation, proceeding from the heat of controversy and the triumph of their adversaries. In this situation, many individuals of high rank and consequence became desirous of restoring the exiled family; and, even when employed in the service of government, did not scruple to betray the secrets of their master; to correspond with the court of Versailles and that of St. Germains;[15] and to promise their assistance to the late king for the recovery of his crown. What is more surprising, it appears, that some persons of distinction among the whigs were induced to hold a correspondence in the same quarter; but with what views, or from what motives, whether from gross corruption, and the effect of discontent and <480> disgust, or from an opinion of the instability of the present government, which led them to provide for their own safety in case of a counter-revolution, it is not easy to determine.*

While many of the leading men in the kingdom were engaged in such crooked and infamous transactions, the inferior partizans of the late king

* The evidence upon this point, adduced by Mr. M'Pherson, in his collection of original papers, is not very distinct. He rests, in a great measure, upon the memoirs of James, and the reports of persons whom he employed in the management of his affairs. But this prince, and his agents, were so credulous and sanguine, as to over-rate and magnify every circumstance in their own favour, and to become the dupes of every impostor. According to their accounts, it is a miracle that the government of King William could subsist for a moment, since both whigs and tories were equally zealous in overturning it, and were only vying with one another in the execution of that enterprise. It is the privilege of every unfortunate adventurer, to weary all his hearers with endless proofs that he has met with uncommonly bad usage, and that his undertaking, in the natural course of things, should have been successful.

15. Versailles was the home of Louis XIV's court; St. Germains-en-Laye was the French royal residence from the time of Francis I to Louis XIII before becoming the home of the exiled Stuarts.

were attempting a more expeditious way to his restoration, by the assassination of William; but these detestable <481> conspiracies were fortunately disappointed and produced no other consequence than to exhibit fresh instances of the courage and magnanimity so conspicuous in the character of that prince, and to excite in the nation a grateful sense of the dangers which he so cheerfully encountered for the preservation of English liberty.

The extensive enterprises in which the crown was involved immediately after the revolution; the settlement of Britain, the reduction of Ireland, the prosecution of the war with France; all these operations were productive of much greater expence than the nation expected, or than parliament could be persuaded to defray. As ministers, therefore, were unable, by the yearly produce of taxes, to answer the demands of government, they were forced to anticipate the supplies, by borrowing money from individuals. To those creditors they granted securities, both for the interest and capital, on branches of the public revenue, believed to be sufficient, in a few years, to repay the loan, and so clear off the incumbrance. Such were the necessities of the crown, that the national debt, contracted in this manner, <482> had risen, before the peace of Ryswick, to above twenty millions; a burden which, at that period, appeared so enormous, that it was thought to threaten the nation with immediate bankruptcy, and became a topic of much clamour, and of bitter invective against the government.

Some politicians, by an over-refinement, affected to consider this national debt as an advantage to the crown, by creating in the monied interest a dependence upon government for the security of their funds. And hence it was inferred, that the procuring of such effectual support had been the great object of William in contracting those burdens. But it is not likely that a king, any more than a private man, is ever induced to borrow, from the consideration that his creditor may become his protector; especially when he must expect that his creditor, as the price of his protection, will acquire over him the authority of a master and governor. The practice of contracting national debt arose from the same causes in Britain, and in all the other opulent nations of Europe; from the dissipation and extravagance which are the usual effects of wealth and luxury; from an increase of activity <483> and ambition, producing enterprises of greater extent than the ordinary revenues of the state are capable of supporting; and, above all, from the facility of borrowing, occasioned by that great circulation of capitals which is the natural consequence of extensive trade and manufactures.

When we contemplate, in every point of view, the important revolution accomplished by the prince of Orange, the hazardous nature of the undertaking, the prudence and vigour with which it was conducted, the solid advantages which have resulted from it to Britain, and to all Europe, we must ever look up to our great deliverer with admiration and with gratitude. It may be questioned who, among statesmen and heroes, have displayed the greatest genius and abilities. It is yet more difficult, perhaps, to determine, who has been actuated by the most pure and genuine principles of patriotism; but who is the monarch that has conferred the most extensive benefits upon mankind, will hardly be doubted, while the actions of William III. shall hold a place in the annals of the world. Had it not been for the active, the persevering, and the <484> single exertions of this prince, it is more than probable, that Britain would have been subjected both to an ecclesiastical and civil tyranny; that Lewis XIV. would have subdued Holland, and the estates in alliance with the Dutch; that the protestant interest would, in a short time, have been annihilated; and that the greater part of Europe would either have been reduced to a vast, unwieldy despotism, like that of ancient Rome, or parceled out among a few absolute sovereigns, who, in the general struggle for dominion, had been able to retain their independence. But the vigorous defence of the United Provinces, against the attacks of the French king, gave time for opening the eyes of many European princes. The revolution in England broke off at once the connection of the kingdom with France, and with the church of Rome; it not only secured her a free government at home, but united her under the same head with the other great maritime state which had arisen in Europe, and this powerful combination was followed by such alliances, and by such military operations as were sufficient to restore the balance of power, and to frustrate <485> those ambitious designs that were so hostile to the peace and tranquillity of Europe. In fine, the revolution in England kept alive that spark which kindled the flame of liberty in other countries, and is now likely to glide insensibly over the whole habitable globe.

The character of William has been scrutinized and censured with a severity and malignity, corresponding to the rage and disappointment of that royal family, and of their numerous and zealous adherents, whose power and projects he overthrew. From the circumstances however which his enemies have laid hold of, as a handle for detraction, we may discover the worst lights in which his conduct was capable of being represented, and thus obtain the most satisfactory evidence of his real integrity and merit.

He obtained the crown of England by dethroning the person who was at the same time his uncle and his father-in-law. Those who form their ideas from the habits acquired in the inferior walks of society are apt to conceive that the domestic affections should have the same influence in the government of kingdoms as in the scenes of private life; not considering that the situa-<486>tion of princes renders them frequently strangers to their own kindred, and that the cares of the public, in which they are necessarily involved, not only exclude them from those friendships, and from that mutual intercourse of good offices which take place among the rest of mankind, but suggest the consideration of peculiar duties which their station has rendered of superior obligation. How seldom are kings prevented from going to war with each other because they happen to be relations? How absurd would it be to suppose that the public interest should yield to so insignificant a motive?

But if ever an individual, in fulfilling his duty to the public, was called upon to overlook family connections, the prince of Orange was undoubtedly the man. Without dethroning his kinsman it was impossible to preserve the English constitution, or even, perhaps, to attain another object which had long engrossed his mind, the independence and security of his native country. Nor had he ever received such treatment from James as laid claim to any peculiar gratitude or affection. In the behaviour of that <487> monarch he experienced nothing but enmity, dissimulation, and falsehood.

Had William lived in the age of Roman virtue, the sacrifice of a domestic relation, in the cause of public liberty, would have been accounted highly meritorious; or if any part of his conduct had been thought blameable, it would have been the sparing of the tyrant's life, by which the country was exposed to future danger. But the manners of the age had introduced milder sentiments of patriotism; and in surveying this great revolution, we cannot overlook one pleasing circumstance, that it was hardly stained with a drop of blood. Though the arbitrary and despotical measures of James had rendered him unworthy of the crown, and drawn upon him the indignation of the people, he was treated with uncommon lenity, and in the very critical period when the popular ferment was raised to the highest pitch, instead of suffering an exemplary punishment, he was merely deprived of that sovereignty which he had shewn a fixed resolution to abuse. It appears, at the same time, that William was not destitute of regard to the family of this unfortunate <488> kinsman. There is now sufficient evidence that he was willing to pay the dowry which had been stipulated to James's queen; and that he even offered to promote the succession of the son, the late prince of Wales, to the throne of England, if proper precautions were taken to secure his education in the protestant religion; a condition which the infatuated bigotry of the father prompted him to reject.*

It has been said, that, in accomplishing the revolution, William was actuated by his ambition, not by motives of public spirit. But such an aspersion, it is evident, may be thrown indiscriminately upon every person who pursues a line of conduct in which his interest happens to coincide with his duty. It would be happy for the world if the ambition of great men was always directed to such actions as tend to the good of society; if the love of power was uniformly exerted in rescuing the human race from slavery and oppression. There can be little doubt, that the prince of Orange, in marrying the eldest daughter of James, who at that time had no sons, considered the eventual succession to the crown as an advantage which <489> might result from the connexion. But that he was guilty of any improper step to hasten or secure the acquisition of this object, cannot with justice be asserted. In the violent political disputes which clouded the reign of his two uncles, he appears to have given some countenance to the party in opposition to the court; but this party was composed of the friends of liberty and the protestant religion, which those two princes, in conjunction with France, had formed a league to destroy. Upon the same account, he favoured the enterprise of the duke of Monmouth; though he knew that this nobleman aspired to the throne, and must therefore have regarded him in the light of a rival.

A late author seems to believe that William artfully suggested to his father in law, those very measures which he afterwards took hold of to ruin that unfortunate monarch. This is a curious hypothesis, requiring no ordinary portion of credulity. One sovereign counsels another to act the part of a tyrant, that this false friend and adviser may have the benefit of deposing him; and the simple king, falling into the snare, is persuaded to forfeit his dominions by a per-<490>son in whom, on no other occasion, he had ever placed any confidence.

To depreciate the military talents of this prince, it has been observed, that in most of his battles he was defeated. But we must remember that he had numberless difficulties to surmount, that originally, with a handful of troops,

* Dalrymple's Memoirs, vol. ii.

he was obliged to cope with the powerful and well-disciplined armies of France, and with the able commanders who had been trained up in the most active and flourishing period of that monarchy; that, after he became king of England, he was continually disturbed by the treachery and the factious disputes of the leaders in parliament, and was neither supplied with money nor with men in proportion to the magnitude of his undertakings. When proper allowance is made for the circumstances in which he was placed, instead of reflecting upon his bad success, we cannot help wondering that he was able to maintain his ground; and we must admire the fertility of his resources by which, like the great admiral Coligni,[16] he rose more formidable upon every defeat, and appeared to derive from it all the advantages of a victory. <491>

His temper and disposition have been represented as cold, haughty, and morose; rendering him disagreeable in all the relations of private life; and proving an inseperable bar to his popularity with the English nation. In reality, whether from natural constitution, or from his being constantly engaged in serious and important pursuits, he was grave and stately in his deportment, reserved and distant in his ordinary demeanour. But that he was incapable of friendship or affection for those who had obtained his good opinion and favour, there is no ground to suppose. Nor was the severity of his adult complexion without intervals of gaiety and cheerfulness. According to the report of those who knew him intimately, he was fond of relaxing from the cares of government, and of dissipating the solitary gloom of a throne by the pleasures of the table, and the free conversation of a few select friends; in whose company, it is said, he was neither destitute of good humour nor of a turn for pleasantry. There can be no doubt, however, that he was more distinguished by a solid understanding and useful talents than by slight and superficial accomplishments. <492> Plain and simple in his manners, he neither studied to disguise his feelings, nor to practise upon the humours and follies of others; but, though an enemy to dissimulation and falsehood, yet, wherever secrecy was necessary, he was perfectly impenetrable. His success in the cabinet was greater than in the field; because he there depended more upon himself, and was in great measure his own agent in those public negociations which he happily concluded. Through the whole

16. Admiral Gaspard de Coligny (1519–72): Huguenot leader in the French Wars of Religion and, like William, a hero of Protestant historiography.

of his life he seems to have adhered invariably to those political principles which, in his early years, he had imbibed; and if he was ambitious, his ambition was entirely subordinate to his public views. To preserve the independence of Holland, and to maintain the balance of Europe, were the great ends which he incessantly pursued, and to which the prosperity of Britain was, perhaps, regarded as a secondary object. It was, in all probability, the suspicion of this, more than his unpopular and forbidding manners, that prevented his gaining the affections of the English. But in the mind of William, and in truth, the interest of the Dutch commonwealth, and that of the British dominions were inseparable; and <493> both were equally promoted, not only by his military exertions before the peace of Ryswick, but also, in the subsequent parts of his reign, by those great alliances and preparations which had led the way to the splendid and successful war of queen Anne, and tended so effectually to diminish the dangerous power of Lewis XIV.[17]

In the administration of Britain, the conduct of this prince was no less uniform and consistent with his principles. Though a friend to religious toleration, he supported the church of England as by law established; and though he never disputed those limitations of the prerogative which were agreeable to the old constitution, as explained by the revolution-settlement, he was averse from all political innovation, and tenacious of what he accounted the ancient rights of the crown.

With respect to the nature of the interesting transaction which produced the accession of William III. though all parties are now disposed to speak of it in the language of approbation, politicians of a certain description have been much disposed to magnify the changes introduced by it. They suppose that the ancient government of <494> England was arbitrary and despotical, and that, from the period of the revolution-settlement, we are to date the first establishment of our limited monarchy.[18]

17. Queen Anne (r. 1702–14) continued English participation in the War of the Spanish Succession.

18. Here, and in what follows, Millar attacks Hume's views. Compare Hume's view of earlier Whig historians: "The Whig party, for a course of near seventy years, has, almost without interruption, enjoyed the whole authority of government, and no honours or offices could be obtained but by their countenance and protection. But this event, which, in some particulars, has been advantageous to the state, has proved destructive to the truth of history, and has established many gross falsehoods, which it is unac-

Were it not for the known influence of party prejudices and passions, it might seem surprising that any one acquainted with the history of the country, should entertain such an opinion, or should expect, by any degree of dexterity or abilities to render it plausible to ordinary readers. The great outlines of the English constitution may be traced back to very remote antiquity. To ascend no higher than the age immediately succeeding the great charters, we find the settled form of a parliament, consisting of a king and two houses; an exclusive power in that assembly to make laws, to impose taxes, and to regulate the order of succession to the crown; an exclusive authority in the house of commons to bring in money bills, and in that of the peers to distribute justice in the last resort. We find also the regular establishment of the chief courts of justice which exist at present; the institution of trials by jury, both in civil and criminal matters; and a specific regulation to prevent the sovereign <495> from the arbitrary imprisonment of individuals. These important branches of the constitution had received the sanction of ancient usage, confirmed by a variety of statutes and public declarations; they had, it is true, been frequently violated by the sovereign, who endeavoured to elude their force by various expedients and evasive practices; but whenever those violations had been so often repeated as to attract the attention of the public, they became the subject of national complaint, and were restrained or punished by new interpositions of the legislature. As new instruments were employed to attack the constitution, a new shield became necessary, and was held out in its defence.

The interposition of greatest importance at the revolution, consisted in deposing the sovereign for his crimes, and in setting aside the lineal heir from considerations of expediency. Though such interpositions of the two houses of parliament were not without example in the English history, they had not occurred in a civilized age; for the trial and execution of Charles I. had been affected without the free determination of the one house, and without any concurrence <496> of the other. The consequence of this deposition was to place the new king in circumstances which prevented him ever after from calling in question those powers of parliament which he had solemnly rec-

countable how any civilized nation could have embraced with regard to its domestic occurrences. Compositions the most despicable, both for style and matter, have been extolled, and propagated, and read; as if they had equalled the most celebrated remains of antiquity." *HE,* 6:533.

ognized. Having received the crown by a parliamentary title, he had no pretence to claim it by hereditary right, or to refuse the performance of those conditions under which it was bestowed upon him. Instead of the vicegerent of heaven, assuming an authority independent of any human controul, he was reduced to be the chief magistrate of a free people, appointed by the community, and possessed of those powers only with which, for the common good, he had been expressly intrusted. The forfeiture, at the same time, which had been incurred by the late king, whatever softening appellation was given to it, proved a formidable precedent to all future sovereigns, proclaiming that they were amenable to public justice, and could not expect, with impunity, to trample upon the laws of their country.

END OF VOL. III.

AN

HISTORICAL VIEW

OF THE

ENGLISH GOVERNMENT

FROM THE

SETTLEMENT OF THE SAXONS IN BRITAIN

TO

THE REVOLUTION IN 1688.

To which are subjoined,

SOME DISSERTATIONS CONNECTED WITH THE

HISTORY OF THE GOVERNMENT,

From the Revolution to the Present Time.

BY JOHN MILLAR ESQ.

Professor of Law in the University of Glasgow

IN FOUR VOLUMES

VOL. IV.

London:

PRINTED FOR J. MAWMAN, NO 22 IN THE POULTRY.

1803.

By T. Gillet, Salisbury-Square

CONTENTS[1]

OF THE FOURTH VOLUME

Book II.

1. The page numbers in the Contents are those of the 1803 edition.

AN HISTORICAL VIEW OF THE ENGLISH GOVERNMENT

Book II

OF THE ENGLISH GOVERNMENT FROM THE REIGN OF WILLIAM THE THIRD TO THE PRESENT TIME.

CHAPTER I

Review of the Government of Ireland.

The connection between England and Ireland, which has now subsisted for many centuries, is a circumstance of great importance in the history of these two countries, and cannot, with propriety, be overlooked in a political survey of Great Britain.

The first invasion of Ireland by the English proceeded from the rapacity of private adventurers; and had no other object but <2> the acquisition of possessions in that country. Though Henry II. under whom the first English settlement was made, claimed the whole island as an accession to his crown, and though he had been at the pains to procure a Papal bull, as a foundation for that claim, he appears to have done very little, either to ascertain and extend the conquest, or to civilize the inhabitants, and reduce them under a regular government. The subsequent monarchs of England were equally inattentive to those objects, or from peculiar embarrassments at home, were incapable of pursuing them; so that the private settlers, in that hitherto rude country, were left, by their own efforts, to maintain their possessions, and to guard against the attacks of the natives. In such a situation, it could not be expected that these two sets of people would live in good neighbourhood. The English were, in reality, a band of robbers, who had stripped the natives of a part of their property; and by means of recruits from England, were endeavouring to avail themselves of every opportunity of seizing on the whole. As the avowed purpose of <3> the former was to invade and plunder, so the provocation, suffered by the latter, must have united them, not only to defend their possessions, but to revenge the injuries they had sustained; and considering the uncultivated state of the one people, with the barbarous ferocity of the other, it is not surprising, that by a long course of mutual depredation, they contracted a bitter and rancorous animosity and hatred, and often conducted their hostilities in a manner equally inconsistent with the faith of treaties, and with the feelings of humanity.

The old and the new inhabitants were thus prevented from incorporating; and a line of separation between them was drawn by their mutual contention and hostile passions. The latter were called the Irish *within the pale:*[1] the former the Irish *without the pale.* The Irish within the pale were accounted subjects of the crown of England; and entitled to receive such protection from the sovereign, as could conveniently be afforded them. The English government considered those without the <4> pale as aliens, from whom it indeed endeavoured to raise a tribute, but whom, in place of protecting, it never failed to treat as enemies, whenever disputes arose between them and the other inhabitants.

The Irish within the pale, from their primitive connection with England, as well as from the influence and authority of her monarchs, fell under a government similar, in every respect, to that of the mother country. They composed, in one view, a sort of English province, over which the sovereign claimed an executive power, and appointed, during pleasure, a governor. These appointments were begun by Henry II. and continued by his successors. The country was divided into districts, and committed to the care of

1. "Within the pale" referred to the region around Dublin, and the name reflected its character as a fortified area of English rule. After 1400 it was broadened to include the lowland region and the medieval counties of Dublin, Meath, Louth, and Kildare.

sheriffs. Superior courts of justice were likewise formed, upon the same plan with those at Westminster-hall.

As the Irish inhabitants of the pale, however, were left, in a great measure, to struggle with the natives, and to follow such measures, for their safety and prosperity, as <5> were suggested by their peculiar circumstances, they required a great council to deliberate upon their affairs, and to regulate the conduct of their executive officers. For this purpose an assembly, after the example of the English parliament, was occasionally convened by the governor; but at what period this establishment was completed is uncertain. Sir John Davies thinks it had no place till the reign of Edward II. about an hundred and forty years after the first settlement; but the opinion of Leland is more probable, that its commencement reaches as high as the reign of Henry II. though it was much later before the institution attained a regular form.[2]

The Irish parliament was early composed of two houses, as in England; the Lords temporal and spiritual having a seat in the one; and the knights of shires, and burgesses, in the other: but for a long time the assembly was far from being numerous. Before the reign of Henry VIII. there were but twelve counties, besides the liberty of Tipperary, and thirty-four boroughs; so <6> that the numbers of the house of commons could not amount to an hundred.*

As this national assembly was called for the same purposes with that of England, it was wont to deliberate upon the same sort of business, and to exercise similar powers. Its interpositions having arisen from a total neglect, or inability, of the English parliament to regulate the government of Ireland, the members of that assembly appear to have early considered themselves, not as acting in any subordinate capacity, but as possessed of an independent authority. In conformity to this idea, we find the states of Ireland as far back as the reign of Edward III. asserting their privilege, according to the ancient custom of holding their own parliaments, and their exemption from the

* See Sir John Davies's speech to the House of Commons, in 1613.

2. Sir John Davies (1569–1626): English poet and politician; attorney general for Ireland 1606–19; author of *A Discovery of the True Causes Why Ireland Was Never Entirely Subdued;* Thomas Leland (1722–85): historian and vicar of St. Anne's, Dublin; author of the *History of Ireland from the Invasion of Henry II., with a Preliminary Discourse on the Antient State of That Kingdom* (1773).

burden of electing and sending any persons to the parliaments, or councils held in England.* <7>

With respect to the native Irish, or to the inhabitants *without the pale,* they seem to be considered, by many writers, as disgraced by a greater portion of barbarity and ferocity, than the rude inhabitants of other countries. But for this opinion it is difficult to discover any real foundation. By their long continued quarrels and hostilities with the English invaders, they became doubtless, inured to bloodshed, and instead of making progress in refinements and the arts, were confirmed in all the vices natural to a people unacquainted with civility and regular government. It must at the same time be acknowledged, that, from the partiality and prejudices of English historians, those vices have been greatly exaggerated.

Before the reign of Henry II. Ireland had been less exposed to foreign invasion than most other European countries; and though the inhabitants had never attained that civilization, which the ancient Romans communicated to their conquered provinces, they had comparatively, for some centuries, enjoyed a degree of tranquillity, which was likely to become the source of improvement. <8> It appears, accordingly, that under the cloud of thick darkness, which hung over Europe in the seventh century, some faint rays of light were discovered in Ireland, where, under the protection of the Christian clergy, a number of schools had been established, and were then in a flourishing condition. We are informed by an historian, of no less authority than Bede,[3] that, about this period, it was usual for persons of distinction, among the Anglo-Saxons, and from the continent of Europe, to retire to that island for the purposes of enjoying the comforts of a sequestered life, and for obtaining the benefit of religious instruction from the Irish clergy, who, at that time, it seems, were distinguished for the purity of their doctrines, and for the strictness of their discipline.

The customs which antiquaries and historians have pointed out and collected, as peculiar to the Irish, are such as indicate no uncommon degree of barbarism and ferocity; but, on the contrary, when compared with those of other nations, exhibit that striking resemblance of lines and features, which

* See the curious record, entitled Memoranda de Hibernia Veriment, referred to by Dr. Leland, and published in the Calendar of Ancient Charters.

3. Bede (673–735), often known as the Venerable Bede: English priest and author of the *Historia Ecclesiastica,* finished in 731.

may be remarked in the inhabitants of every <9> country before the advancement of arts and civilization.[4]

The people were divided into *septs,*[5] or tribes, in a great measure independent of one another. Each of these was under a chief, who conducted the members of his tribe in war, and who endeavoured to protect them, either from the attacks of their neighbours, or from the various acts of injustice arising among themselves. In this latter capacity, the chief, agreeably to the general practice of rude nations, committed the administration of justice to a deputy, who received the appellation of Brehon. The Brehons were the ordinary judges in all those parts of the country, where the authority of the English monarch, in judicial matters, had not been established. Their jurisdiction was of a similar nature, and origin, to that of the *Stewarts,* whom, in the countries under the feudal system, the barons authorised to distribute justice among their tenants and vassals.

Many different *septs,* inhabiting an extensive territory were frequently associated under a common leader, whose authority <10> over this larger division, though much inferior to that of each inferior chief over his own sept, was gradually, by length of time, as well as by occasional circumstances, confirmed and extended. By the confederation of smaller into larger societies, there had arisen five large provinces, into which the whole island was divided. Mention is even made by historians, that these provinces had been occasionally united under a king; but this union was probably so transient and slight as never to have bestowed much real influence upon the nominal sovereign.

The appropriation of land, that great step in the progress of agriculture, appears, among the ancient inhabitants of Ireland, not to have taken place universally, for long after the English invasion, they retained so much of the pastoral manners, as, without confining themselves to fixed residence, to wander, with their cattle, from place to place. This custom known by the name of *boolying,* supposes that large commons, or tracts of unappropriated land, were extended through all the divisions of the country; and that the

4. *Advancement of arts and civilization:* The stadial view of the development of society—an important feature of Smith's *Lectures on Jurisprudence* and Ferguson's *Essay on the History of Civil Society* (1767), as well as of the *Distinction of Ranks*—is deployed here to correct the anti-Irish bias of English historiography.

5. A term used by English and Anglo-Irish writers in the sixteenth and seventeenth centuries for the extended ruling families of Gaelic Ireland.

waste grounds bore a great pro-<11>portion to those, which were employed in tillage. In all countries the acquisition of landed property has arisen from agriculture; for the cultivators of a particular spot become entitled to the immediate produce, as the fruit and reward of their labour; and, after a long course of cultivation, having meliorated the soil, were, upon the same principle, entitled to the future possession of the land itself, by which alone they could reap the advantages, derived from their past improvements. Those lands, therefore, in Ireland, which had been employed solely in pasturage, must have remained in an unappropriated state, open to the promiscuous use of the whole community.

The limited and imperfect state of the appropriation of land in Ireland, may be further illustrated from the Irish customs with relation to succession. It appears that property in land was vested in the chiefs only, or leaders of *septs;* and that the inferior people of the tribe were merely tenants at will. The estates of those chiefs, however, were not transmitted from father to son by hereditary descent, but, upon the death <12> of the proprietor, passed to the eldest of his male relations. This person, by his experience in war, having usually acquired the highest reputation for military skill, was the best qualified to be leader of the tribe, and the most capable of defending that estate, in which they had all a common concern. This is the custom, anciently distinguished, both in Ireland and in Scotland, by the name of *Tanistry;*[6] a name said to be derived from the circumstance, that, in the life time of the predecessor, it was common to ascertain and acknowledge the right of his heir, who, in the Celtic language, received the appellation of the *Tanist,* that is, the second person in the tribe. Traces of this mode of succession are very universally to be found in the early history of mankind. In that situation where the inhabitants of a country are almost continually engaged in predatory expeditions, it may be expedient that the land, possessed by those little societies of kindred, who reside in the same neighbourhood, should remain undivided under the disposal of the chief; and that, in chusing this leader, more regard should be had to <13> his age, experience, and military qualities, than to his blood-relation with the person who formerly enjoyed that office. The plan of transmitting inheritances, by which children, and even families, in a state of infancy, succeed to estates according to such

6. English writers in the sixteenth and seventeenth centuries used the term to mean the whole system of hereditary succession in Ireland.

rules, as are suggested by the inclination of parents, can hardly be made effectual till mankind enjoy a degree of tranquillity, and are, without any exertion of their own, protected by the public, and secured from depredation. The establishment of such a plan therefore, supposes considerable advances in the social intercourse, and a degree of improvement in many of the arts of life.

The inferior tenants, or followers of the chief, appear to have held their lands during his pleasure; though probably these tenants were usually permitted to remain in possession during life; and upon their decease, their estates were divided among the eldest males of the *sept.** This has improperly <14> been called, by some writers, succession by *gavel-kind.*[7]

In that simple age when landed property is, in some measure, retained in common by a whole tribe, there naturally subsists an intimate connection, and strong attachment among the members of that small society. They live much together, are separated from the rest of the world, and assist one another in all their important transactions. Their affections are strengthened by the habits of intimacy, and by their mutual exertions of kindness in promoting their common interest. The chief is commonly attended by a number of his kindred, and tenants, whom he entertains with rustic hospitality and magnificence, as in return, they are ambitious of displaying their attachment, and their own importance, by entertaining their leader. The custom of visiting his tenants, and of his being maintained, on those occasions, at their expence, to which historians have given the appellation of *coshering,*[8] was probably supported likewise by political considerations; as by making frequent progresses through the territories <15> of his tribe, the chief of the *sept* was enabled to prevent disturbance among a disorderly people, and according to the demerits of his tenants to proportion the burden of his maintenance.

The members of every sept were not only subject to the burden of maintaining their chief, when he thought proper to visit them, but were also liable to contributions for defraying the expence of his maintenance when he was employed in defence of the community. Hence a foundation was laid for

* See Davies's Discovery, 1747. p. 169.

7. Legal term used to describe the regionally varied forms of partible inheritance in Ireland before these were abolished in 1606.

8. A custom whereby tenants had to entertain the lord and retinue to a feast periodically throughout the year. Possibly derived from a pre-Norman custom.

arbitrary exactions, distinguished by the names of *coegite* and *livery,* which were originally Irish, but were afterwards adopted by the English settlers, and became the source of great oppression.

The mutual attachment and confidence that subsisted between the chief and the members of his tribe, are most especially remarkable in the practice of what is called *fostering.* It was common for the chief to give out his children, not only to be suckled, but even to be brought up, in the family of some of his tenants. To maintain such children was not looked upon a burden, <16> but as a mark of distinction; it created a new species of relation with the leader of the tribe; and enabled such fosterers to acquire a peculiar interest in those persons, whom the whole society beheld with admiration and respect. The practice, at the same time, shews the general simplicity of manners, which had introduced no idea that the son of a chief required an education superior to what might be obtained in the house of his tenants.

With regard to the laws enforced by the Brehons in the distribution of justice, they were similar to those of the other early European nations. The weakness of government, in rude states, by disabling the injured party from procuring an adequate punishment, has generally produced a pecuniary compensation even for the most atrocious offences, and the same interested motives, which determined the private sufferer to accept of such compositions, have also rendered them agreeable to the public magistrate, who, on the part of the community, levied the fines drawn on those occasions. Such pecuniary punishments are said to have <17> been inflicted by the Brehons for murder, and for the greater part of crimes.

I had formerly occasion to notice that remarkable institution which took place in Ireland, by which the head of every sept was responsible for the conduct of all his followers, in the same manner as in England, a tything man might be called to account for the offences of every member of his tything. It has been supposed, that this law was copied from the English by the inhabitants of Ireland, but, in all probability, it proceeded independent of imitation, from the similarity of circumstances in both countries; and, in reality, it seems agreeable to the notions of justice and expediency suggested by a state of rudeness and barbarism.[9] The estate under the management of a chief, belongs, in some measure, to the whole tribe, and when any member

9. For Smith's views on the collective character of justice in rude nations, see for example *LJ,* 201.

of that society commits a crime, to be expiated by a pecuniary composition, it is not inconsistent with justice, that this penalty should be paid out of the common funds, by the person who represents the community. It is, at the same time, highly expedient, that those who <18> suffer by the injustice of any obscure member of a tribe, should not be under the necessity of prosecuting the particular offenders, but should obtain redress from the person known and distinguished as the head of the community, who could be at no loss to discover the guilty persons, and procure from them an indemnity.

From the reign of Henry II. to the accession of the house of Tudor, the interpositions of the English crown, in the government of Ireland, were feeble and transitory; extending commonly little farther than to the nomination of the chief executive officers. The distresses of King John, and of Henry III.; the schemes of Edward I. for the conquest of Scotland, and for the annexation of that kingdom to his English dominions; the wars carried on by the subsequent princes in France; with the great expence, and the numerous embarrassments of which those imprudent measures were productive; and lastly, the long contention between the rival houses of York and Lancaster, by which England itself became a field of blood, and a continued scene of <19> anarchy and confusion; all this train of vexation, enterprize, disappointment, and disaster, prevented the English monarchs from supporting their authority in Ireland, or taking any vigorous measures for the reduction of that country.*

As the primitive settlers from England derived little or no assistance from the government, they were, on the other hand, subject to no limitation with respect to the extent of their acquisitions. They found no difficulty in obtaining grants of those lands of which they had seized the possession, and even of such territories beyond the pale, as they had formed the project of acquiring. Immense donations were thus <20> nominally made to a few

* So little were the Irish apprehensive of incurring the displeasure of England, that when Richard, Duke of York, with his followers, had been declared rebels, and attainted by the English parliament, they were treated in Ireland with the utmost hospitality; by an express act of parliament, they were taken under the public protection; and some of them being attached, in consequence of the English attainder, the person, who had ventured to execute the king's writ, was condemned and put to death. The same parliament afterwards declared, that Ireland is governed by its own legislature only; and that the inhabitants of that country are not subject to the jurisdiction of any foreign tribunal.—*See Leland's History of Ireland.*

individuals, in so much that while in reality no more than a third part was in possession of the English, the whole kingdom is said to have been parcelled among ten proprietors. Nothing could be more adverse to the cultivation of the country, and the civilization of the inhabitants, than this prodigious extent of property bestowed upon those who had already the chief power in their hands. These great lords not only were incapable of managing the vast estates already in their possession, but were interested to prevent the remainder from being given either to the native Irish, or to such new English planters as might be willing to improve it. In consequence of these grants there came to be in Ireland, at one time, no less than eight counties palatine, each of which was governed by a sort of independent sovereign.*

Notwithstanding these obstacles many desperate English adventurers, at different times, obtained from the crown particular grants of territories beyond the pale, and endeavoured to maintain by force what they had occupied under the colour of a legal <21> sanction. The families of these people, after a long course of war and rapine, degenerated by degrees from the English customs, and by mutual intercourse, were at length so incorporated with their neighbours as to be no longer distinguishable, by any marks of greater civilization. Upon the whole it is observable, that the native Irish, by their power and by their numbers, had more influence in changing the manners of the new inhabitants than the latter, in communicating their improvements to the former; and that the people of English race, whether within or without the pale, were in the course of some centuries, apparently declining to a state of rudeness and barbarism.

The accession of Henry VII. as it restored peace and tranquillity to England, so it enabled the sovereign to plan and execute more effectual measures for the administration of his Irish dominions. It produced, at the same time, an exaltation of the prerogative, the effect of which was distinctly felt in both countries. In Ireland, two objects appear to have been immediately in the view of the crown; to extend a regular policy over the country; and to render the <22> Irish government subordinate to that of England.

To promote the former of these purposes, under the direction of Sir Edward Poynings, the lord-deputy, it was provided by an act of the Irish parliament, that all the statutes lately made in England, of a public nature,

* See John Davies's Discovery.

should be held effectual and valid in Ireland.[10] An extensive improvement was thus introduced at once into the latter country, by assimilating its political system to that of England. It has been justly observed, however, by a late historian, that this adoption of English laws, by the Irish parliament, was not unprecedented, and that in particular, another instance of it occurs in the reign of Edward IV. though it is highly probable that it had proved ineffectual. It has, at the same time, been erroneously supposed by some writers, that this act extended to the whole code of English statutes; whereas, in reality, it refers only to a certain number, which, however inaccurately specified, were under the eye of the Irish legislature.

From this regulation, it may fairly be concluded that the Irish parliament was, at this time, understood to possess an indepen-<23>dent legislative authority. If that assembly was capable of adopting the laws of England, it must have had the power also of rejecting them. And as this act of the legislature sufficiently testifies the exertion of independence upon the part of Ireland, so the assent of the governor, upon the part of the king, leaves no room to doubt of his majesty's approbation and concurrence.

To secure the dependence of the Irish parliament upon the crown, Henry endeavoured to acquire a negative before debate upon all their determinations. For this purpose he procured from that assembly a regulation, that no parliament should be held in Ireland until the lord-deputy and his council should certify to the king and council in England, the causes for which the meeting was to be called, and the bills which were therein to be enacted; and that unless the king's leave were previously obtained, the transactions of any future parliament should be void in law.

The interest of the crown required that all debates in parliament, which might inflame the minds of the people, should be suppressed, and that the king should not be <24> put to the disagreeable necessity of rejecting a bill, which, by a previous discussion, had become a popular measure. Even in England such discussions were often attended with troublesome consequences; and they were likely to be more so in Ireland, where from the distance of the sovereign, his private influence could not be so speedily exerted.

10. Sir Edward Poynings (1459–1521): As lord deputy of Ireland (1494–95), he passed numerous acts restricting Irish independence, especially what became known as Poynings's Law, which required the permission of the lord deputy to summon an Irish parliament.

In the reign of Queen Mary an extension was made of this law, by requiring that not only the acts in contemplation at the calling of parliament, but those also which might be proposed after the meeting of that assembly, should, in like manner, be certified to the king and council in England, and previously to their becoming the subject of deliberation should obtain the royal approbation.

From the progress of an independent spirit at a later period, an expedient for avoiding this law was easily suggested. Though parliament, without the concurrence of the sovereign, could not introduce a bill for a new law, it was thought they were not restrained from deliberating in any case, <25> whether a proposal for such a bill should be certified to the king and council; and, in this view, under the colour of heads of a bill to be proposed in future, every argument that could be advanced in supporting or in opposing the bill itself, might be introduced and considered. By such a preliminary debate, the public attention to the measure proposed might be excited no less effectually, and their opinions and sentiments with regard to it might be discovered no less clearly, than if the bill, after undergoing all the necessary ceremonials, had been regularly presented to the two houses for their determination.

The religious reformation in the reign of Henry VIII. became the source of new animosities in Ireland, more bitter and rancorous than those which had formerly subsisted. In that country, literature had made too little progress to create a spirit of liberty in matters of religion, and a disposition to pull down that edifice, which, in a course of ages, had been reared by ignorance and superstition. The people content to be guided implicitly by their religious teachers, had no disposition to pry into mysteries, or to <26> call in question the ceremonies and observances which a designing priesthood had established among their forefathers. Warmly attached to the ancient system of religion, they were taught to believe that nothing could be more meritorious than to hazard their lives in its defence. The political circumstances at the same time, which, in some other parts of Europe, had begun to promote the freedom and independence of the great body of the people, had hitherto no place in Ireland. Arts and manufactures had not there made such progress as to produce a degree of luxury, and to multiply tradesmen and artificers. Men of great property had not, by an increase in the expence of living, been induced to discard their idle retainers, and with a view of obtaining an advancement of rent, to grant long leases to their tenants. The peasantry were still absolutely dependent upon their masters; the members of every great family, or sept, were invariably attached to their chief. The great wealth in the possession of churchmen, by which, like the temporal lords, they were enabled to maintain a number of dependents, was not squandered in procur-<27>ing luxuries, but expended, the greater part of it, in acts of hospitality and charity, which commanded universal respect and veneration. Their jurisdiction and authority, as barons, not having as yet suffered any diminution, continued to operate in addition to the influence arising from the reputed piety of their lives, the sacred functions committed to them, and their situation as members of that great system of ecclesiastical power, which the Roman pontiff had established. Thus, in Ireland, the religious reformation might be regarded as an exotic, for which the soil, at that time, was totally unprepared, and which could only be raised by artificial and violent means. If, by the utmost care and culture, it had been made to take root, there was reason to fear that, when left to itself, it would immediately decay, and be overgrown and choked up by the native weeds of the country.

The authority, and the violent temper of Henry VIII. were indeed successful in procuring, from the Irish parliament, a renunciation of the papal jurisdiction, an acknowledgment of the King's supremacy, and the <28> suppression of religious houses. But, notwithstanding these compliances with the humour of the king, the people in general, and even a great proportion of both houses of parliament, were zealously attached to the ancient faith. These Roman Catholics, it may easily be supposed, were highly enraged at the late innovations, dissatisfied with every measure of a government so hostile to their religion, and ready to embrace every opportunity of creating disturbances. The emissaries of Rome, in the mean time, were not idle, and spared no pains to cherish and inflame these dispositions. To the inhabitants of English race, it was observed, that their title to settle in the country, was entirely founded upon a donation from the pope. To sooth the vanity, and to excite the superstitious and bigoted zeal of the native Irish, this was represented as the favourite island of his holiness; the peculiar seat of the pure catholic religion, upon the fidelity and steadiness of which, according to ancient prophesies, depended the glory and prosperity of the Christian church. That the enemies of the late innovations, however numerous <29> and hostile to each other, might act in concert, the agents of Rome maintained a regular correspondence with the different *septs,* opened a channel of communication through the remotest parts of the country, and exhorted the leading people to lay aside their private jealousies, and to unite in one great cause, the defence of their common religion.

These dispositions of the Irish gave rise to various combinations and attempts against the government, which, according to circumstances, were more or less formidable; but were uniformly succeeded by forfeitures, calculated to gratify the friends and connections of the ruling party. The reign of Elizabeth produced in Ireland no less than three rebellions; which might be attributed almost entirely to the state of religious differences. The first was excited by John O'Neale, chief of the powerful tribe of that name, who exercised a sort of sovereign power in Ulster.[11] This rebellion was suppressed by the vigour and dexterity of Sir Henry Sidney, the lord-deputy;[12] and, though it occasioned a public declaration of many forfeitures, these were not carried <30> into execution, but suffered to fall into oblivion. Another insurrection, soon after, was produced in the southern part of the island, by the Earl of Desmond,[13] the head of the great family of Fitz-Gerald, a nobleman, whose ancestors had long possessed an authority too great for a subject. The King of Spain, thinking this a proper opportunity for retaliating the assistance given by Queen Elizabeth to his rebellious subjects in the Netherlands, sent a military force to act in concert with the Irish insurgents; but, fortunately, the abilities of Desmond were not equal to such an undertaking, and, after a series of miscarriages, he was deserted by his followers, and lost his life, without the credit of distinguishing himself by any brilliant action. The suppression of this rebellion was attended with forfeitures to a great extent, and drew from England a large colony to settle in Munster. Estates were offered to the settlers at the small rent of three-pence, and, in some cases, of two pence the acre; each purchaser being bound to plant a certain number of families within his domain. Sir Walter <31> Raleigh, Sir Christopher Hatton,[14] and many other persons of distinction, obtained grants of estates upon such terms; but, though they occupied the lands, they were not very scrupulous in fulfilling the conditions.

11. Shane O'Neill (ca. 1530–67): Ulster leader of clan O'Neill and leader of the 1562–67 rebellion.

12. Sir Henry Sidney (1529–86): lord deputy from 1566, he put down the O'Neill rebellion.

13. Rebellions under the fourteenth earl of Desmond (ca. 1533–83) took place 1569–73 and again 1579–83.

14. Sir Christopher Hatton (1540–91): lord chancellor 1587–91.

The last rebellion in this reign, and by far the most formidable, was that conducted by Hugh, another branch of the family of O'Neale, who, together with the chief-ship, had now obtained his father's title, that of Earl of Tirone.[15] This leader, in abilities and education, was much superior to the other chiefs of the mere Irish. He had served in the English army; and, as he had become acquainted with the customs of the English, was equally capable of recommending himself to them, and to his own countrymen, by assuming occasionally the manners and deportment of either. With an insinuating address, joined to the most profound dissimulation, he gained the confidence of the English governors, and even of the Queen herself; while, by secret practices, he inflamed the discontents of his countrymen, and prepared them for an insurrection. Even, after he had recourse to <32> arms, he, by various excuses, by affected complaints of injustice, and by repeated pretences of submission, found means to amuse the government, and to procure the delays necessary for bringing his plans to maturity. The King of Spain sent once more a body of troops to support the rebels;[16] which gave such encouragement to the malcontents, as to render the insurrection almost universal. An army of twenty thousand men from England was thought necessary to support the government; and even over this force the rebels gained many advantages. At length, however, by the activity and judicious conduct of Lord Mountjoy,[17] the governor, their force was broken, and they were completely defeated. Tirone submitted at a very critical period, when the death of Elizabeth was known to the Irish administration, but was still kept a secret from the rest of the inhabitants. Thus the prosperous reign of that princess was terminated by an event of the utmost importance to her subjects, the restoration of peace and tranquillity of Ireland, and the establishment, over all her dominions, of a <33> degree of religious liberty, to which, for many centuries, they had been altogether strangers.

The accession of James I. produced an era no less remarkable, in the his-

15. Hugh O'Neill, earl of Tyrone (ca. 1550–1616), son of Matthew O'Neill, who was murdered by his rival Shane in 1558. Tyrone's Rebellion was part of the Nine Years' War (1593–1603).

16. Phillip II sent Spanish ships with arms and munitions to county Donegal in September 1596; and the "second armada" set sail in October 1597, only to be dispersed by gales four days later.

17. Charles Blount, Lord Mountjoy (1563–1606), put down Tyrone's Rebellion; he was made lord deputy in 1600.

tory of Ireland, than in that of England and Scotland. By the union of the English and Scottish crowns, by the cordial acquiescence of the whole nation in the title of their new sovereign, and, above all, by the entire subjection of the Irish chiefs in the late reign, James found himself in a better condition than any of his predecessors, for communicating the English jurisprudence to Ireland, and for extending the advantages of regular government and civilized manners to that hitherto uncultivated and intractable part of his dominions.

The first step, in the course of these improvements, was to reduce the whole country under tribunals modelled upon the English plan. The authority of the Brehons had still continued in force, in most parts of the kingdom; and their decisions, as might be expected, were agreeable to the ancient Irish customs. To these judges, <34> and to their peculiar forms of procedure, the people were zealously attached, and every attempt to overturn this early institution was treated as a dangerous innovation. So late as the reign of Elizabeth, when Fitz-William,[18] the governor, informed Mac-Guire, the chieftain of Fermanaugh, that he intended to send a sheriff into his territories, the chief replied, without hesitation, "Your sheriff shall be welcome, but let me know his *erie,* that, if my people should cut off his head, I may levy it upon the country." The whole country was now divided into thirty-two counties, which were put under the superintendence of sheriffs, and subjected to the jurisdiction of itinerant courts. By this reformation, people of the lower ranks were protected from those numerous exactions, which their superiors had formerly imposed upon them, and began to taste, in some measure, the blessings of security and freedom. The inhabitants were thus comforted for the loss of their barbarous usages, by the evident advantages resulting from the new regulations; and if they were denied the privilege of plunder-<35>ing their neighbours, had, in return, the satisfaction of being less exposed to theft and robbery, or to personal injury. The change at first, was possibly not relished; but it could not fail in time to become palatable. It resembled the transition from poverty to riches; from hunger and hard fare, to plenty and delicacy.

Another great object, essential to the future tranquillity of Ireland, was

18. Sir William Fitzwilliam (1526–99), lord deputy of Ireland (1571–75; 1588–94), recalled in 1594 after he sparked the Nine Years' War/Tyrone's Rebellion by sending a sheriff into Fermanaugh County.

the settlement of landed property. From the frequency of rebellions and disorders many forfeitures had occurred; and the same estates had passed through a number of different families. In such a situation, there came to be much room for dispute, concerning the property of estates; while, in some cases, the validity of the forfeitures was called in question; in some, the pretended grants from the crown were liable to challenge; and, in others, the right of the present possessor was confirmed by such a length of time, as might appear to supply the defects of the original titles. For putting an end to the numberless controversies that might arise in such cases, certain com-<36>missioners were appointed by the crown to examine defective titles of such persons as held lands by the English forms; and the possessors were invited to surrender their estates into the hands of the governor, in order to obtain a new and more legal grant. The governor was likewise empowered to accept surrenders from those Irish lords, who held their estates by the ancient precarious tenure usual in Ireland, and, under certain precautions and regulations, to re-invest the possessor according to the common law of England, with a full and complete right of property. Care was taken, at the same time, to limit the new grants to the actual possessions of the claimants; as also to secure the inferior tenants, and to convert their former uncertain services and duties into a fixed pecuniary payment. The old custom of *tanistry* was thus abolished, and, according to the new grants, estates became universally transmissible to heirs.

A regulation, somewhat similar to this, had been attempted, by an act of parliament in the reign of Elizabeth; but, from the circumstances of the nation at that period, <37> it could not be made effectual.* The extensive disposal of property, which it now occasioned, and the proportionable influence, which it bestowed upon the crown, may easily be conceived. The determination of the commissioners could so little be subjected to any general rules, that every person must have considered himself as indebted to government, for the estate, which he was allowed to obtain or to preserve, and felt *himself under* the necessity of yielding an implicit submission to such terms as the executive power thought proper to demand.

In this state of the country, Tirone, and his principal adherents, who had formerly submitted to government, were alarmed by the suspicion of some new insurrection, and fled to the Continent; upon which their immense

* Davies.

possessions were confiscated. There fell thus into the hands of the crown an extent of territory, in the six northern counties, amounting to about 500,000 acres, in the settlement of which more moderate portions were assigned to individuals, and <38> more effectual precautions were taken to avoid abuses, than had occurred on former occasions.

The city of London became undertakers in this new settlement, and obtained large grants in the county of Derry. Upon pretence of protecting this infant plantation, though, in reality, with a view of raising money, the King instituted the order of Irish baronets, or knights of Ulster, from each of whom, as was then done in Scotland, with respect to the knights of *Nova Scotia,*[19] he exacted a certain sum, in consideration of the dignity to be conferred.

The regulations, for the security of landed possessions, introduced at this period, and those for the extension of law and regular government, were followed, in Ireland, by the enjoyment of peace and tranquillity for near forty years, during which, considerable advances were made in agriculture and even in manufactures. In the reign of Charles I. the vigorous, though somewhat oppressive administration of Sir Thomas Wentworth, contributed much to the progress of these improvements. By his imme-<39>diate encouragement, and even by his example, the linen manufacture was introduced, and has ever since, though with some interruptions, continued in a state of advancement.

The great object of this able but iniquitous governor, was the improvement of the revenue. As the forfeiture of Desmond had given rise to an extensive English settlement in the southern, and that of Tirone and his adherents in the northern part of Ireland, it was now thought expedient that a similar plantation should be effected in Connaught. For this purpose, the validity of titles to estates, in that part of the island, was called in question; various objections to the right of many individuals were started; and these being referred to the commissioners appointed for the trial of such cases, were very generally sustained. Where the juries employed in trying the facts shewed reluctance, recourse was had to promises, threats, and even to severe punishments, for procuring a verdict in favour of the crown. The arbitrary and tyrannical measures of the governor, on these occasions, were car-

19. The Canadian province of Nova Scotia originated as a chartered colony in 1621. James I offered baronetcies to reputable investors, as he later did to investors in Ulster.

<40>ried to such a pitch, as excited the highest indignation; but, at the same time, they were prosecuted with such impetuosity and steadiness as bore down all opposition, and, in the counties of this western division, brought an extensive territory under the disposal of government.

In the disputes between Charles I. and his people, the Irish parliament took party with the latter, and entered into similar measures with those pursued in England, for preventing the arbitrary exertions of prerogative. In the year 1640, the commons in Ireland refused the subsidies demanded by government, objected to the modes of taxation hitherto practised, and presented to the lord-deputy a remonstrance, complaining of grievances.

Although the inhabitants of Ireland had not, at this period, carried their improvements in trade and manufactures to such a height, as could raise the great body of the people to the same condition of independence as in England, yet the planters of English race, those adventurers, who, by the favour of government, had obtained <41> estates in Ireland, and had been willing to encounter the hazards of settling in that country, amid the rage and resentment of the former possessors, were in general, we may suppose, men of a bold spirit and of independent principles. These were the people, who, by their opulence, and by their powerful connections in England, possessed the chief influence over the determinations of the Irish legislature; and who, as they had caught the enthusiastic love of freedom, which now pervaded the English nation, were chiefly instrumental in diffusing the same sentiments through the sister kingdom.

The same difference of opinion in religious matters, which had arisen in England, and in Scotland, found their way also into Ireland, and contributed to influence their political sentiments. Among those of the protestant persuasion, the two great sects of Presbyterians and Independents, whom their adversaries distinguished by the contemptuous appellation of Puritans, and of whom, the latter rejected all ecclesiastical authority, the former, all subordination of <42> ranks among churchmen, formed a natural alliance with the friends of civil freedom; and their tenets in religion were even adopted by a great part of those individuals, who obtained an ascendency in parliament.

On the other hand, the supporters of the hierarchy, the Roman Catholics, and the members of the established church, who, though differing in many religious tenets, agreed in their ardent zeal for promoting the power of churchmen, and for placing the management and controul of that power in the hands of a single person; all these, by the tenor of their ecclesiastical system, were hostile to the designs of parliament, and willing to exalt the prerogative. As the King could not fail to discover these dispositions, which prevailed among the different classes of the people, he could hardly avoid shewing favour to such as were subservient to his views; and, in particular, affording protection and relief to the Roman Catholics from the hardships of those penal statutes, to which, by their non-conformity, they were exposed. This partiality, naturally became the source of jealousy and <43> disgust in the one party, of gratitude and attachment in the other.

* Such, in both countries, was the state of the two great political parties; but, in Ireland, there was better ground than in England for entertaining an apprehension and jealousy of the Roman Catholics, as, compared with them, the Protestants, though, in some degree, masters of the government, were no more than a handful of people. Their distance from the chief seat of the executive power, and the subor-<44>dinate authority possessed by a lord-deputy, rendered, at the same time, the prevailing party in parliament, less capable of enforcing their determinations, or of keeping their enemies in subjection.

While the popish recusants in Ireland, were so formidable by their numbers, they were highly provoked and irritated against the ruling party. Many of them had been unjustly deprived of their possessions, to make way for the needy favourites of administration; and even those, who had been allowed to retain their estates, were, in return, subjected to such regulations and conditions, as curtailed their ancient privileges, and rendered them dependent upon government. For continuing to profess the religion of their forefathers, they were exposed to endless prosecution, and reduced under the dominion of heretics, whom they abhorred, and whose damnable errors they

* It was the object of Charles to remove, by degrees, the differences that subsisted between the system of the established church and that of the Roman Catholics, and to bestow upon the former that authority, and that influence over the people, which were enjoyed by the latter. For this purpose, with the advice and assistance of Laud, he had introduced in England a new set of ecclesiastical canons, intended to new-model the discipline of the church; and a new liturgy, calculated, by a number of external ceremonies, to impress the multitude with superstitious awe and veneration, and to produce a blind submission to their spiritual guides. The same innovations were extended to Ireland, with a few variations accommodated to the circumstances of the country; and, to render the King absolute in ecclesiastical matters, the convocation was armed with the same powers as in England.

detested. Those hardships they imputed, not to the King, whose disposition to relieve them was abundantly manifest; but to that governing party, in the English and Irish <45> parliaments, which opposed and frustrated his benevolent purposes.

From such views and circumstances proceeded, soon after, the Irish rebellion, planned by the abilities of Roger Moore, in which the rage of disappointed bigotry, under the guidance of a senseless barbarian, Sir Phelim O'Neale, perpetrated that horrid massacre, so disgraceful to the annals of Ireland.[20] The disorders of England, at that time, were such as to prevent the interference of government for suppressing this alarming insurrection. The chief executive power had been committed to two justices, Borlace and Parsons,[21] men totally destitute of the capacity and firmness requisite in the present emergency. There was no military force to stop the progress of the insurgents; who had leisure to collect their whole strength, and to form a regular association over the whole kingdom. Their clergy held a general synod, in which they framed a variety of acts, and declarations, calculated to unite the whole Roman Catholic interest both at home and abroad. They were joined by the nobility and gentry, in con-<46>stituting a permanent national assembly, for the regulation and superintendence of their future concerns.

At the first insurrection, O'Neale pretended, that he was acting by the authority of Charles; and, to gain belief, produced, in writing, an express commission from the King. But the forgery of this deed seems now to be universally admitted. Whether any secret encouragement, however, had been given to this insurrection, by Charles, or by his Queen, a zealous Roman Catholic, it seems more difficult to determine. It is certain, that, in the course of the civil war, the insurgents uniformly professed their intention to support the interest of the crown; and that Charles regarded them as friends, from whom, in his utmost extremity, relief and assistance might be expected. In this view, he employed the Earl of Antrim to raise troops in Ireland; and

20. Sir Phelim O'Neill (ca. 1604–53), member of Parliament for Dungannon, was executed as a traitor in 1653. Irish risings took place 1641–53, with "massacres" of Protestants at Portadwonown Bridge and Armagh in 1641, as well as Drogheda in 1649; Rory O'More (d. ca. 1652–53).

21. Sir John Borlase (1576–1648), lord justice of Ireland (1640–44); Sir William Parsons (1570–1650), lord justice in partnership with Borlase (1640–43). In conjunction, they virtually ruled Ireland after the departure of Strafford in 1640.

that nobleman, having taken the oath prescribed by the confederated rebels, procured a body of 3000 men, who were transported into Britain for the King's service. A commission from Charles, at a later period, was <47> granted to the Earl of Ormond,[22] the lord-deputy, with discretionary powers for entering into a treaty with the Irish rebels, that, in return for the privileges to be bestowed upon them by the crown, they should send into Britain a body of 10,000 troops, to be employed in the royal cause. But that the nature of this transaction might be kept more secret, the King soon after employed the Earl of Glamorgan,[23] a zealous Roman Catholic, to treat with those confederates, promising, upon the word of a king, to ratify and perform whatever terms that nobleman should think proper to grant. The treaty which took place, in consequence of this commission, had been concealed with care, and having been discovered, by an unforeseen accident, was found to contain such concessions to the Roman Catholics, as afforded great scandal to the friends of Charles. Glamorgan was accused of having exceeded his powers, and thrown into prison. But an accusation so improbable was not likely to remove the impression, which the public received from the whole circumstances of the transaction. <48>

The reduction of Ireland, by Oliver Cromwell,[24] and the officers whom he employed, for that purpose, gave rise to new forfeitures, and to a new distribution of lands among English adventurers. By the arrangements attempted on this occasion, it was in view to separate the English from the Irish proprietors; and to confine the latter to the province of Connaught.

In the reign of Charles II. and of James II. the apparent designs of the Monarch, in favour of the Roman Catholics, continued the old prepossession and prejudices among religious parties, and secured the great body of the Irish in the interest of these two princes. The effect of this attachment was evident from the difficulty, with which the nation was reduced under the government of William III.

When the government had been completely settled after the Revolution

22. James Butler, twelfth earl of Ormonde (1610–88), Protestant loyalist and three times the lord lieutenant of Ireland.

23. Edward Somerset, earl of Glamorgan (1601–67), Catholic royalist who from 1644 worked in Ireland on behalf of Charles I, and independently from Ormonde. He was arrested by Ormonde in 1645 and fled to France in 1648.

24. In 1649–50, Cromwell crushed the Catholic and royalist forces in Ireland with the capture of Drogheda, a fortified town on the mouth of the Boyne River.

in 1688, it was to be expected that Ireland, as well as England, would reap the benefit of political freedom, and that it would experience a rapid advancement in the arts. Its advances, however, since that period, though <49> certainly very considerable, have been retarded by a variety of circumstances.

1. The inhabitants of Ireland have been more divided by mutual animosity and discord than those of most other countries. From the invasion of Henry II. to near the end of the last century, the natives were subject to continual depredation from the English government, and from those adventurers of the English race, who had such interest with the government, as enabled them, upon various pretences, to dispossess the ancient proprietors, and to seize their estates. The resentment occasioned by these acts of injustice and oppression, the revenge inflicted by the sufferers, whenever they had an opportunity, the remembrance of past injuries upon either side, and the constant apprehension of the future, could not fail to produce a rooted aversion between the two parties, and to excite the bitterest hatred and rancour.

The religious differences, from the time of Henry VIII. became a fresh ground of dissension, a new source of animosities, which flowed in the same channel with the <50> former. The ruling party in Ireland embraced the doctrines of the reformation. Those, who had little connection with government adhering to the religion of their ancestors, again found themselves, upon this account, oppressed and persecuted, by the same class of people to whom they imputed the loss of their possessions.

As the people, who had thus been subjected to oppression, both in temporal and spiritual matters, were by far the most numerous, they were able to stand their ground, and were always formidable to their adversaries. While the one party were supported by the civil magistrate, the other were superior by their natural strength; whence they maintained a constant struggle, by which their passions were kept awake, and their hopes and fears alternately excited. Their mutual apprehension and distrust, therefore, were too powerful to permit their uniting cordially in any common measures; and their mutual animosity and jealousy rendered them frequently more intent upon distressing and humbling each <51> other, than in prosecuting any scheme of national improvement.

The attention of the Irish was, in this manner, wholly engrossed by political and religious disputes; and their minds embraced those objects with a degree of ardour and vehemence unknown in other countries. The same ardent spirit raised by the continual ferment, which those interesting objects had excited, was, at the same time, diffused through the whole of their constitution, and gave a peculiar direction to the national character. A temper, ardent and vehement, a disposition open, forward, undesigning, and sincere, little corrected by culture, might be expected to produce incorrectness of thought and expression, with a tendency to such inaccuracies and blunders as proceed from speaking without due consideration, and from attempting to convey a first impression, without a full examination of particulars. After all, the strictures of the English upon the character and manners of their neighbours in Ireland, like all other observations tending to gratify national vanity and prejudice, must be <52> received with grains of allowance, and, if not restricted to the lower classes of the people, must be acknowledged, at least, more applicable to the inhabitants of the last century, than to those of the present.

2. At the time when Ireland came to be in a condition to push her trade and manufactures, she was checked by the mercantile regulations of the English government.

The mercantile system of all nations has been built upon the narrow basis of monopoly. Every company, or corporation of merchants or manufacturers, has endeavoured to exclude all their neighbours from their own branches of trade or manufacture. From their situation, living in towns, and capable, with ease, of combining together, they have commonly been enabled, by their own clamours and solicitations, to intimidate or to persuade the government to fall in with their designs, and to make regulations for supporting their interest. When Britain came to have colonies, she endeavoured, by authority, to engross their trade, and to hinder them from trading directly <53> with other nations. With respect to Ireland, she proceeded upon similar principles.

To prevent the Irish from interfering in the woollen manufacture, the great staple of England, the Irish were prohibited from exporting wool or woollen cloth. To the linen trade of Scotland the same attention was not paid, and the exportation of Irish linens was permitted to Britain and her colonies.

By what is called the *Navigation Act,* made in the reign of Charles II. and varied by subsequent statutes, it is provided, that no goods, except victuals, shall be shipped from Ireland for his Majesty's plantations, and that no plantation-goods shall be carried to Ireland without being first landed in

Britain. By a later statute, this prohibition, as to goods not enumerated, was removed.

3. To enforce regulations of so oppressive a nature, it was necessary that the Irish government should be rendered entirely subordinate to that of England; and accordingly, no efforts for that purpose were wanting. By what is called Poyning's law, an attempt <54> was made to invest the crown with a power of controuling and directing the deliberations of the Irish parliament. In critical emergencies, however, the operation of this law, was, afterwards, occasionally suspended; and, at length, as has been formerly hinted, a method was divised of entirely evading its effect, by the practice of debating upon the *heads* of such bills, as were to be transmitted to England for obtaining the consent of the king and council.

How far the inhabitants of Ireland were bound by the acts of the British legislature, was a question, which, from the time of the revolution, came to be much agitated by lawyers and politicians. Those, who maintained the affirmative, among whom we may reckon almost all the English lawyers, appear to have rested their opinion chiefly on what is called the *right of conquest.* By virtue of his conquest of Ireland, Henry II. and his successors, acquired a dominion over that country, and a right of subjecting its government to that of his own kingdom. Such, in fact, was understood to be <55> the nature of the Irish government. Though the nation was allowed to hold parliaments of its own, the English parliament exercised over those assemblies a permanent authority, and claimed the privilege of making statutes for Ireland. Instances, indeed, in early times, of English statutes being extended expressly to Ireland, are not very frequent; but a few such instances occur upon record; and from the year 1641, their number was much encreased. By long custom, the intention of the charters granted to Ireland, and the form of government in that country, are to be explained, and if we rely upon this most infallible interpreter of the meaning of parties, we must conclude that the Irish legislature was, from the beginning, subordinate to that of England.

The friends of Irish independence argued very differently, and with more solidity. The right of conquest, they considered as a right, which has no existence, it being impossible that superior force can ever of itself bestow any right. On the contrary, the employment of force, unless in support of a previous right, is an injury, which <56> becomes the proper object of punishment. If Henry II. had no previous right to invade Ireland, and to settle in that island, he certainly could acquire none by attacking the inhabitants, and stripping them of their property, but rather merited punishment for the crimes, which he committed against them. It is unnecessary to mention that even this right of conquest, supposing it well founded, would not be applicable to a great part of the inhabitants of Ireland, those, at least, who obtained the greatest wealth, and had the principle share in the legislature; for they, instead of being the conquered people, were his English subjects, who had assisted in the conquest, and derived the chief benefit from it.

The nature of the Irish constitution, therefore, is to be inferred, not from the force used by England, but from the acquiescence of the people after this force was withdrawn, and when they could be supposed to have a free choice. At what period the people came to be in those circumstances, it is not very easy to determine. There are <57> here two particulars, which may seem worthy of notice.

First, with respect to the form of government, to which, from long custom, the nation is understood to have consented, this must be determined from the general usage, not from a few singular exertions made upon extraordinary emergencies. In every rude nation, persons invested with authority, are apt to lay hold of opportunities of indulging themselves in arbitrary proceedings; and these irregular acts frequently pass without animadversion or punishment. But, from such abuses, we must not reason concerning what, in the common apprehensions of the people, is legal and constitutional. What is merely overlooked, or is found too troublesome to redress, we must not suppose to be approved. Thus, while the parliament of Ireland was acknowledged to possess a legislative power, and was applied to by the crown in every branch of legislation concerning that country, it is of little moment, that, in some few cases, we also meet with regulations extending to <58> Ireland, enacted by the English parliament. The independence of the Irish legislature, is to be inferred from the general tenor of proceedings; and it would be absurd to draw an opposite conclusion from a few instances of usurpation or inadvertency.

In the second place, it is to be observed, that the effect of old usage must be limited by considerations of public utility, and that the most universal submission of a people, however long continued, will not give sanction to measures incompatible with the great interests of society. Had the Irish parliament, by general practice, been rendered entirely subordinate to that of England, the pernicious tendency of such a constitution, with respect to Ireland, must appear of such magnitude, as to shock our feelings of justice, and, at any distance of time, to justify the inhabitants in asserting their natural rights.

But this point was not to be determined by abstract reasonings, or by general considerations on the principles of justice. The interest of the more powerful country, as commonly happens, was held a sufficient reason for asserting and extending its authority <59> over the weaker, and the system of regulating the trade of Ireland, in subserviency to the views of the mercantile people in England, rendered that interest more obvious and conspicuous. To accomplish this purpose, it was requisite that England should possess a power of controuling the Irish courts of justice. Without this she might command, but had no power to execute; her acts of legislation could be made effectual only by her indirect influence over the Irish judges.

In the year 1719, a private law-suit in Ireland,* gave rise to a controversy whether there lay an appeal from the Irish tribunals to the house of lords in Britain, and this was followed by an act of the British parliament; calculated for the express purpose of securing the dependency of Ireland, upon the crown of Great Britain; and declaring first, "that the King's majesty, by and with the consent of the lords, spiritual and temporal, and the commons of Great Britain, in parliament assembled, had, hath, and of <60> right ought to have full power and authority to make statutes, of sufficient force, and validity, to bind the people and kingdom of Ireland."

Secondly, "that the house of lords of Ireland, have not, nor of right ought to have, any jurisdiction to judge of, affirm or reverse, any judgment, sentence, or decree, given or made in any court within the said kingdom."†

While Britain was thus eager to oppress her sister kingdom, she could not with-hold from this, and from other parts of her empire, that free spirit, which the example of her own constitution, and the general advancement of commerce and manufactures contributed to inspire. The leading men of Ireland saw, with indignation, this narrow-minded policy, and the invidious marks of bondage with which their country was branded. They complained with bitterness of the hard regulations, by which the Irish nation, while they profusely shed their blood in the quarrels of Great Britain, were <61> not only excluded from the commerce of the British colonies, but even denied the privilege of trading with foreign nations. They remonstrated with

* Between Sherlock and Annesly.

† 6 Geo. I. chap. 5.

warmth against the injustice, by which they had been deprived of their national rights, in order to rob them of the fruits of their industry, and by which poverty was entailed upon them as an appendage of that slavery, which they were made to inherit.

In one particular the legislature of Ireland had preserved its independence, the article of taxation. It does not appear that the British parliament ever claimed the privilege of imposing taxes upon that country; and as soon as the Irish began to enjoy the advantages of peace, we find their parliaments discovering a jealousy of this branch of authority, and maintaining it with proper spirit. In the year 1690, the commons of Ireland rejected a money bill, because it had not taken its rise in their house. In 1709, a money bill was returned from England *with alterations;* upon which account it was rejected by the commons. Another instance <62> of a similar exertion occurs in the year 1768.

The exertions of the Irish nation, in favour of liberty and independence, were frequently counteracted and frustrated by the indirect influence of the crown; and nothing contributed more to this abuse, than the duration of their parliament.

According to the early constitution of those assemblies, both in England, and in Ireland, they might be dissolved at the pleasure of the king; but independent of a dissolution by this authority, they remained during the king's life. The first alteration, in this respect, was made in England, in the reign of King William III. when, from the nation having become jealous of the crown-influence over parliaments, their duration was limited to three years; a period, which, in the reign of George I. was extended to seven. But no such limitation had been introduced in Ireland, and parliaments, according to the ancient plan, continued to endure for the king's life. In the year 1768, the voice of the nation demanding a reform, in this particular, became irresistible; <63> and a bill for limiting the duration of parliament to eight years, passed the two houses, and obtained the royal assent. The *octennial* parliaments of Ireland, in place of the *septennial* parliaments of England, were preferred at the suggestion of the English ministry, and were probably recommended to them from the view of preventing the inconvenience to government of attending, at the same time, to the new elections of both countries. This reform was the forerunner of others, yet more decisive, in the cause of liberty. The members of the house of commons became now, in some measure, dependent upon their constituents; and their determinations were, of course, more affected by the general feelings of the people.

Britain was involved in great difficulties, and reduced to the utmost perplexity, by the war with her North American colonies;[25] in the prosecution of which Ireland had cheerfully contributed her assistance. Towards the end of that unsuccessful struggle, the interposition of France had exposed the British empire, at home, to the danger of insult and invasion; and afforded to the <64> Irish a plausible pretence for undertaking the defence of their own country. Volunteers, therefore, in the different parts of the kingdom were associated and embodied for this purpose; and to this exertion, apparently so generous and public spirited, the countenance and approbation of government could not well be refused. In a short time, their number became so great, they acquired so much the confidence of the people, and were animated by such resolution, that they could be neither suppressed nor controuled. Some attempts were made by government to obtain an authority over them, but these were easily discovered and evaded. Thus, while Britain was exhausted by a ruinous war, Ireland had procured an armed force, which nothing could resist, commanded by her own citizens, and firmly determined to procure the redress of her grievances. The consequences were such as might be expected. In 1778, a bill had been brought into the British parliament for the removal of all those restraints, which had been imposed upon the trade of Ireland, but the alarm excited in the trading, and <65> manufacturing towns of Britain rendered the measure unsuccessful. The Irish, however, conscious of their internal strength, were not disheartened. In their address to the throne, they declared, "it is not by temporary expedients, but by a free trade only, that the nation is to be saved from impending ruin." To guard against a prorogation before they should obtain redress, they refused to grant the supply for the usual term of two years, but passed a short money bill, to which the royal assent was obtained. In the English house of commons, the minister, pressed by the difficulties attending his present critical situation, proposed to repeal the restrictive statutes complained of, and to grant the Irish a free trade to the British colonies, as well as to foreign countries. The propositions which he brought into parliament for that purpose were very readily adopted, and obtained the sanction of the legislature.

The joy of the whole people of Ireland, excited by this decisive and important victory, may easily be conceived. It did <66> not, however, prevent them from following the tide of their success, and bearing down every remaining obstacle to their complete independence. They had still the mor-

25. The American War of Independence took place 1775–83.

tifying reflection that they owed this relief to the favour of an English ministry; that it had been procured by the necessity of the times; and that, afterwards, from an alteration of circumstances, it might, very probably, be withdrawn. To secure the permanent enjoyment of present advantages, it was necessary they should depend upon themselves. The volunteers, conscious of having power in their hands, were not negligent in using it to the best advantage. By choosing delegates from different quarters, as a sort of representatives of the whole body, by assembling these delegates on different occasions to act in concert with one another, by publishing resolutions and remonstrances expressing their unalterable purpose to assert their liberties, they spread an universal panic over Great Britain, and a belief that it would be in vain to oppose their demands. In this situation a change of the British <67> ministry took place; and the Marquis of Rockingham,[26] who came to the head of administration, found himself at liberty to comply with his own inclination, and that of his party, by removing those oppressive regulations, which rendered the Irish government subordinate to the British. With this view there passed an act of the British legislature, containing a repeal of Poyning's law; and also a repeal of the statute, by which the parliament of Great Britain is declared to have a power of making laws to bind the Irish nation, and of reviewing the sentences of the Irish tribunals.

At a subsequent period, during the administration of Lord Shelburn,[27] it was suggested, that the repeal of the obnoxious statutes above-mentioned was insufficient, and the British parliament was prevailed upon to renounce the principle upon which they had proceeded, by relinquishing, on the part of Great Britain, all similar claims for the future. The former concession was necessary for the security of Ireland; the latter was merely the effect of popular <68> clamour, which produced a juvenile, though, perhaps, a pardonable degree of triumph and exultation.

By these alterations Ireland became an independent kingdom, connected by a federal union with Britain, but possessing within itself a supreme legislative assembly, and supreme courts for the distribution of justice. <69>

26. Charles Watson-Wentworth, second marquis of Rockingham (1730–82): opposition Whig statesman, briefly a member of a coalition ministry (1765–66), and prime minister in 1782. He supported American independence and internal autonomy for Ireland.

27. Sir William Petty, second earl of Shelburne (1737–1805), led a ministry from July 1782 to April 1783.

CHAPTER II

Political Consequences of the Revolution—Subsequent Changes in the State of the Nation—Influence of the Crown.

The alterations made in the state of the government by what is called the revolution, in 1688, and by the other public regulations in the reign of William III. were judicious, moderate, and prudent. With a perfect adherence to the spirit, and with as little deviation as possible from the ancient forms of the constitution, they were well calculated to restrain the arbitrary conduct of the sovereign, and appeared to establish a limited monarchy upon a solid and permanent basis.

All the avenues and passes, through which the prerogative had formerly invaded the rights of the people, were now apparently guarded and secured. The king could neither maintain troops, nor obtain the necessary supplies, without the annual interposition of the legislature, and therefore was laid <70> under the inevitable necessity of calling regular and frequent meetings of Parliament. The former disputes upon that subject were consequently at an end. Any future injunction upon the sovereign, to perform his duty in this respect, was now superseded. As he could no longer procure money, or carry on the business of government, without parliamentary aid, it was to be expected that no future complaints of his neglecting to convene that assembly would ever be heard. It was no longer prudent for him to hazard the angry dissolution of a parliament for refusing to comply with his demands; a measure tending to engender enmity and resentment in that class of men, whose good will and cordial affection were become indispensibly requisite. In a word, the executive power was rendered completely subordinate to the legislative; which is agreeable to the natural order of things; and without which there can be no free government.

The legislative power was, by the ancient structure of the constitution, lodged in the assembly composed of king, lords, and commons; so that the king, to whom was committed <71> the province of executing the laws, had also a great share in making them. But this regulation, which is justly considered by political writers, as inconsistent with the perfection of a free government, has been, in a great measure, removed by custom. As every bill must pass through the two houses before it can receive the royal assent, and as the king cannot legally interfere in bills depending before either house, the interposition of his negative would be apt to excite such national clamour as no wise prince would choose to incur, and would be repugnant to the principles of the constitution, by evincing greater confidence in the advice of other persons than of the national council.* For a long time, therefore, the exercise of this branch of power in the crown has been entirely disused, and the legislative has been of course, placed in different hands from the executive.[1]

Comparing the two houses of parliament with each other, the commons, consisting of <72> national representatives, sustain the popular part of the legislature, while the peers sustain the aristocratical. From circumstances, which I had formerly occasion to observe, the commons acquired the exclusive power of bringing in all money bills, and the peers have only that of assenting, or interposing their negative to the grant. This part of the constitution, which arose from the ancient forms of deliberation, is now supported by considerations of the highest expediency. The commons represent all the property of the kingdom, that of the peerage alone excepted; and therefore it may be supposed, that from a regard to their own interest, as well as that of the community at large, they will be induced to prevent the imposition of unreasonable taxes. The crown, on the other hand, is interested to augment the public revenue; and the peers, who are created by the crown, and have an immediate connection with the higher offices and places in its disposal, may be suspected of adhering invariably to its interest. The house of peers, therefore, in matters of taxation, is allowed to vote in favour of the <73> people, but not in favour of the crown. It cannot grant supplies,

* See the debates upon this subject soon after the revolution. Hatsell's Proceedings of Parliament.

1. Compare Smith's view of the balance of powers in the English Constitution in *LJ*, 269 and 421–22.

but may interpose a negative upon those which have been suggested by the commons.

As it had long been a maxim in the English government, "that the king can do no wrong," by which is meant, that his ministers are alone responsible for ordinary acts of mal-administration, it was hence inferred, that these ministers must be allowed exclusively to direct and govern the state machine; for it would be the height of injustice to load them with the crimes of another, nor could it be expected that any man of spirit would submit to be a minister upon such terms. Were it even possible to find persons willing to answer for measures which they were not permitted to guide, their nominal administration would not serve the purpose intended; as the responsibility of such mean and servile officers could afford no security to the public, that the abuses of the executive power might be restrained by the terrors of such vicarious punishment.

Thus, by the principles of the constitution, the real exercise of the executive or <74> ministerial power came to be regularly, though tacitly, committed to a set of ministers, appointed by the king during pleasure. Their number, though not accurately fixed, was in some measure circumscribed by that of the chief official situations in the gift of the crown; and the individuals belonging to this body were still more distinctly pointed out, and recognized by the public, from their composing a select, or cabinet council, by whose concurrence and direction the administration was visibly conducted.

These ministers being nominated or displaced at the discretion of the crown, their continuance in office was, of course, brought under the controul of the two houses of parliament, and more especially under that of the commons, upon whom, by their power of granting or withholding supplies, the movements of government ultimately depended. From the nature of the constitution, tending to attract the attention of the public to the conduct of its managers, and from circumstances attending the direction of all political measures, it was to be expected that this controul of the legislature over the ap-<75>pointment of the principal officers of state would be frequently exercised. From the event of a war, not corresponding to the sanguine expectations of the people; from the soliciting and enforcing new taxes, which are usually paid with reluctance, and productive of bad humour; from the unfortunate issue of hazardous transactions, not to mention the errors and blunders which are unavoidable in difficult emergencies, or even the corrupt designs that may be discovered or suspected, every junto[2] of ministers is likely in a course of time, to become, in its turn, unpopular, and even to excite the public indignation and resentment. From the multitude of expectants, compared with those who can possibly enjoy places under government, the number of persons who think themselves not rewarded in proportion to their merits, is apt, at the same time, to be continually encreasing, and to supply the party in opposition with new reinforcements. Thus, in the natural progress of things, it might be expected that the growing clamour and discontent against every ministry which had long remained in power would be such <76> as to clog and obstruct their measures, to entangle them in difficulties more and more inextricable, and at length to produce a parliamentary application for their removal.

By the operation of these combined circumstances the English government seemed, in the executive branch, to possess the anvantages both of a monarchy and a republic, by uniting the dignity and authority of a hereditary monarch, calculated to repress insurrection and disorder, with the joint deliberation of several chief executive officers, and a frequent rotation of their offices, tending to guard against the tyranny of a single person.

In the judicial department, it was the object to give decisions, partly according to the rules of law founded upon long experience and observation, partly upon the feelings of equity and the principles of common sense. In the former view professional judges were appointed by the crown: in the latter, jury-men were selected from among the people. To secure, as far as possible, the independence of judges, they were, for the most part, appointed for life. To hin-<77>der jurymen from acquiring the habits of professional judges, they were chosen for each particular cause. So far as the king had retained the direction of public prosecutions for crimes, various regulations were made to prevent the abuses of this power by arbitrary imprisonment, or other acts of oppression.*

Such were the outlines of that constitution which, through many accidental changes, and by a course of gradual improvements upon the primitive

* The most remarkable of those regulations, which is called the *habeas corpus,* by which any person imprisoned on pretence of a crime, may require that his trial should be commenced and finished within a certain time, originated in the *great charters,* and was rendered more specific in the reigns of Charles I. and Charles II.

2. From Spanish *junta,* a cabal, council, or committee. The term was applied by contemporaries to a small group of aristocratic Whig politicians who wielded great influence in a series of ministries at the turn of the eighteenth century.

system of the European nations, was finally established in the reign of William III. a mixed form of government, but remarkable for its beautiful simplicity, and in which the powers committed to different orders of men were so modelled and adjusted as to become subservient to one great purpose, the preservation of the rights and liberties of the people. <78>

We are not, however, to dream of perfection in any human workmanship. Far less are we to imagine that a government can be so contrived as, for ages, to remain equally suited to a nation whose condition and circumstances are perpetually changing. As the husbandman varies his mode of culture and management, according to the meliorations of the soil, and to the alterations in the state of his farm, or of the markets, the legislator must accommodate his regulations to the progressive changes in the condition of the people for whom they are intended, to their progress in manufactures and commerce, their increase in opulence, and their advances in luxury or in refinement.

In England there were two great changes in the state of society, the remarkable appearance of which may be dated from the revolution, though their commencement was doubtless earlier, and the rapid progress of which may be traced through the whole of the following century. The first is the growing influence of the crown, arising from the patronage which it has acquired, and the <79> correspondent habits of dependence in the people which have thence been produced.

After the government had been settled by the regulations which took place at the revolution, and in the reign of William III. parliament no longer entertained any jealousy of encroachments from the prerogative, and became willing to grant supplies with a liberality of which there was formerly no example. The extensive enterprises in which the crown was engaged, and in which the interest of the nation was deeply involved; the settlement of Britain, the reduction of Ireland, the prosecution of the war with France, were productive of great expence, which the public could not view in any other light than as the price of their liberties, and therefore could not decently, or with any colour of justice, refuse to defray. In a subsequent period, new situations, though less urgent, afforded a plausible pretence for new demands; which, from various reasons, whether of a public or private nature were frequently complied with. England becoming gradually more opulent and powerful, was led, from vanity or am-<80>bition, to take a greater share in the disputes of her neighbours, and to assume a higher rank in the scale of nations. Her civil and military establishments became gradually more extensive; the management and protection of her increasing wealth required a greater variety of regulations; and the number of her officers and magistrates, in all the departments of administration, was, of course, augmented. An augmentation of the public revenue, to supply the growing wants of the state, was thus rendered indispensible.

In a course of time these public burdens became familiar and habitual, both to parliament and to the nation, and the imposition of new taxes, which, in the beginning had often excited alarm and clamour, was at length reduced to an ordinary transaction, requiring little examination or attention, and of which the refusal would betray uncommon suspicion and discontent. It happened in this as it usually happens in cases of private liberality. A donation which has been frequently and regularly bestowed comes, after a length of time, to be regarded as a kind of debt; and to withhold it is looked upon as a <81> species of injury. When parliament had been accustomed to confide in the reports of ministry, and, without much enquiry to acquiesce in their demands, its future confidence and acquiescence were expected; and the money came to be sometimes granted even in cases where the measures of administration, which had occasioned the expence, were condemned and severely censured.

But notwithstanding the readiness of parliament to stretch every nerve in supplying the demands of the executive government, the necessities of administration surpassed, occasionally, what the circumstances of the nation were thought able to afford. Having incurred an expence beyond what the taxes which could be levied within the year were sufficient to repay, the ministry endeavoured to relieve themselves by such an expedient, as in a similar case, has commonly been suggested to individuals. They anticipated the national income, by borrowing the money required, and assigning a particular branch of revenue for the security of the creditor. The funds appropriated to this purpose were not, at first, intended to remain under per-<82>petual mortgage; being sufficient, not only to discharge the yearly interest of the debt, but even to clear the incumbrance in a few years. Successive experiments, however, encouraged ministers to venture upon still more expensive undertakings; the quantity of money in circulation, a consequence of the flourishing state of commerce, enabled them easily to find the sums that were wanted; and by giving to the creditor a high rate of interest, transferrable at pleasure, with other pecuniary emoluments, they had no difficulty in persuading him entirely to sink his capital. In this manner they introduced, what is called, a *debt in perpetuity,* the amount of which, for obvious reasons, has been continually and rapidly encreasing. By this expedient, a minister, whose interest may lead him to spend the whole public income in time of peace, is enabled to draw upon futurity for the additional expence of maintaining a war; and as in countries advancing rapidly in luxury, dissipation, and extravagance, every succeeding war is likely to be more expensive than the former, his <83> draughts can hardly fail to advance in the same proportion.

The public revenue has thus come to be divided into two great branches; that which is intended to defray the annual expence of government, and that which is levied to discharge the annual interest of the national debt. The former is plainly the source of influence in the crown, in proportion to the patronage resulting from the disposal of the money. All who enjoy, or who expect offices, or places of emolument, in the gift of the crown, and even in some degree their kindred and connections, may be expected to court, and to support that interest upon which they depend; to acquire suitable habits, opinions, and prejudices, and in such disputes or differences as occur between prerogative and privilege, to arrange themselves under the ministerial standard.

In the same class with the patronage derived from this ordinary revenue, we may consider that which arises from various other offices, or places of honour and profit, in the gift, or under the controul and direction of administration, though supported <84> by different funds; such as those proceeding from the government of Ireland, or of the British colonies; the higher dignities in the church; the lucrative places in the service of the East India company,[3] and many establishments for education and for charitable purposes. The extent of this patronage cannot easily be calculated; though it is apparently immense, and has been advancing in a highly accelerated *ratio,* from the revolution to the present time.

The other great branch of the public revenue, what is levied to pay the interest of the national debt, ought to be examined in connection with the money borrowed, by which that debt was contracted.

3. Chartered by Elizabeth I in 1600 to challenge the Dutch-Portuguese monopoly of the spice trade, the East India Company became the dominant force in the extension of indirect imperial control of India. From the mid-eighteenth century, the company extended its power in India as a result of wars among Indian powers and with other European nations. The impeachment trial of Warren Hastings (1732–1818), led by Edmund Burke, focused public attention on the alleged corruptions of the company.

The money borrowed for the support of a war is the source of influence to the crown in two different ways. First, by its immediate expenditure, which occasions an immense patronage, from the sudden increase of the army and navy, the employment of numerous contractors and other civil officers, the appendages of war, and the various transactions which that active and violent state of the country may pro-<85>duce. Secondly, from the advantages accruing to those rich individuals, who lend the money to government, and who, by availing themselves of the pressing demands of the public, are enabled to reap more profit from the loan, than could be drawn from any other branch of trade.

In this situation the gain of the money-lenders, and of all who are employed in the service of the state, is evidently so much the greater, as the money is commonly spent, and the transactions of government are made, upon the spur of the occasion, amid the hurry and agitation of strong passions, without leisure to deliberate, and without opportunities of practising the ordinary rules of prudence and economy. In such cases, there is unavoidably a negligent waste, a precipitate rashness, in the public expenditure, from which those vermin, who feed upon the necessities of their country, enjoy a plentiful repast.[4]

Thus a war, though generally hurtful to the community at large, proves often highly beneficial to a portion of its members; to the landed gentlemen, who, by serving in <86> the army and navy, obtain a provision for themselves and their families; and those of the mercantile interest, who, by the extensive loans to government, and by lucrative employments, obtain the means of accumulating princely fortunes. From these private considerations it happens, that so much blood and treasure is frequently consumed in wars, undertaken from trivial causes, and continued without any rational prospect of public advantage.

To be sensible of the extent of this evil we need only consider, that, of the period which has elapsed from the revolution to the present time, between a third and one-half has been employed in wars, prosecuted in this expensive and improvident manner, and producing an incessant and regularly accelerated accumulation of public debt, which now amounts to more

4. Compare Smith's view of public finance and its implications for Britain's "mixed" constitution, *LJ*, 267–69.

than five hundred millions.* It cannot escape observation, that the uncommon influence acquired by the crown, while the nation is in a state of warfare, will not be immediately extin-<87>guished upon the conclusion of a peace, but, from the usual effects of habit, by remembrance of the past, and by anticipation of future emoluments, may in some measure be retained and propagated from one military harvest to another.

With respect to the permanent funds created for paying the interest of the national debt, these give rise to a separate influence of the crown; *first,* by inducing the holders of stock to promote the popularity of ministers, and to support their measures, in order to raise the value of those funds; *secondly,* by the number of public officers, in the nomination of the king, who are employed in collecting or managing this branch of the revenue.

Upon the whole, the ordinary public revenue directly at the disposal of the crown, or indirectly contributing to its influence, which, immediately before the revolution, amounted to about two millions yearly, has, by the gradual expansion of the two great branches already mentioned, risen to the prodigious annual sum of above thirty millions; and thus without including the <88> value of those numerous offices and places, in the gift of the crown, which are supported by other funds than the national taxes.

That the secret influence of the crown has been continually encreasing from this change of circumstances will hardly be doubted. But has it encreased in proportion to the rise of the public revenue, and to the encrease in the value of all the offices and emoluments at the disposal of administration? This appears to merit a particular examination.

To have a full view of this question, it is proper to observe, that the augmentation of the public revenue, since the accession of William III. has proceeded from three different causes.

1. It has proceeded, in part, from the encreasing wealth of the nation. The defence of property is one of the great purposes of government; and according as more wealth has been accumulated by any people, its protection and security will cost more trouble; and, by giving rise to a more intricate system of regulations, will <89> require the employment of a greater number of persons in the service of administration. The encrease of riches in a country has, at the same time, a tendency to raise the price of commodities, as well as, from fashion, to introduce more expensive modes of living; and

* See resolution of the House of Commons, 5th Jan. and 1st Feb. 1801.

this makes it necessary that the different servants of government, to preserve the same rank as formerly, should obtain a suitable advancement of emoluments. An encrease of taxes, in some shape or other, is thus rendered indispensible.

So far as an augmentation of the revenue has arisen from the greater difficulty in the protection of property, producing a more intricate system of management, it must undoubtedly have encreased the influence of the crown; but so far as this augmentation has proceeded from a rise in the expence of living, there seems no ground for ascribing to it any such tendency. Supposing the expence of living to be trebled or quadrupled since the revolution, and that upon this account, the public revenue has been encreased in the same proportion; this encrease will neither enable ministers to <90> hire more servants, nor to reward them better; nor if it were employed even in the direct operation of bribery, would it produce a greater effect.

2. The augmentation of the public revenue has likewise been partly derived from an enlargement of the empire, and from a multiplication of the inhabitants. The greater the number of people included in one system of government, the management of their public concerns will be rendered the more complex, and of consequence more expensive. That this circumstance has contributed greatly to extend the influence of the sovereign is unquestionable.

The larger and more populous any empire becomes, that is, the greater the number of individuals paying taxes, the influence of the king, who has the disposal of the revenue, will, other circumstances being equal, become so much the greater; because that revenue acquires a greater superiority over the wealth of any one of his subjects, and overbalances more decisively that of any junto of the people, who could possibly associate for opposing and <91> controuling his authority. Suppose, for example, a nation composed of no more than 100,000 men, paying taxes at the rate of forty shillings each person. The revenue, which would thence arise, of 200,000 l. a year, would probably not render the Sovereign much richer than a few of his most opulent subjects, and consequently, after deducting the sum requisite for maintaining his family, would be totally inadequate to the support of his rank.

If the state were so enlarged as that the people, paying taxes at the same rate, amounted to a million, it is evident, that by the revenue of two millions yearly, which would thus be levied, the king would be exalted in a much greater proportion, and would have little reason to fear that his influence might be counterbalanced by any casual accumulation of property in the hands of his refractory subjects. By supposing a state to comprehend twenty or thirty millions, we may conceive that the revenue, according to the same rate of taxation, would bear down all opposition, and become perfectly irresistible. <92>

Lastly, the increase of the public revenue, during the period under consideration, may, perhaps chiefly, be imputed to the negligence and mismanagement incident to all extensive undertakings. Whoever considers the waste and bad economy which commonly take place in managing the private estate of a rich individual; the idleness and embezzlement of servants; the inattention, the fraudulent and collusive practices of stewards and overseers, may easily conceive the still greater abuses that are likely to occur in managing the concerns of a great empire. As there a strict oversight is impossible, all the servants in the various departments of government are left in some measure to their own discretion, and are at liberty to practice innumerable expedients for promoting their own interest. They will endeavour, therefore, we may suppose, to improve their situation in two different ways: first, by laying hold of every pretence, and employing every method to encrease their perquisites and emoluments: secondly, by doing as little as they possibly can, without in-<93>curring either punishment or censure; so that, in order to supply their deficiencies, a variety of assistants and inspectors must be appointed. The expence of administration is thus unnecessarily augmented, both by a needless multiplication of the officers in the service of government, and by bestowing upon them a greater income than the performance of their duty gives them any right to demand. To what a monstrous height has this abuse, which has continued for more than a century, been at length carried! How many officers, in church and state, obtain immense fortunes from the public for doing no work, or next to none! How many are often employed to perform the duty which might easily be performed by a single person! The tendency of this to encrease the patronage, and consequently the influence of the crown, is too obvious to require illustration.

It should seem, therefore, that the augmentation of the public revenue, so far as it has proceeded from any other circumstance, except an augmentation in the ge-<94>neral expence of living, has been attended with a proportional encrease in the patronage and influence of the crown, and has contributed to strengthen the monarchical part of the constitution.

We may further remark, that the influence, arising from the causes already specified, is apt to be the greater, as it operates upon the manners and habits of a mercantile people: a people engrossed by lucrative trades; and professions, whose great object is gain, and whose ruling principle is avarice: a people whose distinguishing feature, as a great author observes, is justice; equally opposed to dishonesty on the one hand, and to generosity on the other; not that nice and delicate justice, the offspring of refined humanity, but that coarse, though useful virtue, the guardian of contracts and promises, whose guide is the square and the compass, and whose protector is the gallows. By a people of this description, no opportunity of earning a penny is to be lost; and whatever holds out a view of interest, without violating any <95> municipal law, or incurring any hazard, is to be warmly embraced. *Quaerenda pecunia primum.*[5]

From the time of the revolution, accordingly, we may trace, in some measure, a new order of things; a new principle of authority, which is worthy the attention of all who speculate upon political subjects. Before that period, the friends of liberty dreaded only the direct encroachments of the prerogative: they have since learnt to entertain stronger apprehensions of the secret motives of interest which the crown may hold up to individuals, and by which it may seduce them from the duty which they owe to the public. To what a height, in fact, has this influence been raised in all the departments of government, and how extensively has it pervaded all ranks and descriptions of the inhabitants. In the army, in the church, at the bar, in the republic of letters, in finance, in mercantile and manufacturing corporations. Not to mention pensioners and placemen; together with the various officers connected with the distribution of justice, and the execution of <96> the laws, the corps diplomatique, and the members of the king's confidential council. With what a powerful charm does it operate in regulating opinions, in healing grievances, in stifling clamours, in quieting the noisy patriot, in extinguishing the most furious opposition! It is the great opiate which inspires political courage, and lulls reflection; which animates the statesman to despise the resentment of the people; which drowns the memory of his former professions, and deadens, perhaps, the shame and remorse of pulling down the edifice which he had formerly reared.

Nor is the influence, founded on the numerous offices in the gift of the crown, confined to those who are in possession and in expectation of such

5. "In the first place, money ought to be sought" (Horace, *Epistles,* I, 1, 53).

offices, or even to their numerous relations and friends. In every country, a great majority of the people immersed in pursuits of gain, devoted to pleasure, unaccustomed to political speculation, or destitute of that firmness of character, which enables a man to assert the truth through good report, and through bad, are apt to take their opinions, in a great <97> measure from those around them. Such people are always to be found in the party prevailing for the time, whether the current may run in the channel of prerogative or of freedom; like those who are indifferent in religion, they are always supposed to hold the ruling faith, and counted as members of the established church. It is therefore of infinite consequence to have a number of partisans scattered through the nation, at all times zealous to support the administration, and ready to extol their measures. In this way, placemen, pensioners and expectants are of the most essential service to their employers. Like people stationed in different parts of a theatre to support a new play, they set up such an enthusiastic and noisy applause, as by giving an appearance of general approbation, drowns all opposition, confounds the timid, and secures the concurrence of that immense class of persons who either want leisure or talents to judge for themselves. In this manner it frequently happens that good and bad administrations have nearly an equal appearance of <98> popularity, and that ruinous measures seem to be sanctioned by the opinion of the nation.

The progressive advancement of influence in the crown, has gradually been productive of changes in the methods of conducting the business of the legislature. It was early an essential maxim in the English government, as I formerly observed, that every proposal for a new statute should originate in either house of parliament; and that, it could not come under the consideration of the king, until it had passed through the two houses. The crown, therefore, had merely a negative upon the resolutions of parliament, a power of preventing the state vessel from wandering into a new tract, not that of putting it in motion, or of directing its course. From the circumstances which have been mentioned, this order of proceeding is, in a good measure, inverted. Though the king had no right to interfere in the deliberations of parliament; yet his ministers, as members of either house, might suggest any bill to its consideration; and, from the secret influence of the crown, <99> the bills introduced in this manner were likely to obtain a favourable hearing, and to be most successful. At present almost all bills of importance are thus indirectly brought into parliament by the crown, and in all ordinary cases, are supported and passed by a great majority. Thus while the king no longer exercises his original prerogative of with-holding the royal assent from the determinations of parliament, he has in reality acquired the more important power of proposing the laws, and the privilege of debate which remains in the two houses, is reduced to a mere passive power of controul; that is, to be little more than a negative; a negative too, which, in the ordinary state of political controversy, can rarely be exercised.

Has there occurred nothing on the other side to counterbalance the effect of this growing patronage, and its correspondent influence? Have the progressive changes in the state of society, since the time of the revolution-settlement, contributed uniformly to support the authority of the monarch, <100> and can we discover no circumstances of an opposite nature tending to preserve the former equilibrium, by supporting the popular part of our constitution? The rapid improvements of arts and manufactures, and the correspondent extension of commerce, which followed the clear and accurate limitation of the prerogative, produced a degree of wealth and affluence, which diffused a feeling of independence and a high spirit of liberty, through the great body of the people; while the advancement of science and literature dissipated the narrow political prejudices which had prevailed, and introduced such principles as were more favourable to the equal rights of mankind. This is the other great change in the state of society, to which I alluded in the beginning of this chapter, and of which I shall now proceed to give an account.

In a review of the different reigns, from that of William III. to the present time, I shall afterwards endeavour to trace the struggles between those two opposite principles, of regal influence and popular inde-<101>pendence, and to point out the chief incidents of a constitutional history, lying in a good measure beneath that common surface of events which occupies the details of the vulgar historian. <102>

CHAPTER III

The Advancement of Manufactures, Commerce, and the Arts, since the Reign of William III.; and the Tendency of this Advancement to diffuse a Spirit of Liberty and Independence.

The natural advantages of England, in the cultivation of wool, having promoted her woollen manufacture, it was to be expected that her industry, and her capitals, derived from that source, would be communicated to other branches of labour, in which they might be employed with similar success. Her maritime situation, by extending the benefit of water-carriage over a great part of the island, and by rendering many of the inhabitants acquainted with navigation, was calculated to produce a suitable extension of commerce, and to open a foreign market for such of her commodities as exceeded her internal consumption. The full establishment of a regular and free constitution was alone wanting to improve these favourable <103> circumstances, by exciting that energy and vigour which political liberty, and the secure possession and enjoyment of property are wont to inspire. This was obtained by the memorable Revolution in 1688, which completed, and reduced into practice, a government of a more popular nature, and better fitted to secure the natural rights of mankind, than had ever taken place in a great nation. From this happy period, therefore, commerce and manufactures assumed a new aspect, and, continuing to advance with rapidity, produced innumerable changes in the state of society, and in the character and manners of the people.

It would be superfluous to observe, that these improvements have been attended with correspondent advances in agriculture, and in the arts connected with it. Commerce and manufactures, by encreasing wealth and population, must enhance the demand for provisions; and consequently, by augmenting the profits of the farmer, cannot fail to stimulate his industry and activity. It will be found, accordingly, from the general history of the world, that, in all countries <104> where there is no trade, the cultivation of the ground, if at all known, is performed in a rude and slovenly manner; and that a considerable progress of mercantile improvements has generally preceded an equal degree of skill and dexterity in the several branches of husbandry. The cultivation of the ground, as Dr. Smith justly observes, can never, in any country, approach to perfection, until the price of butcher-meat has, from the diffusion of wealth, risen to such a pitch as will induce the farmer to employ his best grounds, at least occasionally, in the pasturing of cattle; by which he may obtain a constant supply of manure, sufficient to repair that part of his land which has been exhausted by tillage. As England has been long in that situation, her best land is frequently retained for the sole purpose of feeding cattle, or in what is called *meadow;* while in Scotland, whose mercantile and agricultural improvements have been much later, there is no such general practice; and the appellation of *meadow,* is only given to those marshy <105> grounds, which, for want of draining, are unfit for the plough.

The same circumstances, which thus promoted the internal trade of England, were no less favourable to her commercial intercourse with other nations. The encouragement of her foreign trade became a great object as far back as the reign of James I. and of Elizabeth; when trading companies were erected by public authority, and colonies, under the protection of government, were formed in distant parts of the globe. Those great companies were, at the same time, invested with exclusive privileges, calculated to secure them in the monopoly of the several branches of trade for which they had been incorporated. In the infancy of commerce, such regulations were, perhaps, requisite for the encouragement of new and hazardous undertakings; and their apparent equity, inasmuch as they bestowed upon the adventurers the fruit of their own spirited activity, could hardly be disputed. But in a subsequent period, when the progress of commercial improvements had produced large capitals, <106> and a numerous body of merchants, ready to engage in every enterprise which promised an adequate, though, perhaps, a distant return of profit, it began to be perceived that these monopolies were, in every view, inconvenient and pernicious. They contributed to check any competition among the workmen engaged in producing those commodities, which were the subject of the monopoly trade; and, consequently, tended to diminish the *quantity,* as well as to degrade the *quality,* of those commodities.[1] They also prevented all competition in the sale of such commodities, and enabled the monopolists, by starving the market, to advance their price in proportion. Thus the community at large became a sufferer in two respects; first, by procuring goods of an inferior quality to what might otherwise have been expected; secondly, by being obliged to purchase them above their natural rate. Since the Revolution, therefore, these exclusive trading companies have been gradually abolished; and their trade laid open to the whole nation. The monopoly of the East India company has alone <107> been excepted, and continues to be enforced with the utmost rigour. Some authors have endeavoured, from the distance of the country, and from the extent and other peculiarities of the Indian trade, to justify this exception; but, after all, there is little room to doubt, that it has proceeded from political, more than from commercial considerations, and that the strength, not the weakness of this company, is the real ground of the support which it has of late received from government.

The system of imposing restrictions upon commerce has not been directed solely to the purpose of encouraging particular trading companies. Politicians have conceived that individuals, in prosecuting schemes of private interest, were it not for the watchful inspection and controul of government, might be tempted to employ their labour, and their capitals, upon such branches of trade as are less beneficial to the public than others; and that they ought to be restrained and diverted from so doing by numerous regulations; by taxes, prohibitions, and bounties. In particular, the view <108> of preserving a balance of our trade with foreign nations, ought to drive us out of every market in which our imports exceed our exports. Our trade with every foreign country was regarded as profitable, if we sent to it more goods than we received, and, consequently, obtained a surplus in money. If the contrary, it was considered as unprofitable and hurtful. This maxim which runs through the older writers on trade, appears now to be almost universally exploded. When we give to our neighbours money for useful and marketable commodities, we obtain a real value, and an adequate mercantile profit, no less than when we give commodities for their money. To carry on the trade of our country with advantage, and to supply the wants

1. The negative effects of monopolies is a major theme in Smith. See, for example, *LJ,* 363–64, 497–98.

of the inhabitants, it may often be requisite that we should purchase the goods of particular nations, who have not an equal demand for our manufactures; but this will be compensated by our trade with others, who are in opposite circumstances, and who give to us a surplus in money. If our consumption be not greater than our productions; that <109> is, if we are an industrious people; the balance of our trade with all the world, taken complexly, whatever may be the case with particular nations, can never be against us; and, if we have commodities for which there is a general demand, we can seldom remain long without an opportunity of turning them into money.

The quantity of the current species upon the face of the globe is naturally, and without any artificial direction, adjusted to the extent of the circulation in each particular country; for its occasional scarcity, in any one quarter, would raise its value in that place, and make it constantly flow thither until the equilibrium should be restored.

Upon the whole, there is good reason to conclude, that the mercantile people are the best judges of their own interest; and that, by pursuing those lines of trade which they find most beneficial to themselves, they are likely to produce, in most cases, the greatest benefit to the public. The administrators of government can seldom, from their own knowledge, be sufficiently qualified to judge in matters of this kind; and <110> they are likely to be directed by persons who have an interest to mislead them. They have, therefore, frequently contributed more to hurt, than to improve the commercial machine, by their tampering; and their interpositions, besides loading the public with immediate expence, from the bounties bestowed upon the favourite branches of trade, have diverted the mercantile capitals of the nation into channels, very different from their natural course, in which they have been productive of less profit, than they would otherwise have yielded.

For inculcating this truth, and placing it in a great variety of lights, the world is much indebted to the philosophers of a neighbouring country;[2] and still more to the ingenious and profound author of "The Causes of the

2. The reference here is to France, most notably the work of the Physiocrats, a school of writers on political and economic subjects that flourished in the second half of the eighteenth century. They attacked the monopolies, exclusive corporations, vexatious taxes, and various other abuses which had grown up under the mercantile system. François Quesnay (1694–1774), physician to Mme de Pompadour and Louis XV, founded the school (1758).

Wealth of Nations"; by whom the subject is explained and illustrated in a manner that affords the fullest conviction. The universal approbation which this new doctrine has met with in the higher classes of mercantile people, in opposition to a rooted prejudice, connected with the <111> private interests of a numerous body of men, is, of itself, a decisive proof of the high advances of commercial improvement, and of the enlarged views of political economy, by which the present age has become so eminently distinguished.

The great extension of those means, which have been devised to promote and facilitate the circulation of commodities, affords another satisfactory illustration of the great extent, and the rapid encrease, of our commercial dealings.

The introduction of money was a necessary contrivance for producing an exchange between persons, who had no reciprocal demand for the goods of each other. By this expedient, any person, provided with a sufficient quantity of the current species, was in a condition to purchase from every one who had goods to dispose of. But when, in the progress of commerce, merchants came to be engaged in a multiplicity of transactions, the quantity of money which they were obliged, at all times, to keep in their possession, for satisfying their occasional demands, became proportionably <112> large; and the retaining so much dead stock, which yielded no profit, was an inconvenience, from which, we may easily suppose, they endeavoured, by every possible means, to relieve themselves. If they had the reputation of wealth, they might sometimes persuade a creditor to accept of their personal obligation in place of immediate payment; and their promissory note, properly authenticated, might even be regarded as nearly equivalent to ready money, and might therefore pass from hand to hand in the purchase of goods. From an extension of this practice proceeded the establishment of *banks,* or mercantile companies, possessed of sufficient wealth to ensure their good credit, who made it a regular business, upon receiving an equivalent, to issue promissory notes payable on demand; and even, upon a suitable premium, to advance money upon the personal obligation of others. These institutions were introduced into the mercantile countries of Europe, from the interposition of public authority, by which the members of each banking company were incorporated, and exempted from being <113> liable to their creditors beyond the extent of a certain specified capital. Upon this footing, the Bank of England was erected, soon after the accession of William III.; and at a subsequent period, two smaller companies, of a similar nature, were established in the northern part of the island.[3] But the advantages derived from this branch of trade, have since produced innumerable private adventurers over the country, who, without any aid from government, and consequently becoming liable to the amount of their whole fortunes, have engaged in the banking business, and appear to have pushed all its branches to their utmost extent. By the assistance of these banks, whether public or private, the nation has obtained a variety of resources for procuring money upon a sudden demand, and for turning it to an immediate account as soon as the demand is over; so that the quantity of current specie, which must ever lie unemployed in the hands of an individual, has been rendered more and more insignificant.

The same effect has flowed indirectly from the establishment of the funds belong-<114>ing to some great mercantile corporations, and of those created by the public for paying the interest of the national debt; the nature of which I shall have occasion hereafter to consider. As every one is permitted to buy or sell, at his conveniency, greater or smaller shares in those funds, he has thus the command of money for any lucrative undertaking, and may replace it with profit whenever it ceases to be better employed.

In these progressive improvements of our commercial policy, without entering farther into particulars, we cannot fail to recognize the appearances of a nation which has long enjoyed all the advantages of high prosperity in trade and manufactures; and it remains to enquire, how far the uninterrupted possession, and daily encrease of these blessings, have contributed to inspire the people with higher notions of liberty, and more ardent zeal in defence of their privileges.

The spirit of liberty appears, in commercial countries, to depend chiefly upon two circumstances: first, the condition of the people relative to the distribution of pro-<115>perty, and the means of subsistence; secondly, the facility with which the several members of society are enabled to associate and to act in concert with one another.

1. With respect to the former circumstance, the whole property of such a country, and the subsistence of all the inhabitants, may, according to the

3. The national reserve bank was founded in 1694 to support the public debt in the expensive wars of William III. Its notes began to circulate as tender in the eighteenth century. The Bank of Scotland was established in 1695, followed by the Royal Bank of Scotland in 1727.

phraseology of late writers upon political economy, be derived from three different sources; from the rent of land or water; from the profits of stock or capital; and from the wages of labour: and, in conformity to this arrangement, the inhabitants may be divided into landlords, capitalists, and labourers.

Of labourers, who form the lowest class, the situation and way of life must, in every country, render them in some degree dependent upon the person who gives them employment. Having little or no property, and earning a bare subsistence by their daily labour, they are placed in a state of inferiority which commonly disposes them to feel some respect for their master; they have an interest to avoid any difference with him; and in the execution of their work, <116> being constantly required to follow his directions, they are apt, in some degree, to acquire habits of submission to his will.

The relative condition of the labouring people, however, must vary considerably according to the differences which occur in the general state of society. In rude countries, even where domestic slavery is excluded, the chief labourers are either menial servants, or such as cultivate the ground; and, as they generally continue for life in the service of the same person, his influence over them is naturally very great. But, in commercial countries, the bond of union between the workmen and their employer is gradually loosened. There, the most numerous class of labourers are those employed in subserviency to trade or manufactures; and they are so indiscriminately engaged in the service of different persons, that they feel but little the loss of a particular master, with whom they have formed but a slight connection. When a country, at the same time, is rapidly advancing in trade, the demand for labourers is proportionably great; their wages are continually <117> rising; instead of soliciting employment, they are courted to accept of it; and they enjoy a degree of affluence and of importance, which is frequently productive of insolence and licentiousness.

That the labouring people in Britain have, for some time, been raised to this enviable situation, is evident from a variety of circumstances; from the high price of labour, and the difficulty of procuring workmen; from the absurd attempts of the legislature to regulate their wages, and to prevent them from deserting particular employments; from the zeal displayed by the lower orders in the vindication of their political, as well as of their private rights; and, above all, from the jealousy and alarm with which this disposition has, of late, so universally impressed their superiors.

When a labourer has acquired so much property as will enable him, without wages, to subsist until he has manufactured a particular commodity, he may then gain, upon the sale of it, a profit over and above the ordinary value of his labour. In proportion to the enlargement of his capital, his <118> productions, by the employment of subordinate hands will be multiplied, and his profits, of course, extended. Thus, according as the business of producing and disposing of commodities becomes more extensive and complicated, it is gradually subdivided into various departments, and gives rise to the several classes, of manufacturers, tradesmen, and merchants.

To discover the different sources of mercantile profit, we may distinguish two sorts of stock, or capital, belonging to a manufacturer or merchant; the *circulating,* and the *permanent* stock; the former comprehending the goods which he brings to the market; the latter, the houses, the machinery, and the various accommodations which he requires for the manufacture or sale of his goods.

To a manufacturer, the circulating stock affords a profit, by enabling him to unite many different branches of labour upon the same commodity, and, consequently, to save that expence of carriage, which would be incurred if those branches were separately performed in different places, and the <119> amount afterwards collected. If, for example, the several operations requisite in the woollen manufacture were to be performed separately, by workmen at a distance from each other, there would be an expence of carriage necessary to unite the effect of their several productions, which is totally avoided by collecting the different hands in the same neighbourhood, and accumulating their labour upon the same commodity. The manufacturer, therefore, draws a return for his capital, inasmuch as it has been the means of shortening the labour, and consequently of diminishing the expence of his manufacture.

It is unnecessary to observe, that by the saving of carriage there is also a saving of *time,* which is no less valuable; and the manufacturer obtains an additional profit, according as, with the same labour, he can sooner bring his goods to market.

As by collecting many hands in the same manufacture, the undertaker saves an actual expence, he also obtains a direct advantage by having it in his power to divide minutely, the several branches of labour among different <120> workmen, so that each acquires more skill and dexterity in the single branch allotted to him, and is prevented from idling, and losing time, as commonly happens, in passing from one branch to another. The prodigious effect of this division of labour, by increasing the quantity of work done in a given time, as well as by improving its quality, becomes also, like every other circumstance tending to facilitate labour, a separate source of profit to the manufacturer.*

To the merchant, or tradesman, the circulating stock is the source of profit <121> upon similar principles. It enables him to save the purchasers from the trouble and expence of bespeaking the goods before they stand in need of them, and of providing themselves at once with more than they immediately want; while the quantity which he has collected, and the number of his customers, ensure to him the disposal of the whole within a reasonable time. The larger the stock of the merchant, provided it does not exceed the general demand, the saving which he thus procures to his customers, without loss to himself, will be the more complete and certain.

With respect to *permanent* mercantile stock, consisting of the machinery, the houses, and the various accommodations employed by manufacturers or traders, in the course of their business, it is intended for the sole purpose of assisting and promoting the operations upon *circulating* stock; and having therefore, still further a tendency to shorten and facilitate labour, it must, upon that account, be also productive of a suitable profit. <122>

It should seem, therefore, an evident conclusion from these observations, that the benefit resulting from every species of trade or manufacture, is ultimately derived from *labour;* and that the profit arising from every branch of mercantile stock, whether permanent or circulating, is derived from its enabling the merchant, or manufacturer, to produce the same effect with less labour, and consequently with less expence than would otherwise have been required.

It merits attention, however, that the whole revenue drawn by a merchant, or manufacturer, though in a loose way commonly called his profit, does not

* Perhaps part of the profit of a manufacturer may also be drawn from the workman, who, however, will have a full equivalent for what he thus resigns. By working to a master he is sure of constant employment, is saved the trouble of seeking out those who may have occasion for his labour, and avoids the anxiety arising from the danger of being thrown occasionally idle. In return for these advantages, he willingly relinquishes to his master some part of what he can earn while employed. Accordingly in Scotland, where it is still very common for good housewives to manufacture linens for the use of their families, the weavers whom they employ, usually demand wages somewhat higher than the ordinary rates paid by the manufacturers.

with propriety come under this description. Besides the value of his capital, from its effect in shortening, facilitating, and superseding labour, he draws an adequate compensation for his own efforts in putting that capital in motion, for his attention and skill in conducting the several parts of the business, and for the inconvenience he may sustain in waiting a distant, and in some degree, an uncertain return. The former is properly <123> the *rent* of capital: the latter may be called the *wages* of mercantile exertion. These two branches of revenue are frequently separated, inasmuch as the merchant, or manufacturer, borrows a part of the capital with which he trades, and pays for it a regular *interest,* or as the acting partners of the commercial company draw salaries for their personal attendance.

Those who obtain a revenue from capital, therefore, are either monied men who live upon the interest of their money, or mercantile adventurers, who draw, either a profit from their own capital, or a sort of wages from trading with the capital of others. Both of these orders are much more independent in their circumstances than the common labourer: but the former according to the extent of his revenue, is more independent than the latter. The mercantile adventurer draws his revenue from a multiplicity of customers, with whom he is commonly upon equal terms of affluence, and to each of whom he is but little obliged; but the monied man lives entirely upon his <124> property, and is obliged to nobody for any part of his maintenance.

When we consider the changes in this respect, which have taken place in Britain since the period of the revolution; in what proportion both of these orders of capitalists have been multiplied; when we observe the number of common labourers who are daily converted into artificers, frequently vending their own productions; what crowds of people are continually rising from the lower ranks, and disposed of in the various branches of trade; how many have acquired, and how many more are in the high road of acquiring opulent fortunes; how universally mutual emulation, and mutual intercourse, have diffused habits of industry, have banished idleness, which is the parent of indigence, and have put it into the power of almost every individual, by the exertion of his own talents, to earn a comfortable subsistence; when, I say, we attend to the extent of these improvements, which affect the whole mercantile part of the inhabitants, we cannot entertain a doubt of their powerful <125> efficacy to propagate corresponding sentiments, of personal independence, and to instil higher notions of general liberty.

The observations which have been made, with respect to the trader and capitalist, are, in a great measure, applicable to the cultivator and proprietor of land. The farmer, who by his labour and skill, and by the employment of stock, draws a revenue from the cultivation of land, is in circumstances similar to those of the manufacturer. From his cattle, from his tools and instruments of husbandry, and from the money expended in the management of his farm, he derives a profit suitable to their effect, in shortening and facilitating his labour; and the ground itself may be regarded as a part of his permanent stock, contributing, like a loom, or other piece of machinery, to the result of his operations. But as the ground has greater stability, as it appears of much greater importance than all the remaining stock of the farmer, and as in many cases it belongs to a different person, the profit arising from it, which is regularly payable to the landlord, has been commonly <126> distinguished under the name of *rent,* while that which arises from the other part of agricultural stock, is viewed in the same light with mercantile profit. There is, however, no essential difference between those two branches of revenue; they both depend upon the same principles, and bear a regular proportion to the value of the respective funds from which they are drawn.

There is, indeed, one particular in which they require to be distinguished; I mean, with respect to the degree of independence which, in different situations, they bestow upon the possessor. In poor countries, where agriculture is in a low state, the great value of land, compared with the other parts of agricultural stock, renders the employment of the latter in a great measure subordinate to that of the former; and reduces the people who cultivate the ground to be a sort of servants or dependents of the proprietor. But the improvement of husbandry gives more dignity to this useful profession, and raises the condition of those who exercise it. As the operations of the <127> farmer become extensive, his capital must be enlarged; and as he lays out greater expence in improvement, he must obtain a longer lease to afford him the prospect of a return from the lands. He is thus totally emancipated from his former dependence; becomes more enterprising in proportion to his opulence; and upon the expiration of his lease, he finds that it is not more his object to obtain a good farm, than it is the interest of every landlord to obtain a good tenant. This has, for some time, been the general condition of the farmers in England; and to this independent state they are quickly advancing in the more improvable parts of Scotland.

Such are the changes which, in the course of the present century, have taken place, and are still rapidly advancing in Britain, with relation to the different branches of revenue, arising from the wages of labour, and from the employment of stock, either in trade, or in the cultivation of the earth; and with relation to the condition of the respective orders of men by whom those branches of revenue are enjoyed. <128> The tendency of improvement in all the arts of life, and in every trade or profession, has been uniformly the same; to enable mankind more easily to gain a livelihood by the exercise of their talents, without being subject to the caprice, or caring for the displeasure of others; that is, to render the lower classes of the people less dependent upon their superiors.

It must not, however, be imagined, that this independent situation of mankind, with respect to the means of subsistence, will always prevent such inequalities of fortune, as may create in some of the members of society an influence over others. The unequal distribution of property, is a necessary consequence of the different degrees of application or abilities, co-operating with numberless accidents, which retard or promote the pecuniary pursuits of individuals; and the poor will often find their account in courting the favour of the rich. Any attempt, upon the part of the public, to limit the free accumulation of wealth, would be fatal to that industry or exertion which is the foundation of national pros-<129>perity. Sound policy requires that every man should feel a continual spur to his activity from the prospect of enjoying at pleasure, and disposing of the fruits of his labour. But the circumstances of a country, highly advanced in commerce and manufactures, are such as, naturally, and without any interposition of government, have a tendency to moderate those great differences of fortune, which, in a rude age, are usually the source of tyranny and oppression.[4] Where a multitude of people are engaged in lucrative trades and professions, it must commonly happen that a number of competitors, placed in similar circumstances, will meet with nearly equal success; and that their several acquisitions will counterbalance each other, so as to prevent, in any one quarter, the growth of an influence that might be dangerous to the community. The same spirit, being universally, and in some measure equally diffused, and being subject to no obstruction, either from the state of society, or from the injudicious regu-

4. "It is to be observed," said Smith, "that this inequality of fortune in a nation of shepherds occasioned greater influence than in any period after that. Even at present, a man may spend a great estate and yet acquire no dependents. Arts and manufactures are increased by it, but it may make very few persons dependent. In a nation of shepherds it is quite otherwise." *LJ*, 405.

lations of the public, is likely to form such a gradation of opulence, as leaving no <130> chasm from the top to the bottom of the scale, will occasion a continual approximation of the different ranks, and will frequently enable the inferior orders to press upon the superior. "The toe of the peasant comes so near the heel of the courtier, that it galls his kibe."

The effect of superiority in wealth, as I had occasion to shew in a former part of this discourse, is further diminished in commercial countries, by the frequent alienation of estates. As persons of low rank are incited by their situation to better their circumstances, and commonly acquire such habits of industry and frugality, as enable them to accumulate; those who are born to great fortunes, are apt, on the other hand, to become idle and dissipated, and living in all the expence which opulence renders fashionable, are frequently tempted to squander their estates. Hence, opulent families are quickly reduced to indigence; and their place is supplied by professional people from the lower orders; who, by the purchase of land, endeavour to procure that distinction which was the end of their <131> labours. The descendants of these upstarts, in a generation or two, usually go the same round of luxury and extravagance, and finally experience the same reverse of fortune. Property is thus commonly subjected to a constant rotation, which prevents it from conferring upon the owner the habitual respect and consideration, derived from a long continued intercourse between the poor and the rich.

To preserve old families from this destruction became a great object in Britain, and in the other countries of Europe, as soon as commerce began to threaten the dissolution of estates. Entails were invented to arrest and secure the estate; titles of nobility, to preserve the personal dignity of the possessor. But these contrivances were of little avail. When such restrictions became inconsistent with the manners of the age, they could no longer be enforced. In England the fetters of an entail were, by the ingenuity of lawyers, gradually lightened, and at length easily struck off; though in Scotland, a country in which aristocratic government was more firmly rooted, they still remain in full force. <132> The rank of nobility being connected with political distinction, has hitherto maintained its ground, and continues to be the object of ambition; but when separated from the estate which gave it support, so far from being of service to the owner, it operates as an exclusion from almost all the paths of industry, and seems to confer a mock-dignity upon real and hopeless indigence and servility.

The opulence of Britain, in the present century, it is evident, has greatly surpassed that of the preceding ages, in facilitating to the poor the means of accumulation, in multiplying to the rich those artificial wants which produce a rapid circulation of estates, and consequently, in subverting that permanent state of property which is the foundation of all hereditary influence.[5]

2. As the advancement of commerce and manufactures in Britain, has produced a state of property highly favourable to liberty, so it has contributed to collect and arrange the inhabitants in a manner which enables them, with great facility to combine in asserting their privileges. <133>

When government has been so far established as to maintain the general tranquillity, and to introduce peaceable manners; and when a set of magistrates, and rulers, are invested with an authority, confirmed by ancient usage, and supported, perhaps, by an armed force, it cannot be expected that the people, single and unconnected, will be able to resist the oppression of their governors: and their power of combining for this purpose, must depend very much upon their peculiar circumstances. In small states, consisting merely of a capital city, with a narrow adjacent country, like those of ancient Greece and Rome, the inhabitants were necessarily led to an intimate union and correspondence; which appears to have been the chief cause of their being able, at an early period, to expel their petty princes, and establish a popular government. But in large kingdoms, the people being dispersed over a wide country, have seldom been capable of such vigorous exertions. Living in petty villages, at a distance from one another, and having very imperfect means of communication, they are often <134> but little affected by the hardships which many of their countrymen may sustain from the tyranny of government; and a rebellion may be quelled in one quarter before it has time to break out in another. The efforts, which are occasionally made, in different parts of the country, to limit the prerogative, being without union or concert, are commonly unsuccessful; and therefore, instead of producing the effect intended, usually terminate in the exultation of the crown. The unlucky insurgents are obliged to make their peace with the sovereign, by submitting to new encroachments; and to wipe off their former demerits by assisting to reduce their fellow-citizens to obedience. To this want of concert in the members of a wide country, we may ascribe the rise of the greater

5. Both Hume and Smith drew upon similar explanations to explain how the taste for luxury among the aristocracy led to the decline of nobiliar power in the later Middle Ages.

part of rude monarchies; and more especially those of the great Asiatic nations.

From the progress, however, of trade and manufactures, the state of a country, in this respect, is gradually changed. As the inhabitants multiply from the facility of procuring subsistence, they are collected in <135> large bodies for the convenient exercise of their employments. Villages are enlarged into towns; and these are often swelled into populous cities. In all those places of resort, there arises large bands of labourers or artificers, who, by following the same employment, and by constant intercourse, are enabled, with great rapidity, to communicate all their sentiments and passions. Among these there spring up leaders, who give a tone and direction to their companions. The strong encourage the feeble; the bold animate the timid; the resolute confirm the wavering; and the movements of the whole mass proceed with the uniformity of a machine, and with a force that is often irresistible.

In this situation, a great proportion of the people are easily roused by every popular discontent, and can unite with no less facility in demanding a redress of grievances. The least ground of complaint, in a town, becomes the occasion of a riot; and the flames of sedition, spreading from one city to another, are blown up into a general insurrection.

Neither does this union arise merely from local situations; nor is it confined to the <136> lower class of those who are subservient to commerce and manufactures. By a constant attention to professional objects, the superior orders of mercantile people become quick-sighted in discerning their common interest, and, at all times, indefatigable in pursuing it. While the farmer, employed in the separate cultivation of his land, considers only his own individual profit; while the landed gentleman seeks only to procure a revenue sufficient for the supply of his wants, and is often unmindful of his own interest as well as of every other; the merchant, though he never overlooks his private advantage, is accustomed to connect his own gain with that of his brethren, and, is therefore, always ready to join with those of the same profession, in soliciting the aid of government, and in promoting general measures for the benefit of their trade.

The prevalence of this great mercantile association in Britain, has, in the course of the present century, become gradually more and more conspicuous. The clamour and tumultuary proceedings of the populace in the great towns are capable of penetrating <137> the inmost recesses of administration, of intimidating the boldest minister, and of displacing the most presumptuous favourite of the back-stairs. The voice of the mercantile interest, never fails to command the attention of government, and when firm and unanimous, is even able to controul and direct the deliberations of the national councils. The methods which are sometimes practised by ministry to divide this mercantile interest, and to divert its opposition to the measures of the crown, will fall more properly to be considered hereafter.

So much with regard to the progress of trade and manufactures in Britain, since the period of the revolution, and its consequences in rendering the people opulent, as well as independent in their circumstances. I shall now proceed to examine the tendency of this independence and opulence, to promote the cultivation of the liberal arts and sciences, to extend knowledge and literature over the great body of a people, and to introduce opinions and sentiments which may affect the nature of government. <138>

CHAPTER IV

How far the Advancement of Commerce and Manufactures has contributed to the Extension and Diffusion of Knowledge and Literature.

It is natural to suppose that a proficiency in those practical arts, which multiply the necessaries and conveniencies of life will produce corresponding advances in general knowledge, and in the capacity of exercising the intellectual powers. Every practical art proceeds upon certain principles, discovered by experience and observation; and in the process of different arts there are numberless analogies and resemblances, which give rise to various deductions and conclusions, and thus, by a chain of reasoning, lead to new inventions and discoveries. The inexhaustible varieties of analogy and resemblance which occur in the objects around us, whether of art or nature, constitute the great <139> fund of general knowledge; and the faculty of discovering, and of arranging them, is justly regarded as the chief prerogative of the human understanding.

As the great wealth introduced by commerce and manufactures is, at the same time, very unequally divided, there springs up, of course, a numerous class of people, who, being born to affluent fortunes, are exempted from bodily labour, and who choosing to throw aside, in a great measure, the cares of business, indulge themselves in what is called pleasure. Being often destitute of that occupation which is necessary to preserve a relish for enjoyment, and without which the mind sinks into listless apathy and dejection. They seek amusement by artificial modes of occupying their imagination, in sports and diversions, in the collection and embellishment of those objects which are agreeable to the senses, and in those imitations and representations of nature which are calculated to excite admiration, wonder and surprise.[1] Hence the introduction and improvement of the elegant and fine arts, which entertain us by the exhibition of what is grand, new <140> or beautiful, and which afford a delightful exercise to our taste, or a pleasing agitation of our passions.

The pursuits of mankind, however, are not limited to the objects of the common and mechanical, or of the elegant and fine arts. The first aim of every people is to procure subsistence; their next is to defend and secure their acquisitions. Men who live in the same society, or who have any intercourse with one another, are often linked together by the ties of sympathy and affection; as, on the other hand, they are apt, from opposite interests and passions, to dispute and quarrel, and to commit mutual injuries. From these different situations, they become sensible of the duties they owe to each other, and of the rights which belong to them in their various relations and capacities. A system of rules for enforcing those rights is gradually introduced, and the sciences of morality, of law, and of government, being more and more cultivated, give rise to a prodigious diversity of speculations and opinions. From the belief and the sentiments of mankind, in matters of <141> religion, there arises another science, not less intricate than the former, and which has proved even more fertile in disquisition and controversy. The remarkable appearances in the material world, the great changes in nature, the qualities and uses of the several productions of the earth; all these become in like manner, the subjects of attention and inquiry, and afford copious sources of knowledge and speculation.

While arts and sciences are thus advancing, they are gradually separated into different branches, each of which occupies the attention, and becomes the peculiar province of some individuals. The great branches of mechanical labour afford occupation to separate classes of workmen and artificers, who gain a livelihood by their peculiar employments; and according as every species of labour becomes more complicated, the separate classes of the people who derive a maintenance from it, are further subdivided. A similar division follows of course in those elegant and fine arts which become the subject of lucrative employments; as in painting, sculpture, and music. <142> Even in

1. Millar echoes the opening of Smith's essay "The History of Astronomy," where admiration, wonder, and surprise are presented as general categories of human response to intellectual challenge. See Smith, *Essays on Philosophical Subjects,* ed. W. P. D. Wightman and J. C. Bryce (Indianapolis: Liberty Fund, 1982), 33–34.

the cultivation of the sciences, the circumstances of society have commonly occasioned a separation of certain learned professions; and directed, in some measure, the attention of numerous classes of men to particular departments of knowledge. The diseases and accidents by which health is impaired have given rise to the medical profession, with its respective divisions, connected with various branches of natural science. The disputes and quarrels among mankind, with the modes which have been found expedient for settling their contentions without having recourse to arms, the execution of the various deeds requisite for the security and transmission of property, and the direction of those observances and forms which, in most countries, are established for ascertaining and confirming pecuniary transactions; these branches of business have given employment to attornies and lawyers, whose profession leads them to become acquainted with the rules of justice, and with the whole system of legal proceedings. From the belief of a Deity, and the corresponding sentiments which it inspires, has <143> arisen the profession of the clergy; whose business it is to preside over the public acts of religious worship, and who are naturally entrusted with the office of instructing the people in the great duties of morality.

But even in those cases where particular sciences are not immediately connected with any profession, the progress of study and speculation will dispose individuals, according to their peculiar talents or disposition, to give different directions to their inquiries, and to separate the objects of their speculative pursuits.

There can be no doubt that this division in the labours, both of art and of science, is calculated for promoting their improvement.[2] From the limited powers both of the mind and the body, the exertions of an individual are likely to be more vigorous and successful when confined to a particular channel, than when diffused over a boundless expanse. The athlete who limited his application to one of the gymnastic exercises, was commonly enabled to practise it with <144> more dexterity than he who studied to become a proficient in them all.

But though the separation of different trades and professions, together with the consequent division of labour and application in the exercise of them, has a tendency to improve every art or science, it has frequently an

2. Smith remarks that the sciences too benefit from the division of labor. See *WN*, bk. 1, chap. 1, 21.

opposite effect upon the personal qualities of those individuals who are engaged in such employments. In the sciences, indeed, and even in the liberal arts, the application of those who follow particular professions can seldom be so much limited as to prove destructive to general knowledge. In all liberal occupations or scientific professions, there are certain principles to be studied by every person engaged in the practice; principles which admit of an extensive application to a variety of objects, and which, in many cases, cannot be properly applied without exercising the united powers of imagination and judgment. The practitioner, therefore, who is in such cases, engrossed by the objects of his profession, may have an air of pedantry to those who <145> are occupied in different pursuits, but can seldom with justice be regarded as destitute of knowledge or of intellectual exertion. But the mechanical arts admit of such minute divisions of labour, that the workmen belonging to a manufacture are each of them employed, for the most part, in a single manual operation, and have no concern in the result of their several productions. It is hardly possible that these mechanics should acquire extensive information or intelligence. In proportion as the operation which they perform is narrow, it will supply them with few ideas; and according as the necessity of obtaining a livelihood obliges them to double their industry, they have the less opportunity or leisure to procure the means of observation, or to find topics of reflection from other quarters. As their employment requires constant attention to an object which can afford no variety of occupation to their minds, they are apt to acquire an habitual vacancy of thought, unenlivened by any prospects, but such as are derived from the future wages of their labour, or from the <146> grateful returns of bodily repose and sleep. They become, like machines, actuated by a regular weight, and performing certain movements with great celerity and exactness, but of small compass, and unfitted for any other use. In the intervals of their work, they can draw but little improvement from the society of companions, bred to similar employments, with whom, if they have much intercourse, they are most likely to seek amusement in drinking and dissipation.

It should seem, therefore, that in countries highly advanced in commerce and manufactures, the abilities and character of the labouring people, who form the great body of a nation, are liable to be affected by circumstances of an opposite nature. Their continual attention to the objects of their profession, together with the narrowness of those objects, has a powerful tendency to render them ignorant and stupid. But the progress of science and literature and of the liberal arts, among the higher classes, must on the other hand contribute to enlighten the common people, and to spread a degree of the same improvements over the whole <147> community. There is in all mankind a disposition to admire and to imitate their superiors; and the fashions, opinions, and ways of thinking, adopted by men of high rank, are apt to descend very quickly to persons of inferior station. Whenever any branch of learning becomes extensively useful, those who have a common interest in attaining it, are enabled, by joining together, to hire an instructor at an expence moderate to individuals. Schools and seminaries of education are thus introduced, and they are sometimes promoted by the well-meant encouragement and protection of the public. By their industry, different sorts of instruction are brought into a common market, are gradually cheapened by mutual competition, and, being more and more accommodated to the demands of society, become, as far as it is necessary, accessible even to the poor. Thus, in commercial countries, the important accomplishments of reading, writing, and accounting, are usually communicated at such easy rates, as to be within the reach of the lower orders. <148>

The publication of books affords another medium for the circulation of knowledge, the benefit of which must extend, in some degree, to every member of the community. When, among persons in affluent circumstances, who are exempted from bodily labour, reading becomes a common amusement, it is to be expected that their example in this, as in other things, will have an influence upon their inferiors; and, although the publications likely to fall into the hands of the common people will be such as are suited to their taste, and therefore, probably, not the best calculated for conveying instruction, they cannot fail to enlarge the imagination of the readers beyond mere professional objects, and even to communicate, perhaps, something of the opinions which prevail among the higher classes, upon the great popular topics of religion, morality, and government.

The effect of the cultivation proceeding from these different sources, is probably as remarkable at present, in Great Britain, as it has ever been in any commercial country, ancient or modern; but whether, upon the <149> whole, the artificial education thus communicated to the lower orders of the people, be sufficient to counterbalance the disadvantages of their natural situation, there may be good reason to doubt.

In ruder and more simple times, before labour is much subdivided, the whole stock of knowledge existing in a country will be scanty, but it will be more equally diffused over the different ranks, and each individual of the lower orders will have nearly the same opportunities and motives with his superiors, for exerting the different powers of his mind. The rude mechanic, residing in a small town, is forced to bestow his attention, successively, on many objects very different from each other. Not finding constant employment in one branch of manufacture, he exercises several, and furnishes himself with many of the tools requisite for each; he probably makes part of his own clothes, assists in building his own house and those of his neighbours, and cultivates, or directs his wife and children in cultivating, a small patch of ground, on which he raises part of his provisions. As he must <150> buy the materials, and sell or barter the produce of his labour, he is also, in some respects, a merchant; and, in this capacity, he is led to the observation of character, as well as to some speculation respecting the most advantageous times and places, for making his little bargains. When we add, that he is likewise trained to arms, for the purpose of assisting in defending the town of which he is a citizen, we must see that his situation, and consequently, his character, will be very different from that of a mechanic, in a more advanced society.

In this manner, all the members of a rude nation, being forced to exercise a great number of unconnected professions, and individually to provide for themselves, what each stands in need of, their attention is directed to a variety of objects; and their knowledge is extended in proportion. No man relies upon the exertions of his neighbour; but each employs, for the relief of his wants, or in defence of what belongs to him, either the strength of his body or the ingenuity of his mind, all the talents which he has been able to acquire, all the faculties <151> with which nature has endowed him. By experience, therefore, he learns to conduct himself in many different situations, to guard against the dangers to which he is exposed, and to extricate himself from the difficulties and embarrassments in which he may be involved. Unlike the mechanics of a commercial nation, who have each permitted all their talents, except in single and peculiar branches, to lie dormant and useless; but who combine, like the wheels of a machine, in producing a complicated system of operations, the inhabitants of a rude country have separately preserved, and kept in action, all the original powers of man; but in their united capacity, and as members of a community, they have added very little to the independent efforts of every individual.

If we compare the mechanics of different commercial states, we shall probably find that the respective degrees of their knowledge and intellectual attainments correspond with the foregoing observation. In England, and in the other mercantile countries of Europe, it is believed, that, in pro-<152>portion to the advancement of manufactures, the common people have less information, and less curiosity upon general topics; less capacity, beyond the limits of their own employment, of entering into conversation, or of conducting, with propriety and dexterity, the petty transactions which accident may throw in their way.

This is perhaps the chief foundation of the common remark, which is made by the English, concerning the superior sagacity and cunning of their neighbours in the northern part of the island. As in Scotland commerce and manufactures have made less progress than in England, the great body of the people have not acquired the same habits of industry, nor are they so much engrossed by narrow mechanical employments. The man, therefore, has not been so entirely stripped of his mental powers, and converted into the mere instrument of labour. As the same individual often follows a greater variety of occupations, his understanding is more exercised, and his wits are more sharpened, by such different attentions. He is more capable of turning his hand to all <153> kinds of work, but he is much less a proficient in any. In the lower orders of society, where there are fewer restraints from education, it may be expected, that, in proportion as the people are more intelligent and quick-sighted, they will be more apt, in their mutual intercourse, to have their private interest in view, as well as to be more artful and subtle in pursuing it.*

Even in the same country, there is a sensible difference between different professions; and, according as every separate employment gives rise to a greater subdivision of workmen and artificers, it has a greater tendency to withdraw from them the means of intellectual improvement. The business of agriculture, for example, is less capable of a minute subdivision of labour than the greater part of mechanical employments. The same workman has often occasion to plough, <154> to sow, and to reap; to cultivate the ground for different purposes, and to prepare its various productions for the market.

* The inhabitants of the southern counties in Scotland have applied the same remark to those parts of the country which are still further behind in commercial improvements; and they have introduced a proverbial expression to that purpose: they say, "a person is too far north, that we should venture to have dealings with him."

He is obliged alternately to handle very opposite tools and instruments; to repair, and even sometimes, to make them for his own use; and always to accommodate the different parts of his labour to the change of the seasons, and to the variations of the weather. He is employed in the management and rearing of cattle, becomes frequently a grazier and a corn-merchant, and is unavoidably initiated in the mysteries of the horse-jockey. What an extent of knowledge, therefore, must he possess! What a diversity of talents must he exercise, in comparison with the mechanic, who employs his whole labour in sharpening the point, or in putting on the head of a pin![3] How different the education of those two persons! The pin-maker, who commonly lives in a town, will have more of the fashionable improvements of society than the peasant; he will undoubtedly be better dressed; he will, in all probability, have more book-learning, as well as less coarseness in the <155> tone of his voice, and less uncouthness in his appearance and deportment. Should they both be enamoured of the same female, it is natural to suppose, that he would make the better figure in the eyes of his mistress, and that he would be most likely to carry the prize. But in a bargain, he would, assuredly, be no match for his rival. He would be greatly inferior in real intelligence and acuteness; much less qualified to converse with his superiors, to take advantage of their foibles, to give a plausible account of his measures, or to adapt his behaviour to any peculiar and unexpected emergency.

The circumstance now mentioned affords a view not very pleasant in the history of human society. It were to be wished that wealth and knowledge should go hand in hand, and that the acquisition of the former should lead to the possession of the latter. Considering the state of nations at large, it will, perhaps, be found that opulence and intellectual improvements are pretty well balanced, and that the same progress in commerce and manufactures which occa-<156>sions an encrease of the one, creates a proportional accession of the other. But, among individuals, this distribution of things is far from being so uniformly established; and, in the lower orders of the people, it appears to be completely reversed. The class of mechanics and labourers, by far the most numerous in a commercial nation, are apt, according as they attain more affluent and independent circumstances, to be

3. Millar makes use of Smith's famous analysis (itself reflective of a similar discussion in the *Encyclopedie,* Paris, 1751–80) of the division of labor in pin making. See *WN,* bk. 1, chap. 1, 14.

more withdrawn and debarred from extensive information; and are likely, in proportion as the rest of the community advance in knowledge and literature, to be involved in a thicker cloud of ignorance and prejudice. Is there not reason to apprehend, that the common people, instead of sharing the advantages of national prosperity, are thus in danger of losing their importance, of becoming the dupes of their superiors, and of being degraded from the rank which they held in the scale of society?

The separation of a whole people into two great classes, of which the one was distinguished by knowledge and intelligence, <157> the other by the opposite qualities, occurred very remarkably over a great part of Europe, in what are called the dark-ages. A very numerous clergy, who had engrossed all the learning of the times, and whose understandings were whetted by an interested and incessant activity, formed the one class. The laiety, comprehending the military people, continually engaged in war and depredation, and the peasantry, reduced to the state of villainage, both equally sunk in ignorance and superstition, composed the other. In consequence of this unfortunate arrangement, the ministers of a religion which taught men to renounce all considerations of worldly interest, taking advantage of their superior talents, and uniting in a system of deep-laid fraud and deception, persuaded their simple flock to resign so great a proportion of their possessions, and to submit to a series of such extensive encroachments, as at length established an ecclesiastical tyranny, which the efforts of more than two centuries of diffusive science and philosophy, have hardly been able to overturn. <158>

But although commerce and manufactures, have, in like manner, a tendency to form two distinct and separate classes of the learned and the ignorant, there is no reason to suspect that the former will abuse their superiority, by perverting it to the hurt or detriment of the latter. It is plainly the interest of the higher ranks to assist in cultivating the minds of the common people, and in restoring to them that knowledge which they may be said to have sacrificed to the general prosperity. A certain degree of information and intelligence, of acquaintance with the good or bad consequences which flow from different actions, and systems of behaviour, is necessary for suggesting proper motives to the practice of virtue, and for deterring mankind from the commission of crimes. It surely is of the utmost consequence to the public, that men in the lower orders should be sober and industrious, honest and faithful, affectionate and conscientious in their domestic concerns, peaceable in their manners, and averse from riot and disorder. But how can it be expected that they will persevere in the <159> practice of the various duties incumbent upon them, unless they have acquired habits of observation and reflection; unless they have been taught to set a high value upon character and reputation, and are able to discover that such a conduct is no less conducive to their own interest, than to that of others. To render them useful in their several relations, either as men or citizens, it is requisite that they should be in a condition to form a proper estimate of the objects which will promote their true happiness, to detect those false appearances which might frequently mislead them, and to guard against the errors in religion, morality, or government, which designing men may endeavour to propagate. The doctrine maintained by some politicians, that the ignorance of the labouring people is of advantage, by securing their patience and submission under the yoke which their unequal fortune has imposed upon them, is no less absurd, than it is revolting to all the feelings of humanity. The security derived from so mean a source is temporary and fallacious. It is liable to be undermined by the intrigues <160> of any plausible projector, or suddenly overthrown by the casual breath of popular opinion.

As the circumstances of commercial society are unfavourable to the mental improvements of the populace, it ought to be the great aim of the public to counteract, in this respect, the natural tendency of mechanical employments, and by the institution of schools and seminaries of education, to communicate, as far as possible, to the most useful, but humble class of citizens, that knowledge which their way of life has, in some degree, prevented them from acquiring. It is needless to observe how imperfect such institutions have hitherto been. The principal schools and colleges of Europe have been intended for the benefit merely of the higher orders; and even for this purpose, the greater part of them are not very judiciously modelled. But men of rank and fortune, and in general those who are exempted from bodily labour, have little occasion, in this respect, for the aid of the public, and perhaps would be better supplied, if left, in a great measure, to their own <161> exertions. The execution, however, of a liberal plan for the instruction of the lower orders, would be a valuable addition to those efforts, for the maintenance of the poor, for the relief of the diseased and infirm, and for the correction of the malefactor, which have proceeded from the humanity and public spirit of the present age. The parish schools in Scotland, are the only extensive provisions of that nature hitherto known in the island; and though it must be confessed that they are but ill calculated for the purposes of general education, the advantages resulting from them, even in their present state, have been distinctly felt, and very universally acknowledged. <162>

CHAPTER V

The Separation of the different Branches of Knowledge; and the Division of the liberal Arts and of the Sciences.

To explain the political changes, arising in commercial countries, from the progress of liberal education, it may be proper that we should examine more particularly the principal branches of knowledge which are likely to be cultivated, and to consider how far they will probably influence the opinions, the character, and manners of society.

Without entering into any speculation concerning the separate existence of spiritual and corporeal substances, we may observe, that all the objects of knowledge appear naturally to reduce themselves into two great classes; the one relating to the operations of thought and intelligence; the other, to the qualities and operations of inanimate matter. <163>

Men are disposed more easily and readily to survey the corporeal objects around them than to direct their attention to the operations of their own thinking faculties. The study of inanimate nature, or physics, was accordingly the first branch of philosophy, upon which the sages of antiquity employed themselves, and upon which, after the revival of letters, any considerable progress was made. It extended to the revolutions of the heavenly bodies, and to the most remarkable changes produced upon this earth; and it led to an examination of all such natural objects as are calculated to excite admiration or peculiar attention; of the winds and the tides, of thunder and lightening; of the properties of air, of water, of fire, of electricity, of magnetism.

While mere curiosity excited mankind to an examination of the most remarkable changes and appearances upon the great theatre of the universe, an application to the practical arts of life, called them to a more minute investigation of particular objects. The employment of curing diseases and wounds, produced an attentive enquiry into <164> the medical virtues of plants and minerals. The progress of manufactures led to the discovery of the mechanical powers, and to the combination of these in the construction of machines. The vain attempts of an ignorant age to accomplish the transmutation of metals, and the prolongation of life beyond its natural boundaries, gradually suggested many wonderful effects of heat and mixture, and at length produced the modern science of chemistry, which after incurring the ridicule that might be expected from its original pretensions, has made such progress in compounding and analysing the different parts of matter as to be rendered equally subservient to the improvement of the arts, and to the progress of agreeable speculation.

As the several bodies, which were thus to be examined in a variety of lights, became gradually more numerous and complex, the advantage of arranging and reducing them into classes, was proportionally more apparent, and gave rise to the science of natural history with its different subdivisions.

In the investigation of all the general laws of nature, and in many of the practical <165> arts, it is often requisite to enumerate and compare the number, the magnitude, and the figure of different bodies; whence the sciences of geometry and calculation, which contain the conclusions deducible from such relations, were introduced, and applied to all the branches of natural and mechanical knowledge.

Such are the principal branches of science relating to corporeal objects. The sciences founded upon the operation of our mental faculties may be divided into three great classes, in each of which there is room for many subdivisions.

The good or bad behaviour of those who live in society with us, their virtues and vices, cannot fail very early to excite our attention, and to interest our feelings; while we soon perceive that these persons exercise a similar judgment upon us; and this leads us to reflect upon our own conduct, and to regard our own actions in the light in which they appear to others. The speculations, together with the practical rules and observations, arising from this important view of <166> society, form the science of ethics, or morality.

To account for the uncommon events which occur in the affairs of this world, or for the revolutions which happen in the state of natural objects, mankind, in reasoning by analogy, from experience of the movements and changes produced by themselves, have had recourse, almost universally, to the agency of superior beings, possessed of intelligence and powers resembling, but superior in degree to the human. From a belief in the existence of such beings, and from the consideration of their peculiar relations to ourselves, together with that of their capacity or disposition of doing us good or harm, has arisen the science of religion, comprehending a system of religious opinions and duties.

Beside those emotions and passions which lay a foundation for morality and religion, and which appear essential to the comfortable existence of man in the social state, there are other mental operations which contribute to adorn and embellish human society by encreasing its elegant enjoyments. These <167> are the effects of what is beautiful or sublime, either in art or nature;[1] from which are derived the pleasures of taste, and what are called the fine arts. In all these arts, the practical rules give rise to an investigation of the principles upon which they are founded, and to a scientific deduction of the pleasures which are produced from their different sources, and thus the art and the science are made, in each case, to accompany one another; and the pleasure derived from the senses is heightened by an agreeable exercise of the understanding.

As, in these different views, the powers exerted by intelligent beings are highly interesting, as they are numerous, and wonderfully diversified, separated from each other by slender and almost imperceptible boundaries, and frequently combined in producing results which cannot easily be traced to their respective causes, it soon became an important object, to enumerate and to arrange the various operations of our thinking principle, to analyze them, to compare them together, and to discover their several relations. These investigations have been ap-<168>plied, though perhaps with little success, not only to man, but also to superior, and even to inferior orders of intelligence. Hence, the science of metaphysics, which may be regarded as auxiliary and subordinate to morality, religion, and the fine arts, and which, in the sciences founded upon the effects of our various mental exertions, appears to hold the same place that is held by natural history, in the sciences relating to corporeal objects.

With respect to the two great branches of science, of which an outline

1. One of the most important discussions of the sublime and beautiful in aesthetics was Edmund Burke's *Philosophical Inquiry into the Origin of Our Ideas of the Sublime and Beautiful* (1756).

has been suggested, it must be admitted that natural philosophy and the several sciences connected with it, have no immediate effect in extending or improving our ideas with relation to government; further than as all the different branches of knowledge co-operate in dispelling prejudices, in strengthening the intellectual powers, and in promoting an ardent zeal in the discovery of truth. It merits attention, however, that the advancement of natural knowledge, in all its branches, is highly subservient to the improvement of the common arts of life, and consequently, by promoting opu<169>lence and independence in the great body of a people, must contribute, in proportion, to inspire them with sentiments of liberty. To enable the inferior ranks to gain an easy subsistence by their labour is to lay the best foundation of popular government.

The exercise of the practical arts can hardly fail to suggest an investigation of the general principles upon which they are founded, and to produce discoveries which may be useful, in facilitating the different kinds of labour, or in penetrating the secret operations of nature. It seems reasonable to suppose, therefore, that such improvements as take their origin from the higher class of artizans, or from professional men who have had the advantage of a liberal education, would meet with the greatest encouragement in Britain, where manufactures have, for a century past, been more successfully cultivated than in any other part of Europe, and where, of course, a more extensive market has been provided for every profitable invention. Whether this market has been occasionally supplied by natives, or by foreigners, <170> invited into the country by the prospect of emolument, is of little importance.

Those improvements, on the contrary, which are the fruits of mere leisure and curiosity, and which afford occupation to the speculative philosopher, have perhaps, of late, been more successfully cultivated in some other European countries. The great genius of Newton,[2] indeed, about a century ago, produced in this island a rapid advancement of true philosophy; while the high reputation of Des Cartes,[3] in France, gave an unlucky bias to his coun-

2. Sir Isaac Newton (1642–1727): English scientist, mathematician, and chronologist. His principal works include the *Philosophiae Naturalis Principia Mathematica* (1687) and *Opticks* (1703).

3. René Descartes (1596–1650): French philosopher and mathematician. His works include *Discours de la méthode* (1637), *Meditationes de Prima Philosophia* (1641), and the *Principia Philosophiae* (1644).

trymen, and disposed them to adopt his erroneous and chimerical doctrines. But though natural philosophy was thus retarded, it came at length to be more cultivated in France, and in some other parts of Europe, than in Britain; because, from the despotical government in those countries, the inhabitants were, in some measure, debarred from the more generally interesting inquiries upon religion, morality, and politics, and were confined in their speculations, either to matters of taste, and abstracted speculation, or to those de-<171>pending on the nature and operations of corporeal objects. Their exertions, therefore, have been the more conspicuous in that particular sphere to which they were limited; and in mathematical learning, in the several branches of physics, in chemistry, and in natural history, it should seem that their superior proficiency can hardly be disputed.

It cannot, however, escape the observation of those who attend to the history of literature, that, in most countries, after philosophical researches have made a certain progress, they commonly verge more and more to the pursuits of natural knowledge. To be satisfied of this, we need only consult the memoirs of those literary societies, in the different parts of Europe, which have been lately published, as that species of philosophy excited the earliest attention of mankind, so it appears calculated to arrest the curiosity of the most numerous class, in those ages when learning has arrived at full maturity. In our inquiries concerning the faculties and operations of the human mind, it soon becomes difficult to add to the stock of knowledge already acquired, or to exhibit such <172> views and reasonings as will contain much novelty or entertainment. It even requires peculiar acuteness and discernment in treating of those intricate subjects, to attain clear and distinct conceptions of what is already known, and to explain, in a manner sufficiently intelligible, the opinions of preceding philosophers. But the study of external nature, at least in many of its branches, requires no more than common understanding, with an ardent curiosity and perseverance of application. Every man who with the power of divising new experiments can submit to the patient examination of the contents of a crucible; he who can observe the several parts of a plant and assign it its proper place in a general system of classification, or who having made new and accurate inquiries into the economy of animals, can faithfully report and clearly explain the result of his inquiries; every such person is capable of increasing our knowledge of nature, and of acquiring some degree of a literary reputation. We need not be surprised, therefore, that these branches of science, which are adapted to the capacity of the greatest num-<173>ber, and in which the labours of mankind are most likely to be requited with suitable proficiency and information, should be most universally pursued, and become the most popular.

In our present inquiry it would be improper to enter into any further detail concerning the divisions of natural knowledge, which are so remotely connected with the political state of the nation. But in exhibiting a view of the changes in the tide of popular opinions which have taken place during the present century, it seems requisite to examine more particularly the sciences which immediately relate to the faculties and operations of the mind, and to consider how far the progress of speculation, and discussion, in matters of morality, religion, or taste, have influenced the sentiments of the people with relation to government. <174>

CHAPTER VI

The Effects of Commerce and Manufactures, and of Opulence and Civilization, upon the Morals of a People.

That the dispositions and behaviour of man are liable to be influenced by the circumstances in which he is placed, and by his peculiar education and habits of life, is a proposition which few persons will be inclined to controvert. But how far this influence reaches, and what differences are to be found between the morals of rude and of civilized nations, it is not so easy to determine. The fact, I believe, has been seldom examined with that impartiality and deliberation which its importance requires. Moral and religious writers have usually thought proper to treat the subject in the style of satire and invective, and in declaiming against the vices of their own times, have been led to exalt the merit of distant <175> ages. A late celebrated author,* possessed of uncommon powers of eloquence, has gone so far as to maintain, first in a popular discourse, and afterwards in a long serious dissertation, that the rude and savage life is the parent of all the virtues, the vices of mankind being the proper and peculiar offspring of opulence and civilization.[1]

Instead of combating, or of criticising such paradoxical opinions, it is proposed to examine the effects of poverty and riches, of simplicity and refinement, upon practical morality; and to compare the predominant virtues and vices of the different periods of society. We shall thence be enabled

* Rousseau.

1. Jean-Jacques Rousseau (1712–78): French political philosopher, educationist, and novelist. Established himself with his *Discours sur les sciences et les arts* (1750), which argued that civilization had corrupted our natural goodness and decreased our freedom. Other important works include the *Discours sur l'origine et les fondements de l'inégalité parmi les hommes* (1754), *Du contrat social* (1762), and *Emile, ou de l'éducation* (1762).

to discover the influence which the commercial improvements of Great Britain have produced upon the moral character of the nation, and how far this influence has affected the political state of the people.

It should seem that the most remarkable differences, exhibited in the manners of polished and of barbarous nations, relate to <176> the virtues of courage and fortitude, of sobriety and temperance, of justice and generosity.[2]

SECTION I

Of Courage and Fortitude.

Courage and fortitude are virtues, which, though resembling each other in some of the principal features, are easily and clearly distinguished. They are called forth on different occasions; and they do not always exist in the same persons. Courage consists in a steady resolution of submitting to some great evil, which being future, is in some measure uncertain, and takes the name of danger. Fortitude consists in bearing a present pain or uneasiness with firmness and resignation. Courage supposes an active and voluntary exertion: Fortitude, a mere passive suffering. The exertion of courage is opposed and often prevented by the passion of fear, which magnifies and exaggerates all uncertain evils. The exercise of forti-<177>tude is counteracted by that weakness of mind which destroys the power of reflection, and renders us incapable of counterbalancing our present pain, by the recollection of any agreeable circumstance in our condition. Great calamities, and such as are of a personal nature, seem to be the objects of courage; and the most conspicuous triumph of this virtue appears in conquering the fear of death. But fortitude may frequently be displayed in supporting the long continuance of small as well as of great evils; in suffering ridicule, shame, and disappointments, and in submitting with patience and alacrity to the numerous train of vexations "which flesh is heir to."

Both courage and fortitude are promoted by every circumstance which leads to the exercise of those virtues; for here, as in all other cases, men are, by the power of habit, inured to such exertions and sufferings as at first were formidable and difficult.

In another view, those two virtues are improved by opposite circum-

2. In what follows, the same general themes of sympathy and self-command are to be found in Smith's moral philosophy. See *TMS,* 22–26, 238.

stances. A man is excited to expose himself to danger, from <178> the consideration that his neighbours are attentive to his conduct; and that, entering with lively sensibility into his feelings, they will applaud and admire him for his courage, or undervalue and despise him for the want of it. He who fights a duel, upon some trifling punctilio, is instigated to make that exertion, not by the value of the object, which has produced the quarrel, but from a sense of honour; a desire of maintaining the good opinion of others, and of avoiding contempt and disgrace. In all the exertions of courage, it will be found that this forms a weighty consideration; and in many, that it becomes the principal motive.

Our fortitude, on the other hand, is improved by the want of humanity, and is diminished by the exquisite fellow-feeling of those who live with us. In our afflictions, the commiseration and sympathy of our intimate friends awakens our sensibility to our distress, betrays us into unavailing lamentations, and makes us give way to all the weakness of sorrow and despondency. But in the company of our distant acquaint-<179>ance, we are ashamed of such tenderness, we exert ourselves to restrain and to conceal our emotions; if we are able to command our thoughts, we endeavour to suggest indifferent subjects of conversation, and to prevent any expression from escaping us which may be disgusting or disagreeable to those with whom we converse. By thus adapting our behaviour to the general standard of the people around us, we acquire habits, either of indulgence or of restraint. If our companions are kind and affectionate, attentive to our distresses, and eager to relieve them, we are encouraged to lean upon their sympathy and assistance, and losing the firmness and vigour of our minds become unable to stand, alone and unmoved, amid the various trials with which we may be visited. Should we happen, on the contrary, to be cast in the society of persons who are cold and indifferent, "unused to the melting mood," we become proportionably shy and reserved, disdaining, by our complaints, to solicit that pity which we are not likely to obtain, and learning to endure, without repining, and without <180> shrinking, whatever afflictions may befal us. By the continuance of such efforts, we attain more and more the command of our passions, and are enabled to moderate our sensibility to painful or uneasy impressions.*

According as any person is placed, more or less, in either of those two

* Theory of Moral Sentiments.

situations, we may commonly observe, in this respect, a suitable difference of temper and disposition. The child who is constantly indulged by his foolish parents, and taught to expect that every body should run to serve him, is perpetually fretful and peevish, crying at whatever happens to cross his inclination, and keeping the whole family disturbed; while his brother, perhaps, who, from unaccountable caprice, has the good fortune to be a little neglected, becomes hardy and manly, patient under disappointments, and pleased with every attention that is paid to him.

There are many persons whom a long illness, and the constant care of their relations, have reduced to the situation of spoiled children, who are put out of humour by <181> the slightest trifles, are continually wearying their hearers with the dismal catalogue of their complaints, and expect that nobody about them should have any other object but to anticipate their wants.

Many individuals of the female sex, who are, perhaps, advanced in years, or subject to personal infirmities or disadvantages, are apt, on the other hand, to meet with so little attention and sympathy as forces them to endure, in silence and solitude, many of the troubles and vexations of life, and frequently teaches them to submit to their lot, not only with patience and equanimity, but with chearfulness and heroic resignation. If the men have more courage, the women, undoubtedly, are distinguished by superior fortitude.

Considering the general effect of the progress of arts and civilization upon these virtues, it should seem that the circumstances of mankind, in the infancy of society, are more favourable to fortitude than to courage. A savage, who is exposed to many dangers, and who is obliged to <182> undergo many hardships and calamities, becomes, no doubt, in some degree familiar with both, and is rendered constitutionally intrepid, as well as insensible to pain or uneasiness. But though he is not much restrained by the influence of fear, he is little prompted to the exertions of courage by the prospect of procuring admiration or applause from his neighbours; for his neighbours are too much engrossed by their own sufferings to feel much for those of others; while, on the other hand, his patience and constancy under afflictions are confirmed and strengthened by the knowledge that any expression of weakness, instead of obtaining the consolation of sympathy, would expose him to contempt and derision. Savage nations, therefore, in all parts of the world, are said to be cowardly and treacherous. If they can accomplish their end by indirect means, they never make an open attempt upon their enemies. They fight, not from the love of glory, but to gain the advantages of victory, or to gratify a vindictive spirit. They cover their <183> resentment under the mask of friendship; and never seem to harbour malice, till they are prepared to strike.

Their heroic fortitude is universally known. Amid the severest tortures, they disdain to utter a groan; and no artifice can tempt them to betray the secrets which they have an interest to conceal.

The first considerable advancement in the arts which procure subsistence, by pasturing cattle, and by cultivating the ground, has an evident tendency to improve the virtue of courage. From the greater facility of procuring the necessaries of life, men are collected in larger societies; and by finding their own situation more comfortable, they have greater encouragement to indulge and cultivate their social feelings. Different tribes, who happen to be in the same neighbourhood, are almost continually quarrelling and fighting; and as the members, not only of the same, but of opposite parties, become known to each other, they of course become rivals in their martial exploits, and by their mutual emulation acquire a high sense of military honour. The Arabs, and Scythians, <184> or Tartars, the ancient Gauls and Germans, the Gothic tribes who laid the foundation of the modern states of Europe, are all eminent examples of the courage and martial spirit which the pastoral and agricultural ages are wont to inspire.[3] The modern European nations carried those virtues to a still higher pitch; as they continued longer in that situation which gave full scope to the hostilities of neighbouring tribes, and felt more extensively, among different petty societies, that emulation and rivalship which implanted the love of military glory. Their martial spirit at the same time, acquired a peculiar direction, which introduced, among the gentry, an artificial standard of merit, and fantastic modes of behaviour, inconsistent, in some respects, with the dictates of morality. The institutions and customs of chivalry,[4] which arose from that state of things, and of which there are several vestiges remaining at this day, I had formerly occasion to consider.

The improvement of commerce and manufactures, together with that opulence which flows from it, must be productive, it is evident, of great alterations, with respect <185> to the virtues both of courage and fortitude.

3. Smith outlines the stadial view of the development of society in *LJ,* 201–5.
4. See *DR,* 76–81.

By the establishment of regular government, a natural consequence of civilization, mankind are protected from depredation, and those nations who cultivate the arts find it their interest, on ordinary occasions, to avoid mutual hostilities, and to maintain an amicable correspondence. Their modes of life, therefore, which become totally different from those of a rude people, give rise to different habits. Living at ease, and in a state of tranquillity, and engaged in the exercise of peaceable professions, they become averse from every enterprise that may expose them to danger, or subject them to pain and uneasiness. The more secure and comfortable their situation at home, they have the less inclination to exchange it, for the hazards of a campaign, or for the fatigues and hardships with which it may be attended.

The lively sensibility and exquisite fellow-feeling which, in opulent and polished nations, take place among individuals, are, at the same time, peculiarly unfavourable to <186> fortitude. He who, in his distress, meets with indulgence from others, is encouraged to indulge himself. Instead of struggling to repress the appearance of affliction, from an apprehension of incurring contempt or indignation, he gives way to its movements with a view of obtaining the friendly consolation of sympathy. Instead of smothering his feelings by an attempt to conceal them, he awakens and rouses them by an ostentatious display of their magnitude. Thus in a polished nation, people take the advice of the poet, "not to pull their hat upon their brows, but to give their sorrow words."[5] They become loud and clamourous in their grief; and are more desirous of shewing, that they feel with delicacy and vivacity, than that they can bear their misfortunes with firmness and constancy. But it may be supposed, that the same lively sensibility and fellow-feeling, by inspiring a nicer sense of honour, will improve the virtue of courage. By a more intimate communication among the members of society, the manners of mankind are softened, their social dispositions are awakened, and they <187> feel more and more an attraction which leads them to conform their behaviour to the general standard. It may be expected, therefore, that they will be so much the more excited to exertions which, though hazardous, will be rewarded with universal approbation and applause.

But it merits attention, that the standard of approbation in this respect, is apt to vary from this change of situation. In proportion as men live in greater security, and are seldom employed in fighting, they are likely to lower

5. The lines are from Shakespeare, *Macbeth* (1606), act 4.

their estimation of military talents, and to exalt the value of such other accomplishments as, in the ordinary state of society, are found more useful. From the customs of chivalry, indeed, introduced in a former period, certain punctilios of military honour have been transmitted to the present European nations, and are still held indispensibly necessary. Persons of the rank and education of what are called gentlemen must expose their lives, rather than tamely suffer an affront. But these punctilios have been artificially preserved from the force of long usage; they are plainly contrary to the <188> manners of a commercial people, and in the more civilized parts of Europe appear to be daily losing ground. To be forward in seeking occasions to fight a duel, is now generally censured even by those who think it necessary to submit to the custom, or who admit the principles upon which it is understood to be founded.

Independent of this exception, which is restricted to persons of a particular description, and among the greater part of whom it is retained from the tyranny of old custom, the virtue of courage appears, in all the nations of modern Europe, to have declined in proportion to their advancement in commerce and manufactures. The first remarkable effect of this decline was to make the great body of the people discard the military service, and devolve the burden of national defence upon soldiers by profession, gathered promiscuously from the community at large. This practice was introduced by the earliest mercantile countries, and was gradually adopted by others, who followed in the career of commercial improvement. Though <189> it was generally, we may suppose, agreeable to the sovereign, upon whom it bestowed the chief direction of the military force, it could not fail, for the same reason, to excite an alarm upon the part of the people, who found their liberties and rights at the disposal of a set of mercenaries, raised and maintained by their chief magistrate. But whatever patriotic measures have been taken, in some of those countries, for supporting a national militia, to serve as a counterpoise to the standing army, the difficulty of enforcing regulations of this nature, so as to derive much advantage from them, must afford sufficient evidence that they are adverse to the spirit of the times. We may even observe, in the nations most engrossed by trade, a tendency to employ foreign mercenaries, either by hiring to fight their battles the troops of poor states, or subsidizing their sovereigns, and admitting them as nominal allies.

The courage of the mercenary armies of Europe is maintained by discipline; that is, by habits of fighting, and by that *esprit du corps,* which brings home to the breast of <190> each individual a sense of military honour. Art is thus made to supply the deficience of natural circumstances; for men who have undertaken the trade of a soldier must be sensible, that perpetual disgrace will be the punishment of their cowardice; and after being seasoned by a campaign or two, they are commonly able, in the company of one another, to surmount the timidity contracted by their former way of life.

The effect of military discipline is probably greater or less, according to the advances which nations have made in civilization. The armies of a refined and polished people, are likely to acquire from their profession an extreme sensibility to martial reputation, and an enthusiastic ardour to distinguish themselves by their spirited atchievements. Those of a nation but lately emerged from a state of rudeness, will be more apt to possess that constitutional intrepidity, which enables them to remain unshaken and immoveable in the midst of danger, and which disposes them to be contented with a bare obedience to the command of their leaders. The French armies <191> afford a striking pattern of the first; the Russian, a good example of the second. The former are animated with feelings which are calculated to interest us. The latter are merely a powerful instrument.

The decay of the military spirit in the modern commercial nations, has produced a corresponding degradation of the military profession. Among the Romans, and other celebrated nations of antiquity, the only reputable employment seems to have been that of a soldier. The same ideas prevailed, and were even carried to a higher pitch, among our forefathers, in modern Europe, among them, every free man followed the profession of arms, and all other professions were exercised only by slaves. In France there were strong vestiges of these ideas, remaining at the time of the late revolution.[6] A merchant was not a gentleman, and might, by any person of that rank, be affronted with impunity. A physician was nearly in the same predicament. The lawyers, or *long robe,* were in a sort of middle station, between the gentry and commonalty; as who should say half-gentlemen. <192>

The glory attached to superior skill and conduct in war, was of a piece with the exalted notions entertained of the military character. The highest place in the temple of fame has been commonly assigned to an Alexander, or a Caesar;[7] though the one was little more, perhaps, than a daring madman,

6. The French Revolution, customarily dated 1789–99.

7. Alexander the Great (356–23 B.C.); Julius Caesar (100–44 B.C.).

and the other was a profligate, utterly destitute of principle, who destroyed the liberties of his country.

But commerce has at length introduced other notions of personal merit, and taught people to estimate professions by a different scale. Dr. Swift defines a soldier to be "a Yahoo, hired to kill as many of his fellow-creatures, who have never offended him, as he possibly can."[8] This definition is, doubtless, loose and declamatory. A soldier is understood to be hired for the defence of his country, and the professed end of his appointment is laudable. Nor can it with reason be asserted, that the people whom he has undertaken to kill, have never offended him; for they are the enemies of his country, who, though they never injured him in <193> particular, may be considered as the objects of his just resentment.

But though the killing of our enemies may be vindicated from its necessity, it will not thence follow that the performance of this public duty is a desirable service. It is a painful task, barely reconcileable to strict justice, and of which the execution is disgusting to humanity.

It must, at the same time, be taken into consideration, that men who engage for hire in the military profession, are not permitted to call in question the justice of those wars in which they may be employed. To refuse to obey orders, would be mutiny; and to do this in a service of danger, would infer the imputation of cowardice. It is evident, however, that, in every war, the half of those professional men must be fighting in support of injustice; for of two hostile nations, who have resolved to determine their quarrel by the sword, one only can be in the right. But it may easily happen that both should be in the wrong. The greater part of the wars in which nations are engaged, proceed, in reality, from the fault <194> of both parties: they proceed from the avarice, or ambition of princes, or their ministers, who, from motives of private interest, and upon false pretences, embroil their respective states in frivolous and groundless disputes, and scruple not, with unbounded profusion, to waste their blood and their treasure. A mercenary army is often the blind agent of a minister, employed in the most mischievous part of the dirty work, which he finds requisite for the preservation of his power.

8. Jonathan Swift (1667–1745): Anglo-Irish clergyman, poet, satirist, and Tory political pamphleteer. Author of *Gulliver's Travels* (1726), a satire on contemporary European politics, religion, arts, and sciences, in which the term *Yahoo* is applied to humankind in its folly. The passage alluded to is from pt. 4, chap. 5.

As far as Britain has surpassed other European countries in commerce and manufacturers, her inhabitants appear to have declined more conspicuously in their martial dispositions, and in their admiration of military talent. They are more invariably occupied, than most of their neighbours, in those peaceable arts, which require a patient persevering industry, but no exertion of courage. They are more engrossed by gainful pursuits, which present a continual prospect of accumulation, but which would be totally frustrated by a temporary desertion, for the purpose of engaging in military opera-<195>tions. Above all, their superior opulence tends to discourage any enterprise that is likely to be attended with danger and uncertainty. "Let him go fight," says the soldier of Lucullus, "who has lost his purse."[9] The man who is poor is incited to desperate adventures by the consideration that he has much to gain, and little or nothing to lose. He who is rich is in the opposite circumstances. The fall from his present fortune to beggary would occasion more misery, than the rise to any fortune which he can expect to acquire would add to his happiness. Common prudence, therefore seems to require, that he should hazard nothing, that he should be cautious in retaining an existence which admits of so many comforts, and be careful to preserve that brittle thread of life, upon which all his enjoyments depend.

In examining how far these peculiar circumstances have rendered the inhabitants of this island less warlike than their neighbours, there is no question concerning our fleets and armies. The valour and steadiness of mercenary troops depends upon their discipline; at least a great superiority in this <196> respect will overcome every disadvantage; and a deficiency can not be counterbalanced by any favourable circumstance. It was by superior discipline that the armies of the great Prussian monarch[10] became the best in the world. The British sailors, from circumstances which produce a better discipline with regard to the conduct of naval affairs, are an over-match, with exception, perhaps, of the Dutch, for those of any other country; and if the armies of Britain are not equal, in every respect, to some of those upon the Continent; it is partly owing to the situation and manners of their country-

9. Lucius Licinius Lucullus (ca. 117–56 B.C.): Roman soldier and administrator who had a reputation for protracting wars in the interest of his own love of money, and for indolence and luxury in his later years.

10. Frederick II, the Great (r. 1740–86): Prussian ruler and writer of political, military and historical works. By the end of his reign, Prussia had doubled in area and its army was increased to 200,000 strong.

men, which are less favourable to *military pursuits;* and partly to the impediments under which their officers lie, in acquiring a scientific knowledge of their profession.

Neither is there any question concerning that class of persons who are supposed to be under the necessity of maintaining what are called the punctilios of honour at the hazard of their lives. The character of a gentleman, whether in Britain, or in any other civilized country of Europe, is understood, in this respect, to be nearly the same, <197> being formed according to a general standard, with which, however whimsical, every individual of that rank is obliged to comply. The courage of the people of this description depends upon a species of discipline, different from that which is exercised over the military profession, but neither less rigid, nor enforced by punishments less efficacious.

But exclusive of those two classes, the mercenary forces, and persons who by their education and rank are still subjected, in some degree, to the old artificial customs of chivalry, the great body of the people seem to be removed at an extreme distance from all military ideas. They hold the military profession in the lowest estimation. When the son of a tradesman enlists in the army, he is looked upon as a profligate who has been deluded to his ruin; and if he cannot be bought off, he is given up for lost. Even among the gentry, unless where some of the sons shew an early predilection for a military life, those who appear the least qualified to rise by other professions are commonly destined to serve in the army or navy. <198>

Though the mercantile towns in England are much addicted to mobbing, a consequence of their independent circumstances, their mobs are, in most cases, easily quelled by an insignificant body of troops. Thus the bill for extending the privileges of the Roman Catholics, excited a prodigious fury in London and throughout the whole country; but notwithstanding the enthusiasm, with which the populace were actuated in opposing that measure, they were easily intimidated, and, by a mere handful of troops reduced to submission: whereas in Scotland, a poorer and a ruder country, the people persisted in their opposition, and obliged the minister, though he shewed a good deal of reluctance, to abandon his bill.[11]

11. In 1778 the Catholic Relief Act repealed certain anti-Catholic legislation passed in the late seventeenth century. Riots in Edinburgh and Glasgow dissuaded Parliament from extending the bill to Scotland. In 1780 a protest in London led by member of

In the year 1745,[12] a body of Scottish rebels, perfectly undisciplined, and ill-armed, whose numbers did not exceed four or five thousand, marched over a considerable part of England, and, though the country was warmly attached to the house of Hanover,[13] met with no body of men who ventured to oppose them, until the army, which had then been employed in Flanders, was brought <199> home for that purpose. The people of England, though they knew that their religion and liberties were at stake, did not think proper, on that occasion, to shew themselves in the field; imitating the example of that helpless and timid animal which, upon the least approach of external violence, shrinks within its shell, and cannot be drawn from that asylum until the danger is removed.

How often have we seen a great majority of the English nation, fired with indignation at the conduct of administration, loud and clamorous in their complaints, waving the banner of *magna charta* in the face of the minister, and availing themselves of the liberty of the press to annoy him on every side; when by a little steady resolution, by the display of a little timely severity, by a judicious application of the machine of government, *pulveres exigui jactu,*[14] they have been completely subdued, and rendered perfectly submissive?

It is unnecessary to remark that this timidity inspired by overgrown wealth, <200> which renders a rich trading nation vulnerable through the whole of their possessions, and makes them feel an agonizing sensibility to whatever dangers may affect even one shilling of their property, is of great utility in counteracting the excesses of an independent spirit, by strength-

---

Parliament, Lord George Gordon (1751–93), president of the Protestant Association, sparked ten days of anti-Catholic riots (the Gordon Riots).

12. The last significant attempt to restore the Stuart dynasty that had been in exile since the Glorious Revolution of 1688–89. Led by Charles Edward Stuart, the "Young Pretender" (1720–88), and supported by the French, the rebellion attracted popular support in Scotland and among English Catholics (and some Tories) until its suppression at Culloden in 1746.

13. The Electors of Hanover, a small German principality, gained title to the British throne by the Act of Settlement in 1701 (by virtue of being the Protestants closest to the line of succession). When Queen Anne died childless in 1714, Georg Ludwig of Hanover succeeded as George I (r. 1714–27), setting aside the stronger hereditary claim of the Catholic Stuarts.

14. *Pulveres* [[*sic: pulveris*]] *exigui jactu:* "by the tossing of a little dust" (Virgil, *Georgics,* 4.87). See Virgil, *Eclogues, Georgics, Aeneid I–VI,* trans. H. Rushton Fairclough, rev. G. P. Goold (Cambridge, Mass.: Harvard University Press, 1999), 225.

ening the bands of public authority. The wealth of each individual is a pledge for his quiet and orderly behaviour. It may, doubtless, on the other hand, encourage an ambitious monarch to overturn the liberties of his country. But there is ground to expect, that this timidity will not operate beyond certain limits. If the oppression of government should be carried so far as to aim at the destruction of property, the mercantile people would, probably, be the first to burst the bands of fear, and be actuated by a desperate valour in defence of those objects to which they are so immoderately attached. The effect of great commercial opulence, therefore, is to produce caution and long-suffering under the hand of power, but to ensure ultimately a vigorous opposition to such acts of tyranny <201> as are manifestly subversive of the fundamental rights of mankind. This, in reality, seems to point at the due medium of that submission which men owe to their political governors: for nothing is more inconsistent with the happiness of society, than the frequent recurrence of the people to resistance upon slight and trivial grievances; and when there is a real necessity to resist the usurpation of the sovereign, he commonly pulls off the mask in sufficient time to give warning to his subjects, that they may be fully justified for uniting in defence of their privileges.

SECTION II

Of Sobriety and Temperance.

The motives by which men are excited to action may be reduced to two classes: the desire of obtaining what is pleasant or agreeable, and that of avoiding what is painful or disagreeable. By the constitution of our nature, a pleasure that is near makes a stronger impression upon us than <202> one that is distant; whence it frequently happens, that we become unable to estimate properly those different objects; and by yielding to a present or immediate enjoyment, we sacrifice a future happiness of greater importance.

The virtue of temperance consists in correcting this vicious tendency, by balancing our several enjoyments, and by never allowing an inferior to usurp the place of a superior pleasure. Fortitude, which has already been considered, exercises a self-command of another kind, by holding a similar balance between painful or disagreeable objects.

The most violent appetites which often produce the greatest irregularity and inconsistency of conduct, are those of hunger and thirst, and those which relate to the intercourse of the sexes. The virtue of temperance therefore is chiefly employed in restraining the excesses of those two natural propensities.

The appetite for food, it is evident, will assume a different aspect in every country and its gratification will be variously modi-<203>fied, according as the inhabitants experience a greater plenty or scarcity of provisions. Very poor and rude nations, who have collected no regular fund for subsistence, but depend upon their daily exertions for supplying the calls of nature, are often exposed to the extremities of hunger, and when by good fortune they obtain a plentiful repast, are apt to indulge in the excesses of gluttony. Man, in this miserable state, appears to resemble those voracious brute animals who are fitted to endure a long abstinence, and who, by gormandizing sometimes destroy their vital functions.

The arts which enabled men to accumulate a stock of provisions, render them of course careful and provident of the future. Having been exposed to the pain of hunger, they endeavour to guard against that calamity; and the most obvious reflection will teach them to store up the food which they have no immediate occasion to use. The disposition to hoard grows upon them by favourable circumstances, and inspires not only anxiety to acquire, but reluctance to consume. From the slow and gradual pro-<204>gress of those improvements which tend to multiply and accumulate the necessaries of life, the pursuits of mankind are principally directed to the acquisition of daily food, and the want of this continues for a long time to be the chief object of their apprehensions. Frugality, therefore, and even parsimony, in this article, are in early ages considered as indispensible qualities, and profusion as an odious vice. In those European nations who have made considerable advances in opulence, we still find evident vestiges of this primitive way of thinking. To cast away any thing that contributes to the subsistence of man is regarded with superstitious abhorrence, as tending to provoke the resentment of Providence, "You know not what you may come to," is the reproach which an act of this kind commonly excites among the populace in Scotland. To have a small appetite was regarded as a recommendation. "You eat nothing—one would not know what you live upon," were the old-fashioned compliments by which the mistress of the house was accustomed to flatter her guests. <205>

Our fathers praised rank venison, you suppose,
Perhaps, young man! our fathers had no nose,
Not so; a buck was then a week's repast;
And 'twas their point, I ween, to make it last;
More pleased to keep it till their friends should come,
Than eat the sweetest by themselves at home.
Why had not I in those good times my birth,
'Ere coxcomb pies, or coxcombs were on earth?[15]

From the diffusion of wealth by commerce and manufactures, there has arisen in some countries, such a regular and plentiful supply of provisions as among people in the higher and even middling ranks, to banish the idea of scarcity, and to produce, in this respect, a total change of manners. What was formerly a mere necessary expence is now converted into a matter of refinement; and the relief of hunger is lost in the enjoyments of the table. Upon the gratification of the palate, upon the natural hilarity inspired by good cheer, are ingrafted the pleasures of social intercourse; and both corporeal and mental faculties are expected to contribute their share towards an elegant entertainment. As this entertainment is level to every capacity; as it takes hold of propensities which are <206> very universal, and which from the time consumed in their indulgence, are greatly strengthened by the power of habit: as by exhibiting an appearance of wealth, it becomes in many cases a great source of ostentation and vanity; we need not wonder that it should sometimes run into prodigious excess, that it should frequently encroach upon the important business and attentions of mankind, and that it should prove hurtful and even ruinous to the fortunes of many individuals.

By the bountiful disposition of nature, the removal of the painful sensation of thirst is, in most countries and situations, attended with no labour or trouble. But here in the rudest forms of society, mankind have generally introduced a species of luxury; some artificial beverage, to relieve the insipidity of simple water, or rather to obtain the exhilarating effect of intoxication. Some invention for this purpose appears to have taken place in almost every age and country. The poor savage, upon whose mind there are few traces of thought beyond what arise from the few objects which impress his external senses, <207> and who, if not roused to exertion for the relief of

15. The lines are from Alexander Pope's "Second Satire of the Second Book of Horace Imitated," lines 91–98. See note 25 in this chapter.

his wants, passes many a tiresome melancholy hour, flies with avidity to this terrestrial nectar, which creates a new world before his eyes, makes all nature smile and dance around him, and at length steeps his senses in a grateful oblivion of his miserable existence. Our European merchants who traffic in the human species, know sufficiently the effect of this powerful charm, to conquer his affections, or to drown his feelings of humanity; and they scruple not to take advantage of his weakness, by purchasing his wife or his child for a bottle or two of spirituous liquor, or by exciting him for a bribe of the same kind, to kidnap his neighbours, or to join in bloody wars which may give rise to a plentiful harvest of prisoners.

When the use of intoxicating liquors has grown up, and been spread over a country, it is not easily eradicated. The vice of drunkenness, which is universally prevalent among barbarians, is not quickly banished, though in the progress of civilization it may be somewhat modified and restrained. Among the higher ranks, even in countries <208> far advanced in the arts, the bottle continues to be the great enlivener of conversation, the source of gaiety and pleasantry, which, if it does not always produce true wit, never fails to soften criticism, and while it blunts the faculties of the speaker, it augments in a greater proportion, the indulgence and facile applause of the company. The same happy instrument of social mirth bestows upon our failings the garb and aspect of virtue, by inspiring the glow of kindness and affection, by improving the ordinary companion into the bosom friend, and by opening the heart to the overflowings of generosity and benevolence.

We cannot, however, expect that the mirth which rises from the enchanted cup will be always the most refined or polished; or that it will not exceed the bounds of decency and decorum. The same blind and headstrong power which exalts the soul, without the guidance of reason, to sudden friendships and attachments, will also, without cause, provoke and irritate the self-important, the resentful, and discordant passions. The modest Graces wing their <209> flight from the revels of Bacchus, and are succeeded by loose riot and disorder, by rude and boisterous disputes, and by groundless and unmeaning, though sometimes fatal quarrels.

To the lower orders of the community, to the labouring poor, the delusive poison of intoxication is productive of consequences far more pernicious. It affords, indeed, a healing balsam to their toils and cares; and our fellow-feelings must reclaim against that rigid severity which would altogether deny this consolation to a class of men, by whose painful exertions the prosperity of every state is principally supported, and the rest of the society maintained in ease and affluence. But their excesses in this particular are so pregnant with mischief, so destructive of all industry and domestic attention, and lead so directly to complete dissipation, and shameless profligacy, that sobriety, or temperance in the use of intoxicating liquors, has been justly regarded as the leading virtue of the populace, and the contrary, if not the most inexcusable vice, at least the great inlet to every sort of immorality. <210>

It has been commonly thought that the propensity to strong liquors arises from physical causes; and that it is peculiarly prevalent in cold climates. It is probable that the manners of the people in the northern parts of Europe have given rise to this opinion. But it ought to be remembered that the same people, from the nature of the soil, and from the temperature of the weather, lie under great disadvantages with respect to agriculture and the common arts of life, and have therefore long remained in a situation which is favourable to this propensity. As in countries which are exposed to the extremities of cold, the savage life must be the more bitter and uncomfortable, it seems, on that account, to stand more in need of the friendly aid of intoxication; and as the progress of improvement in those countries must be slower and more difficult, so the custom of hard drinking will, in proportion as it has remained longer, be so much the more confirmed.

There is, however, from the history of the world, no ground to believe that the <211> vice of drunkenness is peculiar to cold climates. The ancient Greeks, though living in the southern part of Europe, appear to have been great drinkers. The same circumstance is mentioned as characteristic of the Gauls. It appears that the modern inhabitants of Spain were formerly distinguished by a similar character; for, in the agreeable novel of Gil Blas,[16] so highly celebrated for its pictures of real manners, the fine gentlemen of Madrid are described as passing the whole night in hard drinking, and as reeling home to bed late in the morning, in the very style which is fashionable in the most drunken parts of Europe. It is true, the author has hinted in his preface, that though the scene of his work is laid in Spain, there are frequent allusions to the manners of his own countrymen; but whether we consider this feature as belonging to the Spaniards or the French, it serves equally to

16. French picaresque novel by Alain René Lesage (1668–1747), which appeared in four volumes 1715–35.

prove that even in modern times, the vice of drunkenness has not been confined to the northern parts of Europe.

The ancient inhabitants of Persia, a still warmer country, were notorious drunkards, <212> insomuch that Alexander, a man of universal ambition, could not think to be out-done in this respect by a people whom he had conquered in arms.* It is hardly necessary to add, that the use of opium among the Turks, who are forbid by their religion to drink wine, answers the same purpose, and has been introduced upon the same principle, with the fermented and distilled liquors of Europe.

But though debauchery in drinking may for a long time maintain its ground in those countries where it has once been firmly rooted, we have reason to expect that after a certain pitch of improvement in arts and sciences, it will be expelled from every country. The advancement of knowledge contributes, at least in the higher and middling ranks of life, to supply a fund of ideas, productive of continual amusement, and proves a powerful antidote to melancholy or dejection. To people who are <213> provided with constant resources for entertainment from the powers of imagination and reflection, the aid of intoxication is not necessary to exalt their spirits, or to enliven conversation. From the advancement of taste, they are disgusted with that coarse mirth which is the effect of strong liquors, and with that ferment of delirious joy, which is commonly requited by a subsequent mental depression and bodily indisposition. If they call in a cheerful glass, they are not tempted to such a degree of excess as will disturb the feast of reason, or interrupt the flow of elegant pleasantry. In a word, the use of the bottle is rendered subordinate to the correct enjoyment of social intercourse and becomes merely a branch of that good cheer which constitutes the most learned luxury of the table.

These observations may be illustrated by the change of manners which, in later times, have taken place in Britain and the countries connected with it. In England the custom of hard drinking among people of the better sort, is in a great measure exploded. The inhabitants of Scotland, <214> though they still lie under a bad character in point of sobriety, appear to be rapidly following the footsteps of their southern neighbours, in this as well as in other improvements. If the inhabitants of Ireland discover, in this respect,

* Darius's Epitaph on himself—"That he was a great conquerer and a great drinker." See the facts collected on this subject by Mr. Hume. "Essay of Nat. Characters."

a greater attachment to the ancient usage, it is because the arts in general have made less progress in that country. Though the populace, in any of these countries, are doubtless more invariably under the dominion of those propensities which lead to intoxication, there is ground to hope that from increasing habits of industry and frugality, and from the prevailing fashion among their superiors, they will be more and more disposed to correct a vicious indulgence, which they find so prejudicial to their interest.[17]

With regard to the intercourse of the sexes, the virtue of temperance may be considered in three different aspects. The first is exhibited in early and rude nations.

The instinct which leads to the propagation of the species, is less necessary than the appetite for food, which is directed to the preservation of the individual. The former <215> is more affected by education than the latter, and according to the habits acquired in different situations, puts on a greater variety of aspects. The demands of hunger require a constant and regular supply, while those of the sexual appetite occur only at intervals, and are excluded by numberless wants and cares of greater importance. The former is equally an object of attention in all ages and countries; but the latter must be in great measure overlooked in that miserable state of society where men have made no provision for subsistence, and are engaged in continual struggles for procuring the bare necessaries of life.

It is observed, that the greater part of animals, who have much difficulty in procuring their food, which is remarkably the case of all the carnivorous, are restricted in the intercourse of the sexes to particular seasons; and it is probable that in the human species, when they subsist principally by hunting and fishing, the propensities of nature are usually so feeble as to be consistent with similar restrictions. <216>

Even at this early period, however, some kind of marriage, or permanent union between persons of different sexes, for the purpose of rearing and maintaining their children, has generally taken place. That natural affection which is implanted not only in all mankind, but in the more sagacious of the brute animals, disposes the parents universally to co-operate in maintaining their offspring. In the brute creation, indeed, the union arising from that circumstance is commonly of short duration; because the young animal, soon after the birth, is in a condition to provide for its own subsistence. But the offspring of the human species remains, for so long a period, in a state

17. For a parallel discussion, see *DR,* chap. 1, sec. 4, 67–86.

of perfect imbecillity, that the parents, in the natural course of things, are likely to have propagated several children before their protection and care of the first can be dispensed with. Their connection, therefore, from the same circumstance which gave rise to it is prolonged, not only while the mother is capable of child-bearing, but until the youngest child is able to maintain <217> itself; and the habits which they acquire by living so long in the same family, in the company of each other and of their children, must render it agreeable, and in most cases expedient, that their union should be continued for the rest of their life.

Thus the society produced by marriage, though doubtless, originating in a blind propensity, is promoted and supported by feelings of a superior order. The conjugal, the parental, and filial relations give rise to various modifications of mutual sympathy and benevolence, which, in their range are not the most extensive, but which operating in a sphere adapted to the limited capacities of the human heart, are exerted in such directions as are most conducive to the great purposes of human nature. The good which we can do to mankind at large is commonly inconsiderable; but the benefits which may result from our acting with propriety in the exercise of domestic affections, are above all calculation.

In this early state of society, the manners of mankind, with relation to the intercourse of the sexes, are usually removed at the <218> greatest distance from intemperance. The propensity or instinct which leads to the continuance of the species is commonly no more than sufficient to answer the purpose for which it is implanted in all mankind. In very rude ages, people are so far from being addicted to excess in its indulgence, that upon the slightest degree of refinement in this particular, they become ashamed of its ordinary gratifications. In many barbarous tribes it is a punctilio of decorum that the husband and wife should cohabit by stealth; and if among such people, correct notions of chastity are in a great measure unknown, this proceeds not from habits of debauchery, but from ignorance of those principles which recommend personal fidelity to an individual. It may, at the same time, be remarked, that although the conjugal affection, when joined to the love of offspring, has been capable, at an early period, of cementing families, and thus laying the foundation of political society, it is not of itself sufficient in those times, to give much consideration and dignity to the wife, or even to prevent her, in consequence of her <219> inferiority in strength and courage, from becoming the servant or slave of the husband.

The second aspect of society to which I alluded, is that which arises from the advancement of the useful arts, from the consequent acquisition and extension of property, and from the progress of civil government.

The advancement of a people in the various arts, which procure the progressive accommodations and conveniencies of life, and the accumulation of property in different proportions by individuals, must affect the intercourse of the sexes in two different ways. In the first place, when men are placed in a situation which relieves them from the pressure of immediate want, and supplies them with abundance of whatever is necessary to subsistence, their attention is, of course, directed to other less important gratifications; they obey the suggestions of nature by indulging their various propensities, and become, from the influence of habit, more and more addicted to pleasure. The different degrees of wealth, on <220> the other hand, which arise from the talents or the fortune of individuals, give rise to such differences of rank and condition, as remove different families to a distance from each other, inflame and swell them with family pride and jealousy, and, from an apprehension of unsuitable and degrading alliances, renders them averse from that familiarity and freedom of intercourse which might be attended either with licentious indulgence, or with hasty and inconsiderate matrimonial connections.

The indiscriminate gratification of the propensity between the sexes is further obstructed by the general improvements of society. From a gradual refinement of taste and manners, there is produced a nicer selection of objects, and a stronger preference of those individuals, by whose beauty, or other personal qualities, our desires have been peculiarly exerted. But the same circumstances, which create more diversity of taste, will tend more frequently to prevent a reciprocity of inclination, and consequently, will often render it more difficult <221> for the lover to attain the object of his wishes.

The restraints which are thus laid upon the sexual correspondence, contribute, in a high degree, to improve and augment the pleasures which result from it. The difficulties, the delays, the disappointments, which we experience in pursuit of a favourite gratification, cannot fail to enhance its value, by fixing our attention for a length of time upon the same object, by disposing us to estimate the attainment in proportion to the distress which we feel from the want of it, and by rousing the imagination to paint every circumstance in such colours as may flatter our prevailing inclinations. These are the great expedients of nature, which give rise to peculiar attachments, and by which a simple desire or appetite is often converted into a violent passion.

The effects of mere facility in procuring subsistence, while no difficulties occur in the indulgence of the sexual propensities, may be illustrated by the manners which prevail in Otaheite[18] and those neighbouring islands in the South Sea, with which Euro-<222>pean travellers have lately made us acquainted. Those people, from their singularly happy climate, are without industry or labour, possessed of all the necessaries of life. As they have, at the same time, accumulated little or no wealth, they are, in a great measure, strangers to those distinctions of rank which divide and separate the inhabitants of civilized countries; and, as they have never been roused to active exertions, either of body or mind, they are unacquainted with those refinements of taste and manners which arise from the cultivation of the arts. Living, therefore, in constant ease and idleness, they are strongly addicted to sensual pleasure; but they are debauched without passion, and voluptuous without elegance, or even discrimination of objects.

The effect of uncommon restraints upon the intercourse of the sexes may, on the other hand, be observed in the manners of those Gothic nations, who over-ran and subdued the western provinces of the Roman empire. Those nations, acquiring large possessions by their conquest, and spreading themselves over an extensive territory, were <223> formed into a multitude of separate baronies, under the authority of a sovereign, but so independent, and so feebly united, as to be under little restraint in the exercise of mutual hostilities and depredations. By these peculiar circumstances, which remained for several centuries, neighbouring families contracted such animosities, and entertained such apprehension and jealousy of each other, as became an insuperable bar to their intimate correspondence, and therefore interrupted, in proportion, the communication of the sexes. To this interruption we may ascribe the romantic love, the uncommon purity and delicacy of sentiment, which appear so conspicuously in the manners of that period, and of which there are still very evident and remarkable traces in the turn of thinking, the usages, and the literature of the present European nations.

The ordinary state of civilized society exhibits a medium between those two extremes; with neither the voluptuousness of the former, nor the fan-

18. Former name of Tahiti.

tastic love and admiration of the latter; but with a moderate sensibility to pleasure, derived from the <224> advancement of taste, and with a degree of passion excited by the usual impediments to gratification. Upon the first considerable advances of commerce and the arts, the situation of mankind is rendered so easy and comfortable, as disposes them commonly to enter into marriage whenever they arrive at that period of life which fits them for the discharge of its duties; and in forming this connection, they must frequently, from differences of rank or personal qualities, or from accidental circumstances, meet with various obstacles to the attainment of their wishes, and be engaged in a long courtship, which, by inflaming their desires, and fixing their imagination upon the same object, is likely to create a sincere and lasting attachment; an attachment, upon which all the domestic virtues are easily engrafted, and which is capable of rendering all the cares of the marriage state light and agreeable. The ardour of a blind appetite is thus controuled by feelings of a superior order; and the passion of love becomes the guardian of temperance. <225>

The high cultivation of the elegant arts, and the introduction of immoderate opulence, give rise to a third variety, by which, in relation to the present subject, the manners of society require to be distinguished.

Luxury and expensive living are the natural attendants of great wealth. Excited by mutual emulation, individuals, in proportion to their riches, endeavour more and more to surpass one another in elegance and magnificence, and in supplying those wants by which, from fashionable extravagance, they are continually solicited, must find at length that their income, however large, is inadequate to their demands. They become, of consequence, unwilling to take upon them the additional burden of maintaining a family. While the men, by whose courage and superior exertions property is, in a great measure engrossed, are thus generally disposed to remain in the state of bachelors, a proportional part of the other sex are laid under the necessity of remaining unmarried; and both, from the operation of the same causes, contract, unavoid-<226>ably, such habits as tend to disqualify them from enjoying happiness in the married state. It may, at the same time, be expected that persons, who, notwithstanding these discouragements, are induced to form a matrimonial connection, will endeavour to compensate the inconveniences attending it, by regarding the fortune more than the personal attractions of their yoke-mates. From such a mercenary traffic, it would be vain to look for that harmony which is requisite to promote the welfare of the family. To such marriages may be applied the maxim of the civil law: *Societas est mater discordiarum.*[19]

These observations are illustrated by the manners of ancient Rome about the beginning of her despotical government. The great wealth imported from the conquered provinces had then given rise to such a degree of luxury and expensive living as proved extremely unfavourable to marriage, and induced the Emperor Augustus to encourage that union, by various taxes and penalties upon celibacy, and by bestowing suitable premiums upon married people, <227> and upon those who had produced a number of children. The same circumstance introduced the avowed and very universal practice, among wealthy and unmarried persons, of keeping a concubine, whose children, being of inferior rank, were maintained at less expence, but who, in other respects, was viewed in a light somewhat similar to that of a wife.

So mercenary were the Romans in their matrimonial alliances, that a woman who brought no dower to her husband, was considered in a disgraceful situation; and unless there appeared good evidence of her marriage, she was held to be, not a wife, but a concubine.

The same circumstances which render marriage inconvenient and burdensome, in regard to pecuniary interest, are no less unfavourable to that connection from the general progress of dissipation and voluptuousness.

Among nations possessed of moderate wealth, who are chiefly occupied in the cultivation of the useful arts, the inhabitants are, for the most part, engaged in <228> serious employments, by which they are separated into various departments, and prevented from holding an extensive communication. The members of neighbouring families, the several knots of kindred and acquaintance, whom accidents, or the transactions of business, have collected in small circles, are accustomed to keep company with one another, but little intercourse is held with strangers. Among persons of different sexes, living in this retired situation, the imagination will frequently be led to form a reciprocal and permanent attachment. But the advancement of a people in those arts which are subservient to pleasure and amusement, occasions a more extensive correspondence among the different members of society. Almost all men of fortune, and of liberal education, whose residence admits of their intercourse, become acquainted with each other, and frequently as-

19. "Society is the mother of discord" (or, "Association is the mother of disagreements").

semble in all the fashionable meetings of pleasure and amusement. The more opulent they become, and the more polished in their manners, these meetings become the more numerous; and the com-<229>munication among people of rank and condition is, in proportion, extended and diversified. In these polite circles, the women claim an equal share with the other sex, and by their agreeable accomplishments, by their delicacy and vivacity, as well as by their personal charms, contribute no less to the entertainment.

The unreserved and extensive intercourse of the two sexes has, doubtless, a tendency to divide the attention among a great variety of objects, to efface the impression of one object by that of another; and, consequently, to prevent a strong or lasting attachment to any individual. The sensibility of the heart is thus gradually worn out and exhausted by continual dissipation; and the passion, which formerly excited all the tender affections, is at length converted into a mere vehicle of sensual enjoyment. A spirit of gallantry and intrigue, totally inconsistent with the duties of domestic society, is of course introduced in the higher ranks; to whom it affords that occupation and amusement which their inferiors derive from the pursuits of industry. In the natural <230> course of things, the dissipated manners of the rich are, by the force of example, communicated to the lower orders, among whom they lose that appearance of refinement in which they were enveloped, and appear in the undisguised form of gross debauchery and common prostitution.

This progress of dissipation and voluptuousness may be observed in all countries where the people have made great advances in the accumulation of wealth, and in the arts which administer to luxury and extravagance. In ancient Rome, in the great Asiatic nations, in modern Italy, France, and England, a dissoluteness of manners, in relation to the intercourse of the sexes, appears to have been the inseparable attendant of great opulence; though from peculiar circumstances in these different countries, it has been exhibited under various modifications.

The ancient Romans passed very suddenly from poverty and barbarism to immoderate wealth and luxury; and, between these two extremes, there seems to have passed no interval which was calculated to refine and <231> exalt the passion between the sexes. When they advanced, therefore, into the latter situation, about the end of the commonwealth, they had acquired no previous habits, to prevent them from sinking at once into a degree of sensuality, and gross debauchery, of which there is no example. Among them, the shameless profligacy of a Messalina, was understood to exhibit the behaviour of a woman of rank, immoderately addicted to the pursuits of gallantry and pleasure.[20]

In the present opulent nations of Europe, the vestiges which remain of the refined sentiments of a former period, have produced in the higher ranks, a more elegant species of licentiousness; at the same time that the Christian religion, by exalting the merit of restraint, and even of total abstinence, in relation to the sexual correspondence, has contributed, no doubt, to retard a general relaxation of manners. In particular, the authority of the church, which was exerted to render marriage an indissoluble tie, has prevented parents, in many cases, from being led by caprice, or bad humour, to <232> form such connections as were incompatible with the interest of their children. The regulations to this effect have not, indeed, entirely maintained their ground, in opposition to the spirit of the later age. In some parts of Europe they have been subjected to limitations; in others they have been evaded; in France they have been wholly repealed.

In the great eastern nations, the practice of polygamy, though calculated to promote, in the one sex, an unlimited indulgence in sensual pleasure, is equally adverse, on the one hand, to gross prostitution; and, on the other, to the refinements of sentimental passion. The harams and seraglios of the east are said to exhibit an assemblage of beauty in the utmost variety of elegant forms; but they leave their indolent master nothing to desire except the capacity of enjoyment.

Some benevolent philosophers have indulged the pleasing speculation, that the faculties and virtues of mankind are universally improved by the progress of the arts and sciences; and that human nature, by <233> culture and education, is led to endless degrees of perfection.[21] To this flattering, and perhaps generally well-founded hypothesis, the circumstance now suggested appears to form a remarkable exception. Nothing can be more inconsistent with the finer feelings of the heart; nothing more incompatible with the order of society; nothing more destructive of those bands which unite men together, and enable them to live in mutual confidence and security, than debauchery and dissolute manners. The indiscriminate volup-

20. Valeria Messalina (ca. A.D. 24–48): third wife of emperor Claudius I (r. 41–54), notorious for her many affairs. She was executed by Claudius in 48.

21. Millar's reference is very likely to the perfectibilist philosophies of William Godwin (1756–1836) and Marie Jean Antoine Nicolas de Caritat Condorcet (1743–94).

tuousness of the one sex cannot fail to produce a still greater depravity of the other, by annihilating the female point of honour, and introducing universal prostitution. The rank of the women is thus degraded; marriage becomes hardly the source of a peculiar connection; and the unhappy child who is born in a family, instead of reaping advantage from the natural prepossessions and affections of its parents, is doomed to suffer the fatal consequences of their jealousy and discord. The effect of their negligence, in such a <234> situation, may easily be conceived, when we consider the hard fortune which is commonly experienced by the issue of an illegitimate correspondence.

Nature has wisely provided, that the education and even the maintenance of the human offspring, should not depend upon general philanthropy or benevolence, deduced from abstracted philosophical principles; but upon peculiar passions and feelings, which have a more powerful and immediate influence on the conduct of mankind: and, when these passions are weakened, these feelings destroyed, we shall in vain expect their place to be supplied by general views of utility to mankind, or particular interpositions of the legislature. <235>

SECTION III

Of Justice and Generosity.

The virtues and vices of mankind relate more immediately, either to the interest of the agent himself or to the interest of others. Of the former class are those which have been already considered. The latter may deserve a separate examination.

When our actions tend to promote the happiness of our neighbours, or when they have a contrary tendency, it may frequently happen, that, while every spectator approves or disapproves of our conduct in these different cases, yet no person imagines we could, with propriety, be compelled to act in the one way, or to abstain from acting in the other. To requite a favour with gratitude, to hazard our fortune in behalf of a friend, to relieve the distress of those with whom we have no particular connection, are actions of this nature. There are many cases, on the other hand, where our behaviour in relation to our neighbours becomes <236> a matter of strict obligation, and where we may be compelled to follow one course of action, and punished for the contrary. Thus we may be forced to fulfil our promises, and to abstain from doing hurt to others. Actions of the latter sort belong to what, in a strict sense, are called the rules of justice. Those of the former belong to generosity or benevolence.

That the advancement of arts, manufactures, and commerce, has a tendency to improve the virtue of justice in all its branches, appears indisputable.

Mankind are induced to abstain from injustice by the feelings of humanity, which dispose them to avoid hurting their neighbours, as well as by the consideration that such a conduct will be highly conducive to their own interest; and both of these principles operate with peculiar force from the circumstances in which a commercial people is placed. By commerce and manufactures, the contracts and transactions of a country are multiplied almost without end; and the possessions of individuals are extended and varied in proportion; whence the injuries <237> arising from the breach of promise, from dishonesty and fraud, or from any violation of property, are more sensibly felt, and productive of more sympathy and regret. The advantages, at the same time, which every individual derives from a strict observance of the rules of justice, become also proportionably greater and more manifest. According as the intercourse of society is extended, it requires more and more a mutual trust and confidence, which cannot be maintained without the uniform profession and rigid practice of honesty and fair-dealing. Whoever is unable, in this respect, to maintain a fair character, finds himself universally reprobated, is of course disqualified for the exercise of any lucrative profession, and becomes a sort of outcast, who, like the stricken deer, is carefully avoided by the whole herd. Compared with so dreadful a misfortune, the gain which is likely to accrue from the most artful knavery is a mere trifle.

In such a situation it becomes the object of early education to recommend and inculcate the rules of justice. Children are deterred from any failure in this respect, by <238> timely correction, and by the disgrace which attends it. At a more advanced period of life, the principles of honour, dictated by the general sentiments of mankind, and communicated through the different ranks and orders of society, confirm the same doctrine. In addition to these considerations, religion bestows her aid, by representing what is infamous among men, as offensive to the Deity, and as incurring the effects of his displeasure; while the sanctions of civil government are employed in repressing such disorders, by the salutary example of human punishments.

These principles and habits which characterize a mercantile age and country, are apt to appear most conspicuous in that part of the inhabitants who are actually engaged in trade; because they feel most powerfully the influence of the various motives which have been mentioned. In the most commercial nations of Europe, it is not, indeed, considered as inconsistent with the rules of fair trade, to lay hold of an accidental scarcity for enhancing the price of any commodity; but a merchant of credit is accus-<239>tomed to deal at a word, and to take no advantage of the ignorance of his customer. Among the rest of the inhabitants, who traffic occasionally, the same scrupulous punctuality is not required; and it is not unusual to chaffer, or even to overreach in a bargain. This is particularly the case in the sale of commodities, which have, in some degree, an arbitrary value; as of horses, where even the country gentleman is frequently not ashamed to become a species of horse-jockey.

The manners of rude nations are, in the present view, diametrically opposite to those of a commercial people. Barbarians, whatever may be their other virtues, are but little acquainted with the rules of justice; they have seldom any regard to their promises, and are commonly addicted to theft and rapine. This is evident from the history of all early nations. In Captain Cook's first voyage to Otaheite,[22] the inhabitants of that island were so far from being ashamed of their thefts, that upon being challenged, they held up the stolen goods in triumph at their success. In Kamtschatska,[23] it is said, <240> that a young woman has difficulty to procure a husband, until she has given proof of her dexterity in filching.* Among the ancient Egyptians there was no punishment for theft;† nor among the Gauls, when the crime was committed between the members of different tribes.‡

In the highlands of Scotland, stealing of cattle was denominated *lifting;* a term to which no blame appears to have been attached; and it is a well-

* See the accounts of the Russian emissaries.

† Aul. Gell. Noct. Att. lib. II. 58.

‡ Caesar. de bell. Gall. lib. 6. 5. 23.

22. James Cook (1728–79), British navigator and explorer, commanded a voyage on behalf of the Royal Society to make astronomical observations in Tahiti [Otaheite] 1768–71. He charted New Zealand, the eastern coast of Australia, Hawaii, some of Antarctica, and the northwest coast of North America.

23. First visited by Russians in the late seventeenth century, Kamchatka is a northeastern Russian peninsula extending south between the Sea of Okhotsk and the Bering Sea.

known fact, that an inhabitant of that country, who, upon the suppression of the rebellion, 1745, had the Pretender under his protection, and who had not been tempted to deliver him up by the great premium offered by government, was at a subsequent period tried at Inverness, and condemned to a capital punishment for horse-stealing.

As in countries highly advanced in trade and manufactures, the trading part of the inhabitants are the fairest and most punctual in their dealings, they are, in the infancy <241> of commerce, the most knavish and dishonest.

In a rude and military age, mechanics and tradesmen, who follow sedentary professions, are despised on account of their unwarlike dispositions, and from the low estimation in which they are held, become degraded in their own eyes, and regardless of their character and behaviour. The first merchants, who are a sort of pedlars, wandering from place to place, and frequently reduced to the necessity of begging their bread and their lodging among strangers, are even in a meaner condition than artificers, or labourers, who enjoy a fixed residence in the midst of their kindred and acquaintance. When Ulysses,[24] in Homer, is twitted with being a wandering merchant, the patient hero is unable to bear this unmerited reproach; and though he had before determined to conceal his rank, he starts up immediately, to wipe off the aspersion, by distinguishing himself in the athletic exercises.

So long as the ancient Romans preserved their military character, they considered the <242> profession of a merchant as disgraceful to a free citizen. In modern Europe, trade and manufactures were also, for many centuries, confined to that class of the people who remained in a species of servitude.

From the want of a regular market, for ascertaining the price of commodities, it is also more difficult, in the first dawn of mercantile improvements, to discover and restrain the fraud of individuals. The pedlar, who provides a stock of goods from different quarters, and retails the various articles to persons at a distance from each other, may almost always impose upon his customers with little hazard of detection, and is laid under strong temptation to avail himself of contingencies for increasing his profits.

The mercantile profession seems, accordingly, in all countries where trade is in a low state, to be considered as peculiarly connected with knavery and injustice. Among the early Greek nations, a merchant, and a private, were understood to be nearly synonimous terms; and the same tutelary deity, who

24. Ulysses is the Latin form of Odysseus, the hero of the *Odyssey.*

presided over merchants, became <243> also the patron of cheats and pickpockets.

Cicero, whose opinion we may suppose was founded upon the manners of his countrymen, declares that a great wholesale merchant, who imports goods from every quarter, may have a tolerable character; but that a retailer, who buys with a view of selling immediately, is engaged in a very mean employment; because he can make no profit, unless he becomes a great liar.* Mr. Pope appears to have rather injudiciously transferred this thought to the tradesmen of his own country.

"The next a tradesman, meek, and much a liar."[25]

In Armenia, Persia, and many other eastern regions, commerce is managed, in a <244> great measure, by a set of wandering merchants, who are not only destitute of protection, but even liable to be frequently plundered by government. It can hardly be expected that these people, who are often obliged to bury a part of their stock, and to invest a part of it in jewels, that they may be able to conceal, or suddenly to withdraw their effects, will be scrupulously punctual in their transactions, or that they will not, by exorbitant profit in some cases, endeavour to compensate the losses and hazards which they sustain in others.

The Jews were a people, who, on account of their singular manners and customs, and their uncommon religious rites and ceremonies, had incurred the ridicule, and even in some degree the hatred of other nations. In these

* "Mercatura antem [[*sic: autem*]], si tennis [[*sic: tenuis*]] est, sordida putanda est: sin magna et copiosa, multa undique apportans, multisque sine vanitate impartiens, non est admodum vituperanda."—"Sordidi etiam putandi qui mercantur a mercatoribus quod statim vendant. Nihil enim proficiunt nisi admodum mentcantur" [[*sic:* mentiantur]]. [*Cicero de offic. Lib.* I. § 42.] [["Trade, if it is on a small scale, is to be considered vulgar; but if wholesale and on a large scale, importing large quantities from all parts of the world and distributing to many without misrepresentation, it is not to be greatly disparaged."—"Vulgar we must consider those also who buy from wholesale merchants to retail immediately; for they would get no profits without a great deal of downright lying." Cicero, *De Officiis,* 1.42. See Marcus Tullius Cicero, *De Officiis,* trans. Walter Miller (Cambridge, Mass.: Harvard University Press, 1913), 155, 153. (These page numbers are not reversed: a later text has been placed before an earlier.)]]

25. Alexander Pope (1688–1744): English poet, a member of Swift's circle. His major works include *The Rape of the Lock* (1712), the *Dunciad* (1712; enlarged 1729, 1742), translations of the Homeric epics, and the *Essay on Man* (1733). The line quoted by Millar is from Pope's "Epistle to Sir Richard Temple, Lord Viscount Cobham."

unfortunate circumstances, they found little degradation in a mean employment, and therefore betook themselves very generally to merchandize, in those periods and countries where it was held in some degree ignominious. This was more especially the case after the Christian religion had spread itself over Europe, and had over-<245>whelmed that once chosen people in recent odium and aversion. The Jews became early the principal traders of the modern European nations; and in that capacity acquired immense riches; while in conformity to the state of commerce at that period, they obtained universally the character of knavery and dishonesty; a character which they appear to have long borne without murmuring, and which, even at this day, notwithstanding the great revolution in the rank and behaviour of mercantile people, they have never been able fully to obliterate.

But the circumstances of a nation which has been enriched by trade are not more friendly to justice, than unfavourable to generosity, and to the higher exertions of benevolence.

That a man should be induced to a constant observance of the rules of justice, nothing further is commonly requisite than to understand his own pecuniary interest; but before he can become eminently generous or benevolent, he must resolve to sacrifice that interest to the good of others. Justice <246> is the result of a deliberate purpose to reject an incidental advantage for obtaining an ultimate, and much greater profit. Generosity is the fruit of a violent impulse, which overlooks all private and selfish considerations. The careful and penurious tradesman, the industrious and active manufacturer, or merchant, can have little temptation to desert the one, but in the course of his professional views, he meets with as little incitement to practice the other. To be just is to breathe his natural element; to require that he should be generous is to invert his ordinary functions, and to make him subsist by organs to which he has not been accustomed.

In a commercial country, the mercantile spirit is not confined to tradesmen or merchants; from a similarity of situation it pervades, in some degree, all orders and ranks, and by the influence of habit and example, it is communicated, more or less, to every member of the community. Individuals form their notions of propriety according to a general standard, and fashion their morals in conformity to the prevailing taste of the times. By living much in society, and <247> maintaining an intimate correspondence, they are led also to a frequent and ready communication of their thoughts and sentiments. They learn by experience to do this, without hurting the feelings of one another; to conceal their own selfishness or contempt of others; to assume a tone of moderation, deference, and respect; and, without apparent restraint or effort, to accommodate their behaviour to the disposition and temper of their company, while in this manner, they improve in the arts of civility and politeness, they can hardly fail to cultivate their social feelings, by participating in the pleasures and pains of each other, and by mutual endeavours to promote the former, and to relieve or soften the latter. But this intercourse is often little more than a petty traffic, which aims merely at the purchase of reciprocal good offices; or when it proceeds from better motives, it is the offspring of a subordinate, and in some measure a speculative humanity, which in the case of any serious distress, contents itself with weeping and lamenting over the afflicted, but never thinks of sacrificing any great interest to afford him relief. <248>

Even this tinsel reciprocation of small benefits, which people are apt to value more than it deserves, but which in reality is of signal utility in removing the inconveniences, and improving the comforts which attend our journey of human life, is frequently interrupted by those opposite and jarring passions which arise amid the active pursuits of a commercial nation. In a rude age, where there is little industry, or desire of accumulation, neighbouring independent societies are apt to rob and plunder each other; but the members of the same society are attracted by a common interest, and are often strongly united in the bands of friendship and affection, by mutual exertions of benevolence, or by accidental habits of sympathy. But in a country where no body is idle, and where every person is eager to augment his fortune, or to improve his circumstances, there occur innumerable competitions and rivalships, which contract the heart, and set mankind at variance. In proportion as every man is attentive to his own advancement, he is vexed and tormented by every obstacle to his prosperity, and <249> prompted to regard his competitors with envy, resentment, and other malignant passions.

The pursuit of riches becomes a scramble, in which the hand of every man is against every other. Hence the dissentions among persons of the same trade or profession, which are more conspicuous according as the opposition of interest is more direct and pointed. The physicians, the apothecaries, and the lawyers of a small town are commonly not in speaking terms; they are not more instigated to advance their own success than to thwart and oppose that of each other; and even the customers of each party are frequently involved in the quarrel. The same principles exhibit themselves with less indecorum, perhaps, or violence, but not less invariably, through the whole commercial world. That there is no friendship in trade is an established maxim among traders. Every man for himself, and God Almighty for us all, is their fundamental doctrine.

Among an active and polished people, the desire of fame and distinction is productive of competitions and jealousies yet more ex-<250>tensive. Neither age, nor sex, nor condition; neither wisdom, nor folly; neither learning, nor ignorance, is exempted from the serious, and the ludicrous discord which originates in this universal passion, or from the acrimony and malice which it often inspires; whether it appears in the light airy shape of vanity, which glides through every corner of society, and presents the aspect of a rival in every accomplishment or agreeable talent; from that of the well-dressed coxcomb who figures at a ball, to that of the eloquent speaker who shakes an admiring senate: or whether it assumes the graver form of ambition, which divides mankind into parties, inflames their party zeal, and their party animosities, and sheltering itself under the multitude of associates, bids defiance to the sense of shame, and becomes deaf to the voice of humanity. Of this passion, the jealousy among authors, will, perhaps, be regarded as the most remarkable instance; but it seems to be so, chiefly because the parties have more the capacity of publishing their disputes, and of circulating the bitter animosities by which they are agitated. <251>

As the pursuit of wealth, the great object of a mercantile nation, contributes to scatter the seeds of envy and selfishness, the luxurious and voluptuous habits, which, as I formerly observed, become also prevalent among the same people, tend to nourish and strengthen those baneful productions.

Sensual pleasures, whether founded upon the enjoyments of the table, or upon the propensity which unites the sexes, are all of a selfish nature; however they may be connected in many cases, with the exercises of social dispositions. The mirth and festivity of the epicure[26] terminates in the gratification of his palate; and the boon companion of a luxurious age will commonly prefer the company where he finds the best dinner. The pleasure of a love-intrigue supposes a communication of sentiments; but the voluptuary scruples not to procure it at the expence of ruin to the object of his wishes.

26. The Greek philosopher Epicurus (341–270 B.C.) was the founder of the Epicurean school of philosophy, which aimed to achieve a life free from anxiety.

But what more especially merits attention, is, that the fashionable pleasures of an opulent nation become the source of enormous expence, by which multitudes are led to exceed their income, and become embarrassed <252> in their circumstances. To men who are, at the same time, addicted to expensive habits, and forced to struggle with pecuniary difficulties, wealth is the constant idol, the sovereign dispenser of happiness; and poverty, a dreadful spectre, usurping the place of an awakened conscience, to haunt and terrify the disordered imagination.

While the peculiar habits of an opulent people are thus calculated to increase the bias which is already too strong, by fortifying the love of money, they give unavoidably a particular turn and direction to that passion. They afford a spur to the acquisition of riches, but they encourage, at the same time, and promote the expenditure. The avarice of a frugal, and that of a luxurious age, assume very frequently, a different, and in some respects, an opposite character. The character of the former is that of a miser, who scruples not to practise the meanest arts of accumulation, is unable to take any use of what he has gathered, but living in constant terror of poverty, is afraid to lend out his money at interest, and has recourse to the wretched precaution of con-<253>cealing it in the earth. Such are the leading features of the miser, as represented by the poets of antiquity, which have been copied by Moliere[27] with more fidelity and humour, than discernment in applying them to the manners of his own age; for the original of this picture is now rarely to be found. The modern usurer is not less rapacious, nor less absorbed in the constant pursuit of gain than the ancient; but he is more enterprising, and less ready to forget the end of his labours. He never loses a penny by hugging his treasure in secret, or by hiding it in the ground. Goaded, on either side, by the love of money, and by the love of pleasure, he obeys alternately the dictates of these opposite passions, and hoards that he may spend to the best advantage. He is covetous and profuse;* but his profusion is merely the avarice of sensual gratification.

From these observations it may be concluded, that the manners of an

* Sui profusus, alieni cupictus [[*sic:* cupidus]]. SALUST. [["Covetous of others' possessions, he was prodigal of his own." Sallust, *Catalina,* 5. See *Sallust,* trans. J. C. Rolfe (Cambridge, Mass.: Harvard University Press, 1921, rev. 1931), 9.]]

27. Molière: The stage name of the French dramatist and theater manager Jean Baptiste Poquelin (1622–73). His major plays include *Le Festin de Pierre* [Don Juan] (1665) and *Le Misanthrope* (1666).

opulent and luxurious age, are, upon the whole, favourable to the general intercourse of society. <254> In the common relations of neighbourhood and acquaintance, it is not expected that individuals will make any great sacrifice of their own interest to that of others. If men abstain from the commission of crimes, if they observe the rules of justice in their various transactions, if they are punctual to their word, so as to create a mutual confidence in their probity and good faith, and if to these virtues they add the constant exercise of those inferior good offices which are dictated by humanity and the desire of pleasing, they are likely to communicate to each other, and to enjoy, all that security, ease, and tranquillity, all that comfort and satisfaction which can reasonably be desired. The practice of these common virtues will be sufficient to facilitate the accumulation of wealth, or to secure the fruits of industry, to those who are in ordinary prosperous circumstances; and at the same time to afford a moderate relief or assistance to those who may be reduced to indigence or distress. The higher exertions of benevolence are out of the question; but a limited and regulated charity is perfectly <255> consistent with the manners of a refined and polished people; and it may, perhaps, be affirmed with reason, that, from prudent and well-directed interpositions of that nature, more diffusive benefit is likely to arise, both to the public and to individuals, than from the warmest occasional ebullitions of tender-hearted and thoughtless generosity. This, at least, is indisputable, that mere generosity without the punctual observance of the rules of justice, is of less consequence to the prosperity and good order of society, than the latter, though without any considerable share of the former.

But although the spirit of opulent and trading nations tends evidently to improve the intercourse of mankind, in their more general and distant connections, it must be confessed, that when we turn our eyes to the private and intimate relations of human life, we are led, in some respects, to a different conclusion. In their domestic relations, the happiness of mankind seems to depend more upon the warmth of friendship and benevolence, than upon the alderman-like virtue of justice.[28] A fond husband expects <256> more from his wife than merely that she will not steal from him. Much more is required from the father of a family, than that he should do no injury to his

28. "To a Cromwell, perhaps, or a De Retz, discretion may appear an alderman-like virtue, as Dr Swift calls it." Hume, *Enquiry Concerning the Principles of Morals,* ed. T. Beauchamp (Oxford: Oxford University Press, 1998), 121.

children, or that he should bestow small charities upon them. The domestic affections, which constitute the chief happiness of private life, are nothing but various modifications of sympathy and friendship; and these, it is to be feared, are not likely to be improved by the peculiar manners of a mercantile and luxurious age. Marriage becomes then almost always an interested connection, in which those pecuniary considerations by which it was formed are likely to keep the ascendant during the whole of its course. On the part of the husband, it is frequently a mercenary bargain calculated to gain a livelihood, or to plaster a broken fortune, by yoking himself with folly, age, or decrepitude. On the part of the wife, it is as frequently the successful issue of a decoy, by which, under the auspices of a careful and experienced mother, she has contrived to recommend her personal attractions, and factitious accomplishments, to the highest bidder. The effects of <257> opulence and luxury are no less hurtful to the parental and filial affections. The father, immersed in the sordid pursuits of the world, is apt to look upon his family as a tax upon his pleasures, and to find himself elbowed by children; who, as they grow up in years, require from their increasing demands, a suitable retrenchment of his own personal expences. If even the parents are more conscientious, and less tainted with the vices of the age, they are likely to meet with miserable disappointments and mortifications from the behaviour of their children, who frequently corrupted by bad example and by the selfish maxims which prevail around them, correspond so little to the partial hopes and anxious cares of parental fondness, as to waste their time in idleness and dissipation, and even to wait with impatience for the full possession of that hereditary fortune which will render them their own masters. The future distribution of that fortune may also become a source of discontent among the children themselves, to poison their mutual affections, and to interrupt that agreeable <258> intercourse which their situation has otherwise a tendency to produce.

The same commercial spirit is adverse to that peculiar attachment which arises among friends, united by particular habits of intimacy, and by similarity of taste and dispositions. The situation of mankind in a rude age, which prevents them from being engrossed by objects of pecuniary interest, and which prompts them to frequent exertions for the protection and defence of each other, is highly favourable to such peculiar connections. The learned father, L'Afitau,[29] observes, that among the American savages, it is

29. Joseph-François Lafitau (1681–1746): French Jesuit missionary and ethnologist

usual for individuals to form such intimate friendships as give rise to a perfect community of goods; insomuch that they have no separate interest, and even think it incumbent on them to abstain from intermarriages between their respective families, as if they were near relations. To sacrifice their lives for each other is regarded as a duty which these generous and simple-hearted friends are never backward to fulfil. When a warrior is made captive by his enemies, and put to death, as he commonly is by the most excru-<259>ciating tortures, he frequently pronounces the name of a particular person, and calls upon him to avenge his torments. This person is the friend of his bosom, who is rendered so eager for vengeance, and so careless of life, that hovering about the place where the bloody tragedy has been acted, he commonly soon falls into the hands of the same people. That ingenious author compares the friendships of those barbarians with the connections of a similar nature which have been so highly celebrated in the early history of the Greeks; of Hercules and Iolas, of Theseus and Peritheus, of Achilles and Patroclus, of Orestes and Pylades,[30] and of several other distinguished warriors of antiquity; whose attachment has appeared so little conformable to the manners of a later age as to be frequently misunderstood and misrepresented.

The friendships of a luxurious and mercantile country are of a different complexion. They are cool and sober, breathing no ardour of enthusiasm, producing no unreserved confidence, requiring no sacrifice either of life or fortune. It is enough that you should rejoice in your friend's prosperity; that you <260> should relieve his distress when it can be done without inconvenience to yourself; and that you should be always ready to assist him with your good advice. But you ought never to forget the famous prudential maxim, of constantly behaving to him as if he were one day to become your

---

who wrote *Moeurs des sauvages ameriquains, comparées aux moeurs des premiers temps* (1724), a comparative ethnology of Iroquois and Hurons in relation to ancient Europeans.

30. Hercules is the Latin form of Heracles, the most celebrated hero of ancient Greek legend and, according to tradition, the son of the god Zeus. Iolas was the younger companion and helper of Heracles. Theseus was a legendary king of Athens whose major exploit was the journey to Crete and the killing of the Minotaur. A close friend of Theseus, Peritheus was a mythical king of the Lapiths, a Thessalian clan who warred against the legendary centaurs. Achilles was the central character of Homer's *Iliad* who heroically avenged the death of his friend Patroclus. Orestes was the son of Agamemnon (king of Mycenae and leader of the Greeks during the Trojan War) who was raised by Agamemnon's brother-in-law and befriended his son, Pylades.

enemy. Your friend, as friends go in the present age, is a person whom you esteem, in whose company you receive peculiar pleasure, whose conduct in his absence you endeavour to defend, whose party you embrace in his quarrels or disputes with others, and upon whom, in a word, you confer a double portion of those good offices and civilities which pass current in the intercourse of common acquaintance.

After all, though the virtue of justice commonly maintains the ascendant in opulent and luxurious nations, there may occur particular situations where this order of things is completely reversed. Among such a people, the strict observance of the rules of justice proceeds chiefly from considerations of interest, and from the establishment of a general standard of behaviour, which has been founded on those considera-<261>tions, and with which individuals, if they wish to preserve their character, find it necessary to comply. This may be considered as the effect of artificial discipline, tending to restrain and controul the feelings of avarice, which, in that state of society, are commonly wound up to a high pitch, and are apt to form the ruling principle. It may happen, therefore, in singular circumstances, where many persons are tempted in conjunction to the same acts of injustice, where they have an opportunity of acquiring suddenly an immense profit by their transgression, and where the delinquents are so numerous, and of such rank as in some measure to keep one another in countenance, that they should give way to the immediate impulse of their passions, and that having once broken through the restraints to which they were formerly subjected, they should run into very great enormities.[31]

The officers who governed the ancient Roman provinces were in this tempting situation. They possessed an almost unlimited authority over the inhabitants, and were subject to no other controul but that <262> of the senate, the members of which, having either enjoyed, or expecting to enjoy, similar offices, had commonly a fellow-feeling with their situations, and were, therefore, not likely to take a strict account of their abuses. Their number was, at the same time, so great, as to lighten the share of censure which might fall upon individuals; while their distance from the capital obscured their behaviour, or concealed it entirely from their friends at home. In these

31. Millar's reference here and in subsequent pages is to the corruptions of the East India Company.

circumstances, and inflamed with the rage of accumulation, they seem, as with one consent, to have burst through the restraints of justice and humanity, and to have put in practice every engine of extortion, fraud, and oppression. As the same set of officers did not commonly remain above a year or two in the same province, no time was to be lost; and when having amassed enormous wealth, they returned to Rome, to enjoy the fruits of their industry, they found another expedient for the improvement of their fortunes, by lending money at exorbitant interest, to the very <263> people whom they had already pillaged. This kind of trade became so universal, that, however prohibited by the laws, it was not held, it seems, to be disgraceful; and, though the legal interest was restricted to about twelve per cent. more than forty or fifty per cent. appears to have been frequently exacted even by the most respectable citizens.

The great mercantile companies, established by the modern European nations in very distant countries, and invested with the privileges of monopoly, may be regarded, in the present question, as in a situation similar to that of the ancient rulers of the Roman provinces; with this additional circumstance, that accumulation being in the direct line of their profession, we may expect that it will be prosecuted by them in a more systematic and regular manner. If a company of this kind shall acquire an extensive territory, and be placed at such a distance from the mother-country as to be, in some measure, emancipated from her jurisdiction, it is likely that pecuniary profit <264> will be the great object in exercising the powers of government; and if the servants of this company, from the extent of their business, and from the implicit confidence necessarily reposed in them, shall become independent of their masters, there is ground to apprehend, that the interest of the public will be assumed as a pretence, to justify the most oppressive measures; and that a set of merchants, acting in concert with one another, and provided with an excuse for their abuses, will proceed, without fear or shame, in plundering the inhabitants, and in building up such fortunes as may enable them, in another hemisphere, not only to appear with dazzling splendour, but secure them from any inquiry into the means by which their wealth has been procured.

There can be little doubt that report has often greatly exaggerated and misrepresented the abuses committed on such occasions. But every exaggeration supposes a foundation in reality. Every one must be convinced, that, if the merchants of a country are invested with unlimited authority, <265> their profits will be commensurate to their desires.

Quid non mortalia pectora cogis,
Auri sacra fames?* <266>

* In a striking picture, exhibited by an eloquent speaker of the present day, a supreme judge is represented as acting in subserviency to that "sacred thirst," and as making a solemn progress over the country, "carrying a bloody standard in one hand, and picking pockets with the other." [[*Quid non mortalia pectora cogis / Auri sacra fames?:* "To what do you not compel mortal hearts / Accursed hunger for gold?" (Virgil, *Aeneid,* bk. 3, lines 56–57). The phrase "sacred thirst," adapted from Psalm 42, was often used as an ironic reference to desire for gold. It is used by Smith in a context very similar to Millar's in the section "Of Colonies" in *WN,* vol. 2, bk. 4, chap. 7.]]

CHAPTER VII

The Progress of Science relative to Law and Government.

As the advancement of commerce and civilization tends to promote the virtue of strict justice, it of course disposes mankind to cultivate and improve the science of law. By attention and experience, and by a gradual refinement of their feelings, men attain a nicer discrimination in matters of right and wrong, and acquire more skill and dexterity in settling the claims and disputes of individuals, or in proportioning punishments to the various offences which may invade the peace of society.

There is this remarkable difference between justice and the other virtues, that the former can be reduced under general rules, capable, in some degree, of accuracy and precision; while the latter, more uncertain and variable in their limits, can frequently <267> be no otherwise determined than from a complex view of their circumstances, and must, in each particular case, be submitted to the immediate decision of taste and sentiment.[1] Justice requires no more than that I should abstain from hurting my neighbour, in his person, his property, or his reputation; that I should pay the debts, or perform the services, which by my contracts, or by the course of my behaviour, I have given him reason to expect from me; and that, if I have ever transgressed in any of these particulars, I should make a suitable compensation and reinstate him, as far as possible, in those advantages of which I have unwarrantably deprived him. The line of duty suggested by this mere negative virtue, can

1. Millar's discussion in this chapter of morality as a cultivation of sentiments, his sharp distinction between justice and the other virtues, and his account of justice as the basis for the legal system is an epitome of the theory developed by Smith in reaction to premises laid down by Hume. Nearly every paragraph of the chapter can be seen as an echo or discussion of parts of Smith's *TMS* and *LJ.*

be clearly marked, and its boundaries distinctly ascertained. It resembles a matter of calculation, and may, in some sort, be regulated by the square and the compass.

But the other virtues, those more especially which lead us to promote the positive happiness of our neighbours, admit of a greater variety of aspects, and are of a more delicate nature. What is the precise beha-<268>viour consistent with the most perfect friendship, generosity, gratitude, or other benevolent affections, may often be a difficult question; and the situations which give rise to the complete exercise of those virtues are so diversified by a multiplicity of minute circumstances, that there seldom occur two instances altogether alike; and there is no room for determining any number of cases according to the same general view.

Though mankind, therefore, have in all ages, given a very universal attention to morality, though their constant aim and endeavour has been to recommend themselves, one to another, by practising, or by seeming to practice, those virtues which procure esteem, or affection and confidence—they have made, after all, but slender advances in digesting their knowledge upon the subject, and in reducing it to a regular system. Philosophers have been able to do little more than to exhibit a description or picture, more or less animated, of the principal virtues and vices, together with their various combinations in the characters of individuals, and at the same time to suggest <269> considerations and views, which, from the condition of human nature, are likely to produce an admiration and love of virtue, as well as a detestation and abhorrence of vice.

The first moralists, among an ignorant and simple people, were contented with giving general advices, for the benefit of such as were destitute of experience, to guard against the temptations to vice, and the irregular influence of the passions. Parents, desirous of promoting the welfare of their children, men of sagacity, who, in the course of a long life, had surveyed the vicissitudes of human affairs, were induced to communicate the fruits of their experience, and to inculcate such observations and maxims as might correct the errors and imprudencies to which mankind are peculiarly liable. Hence the numerous proverbs which have been circulated in all nations, containing such moral and prudential maxims, as, from an apparent shrewdness of remark, from strength or felicity of allusion, or from any peculiar point of expression, were thought worthy of atten-<270>tion, and frequently repeated. Of a similar nature, but uniting, in some cases, a train of reflections upon the same subject, are those observations, and advices, relating to the conduct of life, which have been collected by early writers, or delivered by ancient sages of high reputation; such as, the proverbs of Solomon, the words of Agur, the wisdom of the son of Sirah, a part of the writings of Hesiod, and the sayings of those who are denominated the wise men of Greece.[2]

Succeeding writers endeavoured to explain and enforce these observations and maxims by historical events, real or fictitious; and to illustrate their truth, by allegorical representations, taken from the brute creation, or from those different parts of nature in which we may trace any resemblance to human actions and passions. Of this latter sort are the parables of Scripture, the fables known to us by the name of Pilpay,[3] which appear to have enjoyed a very ancient and extensive reputation in the eastern world; and those of equal celebrity in Europe, which are ascribed to Aesop, <271> and which have been translated, paraphrased, and embellished by such a multitude of eminent authors. Even after those early observations, from the general diffusion of knowledge, have ceased to convey much instruction, the apologue or fable, has continued, with several men of genius, to be a favourite mode of composition, on account of the delicate strokes with which it is capable of exhibiting the follies and foibles of human life.[4]

When men had been accustomed to consider in detail the several branches

2. Solomon was king of the Hebrews ca. 970–ca. 930 B.C.; his wisdom is proverbial. Proverbs and Ecclesiastes are ascribed to him. Agur was a contributor of proverbs mentioned in Prov. 30:1, and the Prayer of Agur in Prov. 30:7–9 is the best-known part of his writing. The Wisdom of Jesus, the Son of Sirach is another name for an apocryphal book of the Old Testament, and its main themes are the excellence and teaching of wisdom. Hesiod is one of the earliest-known Greek poets; he was active around 700 B.C. He wrote the *Theogony,* an epic poem on the origin of the gods and the earth, and *Works and Days,* which through myths and proverbial maxims offered advice for living a life of honest work.

3. The Fables of Bidpai (Pilpay) was the European title for the collection of animal fables known in Sanskrit as *Panca-tantra* that offered instruction in statecraft to the king's sons. The collection dates from ca. A.D. 200, and Millar is referring to the Persian version, which was translated into several European languages as the Fables of Bidpai (or Pilpay), a corruption of Vidyapati, a wise Brahmin who figures in them. Aesop was a legendary Greek fabulist usually placed as a Phrygian slave in the sixth century B.C.

4. Jean de la Fontaine's *Fables* (1668–94) were basic to the modern fashion, e.g. Bernard Mandeville's *Fable of the Bees* (1714; 1723), Jonathan Swift's *Gulliver's Travels* (1726), John Gay's *Fables* (1727; 1738), and many others.

of human conduct, they were led by degrees to more connected views, and extensive reasonings. They were led to enumerate and arrange the principal virtues and vices, and to distribute them into different classes, according to the various feelings or passions, from which they proceed, or the different ends to which they are directed. The celebrated and well known division of the virtues into four great classes, usually denominated the four cardinal virtues,[5] which has been handed down to us by the Greek and Roman writers, and which is reported to have been <272> brought by Pythagoras[6] from the east, appears to be a very ancient, and at the same time, a successful attempt of this nature.

The arrangement and classification of the several virtues, could hardly fail to occasion enquiries and discussions concerning the peculiar character of each; and more especially to suggest an examination of the circumstances by which all the virtues are distinguished from the opposite vices. This gave rise to the far-famed question, *Wherein consists virtue?*

The great distinction between virtue and vice appears to consist in the different sentiments which they excite in the beholders, and in their opposite tendency, to produce *happiness* or *misery* to mankind.

There is in virtue a native beauty and excellence, which is felt and acknowledged by all the world; which, from the immediate contemplation of it, and without regard to its consequences, is the genuine source of pleasure and satisfaction; and which procures to the person in whom it is discovered, universal love and esteem, with various modifications of benevolence. The natural <273> deformity of vice; the disgust and aversion with which it is regarded; and the contempt and abhorrence, or the indignation and resentment which it excites, are no less conspicuous. That these feelings exist in the human mind is indisputable: but whether they are simple and original feelings, intended by nature for this purpose alone; or whether they are excited from different views and reasonings, and consequently, are capable of explanation and analysis, has been the subject of much philosophical disquisition; a disquisition highly curious and interesting to the lovers of meta-

5. The moral virtues on which other virtues hinge. The four cardinal virtues are prudence, temperance, fortitude, and justice. They are distinguished from the theological virtues in that they are attainable by our natural powers and do not require an infusion of divine grace.

6. Pythagoras (ca. 582–ca. 507 B.C.) was a pre-Socratic Greek philosopher.

physical knowledge; though, in relation to practical morality, of little or no importance.

The tendency of all virtuous actions to produce happiness, either to the person who performs them or to others, and the contrary tendency of all vicious actions, are considerations, which, to the bulk of mankind, will appear of still greater magnitude, in creating a preference of the former to the latter. In this view, those virtuous actions which promote a man's own good, are agreeable to a spectator, from those bene-<274>volent feelings which render him pleased with the happiness of the person who performs them; while those actions which promote the good of others, gratify the selfish feelings of the spectator, and call forth a sort of gratitude from every person who conceives himself within the sphere of their beneficial influence. We need not be surprised, therefore, that men should universally bestow much higher applause upon the benevolent, than upon the selfish virtues; or that some eminent philosophers have considered the latter in the light merely of useful qualities, which are not the proper objects of moral approbation. The person who performs a benevolent action appears in the light of a benefactor; and, as we readily suppose ourselves to be the objects of his beneficence, we feel, upon that account, a disposition to make a suitable return of good offices; we look upon him as peculiarly worthy of our good will and affection; and are thence led to form a notion of his meriting a reward.

From considering the beneficial tendency of all the virtues, philosophers proceeded <275> to a more general enquiry, concerning the supreme good or happiness of mankind, and the circumstances by which it is produced; whether it be produced by virtue alone, or by what is called pleasure, or from the union and co-operation of both?

Such appear to be the principal steps by which men have advanced in cultivating the general science of morality, which have undoubtedly been of great utility in presenting such views and considerations as were fitted to awaken the noblest and best affections of the heart; but which often terminating in vague reflection, or speculative disquisition afford no specific information, no precise land-marks for the regulation of our conduct. If we do not miss our way in the journey of life, it is more from our general knowledge of the compass, than from any directions we receive concerning the several windings and turnings of the road.

But in relation to strict justice, the attention of mankind has been excited and directed in a different manner, and has produced an examination of particulars much more minute and accurate. As individuals who <276> have much intercourse, are likely, on many occasions, to experience an opposition of interest, and if they are independent of each other, must be liable to numerous disputes in matters of right, they have in the infancy of society, no other method of terminating any difference which cannot be amicably adjusted than either by fighting, or by referring it to the decision of a common arbiter; and this latter mode of accommodation, which flatters the sanguine expectations of either party, and which, by preventing a quarrel, must commonly be agreeable to their private friends, as well as to the friends of good order and public tranquillity, is likely to be more frequently adopted in proportion as, by the habits of living in society, people become less quarrelsome in their temper, and more under the guidance of prudence and discretion.

The arbiters most frequently chosen on those occasions, will probably be persons who from their eminent reputation for wisdom and integrity, possess the confidence of both parties, and by their high station, and superior influence, are capable of giving <277> weight to their decisions. The longer these men have officiated in the same employment, provided they have acted with tolerable propriety, the respect paid to their opinions will be the greater, and the disposition to treat them with deference and submission, will become the more habitual. Their own efforts to render their sentences effectual will also, from considerations of expediency, be supported by the general voice of the community; till at length, by the assignment of an armed force to assist them in enforcing obedience, they are invested with power to determine law-suits independent of any reference of parties, and thus, in the natural progress of things, are converted into regular and permanent judges.

Corresponding to the advices and prudential maxims which are circulated by men of experience and observation, in the primitive cultivation of morality, are the decisions of arbiters and judges, which constitute the foundation of the science of law. From the various disputes of individuals, and from the various claims that are successively decided <278> and enforced, there is formed a set of practical rules of justice, which are gradually multiplied, and according to the different situations and relations of mankind in society, gradually extended and diversified.

The disputes among mankind are innumerable; but as one dispute is often very like another, it is apt to be decided in a similar manner; and when a number of cases have been determined upon the same grounds, there is introduced a general rule, which from the influence of habit and of analogy, is extended, even without examination to other cases of the same kind. Though this procedure originates in a propensity natural to all mankind, it is doubtless recommended and confirmed by its utility. The general rules of law are of signal service, by enabling every person to simplify his transactions, as well as to ascertain the tenor of conduct which he is bound to maintain, and by proving at the same time, a check to the partiality of judges, who must be ashamed or afraid to deviate from <279> that beaten path, which is universally known, and easily distinguished.

The advantages, however, arising from the general rules of justice, are not without limitations. When a great number of claims are decided from the consideration of those outlines in which they all agree, the smaller circumstances in which they happen to differ must of course be overlooked; and the decision may, therefore, in some instances, be productive of injustice. This is the foundation of that old complaint, which, in every country, has been made against the *extremity of the law.* It is necessary, for this reason, to forego in many cases, the benefit of that uniformity and certainty derived from the strict observance of a general rule, and by introducing an exception from the consideration of what is equitable in particular circumstances, to avoid the hardship which would otherwise fall upon individuals. We must on this as on many other occasions, compare and balance the inconveniencies which present themselves on opposite sides, and be contented with submitting to those which are of the least importance. <280>

The interpositions of equity, which are made in detached and singular circumstances, are at first regarded as extraordinary deviations from that legal maxim, which however just and expedient in other cases, is found in some particular instance, to be hard and oppressive. But when these interpositions have been often repeated in similar situations, they become familiar and habitual; and such of them as depend upon a common principle, are reduced into the same class, the boundaries of which are precisely determined.

In this manner, by the successive litigation of individuals, and by the continued experience and observation of judges, the science of law grows up in society, and advances more and more to a regular system. Particular decisions become the foundation of general rules, which are afterwards limited by particular exceptions; and these exceptions being also generalized, and reduced into different classes, are again subjected to future limitations. From a few parent stems, there issue various branches; and <281> these are succeeded by subordinate ramifications; diminishing gradually in size, while they increase in number; separated from each other by endless divisions and subdivisions; exhibiting a great multiplicity and variety of parts, uniformly and regularly adjusted; and which may, therefore, be easily and readily traced through all their different connections.

But though the rules of justice derive their origin from the business of the world, and are introduced by the actual decisions of judges, their extensive utility is likely to attract the notice of speculative reasoners, and to render them the subject of criticism and philosophical discussion. As from various causes the practical system of law in any country is apt, in many respects, to deviate from that standard of perfection which nature holds up to the speculative mind, the detecting of its errors and imperfections, and the display of its peculiar advantages, become an agreeable exercise to men of ingenuity and reflection; and from such disquisitions, it is reasonable to expect that the <282> knowledge of mankind will be extended, their prejudices corrected, and useful improvements suggested.

In speculating upon the system of law in any country, it is natural to compare it with other systems, and by examining and contrasting the respective advantages or disadvantages of each, to explain and illustrate the nature and tendency of different regulations. From these comparisons, pursued extensively, and accompanied by such reflections as they must naturally suggest, philosophers at length conceived the idea of delivering a system of law, free from the defects which occur in every practical establishment, and which might correspond in some measure, with our views of absolute perfection; a noble idea which does not appear to have entered into the imagination of any Roman or Greek writer, and which may be regarded as one of the chief improvements in the philosophy of modern Europe. Hence the system of *jurisprudence,* which, after the revival of letters, has occurred in such multitudes, and which has been dressed in different shapes, and with <283> different degrees of accuracy by Grotius and other speculative lawyers.[7]

It must be acknowledged, that the execution of those works has not equalled the merit of the attempt. Although they profess to deliver the rules

7. Hugo Grotius (1583–1645): Dutch diplomat, jurist, and theologian. His main work, *De Jure Belli ac Pacis* (1625), was fundamental to the development of natural law theory in the seventeenth and eighteenth centuries. A second key figure was Samuel Pufendorf (1632–94), author of *De Jure Naturae et Gentium* (1672) and *De Officio Hominis et Civis* (1673).

of justice, abstracted from the imperfections of every particular establishment, they appear, for the most part, to follow implicitly, at least, in several particulars, the ancient Roman system, which, notwithstanding the consideration and celebrity it had very deservedly attained, is in many of its doctrines erroneous, and in some of its principles narrow and illiberal.

A more material defect in most of the writers on jurisprudence is their not marking sufficiently the boundaries between strict law and mere morality. They seem to consider, what a good man, from the utmost propriety of feelings and scruples of conscience, would be disposed to do, rather than what an upright judge would compel him to perform, and are thus led frequently to confound what is properly called justice (which requires that we should avoid hurting our neighbours,) with generosity or benevolence, <284> which prompts us to increase their positive happiness.

The attempts to delineate systems of jurisprudence, which have been so often repeated with more or less perspicuity or conciseness, but with little variation in substance, opened at length a new source of speculation, by suggesting an enquiry into the circumstances which have occasioned various and opposite imperfections in the law of different countries, and which have prevented the practical system, in any, from attaining that improvement which we find no difficulty in conceiving.[8] In the prosecution of this inquiry, more especially by President Montesquieu, by Lord Kames,[9] and by Dr. Smith, the attention of speculative lawyers has been directed to examine the first formation and subsequent advancement of civil society; the rise, the gradual developement, and cultivation of arts and sciences; the acquisition and extension of property in all its different modifications, and the combined influence of these and other political causes, upon the manners and

8. In this passage Millar gives a brief genealogy of his own profession as a teacher of law, drawing a line between the earlier speculations of Grotius and Pufendorf and the new, more historically framed works of Montesquieu, Kames, and Smith, who were his own great teachers. The remainder of this chapter is replete with the influence of these thinkers and is particularly close to Smith's lectures on jurisprudence (which Millar audited twice).

9. Henry Home, Lord Kames (1696–1782): Scottish judge and author of works on philosophy, jurisprudence, theology, education, literary criticism, history, antiquities, and agriculture. He was a mentor to Millar, who had served as tutor in his home as a young man. His major works include *Essays on the Principles of Morality and Natural Religion* (1751), *Historical Law-Tracts* (1758), *Principles of Equity* (1760), *Elements of Criticism* (1762), and *Sketches of the History of Man* (1774).

customs, the institutions and laws of any people. By tracing in this <285> manner the natural history of legal establishments, we may be enabled to account for the different aspect which they assume in different ages and countries, to discover the peculiarity of situation which has, in any case, retarded or promoted their improvement, and to obtain, at the same time, satisfactory evidence of the uniformity of those internal principles which are productive of such various and apparently inconsistent operations.

The system of law, in every country is divided into that part which regulates the powers of the state, considered as a corporation or body politic; and that which regulates the conduct of the several members of which this corporation is composed. The former is the government, the law which *constitutes;* the latter, the law which is *constituted.* The former may with propriety, though not in the common acceptation be called the *public;* the latter the *private* law.

To government belongs the province of appointing judges for the determination of law-suits; of establishing an armed force, <286> to secure internal tranquillity as well as for defence against foreign enemies; and also, in cases where the dictates of justice are silent, that of superadding to the private law such positive regulations or statutes, as peculiar conjunctures may render necessary or expedient. It is evident, therefore, that the state of the private law in any country must be entirely subordinate to the nature of its government; and that according to the merit or demerit of the latter, will be the excellence or deficiency of the former. The origin and progress of different public institutions, and the manner in which they have arisen, and been variously modified, from the circumstances of mankind, and from the different improvements in society, are on this account, objects of great curiosity, which present an important and leading speculation in the natural history of law.

All government appears to be ultimately derived from two great principles. The first which I shall call *authority,* is the immediate effect of the peculiar qualities or circumstances, by which any one member of society may be exalted above another. The <287> second is the consideration of the advantages to be derived from any political establishment.

1. Superior bodily qualities, agility, strength; dexterity of hand, especially in using the weapons employed in fighting; as well as uncommon mental endowments; wisdom, knowledge, fidelity, generosity, courage, are the natural sources of admiration and respect, and consequently of deference and

submission. A school-boy, superior to his companions in courage and feats of activity, becomes often a leader of the school, and acquires a very despotic authority. The strongest man of a parish assumes a pre-eminence in their common diversions, and is held up as their champion in every match or contest with their neighbours. The patriarchal government in the primitive ages of the world, and the authority possessed by the leaders of barbarous tribes in those periods which preceded the accumulation of property, are known to have arisen from similar circumstances. The heroes and demi-gods of antiquity, were indebted solely to their valour, and their <288> wonderful exploits, for that enthusiastic admiration which they excited, and for that sovereign power to which they were frequently exalted.

The acquisition of property, whether derived from occupancy and labour in conformity to the rules of justice, or from robbery and oppression, in defiance of every law, human and divine, became another and a more extensive source of authority. Wealth, however improperly in the eye of a strict moralist, seldom fails to procure a degree of admiration and respect. The poor are attracted and dazzled by the apparent happiness and splendour of the rich; and they regard a man of large fortune with a sort of wonder, and partial prepossession, which disposes them to magnify and over-rate all his advantages.[10] If they are so far beneath him as not to be soured by the malignity of envy, they behold with pleasure and satisfaction the sumptuousness of his table, the magnificence of his equipage, the facility and quickness with which he is whirled from place to place, the number of his attendants, the readiness with which they <289> observe all his movements, and run to promote his wishes. Delighted with a situation which appears to them so agreeable, and catching from each other the contagion of sympathetic feelings, they are often prompted by an enthusiastic fervor, to exalt his dignity, to promote his enjoyments, and to favour his pursuits. Without distinguishing the objects which figure in their imagination, they transfer to his person that superiority which belongs properly to his condition, and are struck with

10. The esteem with which the poor regard the rich is a major theme in Smith's *Theory of Moral Sentiments:* "When we consider the condition of the great, in those delusive colours in which the imagination is apt to paint it, it seems to be almost the abstract idea of a perfect and happy state. It is the very state which, in all our waking dreams and idle reveries, we had sketched out to ourselves as the final object of all our desires. We feel, therefore, a peculiar sympathy with the satisfaction of those who are in it. We favour all their inclinations and forward all their wishes." See *TMS,* 51–52.

those accomplishments, and modes of behaviour, which his education has taught him to acquire, and which his rank and circumstances have rendered habitual to him. They are of course embarrassed in his presence by impressions of awe and reverence, and losing sometimes the exercise of their natural powers are sunk in abasement and stupidity.*

The authority, however, of the rich over the poor is, doubtless, chiefly supported by selfish considerations. As in spending a <290> great fortune, the owner gives employment, and consequently subsistence to many individuals, all those who, in this manner, obtain or expect any advantage have more or less an interest in paying him respect and submission. The influence which may be traced from this origin, operates in such various directions, is distributed in such different proportions, and so diffused through every corner of society, that it appears in its degree and extent to be incalculable. Uncommon personal talents occur but seldom; and the sphere of their activity, so to speak, is often very limited. But the inequalities in the division of wealth are varied without end; and though their effect is greater in some situations of mankind than in others, they never cease, in any, to introduce a correspondent gradation and subordination of ranks.

These original circumstances, from which authority is derived, are gradually confirmed and strengthened by their having long continued to flow in the same channel. The force of habit, the great controuler and governor of our actions, is in nothing more <291> remarkable than in promoting the respect and submission claimed by our superiors. By living in a state of inferiority and dependence, the mind is inured to subjection; and the ascendant which has been once gained is gradually rendered more complete and powerful.

But the force of habit is much more effectual in confirming the authority derived from wealth, than that which is founded on personal qualities. The superior endowments, either of the body or of the mind, can seldom operate very long in the same direction. The son of an eminent general, or poet, or statesman, is most commonly remarkable for none of the splendid abilities by which the father was distinguished; at the same time, that we behold him in a contrasted light, which deepens the shade of his deficiency. The case is different with relation to wealth, which, in the ordinary course of things, is transmitted, by lineal succession, from father to son; and remains for many

* Theory of Moral Sentiments.

generations in the same family. The possessor of that estate, therefore, who <292> bears the name, and who exercises the powers which belonged to his ancestors, obtains not only the original means of creating dependence which they enjoyed, but seems to inherit, in some degree, that consideration and respect, that influence or attachment, which, by their high station, and by the distribution of their favours during a long period they were able to accumulate.[11] This is the origin of what is called *birth,* as the foundation of authority, which creates a popular prepossession for the representative of an ancient family, giving him the preference to an upstart, though the latter should possess greater abilities and virtues.

From the operation of these different circumstances; from the accidental superiority of personal qualities, and from the unequal distribution of wealth, aided and confirmed by the force of habit, systems of government have grown up, and been variously modified, without exciting any inquiry into their consequences, and without leading the people to examine the grounds of their submission to the constituted authorities. <293>

2. But when, in the course of political transactions, particular persons grossly abuse their powers, or when competitions arise among individuals possessing influence and authority, and of consequence parties are formed, who espouse the interest of the respective leaders, the public attention is roused to scrutinize the pretensions of the several candidates, to compare the different modes of government which they may propose to introduce, and to examine their title to demand obedience from the rest of the community.

In such inquiries, it is hardly possible to avoid suggesting another principle, more satisfactory than that of mere authority; the general *utility* of government; or rather its absolute necessity, for preventing the disorders incident to human society. Without a subordination of ranks, without a power, vested in some men, to controul and direct the behaviour of others, and calculated to produce a system of uniform and consistent operations, it is impossible that a multitude of persons, living together, should be induced to resign their own pri-<294>vate interest, to subdue their opposite and jarring passions, and regularly to promote the general happiness.

11. See Hume on "long possession" as "that which gives authority to almost all the establish'd governments of the world." *A Treatise of Human Nature,* ed. David Fate Norton and Mary J. Norton (Oxford: Oxford University Press, 2000), 356.

There are natural rights, which belong to mankind antecedent to the formation of civil society. We may easily conceive, that, in a state of nature, we should be entitled to maintain our personal safety, to exercise our natural liberty, so far as it does not encroach upon the rights of others; and even to maintain a property in those things which we have come to possess, by original occupancy, or by our labour in producing them. These rights are not lost, though they may be differently modified when we enter into society. A part of them, doubtless, must be resigned for the sake of those advantages to be derived from the social state. We must resign, for example, the privilege of avenging injuries, for the advantage of being protected by courts of justice. We must give up a part of our property, that the public may be enabled to afford that protection. We must yield obedience to the legislative power, that we may enjoy that good order and tranquillity to be expected from its cool and <295> dispassionate regulations. But the rights which we resign, ought, in all these cases, to be compensated by the advantages obtained; and the restraints, or burdens imposed, ought neither to be greater, nor more numerous, than are necessary for the general prosperity and happiness.

Were we to examine, according to this criterion, the various political systems which take place in the world, how many might be weighed in the balance and found wanting? Some are defective by too great strictness of regulation, confining and hampering natural liberty by minute and trivial restraints; more have deviated widely from the purpose by too great laxity, admitting, an excessive license to the various modifications of knavery and violence; but the greatest number have almost totally failed in producing happiness or security, from the tyranny of individuals, or of particular orders and ranks, who, by the accidental concurrence of circumstances, acquiring exorbitant power, have reduced their fellow-citizens into a state of servile subjection. It is a mortifying reflection, to observe, that, <296> while many other branches of knowledge have attained a high degree of maturity, the master-piece of science, the guardian of rights, and of every thing valuable, should, in many enlightened parts of the world, still remain in a state of gross imperfection. Even in countries where the people have made vigorous efforts to meliorate their government, how often has the collusion of parties, the opposite attraction of public and private interest, the fermentation of numberless discordant elements, produced nothing at last but a residue of despotism.

It may here be remarked, that, when a political constitution is happily constructed, it not only excites approbation from the ultimate view of its beneficial tendency, but, like a complex machine, in which various wheels and springs are nicely adjusted, it affords additional pleasure, from our sense of order and beautiful arrangement.[12] If we are pleased with the survey of a well-regulated farm or workhouse, in which there is nothing slovenly or misplaced, nothing lost or superfluous, but in which every opera-<297>tion, and every article of expence, is directed to the best advantage, how much greater satisfaction must we receive, in beholding the same regular disposition of parts, the same happy adjustment of means to a beneficial purpose, exhibited in a system so complicated and extensive, as to comprehend the moral and political movements of a great nation?

In England, where the attention of the inhabitants has been long directed to speculations of this nature, the two original principles of government, which I have mentioned, were distinguished by political writers as far back, at least, as the commencement of the contest between the king and the people, upon the accession of the House of Stewart, and were then respectively patronized and adopted by the two great parties into which the nation was divided. The principle of *authority* was that of the tories; by which they endeavoured to justify the pretensions of the sovereign to absolute power.[13] As the dignity of the monarch excited universal respect and <298> reverence, and as it was not conferred by election, but had been immemorially possessed by a hereditary title, it was understood to be derived from the author of our nature, who has implanted in mankind the seeds of loyalty and allegiance. The monarch is, therefore, not accountable to his subjects, but only to the Deity, by whom he is appointed; and consequently his power, so far as we

12. Smith similarly emphasized the combination of aesthetic and utilitarian motives in the "machine" of government: "The perfection of police, the extension of trade and manufactures, are noble and magnificent objects. The contemplation of them pleases us, and we are interested in whatever can tend to advance them. They make part of the great system of government, and the wheels of the political machine seem to move with more harmony and ease by means of them. We take pleasure in beholding the perfection of so beautiful and grand a system, and we are uneasy till we remove any obstruction that can in the least disturb or encumber the regularity of its motions. All constitutions of government, however, are valued only in proportion as they tend to promote the happiness of those who live under them. This is their sole use and end." See *TMS,* 185.

13. Millar's outline of the principles of authority vs. utility as the leading doctrines of the Tory and Whig parties can be compared with his more historical discussion of these same divisions in vol. 3.

are concerned, is absolute; requiring, on our part, an unlimited passive obedience. If guilty of tyranny and oppression, he may be called to an account in the next world, for transgressing the laws of his Maker; but, in this life, he is totally exempted from all restraint or punishment; and the people, whom heaven in its anger has visited with this affliction, have no other resource than prayers and supplications.

The whigs, on the other hand, founded the power of a sovereign, and of all inferior magistrates and rulers, upon the principle of *utility.* They maintained, that as all government is intended for defending the natural rights of mankind, and for promoting the happiness of human society, every <299> exertion of power in governors, inconsistent with that end, is illegal and criminal; and it is the height of absurdity to suppose, that, when an illegal and unwarrantable power is usurped, the people have no right to resist the exercise of it by punishing the usurper. The power of a king is no otherwise of Divine appointment than any other event which happens in the dispositions of Providence; and, in the share of government which is devolved upon him, he is no more the vicegerent of God Almighty than any inferior officer, to whom the smallest or meanest branch of administration is committed.

At the same time that the whigs considered the good of society as the foundation of our submission to government, they attempted to modify and confirm that principle by the additional principle of *consent.* As the union of mankind in society is a matter of choice, the particular form of government introduced into any country depends, in like manner, upon the inclination of the inhabitants. According to the general current of popular opinion, they adopt certain <300> political arrangements, and submit to different rulers and magistrates, either by positive regulation and express contracts, or by acting in such a manner as gives room to infer a tacit agreement. As government, therefore, arose from a contract, or rather a number of contracts, either expressed or implied, among the different members of society, the terms of submission between the governors and the governed, as well as the right of punishing either party, upon a violation of those original agreements, may thence be easily and clearly ascertained.

With respect to this origin of the duty of allegiance, which has been much insisted on by the principal writers in this country, and which has of late been dressed and presented in different shapes by politicians on the continent,[14] it seems rather to be a peculiar explanation and view of the former principle of utility, than any new or separate ground of our submission to government; and even, when considered in this light, it must be admitted with such precautions and limitations, that very little advantage is gained by it. <301>

The obligation of a contract is liable in all cases, to be controuled and modified by considerations of general utility; and a promise inconsistent with any great interest of society is not productive of moral obligation. In reality, men, when they come into society, are bound to preserve the natural rights of one another; and, consequently, to establish a government conducive to that end. Good government is necessary to prevent robbery, murder, and oppression; and if a man be supposed to have promised, that he would support or obey a government of an opposite tendency, it would be his duty to break such an illegal compact, and to reform such an unjust constitution.

The addition of a promise, at the same time, appears but little to increase the weight of that previous obligation. The obligation to abstain from murder, receives but little additional strength by our giving a promise to that effect.

It seems, indeed, to be a maxim universally admitted, that every nation is entitled to regulate its own government; but this <302> proceeds upon the presumption that every nation is the best judge of what is expedient in its peculiar circumstances, and is likely to receive most benefit from that peculiar constitution which is introduced by the voice of the majority. The maxim, therefore, must be understood with exception of such political arrangements as are evidently tyrannical, and is applicable to such forms of government only, as in point of expediency, admit of different opinions.

It is understood, on the other hand, that no foreign state is entitled to controul or restrain its neighbours, in modelling and establishing their own political system; because, whatever pretences for such interference may be assumed, it never is dictated by a benevolent purpose, but commonly proceeds from selfish and sinister motives. As different states have always a separate, and very frequently an opposite interest, it must be expected that each

14. Millar is referring to the use of contract ideas and rhetoric in the French Revolution.

will invariably pursue its own; and that, in seeking to aggrandize itself, the constant object of its policy, whether professed or concealed, will be to limit the power, and prevent the <303> aggrandizement of its neighbours. There could not, therefore, exist a more fatal calamity to any country, than that its administration and government should be settled under the direction of its neighbours.[15]

There occur, at the same time, a variety of circumstances, in which it should seem, that the inhabitants of a country, by living under the protection of its laws, give no good reason to infer a tacit promise of submission to its government.

It would be absurd to suppose, that the inhabitants of Turkey have given a free consent to support that government under which they live. Even in other countries, less benumbed with ignorance and stupidity, or sunk in the lethargy of despotism, a great part of the inhabitants feel themselves under a sort of necessity to remain, where the language and habits of life are familiar to them, where they enjoy the comfortable intercourse of their friends, and where they have already secured the regular means of subsistence. Their submission to the government is, therefore, extorted by the prospect of those inconveniences which would attend <304> their emigration; and if it were at all to be regarded in the light of a promise, would be such a one as ought to be set aside from equitable considerations.

When we examine historically the extent of the tory, and of the whig principle, it seems evident, that from the progress of arts and commerce, the former has been continually diminishing, and the latter gaining ground in the same proportion. In England, so late as the year 1688—

> "The right divine of kings to govern ill,"[16]

was a doctrine still embraced in general by the landed gentry, by the church, and by a great part of the nation; and had it not been for the terror of popery, the revolution at that time would not have taken place. Since that period, however, there has been a gradual progress of opinions. Philosophy has been constantly advancing in all the departments of science; has been employed

15. Millar's argument here echoes his charge in the *Letters of Crito* (1796) against the hypocrisy of the British government's attempt to overthrow the revolutionary regime in France.

16. Alexander Pope, *Dunciad,* bk. 4, line 188.

in reducing all the works of art, all the appearances of nature, to their principles; and has not neglected to push her researches into political, as well as other branches of specu-<305>lation. The mysteries of government have been more and more unveiled; and the circumstances which contribute to the perfection of the social order have been laid open. The degrees of power committed to individuals, have been placed on their proper basis; and the chief magistrate, when stript of his artificial trappings, and when the mist of prepossession which had surrounded him is dispelled, appears naked, and without disguise, the real servant of the people, appointed for the important purpose of superintending, and putting in motion the great political machine. The blind respect and reverence paid to ancient institutions has given place to a desire of examining their uses, of criticising their defects, and of appreciating their true merits. The fashion of scrutinizing public measures, according to the standard of their utility, has now become very universal; it pervades the literary circles, together with a great part of the middling ranks, and is visibly descending to the lower orders of the people.

During the rebellion in 1745, a gentleman of some eminence, who had embarked <306> in that ridiculous project, is said to have distinguished himself, by defending the measure upon what were called whig principles. This was, at that time regarded as a novelty, and was far from being well received by his associates; but so great has been the progress of opinion since that period, that the more liberal part of the tories have now caught universally the mode of reasoning employed by their adversaries, and are accustomed to justify the degree of monarchical power which they wish to establish, not by asserting that it is the inherent birthright of the sovereign, but by maintaining that it is necessary for the suppression of tumult and disorder.

Even that hardy race,[17] who formerly issued from their mountains to attack him whom they considered as the usurper of the throne, are long since fully reconciled to the beneficial government of a German elector, raised by an act of parliament to the sovereignty of a free people.* <307>

The whigs themselves have not been exempted from the progressive operation of the same circumstances, which have gradually exalted their speculative principles, and occasioned a proportional change in their prac-

* See Addison's verses to Sir Godfrey Kneller.

17. The Scottish Highlanders, who long retained their Jacobite loyalty to the exiled Stuarts.

tical system. It cannot be overlooked, that the disposition to pry into the abuses of government is likely to suggest limitations in the power of rulers; and when a people at large employ themselves in discussing the advantages arising from different political arrangements, they must feel a bias in favour of that system, which tends to the equalization of ranks, and the diffusion of popular privileges.*

The despotism, which had long been deeply rooted upon the neighbouring continent, checked the progress of political speculation, and taught the people, not only to suffer, but even to exult in their fetters. <308> Philosophy, however, triumphed at length over ancient customs; and the light of science, which had long been diffused in every other department, discovered the rights of man, and the true principles of government.[18] The nation awoke, as from a dream of horror and distress. Their enthusiasm in correcting abuses and in propagating the new system, rose to a height proportioned to the danger which they had escaped, and the obstacles which they had to surmount. It bore down all opposition; it swept away those corrupt institutions which had been the work of ages; it levelled with the dust those bulwarks which avarice and ambition had erected for maintaining their encroachments; but unhappily, in the general wreck of opinions, it overthrew those banks and landmarks, which while they defended the civil rights of the inhabitants, might have contributed to direct and regulate the new establishment.

It seems worthy of remark, that when the new system in France appeared likely to spread over the rest of Europe, the alarm and panic which it struck among the in-<309>habitants of this country, was chiefly excited by a prospect of the dangers with which they were threatened, and the arguments employed in opposing and combating that system, were drawn entirely from the anarchy and confusion, the destruction of all rights and liberties, religious and civil, with which it would be attended; and the chief alarmists were taken from that class of men who had been denominated whigs.

Upon the whole, it is evident that the diffusion of knowledge tends more

* Hence the distinction between the *old* and the *new* whigs, by which a famous political character endeavoured lately to cover the desertion of his former tenets; and hence too a pretty general suspicion, that many nominal adherents of that party have become secret admirers of democracy.

18. Millar is referring, of course, to the outbreak of the French Revolution and the framing of the Declaration of the Rights of Man (1789).

and more, to encourage and bring forward the principle of utility in all political discussions; but we must not thence conclude that the influence of mere authority, operating without reflection, is entirely useless. From the dispositions of mankind to pay respect and submission to superior personal qualities, and still more to a superiority of rank and station, together with that propensity which every one feels to continue in those modes of action to which he has long been accustomed, the great body of the people, who have commonly neither leisure nor capacity to weigh the advantages of public regulations, are <310> prevented from indulging their unruly passions, and retained in subjection to the magistrate. The same dispositions contribute in some degree to restrain those rash and visionary projects, which proceed from the ambition of statesmen, or the wanton desire of innovation, and by which nations are exposed to the most dreadful calamities. Those feelings of the human mind, which give rise to authority, may be regarded as the wise provision of nature for supporting the order and government of society; and they are only to be regretted and censured, when, by exceeding their proper bounds, they no longer act in subordination to the good of mankind, but are made, as happens, indeed, very often, the instruments of tyranny and oppression. <311>

CHAPTER VIII

The gradual Advancement of the Fine Arts—Their Influence upon Government.

The diversions and amusements of any people are usually conformable to the progress they have made in the common arts of life. Barbarians, who are much employed in fighting, and are obliged to procure subsistence, as well as to defend their acquisitions, by vigorous corporeal exertions, amuse themselves with mock fights, and with such contentions as display their strength, agility, and courage. Long after mankind have made such advances in rearing cattle, and in agriculture, as to derive their principal maintenance from those arts, they continue to follow hunting and fishing, with all the varieties of rural sport, as their chief recreation and pastime. But when, in consequence of their improvement in useful arts, the bulk of a people are engaged in peaceable professions, and from <312> their advancement in opulence and civilization, have become averse from hazardous exertions, and desirous of repose and tranquillity, it may be expected that a suitable variation will take place in the style of their amusements. Instead of engaging in the athletic exercises, they will hire others to exhibit spectacles of that nature, and will become sedentary spectators of the struggle. Or if they have attained a higher degree of refinement, they will invent games which admit the display of mental address and ingenuity; and will at length introduce entertainments calculated to gratify the taste of whatever is beautiful in the compass of art or of nature. In some countries, no doubt, accidental circumstances have retarded the improvement of these elegant pleasures, and preserved, in the midst of opulence and civilization, an uncommon attachment to the primitive amusements of a rude age. The Romans, in consequence of early and deep impressions which they had received from their long and constant employment in war, were disgraced, even at the most exalted period of their philosophy and litera-<313>ture, by the fondness which they retained for the barbarous exhibitions of the amphitheatre. The inhabitants of this island, among whom the lower orders have considerable influence in directing the fashions, have incurred the ridicule of their neighbours, for their strong partiality to the inelegant amusements of the cock-pit, and the bear-garden. But whatever exceptions may occur in particular cases, it is commonly observed, that the refinements of taste, and the cultivation of the elegant arts, among a people, are in proportion to those improvements which multiply the comforts and conveniencies of life, and give rise to extensive affluence and luxury.

That the degree of barbarism, or of refinement, in this particular, which happens to prevail in a country, must have a powerful effect upon the character and manners of the inhabitants, will be readily admitted, when we consider what a large proportion of time is frequently spent in amusements and diversions; what a multiplicity of ideas these are capable of suggesting; and what a deep impression they make, more especially <314> in the higher ranks, and in the early periods of life!

In examining, therefore, the improvements which have taken place, in this country, since the revolution, it would be improper to overlook that progressive culture of the fine arts which has been so conspicuous, and from which the inhabitants of the higher, and even middling ranks, derive so great a share of their amusement.[1] Upon this subject, I shall throw together a few observations, concerning the history of these arts, and concerning their influence upon the government of a people; beginning with that extensive branch which is communicated by language, or literary composition. This

1. Millar's view that the development of the practical and fine arts should be an important part of the historical narrative was shared by a number of historians of this period. See, for example, Robert Henry's *History of Great Britain* (1771–93), which surveyed all epochs of British history in terms of several parallel narratives, including the history of the arts and of literature. Millar's most important predecessor, however, was undoubtedly Hume, who famously gathered such material into his appendixes: "It may not be improper, at this period, to make a pause: and to take a survey of the state of the kingdom, with regard to government, manners, finances, arms, trade, learning. Where a just notion is not formed of these particulars, history can be little instructive, and often will not be intelligible" (appendix to the Reign of James I, *HE,* 5:124). Though Hume's appendixes are evidently briefer and less developed, the parallel suggests that Millar may have seen the dissertations that now form vol. 4 of this work as a kind of extended version of Hume's earlier efforts.

may be divided into two classes: the first comprehending those compositions which are primarily calculated for mere entertainment, and to which, in a large sense, the denomination of *poetry* may be given: the second, including those in which entertainment is but a secondary object, and which may come under the general description of *eloquence.* <315>

SECTION I

Of Poetry; or those Compositions which are primarily calculated for mere Entertainment.

We find that from the original constitution of our nature, we derive pleasure from the utterance of certain measured and modulated sounds; and are still more delighted when by the contrivance of language, these pleasing sounds are made to represent or convey the ideas or images of former sensations. These two sources of pleasure, the melody of sounds, and the agreeable representation of ideas or images by words, concur in singing, which, with the accompaniment of dancing, constitutes one of the great amusements of early nations.

A song contains the rudiments of poetry and music, two arts, which, in a state of extreme simplicity, are commonly united. But when the musician on the one hand has <316> invented a rich and varied melody, and the poet, on the other hand has acquired so much experience and knowledge as to introduce a long and intricate series of thoughts, it is no longer possible to enjoy at once the result of their different improvements, and it becomes necessary that the two arts should be separated. The consequence of that separation is the superior cultivation and improvement of each, with regard to all those effects which they are separately capable of producing. As music is thus gradually rendered more intricate, and of more difficult execution, the mechanical part of it requires a longer and more intense application for acquiring a proficiency in the performance, and surpassing more and more the patience and perseverance of the ordinary gentleman performer, is at length abandoned in a great measure to the mere artist, who follows that profession for hire; while poetry, of which the mechanism is more simple and easy, and in which the powers of imagination are less confined in the trammels of art, becomes not so much a professional object as the occa-<317>sional exercise of all those persons to whom inclination or genius happens to recommend that species of amusement.

The pleasure which poetry affords appears to arise primarily from the representation of those natural objects which are great, new, or unexpected, and which are fitted to excite admiration, wonder, and surprise. These emotions are produced in us, not only from the nature of the objects represented, but still more from the mode of representation, which through the surprising medium of language, by an operation like that of enchantment, conveys an exact and lively image of every possible existence.

That admiration, wonder, and surprise, are agreeable feelings, which in different shapes and directions, become the source of a delightful occupation to the mind, is consistent with universal experience. The impressions of admiration are the deepest and most violent. Those of wonder and surprise, are slighter and more transient, but in return, they are more numerous and varied, more susceptible of different forms and mo-<318>difications, and enter more intimately into the ordinary train of our ideas and amusements.

The images communicated by the poet may relate either to external nature or to the passions and operations of the mind. The former are agreeable from the circumstances already suggested. But the latter afford a separate pleasure, which is frequently of much higher importance. When the passions and sentiments of our fellow-creatures correspond with our own, they excite that pleasing sympathy which is the great source of benevolence and friendship; when they are on the other hand, remarkably contrasted with our own feelings, they contribute, in some cases, to our entertainment, by provoking ridicule, and exciting the grateful sensation of laughter. <319>

PART I

Of Epic Poetry; or what is related by the Poet in his own Person.

Though the imagery arising from views of external nature, is unavoidably blended with that which springs from the representation of human sentiment, they have given rise to two different forms of poetical composition, more peculiarly adapted to the one or the other, the epic and the dramatic. The former in which the incidents are constantly related by the poet himself, and are thus thrown into a sort of shade and distance, favourable to the exaggerating emotions of admiration, wonder, and surprise, is peculiarly suited to the description of external nature. The latter, in which events are not supposed to be communicated by the intervention of the poet, but to pass in the immediate presence of the spectator, is better calculated to produce that vivacity of colouring, and that visionary conception of <320> reality, without which it is impossible to awaken our sympathetic affections.[2]

The sublime genius of epic poetry is peculiarly favoured by the manners of that rude and barbarous period which precedes the cultivation of the common arts of life. In proportion as men are ignorant and destitute of civilization, they are the more liable to be impressed with admiration, wonder, and surprise; and the more likely, though without skill or management, to communicate those feelings in their genuine simplicity and force. They are in a world where almost every thing is new and unaccountable, and where their observation is confined to a small number of objects. The great scenes of nature are spread before them, and successively recur in all the various forms which they assume in different seasons and situations. These, dwelling upon the imagination of the uninstructed beholder, and surveyed in a variety of aspects, present new and striking images of grandeur and terror, of contrast, and of resemblance, of unknown causes, magnified and misconceived by fear, <321> or of strange and unexpected events, misrepresented by delusive prepossession. At the approaching light of knowledge, these wonders disappear; the gigantic vanishes; and the multiplied pursuits of society render mankind acquainted with the new, familiar with the great, and conversant in the minute parts of nature. Their poetic imagery of course changes its character, and losing its enthusiastic ardour, sinks gradually into the temper of cool thought and reflection.

In the oriental poetry of a remote period, which is handed down to us, we discover evident proofs of that peculiar style and manner, by which the poetry of a rude people appears to be distinguished. Great force of conception, with little taste or judgment in the distribution of parts: a few features, boldly delineated, without skill or perseverance to finish the picture: grand and sublime images, loosely combined, and often ill asserted: comparisons far-fetched, but lofty and magnificent; with strong, but harsh metaphors, frequently broken and inconsistent; and with language highly figurative rather from a penury of <322> appropriated expression, than from exuberance of fancy, and therefore, in many cases, hyperbolical and uncouth.

2. Millar's discussion of "vivacity of colouring" and its ability to produce "sympathetic affections" echoes Kames's doctrine of "ideal presence" in his *Elements of Criticism* (1762).

The same character of sublimity may be recognised in those relicts of Celtic poetry, ascribed to Ossian; which no credulity can believe to be an entire forgery of the publisher; but from which we may easily suppose that he has removed a great part of their original imperfections.[3]

That the sublime genius of Homer was greatly indebted to the character of the age in which he lived, will readily be admitted; but the difficulty lies in conceiving, by what means, in so rude an age, he could acquire that correctness of taste and judgment for which he is so conspicuous. What an astonishing phenomenon is the Iliad, if we survey the extensive and regular plan upon which it is composed, the skill and experience with which it is executed, together with the purity of expression, and the harmony of numbers, which every where prevail in that immortal work; and if, at the same time, we consider that the author must have lived before the return of the Heraclidae into Peloponesus <323> otherwise he would undoubtedly have made some allusion to that event of so much importance to all Greece;[4] that is, he must have lived within eighty years of the Trojan war,[5] when the art of writing was hardly known to the Greeks, and more than three hundred years before their oldest prose-writer, of whom we have any accounts! How much more advanced was the state of arts and sciences in England during the life of Spenser[6] than in Greece, during the period when Homer is understood to have lived; but how obsolete is the language of the former compared with that of the latter? If we consider the chronology of Homer's life to be sufficiently established, one would be tempted to believe that his rhapsodies, as they were called, have not only been arranged and digested in a subsequent period, as has been asserted upon good authority, but have even

3. Millar's continued desire to believe in the fundamental authenticity of Macpherson's Ossianic publications no doubt owed something to his interest in the poem as a portrait of early manners.

4. The myth of the return of the descendants of Heracles to the Peloponnese functioned as a charter myth for the division of the Peloponnese between different Dorian states. According to the myth, Zeus granted Sparta to the Heraclidae who had left the Dorian heartland of northern Greece.

5. The assumed date of the Trojan War falls in the thirteenth century B.C., toward the end of the Mycenean Age, thus leaving a gap of some four and a half centuries between the date of composition of the *Iliad* and the legendary past in which it is set.

6. Edmund Spenser (1552?–99): Elizabethan poet, author of *The Faerie Queen,* begun ca. 1579 and published 1590–96.

undergone something similar to the *refacciamento,* by Berni, of Bogardo's *Orlando.*[7]

The improvement of poetry as an art, so far as it depends upon culture and experience, is naturally progressive; but when this art has attained a certain degree of perfec-<324>tion, like all others derived from the mere exercise of imagination, it is rendered stationary; after which it begins to decline, and hastens to its final extinction, while the impressions of the poet are weakened by the progress of knowledge, and by a familiar acquaintance with the objects of nature, his powers are, doubtless, in another view, increased by storing his mind with a greater number of ideas, by collecting and combining a greater diversity of images and events, and by the capacity he acquires of arranging and disposing them to the best advantage. The poetry of rude nations consists of separate lineaments, and of unconnected incidents; but from the natural advancement of the art, in a civilized and refined age, these disjointed members are united in a regular system, and produce a finished performance. The volume of nature is expanded; the range of imagination is enlarged; the discrimination of what is interesting and agreeable is improved; and by the union and co-operation of many beautiful parts, the mind is detained in a labyrinth of pleasing emotions. But in pro-<325>portion to the degree of excellence that has been attained, the standard of perfection is exalted; and the readers of poetry, tired with the repetition of similar objects and exhibitions, become severe and fastidious critics, quick and expert in discovering and censuring blemishes. Conscious, therefore, of what is expected, every succeeding candidate for fame must endeavour to surpass his predecessors by new images or combinations; by adorning each part with a greater accumulation of beauties, and by enriching the whole with a greater variety of parts. But there is a certain point beyond which the progress of embellishment ceases to be agreeable, and more is lost by deviation from simplicity than is gained by additional decoration. By crowding together a number, even of beautiful objects, the impression of

7. Matteo Maria Boiardo (Bojardo) (1440?–94): Italian humanist, poet, and aristocrat, best known for his *Orlando innamorato* (Roland in Love), a chivalric romance. After its initial appearance in the late fifteenth century, it was reworked by the Florentine poet Francesco Berni (1497?–1535) in an attempt to bring it up to the (Tuscan) purity of Lodovico Ariosto's (1474–1533) *Orlando furioso,* a more celebrated continuation which first appeared in 1516.

each is diminished, the attention is dissipated in a multiplicity of particulars, and the general effect is proportionably impaired. By excessive ornament, the figures appear loaded with artificial trappings; and the piece becomes gaudy and inelegant. The more interesting and genuine appearances <326> of nature are, at the same time exhausted; and it becomes necessary to substitute others of inferior value. The grand and the sublime are deserted in the pursuit of mere novelty and variety; and a corrupted taste becomes more habituated to factitious and sophisticated embellishments. Despairing to rival the models of a former period, the followers of the muses are at length induced to abandon the higher flights of imagination, and steering, without hazard, in a level and equable course, are content with the humbler attainments of smooth versification, and pointed expression; with figurative language, coined and carefully collected from every quarter; in a word, with prosaic tameness and languor, arrayed according to the fashion of the times, in a pompous artificial diction. In this declining state of poetry, it becomes a natural improvement, to throw aside the mechanism of verse, and in more natural and easy expression, to exhibit such pictures of life and manners as are calculated to please the understanding, and to interest the passions. Compositions of this nature, which, considering that their <327> chief object is mere entertainment, may be called poetical, are capable of being extended and diversified without end; and they seem peculiarly adapted to that combined exercise of the imagination and judgment which is agreeable to a refined and philosophical age.

These observations are confirmed by the history of all those nations who have made progress in the arts, and in polite literature. The sublimity of the poetical genius among the early Greeks, not only in what is commonly called epic poetry, but in the serious compositions intended for the accompaniment of music, has been universally acknowledged; and its decline in the later periods, after it had risen to a high degree of eminence, is not less conspicuous.

When the poetical talent, from despair of equalling the models already exhibited, and from the corruption of taste produced by the incessant study of novelty and variety, has been extinguished in one country, it is not likely, ever after, to revive among the same people; but it may easily be introduced into another country, where the <328> same natural beauties, not yet faded by time, are still fresh and agreeable; and where those images and descriptions, which had become tiresome by repetition, assume, when imitated in a different language, a new and interesting appearance, and may even acquire, in some degree, an air of originality.[8] Thus the Roman poets, towards the end of the commonwealth, and about the beginning of the despotism, rose to high reputation by a judicious imitation of the Greek writers; though, in the latter period, the career of Roman poetry was very similar to that of the Grecian; with this difference, that, as the Roman government lasted longer, it afforded more time to mark the steps of descending genius, and those affectations which the growing corruption of taste had a tendency to produce.

When the nations of modern Europe, after a long interval of desolation and disorder, had begun to enjoy peace and tranquillity, and acquired some degree of opulence, they applied themselves to the arts of entertainment, and imitated with success the poetical compositions of the <329> Greeks and Romans. Their attempts of this nature were, however, peculiarly modified by two circumstances.

In imitating the Greek and Roman writers, they at first preferred the affected brilliancy, and tinsel ornaments of a later age, to the simple and genuine beauties of the preceding period. Though, in the infancy of the fine arts, mankind, as has been remarked by Mr. Hume, when left without direction or instruction, will commonly follow the dictates of nature and truth; and, in their compositions, will endeavour to express their thoughts with plainness and simplicity, yet they are easily misled by false guides, and have too little experience and taste to reject the gaudy and affected embellishments of a vitiated style. From this injudicious imitation of ancient models, the first poetical compositions of modern Italy, and of other European countries, exhibited all those defects which are usual in a declining state of the fine arts. The tendency, however, of subsequent improvements, was not only to produce that correctness which is derived from observa-<330>tion, and from rules of criticism, but to restore that simplicity which is commonly the peculiar character of early compositions.

The Gothic manners, on the other hand, by introducing such romantic love, and such exalted notions of military honour, as were unknown to the Greeks and Romans, afforded a new and rich field for the display of heroic

8. As Millar indicates more clearly below, he has in mind the modern novel as the successor of the epic.

sentiments, and of striking adventures. The admiration and gallantry of which, in the age of chivalry, the ladies were uniformly the objects, and the humanity and generosity, with which all those gentlemen, who had acquired distinction in arms, thought it incumbent on them to behave towards one another, furnish a remarkable contrast with the spirit and behaviour of the principal personages in the Iliad; where a country is praised, in the same breath, for producing fine horses and beautiful women; and where Hector,[9] who first runs away from Achilles, is afterwards dragged at the chariot wheels of that brutal conqueror. The advantages, however, derived from this modern refinement, were so counteracted by the false taste which pre-<331>vailed, as to render the poetical compositions, which appeared upon the revival of letters, a set of motley performances, not less disgraced by childish and extravagant conceits, than they were often distinguished by uncommon strength of imagery and wildness of imagination. The Italian poets, who set the example to all Europe, were most remarkable both for the beauties and the defects which have been mentioned;[10] though, in the course of near two centuries, when they continued to flourish, they seem to have availed themselves more and more of an acquaintance with the purer classics of Greece and Rome. The French, who, after the states of Italy, came next into the situation of a polished people, appear to have turned their chief attention to supply the defect which was most wanting in the Italian poets, by substituting order, method, and regularity; and, as every new attempt is commonly pushed into extremities, the exuberance of imagination in the latter gave rise, in the former, to excessive restraints, to a rigid observance of critical rules, and to feeble and languid compositions. In <332> England, the progress of civilization was much later than in France; and as the people, for this reason, advanced more slowly in their ideas of correctness, the poets did not abandon the Italian models until, by the force of custom, and by the practice of several eminent writers, the national taste was invariably fixed and determined. The irregularity and bold imagery of Spenser, and the sublime genius of Milton, not to mention our great writer in the dramatic

9. In Greek myth, the son of Priam, king of Troy, and the greatest of the Trojan warriors described in the *Iliad.* He is killed by Achilles in vengeance for the slaying of Patroclus.

10. Millar presumably has in mind the excesses of European Petrarchism, with its taste for extravagant oxymorons and far-fetched love imagery.

walk,[11] who has no pretensions to correctness, have given a peculiar bias to the poetical taste of Englishmen, and directed their admiration almost exclusively to the powers of invention and fancy.

In all these European countries however, it should seem, that the poetic spirit has greatly declined, and that in two of them it is almost extinct. In Italy, the Gierusalemmé Liberata[12] may be accounted the last great exertion of the epic muse. In France, the Henriade of Voltaire,[13] which is, in that country, the most considerable poem of the same class, appears, notwithstanding the <333> celebrity of its author, to have sunk into the shade.

That in England too, epic poetry is already long past its summit, and has been declining for more than half a century, will, from the slightest examination, appear abundantly evident. The late adventurers in this field discover, indeed, few marks of a corrupted taste; but they seem greatly inferior to their predecessors, in original genius, in fertility of invention, and in richness of imagery. They are a sort of minor poets, destitute of that creative power which enlivens every object, and without effort converts all nature to their purposes; but straining to be sublime, tiring their fancy by endless and rapid excursions to the most remote and opposite corners of the universe, painfully collecting and skilfully appropriating the labours of preceding authors, and after all producing, at best, a few fragments of beautiful passages.

In reality, considering the state of society at present, both in France and England, it may be doubted, whether an epic poem, of great length, and highly finished in all its <334> parts, embellished with the harmony of versification, and the splendour of diction, and enriched with metaphors and figures of all sorts, be an entertainment suited to the general taste of the people. It should seem, that a short composition of this nature may give a delightful exercise to the imagination; but that a long work becomes tedious, and demands from the reader an alertness, and intensity of application, which few persons are capable of maintaining. We find, accordingly, that the modern novels, which, in a plainer style, comprehend a wider field of

11. William Shakespeare (1564–1616): the contrast between the "incorrectness" of Shakespeare and the rule-bound classicism of the great French dramatic poets (especially Jean Racine, 1639–99) was a frequent theme of eighteenth-century criticism.

12. Torquato Tasso (1544–95) published *Gerusalemme liberata* (Jerusalem Delivered) in 1581.

13. The *Henriade,* an epic poem on Henry IV, was begun in 1717 and published 1726–29.

adventures, have now, in great measure, superseded the ancient modes of epic poetry, and become the chief amusement of almost all those individuals who are exempted from bodily labour. The multiplication of these compositions, which were scarcely known to the Greeks and Romans, and their endless diversity of shapes, whether serious or comic, in which they have appeared, may be regarded as one of the great varieties in the history of polite literature. <335>

PART II

Of Dramatic Poetry.

Dramatic performances are, in all countries, of a later origin than epic. It is a more natural and obvious thought, that one should express his own ideas and sentiments, than that, by means of actors, or representatives, he should endeavour to communicate the ideas and sentiments of others. The latter supposes two very difficult, and, in some degree, inconsistent operations: First, that, by the warmth of sympathetic emotion, a man should enter so completely into the mind of others, as to conceive in what manner they will be affected on any particular occasion; and, in the second place, that he should distinguish and discriminate so nicely their peculiar feelings and affections, as never to confound them with his own. The exhibition of dramatic representations is, at the same time, attended with an expence, which may suit the cir-<336>cumstances of an opulent nation, but in which a rude people have neither the inclination nor the capacity to indulge.

This observation is confirmed both by the ancient and modern history of the drama. Sophocles and Euripides, among the Greeks, as well as Menander, and the other writers of the new comedy, flourished at the time of the highest Athenian opulence and politeness.[14] The Romans, indeed, in a ruder age, appear to have made considerable exertions in comedy; but they were little more than mere translators from the Greeks, and imported those foreign productions when the state of Rome did not permit the rearing of

14. Sophocles (ca. 496–405 B.C.): Athenian tragedian who wrote over a hundred satirical plays, as well as seven major tragedies including *Antigone* and *Oedipus Tyrannus;* Euripides (ca. 480–406 B.C.): the latest of the prominent Greek tragedians; his major plays included *Medea, Hippolytus, Andromache, Orestes,* and *The Bacchae;* Menander (ca. 343–291 B.C.): Athenian poet, the greatest writer of Attic comedy.

them at home. The Roman taste began to degenerate before there was leisure for much internal improvement in theatrical representations. This was likewise the fate of modern Italy. In France, the flourishing state of the theatre was not prior to the age of Lewis XIV.; nor in England to that of William III.

With respect to *tragedy* in particular, of which the great object is to excite compassion, by a display of the natural feelings of <337> distress, we may remark, that its improvement has been chiefly retarded from the difficulty of separating the ideas and sentiments, proper to the persons introduced, from those of the poet himself. To that source we may trace the most conspicuous blemishes which are discernible in this kind of composition.

In a dramatic representation, though the incidents are in reality intended to pass before a set of spectators, they are supposed to be carried on without any witnesses. But this fundamental supposition the poet is frequently tempted to overlook, by making the persons of the drama explain to the audience those parts of the plot which he finds himself unable otherwise to communicate. This indirect address to the spectators is to be met with, less or more, in the best tragedies of every country; but, in the infancy of the drama, a great part of the plot is unfolded in that manner. In the fragments of a Chinese tragedy, published by Du Halde,[15] every person informs the spectators who he is, what he has done, and what he intends to do. In the tragedies <338> of Euripides, the author generally supersedes the necessity of this, by employing some deity, or intelligent person, at the outset of the performance, to give the audience a full account of whatever is to happen. As, in the regular compositions of modern Europe, this clumsy contrivance is totally rejected; the information of this nature which they sometimes contain, appears to escape the writer from mere inadvertence, and from his confounding, in some measure, his own situation and views with those of the persons whom he exhibits.

From a similar inadvertence, we may account for those formal and set speeches, of unnatural, and apparently measured length, which abound in our most correct tragedies. In the conduct of his plot, the poet has occasion

15. The French Jesuit Jean-Baptiste du Halde (1674–1743) wrote the hugely influential *Description geographique, historique, chronologique, politique, et physique de l'Empire de la Chine* (1735; English trans. 1736), based upon seventeenth-century Jesuit missionaries' reports, in which he has an account of a thirteenth-century opera, *L'orphelin de la famille Zhao,* by Ji Junxiang, a work that inspired Voltaire's *L'orphelin de la Chine* (1755).

to introduce a certain train of ideas and sentiments, but, losing sight of the characters to whom they should be appropriated, he becomes himself the speaker, and endeavouring to do full justice to his friends, is anxious that they should omit no topic which the occasion may suggest. Hence, instead of the natural <339> turns of conversation, with such various and sudden reciprocations of dialogue, as frequently occur in real life, the piece is loaded with verbose and tedious harangues, resembling the declamatory pleadings of hireling orators. It is wonderful, how universally this unnatural style has become prevalent both in France and England, and how much the influence of custom has prevented even the most fastidious critics from being disgusted with it.

These defects are so gross and palpable, that they might easily be avoided; but there is another, derived from the same source, where the difficulty appears much greater. The person who is violently affected by any particular event, is apt to feel and act very differently from another who is merely a witness of his situation and emotions; and the passions excited in the former may not only be dissimilar, but often perfectly repugnant, to those which are produced in the latter. Thus, he who is under the dominion of anger, or of resentment, gives way to the boisterous expression of those passions, while the spectators may be affected <340> with apprehension or disgust;[16] and he who is instigated, by avarice or ambition, to commit an act of injustice, is probably buoyed up with the immediate prospect of gratifying his desires, and disposed to palliate or justify the measure; while those who behold the commission of the crime, are likely to feel indignation, hatred, or contempt. When a poet, therefore, endeavours to represent the behaviour of his dramatic personages, he must, by an effort of imagination, enter, as it were, into their situation, in order to conceive the feelings that are suited to their character and circumstances. It is extremely difficult, however, to remain in this artificial station, and steadily to retain that view of things which it is calculated to present. His own situation incessantly obtrudes itself upon him,

16. Millar makes use of Smith's observations on the differences between the emotions of the agent and those of the spectator—a difference which Smith argues is a force for moderation in social exchange. "But he can only hope to obtain this [i.e., the sympathy of spectators] by lowering his passion to that pitch, in which the spectators are capable of going along with him. He must flatten, if I may be allowed to say so, the sharpness of its natural tone, in order to reduce it to harmony and concord with the emotions of those who are about him." *TMS,* 22.

and shifting the visionary scene, disposes him to regard the several incidents through the medium of a by-stander. Thus the persons exhibited in tragedy, instead of expressing the passions natural to their situation, are made to describe those passions, to explain their various appearances, to <341> point out the movements which they have a tendency to produce, to moralize upon their consequences; in a word, to become a sort of spectators of their own conduct.

The imperfections and blemishes in this respect, which occur in the best dramatic performances, are innumerable. Few poets appear to have conceived the idea of avoiding them; but the immortal Shakespear, from the mere force of his genius, has done so more successfully than any other writer, ancient or modern; and it is this circumstance alone, which, in the midst of a thousand irregularities and defects, forms the great superiority of his dramas.[17]

To the difficulties which are unavoidable in dramatical compositions, there was added, in modern Europe, another, from those forms of versification which fashion had introduced and established. The melody arising from the recurrence of similar sounds, with which modern ears were peculiarly delighted, gave birth, first of all, to the *stanza,* which became fashionable in Italy, and in those other European nations who made any progress in the fine arts. But <342> the intricacy of this measure was found so inconsistent with the form of dialogue required in dramatic writings, that in these it was abandoned, and gave place to a more manageable kind of verse, by the regular adoption of couplet-rhymes. Even this versification, however, according to the mode which it assumed, more especially in France, with a pause constantly in the middle of each line, with alternate male and female couplets, and with the indispensible requisite, that every speaker shall finish the verse left incomplete by his predecessor, proved a considerable incumbrance to the poet, and, by demanding so much attention to the mere form of expression, exhausted, in some degree, that vigour which ought to be employed in the more important parts of the composition. To write good verses came thus to be held a distinct species of excellence, capable of compensating, in many cases, and even concealing the poverty of the matter

17. Drawing on Kames's doctrine of "ideal presence," Millar voices a view of Shakespeare that resembles what the Romantic poet John Keats (1795–1821) would later call "negative capability."

contained in them; and an artificial diction, like the gait of a man walking upon stilts, was preferred to the <343> plain easy movements of a more natural expression.

The English, among whom a critical taste in poetry advanced more slowly than in France, and who began to study the art at a period when old prejudices were more dissipated by the light of knowledge, were less attached to the Gothic beauty of rhyme; and in tragedy, as well as in other kinds of poetical composition, were led to indulge themselves in a species of verse which admitted greater freedom and variety. The fortunate example of an Italian writer, which, in a short time, found a successful imitator in England, delivered the dramatic poets of this country from the fetters of the rhyming couplet, and introduced the measure of blank verse, which is at once capable of approaching the looseness and facility of prose, and of being adapted to the most exalted and heroic sentiments.[18] The consequences were such as might be expected; and if the English writers of tragedy have been commonly more happy than their neighbours upon the Continent, in delineating the simple and genuine feelings of the <344> human heart, it may be attributed more to the convenient mode of their versification than to any other circumstance.

Their merit in this respect has also taught their countrymen to distinguish and to admire this particular excellence, and to undervalue any other where this is wanting. It should seem, therefore, that in this instance, the standard of taste, in France and in Britain, has become remarkably different; and to those who adopt the one or the other, it appears equally inconceivable that the merit of Racine and of Shakespear should admit of a comparison. Voltaire observes, that the question is decided by the other countries of Europe, who may be considered as impartial, and who unanimously give the preference to Racine.[19] But French literature is better understood through the greater part of Europe, and is more fashionable than English. Besides, a foreigner is better qualified to judge of merit in the conduct of the plot, in which the superiority of the French writers is admitted, than with regard to

18. Millar presumably has in mind the blank verse translation of Virgil's *Aeneid* by Henry Howard, earl of Surrey (1517–47).

19. Jean Racine (1639–99): French dramatist and poet; his major works include *Andromaque* (1667), *Iphigénie* (1675), and *Phèdre* (1677). Voltaire's strictures on Shakespeare had become notorious among British writers; see his *Dissertation sur la tragédie* (1748).

the natural expression of sentiment and passion, which constitutes the peculiar excellence of <345> the English. Thus the Italians are said to look upon the *Orlando Furioso* as their greatest epic poem, while foreigners generally prefer the *Gierusalemmé liberata;* because the merit of the former, which consists in its fine verses, none but a native of Italy can feel; but the regularity and good conduct of the fable, which forms the chief recommendation of the latter, is perceived by every smatterer in the language. It was perhaps, for a similar reason, that Euripides, was the favourite writer of tragedy among the Greeks themselves, and that Sophocles is more commonly admired by the moderns.

Among the other differences between epic and dramatical compositions, we may remark, that the latter, being the subject of public spectacles, in which mankind become highly interested, are easily modified into a variety of shapes, to suit the prevailing inclination; and consequently, they are less liable, by length of time, or frequent repetition, to be exhausted, or to lose their attractions. Of this a striking instance occurred not long since in France; where, though the general style of tragedy had been long settled by <346> custom, an entirely new species of drama, under the name of the *weeping comedy,** has been introduced; as in *cenie,* Le Pere de Famille, Le Philosophe sans scavoir, and the dramatic works of Mercier.[20] In these compositions, by laying aside altogether the restraints of versification, together with all pomp of imagery or of expression, and by founding the plot, not upon the misfortunes peculiar to princes and heroes, but upon such domestic afflictions and calamities as are incident to the greater part of mankind, there is opened a direct avenue to the heart, equally inviting and attractive to every spectator. By this improvement, tragedy being stript of all foreign ornaments, and exhibiting a more simple and genuine picture of nature, is likely to excite more powerfully the movements of pity and sympathy, and consequently to attain more completely her proper object.

Some attempts of the same nature have of late been made successfully in

* Comedie Larmayante. [[*Comédie larmoyante:* a form of sentimental and domestic tragedy in which the traditional boundaries between the genres of tragedy and comedy were blurred.]]

20. *Cénie* (1750) by Mme. de Graffigny (1695–1758); *Le père de famille* (1758) by Denis Diderot (1713–84); *Le philosophe sans savoire* (1765) by Michel-Jean Sedaine (1719–97); Louis Sebastien Mercier (1740–1814): author of *An 2440* (1770) and the plays *Jean Hennuyer* (1772) and *La destruction de la ligue* (1782).

England, <347> though in this country they are not so absolutely necessary, as the old models, in that species of composition which had deviated less from the true standard. But in Germany, where the drama has hitherto made but small advances, and where the writers of this class are therefore, less hampered by former habits and prejudices, the late examples of a new composition in France have produced a general imitation, and have had suitable influence in forming the national taste.

The end of comedy, properly so called, is to excite laughter; an emotion arising from a contrast in the mind between certain objects of an opposite description. Grand, solemn, or important objects are beheld with admiration, and with respect, or at least with serious attention. Mean, light, or trivial objects appear contemptible, insignificant, or frivolous. The ideas and sentiments, therefore, which arise from these two sources are so totally inconsistent and repugnant, that they cannot be blended together in our thoughts; and even when they are forced upon us in succession, we find a difficulty in passing very quickly from the one to the <348> other. The respective impressions appear to contend for the preference; and while they rouse our attention to alternate and opposite views, we are conscious of an effort or struggle, which occasions the pleasant, but somewhat uneasy convulsion of laughter.

To produce this emotion, therefore, a sudden contrast of dignity and meanness is always necessary. But it makes no difference, whether this contrast occur in the several parts of an idea presented to us, or from comparing what is presented, with something suggested by the previous train of our own thoughts. Provided there be a sudden transition from the one sort of impression to the other, the manner in which it is produced is of no consequence. Even in the ordinary course of our thoughts, the sudden occurrence of a light and trivial incident will frequently excite mirth. The mind passes readily, by a natural spring, from grave and solemn occupations, to the utmost levity and frivolity; but the transition in the opposite direction is more slow and difficult. The most insignificant avocation at church will sometimes discompose our gravity, and <349> mar our devotions by an ill-timed jocularity; but in our idle amusements, and in a playful humour, we are seldom provoked to laughter by the intrusion of an important and wise reflection.*

* See Akenside's Pleasures of Imagination. Note on Book III.

From the immense number of ideas, of different sorts, which pass through the mind, and frequently in rapid succession, there cannot fail to arise numerous instances of that contrast which tends to mirth and pleasantry. These are varied without end in the degree of their intensity, from such as produce the most violent horse-laugh, to such as awaken a mere smile that is hardly perceptible, and which may be considered as expressing little more than the simple feeling of pleasure, a feeling, however, which is light and volatile, in contra-distinction to what is important and solemn.[21]

—Olli subridens pater hominumque deumque.

———As Jupiter on Juno smiles,
When he impregns the clouds.[22] <350>

It may not be unworthy of remark, that, as the pleasurable convulsion of laughter arises not only from the influence of certain mental emotions, but also from the mechanical operations of corporeal objects, it is attended, in this latter case, with circumstances a good deal analogous to those which take place in the former. When, by the rubbing of certain irritable parts of the body, we become no longer able to suppress the risible agitation, we are sensible of a conflict between opposite sensations, resembling what arises from a contrast of ideas or sentiments; and are with difficulty able to resist the attacks of pleasure and pain, which appear alternately to obtain the superiority.

Of all the examples of contrast which are conducive to laughter, the richest and most extensive is, that which appears in the character and manners of men. As nothing is more constantly the object of attention than the behaviour of our fellow-creatures, there is no subject which more frequently employs our judgment, and awakens our feelings. When their behaviour is consistent with <351> propriety, it excites approbation and esteem, and is always attended with the appearance of dignity in the person in whom it is displayed. As every man wishes to be esteemed by others, he endeavours on all occasions, to exhibit such a view of himself as will tend to that purpose.

21. Millar ascribes his thoughts on incongruity and comic effect to Akenside's very popular poem "Pleasures of the Imagination" (1744), a poetic reworking of Addison's famous consideration of the same subject in the *Spectator.*

22. "This smiling father of both men and gods," Virgil, *Aeneid,* bk. 12, line 829; the English is from Milton's *Paradise Lost,* bk. 4, line 499.

This we know, from experience, to be the general aim of mankind; and according to this standard we examine the behaviour of each individual. When it happens, therefore, that the conduct of our fellow-creatures, instead of exhibiting that propriety which we look for, and which we suppose to be intended, is foolish, absurd and despicable, and when this conduct is presented to our view in a manner so unexpected as to excite surprise; it affords a strong and sudden contrast of dignity and meanness, and becomes the natural object of scorn and ridicule.

It is unnecessary to add, that such improprieties of conduct as fall under the denomination of *crimes,* or *great vices,* are not properly ridiculous; as they do not excite contempt but indignation and resentment; <352> feelings which have no resemblance to such as are produced by mean or trivial objects.

The talent of exciting laughter, by the exhibition of any impropriety or absurdity in human character and conduct, seems to be what is properly called *humour;* as *wit* seems to be the talent of exciting mirth by any contrast which has no dependence on the behaviour of mankind.

Considering humour and wit as distinguished in this manner, it must be evident that the former has a much greater tendency than the latter, to excite hearty and violent laughter; and constitutes, for that reason, the chief province of comedy. The ideas of dignity, which we not only refer to every rational creature, but which we see that he still more strongly refers to himself, render us peculiarly sharp-sighted in marking every instance of absurdity, weakness, or impropriety of which he is guilty, and dispose us to exaggerate those imperfections, from the secret gratification which our vanity obtains by diminishing the rank and consequence of others. Human nature is a great laughing-<353>stock, which we are pleased to see tossed about, and turned in all shapes, and with whose ridiculous appearance we are never tired. The pleasure we derive from the ludicrous combinations of other objects is more slight and transitory. The flushes of wit excite commonly no more than a smile, and are not so much the objects of mirth, as of admiration and surprise.[23]

23. Compare Smith's discussion of ridicule in *Lectures on Rhetoric:* "Whatever we see that is great or noble excites our admiration and amazement, and whatever is little or mean on the other hand excites our contempt. A great object never excites our laughter, neither does a mean one, simply as being such. It is the blending and joining of those

From what has been observed, it should seem, that, though comic writing cannot be successfully cultivated until the liberal arts and sciences have, in general, made considerable progress, it is likely to attain its highest improvement, at a period which precedes the most refined and correct state of taste and literature.

Among simple and ignorant people, it is not difficult to provoke laughter, because they have too little experience and reflection to distinguish what has real dignity or meanness from what may assume the appearance of either; and because they are so little acquainted with the various connections of objects, that any assemblage, in the least out of the common road, is apt to surprise them. <354>

> The simple joke that takes the shepherd's heart,
> Easily pleased, the long loud laugh sincere.
>
> THOMSON.[24]

According as men acquire comprehensive and liberal views of things, they become fastidious and sparing of their merriment. They are more discriminating in regard to the objects which afford the necessary contrast, and they are more capable of preconceiving those occasions and situations which give rise to it. A man is never much tickled with a story which he has heard before, and which he distinctly remembers; and upon the same principle he is not apt to laugh heartily at those pleasantries which depend upon associations already familiar to him, or which have a great similarity to those which he has foreseen or imagined.[25]

In Turkey, and in some other eastern countries, the contrast between a tall and short man is thought to be a reasonable cause of laughter; and a dwarf is, therefore, a necessary appendage in the retinue of princes.

False and inconsistent reasonings which have an air of speciousness, bulls and blunders of expression, even errors of pronuncia-<355>tion, or impro-

---

two ideas which alone causes that Emotion. The foundation of Ridicule is either when what is in most respects Grand or pretends to be so or is expected to be so, has something mean or little in it." *Lectures on Rhetoric and Belles Lettres,* ed. J. C. Bryce (Indianapolis: Liberty Fund, 1985), 43.

24. James Thomson (1700–48): Anglo-Scottish poet and dramatist. The line is from *The Seasons* (1730), lines 622ff.

25. In the "Deserted Village" (1770), Oliver Goldsmith (1730?–74) famously wrote of "The loud laugh that spoke the vacant mind."

prieties of dress unperceived by the wearer, are sources of mirth and jocularity in all countries.

Among our forefathers in Europe, the behaviour of a mere idiot was viewed in a similar light; and a person in those unfortunate circumstances was commonly kept by men of wealth, as an object of ridicule. When people become too polite to laugh at a real idiot, they substitute in his place an artificial one with a motley coat, and with a cap and bells, to imitate the behaviour of a simpleton, but with occasional strokes of shrewdness and sagacity. This personage afforded entertainment, by appearing, according to the proverb, more knave than fool; and became at last a professed jester, upon whom the family in which he lived, and their guests, were accustomed to exercise their talents; but who, at the same time, like the clown of a pantomime could shew by his occasional sallies, that he was himself no mean performer in the scene.

Persons of education, however, becoming gradually more expert in this kind of diversion, began to undervalue the studied jokes <356> of these pretended fools, and endeavoured to improve the entertainment by jesting with one another, and by assuming upon occasion any sort of character which might contribute to the mirth of the company. The practice of *masquerading,* which came to be universal through a great part of Europe, arose from this prevailing disposition, and gave individuals a better opportunity of exercising their talents, by enabling them to use more freedom with each other, and to appear unexpectedly in a variety of situations. Such was the style of amusement, which having prevailed in that period of European manners described by Shakespear, makes a conspicuous figure in the comic works of that author. As fashion is apt to produce fantastical imitation, it appears that the folly of individuals led them, in those times, to assume or counterfeit those humours in real life; an affectation which had become so general as to fall under the notice of the stage, and to produce a ridicule of the *cheating* humour, the *bragging* humour, the *melancholy* humour, the *quarrelling* humour, exhibited by Shakespear and John-<357>son, in the characters of Nym, of Pistol, of Master Stephen, or Master Matthew, and the Angry Boy.[26]

26. Pistol and Nym are from Shakespeare's *Henry V* and *Merry Wives of Windsor.* Master Stephen is from Ben Jonson's (1572–1637) *Every Man in His Humour.* The Angry Boy is from Jonson's *The Alchemist.*

The higher advances of civilization and refinement contributed, not only to explode these ludicrous pastimes which had been the delight of a former age, but even to weaken the propensity to every species of humorous exhibition. Although humour be commonly productive of more merriment than wit, it seldom procures to the possessor the same degree of respect. To shew in a strong light the follies, the defects, and the improprieties of mankind, they must be exhibited with peculiar colouring. To excite strong ridicule, the picture must be changed; and the features, though like, must be exaggerated. The man who in conversation, aims at the display of this talent, must endeavour to represent with peculiar heightening the tone, the aspect, the gesture, the deportment of the person whom he ridicules. To paint folly, he must for the time, appear foolish. To exhibit oddity and absurdity, he must himself become odd and absurd. There is, in this attempt, something low and buf-<358>foonish; and a degree of that meanness which appeared in the person thus exposed, is likely by a natural association, to remain with his representative. The latter is beheld in the light of a player, who degrades himself for our entertainment, and whom nothing but the highest excellence in his profession can save from our contempt.

But though the circumstances and manners of a polished nation are adverse to the cultivation of humour, they are peculiarly calculated to promote the circulation and improvement of wit. The entertainment arising from the latter has no connection with those humiliating circumstances which are inseparable from the former; but is deviated from such occasional exertions of the fancy as may be consistent with the utmost elegance and correctness. The man of wit has no occasion to personate folly, or to become the temporary butt of that ridicule which he means to excite. He assumes no grotesque attitude; he employs no buffoonish expression; nor appears in any character but his own. Unlike the man of humour, he is never prolix or tedious, but <359> passing with rapidity from one object to another, selects from the group whatever suits his purpose. He sees with quickness those happy assemblages, those unexpected oppositions and resemblances with which the imagination is delighted and surprised; and by a sudden glance, he directs the attention to that electrical point of contact by which the enlivening stroke is communicated.

Persons in the higher sphere of life, who are exempted from manual labour, and spend a great part of their time in meetings of pleasure and amusement, are captivated by the brilliancy of this talent, and become fond of displaying it. By reciprocal efforts to entertain one another, and by hazarding the free exercise of their mental powers, their understandings are sharpened, their knowledge is extended, the range of their fancy is enlarged, their conceptions become clear and lively, and they acquire a facility and command of expression. As their minds are thus filled with a greater store of ideas and sentiments, and as their habits of communication are improved in proportion; their conversation is, of course, enriched and <360> diversified; it assumes a higher tone of sprightliness and vivacity, and is more productive of those new and uncommon turns of thought which are the sources of wit and pleasantry.

While true comedy, therefore, which is conversant in theatrical representation, and which is possessed of the higher powers of ridicule, experiences the discouraging influence of refined and elegant manners, it is apt, in most countries, to be succeeded by a kindred species of composition, more airy and volatile, but less forcible; which is equally calculated to exhibit the mere playfulness of a sportive imagination, and to become the pointed instrument of satire and invective.

It may, however, be remarked that the display of comic humour, in any country, will depend very much on the varieties which occur in the characters of the inhabitants. According to the diversity which prevails in the real characters of mankind, more numerous instances of impropriety and absurdity will arise, and a wider field of ridicule will be presented to those who have the capacity to make use of it. <361>

One of the chief causes of this diversity is the advancement of commerce and manufactures, and the consequent separation and multiplication of trades and professions. In commercial and manufacturing countries, all the active and industrious part of the inhabitants, that is, the great body of the people are divided and subdivided, by an endless variety of occupations, which produce corresponding differences, in their education and habits, in their sentiments and opinions, and even in the configuration of their bodies as well as in the temper and disposition of their minds.

It also merits attention, that the same varieties in character and situation, which furnish the materials of humour and ridicule, dispose mankind to employ them for the purpose of exciting mirth. The standard of dignity and propriety is different according to the character of the man who holds it, and is therefore contrasted with different improprieties and foibles. Every person, though he may not be so conceited as to consider himself in the light of a perfect model, <362> is yet apt to be diverted with the apparent oddity of that behaviour which is very different from his own. Men of robust professions, the smith, the mason, and the carpenter, are apt to break their jests upon the weakness and effeminacy of the barber, the weaver, or the taylor. The poet, or the philosopher in his garret, condemns the patient industry, and the sordid pursuits of the merchant. The silent, mysterious, practitioner in physic, is apt to smile at the no less formal but clamorous ostentation of the barrister. The genteel military man, who is hired, at the nod of his superior, to drive his fellow-creatures out of this world, is ready to sneer at the zeal, and starch-deportment of the Divine, whose profession leads him to provide for their condition and enjoyments in the next. The peculiarities of each individual are thus beheld through a mirror, which magnifies their ludicrous features, and by continually exciting that "itching to deride," of which all mankind are possessed, affords constant exercise to their humorous talents. <363>

Rude and barbarous nations are placed in opposite circumstances. They have no such division of labour as gives rise to separate employments and professions, but are engaged, promiscuously and successively, in all those kinds of work with which they are acquainted. Having all, therefore, the same pursuits and occupations, and consequently the same objects of attention, they undergo a similar education and discipline, and acquire similar habits and ways of thinking. From the accounts of travellers and historians, we accordingly find, that however such people may happen to be distinguished by singular institutions and whimsical customs, they discover a wonderful uniformity in the general outline of their character and manners; an uniformity no less remarkable in different nations the most remote from each other, than in the different individuals of the same tribe or nation. As barbarians and savages have, at the same time, little opportunity for cultivating the powers of imagination, they are apt to be no less destitute of the inclination, than of the materials, for the exercise of humour. They <364> have, it is said, no turns of mirth and pleasantry. Their aspect is gloomy and severe. Their complexion, adust, and melancholy.

From the different circumstances attending the cultivation of the arts in different countries we may discover, in the article now under consideration, some varieties that seem worthy of notice. Among the ancient Greek states, the advancement of commerce and manufactures was, doubtless, much inferior to that which, during the present century, has taken place in modern

Europe. But even so far as it went, its effects, in occasioning a diversity of characters among the people, were limited by the institution of domestic slavery, which was pushed to a great extent. The character of a slave, whatever be the employment in which he is engaged, must always be affected by his degrading situation, and by the arbitrary treatment to which he is exposed. "The world is not his friend, nor the world's law."[27] It is no wonder that he should endeavour to elude those rules of justice, which appear to be established for the advantage merely of the free people, and from the benefit of <365> which he is totally excluded. It is no wonder that he should study to over-reach an unfeeling master, by whom he is regarded as no better than a brute animal, and denied the common rights and privileges of humanity; or that he should boil with indignation and resentment at those injuries to which he is continually subjected, and, when restrained by fear from expressing a sense of his wrongs, should be disposed to treasure up vengeance against his cruel oppressors. The greater part of slaves, therefore, are unable to resist the powerful contagion of the vices which are engendered in their miserable and humiliating circumstances; and the entire destruction of their morals is not the least injury of which they have reason to complain. In all ages and countries they discover nearly the same temper and dispositions—jealous, vindictive, and cruel; weak, fickle, and pusillanimous; cunning, selfish, and dishonest.

As in the most commercial of the Greek states, almost all the departments of trade and manufactures, and even many of those <366> which in modern times are accounted liberal, were filled with slaves, the uniformity of character so prevalent in that class of men, was, in a great measure, extended to the whole body of the people, and produced a proportional deficiency of those objects which afford the chief materials, as well as the chief excitements of humour and ridicule. This was probably the reason why the Athenians, notwithstanding their eminence in all the other productions of genius, discover so remarkable a deficiency in comic or ludicrous compositions. The comedies of Aristophanes,[28] written at a period when the nation had attained a high pitch of civilization, are mere farces, deriving the whole of their pleasantry, not from nicely discriminated and well-supported charac-

27. Shakepeare's *Romeo and Juliet,* act 5, scene 1.

28. Aristophanes (ca. 448–ca. 388 B.C.): Greek comic playwright, best known for *The Acharnians, The Knights, The Clouds, Lysistrata,* and *The Frogs.*

ters, but from the droll and extravagant situations in which the persons of the drama are exhibited. It is true that the style of what is called the *new comedy,* is said to have been very different; but of this we can form no judgment, unless from the translations or imitations of it by Plautus and Terence;[29] from <367> which the originals, in the article which we are now considering, do not appear in a very favourable light.

The comedies of those two Roman writers are also very deficient in the representation of character. An old avaricious father, a dissolute extravagant son, a flattering parasite, a bragging cowardly soldier, a cunning intriguing rascal of a slave; these, with a few trifling variations, make the *dramatis personae* in all the different compositions of those authors. But though neither Plautus nor Terence appear to have much merit in describing those nice combinations of affectation and folly, which may be regarded as the foundation of true comedy, they seem happy in the expression of common feelings, and in exhibiting natural pictures of ordinary life.

The Romans, independent of their close imitation of the Greeks, had scarce any comic writing of their own. After the destruction of the commonwealth, we meet with few writers in this department; and none of any eminence. The age of elegant literature at Rome was very short: there <368> was no commerce: the number of slaves was immense, as no free citizen would engage in any profession but those of the camp or the bar; and therefore it is probable that the Romans were still more deficient, than the Greeks, in that variety of original characters which is the great spur to ridicule.

In modern Italy, the rise of mercantile towns was followed by the revival of letters, and by the introduction of ludicrous and somewhat licentious compositions; but the Italians lost their trade, and their literature began to decline, before it had risen to that height at which the improvement of comedy was to be expected. They displayed, however, in a sort of pantomimic entertainments, a vein of low humour, by grotesque exhibitions, which are supposed to characterize the citizens of different states; and in this inferior

29. Greek comedy written from the last quarter of the fourth century B.C. onward, but generally regarded as ending its creative heyday in the mid-third century B.C. Titus Maccius Plautus (ca. 250–184 B.C.): Roman comic dramatist, author of the *Amphytryon, Bacchides, Trinummus,* and other works. Most of his plays are held to be revisions and improvements of earlier works, particularly the Attic New Comedy. Terence, or Publius Terentius Afer (ca. 190–159 B.C.): Roman comic dramatist and a freed Carthaginian slave whose plays were based mostly on Menander.

species of drama, they are said to possess irresistible powers of exciting laughter.[30]

In France, the country which, after Italy made the first advances in civilization, the state of society has never been very favourable to humorous representation. In <369> that country, the fashion has had more influence, than in any other part of Europe to suppress the oddities and excentricities of individuals. The gentry, by their frequent intercourse, are induced to model their behaviour according to a common standard; and the lower orders think it incumbent upon them to imitate the gentry. Thus a greater degree of uniformity of character and behaviour is propagated through all ranks, from the highest to the lowest; and a French beggar is a gentleman in rags. Individuals, at this rate, have little temptation to laugh at each other; for this would be nearly the same thing as to laugh at themselves. From refinement of manners, at the same time, their attention has been directed to elegant sallies of pleasantry, more than to ludicrous and buffoonish representation; and the nation has at length come to occupy the superior regions of wit, without passing through the thicker and more vulgar medium of humour.

It may, accordingly, be remarked, that among the numerous and distinguished men <370> of genius whom France has produced, Le Sage, and Moliere, are perhaps the only examples that can be adduced of eminent humourous writers. The high and deserved reputation of the latter, as a writer of comedy, is universally admitted; though I think it can hardly be denied, that his characters are commonly overcharged and farcical.

There is, perhaps, no country in which manufactures and commerce have been so far extended as in England, or consequently in which the inhabitants have displayed such a multiplicity and diversity of characters. What is called a *humourist,* that is, a person who exhibits particular whims and oddities, not for the sake of producing mirth, but to gratify his own inclination, is less known in any other country. The English are regarded by their neighbours as a nation of humourists; a set of originals, moulded into singular shapes, and as unlike the rest of mankind as each other.

Political reasoners have ascribed this wonderful diversity of character

30. *Commedia dell'arte* ("comedy of art" or "comedy of the profession") means unwritten drama; it was a form of improvisational comedy which began in Italy and flourished in the sixteenth and seventeenth centuries.

among the <371> English to the form of their government, which imposes few restraints upon their conduct. It is obvious, however, that, though an absolute government may prevent any great singularity of behaviour, a free constitution will not alone produce it. Men do not acquire an odd or whimsical character, because they are at liberty to do so, but because they have propensities which lead them to it. In the republican states of antiquity, which enjoyed more political freedom, and among mere savages, who are almost under no government at all, nothing of this remarkable excentricity is to be observed.

But, whatever be the cause of that endless diversity of characters which prevails in England, it certainly gives encouragement to sarcastic mirth and drollery, and has produced a general disposition to humour and raillery, which is the more conspicuous from the natural modesty, reserve, and taciturnity of the people. In delineating the most unaccountable and strange appearances of human nature, they require not the aid of fiction; to conceive what is ridiculous, <372> they have only to observe it. Each individual, according to the expression of a famous buffoon, is not only humourous in himself, but the cause of humour in other men. The national genius, as might be expected, has been moulded and directed by these peculiar circumstances, and has produced a greater number of eminent writers, in all the branches of comic and ludicrous composition, than are to be found in any other country. To pass over the extraordinary genius of Shakespeare, in this as well as in other departments, with those other comic writers who lived about the commencement of English manufactures; and to mention only a few instances, near our own times, it will be difficult for any country, at one period, to match the severe and pointed irony of Swift; the lighter, but more laughable satire of Arbuthnot; the gentle raillery of Gay; the ludicrous and natural, though coarse, representations of low life, by Fielding; the strong delineations of character, together with the appropriate easy dialogue of Vanbrugh; the rich vein of correct pleasantry, in ridiculing the va-<373>rieties of studied affectation, displayed by Congreve; and, above all, the universal, equable, and creative humour of Addison.[31]

31. John Arbuthnot (1667–1735): Scottish physician and writer, a member of Pope and Swift's circle; he wrote *The History of John Bull* (1712), an allegorical satire which originated the popular image of John Bull as the typical Englishman, and he was the main author of the *Memoirs of Martin Scriblerus* (1741); John Gay (1685–1732): English

It cannot, however, escape observation, that the number of adventurers in this province, has of late been greatly diminished; and few of them have risen to eminence. With all the partiality which national prepossession can inspire, we are unable to name above one comic writer of the present day, who deserves to be mentioned along with his illustrious predecessors. Our late theatrical exhibitions, under the title of comedy, are, for the most part, either decent and regular, but cold and spiritless performances, or poor farces, interlarded with common place sentiment, and often accompanied by music, which creates a sort of interest with the greater part of an audience.

Whether this alteration is merely accidental, or proceeds from permanent causes; whether it is produced by the mere love of novelty, or by a general decline in the powers of exciting laughter, it is not easy to determine. That the present deficiency of talents may originate in permanent cir-<374>cumstances, depending upon gradual changes in the state of society, is far from being improbable. Though, in a country where trade and manufactures continue to flourish, the divisions of labour are endless, yet the new professions to which they give occasion come, at length, to be so minutely separated from each other, as to produce very little peculiarity of temper or disposition in those who exercise them. The person who rounds the head, and he who sharpens the point of a pin, though labouring in separate departments, present nothing different to the view of the comic observer. The field of humour and ridicule, therefore, ceases to encrease; while, by constant employment, it may be worn out and exhausted.

On the other hand, it cannot be doubted, that the inhabitants of this island, though they have long retained the "vestigia ruris," are now, from an intercourse with their neighbours, and in the natural course of things, laying aside their former prejudices, and advancing with rapidity in all those refinements which contribute to the embellishment of society; and it may be expected <375> that when they attain a certain pitch of elegance and correctness of manners, they will become less desirous of figuring in the walks

---

poet and dramatist, author of *Fables* (1727) and *The Beggar's Opera* (1728); Henry Fielding (1707–54): English novelist, playwright, journalist and magistrate, author of *Joseph Andrews* (1742) and *The History of Tom Jones* (1749); Sir John Vanbrugh (1664–1726): English playwright and architect who was comanager of Haymarket Theatre; William Congreve (1670–1729): English dramatist and manager of Haymarket with Vanbrugh; Joseph Addison (1672–1719): English essayist, dramatist, and politician who cofounded the *Spectator.*

of humourous representation. Whether they are likely to become eminent in wit, in proportion as they decline in humour, may still be a question. There may be some reason to apprehend, that their application to serious business will preserve that saturnine complexion by which they have long been distinguished, and prevent their acquiring that quickness and flexibility of imagination, that never-failing vivacity and pleasantry, which are so conspicuous in their more volatile neighbours.

THE END.

APPENDIX I

Authorities Cited in the Text and in Millar's Notes

Addison, Joseph. *To Sir Godfrey Kneller, on His Picture of His Sacred Majesty King George.* London, 1716.

Akenside, Mark. *The Pleasures of Imagination: A Poem, in Three Books.* London, 1744.

Anderson, Adam. *An Historical and Chronological Deduction of the Origin of Commerce, from the earliest accounts to the present time.* 2 vols. London, 1764.

Anderson, James. *Observations on the means of exciting a spirit of national industry, chiefly intended to promote the agriculture, commerce, manufactures, and fisheries, of Scotland.* Edinburgh, 1777.

Asser (Joannes, Menevensis, bishop of Sherburn). *Aelfredi Regis Res Gestae.* London, 1574.

Atkyns, Sir Robert. *The Power, Jurisdiction, and Priviledge of Parliament; and the Antiquity of the House of Commons Asserted.* London, 1689.

Atwood, William. *Jani Anglorum Facies Nova: Or, Several Monuments of Antiquity touching the Great Councils of the Kingdom, and the Court of the Kings immediate tenants and officers from the first of William the First, to the forty ninth of Henry the Third.* London, 1680.

———. *Jus Anglorum ab Antiquo.* London, 1681.

Bacon, Francis. *The Historie of the Raigne of King Henry the Seuenth.* London, 1622.

Bacon, Nathaniel. *An Historical and Political Discourse of the Laws and Government of England, from the first times to the end of the reign of Queen Elizabeth. Collected from some manuscript notes of John Selden, Esq.* 4th ed. London, 1739.

Balfour, Sir James. *Practicks: or, a System of the More Ancient Law of Scotland.* Edinburgh, 1754.

Bede. *Historia Ecclesiastica Gentis Anglorum.* [Completed 731].

Blackstone, Sir William. *Commentaries on the Laws of England.* 4 vols. London, 1765–69.

———. *The Great Charter and Charter of the Forest, with other authentic instruments; to which is prefixed, an introductory discourse, containing the history of the charters.* Oxford, 1759.

Bolingbroke, Henry St. John, Viscount [as "Humphrey Oldcastle"]. *Remarks on the History of England.* London, 1743.

Boulainvilliers, Henri de, Compte. *Histoire de l'ancien gouvernement de la France. Avec XIV. lettres historiques sur les parlemens ou états-généraux.* La Haye & Amsterdam, 1727.

Bracton, Henri de. *De Legibus et Consuetudinibus Angliae.* London, 1569.

Brady, Robert. *A Complete History of England.* London, 1685.

———. *A Full and Clear Answer to a Book Written by William Petit, Esq.* London, 1681.

———. *An Historical Treatise of Cities and Burghs.* 2nd edition. London, 1704.

———. *An Introduction to the Old English History.* London, 1684.

Burke, Edmund. *An appeal from the new to the old Whigs, in consequence of some late discussions in Parliament relative to the Reflections on the French revolution.* London, 1791.

Burman, Pieter. *De Vectigalibus populi Romani dissertatio.* Leiden, 1714.

Burn, Richard. *The Ecclesiastical Law.* 2 vols. London, 1763.

Burnet, Gilbert. *History of the Reformation of the Church of England.* 3 vols. London, 1679–1715.

———. *History of His Own Time.* 2 vols. London, 1724–34.

Caesar, Julius. *De Bello Gallico.*

Carte, Thomas. *A General History of England.* 4 vols. London, 1747–55.

Cicero, Marcus Tullius. *De Officiis.*

Clarendon, Edward Hyde, Earl of. *The History of the Rebellion and Civil Wars in England.* 3 vols. Oxford, 1702–4.

Coke, Sir Edward. *Institutes of the Laws of England.* London, 1628–44.

Coleman, Edward. *A Collection of Letters . . . Relating to the . . . Popish Plot.* Edited by Sir George Treby. London, 1681.

Cooke, Edward. *Argumentum Anti-Normanicum.* London, 1680.

Dalrymple, Sir John. *Memoirs of Great Britain and Ireland. From the Dissolution of the Last Parliament of Charles II until the Sea Battle off La Hogue.* 3 vols. London and Edinburgh, 1771–73.

Daniel, Samuel. *The Collection of the Historie of England.* London, 1618.

Davies, Sir John. *A Discovery of the True Causes Why Ireland Was Never Entirely Subdued . . . Printed exactly from the edition of 1612.* London, 1747.

———. "A speech to the Lord-Deputy in 1613, tracing the ancient constitution of Ireland." In *Historical Tracts,* ed. George Chalmers. London, 1786.

Du Bos, Jean-Baptiste. *Histoire critique de l'établissement de la monarchie françoise dans les Gaules.* 3 vols. Paris, 1734.

———. *Réflexions critique sur la poésie et sur la peinture.* 2 vols. Paris, 1719.

Du Cange, Charles Du Fresne. *Glossarium ad Scriptores Mediae et Infimae Latinitatis.* 6 vols. Paris, 1766.

Duck, Sir Arthur. *De Usu et Authoritate Juris Civilis Romanorum, in Dominiis Principum Christianorum.* London, 1653.

Dugdale, Sir William. *The Baronage of England.* 2 vols. London, 1675.

Farley, Abraham, and Sir Henry Ellis, eds. *Domesday-book.* 2 vols. London, 1783.

Forbes, William. *A Treatise of Church Lands and Tithes.* Edinburgh, 1705.

Fortescue, Sir John. *De Laudibus Legum Angliae.* London, 1600.

Gellius, Aulus. *Noctes Atticae.*

Giannone, Pietro. *The Civil History of the Kingdom of Naples.* Trans. J. Ogilvie. 2 vols. London, 1729–31.

Gibson, Edmund, ed. *Chronicon Saxonicum.* Oxford, 1692.

Gilbert, Sir Geoffrey. *The History and Practice of the High Court of Chancery.* London, 1758.

Gildas. *De Excidio Britannae Liber Querulus.* London, 1568.

Goodwin, Thomas. *Moses and Aaron. Civil and Ecclesiastical Rites, Used by the Ancient Hebrews.* London, 1625.

Gurdon, Thornhaugh. *The History of the High Court of Parliament.* 2 vols. London, 1731.

Hailes, Sir David Dalrymple, Lord. *Annals of Scotland. From the Accession of Malcolm III, Surnamed Canmore, to the Accession of Robert I.* 2 vols. Edinburgh and London, 1776.

———. *An Examination of some of the Arguments for the High Antiquity of Regiam Majestatem; and an enquiry into the authenticity of Leges Malcolmi.* Edinburgh, 1769.

Hale, Matthew. *The History of the Common Law of England.* London, 1713.

Halhed, Nathaniel Brassey. *A Code of Gentoo Laws; or, Ordinations of the Pundits.* London, 1776.

Harris, William. *An Historical and Critical Account of the Life and Writings of Charles I.* London, 1758.

———. *An Historical and Critical Account of the Life of Charles II.* 2 vols. London, 1746.

Hatsell, John. *Precedents of Proceedings in the House of Commons.* Vol. 3. London, 1785.

Hawkins, William. *A Treatise of the Pleas of the Crown.* 2 vols. London, 1716–21.

Hearne, Thomas. *The Antiquities of Great Britain.* 2 vols. London, 1786–1807.

———. *A Collection of Curious Discourses, Written by Eminent Antiquaries upon Several Heads in Our English Antiquities.* London, 1720.

Hénault, Charles Jean François. *A New Chronological Abridgement of the History of France.* Translated by Thomas Nugent. 2 vols. London, 1762.

Henry, Robert. *The History of Great Britain, from the First Invasion of It by the Romans Under Julius Caesar. Written on a New Plan.* 6 vols. London, 1771–93.

Higden, Ranulf. *Polychronicon.* Southwark, 1482.

Holles, Denzil, Baron. *Memoirs of Denzil Lord Holles . . . from . . . 1641 to 1648.* London, 1699.

Horne, Andrew. *The Booke called the Mirrour of Justices . . . translated out of the old French into the English tongue. By W[illiam] H[ughes] of Grays Inne, Esquire.* London, 1646.

Horsley, John. *Britannia Romana; or, The Roman Antiquities of Britain: in Three Books.* London, 1732.

Hoveden, Roger de. *Annalium.* London, 1596.

Hume, David. *Essays, Moral and Political.* 2 vols. Edinburgh, 1741–42.

———. *The History of England, from the Invasion of Julius Caesar to the Revolution in 1688.* 6 vols. London, 1754–62.

James I, king of Great Britain and Ireland. *The Workes of the Most High and Mightie Prince, James . . . King of Great Britaine.* London, 1616.

Juvenal. *Satires.*

Kames, Henry Home, Lord. *Essays upon Several Subjects Concerning British Antiquities.* 2nd ed. Edinburgh, 1749.

———. *Historical Law-Tracts.* 2 vols. Edinburgh, 1758.

———. *Principles of Equity.* Edinburgh, 1760.

Kennet, Basil. *Romae Antiquae Notitia; or, The Antiquities of Rome.* London, 1696.

Lambarde, William. *Archaionomia.* Cambridge, 1644.

Leland, Thomas. *The History of Ireland, from the Invasion of Henry II., with a Preliminary Discourse on the Antient State of That Kingdom.* 3 vols. London, 1773.

Lewis, Thomas. *Origines Hebraeae: The Antiquities of the Hebrew Republic.* London, 1724.

Lightfoot, John. *The Harmony, Chronicle, and Order of the Old Testament.* London, 1647.

Ludlow, Edmund. *Memoirs.* 3 vols. Vivay, 1698.

Lyttelton, George, Lord. *The History of the Life of King Henry the Second.* 3rd ed. 4 vols. London, 1769.

Mably, Abbé de. *Observations sur l'histoire de France.* 2 vols. Genève, 1793.

Macaulay, Catherine. *The History of England from the Accession of James I to That of the Brunswick Line.* 8 vols. London, 1763–81.

Macpherson, James. *An Introduction to the History of Great Britain and Ireland.* London, 1771.

———. *Original Papers; containing the secret history of Great Britain, from the Restoration, to the accession of the House of Hanover; to which are prefixed extracts from the life of James II, as written by himself.* 2 vols. London, 1775.

Madox, Thomas. *Firma Burgi, or, An Historical Essay Concerning the Cities, Towns and Buroughs of England.* London, 1726.

———. *The History and Antiquities of the Exchequer of the Kings of England.* London, 1711.

Millar, John. *The Origin of the Distinction of Ranks.* 3rd ed., corr. London, 1779.

Montesquieu, Charles Louis de Secondat, Baron de. *De l'esprit des loix.* 2 vols. Geneve, 1748.

Moore, John. *A Journal during a Residence in France, from the beginning of August, to the middle of December, 1792.* London, 1793.

Muratori, Ludovico Antonio. *Antiquitates Italicae Medii Aevi.* 6 vols. Milano, 1738–42.

Nennius. *Nennii Banchorensis Coenobiarchiae Eulogium Britanniae sive Historia Britonum.* Edited by Thomas Gale and Charles Bertram. The Hague, 1758.

Noble, Mark. *Memoirs of the Protectorate-House of Cromwell.* 2 vols. London, 1784.

The Parliamentary or Constitutional History of England. 24 vols. London, 1751–61.

Pasquier, Etienne. *Les recherches de la France.* Paris, 1621.

Petyt, William. *The Antient Rights of the Commons of England Asserted.* London, 1680.

Pfeffel, Christian Friedrich. *Nouvel abrégé chronologique de l'histoire et du droit public d'Allemagne.* Paris, 1777.

Prynne, William. *Preface to An Exact Abridgement of the Records in the Tower of London . . . Collected by Sir R. Cotton.* London, 1657.

Rapin-Thoyras, Paul de. *The History of England.* Translated by Nicholas Tindal. 15 vols. London, 1725–31.

[Ridpath, George]. *A Discourse upon the Union of Scotland and England; . . . Humbly submitted to the Parliament of Scotland by a Lover of his Country.* Edinburgh, 1702.

———. *An Historical Account of the Antient Rights and Power of the Parliament of Scotland.* Edinburgh, 1703.

Robertson, William. *History of the Reign of the Emperor Charles V.* 3 vols. London, 1769.

Rousseau, Jean-Jacques. *Discours sur l'origine et les fondemens de l'inégalité parmi les hommes.* Amsterdam, 1755.

———. *Discours sur les sciences et les arts.* Genève, 1750.

Rushworth, John. *Historical Collections.* 8 vols. London, 1659.

Russell, Rachel, Lady. *Letters of Lady Rachel Russell.* London, 1773.

Sale, George, et al. *The Modern Part of an Universal History.* 44 vols. London, 1759–66.

Sarpi, Paulo. *A Treatise of Beneficiary Matters: or, A history of ecclesiastical benefices and revenues. Translated from the most correct copy in Italian extant.* Westminster, 1727.

Selden, John. *A Brief Discourse Touching the Office of Lord Chancellor of England.* London, 1672.

———. *Eadmeri Monachi Cantuariensis Historiae Novorum.* London, 1623.

———. *Table-Talk: Being the Discourses of John Selden, Esq.* London, 1689.

———. *Titles of Honour.* 2nd ed. London, 1614.

Skene, Sir John. *De Verborum Significatione. The Exposition of the Termes and Difficill Wordes, Contained in the Foure Buikes of Regiam Majestatem, and Vthers, etc.* Edinburgh, 1681.

———. *Regiam Majestatem: The Auld Lavves and Constitvtions of Scotland.* Edinburgh, 1609.

Smith, Adam. *An Inquiry into the Nature and Causes of the Wealth of Nations.* 2 vols. London, 1776.

———. *The Theory of Moral Sentiments.* London, 1759.

Smith, Sir Thomas. *The Commonwealth of England.* London, 1612.

———. *De Republica Anglorum.* London, 1583.

Somner, William. *Dictionarium Saxonico-Latino-Anglicum.* Oxford, 1659.

Spelman, Sir Henry. *Concilia, Decreta, Leges, Constitutiones, in Re Ecclesiarum Orbis Britannici.* Edited by J. Stephens. London, 1639.

———. *Glossarium Archaiologium.* London, 1687.

———. *Reliquiae Spelmannianae: The posthumous works of Sir Henry Spelman, Kt., Relating to the Laws and Antiquities of England.* Edited by Edmund Gibson. Oxford, 1698.

———. *Treatise of Feuds and Tenures by Knight-Service.* Vol. 2 (1639) of *The English Works of Sir Henry Spelman.* London, 1723.

Spenser, Edmund. *A View of the State of Ireland.* Dublin, 1633.

Stillingfleet, Edward. *Origines Brittanicae; or, the Antiquity of the British Churches.* London, 1685.

Stuart, Gilbert. *The History of Scotland, from the Establishment of the Reformation, till the Death of Queen Mary.* 2 vols. London, 1782.

Tacitus. *Agricola.*

———. *Germania.*

Tindal, Nicholas. *The Continuation of Mr. Rapin de Thoyras's History of England, from the Revolution to the Accession of King George II.* 2nd ed. 2 vols. London, 1787.

Tyrrell, James. *Bibliotheca Politica: Or, an Enquiry into the Ancient Constitution of the English Government.* London, 1694.

———. *The General History of England, Both Ecclesiastical and Civil.* 3 vols. London, 1696–1704.

Velly, Paul François. *Histoire de France.* Continued by Claude Villaret and Jean-Jacques Garnier. 30 vols. Paris, 1755–86.

Vitringa, Campegius. *Archisynagogus Observationibus Novis Illustratus.* Franeker, 1685.

Wallingford, John of. *Chronicles.* [Completed thirteenth century].

Whitaker, John. *The History of Manchester.* 2 vols. London, 1771–75.

Whitelocke, Bulstrode. *Memorials of the English Affairs.* London, 1682.

Wight, Alexander. *An Inquiry into the Rise and Progress of Parliaments, Chiefly in Scotland.* Edinburgh, 1784.

Wilkins, David. *Leges Anglo-Saxonicae Ecclesiasticae et Civiles.* London, 1721.

William of Malmesbury. *Gesta Regum Anglorum: The History of the English Kings.* Edited and translated by R. A. B. Mynors, R. M. Thomson, and M. Winterbottom. Oxford: Clarendon Press, 1998.

Willis, Browne. *Notitia Parliamentaria: or, An History of the Counties, Cities and Boroughs in England and Wales.* 2nd ed. 3 vols. London, 1730.

Xiphilinus, Johannes. *Epitome of Dio Cassius* [Roman history, bks. 36–80]. [Completed late eleventh century].

APPENDIX 2

Main Historiographical Sources for Millar's Narrative to 1688

Volume 1

Bacon, Nathaniel (1593–1660): *An Historical and Political Discourse of the Laws and Government of England, from the first times to the end of the reign of Queen Elizabeth. Collected from some manuscript notes of John Selden, Esq.* (London, 1689).

Bacon was a Puritan and supporter of Oliver Cromwell, and accordingly his historical writings are pervaded by a strong spirit of hostility to the claims of the royal prerogative and to hierarchical pretensions. The *Historical Discourse,* originally published in 1665, was suppressed by the Restoration government and reissued in 1689 with the addition of a new title page, claiming the work to have been "collected" from some notes by John Selden (on Selden, see below).

Bede, the Venerable (ca. 672–735): *Historia Ecclesiastica Gentis Anglorum* (731).

Characterized as the "father of English history," Bede spent most of his life in the monastery of Jarrow. Combining church history with other facets of British history up to 731, the *Historia* provides a narrative based upon both written documents and oral tradition. It is the primary source of historical knowledge for the early Anglo-Saxon period.

Robert Brady (d. 1700): *A Complete History of England* (1685).

A historian and physician, Brady was appointed regius professor of physics at Cambridge and twice represented the university in the House of Commons. As keeper of the records at the Tower of London, he developed a profound interest in studying the documents under his charge. His historical works are marked by a sympathy with the royal prerogative and a positive account of the feudal state, a political structure that in his view was introduced by the Normans.

Henry, Robert (1718–90): *The History of Great Britain, from the First Invasion of It by the Romans Under Julius Caesar. Written on a new plan.* 6 vols. (London, 1771–93).

Henry's "new plan" involved an ambitious narrative structure that attracted attention well into the nineteenth century. While divided by time period, it is further subdivided into seven thematic narratives that parallel each epoch of British history to the Tudor period. Each of the seven narratives relates a particular strand of history, namely the history of politics, the church, the law and the constitution, learning, the arts, commerce, and manners.

Spelman, Sir Henry (ca. 1564–1641): *Glossarium Archaiologium* (London, 1664).

Spelman was an antiquarian and historian whose works concentrated on the Anglo-Saxon and early medieval periods. He attempted to write a history of English law from original records but was forced to abandon the exercise due to the difficulty of assigning proper meanings to Anglo-Saxon terms. Out of this experience he wrote his *Glossarium,* a dictionary of Anglo-Saxon and Latin legal terms. Spelman argued that feudal law was introduced to England in fully developed form only by the Norman Conquest, and that English law had not developed without interruption since the Anglo-Saxon period.

Wilkins, David (1685–1745): *Leges Anglo-Saxonicae* (London, 1721).

Wilkins, who became archdeacon of Suffolk in 1724, was a scholar of wide-ranging interests with a facility in a number of languages, including Arabic and Hebrew. His knowledge of Anglo-Saxon was put to use in his *Leges Anglo-Saxonicae,* a collection and translation of Anglo-Saxon laws.

Volume 2

Bacon, Francis (1561–1626): *The Historie of the Raigne of King Henry the Seuenth* (London, 1622).

The philosopher and politician's only completed political history was a flattering portrait of the first Tudor monarch. The work was dedicated to James

I and intended as a model of virtuous political conduct for Prince Charles. As a work of historical analysis, it long remained a fundamental source for the history of the early Tudor period.

Blackstone, Sir William (1723–80): *Commentaries on the Laws of England.* 4 vols. (London, 1765–69).

A jurist and professor of law at Oxford, Blackstone wrote commentaries that cover the whole field of law, including a chapter on the "rise, progress and gradual improvements of the laws of England." The most influential of eighteenth-century English legal texts, it ran to some nine editions during the author's own lifetime. Blackstone also prepared important editions of the Magna Carta and other charters for the Clarendon Press at Oxford.

Burnet, Gilbert (1643–1715): *History of the Reformation of the Church of England.* 3 vols. (London, 1679–1715).

A Scottish theologian and historian, the staunchly Protestant Burnet was appointed bishop of Salisbury in 1689 after returning from exile during the reign of James II. His *History of the Reformation* was one of the first accounts of the English Reformation based on primary sources, and was written largely as an answer to Nicholas Sanders's *De Origine ac Progressu Schismatis Anglicani* (Cologne, 1585), a work that had formed the basis of most Roman Catholic histories of the English Reformation.

Carte, Thomas (1686–1754): *A General History of England.* 4 vols. (London, 1747–55).

Carte was a historian of decidedly Jacobite sympathies, and these inform parts of his *History.* While not very well known during his lifetime, the work remains a careful and important collection of information and documentary material.

Fortescue, Sir John (ca. 1385–1476): *De Laudibus Legum Angliae* (London, 1600).

Fortescue was chief justice of the King's Bench and an ardent adherent of the house of Lancaster. Having been attainted for treason by Edward IV, he was in exile 1463–71. *De Laudibus Legum Angliae,* though concerned more with politics than with law, sheds much light on trial by jury and other English legal institutions. It was written 1468–70 in the form of a dialogue for the instruction of Edward, son of Henry VI, and it compares the law of England favorably with the civil law of France. His chief object was to emphasize the advantages of a mixed constitution and a limited monarchy.

Gilbert, Sir Geoffrey (1674–1726): *The History and Practice of the High Court of Chancery* (London, 1758).

Published from Gilbert's private papers, the *History* is a treatise on the origins and workings of chancery, and includes a discussion of Roman law. Gilbert was a Whig lawyer, serving as lord chief baron of the Court of Exchequer in Ireland 1714–22. He was appointed to a seat on the English Exchequer Bench in 1722 and then elevated to lord chief baron of the Court of Exchequer in 1724.

Hume, David (1711–76): *The History of England.* 6 vols. (London, 1754–62).

In this work by the foremost philosopher and historian of eighteenth-century Britain, Hume's initial concentration was on the reigns of the Stuart monarchs James I and Charles I, because this was when the "great constitutional struggle had first manifested itself." Hume's philosophically polished *History* was wildly successful and became the standard history of England, even if disliked by many Whigs for its apparent royalism and sharp critique of Puritanism.

Madox, Thomas (1666–1727): *The History and Antiquities of the Exchequer of the Kings of England* (London, 1711).

Madox was an English antiquarian and historian. His *History and Antiquities of the Exchequer* was the first serious study of that institution and shed much light on the financial structure of medieval England. Before his death in 1727, Madox had been compiling a general history of medieval England, the remains of which are now in the British Library.

Selden, John (1584–1654): *Eadmeri Monachi Cantuariensis Historiae Novorum* (London, 1623).

Selden, an English antiquary and jurist, edited the six books of Eadmer (a twelfth-century monk and chronicler), giving an account of the courts of the first two Williams and Henry I. To this text he appended his *Notae et Spicilegium,* a commentary on Eadmer's writings. Selden was also the author of several legal and constitutional works, including an edition of Fortescue's *De Laudibus Legum Angliae,* and *A Brief Discourse Touching the Office of Lord Chancellor.*

Smith, Sir Thomas (1513–77): *De Republica Anglorum* (London, 1583).

Smith's work was the most important and influential description of the constitution and government of England produced during the Tudor period—indeed produced from within the system which it described. Smith was a moderate Protestant, a scholar (appointed regius professor of civil law at Cambridge in 1543 and vice-chancellor in 1545), and statesman (a member of the Privy Council 1548–50 and 1570–77).

Tyrrell, James (1642–1718): *Bibliotheca Politica* (London, 1694).

Conceived as a series of fourteen political dialogues, the *Bibliotheca* deals with parliamentary rights and the royal prerogative through a careful examination of the constitutional questions raised during the reigns of the later Stuarts. The dialogues form a valuable part of the Whig theory of the English constitution.

Willis, Browne (1682–1760): *Notitia Parliamentaria.* 3 vols. (London, 1730).

Willis was an antiquarian who published widely, including a series of works on English cathedrals. The first two volumes of the *Notitia* treat parliamentary representation in a very detailed way, addressing the counties alphabetically (but reaching only as far as Durham). The third volume provides brief notes for borough representation, as well as valuable lists of members of Parliament 1542–1660.

Volume 3

Clarendon, Edward Hyde, Earl of. *The History of the Rebellion and Civil Wars in England.* 3 vols. (Oxford, 1702–4).

A staunch supporter of Charles I upon the outbreak of the Civil War in 1642, Hyde was made an earl after the Restoration. After serving as lord chancellor, he was exiled in the aftermath of the Dutch War. His *History* was a contemporary account of the Civil War that was originally written during the 1640s, augmented in exile, and published posthumously early in the eighteenth century as the standard royalist account of the conflict.

Dalrymple, Sir John (1726–1810): *Memoirs of Great Britain and Ireland.* 3 vols. (London, 1771–73).

A lawyer trained in both Scottish and English law, Dalrymple served as baron of the exchequer 1776–1807. His *Memoirs of Great Britain and Ireland,* which were illustrated by collections of state papers from Versailles and London, were criticized by David Hume for being too concerned with the "biographical and anecdotical."

Hailes, Sir David Dalrymple, Lord (1726–92): *Annals of Scotland.* 2 vols. (Edinburgh, 1776) and *An Examination of some of the Arguments for the High Antiquity of Regiam Majestatem; and an enquiry into the authenticity of Leges Malcolmi* (Edinburgh, 1769).

A Scottish judge, Dalrymple was a friend and correspondent of both Edmund Burke and Samuel Johnson. His publications were chiefly related to early Scotland, as well as to Christian antiquities, which he deemed the best defense against the skeptical tendencies of the age. The *Annals of Scotland,* which soon became a standard work on the subject, lamented the loss of Scottish independence, while his *Examination* delved into early Scottish law, particularly the extent to which it was borrowed from English sources.

Harris, William (1720–70): *An Historical and Critical Account of the Life and Writings of Charles I* (London, 1758) and *An Historical and Critical Account of the Life of Charles II.* 2 vols. (London, 1746).

Harris was the son of a Nonconformist tradesman in Salisbury, and himself became a Nonconformist minister in Devonshire. His biographies of the Stuart kings are chiefly concerned with detailing the struggles of the Nonconformists and the establishment of various dissenting churches during the early seventeenth century.

Hume, David (1711–76): *The History of England.* 6 vols. (London, 1754–62).

(See entry on p. 850.) Millar's narrative of the Stuart period engages heavily with Hume's account in the first two volumes of his *History.*

Rapin-Thoyras, Paul de (1661–1725): *History of England.* Translated by Nicholas Tindal. 15 vols. (London, 1725–31).

A Huguenot (French Protestant), Rapin left France to avoid persecution following the revocation of the Edict of Nantes in 1685. He soon joined the armies of William of Orange and was involved in the invasion of 1688 as well as the Irish campaigns. Early in the eighteenth century he began to write his *Histoire,* and it became the standard Whig account of English history from the Anglo-Saxons to the Glorious Revolution of 1688 (until Hume's *History*). In later translations, Tindal continued the narrative to the accession of George I in 1727.

Rushworth, John (1612?–90): *Historical Collections.* 8 vols. (London, 1659).

A lawyer, member of Parliament, and historian, Rushworth was appointed secretary to General Fairfax. His *Historical Collections* is composed, for the most part, of his own notes of speeches and debates over the period 1640–48. It was vehemently attacked by royalist writers for its partiality and inaccuracy, but for later historians, his notes were a valuable source for the later years of the reign of Charles I.

INDEX

This book is set in Adobe Garamond, a modern adaptation by Robert Slimbach of the typeface originally cut around 1540 by the French typographer and printer Claude Garamond. The Garamond face, with its small lowercase height and restrained contrast between thick and thin strokes, is a classic "old-style" face and has long been one of the most influential and widely used typefaces.

Printed on paper that is acid-free and meets the requirements of the American National Standard for Permanence of Paper for Printed Library Materials, z39.48-1992. ♾

Book design by Louise OFarrell
Gainesville, Florida
Typography by Apex Publishing, LLC
Madison, Wisconsin
Printed and bound by Edwards Brothers, Inc.
Ann Arbor, Michigan